Accounting Cycle Roadmap:

Start

1. Business transactions occur and generate documents.

2. Analyze and record business transactions into a journal.

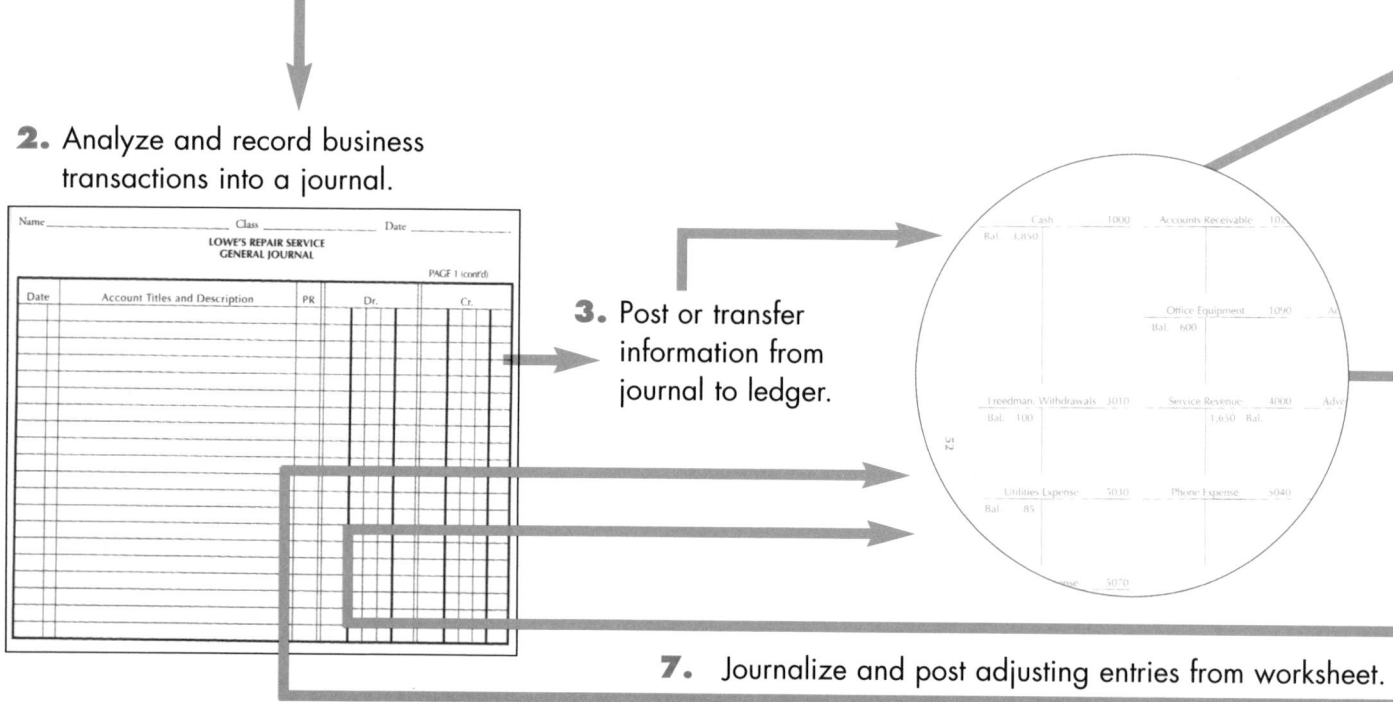

3. Post or transfer information from journal to ledger.

7. Journalize and post adjusting entries from worksheet.

Roadmap TIPS:

(2) Here are the rules to analyze debits and credits:

ASSETS	=	LIABILITIES	+	OWNER'S EQUITY							
Dr. Cr.		Dr. Cr.	+	Capital	– Withdrawals	+	Revenue	–	Expenses		
+ –		– +		Dr. Cr.	Dr. Cr.		Dr. Cr.		Dr. Cr.		
				– +	+ –		– +		+ –		

(3) Reference column in ledger shows what page of the journal that the transaction came from. Reference column in journal tells what account number the information has been transferred to.

(4) Trial balance is a list of the ledger balances:
Debit + Debit = Debit (Dr.)
Credit + Credit = Credit (Cr.)
Debit + Credit: Take the difference of both sides. The balance is placed on the side that has the larger balance.

(5) Worksheet not needed in a computerized system. Analyzing the adjustments column:
- Supplies "used up"
- Insurance expired
- Depreciation expense builds up a contra asset called Accumulated Depreciation (Cr. Balance)
- Salaries earned but not paid

(6) Formal statements do NOT have debits or credits.

A Reference Guide: When Do I Do What?

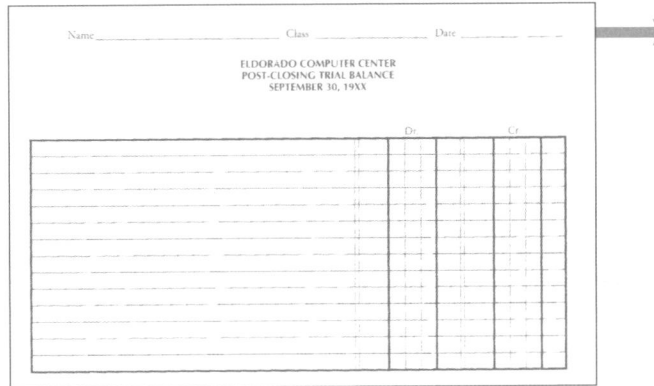

9. Prepare a post-closing trial balance.

→ **End**

4. Prepare a trial balance.

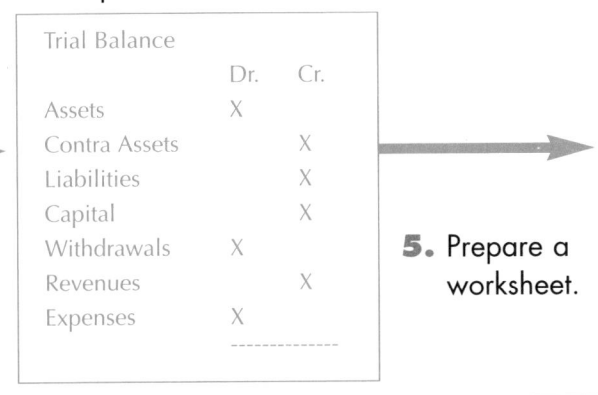

Trial Balance

	Dr.	Cr.
Assets	X	
Contra Assets		X
Liabilities		X
Capital		X
Withdrawals	X	
Revenues		X
Expenses	X	

5. Prepare a worksheet.

WORKSHEET

CLARK'S WORD PROCESSING SERVICES
WORKSHEET
FOR MONTH ENDING MAY 31, 19XX

Account Titles	Trial Balance Dr.	Trial Balance Cr.	Adjustments Dr.	Adjustments Cr.	Adjusted Trial Balance Dr.	Adjusted Trial Balance Cr.	Income Dr.
Cash	6 1 5 5 00						
Accounts Receivable	5 0 0 0 00						
Office Supplies	6 0 0 00						
Prepaid Rent	1 2 0 0 00						
Word Processing Equipment	6 0 0 0 00						
Accounts Payable		3 3 5 0 00					
Brenda Clark, Capital		10 0 0 0 00					
Brenda Clark, Withdrawals	6 2 5 00						
Word Processing Fees		8 0 0 0 00					
Office Salaries Expense	1 3 0 0 00						
Advertising Expense	2 5 0 00						
Telephone Expense	2 2 0 00						
	21 3 5 0 00	21 3 5 0 00					

8. Journalize and post closing entries from worksheet.

6. Prepare the financial statements from worksheet.

Income Statement	Statement of Owners equity	Balance Sheet
Revenues - expenses = net income	Begining Capital + net income - withdrawals = Ending Capital	Assets Liabilities Owner's equity Ending Capital

(7) Adjustments from the worksheet are journalized in the SAME JOURNAL as Step 2 and posted to SAME LEDGER as Step 3.

(8) All closing entries are recorded in SAME JOURNAL (Step 2) and posted to SAME LEDGER (Step 3).

(9) After closing entries have been journalized and posted, only PERMANENT accounts will have balances left in the ledger to carry over to the next period.

Account Title	Normal Balance	Financial Report Found On	Category	Permanent or Temporary
Accounts Payable	Credit	Balance Sheet	Current Liability	Permanent
Accounts Receivable	Debit	Balance Sheet	Current Asset	Permanent
Accumulated Depreciation	Credit	Balance Sheet	Contra Plant & Equipment	Permanent
Advertising Expense	Debit	Income Statement	Operating Expense	Temporary
Allowance for Doubtful Accounts	Credit	Balance Sheet	Contra Current Asset	Permanent
Bad Debts Recovered	Credit	Income Statement	Other Income	Temporary
Bad Debts Expense	Debit	Income Statement	Operating Expense	Temporary
Bond Interest Expense	Debit	Income Statement	Operating Expense	Temporary
Bond Interest Payable	Credit	Balance Sheet	Current Liability	Permanent
Bonds Payable	Credit	Balance Sheet	Long-Term Liability	Permanent
Building	Debit	Balance Sheet	Plant & Equipment	Permanent
Capital	Credit	Statement of Owner's Equity; Balance Sheet	Owner's Equity	Permanent
Cash	Debit	Balance Sheet	Current Asset	Permanent
Cash Short and Over (Assume Short)	Debit	Income Statement	Miscellaneous Expense	Temporary
(Assume Over)	Credit	Income Statement	Other Income	Temporary
Change Fund	Debit	Balance Sheet	Current Asset	Permanent
Commissions Earned	Credit	Income Statement	Revenue	Temporary
Common Stock	Credit	Balance Sheet	Stockholders' Equity	Permanent
Common Stock Subscribed	Credit	Balance Sheet	Stockholders' Equity	Permanent
Common Stock Dividend Distributable	Credit	Balance Sheet	Stockholders' Equity	Permanent
Copyright	Debit	Balance Sheet	Intangible Asset	Permanent
Credit Card Expense	Debit	Income Statement	Other Expense	Temporary
Depletion Expense	Debit	Income Statement	Operating Expense	Temporary
Depreciation Expense	Debit	Income Statement	Operating Expense	Temporary
Discount on Bonds Payable	Debit	Balance Sheet	Contra Long-Term Liability	Permanent
Discount on Notes Payable	Debit	Balance Sheet	Contra Current Liability	Permanent
Dividends Payable	Credit	Balance Sheet	Current Liability	Permanent
Equipment	Debit	Balance Sheet	Plant & Equipment	Permanent
Federal Income Tax Payable	Credit	Balance Sheet	Current Liability	Permanent
FICA Tax Payable	Credit	Balance Sheet	Current Liability	Permanent
Freight-In	Debit	Income Statement	Cost of Goods Sold	Temporary
FUTA Tax Payable	Credit	Balance Sheet	Current Liability	Permanent
Gain on Sale of Asset	Credit	Income Statement	Other Income	Temporary
Goodwill	Debit	Balance Sheet	Intangible Asset	Permanent
Income Summary	—	—	Owner's Equity	Temporary
Insurance Expense	Debit	Income Statement	Operating Expense	Temporary
Interest Earned	Credit	Income Statement	Other Income	Temporary
Interest Expense	Debit	Income Statement	Other Expense	Temporary
Interest Payable	Credit	Balance Sheet	Current Liability	Permanent
Land	Debit	Balance Sheet	Plant & Equipment	Permanent
Land Improvement	Debit	Balance Sheet	Plant & Equipment	Permanent
Loss from Fire	Debit	Income Statement	Other Expense	Temporary
Loss on Sale of (Asset)	Debit	Income Statement	Other Expense	Temporary
Loss or Gain from Realization (Assume Loss)	Debit	Income Statement	Other Expense	Temporary
(Assume Gain)	Credit	Income Statement	Other Income	Temporary
Machinery	Debit	Balance Sheet	Plant & Equipment	Permanent

Account Title	Normal Balance	Financial Report Found On	Category	Permanent or Temporary
Medicare Tax Payable	Credit	Balance Sheet	Liability	Permanent
Merchandise Inventory	Debit	Balance Sheet; Income Statement	Current Asset; Cost of Goods Sold	Permanent
Mortgage Payable	Credit	Balance Sheet	Long-Term Liability	Permanent
Notes Payable	Credit	Balance Sheet	Current Liability	Permanent
Notes Receivable	Debit	Balance Sheet	Current Asset	Permanent
Organization Costs	Debit	Balance Sheet	Intangible Asset	Permanent
Patents	Debit	Balance Sheet	Intangible Asset	Permanent
Paid-In Capital from Treasury Stock	Credit	Balance Sheet	Stockholders' Equity	Permanent
Paid-In Capital in Excess of (. . .)	Credit	Balance Sheet	Stockholder's Equity	Permanent
Payroll Tax Expense	Debit	Income Statement	Operating Expense	Temporary
Petty Cash	Debit	Balance Sheet	Current Asset	Permanent
Premium on Bonds Payable	Credit	Balance Sheet	Long-Term Liability	Permanent
Prepaid Insurance	Debit	Balance Sheet	Current Asset	Permanent
Prepaid Rent	Debit	Balance Sheet	Current Asset	Permanent
Preferred Stock	Credit	Balance Sheet	Stockholders' Equity	Permanent
Purchases	Debit	Income Statement	Cost of Goods Sold	Temporary
Purchases Discount	Credit	Income Statement	Contra Cost of Goods Sold	Temporary
Purchases Returns and Allowances	Credit	Income Statement	Contra Cost of Goods Sold	Temporary
Retained Earnings	Credit	Statement of Retained Earnings; Balance Sheet	Stockholders' Equity	Permanent
Salaries Expense	Debit	Income Statement	Operating Expense	Temporary
Salaries Payable	Credit	Balance Sheet	Current Liability	Permanent
Sales	Credit	Income Statement	Revenue	Temporary
Sales Discount	Debit	Income Statement	Contra Revenue	Temporary
Sales Returns and Allowances	Debit	Income Statement	Contra Revenue	Temporary
Sales Tax Payable	Credit	Balance Sheet	Current Liability	Permanent
Social Security Tax Payable	Credit	Balance Sheet	Liability	Permanent
Stock Dividend Distributable	Credit	Balance Sheet	Stockholders' Equity	Permanent
Stock Subscriptions Receivable	Debit	Balance Sheet	Current Asset	Permanent
Supplies	Debit	Balance Sheet	Current Asset	Permanent
Treasury Stock	Debit	Balance Sheet	Contra Stockholder's Equity	Permanent
Unearned Revenue	Credit	Balance Sheet	Current Liability	Permanent
Vouchers Payable	Credit	Balance Sheet	Current Liability	Permanent
Withdrawals	Debit	Statement of Owner's Equity; Balance Sheet	Owners' Equity	Temporary

KEY TO USE OF COLOR IN TEXT

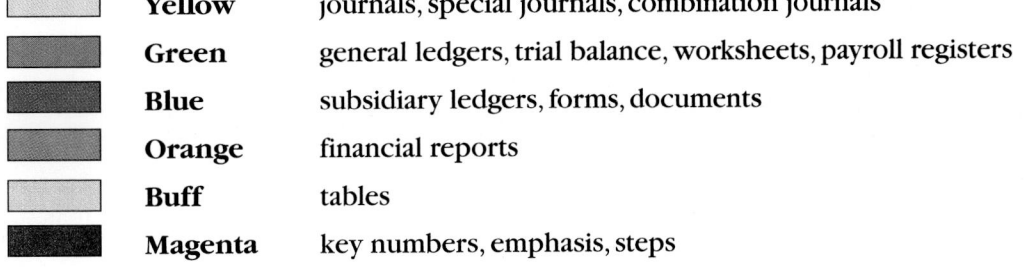

	Yellow	journals, special journals, combination journals
	Green	general ledgers, trial balance, worksheets, payroll registers
	Blue	subsidiary ledgers, forms, documents
	Orange	financial reports
	Buff	tables
	Magenta	key numbers, emphasis, steps

College Accounting

A Practical Approach

Chapters 1–12
Ninth Edition

Jeffrey Slater

North Shore Community College
Danvers, Massachusetts

Prentice Hall
Upper Saddle River, New Jersey 07458

Library of Congress Cataloging-in-Publication Data

Slater, Jeffrey, 1947–
    College accounting: a practical approach, chapters 1–12 / Jeffrey
Slater.—9th ed.
        p. cm.
Includes index.
    ISBN 0-13-143963-4
    1. Accounting.   I. Title.

HF5635.S6315 2003c
657′.044—dc22

2003064998

Editor-in-Chief: PJ Boardman
Managing Editor (Editorial): Alana Bradley
Assistant Editor: Sam Goffinet
Senior Editorial Assistant: Jane Avery
Senior Media Project Manager: Nancy Welcher
Executive Marketing Manager: Beth Toland
Marketing Assistant: Melissa Owens
Managing Editor (Production): Cynthia Regan
Production Editor: Kerri M. Tomasso
Manufacturing Buyer: Diane Peirano
Design Manager: Maria Lang
Interior Designer: Blair Brown
Cover Design: Blair Brown
Cover Illustration/Photo: Courtesy of Rob Casey & Getty Images, Inc.
Photo Researcher: Teri Stratford
Image Permission Coordinator: Tara Gardner
Manager, Multimedia Production: Christy Mahon
Composition/Full-Service Project Management: Progressive Publishing Alternatives
Printer/Binder: Courier–Kendallville

Pearson Education LTD.
Pearson Education Singapore, Pte. Ltd
Pearson Education, Canada, Ltd
Pearson Education–Japan

Pearson Education Australia PTY, Limited
Pearson Education North Asia Ltd
Pearson Educación de Mexico, S.A. de C.V.
Pearson Education Malaysia, Pte. Ltd

10 9 8 7 6 5 4
ISBN 0-13-143963-4

To

Matthew (Matty) and to Samuel
(Sam): Welcome to our family

with love ... Grumpa JEFF

Brief Contents

Contents

3 Beginning the Accounting Cycle   70

4 The Accounting Cycle Continued   118

Subway Case Boxes

Peachtree® Computer Workshops

A Note to Faculty from Jeff Slater . . .

We share common goals. We want to motivate our students to be interested in accounting and to see accounting as the most dynamic tool of business. We want to introduce students to the accounting cycle and to learn double entry accounting. We want our students to see the critical role accounting plays in making business decisions. And, along the way, we want students to develop skills that will enable them to succeed in the workforce.

These are my goals for each edition of **College Accounting.** Nothing has changed and yet everything has changed. Now we have the opportunity to utilize the excitement of a new text design, provide a wealth of pedagogical tools, and exploit the learning mediums and available technologies to enhance your teaching environment and your students' learning experience.

Thank you for your interest in the Ninth Edition of **College Accounting** and, as you peruse the remainder of this preface, I encourage you to *Taste the Slater Difference!*

UNIQUE SLATER LEARNING SYSTEM

Three Text Versions!

Three versions of **College Accounting 9e** are available to enable faculty to customize the text to fit their individual course need.

Learning Units with Immediate Application

A Slater hallmark! Unlike other texts that require students to read 30+ pages before they have a chance to test their understanding, **College Accounting 9e** organizes each chapter into small, bite-sized units. Students are introduced to new concepts in the **Learning Unit** and then immediately have the opportunity to test their understanding in the **Learning Unit Reviews.**

Study Guide and Working Papers

The Study Guide and Working Papers are available for each of the three text versions. All of the forms needed to solve the chapter problems are included in the working papers and are referenced by page to the text.

Unique Presentation of Perpetual and Periodic Inventory

Slater has an appendix to Chapter 9 that provides an introduction to merchandising through general journals for a perpetual inventory system instead of special journals. **College Accounting 9e** completes the merchandise cycle by Chapter 12 and then provides the OPTION to cover perpetual inventory for a merchandise company in the Appendices.

In-Text Practice Set

The in-text Valdez Realty Practice Set (Chapter 5) enables students to complete two cycles of transactions (in your choice of manual or electronic formats). And source documents to complete the practice set are now included.

END-OF-CHAPTER ASSIGNMENT MATERIAL INCLUDES:

Key Terms/Blueprint

This feature is designed to highlight the key terms that students should know for each chapter, and the blueprint highlights important accounting processes they should know.

YOU make the call

These action-oriented exercises encourage students to put themselves in the decision-maker's seat.

Internet Exercises

These exercises provide students with the opportunity to use the Internet to solve specific accounting problems.

Continuing Problem

Throughout the book, students will read about a single company, called El Dorado Computer Company. At the end of each chapter, students will apply concepts you have learned to solve a specific accounting problem. In the next chapter, students will see the next evolution in the organization.

Comprehensive Problem

This problem helps students recall concepts from previous chapters as they pull upon all of their knowledge to solve these problems.

Unique In-Text Computer Workshops

These Workshops (beginning at the end of Chapter 3) enable students to use the latest release of Peachtree Complete Accounting Software in order to solve specific accounting problems. *Note that the full version of this software may be packaged with new copies of the text at a minimal charge.*

NEW FOR THE NINTH EDITION

New Text Versions!

The Slater text is available in three text versions: Chapters 1–8, 1–12, or 1–25. *Note that Working Papers and Study Guides are packaged free with the briefer texts.*

New! Subway Boxes

This unique feature appears at the ends of many chapters (13 boxed inserts) and shows students how this well-known company uses accounting information to make business. A **new** video (on the DVD) takes students inside Subway to review accounting concepts.

New Content Enhancements

The key content enhancements for **College Accounting 9e** include: eliminating Chapter 11 on Combined Journals from the previous edition, updating all payroll chapters, including updated bank statements reflecting current banking trends (Chapter 4), and a new presentation (Chapter 4) to show adjustments one at a time.

New Chapter-Opening Stories

The chapter-opening stories show students how accounting issues touch their lives each day and motivate students with the topics to be covered in each chapter.

Margin Notes

These "coaching tips" appear in the side margins of each chapter to provide extra insights for students.

NEW TECHNOLOGY RESOURCES FOR THE NINTH EDITION

New! Accounting in the Reel World Video Cases

These in-text video cases are designed to show students how accounting is relevant to the things they are interested in and care about: dating, shopping, sports, dining, and so forth. These are linked to the Slater custom-crafted *On Location! Videos* on the DVD.

New DVD Icons

The icon signals faculty and students that there are resources available to use with the **FREE DVD packaged only with New Student Texts!** These include:

Videos

- **New!** Subway *On Location! Video* linked to the new Subway in-text boxes
- **New!** *On Location! Videos!* linked to the new in-text video cases
- **New!** Jeff Slater Learning Unit Review Video for Chapters 1–5
- **New!** 5 Steps in Accounting Cycle Video

Software

- General Ledger Software
- Data files for the latest releases of the Getting Started Series (Peachtree, QuickBooks, Simply Accounting)
- PowerPoint® slides
- Links to the Slater Website and online courses

SUPPLEMENTS:

Technology Resources

INNOVATION! **Instructor Resource CD-ROM**   This unique tool enables faculty to **save time** and **quickly prepare highly effective and interactive multimedia classroom presentations.** Using a **highly accessible menu,** faculty can easily customize their lectures using an interactive library of video, PowerPoints, and additional resources by simply clicking on a chapter or key word.

Enjoy the freedom to transport the entire package from office, to home, to classroom. The Instructor CD-ROM enables you to customize any of the ancillaries, print only the chapters or materials you wish, or access any item from the package within the classroom!

***INNOVATION!* Getting Started Series**   Upon request, faculty may package your choice of one of these approximately 90-page manuals on the latest professional accounting software packages with **College Accounting 9/e** at no charge. Each manual introduces students to the concepts of Excel, Peachtree, QuickBooks, or Simply Accounting.

***INNOVATION!* Special Offers — Professional Accounting Software Packages**
Package your choice of the latest software releases of Peachtree or Simply Accounting at $11.00 net with new text purchase.

General Ledger Software   The General Ledger software enables students to complete homework assignments using a general ledger software package. Students may also enter and solve their own problems. Available on the Student DVD, Instructor CD-ROM, and downloadable from the Companion Website.

***INNOVATION!* Standard Online Courses in WebCT, CourseCompass, and BlackBoard**   Teach a complete online course or a Web-enhanced course. Add your own course materials, take advantage of online testing and Gradebook opportunities, and utilize the bulletin board and discussion board functions. Free upon request. This is an excellent time to build your own course using our CD-ROMs with your choice of platform. (The courses will not be "robust".)

Companion Website at www.prenhall.com/slater   Prentice Hall's Learning on the Internet Partnership offers extensive Internet-based support. Our Website provides a wealth of resources for students and faculty resources, including an Online Study Guide with Quizzes, Internet Exercises, PowerPoint slides, software downloads, complete faculty supplements, and much more.

Instructor Supplements

***INNOVATION!* Instructor CD-ROM**   The **IRCD** contains all print and technology (e.g., videos, data files, PowerPoint slides) supplements on a single CD-ROM.

Instructor's Solutions Manual   Each chapter of this comprehensive resource consists of a list of the student learning objectives and the fully worked-out solutions to the chapter problems.

Test Item File and Achievement Tests   The printed Test Item File consists of hundreds of premade questions, including true/false questions, conceptual and quantitative multiple-choice questions, critical thinking problems, and exercises. Each question identifies the difficulty level and the corresponding learning objective. The Achievement Tests give faculty the flexibility to pop a quiz with little effort. **Prentice Hall TestGenEQ** can create exams and evaluate and track student results.

Solutions and Teaching Transparencies   Every page of the Solutions Manual has been reproduced in acetate form for use on the overhead projector. These acetates have been enhanced for easier viewing.

On Location! Videos   These eight brief videos take students "on location" to real companies where real accounting situations are discussed and explained.

Student Supplements

New! **Computerized Accounting Practice Sets** The **A-1 Photography and Runners Corporation** practice sets are available complete with data files for Peachtree, QuickBooks, and Simply Accounting. Each practice set also includes business stationary for manual entry work. In addition, the Who-Dun-It Bookstore practice set (for use with Chapters 12–25) has been revised and updated.

INNOVATION! **Student DVD** The **Student DVD** is free with every new text purchased from Prentice Hall (it can also be purchased separately) and contains the General Ledger software package, PowerPoints, Getting Started data files, On Location! videos, Learning Unit Review videos (for Chapters 1–5), and 5 Steps in the Accounting Cycle videos.

Study Guide with Working Papers This chapter-by-chapter learning aid systematically and effectively helps students study college accounting and get the maximum benefit from their study time. Each chapter provides a Summary Practice Test with fill-in-the-blanks, multiple choice, and true/false problems AND solutions to all the questions, and the Working Papers contain tailor-made spreadsheets to all end-of-chapter problems.

Who-Dun-It Practice Set A case study (with solutions available for instructors) that follows a sole proprietorship throughout end-of-year transactions, cash sales, sales tax, payroll, purchases, and other year-end processes. This practice set is most effectively used with Chapters 12–25 of the text.

ACKNOWLEDGMENTS

Reviewers

I wish to thank the following reviewers for their suggestions, many of which made their way into this text, and for their support, without which this text would not be the success that it is today.

Kevin Bess, Florida Metropolitan, Melbourne

Janell Spencer, College of the Sequoias

Susan Davis, Green River Community College

James Mann, Huntington Junior College

Michael Farina, Cerritos College

Thomas Milligan, St. Philip's College

Harry Gray, Ivy Tech State College, Indianapolis

Claire Moore, Heald College, Roseville

Scott Steinhamp, College of Lake County

Richard Williams, Nashville State Technical Community College

Marjorie Ashton, Truckee Meadows Community College

Thea Hosselrode, Allegany College

Julie Dailey, Tidewater Community College

Beverly Bugay, Tyler Junior College

Mark Preising, Florida Metropolitan, Orlando

William Hood, Central Michigan University

Brenda Bindschatel, Spokane Falls Community College

Elaine Anes, Heald College, Fresno

Cornelia Alsheimer, Santa Barbara City College

Michelle Berube, Florida Metropolitan, Clearwater

Dorenda Haynes, Heald College, San Jose

Tom Snavely, Yavapai Community College

Angela Harper, Indiana Business College, Evansville

Wayne Smith, Indiana Business College, Lafayette

Ruth Turner, National College of Business & Technology, Lynchburg

Brennan Randolph, Indiana Business College, Terre Haute

Brenda Jenkins, National College of Business & Technology, Bluefield

Sara Bottomley, Indiana Business College, Terre Haute

John Hudson, National College of Business & Technology, Bluefield

Michael Kulper, Santa Barbara City College

SUPPLEMENT AUTHORS

Test Bank/Achievement Tests—Patti Holmes, Des Moines Area CC

Online Study Guide—Tim Carse

Who-Dun-It Practice Set—Shari DeMarco

PowerPoints—Olga Quintana, University of Miami

Getting Started with Peachtree Complete Accounting 2003—Errol Osteraa, Heald College

Getting Started with Simply Accounting 2003—Jean Insinga, Middlesex Community College

Getting Started with QuickBooks Pro 2003—Janet Horne, Los Angeles Pierce College

Transparency Acetates—Jeff Slater

Instructor Solutions Manual—Jeff Slater

Study Guide w/Working Papers—Jeff Slater

On Location! Videos—Beverly Amer, Northern Arizona University

Subway Case Videos—Beverly Amer, Northern Arizona University

5 Steps in the Accounting Cycle Videos—Beverly Amer, Northern Arizona University

Jeff Slater's One on One Videos—Beverly Amer, Northern Arizona University

Additionally, there are a few people who need to be mentioned for their help with this edition: Nancy Brandwein, for writing the Subway Cases for me; Les Winograd, of Subway World Headquarters, who worked closely with Nancy Brandwein as she created our Subway Cases; and Jim Hatfield, owner of Subway of Upstate South Carolina, who provided real-world examples and first-hand knowledge for the Cases. Tim Carse did a great job as he wrote the chapters on Payroll and worked closely with Errol Osteraa, who once again did an outstanding job writing the Computer Workshops (and the *Getting Started with Peachtree Complete Accounting 2003*). Their effort and expertise are most valuable and much appreciated. Abby Kaminsky did a wonderful job checking proofs, paging the study guide, and coordinating all text reviews. All these people helped me write the text, and I couldn't have done it without them.

The people at Prentice Hall who worked together to make this text a reality also deserve a heartfelt thank you: Kerri Tomasso, for her careful eye on the production of the text; Blair Brown, for his excellent design work both interior and on the cover; Beth Toland; for her non-stop marketing efforts, Sam Goffinet, for all his dedication in getting the supplements out on time AND done right; and to wonderful Jane Avery for keeping us honest at all times. Special thanks to Alana Bradley, my editor, who has shown patience beyond the call of duty. Thanks for always finding a way to resolve my many requests. You are a real jewel.

A Note to Students from Jeff Slater . . .

Welcome! **College Accounting 9e** will introduce you to Accounting, the most dynamic tool of business. This textbook focuses on real-world applications designed to help you see the critical role accounting plays in the business world. Each text chapter opens with a real-life situation where an individual learns how accounting is a part of the everyday world. In every instance, I have tried to think of the most interesting and applicable examples for you . . . including selecting Subway, the largest franchised business in the world as the spotlight business for this edition of the text. I hope you will enjoy learning about this tasty business as you devour new accounting concepts.

Please take a few moments to "walk through" the features of the Ninth Edition to see all of the tools that are available to assist you in this course.

New Chapter-Opening Stories

The chapter-opening stories show how accounting issues touch your life each day and motivate topics to be covered in each chapter.

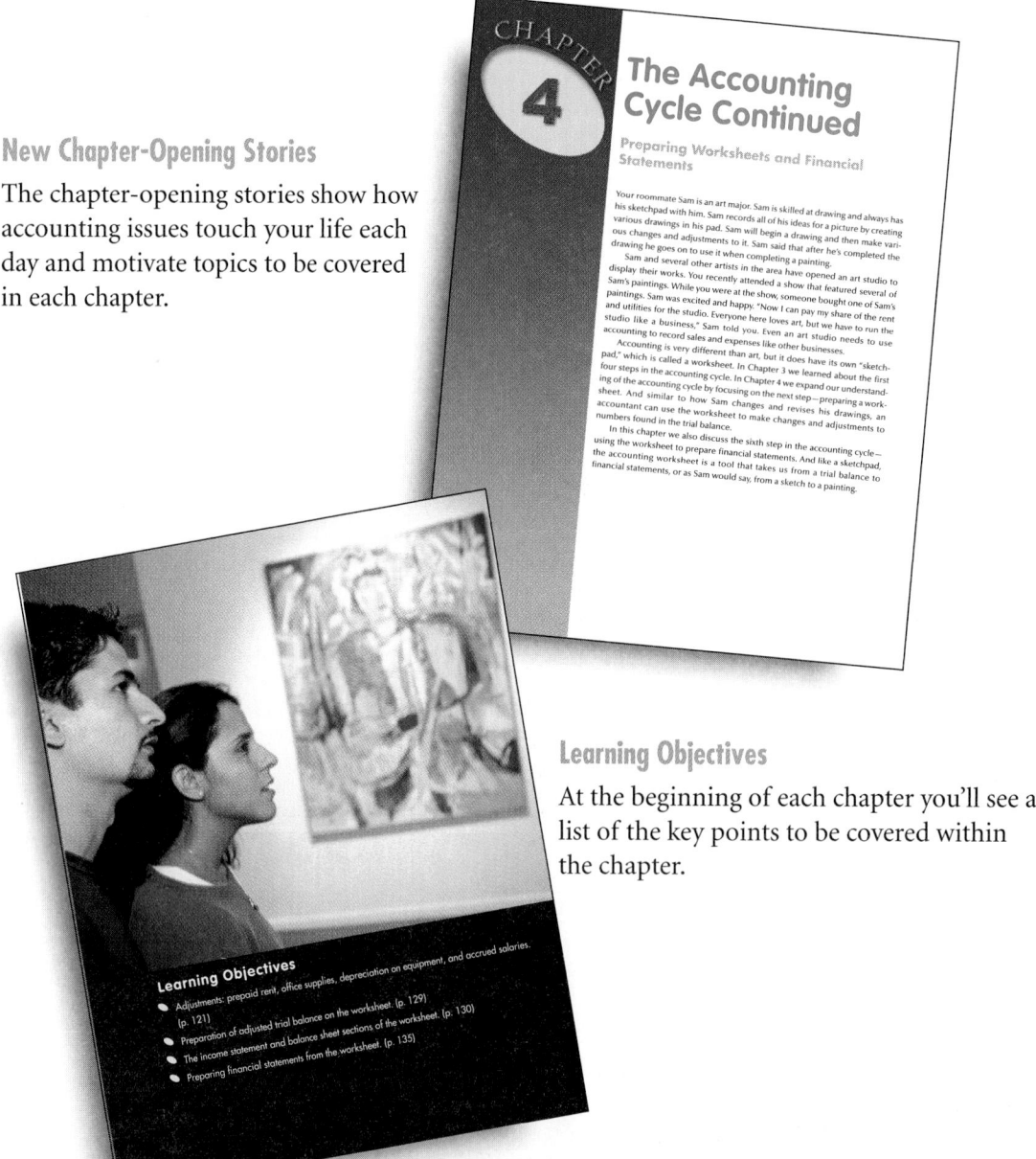

CHAPTER 4

The Accounting Cycle Continued

Preparing Worksheets and Financial Statements

Your roommate Sam is an art major. Sam is skilled at drawing and always has his sketchpad with him. Sam records all of his ideas for a picture by creating various drawings in his pad. Sam will begin a drawing and then make various changes and adjustments to it. Sam said that after he's completed the drawing he goes on to use it when completing a painting.

Sam and several other artists in the area have opened an art studio to display their works. You recently attended a show that featured several of Sam's paintings. While you were at the show, someone bought one of Sam's paintings. Sam was excited and happy. "Now I can pay my share of the rent and utilities for the studio. Everyone here loves art, but we have to run the studio like a business," Sam told you. Even an art studio needs to use accounting to record sales and expenses like other businesses.

Accounting is very different than art, but it does have its own "sketchpad," which is called a worksheet. In Chapter 3 we learned about the first four steps in the accounting cycle. In Chapter 4 we expand our understanding of the accounting cycle by focusing on the next step—preparing a worksheet. And similar to how Sam changes and revises his drawings, an accountant can use the worksheet to make changes and adjustments to numbers found in the trial balance.

In this chapter we also discuss the sixth step in the accounting cycle—using the worksheet to prepare financial statements. And like a sketchpad, the accounting worksheet is a tool that takes us from a trial balance to financial statements, or as Sam would say, from a sketch to a painting.

Learning Objectives

- Adjustments: prepaid rent, office supplies, depreciation on equipment, and accrued salaries. (p. 121)
- Preparation of adjusted trial balance on the worksheet. (p. 129)
- Preparation of the income statement and balance sheet sections of the worksheet. (p. 130)
- The income statement and balance sheet sections of the worksheet. (p. 135)
- Preparing financial statements from the worksheet.

Learning Objectives

At the beginning of each chapter you'll see a list of the key points to be covered within the chapter.

Key Content Changes

- Eliminated Chapter 11 on Combined Journals from the previous edition

- Updated all payroll chapters

- Include updated bank statements reflecting trends in banking (Chapter 4)

- Shows adjustments one at a time (Chapter 4). No other book takes this much time to reinforce learning

- In-text Valdez practice set (manual & computerized) now includes source documents

- Slater covers perpetual inventory with general journal entries (along with samples of perpetual inventory for special journals and worksheets)

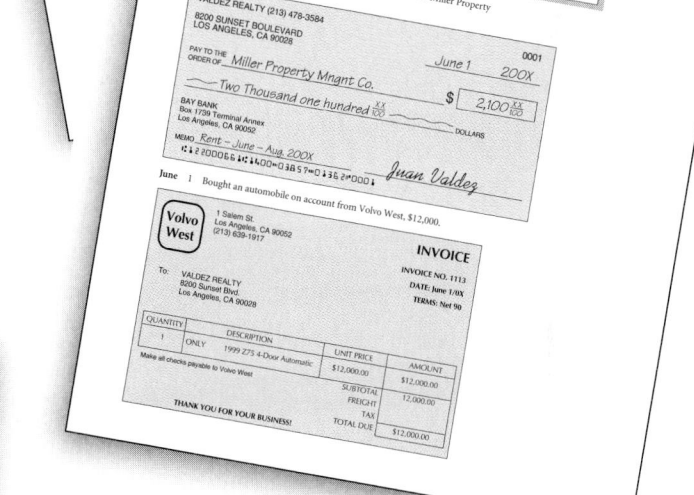

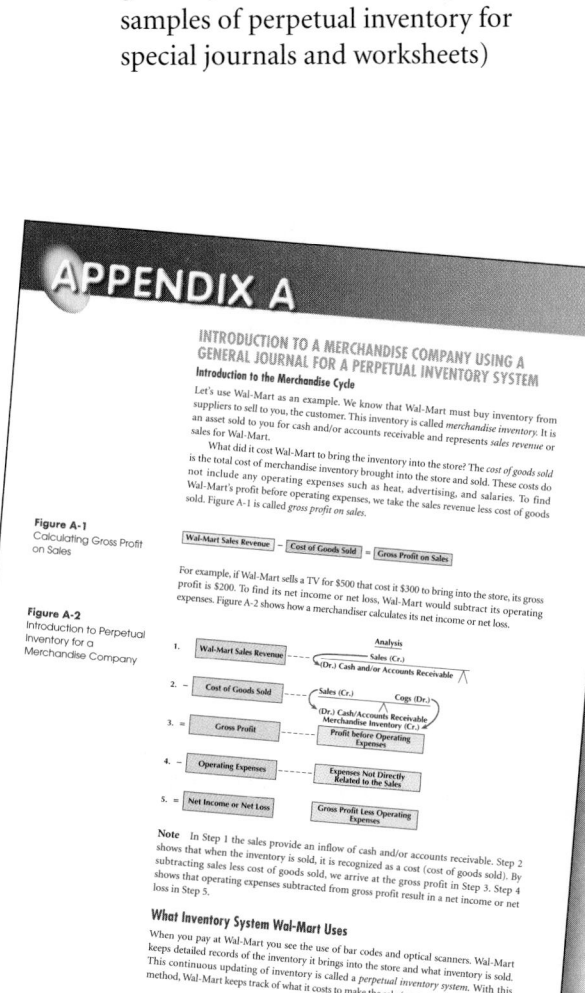

Hallmark Features

Covers both Perpetual and Periodic Inventory

College Accounting 9e has an appendix to Chapter 9 that provides an introduction to merchandizing through general journals for a perpetual inventory system instead of special journals. This edition completes the merchandise cycle by Chapter 12 and then provides the OPTION to cover perpetual inventory for a merchandise company in the Appendices.

Learning Unit

A Slater hallmark! Jeff Slater organizes each chapter into small, bite-sized units. First you are introduced to new concepts and then you have the opportunity to test your understanding in the **Learning Unit Reviews.**

Margin Notes

These "coaching tips" appear in the side margins of each chapter to provide extra insights.

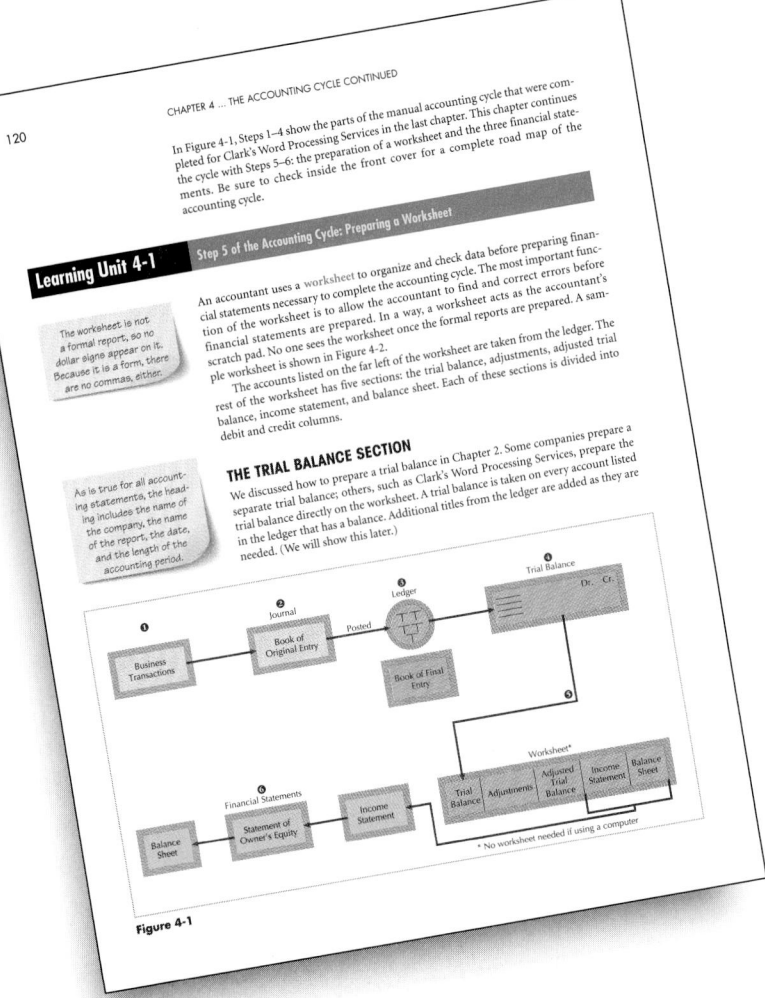

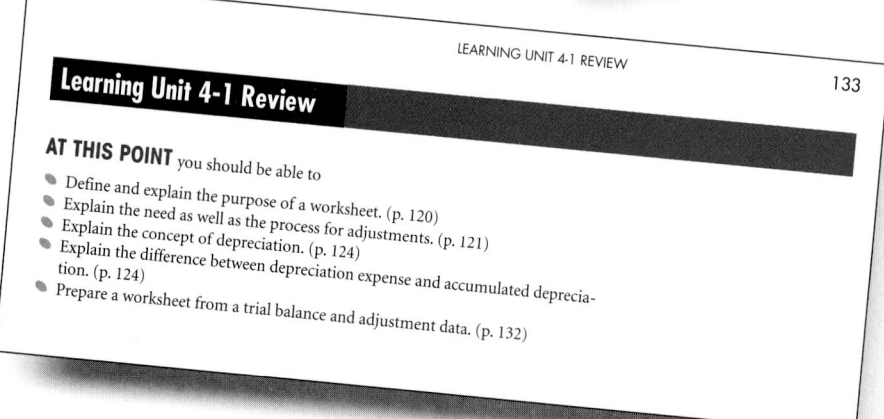

Learning Unit Reviews

A Slater hallmark! Unlike others texts which make you read 30+ pages before you have a chance to test your understanding, Jeff Slater organizes each chapter into small, bite-sized units. After you are introduced to new concepts in the **Learning Unit,** you have the opportunity to test your understanding in the **Learning Unit Reviews.**

   Check your understanding by viewing the author's video in which he walks the viewer through the Learning Unit Reviews for the first five chapters.

New! Subway Boxes

This unique feature appears at the end of twelve chapters and shows you how this student-recognizable company uses accounting information to make business decisions. A new video (on the DVD) takes you inside Subway to review accounting concepts.

New! Accounting in the Reel World Video Cases

These in-text video cases are designed to show you how accounting is relevant to the things you care about: dating, shopping, sports, dining, etc. These are linked to our custom-crafted *On Location! Videos* on the DVD.

New DVD Icons

The icon signals to you that there are resources available to use with the *FREE DVD packaged only with New Student Texts*. These include:

Videos

- **New!** Subway *On Location! Videos* linked to the new Subway in-text boxes
- **New!** *On Location! Videos!* linked to the new in-text video cases
- **New!** Jeff Slater Learning Unit Review Video for Chapters 1–5
- **New!** 5 Steps in Accounting Cycle Video

Software

- General Ledger Software
- Data files for the latest releases of the Getting Started Series (Peachtree, QuickBooks, Simply Accounting)
- PowerPoints
- Links to the Slater Website and online courses

Continuing Problem

Throughout the book, you will read about Eldorado Computer Center. At the end of each chapter, you will apply concepts you have learned to solve a specific accounting problem. In the next chapter, you will see the next evolution in the organization.

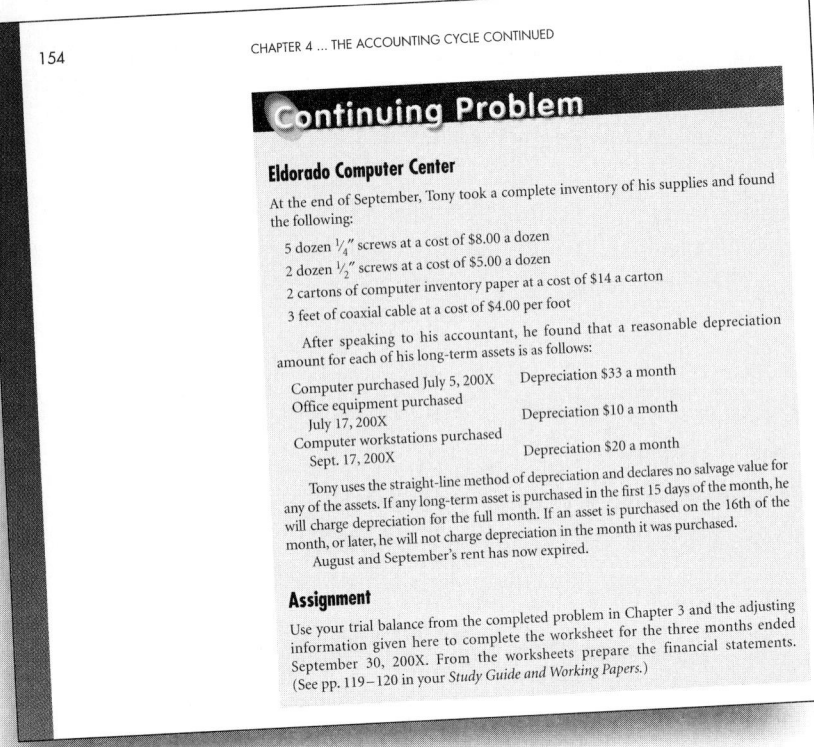

154   CHAPTER 4 ... THE ACCOUNTING CYCLE CONTINUED

Continuing Problem

Eldorado Computer Center

At the end of September, Tony took a complete inventory of his supplies and found the following:

5 dozen ¼″ screws at a cost of $8.00 a dozen

2 dozen ½″ screws at a cost of $5.00 a dozen

2 cartons of computer inventory paper at a cost of $14 a carton

3 feet of coaxial cable at a cost of $4.00 per foot

After speaking to his accountant, he found that a reasonable depreciation amount for each of his long-term assets is as follows:

Computer purchased July 5, 200X	Depreciation $33 a month
Office equipment purchased July 17, 200X	Depreciation $10 a month
Computer workstations purchased Sept. 17, 200X	Depreciation $20 a month

Tony uses the straight-line method of depreciation and declares no salvage value for any of the assets. If any long-term asset is purchased in the first 15 days of the month, he will charge depreciation for the full month. If an asset is purchased on the 16th of the month, or later, he will not charge depreciation in the month it was purchased.

August and September's rent has now expired.

Assignment

Use your trial balance from the completed problem in Chapter 3 and the adjusting information given here to complete the worksheet for the three months ended September 30, 200X. From the worksheets prepare the financial statements. (See pp. 119–120 in your *Study Guide and Working Papers*.)

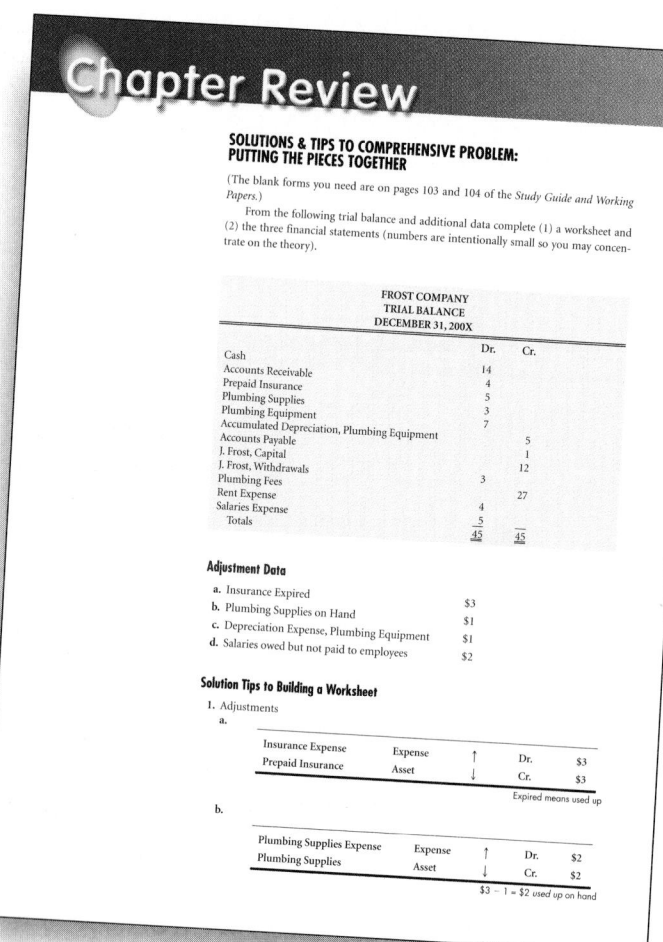

Chapter Review

SOLUTIONS & TIPS TO COMPREHENSIVE PROBLEM: PUTTING THE PIECES TOGETHER

(The blank forms you need are on pages 103 and 104 of the *Study Guide and Working Papers*.)

From the following trial balance and additional data complete (1) a worksheet and (2) the three financial statements (numbers are intentionally small so you may concentrate on the theory).

FROST COMPANY TRIAL BALANCE DECEMBER 31, 200X		
	Dr.	Cr.
Cash	14	
Accounts Receivable	4	
Prepaid Insurance	5	
Plumbing Supplies	3	
Plumbing Equipment	7	
Accumulated Depreciation, Plumbing Equipment		5
Accounts Payable		1
J. Frost, Capital		12
J. Frost, Withdrawals	3	
Plumbing Fees		27
Rent Expense	4	
Salaries Expense	5	
Totals	45	45

Adjustment Data

a. Insurance Expired $3

b. Plumbing Supplies on Hand $1

c. Depreciation Expense, Plumbing Equipment $1

d. Salaries owed but not paid to employees $2

Solution Tips to Building a Worksheet

1. Adjustments

a.

Insurance Expense	Expense	↑	Dr.	$3
Prepaid Insurance	Asset	↓	Cr.	$3

Expired means used up

b.

Plumbing Supplies Expense	Expense	↑	Dr.	$2
Plumbing Supplies	Asset	↓	Cr.	$2

$3 − 1 = $2 used up on hand

Comprehensive Problem

This problem helps you recall concepts from previous chapters as you pull upon all of your knowledge to solve these problems.

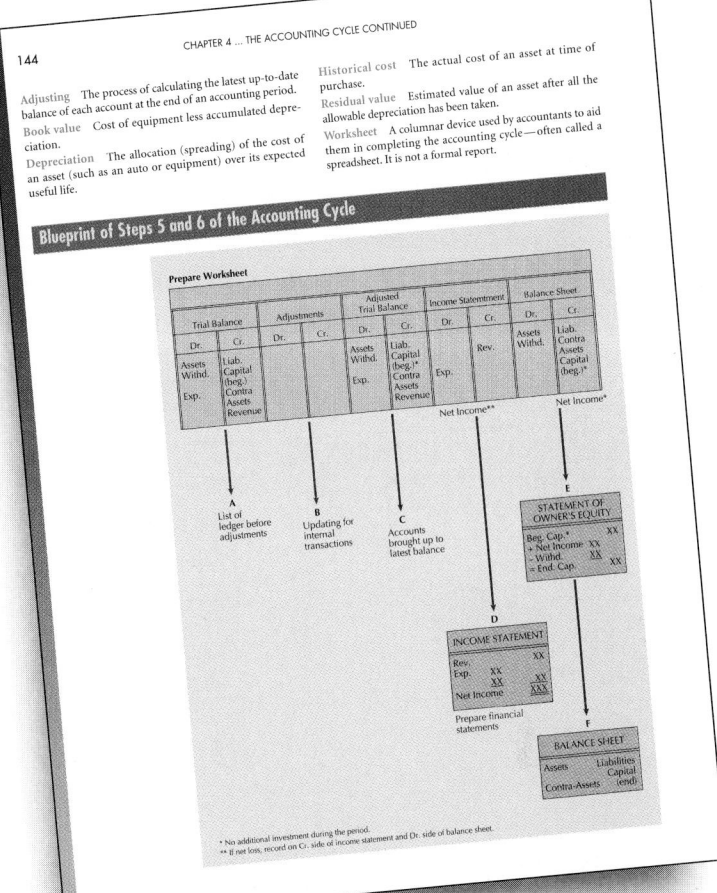

Key Terms/Blueprint

This feature is designed to highlight the key terms you should know for each chapter and the blueprint highlights important accounting processes you should know.

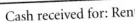

Cash received for: Rent   2,300

As his best friend, could you help Harry show the amounts that are to be reported on the income statement for (a) Advertising Expense, (b) Interest Expense, and (c) Rent Fees Earned. Please explain in writing why Unearned Rent is considered a liability.

YOU make the call

Critical Thinking/Ethical Case

4R-3. Janet Fox, President of Angel Co., went to a tax seminar. One of the speakers at the seminar advised the audience to put off showing expenses until next year because doing so would allow them to take advantage of a new tax law. When Janet returned to the office, she called in her accountant, Frieda O'Riley. She told Frieda to forget about making any adjustments for salaries in the old year so more expenses could be shown in the new year. Frieda told her that putting off these expenses would not follow generally accepted accounting procedures. Janet said she should do it anyway. You make the call. Write your specific recommendations to Frieda.

Internet Exercises: Office Max

EX-1. [www.officemax.com]   On the Web site look for "General Information," then click on "Corporate Information." Under "Investor Information" look up Annual Reports and find the Consolidated Balance Sheet for 2001.

1. Under the caption "other current assets," what accounts do you think could be there that required end-of-period adjustments?
2. If Office Max rented the property where its stores are located and paid the rent in advance for 24 months, how would adjustments have been made in its financial statements?
3. What effect would these adjustments have on (a) Total Assets, and (b) Net Income?
4. Look at "current liabilities" in the balance sheet. Which accounts there seem most susceptible to the adjustment process, and why did you choose these accounts?

EX-2. [www.officemax.com]   Click on "CEO Sworn Statement." Why do you think the CEO is required to report this information?

YOU make the call

These action-oriented exercises encourage you to put yourself in the decision-marker's seat.

Internet Exercises

These exercises give you the opportunity to use the Internet to solve specific accounting problems.

Unique In-Text Computer Workshops

These Workshops enable the use of the latest release of Peachtree Complete Software in order to solve specific accounting problems. *Note that the full educational version of this software may be packaged with new copies of the text at a minimal charge.*

COMPUTERIZED ACCOUNTING APPLICATION FOR CHAPTER 4
PART A: *Compound Journal Entries, Adjusting Entries, and Financial Reports*
PART B: *Backup Procedures*

Before starting on this assignment, read and complete the tasks discussed in Parts A, B, and F of the Computerized Accounting appendix at the back of this book and complete the Computerized Accounting Application assignment at the end of Chapter 3.

PART A: COMPOUND JOURNAL ENTRIES, ADJUSTING ENTRIES, AND FINANCIAL REPORTS

How to Open the Company Data Files

1. Click on the Start button. Point to Programs; point to the Peachtree folder and select Peachtree Complete Accounting. Your desktop may have the Peachtree icon allowing for a quicker entrance into the program.
2. Follow the "Open a File" instructions in Part A of the Computerized Accounting appendix at the back of this book to open **The Zell Company.** You may be initially presented with the Peachtree Today window. If so, simply close it. If you are missing the navigation aids at the bottom of the screen and want them, you can activate them under the **Options** menu. Select **View Navigation Aid.** It will remain on until you turn it off. This feature offers an alternative way to access the different features of Peachtree.
3. Click on the **Maintain** menu option. Then select **Company Information.** The program will respond by bringing up a dialogue box allowing the user to edit/add information about the company.

How to Add Your Name to the Company Name

4. Click in the **Company Name** entry field at the end of **The Zell Company.** If it is already highlighted, press the right arrow key. Add a dash and your name "**-Student Name**" to the end of the company name. Click on the OK button to return to the Menu Window.
5. In the computerized accounting application assignment in Chapter 3 you learned how to record journal entries in the General Journal dialog box. Compound journal entries can also be recorded in the General Journal dialog box. The owner of The Zell Company has made an investment in the business consisting of $5,000 in cash and an automobile valued at $12,000. Select **General Journal Entry** from the **Tasks** menu to open the General Journal dialog box. Enter the date 1/1/04 into the **Date** field; press the TAB key; enter "Memo" into the **Reference** field and press TAB.

How to Record a Compound Journal Entry

6. With the flashing insertion point positioned in the **Account No.** field, click on the pull down menu (magnifying glass icon) and double click on "1110 Cash". The program will enter the account number and name into the **Account No.** field and the flashing insertion point will move to the **Description** field. Enter "Initial investment by owner" into this field and press TAB to move to the **Debit** field. Enter "5000" and press TAB three times to move back to the **Account No.** field.
7. With the flashing insertion point positioned in the **Account No.** field, click on the pull down menu (magnifying glass icon) and double click on "1230 Automobile". Press TAB to move to the **Description** field. This should repeat the information entered in step 6 by default. Press the TAB key again to move to the **Debit** field. Enter "12000". Hit TAB three times to move the cursor back to the **Account No.** field. You should now have two debit entries.

Learning accounting means familiarizing yourself with many new terms and concepts. Don't let the temptation to cut corners and take shortcuts fool you. It is to your advantage to follow the detailed step-by-step directions provided in the text so that you can learn good habits from the start. Once you have learned basic terms and concepts the rest will quickly fall into place. I've enclosed my own **Tips to Success** that I share with my students when I teach the course. I encourage you to read these Tips and apply them in your daily reading and classwork:

TIPS TO SUCCESS . . . FROM JEFF SLATER

1. **Read each chapter by Learning Unit**. Don't try to read a chapter all at once, but instead, focus just on the learning unit, and don't overdo it.

2. **Complete each self-review quiz** given at the end of each learning unit to immediately assess your understanding of the material.

Remember! In **College Accounting 9e,** *each chapter builds on the previous chapter. You need to build a solid foundation before going on to the next chapter. Accounting is one discipline where you can only learn by doing, so follow this advice!*

3. **Utilize the DVD** to review core accounting concepts: the Self Review Quiz videos and the Accounting Cycle videos will give you the best foundation available.

4. **Use the Website** at www.prenhall.com/slater for extra help in drill and practice.

5. **Review the Comprehensive Review Problems** with worked-out solutions that are at the end of the first five chapters in the text. These special problems are great for putting all the learning units together to give you an overview of how accounting works. All the forms are available in your study guide/working papers.

As you can see, I really enjoy teaching accounting and providing my students with every possible resource to maximize their learning experience. I wish you the best of luck in your class and I welcome your input as you use the text. You may feel free to contact me at jeffslater@aol.com.

CHAPTER 1

Accounting Concepts and Procedures

An Introduction

When you stop to think about accounting, it surrounds you, every day.

You go to the school bookstore and buy your textbooks for the new term. The cashier rings up your purchase by scanning the bar codes on each book. The electronic register keeps track of the sale, adds the tax, and bills you a total of $342.28. You present the cashier with your credit card, sign your name on an electronic touch pad with a special pen, and then take your receipt and your books. While standing in the checkout line you hear one bookstore employee tell another that she's going to be working an extra shift this weekend and that she'll be paid overtime for the extra hours.

It's simple to use your credit card to buy books, but how does the bookstore keep track of book sales, book orders, and paying its employees? What process does a business like a bookstore use to keep it operating efficiently? It's all tracked through accounting, the language of business.

Throughout this text we will be looking at how accounting helps businesses like the bookstore keep track of book orders and sales and paying its employees. In this chapter we discuss the types of business organizations and how accounting differs from bookkeeping. We will look at the basics of recording business events using accounting. We will learn that accounting starts with a basic set of rules that make up the accounting equation. Then we build on the accounting equation to learn how a business records its events and reports them. We conclude this chapter by discussing how to summarize the results of accounting using financial statements such as the balance sheet, income statement, and statement of owner's equity.

The world of business surrounds us, and accounting is the language spoken in the world of business.

Learning Objectives

- Defining and listing the functions of accounting. (p. 4)

- Recording transactions in the basic accounting equation. (p. 4)

- Seeing how revenue, expenses, and withdrawals expand the basic accounting equation. (p. 11)

- Preparing an income statement, a statement of owner's equity, and a balance sheet. (p. 17)

Accounting is the language of business; it provides information to managers, owners, investors, governmental agencies, and others inside and outside the organization. Accounting provides answers and insights to questions like these:

- Should I invest in Disney stock?
- Will McDonald's show good returns in the future?
- Can American Airlines pay its debt obligations?
- What percentage of Apple's marketing budget is for e-business? How does that percentage compare with the competition? What is the overall financial condition of Apple?

Smaller businesses also need answers to their financial questions:

- At a local Pizza Hut did business increase enough over the last year to warrant hiring a new assistant?
- Should Eatons Drug-Store spend more money to design, produce, and send out new brochures in an effort to create more business?
- What role should the Internet play in our business?

Accounting is as important to individuals as it is to businesses; it answers questions like these:

- Should I take out a loan to buy a new Volvo SUV or wait until I can afford to pay cash for it?
- Would my money work better in a money market or in the stock market?

Accounting is the process that analyzes, records, classifies, summarizes, reports, and interprets financial information to decision makers—whether individuals, small businesses, large corporations, or governmental agencies—in a timely fashion. It is important that students understand the "whys" of the accounting process. Just knowing the mechanics is not enough.

There are three main categories of business organization: (1) sole proprietorships, (2) partnerships, and (3) corporations. Let's define each of them and look at their advantages and disadvantages. This information also appears in Table 1-1.

Sole Proprietorship

A **sole proprietorship**, such as Gracie's Nail Care, is a business that has one owner. That person is both the owner and the manager of the business. An advantage of

> The Internet is creating many new opportunities and challenges for all forms of business organizations.

TABLE 1-1 Types of Business Organizations

	Sole Proprietorship (Gracie's Nail Care)	Partnership (Matthew and Jones)	Corporation (Home Depot)
Ownership	Business owned by one person.	Business owned by more than one person.	Business owned by stockholders.
Formation	Easy to form.	Easy to form.	More difficult to form.
Liability	Owner could lose personal assets to meet obligations of business.	Partners could lose personal assets to meet obligations of partnership.	Limited personal risk. Stockholders' loss is limited to their investment in the company.
Closing	Ends with death of owner or closing of business.	Ends with death of partner or exit of a partner.	Can continue indefinitely.

a sole proprietorship is that the owner makes all the decisions for the business. A disadvantage is that if the business cannot pay its obligations, the business owner must pay them, which means that the owner could lose some of his or her personal assets (e.g., house or savings).

Sole proprietorships are easy to form. They end if the business closes or when the owner dies.

Partnership

A partnership, such as Matthew and Jones, is a form of business ownership that has at least two owners (partners). Each partner acts as an owner of the company, which is an advantage because the partners can share the decision making and the risks of the business. A disadvantage is that, as in a sole proprietorship, the partners' personal assets could be lost if the partnership cannot meet its obligations.

Partnerships are easy to form. They end when a partner dies or leaves the partnership.

Corporation

A corporation, such as Home Depot, is a business owned by stockholders. The corporation may have only a few stockholders, or it may have many stockholders. The stockholders are not personally liable for the corporation's debts, and they usually do not have input into the business decisions.

Corporations are more difficult to form than sole proprietorships or partnerships. Corporations can exist indefinitely.

> eBay is an example of a corporation.

CLASSIFYING BUSINESS ORGANIZATIONS

Whether we are looking at a sole proprietorship, a partnership, or a corporation, the business can be classified by what the business does to earn money. Companies are categorized as service, merchandise, or manufacturing businesses.

A limo service is a good example of a service company because it provides a service. The first part of this book focuses on service businesses.

Gap and J.C. Penney sell products. They are called merchandise companies. Merchandise companies can either make their own products or sell products that are made by another supplier. Companies like Mattel and Ford Motor Company that make their own products are called manufacturers. (See Table 1-2.)

TABLE 1-2 Examples of Service, Merchandise, and Manufacturing Business

Service Businesses	Merchandise Businesses	Manufacturing Businesses
Lou's Detailing Co.	L.L. Bean	GE
eBay	J.C. Penney	Ford
Dr. Wheeler, M.D.	Amazon.com	Toro
Accountemps	Home Depot	Levi's
CellularOne Paging Services	Staples	Intel

DEFINITION OF ACCOUNTING

Accounting (also called the accounting process) is a system that measures the activities of a business in financial terms. It provides various reports and financial statements that show how the various transactions the business undertook (e.g., buying and selling goods) affected the business. It does this by performing the following functions:

- **Analyzing**: Looking at what happened and how the business was affected.
- **Recording**: Putting the information into the accounting system.
- **Classifying**: Grouping all the same activities (e.g., all purchases) together.
- **Summarizing**: Explaining the results.
- **Reporting**: Issuing the statements that tell the results of the previous functions.
- **Interpreting**: Examining the statements to determine how the various pieces of information they contain relate to each other.

The system communicates the reports and financial statements to people who are interested in the information, such as the business's decision makers, investors, creditors, and governmental agencies (e.g., the Internal Revenue Service).

As you can see, a lot of people use these reports. A set of procedures and guidelines were developed to make sure that everyone prepares and interprets them the same way. These guidelines are known as generally accepted accounting principles (GAAP).

Now let's look at the difference between bookkeeping and accounting. Keep in mind that we use the terms *accounting* and the *accounting process* interchangeably.

DIFFERENCE BETWEEN BOOKKEEPING AND ACCOUNTING

Confusion often arises concerning the difference between bookkeeping and accounting. Bookkeeping is the recording (recordkeeping) function of the accounting process; a bookkeeper enters accounting information in the company's books. An accountant takes that information and prepares the financial statements that are used to analyze the company's financial position. Accounting involves many complex activities. Often, it includes the preparation of tax and financial reports, budgeting, and analyses of financial information.

Today, computers are used for routine bookkeeping operations that used to take weeks or months to complete. The text takes this into consideration by explaining how the advantages of the computer can be applied to a manual accounting system by using hands-on knowledge of how accounting works. Basic accounting knowledge is needed even though computers can do routine tasks. QuickBooks and Peachtree are two popular software packages in use today.

Learning Unit 1-1   The Accounting Equation

ASSETS, LIABILITIES, AND EQUITIES

Let's begin our study of accounting concepts and procedures by looking at a small business: Cathy Hall's law practice. Cathy decided to open her practice at the end of August. She consulted her accountant before she made her decision. The accountant told her some important things before she made this decision. First, he told her the new business would be considered a separate business entity whose finances had to be kept separate and distinct from Cathy's personal finances. The accountant went on to say that all transactions can be analyzed using the basic accounting equation: Assets = Liabilities + Owner's Equity.

Cathy had never heard of the basic accounting equation. She listened carefully as the accountant explained the terms used in the equation and how the equation works.

Assets

Cash, land, supplies, office equipment, buildings, and other properties of value *owned* by a firm are called assets.

Equities

The rights of financial claim to the assets are called equities. Equities belong to those who supply the assets. If you are the only person to supply assets to the firm, you have the sole rights, for financial claims, to them. For example, if you supply the law firm with $5,000 in cash and $4,000 in office equipment, your equity in the firm is $9,000.

Relationship Between Assets and Equities

The relationship between assets and equities is

Assets	=	Equities
(Total value of items *owned* by business)		**(Total claims against the assets)**

The total dollar value of the assets of your law firm will be equal to the total dollar value of the financial claims to those assets, that is, equal to the total dollar value of the equities.

The total dollar value is broken down on the left-hand side of the equation to show the specific items of value owned by the business and on the right-hand side to show the types of claims against the assets owned.

Liabilities

A firm may have to borrow money to buy more assets; when this occurs it means the firm is *buying assets on account* (buy now, pay later). Suppose the law firm purchases a new computer for $2,300 on account from Gateway, and the company is willing to wait 10 days for payment. The law firm has created a liability: an obligation to pay that comes due in the future. Gateway is called the creditor. This liability—the amount owed to Gateway—gives the store the right, or the financial claim, to $2,300 of the law firm's assets. When Gateway is paid, the store's rights to the assets of the law firm will end, because the obligation has been paid off.

Basic Accounting Equation

To best understand the various claims to a business's assets, accountants divide equities into two parts. The claims of creditors—outside persons or businesses—are labeled *liabilities*. The claim of the business's owner are labeled owner's equity. Let's see how the accounting equation looks now.

Elements of basic accounting equation

Assets =   **Equities**

1. Liabilities: rights of creditors
2. Owner's equity: rights of owner

Assets = Liabilities + Owner's Equity

The total value of all the assets of a firm equals the combined total value of the financial claims of the creditors (liabilities) and the claims of the owners (owner's equity). This is known as the **basic accounting equation.** The basic accounting equation provides a basis for understanding the conventional accounting system of a business. The equation records business transactions in a logical and orderly way that shows their impact on the company's assets, liabilities, and owner's equity.

Importance of Creditors

Another way of presenting the basic accounting equation is

$$\text{Assets} - \text{Liabilities} = \text{Owner's Equity}$$

This form of the equation stresses the importance of creditors. The owner's rights to the business's assets are determined after the rights of the creditors are subtracted. In other words, creditors have first claim to assets. If a firm has no liabilities—and therefore no creditors—the owner has the total rights to assets. Another term for the owner's current investment, or equity, in the business's assets is **capital.**

As Cathy Hall's law firm engages in business transactions (paying bills, serving customers, and so on), changes will take place in the assets, liabilities, and owner's equity (capital). Let's analyze some of these transactions.

> **Transaction A   Aug. 28:** Cathy invests $7,000 in cash and $800 of office equipment into the business.

On August 28, Cathy withdraws $7,000 from her personal bank account and deposits the money in the law firm's newly opened bank account. She also invests $800 of office equipment in the business. She plans to be open for business on September 1. With the help of her accountant, Cathy begins to prepare the accounting records for the business. We put this information into the basic accounting equation as follows:

	Assets		= Liabilities +	Owner's Equity
Cash	+	**Office Equipment**	=	**Cathy Hall, Capital**
$7,000	+	$800	=	$7,800
			$7,800 = $7,800	

Note that the total value of the assets, cash, and office equipment—$7,800—is equal to the combined total value of liabilities (none, so far) and owner's equity ($7,800). Remember, Hall has supplied all the cash and office equipment, so she has the sole financial claim to the assets. Note how the heading "Cathy Hall, Capital" is written under the owner's equity heading. The $7,800 is Cathy's investment, or equity, in the firm's assets.

> **Transaction B   Aug. 29:** Law practice buys office equipment for cash, $900.

From the initial investment of $7,000 cash, the law firm buys $900 worth of office equipment (such as a computer desk), which lasts a long time, whereas **supplies** (such as pens) tend to be used up relatively quickly.

Sidebar notes:

Assets
− Liabilities
= Owner's Equity

In accounting, capital does not mean cash. Capital is the owner's current investment, or equity, in the assets of the business.

Note:
Capital is part of owner's equity; it is not an asset. In our analyses, assume that any number without a sign in front of it is a +.

	Assets		= Liabilities +	Owner's Equity	
Cash	+	Office Equipment	=	Cathy Hall, Capital	
$7,000	+	$800	=	$7,800	BEGINNING BALANCE
−900		+900			TRANSACTION
$6,100	+	$1,700	=	$7,800	ENDING BALANCE

$$\$7,800 = \$7,800$$

Shift in Assets

As a result of the last transaction, the law office has less cash but has increased its amount of office equipment. This is called a **shift in assets;** the makeup of the assets has changed, but the total of the assets remains the same.

Suppose you go food shopping at Wal-Mart with $90 and spend $60. Now you have two assets, food and money. The composition of the assets has been *shifted*—you have more food and less money than you did—but the *total* of the assets has not increased or decreased. The total value of the food, $60, plus the cash, $30, is still $90. When you borrow money from the bank, on the other hand, you have an increase in cash (an asset) and an increase in liabilities; overall there is an increase in assets, not just a shift.

An accounting equation can remain in balance even if only one side is updated. The key point to remember is that the left-hand-side total of assets must always equal the right-hand-side total of liabilities and owner's equity.

> **Transaction C   Aug. 30: Buys additional office equipment
> on account, $400.**

The law firm purchases an additional $400 worth of chairs and desks from Wilmington Company. Instead of demanding cash right away, Wilmington agrees to deliver the equipment and to allow up to 60 days for the law practice to pay the invoice (bill).

This liability, or obligation to pay in the future, has some interesting effects on the basic accounting equation. Wilmington Company has accepted as payment a partial claim against the assets of the law practice. This claim exists until the law firm pays off the bill. This unwritten promise to pay the creditor is a liability called **accounts payable.**

	Assets		=	Liabilities	+	Owner's Equity	
Cash	+	Office Equipment	=	Accounts Payable	+	Cathy Hall, Capital	
$6,100	+	$1,700	=			$7,800	BEGINNING BALANCE
		+400		+$400			TRANSACTION
$6,100	+	$2,100	=	$400	+	$7,800	ENDING BALANCE

$$\$8,200 = \$8,200$$

When this information is analyzed, we can see that the law practice has increased what it owes (accounts payable) as well as what it owns (office equipment) by $400. The law practice gains $400 in an asset but has an obligation to pay Wilmington Company at a future date.

The owner's equity remains unchanged. This transaction results in an increase of total assets from $7,800 to $8,200.

Finally, note that after each transaction the basic accounting equation remains in balance.

Learning Unit 1-1 Review

AT THIS POINT you should be able to

- Define and explain the differences between sole proprietorships, partnerships, and corporations. (p. 2)
- List the functions of accounting. (p. 4)
- Compare and contrast bookkeeping and accounting. (p. 4)
- Explain the role of the computer as an accounting tool. (p. 4)
- State the purpose of the accounting equation. (p. 5)
- Explain the difference between liabilities and owner's equity. (p. 5)
- Define capital. (p. 6)
- Explain the difference between a shift in assets and an increase in assets. (p. 7)

To test your understanding of this material, complete Self-Review Quiz 1-1. The blank forms you need are in the *Study Guide and Working Papers* for Chapter 1. The solution to the quiz immediately follows here in the text. If you have difficulty doing the problems, review Learning Unit 1-1 and the solution to the quiz. The DVD has worked out solutions for Chapters 1–5 for these Quizzes. Be sure to check the Slater Web site for student study aids. Check with your instructor on availability.

Keep in mind that learning accounting is like learning to type: The more you practice, the better you become. You will not be an expert in one day. Be patient. It will all come together.

Quiz Tip:
Note that transaction 2 below is a shift in assets, whereas transaction 3 is an increase in assets. Keep asking yourself, What did the business get and who supplied it to the business? Remember, capital is not cash. Cash is an asset, whereas capital is part of owner's equity.

SELF-REVIEW QUIZ 1-1

(The blank forms you need are on page 1 of the *Study Guide and Working Papers*. See your DVD for worked-out solutions.)

Record the following transactions in the basic accounting equation:

1. Gracie Ryan invests $17,000 to begin a real estate office.
2. The real estate office buys $600 of computer equipment from Wal-Mart for cash.
3. The real estate company buys $800 of additional computer equipment on account from Circuit City.

SOLUTION TO SELF-REVIEW QUIZ 1-1

	Cash	+	Computer Equipment	=	Accounts Payable	+	Gracie Ryan, Capital
			Assets	**=**	**Liabilities**	**+**	**Owner's Equity**
1.	+$17,000						+$17,000
BALANCE	17,000			=			17,000
2.	−600		+$600				
BALANCE	16,400	+	600	=			17,000
3.			+800		+$800		
ENDING BALANCE	$16,400	+	$1,400	=	$800	+	$17,000

$$\$17,800 = \$17,800$$

Accounting in the Reel World

Happy Ice Cream Memories = A Cool $3.5 Million

Many people think of ice cream as fleeting pleasure—something you enjoy in the few minutes it takes to lick up a scoop and keep it from dripping onto your lap. Not Amy Miller, the founder of the Austin, Texas-based Amy's Ice Creams of Austin. At her nine stores she not only dishes out super-premium flavors like Mexican Vanilla with crushed strawberries, but she also seeks to create "happy ice cream memories." For instance, her exhuberant, creative employees host theme nights, spoon out samples, and host events for local charities.

While the values Amy's Ice Creams espouses are warm and fuzzy, there's nothing remotely fuzzy about the figures.

Amy Miller's privately held corporation pulls in $3.5 million a year, and she and her fellow investors must wrestle with tough business decisions every day. As you watch the Amy's Ice Creams on-location video on your DVD, think about the formal business structure behind the informal, vibrant atmosphere at Amy's Ice Creams stores.

1. Why do you think that Amy decided to form a corporation instead of a partnership?
2. What are some of the assets and liabilities of Amy's Ice Creams?
3. Do you think corporations can be as creative as sole proprietorships or partnerships? Why or why not?

Learning Unit 1-2   The Balance Sheet

In the first learning unit, the transactions for Cathy Hall's law firm were recorded in the accounting equation. The transactions we recorded occurred before the law firm opened for business. A statement called a **balance sheet** or **statement of financial position** can show the history of a company before it opened. The balance sheet is a formal statement that presents the information from the ending balances of both sides of the accounting equation. Think of the balance sheet as a snapshot of the business's financial position as of a particular date.

Let's look at the balance sheet of Cathy Hall's law practice for August 31, 200X, shown in Figure 1-1. The figures in the balance sheet come from the ending balances of the accounting equation for the law practice as shown in Learning Unit 1-1.

Note in Figure 1-1 that the assets owned by the law practice appear on the left-hand side and that the liabilities and owner's equity appear on the right-hand side.

> The balance sheet shows the company's financial position as of a particular date. (In our example, that date is at the end of August.)

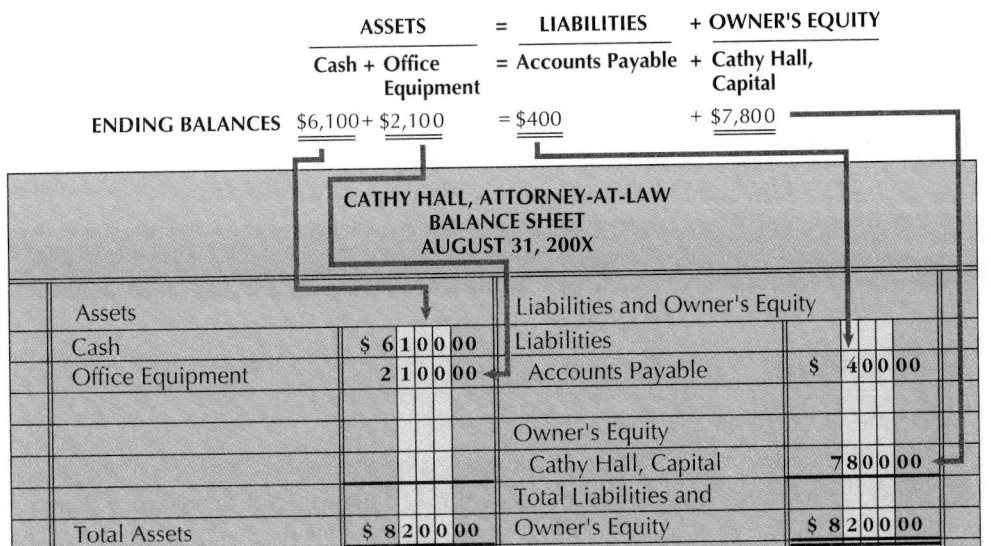

Figure 1-1
The Balance Sheet

> Remember:
> The balance sheet is a formal statement.

Figure 1-2 Partial Balance Sheet

Both sides equal $8,200. This *balance* between left and right gives the balance sheet its name. In later chapters we look at other ways to set up a balance sheet.

POINTS TO REMEMBER IN PREPARING A BALANCE SHEET

The Heading

The heading of the balance sheet provides the following information:

- The company name: Cathy Hall, Attorney-at-Law.
- The name of the statement: Balance Sheet.
- The date for which the report is prepared: August 31, 200X.

> Do you remember the three elements that make up a balance sheet? Assets, liabilities, and owner's equity.

Use of the Dollar Sign

Note that the dollar sign is not repeated each time a figure appears. As shown in Figure 1-2, the balance sheet for Cathy Hall's law practice, it usually is placed to the left of each column's top figure and to the left of the column's total.

Distinguishing the Total

When adding numbers down a column, use a single line before the total and a double line beneath it. A single line means that the numbers above it have been added or subtracted. A double line indicates a total. It is important to align the numbers in the column; many errors occur because these figures are not lined up. These rules are the same for all accounting reports.

The balance sheet gives Cathy the information she needs to see the law firm's financial position before it opens for business. This information does not tell her, however, whether or not the firm will make a profit.

Learning Unit 1-2 Review

AT THIS POINT you should be able to

- Define and state the purpose of a balance sheet. (p. 9)
- Identify and define the elements making up a balance sheet. (p. 9)
- Show the relationship between the accounting equation and the balance sheet. (p. 9)
- Prepare a balance sheet in proper form from information provided. (p. 9)

SELF-REVIEW QUIZ 1-2

(The blank forms you need are on page 2 of the *Study Guide and Working Papers.* See your DVD for worked-out solutions)

The date is November 30, 200X. Use the following information to prepare in proper form a balance sheet for Janning Company:

Accounts Payable	$40,000
Cash	18,000
A. Janning, Capital	9,000
Office Equipment	31,000

> **Quiz Tip:**
> The heading of a balance sheet answers the questions *who, what,* and *when.* November 30, 200X is the particular date.

SOLUTION TO SELF-REVIEW QUIZ 1-2

JANNING COMPANY
BALANCE SHEET
NOVEMBER 30, 200X

Assets		Liabilities and Owner's Equity	
Cash	$18 000 00	Liabilities	
Office Equipment	31 000 00	Accounts Payable	$ 40 000 00
		Owner's Equity	
		A. Janning, Capital	9 000 00
		Total Liabilities and	
Total Assets	$ 49 000 00	Owner's Equity	$ 49 000 00

Capital does not mean cash. The capital amount is the owner's current investment of assets in the business.

Figure 1-3 Balance Sheet

Learning Unit 1-3   The Accounting Equation Expanded: Revenue, Expenses, and Withdrawals

As soon as Cathy Hall's office opened, she began performing legal services for her clients and earning revenue for the business. At the same time, as a part of doing business, she incurred various expenses, such as rent.

When Cathy asked her accountant how these transactions fit into the accounting equation, he began by defining some terms.

Revenue   A service company earns revenue when it provides services to its clients. Cathy's law firm earned revenue when she provided legal services to her clients for legal fees. When revenue is earned, owner's equity is increased. In effect, revenue is a subdivision of owner's equity.

Assets are increased. The increase is in the form of cash if the client pays right away. If the client promises to pay in the future, the increase is called accounts receivable. When revenue is earned, the transaction is recorded as an increase in revenue and an increase in assets (either as cash and/or as accounts receivable, depending on whether it was paid right away or will be paid in the future).

Expenses   A business's expenses are the costs the company incurs in carrying on operations in its effort to create revenue. Expenses are also a subdivision of owner's equity; when expenses are incurred, they *decrease* owner's equity. Expenses can be paid for in cash or they can be charged.

> Accounts receivable is an asset. The law firm expects to be able to receive amounts owed from customers at a later date.

> *Remember:*
> Accounts receivable results from earning revenue even when cash is not yet received.

> Record an expense when it is incurred, whether it is paid then or is to be paid later.

Figure 1-4
Owner's Equity

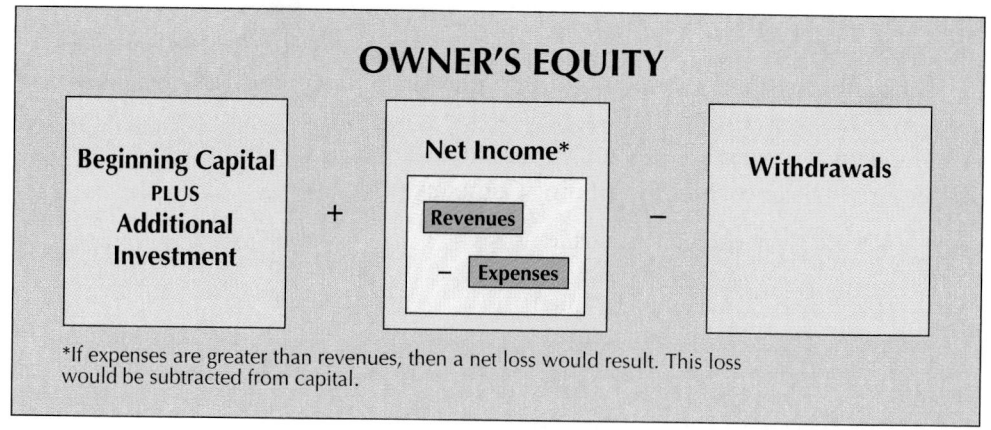

Net Income/Net Loss   When revenue totals more than expenses, net income is the result; when expenses total more than revenue, net loss is the result.

Withdrawals   At some point Cathy Hall may need to withdraw cash or other assets from the business to pay living or other personal expenses that do not relate to the business. We will record these transactions in an account called withdrawals. Sometimes this account is called the *owner's drawing account*. Withdrawals is a subdivision of owner's equity that records personal expenses not related to the business. Withdrawals decrease owner's equity (see Fig. 1-4).

It is important to remember the difference between expenses and withdrawals. Expenses relate to business operations; withdrawals are the result of personal needs outside the normal operations of the business.

Now let's analyze the September transactions for Cathy Hall's law firm using an expanded accounting equation that includes withdrawals, revenues, and expenses.

EXPANDED ACCOUNTING EQUATION

> Transaction D   Sept. 1–30: Provided legal services for cash, $3,000.

Transactions A, B, and C were discussed earlier, when the law office was being formed in August. See Learning Unit 1-1.

	Assets			= Liabilities +			Owner's Equity	
	Cash	+ Accts. Rec.	+ Office Equip.	= Accts. Pay.	+ C. Hall, Capital	− C. Hall, Withdr.	+ Revenue	− Expenses
BALANCE FORWARD TRANSACTION	$6,100 +3,000		+ $ 2,100	= $ 400	+ $7,800		+$3,000	
ENDING BALANCE	$9,100		+ $ 2,100	= $ 400	+ $7,800		+ $3,000	

$$\$11,200 = \$11,200$$

In the law firm's first month of operation, a total of $3,000 in cash was received for legal services performed. In the accounting equation, the asset Cash is increased by $3,000. Revenue is also increased by $3,000, resulting in an increase in owner's equity.

A revenue column was added to the basic accounting equation. Amounts are recorded in the revenue column when they are earned. They are also recorded in the assets column, either under Cash and/or under Accounts Receivable. Do not think of revenue as an asset. It is part of owner's equity. It is the revenue that creates an inward flow of cash and accounts receivable.

Transaction E   Sept. 1–30: Provided legal services on account, $4,000.

Assets			= Liabilities +		Owner's Equity			
Cash +	Accts. Rec.	+ Office Equip.	= Accts. Pay.	+ C. Hall, Capital	− C. Hall, Withdr.	+ Revenue	− Expenses	
$9,100		+ $ 2,100	= $ 400	+ $7,800		+ $3,000		BAL. FOR. TRANS.
	+4,000					+4,000		
$9,100 +	$4,000	+ $ 2,100	= $ 400	+ $7,800		+ $7,000		END. BAL.

$$\$15,200 = \$15,200$$

Cathy's law practice performed legal work on account for $4,000. The firm did not receive the cash for these earned legal fees; it accepted an unwritten promise from these clients that payment would be received in the future.

Transaction F   Sept. 1–30: Received $700 cash as partial payment from previous services performed on account.

During September some of Cathy's clients who had received services and promised to pay in the future decided to reduce what they owed the practice by $700 when their bills came due. This is shown as follows on the expanded accounting equation.

Assets			= Liabilities +		Owner's Equity			
Cash +	Accts. Rec.	+ Office Equip.	= Accts. Pay.	+ C. Hall, Capital	− C. Hall, Withdr.	+ Revenue	− Expenses	
$9,100 +	$4,000	+ $ 2,100	= $ 400	+ $7,800		+ $7,000		BAL. FOR. TRANS.
+700	−700							
$9,800 +	$3,300	+ $ 2,100	= $ 400	+ $7,800		+ $7,000		END. BAL.

$$\$15,200 = \$15,200$$

The law firm increased the asset Cash by $700 and reduced another asset, Accounts Receivable, by $700. The *total* of assets does not change. The right-hand side of the expanded accounting equation has not been touched because the total on the left-hand side of the equation has not changed. The revenue was recorded when it was earned, and the *same revenue cannot be recorded twice*. This transaction analyzes the situation *after* the revenue has been previously earned and recorded. Transaction F shows a shift in assets: more cash and less accounts receivable.

Transaction G   Sept. 1–30: Paid salaries expense, $600.

	Assets			= Liabilities +		Owner's Equity		
	Cash	+ Accts. Rec.	+ Office Equip.	= Accts. Pay.	+ C. Hall, Capital	− C. Hall, Withdr.	+ Revenue	− Expenses
BAL. FOR. TRANS.	$9,800 −600	+ $3,300	+ $ 2,100	= $ 400	+ $7,800		+ $7,000	+$600
END. BAL.	$9,200	+ $3,300	+ $ 2,100	= $ 400	+ $7,800		+ $7,000	− $600

$$\$14,600 = \$14,600$$

As expenses increase, they decrease owner's equity. This incurred expense of $600 reduces the cash by $600. Although the expense was paid, the total of our expenses to date has *increased* by $600. Keep in mind that owner's equity decreases as expenses increase, so the accounting equation remains in balance.

Transaction H   Sept. 1–30: Paid rent expense, $700.

	Assets			= Liabilities +		Owner's Equity		
	Cash	+ Accts. Rec.	+ Office Equip.	= Accts. Pay.	+ C. Hall, Capital	− C. Hall, Withdr.	+ Revenue	− Expenses
BAL. FOR. TRANS.	$9,200 −700	+ $3,300	+ $ 2,100	= $ 400	+ $7,800		+ $7,000	− $ 600 +700
END. BAL	$8,500	+ $3,300	+ $ 2,100	= $ 400	+ $7,800		+ $7,000	− $1,300

$$\$13,900 = \$13,900$$

During September the practice incurred rent expenses of $700. This rent was not paid in advance; it was paid when it came due. The payment of rent reduces the asset Cash by $700 as well as increases the expenses of the firm, resulting in a decrease in owner's equity. The firm's expenses are now $1,300.

Transaction I   Sept. 1–30: Incurred advertising expenses of $300, to be paid next month.

	Assets			= Liabilities +		Owner's Equity		
	Cash	+ Accts. Rec.	+ Office Equip.	= Accts. Pay.	+ C. Hall, Capital	− C. Hall, Withdr.	+ Revenue	− Expenses
BAL. FOR. TRANS.	$8,500	+ $3,300	+ $2,100	= $ 400 +300	+ $7,800		+ $7,000	− $1,300 +300
END. BAL.	$8,500	+ $3,300	+ $2,100	= $ 700	+ $7,800		+ $7,000	− $1,600

$$\$13,900 = \$13,900$$

Cathy ran an ad in the local newspaper and incurred an expense of $300. This increase in expenses caused a corresponding decrease in owner's equity. Because Cathy has not paid the newspaper for the advertising yet, she owes $300. Thus her liabilities (Accounts Payable) increase by $300. Eventually, when the bill comes in and is paid, both Cash and Accounts Payable will be decreased.

Transaction J   Sept. 1–30: Cathy withdrew $200 for personal use.

Assets			= Liabilities +		Owner's Equity			
Cash	+ Accts. Rec.	+ Office Equip.	= Accts. Pay.	+ C. Hall, Capital	− C. Hall, Withdr.	+ Revenue	− Expenses	
$8,500 +	$3,300	+ $ 2,100 =	$ 700	+ $7,800		+ $7,000	− $1,600	BAL. FOR. TRANS.
−200					+$200			
$8,300 +	$3,300	+ $ 2,100 =	$ 700	+ $7,800 −	$200	+ $7,000	− $1,600	END. BAL
		$13,700 = $13,700						

By taking $200 for personal use, Cathy has *increased* her withdrawals from the business by $200 and decreased the asset Cash by $200. Note that as withdrawals increase, the owner's equity *decreases*. Keep in mind that a withdrawal is *not* a business expense. It is a subdivision of owner's equity that records money or other assets an owner withdraws from the business for *personal* use.

Subdivision of Owner's Equity

Take a moment to review the subdivisions of owner's equity:

- As capital increases, owner's equity increases (see transaction A).
- As withdrawals increase, owner's equity decreases (see transaction J).
- As revenue increases, owner's equity increases (see transaction D).
- As expenses increase, owner's equity decreases (see transaction G).

Cathy Hall's Expanded Accounting Equation

The following is a summary of the expanded accounting equation for Cathy Hall's law firm.

Cathy Hall
Attorney-at-Law
Expanded Accounting Equation: A Summary

Assets			= Liabilities +		Owner's Equity				
Cash	+ Accts. Rec.	+ Office Equip.	= Accts. Pay	+ C. Hall, Capital	− C. Hall, Withdr.	+ Revenue	− Expenses		
$7,000		+$800 =		+$7,800					A.
7,000	+	800 =		7,800					BALANCE
−900		+900							B.
6,100	+	1,700 =		7,800					BALANCE
		+400	+$400						C.
6,100	+	2,100 =	400	+ 7,800					BALANCE
+3,000						+$3,000			D.
9,100	+	2,100 =	400	+ 7,800		+ 3,000			BALANCE
	+ $4,000					+4,000			E.
9,100 +	4,000	+ 2,100 =	400	+ 7,800		+ 7,000			BALANCE
+700	−700								F.
9,800 +	3,300	+ 2,100 =	400	+ 7,800		+ 7,000			BALANCE
−600							+$600		G.
9,200 +	3,300	+ 2,100 =	400	+ 7,800		+ 7,000	− 600		BALANCE
−700							+700		H.
8,500 +	3,300	+ 2,100 =	400	+ 7,800		+ 7,000	− 1,300		BALANCE
			+300				+300		I.
8,500 +	3,300	+ 2,100 =	700	+ 7,800		+ 7,000	− 1,600		BALANCE
−200					+$200				J.
$8,300 +	$3,300	+ $ 2,100 = $	700	+ $7,800 −	$200	+ $7,000	− $1,600		END BALANCE
		$13,700 = $13,700							

Learning Unit 1-3 Review

AT THIS POINT you should be able to

- Define and explain the difference between revenue and expenses. (p. 11)
- Define and explain the difference between net income and net loss. (p. 12)
- Explain the subdivisions of owner's equity. (p. 15)
- Explain the effects of withdrawals, revenue, and expenses on owner's equity. (p. 15)
- Record transactions in an expanded accounting equation and balance the basic accounting equation as a means of checking the accuracy of your calculations. (p. 15)

SELF-REVIEW QUIZ 1-3

(The blank forms you need are on page 3 of the *Study Guide and Working Papers*. See your DVD for worked-out solutions.)

Record the following transactions into the expanded accounting equation for the Bing Company. Note that all titles have a beginning balance.

1. Received cash revenue, $4,000.
2. Billed customers for services rendered, $6,000.
3. Received a bill for telephone expenses (to be paid next month), $125.
4. Bob Bing withdrew cash for personal use, $500.
5. Received $1,000 from customers in partial payment for services performed in transaction 2.

> *Quiz Tip:*
> Think of expenses and withdrawals as *increasing*. As they increase, they will reduce the owner's rights. For example, Transaction 4 withdrawals increased by $500, resulting in withdrawals increasing from $800 to $1,300. This represents a $500 decrease to owner's equity.

SOLUTION TO SELF-REVIEW QUIZ 1-3

	Cash	+	Accts. Rec.	+	Cleaning Equip.	=	Accts. Pay.	+	B. Bing, Capital	−	B. Bing, Withdr.	+	Revenue	−	Expenses
BEG. BALANCE	$10,000	+	$2,500	+	$6,500	=	$1,000	+	$11,800	−	$800	+	$9,000	−	$2,000
1.	+4,000														
BALANCE	14,000	+	2,500	+	6,500	=	1,000	+	11,800	−	800	+	13,000	−	2,000
2.			+6,000												
BALANCE	14,000	+	8,500	+	6,500	=	1,000	+	11,800	−	800	+	19,000	−	2,000
3.							+125								+125
BALANCE	14,000	+	8,500	+	6,500	=	1,125	+	11,800	−	800	+	19,000	−	2,125
4.	−500										+500				
BALANCE	13,500	+	8,500	+	6,500	=	1,125	+	11,800	−	1,300	+	19,000	−	2,125
5.	+1,000		−1,000												
END BALANCE	$14,500	+	$7,500	+	$6,500	=	$1,125	+	$11,800	−	$1,300	+	$19,000	−	$2,125

$$\$28,500 = \$28,500$$

Learning Unit 1-4   Preparing Financial Statements

Cathy Hall would like to be able to find out whether her firm is making a profit, so she asks her accountant whether he can measure the firm's financial performance on a monthly basis. Her accountant replies that there are a number of financial statements that he can prepare, such as the income statement, which shows how well the law firm has performed over a specific period of time. The accountant can use the information in the income statement to prepare other reports.

THE INCOME STATEMENT

An income statement is an accounting statement that shows business results in terms of revenue and expenses. If revenues are greater than expenses, the report shows net income. If expenses are greater than revenues, the report shows net loss. An income statement can cover one, three, six, or twelve months. It cannot cover more than one year. The statement shows the result of all revenues and expenses throughout the entire period and not just as of a specific date. The income statement for Cathy Hall's law firm is shown in Figure 1-5.

> The income statement is prepared from data found in the revenue and expense columns of the expanded accounting equation.

Points to Remember in Preparing an Income Statement

Heading   The heading of an income statement tells the same three things as all other accounting statements: the company's name, the name of the statement, and the period of time the statement covers.

The Setup   As you can see on the income statement, the inside column of numbers ($600, $700, and $300) is used to subtotal all expenses ($1,600) before subtracting them from revenue ($7,000 − $1,600 = $5,400).

Operating expenses may be listed in alphabetical order, in order of largest amounts to smallest, or in a set order established by the accountant.

> The inside column of numbers ($600, $700, $300) is used to subtotal all expenses ($1,600) before subtracting from revenue.

THE STATEMENT OF OWNER'S EQUITY

As we said, the income statement is a business statement that shows business results in terms of revenue and expenses, but how does net income or net loss affect owner's

Figure 1-5
The Income Statement

CATHY HALL, ATTORNEY-AT-LAW INCOME STATEMENT FOR MONTH ENDED SEPTEMBER 30, 200X		
Revenue:		
Legal Fees		$ 7 0 0 0 00
Operating Expenses:		
Salaries Expense	$ 6 0 0 00	
Rent Expense	7 0 0 00	
Advertising Expense	3 0 0 00	
Total Operating Expenses		1 6 0 0 00
Net Income		$ 5 4 0 0 00

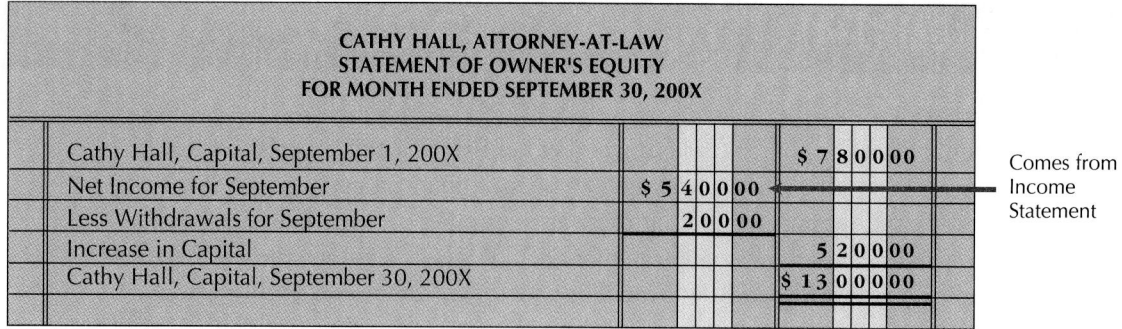

Figure 1-6 Statement of Owner's Equity

equity? To find that out we have to look at a second type of statement, the **statement of owner's equity**.

The statement of owner's equity shows for a certain period of time what changes occurred in Cathy Hall, Capital. The statement of owner's equity is shown in Figure 1-6 above.

The capital of Cathy Hall can be

Increased by:	Owner Investment Net Income (Revenue − Expenses)
Decreased by:	Owner Withdrawals Net Loss (Expenses Greater than Revenue)

Remember, a withdrawal is *not* a business expense and thus is not involved in the calculation of net income or net loss on the income statement. It appears on the statement of owner's equity. The statement of owner's equity summarizes the effects of all the subdivisions of owner's equity (revenue, expenses, withdrawals) on beginning capital. The ending capital figure ($13,000) will be the beginning figure in the next statement of owner's equity.

Suppose Cathy's law firm had operated at a loss in the month of September. Suppose instead of net income there was a $600 net loss and an additional investment of $800 was made on September 15. Figure 1-7 shows how the statement would look if that had happened.

Figure 1-7

CATHY HALL, ATTORNEY-AT-LAW STATEMENT OF OWNER'S EQUITY FOR MONTH ENDED SEPTEMBER 30, 200X		
Cathy Hall, Capital, September 1, 200X		$ 7 8 0 0 00
Additional Investment, September 15, 200X		8 0 0 00
Total Investment for September		$ 8 6 0 0 00
Less: Net Loss for September	$ 6 0 0 00	
Withdrawals for September	2 0 0 00	
Decrease in Capital		8 0 0 00
Cathy Hall, Capital, September 30, 200X		$ 7 8 0 0 00

THE BALANCE SHEET

Now let's look at how to prepare a balance sheet from the expanded accounting equation (see Fig. 1-8). As you can see, the asset accounts (cash, accounts receivable, and office equipment) appear on the left side of the balance sheet.

Accounts payable and Cathy Hall, Capital appear on the right side. Notice that the $13,000 of capital can be calculated within the accounting equation or can be read from the statement of owner's equity.

MAIN ELEMENTS OF THE INCOME STATEMENT, THE STATEMENT OF OWNER'S EQUITY, AND THE BALANCE SHEET

In this chapter we have discussed three financial statements: the income statement, the statement of owner's equity, and the balance sheet. A fourth statement, called the statement of cash flows, will not be covered at this time. Let us review what elements of the expanded accounting equation go into each statement and the usual order in which the statements are prepared. Figure 1-8 presents a diagram of the accounting equation and the balance sheet. Table 1-3 summarizes the following points:

- The income statement is prepared first; it includes revenues and expenses and shows net income or net loss. This net income or net loss is used to update the next statement, the statement of owner's equity.
- The statement of owner's equity is prepared second; it includes beginning capital and any additional investments, the net income or net loss shown on the income statement, withdrawals, and the total, which is the ending capital. The balance in Capital comes from the statement of owner's equity.
- The balance sheet is prepared last; it includes the final balances of each of the elements listed in the accounting equation under Assets and Liabilities. The balance in Capital comes from the statement of owner's equity.

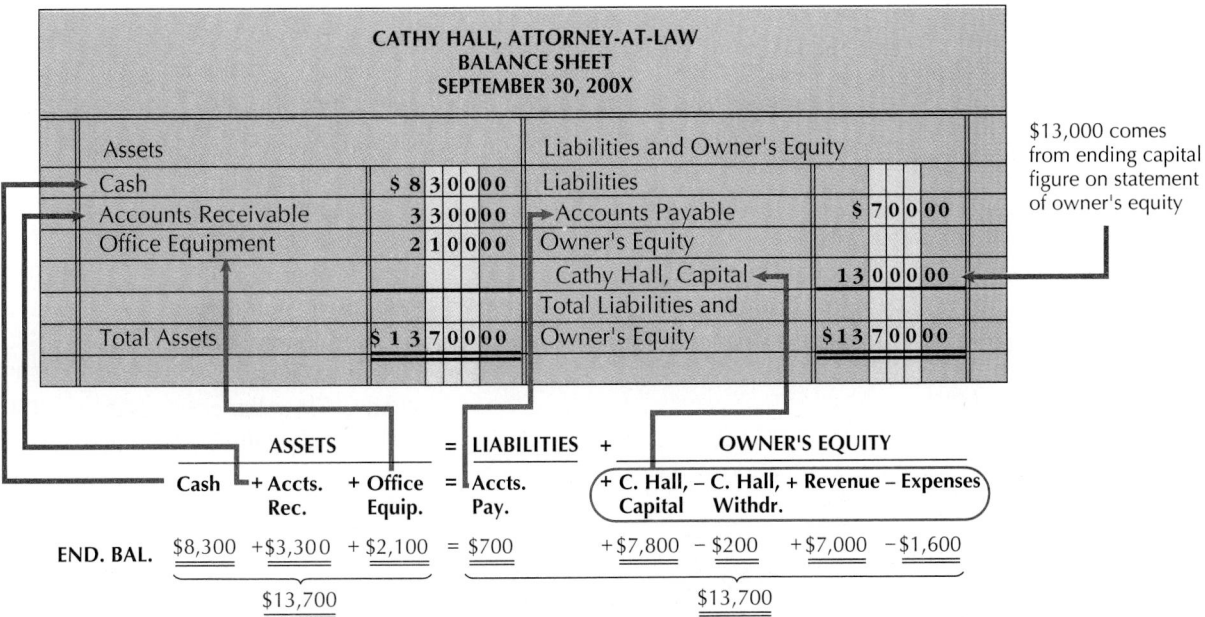

Figure 1-8 The Accounting Equation and the Balance Sheet

TABLE 1-3 What Goes on Each Financial Statement

	Income Statement	Statement of Owner's Equity	Balance Sheet
Assets			X
Liabilities			X
Capital* (beg.)		X	
Capital (end)		X	X
Withdrawals		X	
Revenues	X		
Expenses	X		

Note: Additional Investments go on the Statement of Owner's Equity.

Learning Unit 1-4 Review

AT THIS POINT you should be able to

- Define and state the purpose of the income statement, the statement of owner's equity, and the balance sheet. (p. 17)
- Discuss why the income statement should be prepared first. (p. 17)
- Show what happens on a statement of owner's equity if there is a net loss. (p. 18)
- Compare and contrast these three financial statements. (p. 19)
- Calculate a new figure for capital on the statement of owner's equity and the balance sheet. (p. 19)

SELF-REVIEW QUIZ 1-4

(The blank forms you need are on pages 4 and 5 of the *Study Guide and Working Papers*. See your DVD for worked-out solutions.)

From the following balances for Rusty Realty prepare:

1. Income statement for the month ended November 30, 200X.

2. Statement of owner's equity for the month ended November 30, 200X.

3. Balances as of November 30, 200X.

Cash	$4,000	R. Rusty, Capital	
Accounts Receivable	1,370	November 1, 200X	$5,000
Store Furniture	1,490	R. Rusty, Withdrawals	100
Accounts Payable	900	Commissions Earned	1,500
		Rent Expense	200
		Advertising Expense	150
		Salaries Expense	90

SOLUTION TO SELF-REVIEW QUIZ 1-4

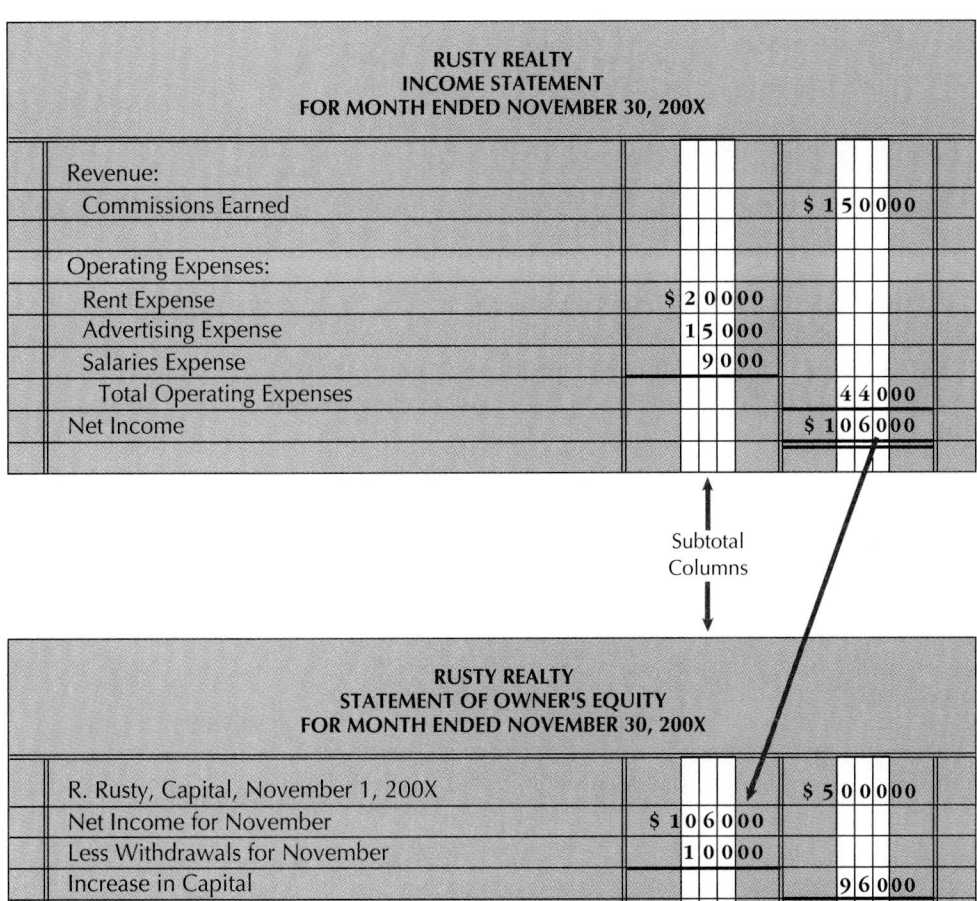

Figure 1-9
Financial Reports

Quiz Tip:
Note that the inside column is only used for subtotaling.

The net income from the income statement is used to help build the statement of owner's equity.

The new figure for capital from the statement of owner's equity is used as the capital figure on the balance sheet.

RUSTY REALTY
INCOME STATEMENT
FOR MONTH ENDED NOVEMBER 30, 200X

Revenue:		
Commissions Earned		$ 1 50 0 00
Operating Expenses:		
Rent Expense	$ 2 0 0 00	
Advertising Expense	1 5 0 00	
Salaries Expense	9 0 00	
Total Operating Expenses		4 4 0 00
Net Income		$ 1 06 0 00

Subtotal Columns

RUSTY REALTY
STATEMENT OF OWNER'S EQUITY
FOR MONTH ENDED NOVEMBER 30, 200X

R. Rusty, Capital, November 1, 200X		$ 5 00 0 00
Net Income for November	$ 1 06 0 00	
Less Withdrawals for November	1 0 0 00	
Increase in Capital		9 6 0 00
R. Rusty, Capital, November 30, 200X		$ 5 96 0 00

RUSTY REALTY
BALANCE SHEET
NOVEMBER 30, 200X

Assets		Liabilities and Owner's Equity	
Cash	$ 4 00 0 00	Liabilities	
Accounts Receivable	1 37 0 00	Accounts Payable	$ 9 0 00
Store Furniture	1 49 0 00		
		Owner's Equity	
		R. Rusty, Capital	5 96 0 00
		Total Liabilities and	
Total Assets	$ 6 86 0 00	Owner's Equity	$ 6 86 0 00

SOLUTIONS & TIPS TO COMPREHENSIVE PROBLEM: PUTTING THE PIECES TOGETHER

(The blank forms you need are on pages 6 and 7 of the *Study Guide and Working Papers*.)

Michael Brown opened his law office on June 1, 200X. During the first month of operations, Michael conducted the following transactions:

1. Invested $6,000 in cash into the law practice.
2. Paid $600 for office equipment.
3. Purchased additional office equipment on account, $1,000.
4. Received cash for performing legal services for clients, $2,000.
5. Paid salaries, $800.
6. Performed legal services for clients on account, $1,000.
7. Paid rent, $1,200.
8. Withdrew $500 from his law practice for personal use.
9. Received $500 from customers in partial payment for legal services performed, transaction 6.

Assignment

a. Record these transactions in the expanded accounting equation.
b. Prepare the financial statements at June 30 for Michael Brown, Attorney-at-Law.

Solution to Comprehensive Problem

	Assets			= Liabilities +		Owner's Equity			
A.	Cash +	Accts. Rec.	+ Office Equip.	= Accounts Payable	+ M. Brown, Capital	− M. Brown, Withdr.	+ Legal Fees	− Expenses	
1.	+$6,000				+$6,000				
BAL.	6,000		=		6,000				
2.	−600		+$600						
BAL.	5,400	+	600 =		6,000				
3.			+1,000	+$1,000					
BAL.	5,400	+	1,600 =	1,000 +	6,000				
4.	+2,000						+$2,000		
BAL.	7,400	+	1,600 =	1,000 +	6,000		+ 2,000		
5.	−800							+$800	
BAL.	6,600	+	1,600 =	1,000 +	6,000		+ 2,000 −	800	
6.	+$1,000						+1,000		
BAL.	6,600 +	1,000 +	1,600 =	1,000 +	6,000		+ 3,000 −	800	
7.	−1,200							+1,200	
BAL.	5,400 +	1,000 +	1,600 =	1,000 +	6,000		+ 3,000 −	2,000	
8.	−500					+$500			
BAL.	4,900 +	1,000 +	1,600 =	1,000 +	6,000 −	500	+ 3,000 −	2,000	
9.	+500	−500							
END BAL.	$5,400 +	$ 500 +	$1,600 =	$1,000 +	$6,000 −	$500	+ $3,000 −	$2,000	

$$\$7,500 = \$7,500$$

Solution Tips to Expanded Accounting Equation

A.

- **Transaction 1:** The business increased its Cash by $6,000. Owner's Equity (capital) increased when Michael supplied the cash to the business.
- **Transaction 2:** There was a shift in assets when the equipment was purchased. The business lowered its Cash by $600, and a new column—Equipment—was increased for the $600 of equipment that was bought. The amount of capital is not touched because the owner did not supply any new funds.
- **Transaction 3:** When creditors supply $1,000 of additional equipment, the business Accounts Payable shows the debt. The business had increased what it *owes* the creditors.
- **Transaction 4:** Legal Fees, a subdivision of Owner's Equity, is increased when the law firm provides a service even if no money is received. The service provides an inward flow of $2,000 Cash, an asset. Remember that Legal Fees are *not* an asset. As Legal Fees increase, Owner's Equity increases.
- **Transaction 5:** The salary paid by Michael shows an $800 increase in Expenses and a corresponding decrease in Owner's Equity.
- **Transaction 6:** Michael did the work and earned the $1,000. That $1,000 is recorded as revenue. This time the Legal Fees create an inward flow of assets called Accounts Receivable for $1,000. Remember that Legal Fees are *not* an asset. They are a subdivision of Owner's Equity.
- **Transaction 7:** The $1,200 rent expense reduces Owner's Equity as well as Cash.
- **Transaction 8:** Withdrawals are for personal use. Here, the business decreases Cash by $500 while Michael withdrawals increase $500. Withdrawals decrease the Owner's Equity.
- **Transaction 9:** This transaction does not reflect new revenue in the form of Legal Fees. It is only a shift in assets: more Cash and less Accounts Receivable.

B-1.

MICHAEL BROWN, ATTORNEY-AT-LAW
INCOME STATEMENT
FOR MONTH ENDED JUNE 30, 200X

Revenue:		
Legal Fees		$3,000
Operating expenses:		
Salaries expense	$ 800	
Rent expense	1,200	
Total operating expenses		2,000
Net income		$1,000

B-2.

MICHAEL BROWN, ATTORNEY-AT-LAW
STATEMENT OF OWNER'S EQUITY
FOR MONTH ENDED JUNE 30, 200X

Michael Brown, Capital, June 1, 200X		$6,000
Net income for June	$1,000	
Less withdrawals for June	500	
Increase in Capital		500
Michael Brown, Capital, June 30, 200X		$6,500

B-3.

MICHAEL BROWN, ATTORNEY-AT-LAW
BALANCE SHEET
JUNE 30, 200X

Assets		Liabilities and Owner's Equity	
Cash	$5,400	Liabilities	
Accounts Receivable	500	Accounts Payable	$1,000
Office Equipment	1,600	Owner's Equity	
		M. Brown, Capital	6,500
Total Assets	$7,500	Total Liabilities and Owner's Equity	$7,500

Solution Tips to Financial Statements

B-1. The income statement lists only Revenues and Expenses for a period of time. The inside column is for subtotaling. Withdrawals are not listed here.

B-2. The statement of Owner's Equity takes the net income figure of $1,000 and adds it to Beginning Capital less any withdrawals. This new capital figure of $6,500 will go on the balance sheet. This statement shows changes in Capital for a period of time.

B-3. The $5,400, $500, $1,600, and $1,000 came from the totals of the expanded accounting equation. The Capital figure of $6,500 came from the statement of Owner's Equity. This balance sheet reports Assets, Liabilities, and a new figure for Capital at a specific date.

Summary of Key Points

Learning Unit 1-1

1. The functions of accounting involve analyzing, recording, classifying, summarizing, reporting, and interpreting financial information.
2. A sole proprietorship is a business owned by one person. A partnership is a business owned by two or more persons. A corporation is a business owned by stockholders. All forms of business organizations are found in Internet businesses.
3. Bookkeeping is the recording part of accounting.
4. The computer is a tool to use in the accounting process.
5. Assets = Liabilities + Owner's Equity is the basic accounting equation that aids in analyzing business transactions.
6. Liabilities represent amounts owed to creditors, whereas capital represents what is invested by the owner.
7. Capital does not mean cash. Capital is the owner's current investment. The owner could have invested equipment that was purchased before the new business was started.
8. In a shift of assets, the composition of assets changes, but the total of assets does not change. For example, if a bill is paid by a customer, the firm increases Cash (an asset) but decreases Accounts Receivable (an asset), so there is no overall increase in assets; total assets remain the same. When you borrow money from a bank, you have an increase in cash (an asset) and an increase in liabilities; overall there is an increase in assets, not just a shift.

Learning Unit 1-2

1. The balance sheet is a statement written as of a particular date. It lists the assets, liabilities, and owner's equity of a business. The heading of the balance sheet answers the questions *who, what,* and *when* (as of a specific date).
2. The balance sheet is a formal statement of a financial position.

Learning Unit 1-3

1. Revenue generates an inward flow of assets. Expenses generate an outward flow of assets or a potential outward flow. Revenue and expenses are subdivisions of owner's equity. Revenue is not an asset.
2. When revenue totals more than expenses, net income is the result; when expenses total more than revenue, net loss is the result.
3. Owner's equity can be subdivided into four elements: capital, withdrawals, revenue, and expenses.
4. Withdrawals decrease owner's equity, revenue increases owner's equity, and expenses decrease owner's equity. A withdrawal is not a business expense; it is for personal use.

Learning Unit 1-4

1. The income statement is a statement written for a specific period of time that lists earned revenue and expenses incurred to produce the earned revenue. The net income or net loss will be used in the statement of owner's equity.
2. The statement of owner's equity reveals the causes of a change in capital. This statement lists any investments, net income (or net loss), and withdrawals. The ending figure for capital will be used on the balance sheet.
3. The balance sheet uses the ending balances of assets and liabilities from the accounting equation and the capital from the statement of owner's equity.
4. The income statement should be prepared first because the information on it about net income or net loss is used to prepare the statement of owner's equity, which in turn provides information about capital for the balance sheet. In this way one statement builds upon the next, beginning with the income statement.

Key Terms

Accounting   A system that measures the business's activities in financial terms, provides written reports and financial statements about those activities, and communicates these reports to decision makers and others.

Accounts payable   Amounts owed to creditors that result from the purchase of goods or services on account: a liability.

Accounts receivable   An asset that indicates amounts owed by customers.

Assets   Properties (resources) of value owned by a business (cash, supplies, equipment, land).

Balance sheet   A statement, as of a particular date, that shows the amount of assets owned by a business as well as the amount of claims (liabilities and owner's equity) against these assets.

Basic accounting equation   Assets = Liabilities + Owner's Equity.

Bookkeeping   The recording function of the accounting process.

Capital   The owner's investment of equity in the company.

Corporation   A type of business organization that is owned by stockholders. Stockholders usually are not personally liable for the corporation's debts.

Creditor   Someone who has a claim to assets.

Ending capital   Beginning Capital + Additional Investments + Net Income − Withdrawals = Ending Capital. Or: Beginning Capital + Additional Investments − Net Loss − Withdrawals = Ending Capital.

Equities   The interest or financial claim of creditors (liabilities) and owners (owner's equity) who supply the assets to a firm.

Expanded accounting equation   Assets = Liabilities + Capital − Withdrawals + Revenue − Expenses.

Expense   A cost incurred in running a business by consuming goods or services in producing revenue; a subdivision of owner's equity. When expenses increase, there is a decrease in owner's equity.

Generally accepted accounting principles (GAAP)   The procedures and guidelines that must be followed during the accounting process.

Income statement   An accounting statement that details the performance of a firm (revenue minus expenses) for a specific period of time.

Liabilities   Obligations that come due in the future. Liabilities result in increasing the financial rights or claims of creditors to assets.

Manufacturer   Business that makes a product and sells it to its customers.

Merchandise company   Business that buys a product from a manufacturing company to sell to its customers.

Net income   When revenue totals more than expenses, the result is net income.

Net loss   When expenses total more than revenue, the result is net loss.

Owner's equity   Rights or financial claims to the assets of a business (in the accounting equation, assets minus liabilities).

Partnership   A form of business organization that has at least two owners. The partners usually are personally liable for the partnership's debts.

Revenue   An amount earned by performing services for customers or selling goods to customers; it can be in the form of cash and/or accounts receivable. A subdivision of owner's equity: As revenue increases, owner's equity increases.

Service company   Business that provides a service.

Shift in assets   A shift that occurs when the composition of the assets has changed, but the total of the assets remains the same.

Sole proprietorship   A type of business ownership that has one owner. The owner is personally liable for paying the business's debts.

Statement of financial position   Another name for a balance sheet.

Statement of owner's equity   A financial statement that reveals the change in capital. The ending figure for capital is then placed on the balance sheet.

Supplies   One type of asset acquired by a firm; it has a much shorter life than equipment.

Withdrawals   A subdivision of owner's equity that records money or other assets an owner withdraws from a business for personal use.

Blueprint: Financial Statements

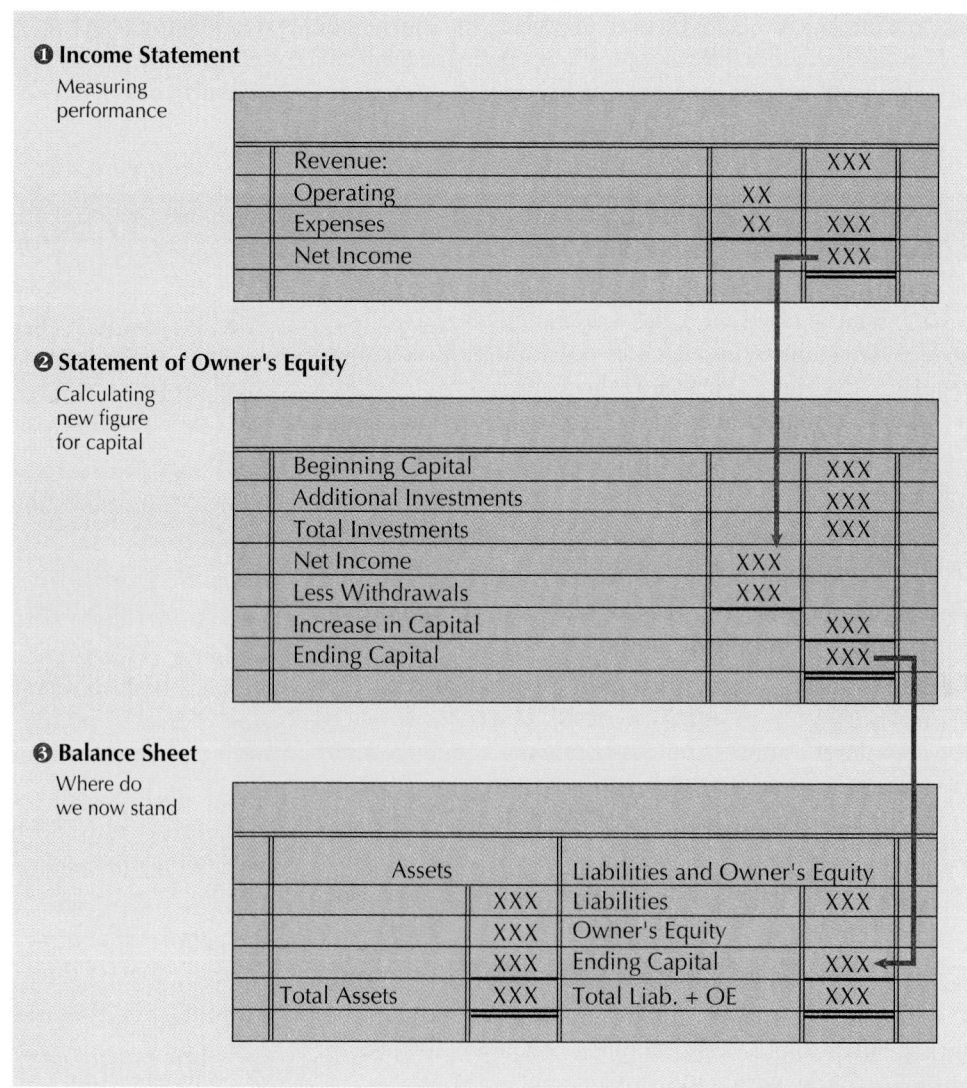

Questions, Mini Exercises, Exercises, and Problems

Discussion Questions

1. What are the functions of accounting?
2. Define, compare, and contrast sole proprietorships, partnerships, and corporations.
3. How are businesses classified?
4. What is the relationship of bookkeeping to accounting?
5. List the three elements of the basic accounting equation.
6. Define capital.
7. The total of the left-hand side of the accounting equation must equal the total of the right-hand side. True or false? Please explain.
8. A balance sheet tells a company where it is going and how well it will perform. True or false? Please explain.
9. Revenue is an asset. True or false? Please explain.
10. Owner's equity is subdivided into what categories?
11. A withdrawal is a business expense. True or false? Please explain.
12. As expenses increase they cause owner's equity to increase. Defend or reject.
13. What does an income statement show?
14. The statement of owner's equity only calculates ending withdrawals. True or false? Please explain.

Mini Exercises

(The blank forms you need are on page 9 of the *Study Guide and Working Papers.*)

Classifying Accounts

1. Classify each of the following items as an Asset (A), Liability (L), or Part of Owner's Equity (OE).

   a. Panasonic DVD   _____
   b. Accounts Payable   _____
   c. B. Aster, Capital   _____
   d. Office Supplies   _____
   e. Cash   _____
   f. Sony Digital Camera   _____

The Accounting Equation

2. Complete the following statements.

   a. A _____ _____ _____ results when the total of the assets remains the same but the makeup of the assets has changed.
   b. Assets − _____ = Owner's Equity.
   c. Capital does not mean _____.

Shift Versus Increase in Assets

3. Identify which transaction results in a shift in assets (S) and which transaction causes an increase in assets (I).

   a. Office Max bought computer equipment for cash.
   b. The Gap bought office equipment on account.

The Balance Sheet

4. From the following, calculate what would be the total of assets on the balance sheet.

H. Sung, Capital	$11,000
Word Processing Equipment	1,000
Accounts Payable	2,000
Cash	12,000

The Accounting Equation Expanded

5. From the following, which are subdivisions of Owner's Equity?

   a. Land _____   e. Accounts Payable _____
   b. M. Kaminsky, Capital _____   f. Rent Expense _____
   c. Accounts Receivable _____   g. Office Equipment _____
   d. M. Kaminsky, Withdrawals _____   h. Hair Salon Fees Earned _____

Identifying Assets

6. Identify which of the following are *not* assets.

   a. Fax Machines _____   c. Legal Fees Earned _____
   b. Accounts Payable _____   d. Accounts Receivable _____

The Accounting Equation Expanded

7. Which of the following statements are false?

   a. _____ Revenue is an asset.
   b. _____ Revenue is a subdivision of Owner's Equity.
   c. _____ Revenue provides an inward flow of Cash and/or Accounts Receivable.
   d. _____ Withdrawals are part of Total Assets.

Preparing Financial Statements

8. Indicate whether the following items would appear on the income statement (IS), statement of owner's equity (OE), or balance sheet (BS).

   a. _____ B. Clo, Withdrawals   e. _____ Commission Fees Earned
   b. _____ Office Supplies   f. _____ Salaries Expense
   c. _____ Accounts Payable   g. _____ B. Clo, Capital (Beg.)
   d. _____ Computer Equipment   h. _____ Accounts Receivable

Preparing Financial Statements

9. Indicate next to each statement whether it refers to the income statement (IS), statement of owner's equity (OE), or balance sheet (BS).

   a. _____ Calculate new figure for Capital
   b. _____ Prepared as of a particular date
   c. _____ Statement that is prepared first
   d. _____ Statement listing Revenues and Expenses

Exercises

(The forms you need are on pages 10–12 of the *Study Guide and Working Papers*.)

1-1. Complete the following table:

The accounting equation.

	Assets	=	Liabilities	+	Owner's Equity
a.	10,000	=	?	+	$2,000
b.	?	=	$6,000	+	$8,000
c.	$10,000	=	$4,000	+	?

1-2. Record the following transactions in the basic accounting equation. Treat each one separately.

Assets = Liabilities + Owner's Equity

a. Ron invests $90,000 in company.
b. Bought equipment for cash, $600.
c. Bought equipment on account, $900.

1-3. From the following, prepare a balance sheet for Avon's Cleaners at the end of November 200X: Cash, $40,000; Cleaning Equipment, $8,000; Accounts Payable, $19,000; A. Avon, Capital.

1-4. Record the following transactions into the expanded accounting equation. The running balance may be omitted for simplicity.

Assets			= Liabilities +			Owner's Equity		
Cash +	Accounts Receivable	Computer Equipment	= Accounts Payable	+ B. Wong, Capital	− B. Wong, Withdrawals	+ Revenues	− Expenses

a. Bill invested $60,000 in a computer company.
b. Bought computer equipment on account, $7,000.
c. Bill paid personal telephone bill from company checkbook, $200.
d. Received cash for services rendered, $14,000.
e. Billed customers for services rendered for month, $30,000.
f. Paid current rent expense, $4,000.
g. Paid supplies expense, $1,500.

1-5. From the following account balances, prepare in proper form for June (a) an income statement, (b) a statement of owner's equity, and (c) a balance sheet for French Realty.

Cash	$3,310	S. French, Withdrawals	$ 40
Accounts Receivable	1,490	Professional Fees	2,900
Office Equipment	6,700	Salaries Expense	500
Accounts Payable	2,000	Utilities Expense	360
S. French, Capital, June 1, 200X	8,000	Rent Expense	500

Group A Problems

(The forms you need are on pages 13–19 of the *Study Guide and Working Papers.*)

1A-1. Lee Stone decided to open Lee's Nail Care Center. Lee completed the following transactions:

a. Invested $18,000 cash from her personal bank account into the business.
b. Bought equipment for cash, $4,000.
c. Bought additional equipment on account, $1,000.
d. Paid $400 cash to partially reduce what was owed from transaction C.

Based on this information, record these transactions into the basic accounting equation.

1A-2. Joyce Hill is the accountant for Green's Advertising Service. From the following information, her task is to construct a balance sheet as of September 30, 200X, in proper form. Could you help her?

Building	$35,000	Cash	$10,000
Accounts Payable	30,000	Equipment	14,000
Green, Capital	29,000		

Recoding transactions into the expanded accounting equation.

Preparing a balance sheet.

Recording transactions into the accounting equation.

Preparing the income statement, statement of owner's equity, and balance sheet.

The accounting equation.

Check Figure:
Total Assets $18,600

Preparing a balance sheet.

Check Figure:
Total Assets $59,000

Recording transactions in the expanded accounting equation.

Check Figure:
Total Assets $15,640

1A-3. At the end of November, Rick Fox decided to open his own typing service. Analyze the following transactions he completed by recording their effects into the expanded accounting equation.

  a. Invested $10,000 in his typing service.
  b. Bought new office equipment on account, $4,000.
  c. Received cash for typing services rendered, $500.
  d. Performed typing services on account, $2,100.
  e. Paid secretary's salary, $350.
  f. Paid office supplies expense for the month, $210.
  g. Rent expenses for office due but unpaid, $900.
  h. Withdrew cash for personal use, $400.

Preparing the income statement, statement of owner's equity, and balance sheet.

Check Figure:
Total Assets $3,385

1A-4. Jane West, owner of West Stenciling Service, has requested that you prepare from the following balances (a) an income statement for June 200X, (b) a statement of owner's equity for June, and (c) a balance sheet as of June 30, 200X.

Cash	$2,300	Stenciling Fees	$3,000
Accounts Receivable	400	Advertising Expense	110
Equipment	685	Repair Expense	25
Accounts Payable	310	Travel Expense	250
J. West, Capital, June 1, 200X	1,200	Supplies Expense	190
J. West, Withdrawals	300	Rent Expense	250

Comprehensive problem.

1A-5. John Tobey, a retired army officer, opened Tobey's Catering Service. As his accountant, analyze the transactions listed next and present them in proper form.

  a. The analysis of the transactions by using the expanded accounting equation.
  b. A balance sheet showing the position of the firm before opening for business on October 31, 200X.
  c. An income statement for the month of November.
  d. A statement of owner's equity for November.
  e. A balance sheet as of November 30, 200X.

200X
Oct. 25 John Tobey invested $20,000 in the catering business from his personal savings account.

Check Figure:
Total Assets,
Nov. 30 $24,060

       27 Bought equipment for cash from Munroe Co., $700
       28 Bought additional equipment on account from Ryan Co., $1,000.
       29 Paid $600 to Ryan Co. as partial payment of the October 28 transaction.

(You should now prepare your balance sheet as of October 31, 200X)
Nov. 1 Catered a graduation and immediately collected cash, $2,400.
       5 Paid salaries of employees, $690.
       8 Prepared desserts for customers on account, $300.
     10 Received $100 cash as partial payment of November 8 transaction.
     15 Paid telephone bill, $60.
     17 Paid his home electric bill from the company's checkbook, $90.
     20 Catered a wedding and received cash, $1,800.
     25 Bought additional equipment on account, $400.
     28 Rent expense due but unpaid, $600.
     30 Paid supplies expense, $400.

Group B Problems

(The forms you need are on pages 13–19 of the *Study Guide and Working Papers*.)

The accounting equation.

1B-1. Lee Stone began a new business called Lee's Nail Care Center. The following transactions resulted:

  a. Lee invested $21,000 cash from her personal bank account into the Nail Care Center.

b. Bought equipment on account, $1,800.

c. Paid $800 cash to partially reduce what was owed from transaction B.

d. Purchased additional equipment for cash, $3,000.

Record these transactions into the basic accounting equation.

Check Figure:
Total Assets $22,000

1B-2. Joyce Hill, accountant, has asked you to prepare a balance sheet as of September 30, 200X, for Green's Advertising Service. Could you assist Joyce?

Preparing a balance sheet.

R. Green, Capital	$19,000
Accounts Payable	70,000
Equipment	41,000
Building	16,000
Cash	32,000

Check Figure:
Total Assets $89,000

1B-3. Rick Fox decided to open his own typing service company at the end of November. Analyze the following transactions by recording their effects on the expanded accounting equation:

Recording transactions in the expanded accounting equation.

a. Rick invested $9,000 in the typing service.

b. Purchased new office equipment on account, $3,000.

c. Received cash for typing services rendered, $1,290.

d. Paid secretary's salary, $310.

e. Billed customers for typing services rendered, $2,690.

f. Paid rent expense for the month, $500.

g. Rick withdrew cash for personal use, $350.

h. Advertising expense due but unpaid, $100.

Check Figure:
Total Assets $14,820

1B-4. Jane West, owner of West Stenciling Service, has requested that you prepare from the following balances (a) an income statement for June 200X, (b) a statement of owner's equity for June, and (c) a balance sheet as of June 30, 200X.

Preparing an income statement, statement of owner's equity, and balance sheet.

Cash	$2,043	Stenciling Fees	$1,098
Accounts Receivable	1,140	Advertising Expense	135
Equipment	540	Repair Expense	45
Accounts Payable	45	Travel Expense	90
J. West, Capital, June 1, 200X	3,720	Supplies Expense	270
J. West, Withdrawals	360	Rent Expense	240

Check Figure:
Total Assets $3,723

1B-5. John Tobey, a retired army officer, opened Tobey's Catering Service. As his accountant, analyze the transactions and present the following information in proper form:

a. The analysis of the transactions by using the expanded accounting equation.

b. A balance sheet showing the financial position of the firm before opening on November 1, 200X.

Comprehensive problem.

c. An income statement for the month of November.

d. A statement of owner's equity for November.

e. A balance sheet as of November 30, 200X.

Check Figure:
Total Assets,
Nov. 30 $25,005

200X

Oct. 25 John Tobey invested $17,500 in the catering business.

27 Bought equipment on account from Munroe Co., $900.

28 Bought equipment for cash from Ryan Co., $1,500.

29 Paid $300 to Munroe Co. as partial payment of the October 27 transaction.

Nov. 1 Catered a business luncheon and immediately collected cash, $2,000.

5 Paid salaries of employees, $350.

8 Provided catering services to Northwest Community College on account, $4,500.

10   Received from Northwest Community College $1,000 cash as partial payment of November 8 transaction.
15   Paid telephone bill, $95.
17   John paid his home mortgage from the company's checkbook, $650.
20   Provided catering services and received cash, $1,800.
25   Bought additional equipment on account, $300.
28   Rent expense due but unpaid, $750.
30   Paid supplies expense, $600.

Real-World Applications

1R-1. You have just been hired to prepare, if possible, an income statement for the year ended December 31, 200X, for Roger's Window Washing Company. The problem is that Roger Smith kept only the following records (on the back of a piece of cardboard):

Figure 1-10

Dollars in:
    My investment $ 1,200
    Window cleaning   11,376
    Loan from brother-in-law   4,000

Dollars out:
    Salaries $5,080
    Withdrawals   6,200
    Supplies expense   1,400

What I owe or they owe me
A. People who work for me but I still owe salaries to $1,800
B. Owe bank interest of $300
C. Work done but clients still owe me $2,900
D. Advertising bill due but not paid $95

Assume that Roger's Window Washing Company records all revenues when earned and all expenses when incurred.

You feel that it is part of your job to tell Roger how to organize his records better. What would you tell him?

1R-2. While Jon Lune was on a business trip, he asked Abby Slowe, the bookkeeper for Lune Co., to try to complete a balance sheet for the year ended December 31, 200X. Abby, who had been on the job only two months, submitted the following:

Figure 1-11

LUNE CO. FOR THE YEAR ENDED DECEMBER 31, 200X			
Building	$446 000 00	Accounts Payable	$127 604 00
Land	729 35 00	Accounts Receivable	104 337 00
Notes Payable	753 28 00	Auto	14 268 00
Cash	100 16 00	Desks	6 825 00
J. Lune, Capital	?	Total Equity	$250 034 00

1. Could you help Abby fix as well as complete the balance sheet?

2. What written recommendations would you make about the bookkeeper? Should she be retained?

3. Suppose that (a) Jon Lune invested an additional $20,000 in cash as well as additional desks with a value of $8,000 and (b) Lune Co. bought an auto for $6,000 that was originally marked $8,000, paying $2,000 down and issuing a note for the balance. Could you prepare an updated balance sheet?

YOU make the call

Critical Thinking/Ethical Case

(The forms you need are on page 8 of the *Study Guide and Working Papers.*)

1R-3. Paul Kloss, accountant for Lowe & Co., traveled to New York on company business. His total expenses came to $350. Paul felt that because the trip extended over the weekend he would "pad" his expense account with an additional $100 of expenses. After all, weekends represent his own time, not the company's. What would you do? Write your specific recommendations to Paul.

Internet Exercises: Microstrategy: Best in Business Intelligence

EX-1. [www.microstrategy.com]   In the financial statements for Microstrategy, amounts received from customers for service policies are reported in two dimensions. One dimension is actual revenue, or amounts earned from providing a service or a product to its customers. The other dimension is that of receiving cash, which represents services to be provided in future accounting periods. Suppose that, in 2003, Microstrategy received $200,000 from customers. That $200,000 represented $125,000 that was amounts for products sold or services actually rendered. The remaining $75,000 represents services to be provided later.

1. What is the company's addition to revenue if the full amount is recorded all in one year?

2. How is the revenue number different if the amount for future services is recorded as a liability?

3. What is the justification of reporting these amounts in two separate segments?

4. Explain how reporting the revenue all at one time could mislead the reader of the company's financial statements.

EX-2. [www.microstrategy.com]   In this chapter you have been introduced to the basic concepts of assets and liabilities. Go to the Microstrategy Web site and read about the company and its operations. After reading about the company, consider these questions:

1. What are three assets you would expect it to have, other than cash?

2. What are three liabilities you would expect it to have, other than accounts payable?

3. How do liabilities represent equities, or claims?

4. In the accounting equation, why do you think the liabilities (claims of creditors) are listed before the stockholders' equity (claims of owners)?

Continuing Problem

Eldorado Computer Center

The following problem continues from one chapter to the next, carrying the balances of each month forward. Each chapter focuses on the learning experience of the chapter and adds additional information as the business grows. Forms are on page 23 of the *Study Guide and Working Papers*.

Assignment

1. Set up an expanded accounting equation spreadsheet using the following accounts:

Assets	Liabilities	Owner's Equity
Cash	Accounts Payable	Freedman, Capital
Supplies		Freedman, Withdrawal
Computer Shop Equipment		Service Revenue
Office Equipment		Expenses (notate type)

2. Analyze and record each transaction in the expanded accounting equation.
3. Prepare the financial statements ending July 31 for Eldorado Computer Center.

On July 1, 200X, Tony Freedman decided to begin his own computer service business. He named the business the Eldorado Computer Center. During the first month Tony conducted the following business transactions:

a. Invested $4,500 of his savings into the business.
b. Paid $1,200 (check #8095) for the computer from Multi Systems, Inc.
c. Paid $600 (check # 8096) for office equipment from Office Furniture, Inc.
d. Set up a new account with Office Depot and purchased $250 in office supplies on credit.
e. Paid July rent, $400 (check # 8097).
f. Repaired a system for a customer; collected $250.
g. Collected $200 for system upgrade labor charge from a customer.
h. Electric bill due but unpaid, $85.
i. Collected $1,200 for services performed on Taylor Golf computers.
j. Withdrew $100 (check # 8098) to take his wife, Carol, out in celebration of opening the new business.

SUBWAY Case

A FRESH START

"Hey, Stan the man!" a loud voice boomed. "I never thought I'd see you making sandwiches!" Stan Hernandez stopped layering lettuce in a foot-long submarine sandwich and grinned at his old college buddy, Ron.

"Neither did I. But then again," said Stan, "I never thought I'd own a profitable business either."

That night, catching up on their lives over dinner, Stan told Ron how he became the proud owner of a Subway sandwich restaurant.

"After working like crazy at Xellent Media for five years and *finally* making it to marketing man-

ager, then wham . . . I got laid off," said Stan. "That very day I was having my lunch at the local Subway as usual, when. . . ."

"Hmmm, wait a minute! I did notice you've lost quite a bit of weight," Ron interrupted and began to hum the bars of Subway's latest ad featuring Clay Henry, yet another hefty male who lost weight on a diet of Subway sandwiches.

"Right!" Stan quipped, "Not only was I laid off, but I was 'downsizing!' *Anyway*, I was eating a Dijon horseradish melt when I opened up an *Entrepreneur* magazine someone had left on the table—right to the headline 'Subway Named #1 Franchise in All Categories for 11th Time in 15 Years.'"

Well, to make a foot-long submarine sandwich story short, Stan realized his long-time dream of being his own boss by owning a business with a proven product and highly successful business model. When you look at Stan's restaurant, you are really seeing two businesses. While Stan is the sole proprietor of his business, he operates under an agreement with Subway of Milford, Connecticut. Subway supplies the business know-how and support (like training at Subway University, national advertising, and gourmet bread recipes). Stan supplies capital (his $12,500 investment) and his food preparation, management, and elbow grease. Subway and Stan operate interdependent businesses, and both rely on accounting information for their success.

Subway, in business since 1965, has grown dramatically over the years and now has over 18,000 locations in 73 countries. It has even surpassed McDonald's in the number of locations in the United States and Canada. To manage this enormous service business requires very careful control of each of its stores. At a Subway regional office, Mariah Washington, a field consultant for Stan's territory, monitors Stan's restaurant closely. In addition to making monthly visits to check whether Stan is complying with Subway's model in everything from décor to uniforms to food quality and safety, she also looks closely at Stan's weekly sales and inventory reports. When Stan's sales go up, Subway's do too, because each Subway franchisee, like Stan, pays Subway, the franchiser, a percentage of sales in the form of royalties.

Why does headquarters require accounting reports? Accounting reports give the information both Stan and the company need to make business decisions in a number of vital areas. For example:

- Before Stan could buy his Subway restaurant, the company needed to know how much cash Stan had and his assets and liabilities (such as credit card debt). Stan prepared a personal balance sheet to give them this information.
- Stan must have the right amount of supplies on hand. If he has too few, he can't make the sandwiches. If he has too many for the amount he expects to sell, items like sandwich meats and bread dough may spoil. The inventory report tells Mariah what supplies are on hand. In combination with the sales report, it also alerts Mariah to potential red flags: If Stan is reporting that he is using far too much bread dough for the amount of sandwiches he is selling, then there is a problem.
- Although Subway does not require its restaurant owners to report operating costs and profit information, Subway gives them the option and most franchisees take it. Information on profitability helps Mariah and Stan make decisions like whether and when to remodel or buy new equipment.

So that its restaurant owners can make business decisions in a timely manner, Subway requires them to submit the weekly sales and inventory report to headquarters electronically every Thursday by 2:00 P.M. Stan has his latest report in mind as he makes a move to pay the bill for his dinner with Ron. "We had a great week. Let me get this," he says. "Thanks Stan the Man. I'm going to keep in touch because I may just be ready for a business opportunity of my own!"

Discussion Questions

1. What makes Stan a sole proprietor?
2. Why are Stan and Subway interdependent businesses?
3. Why did Stan have to share his personal balance sheet with Subway? Do you think most interdependent businesses do this?
4. What does Subway learn from Stan's weekly sales and inventory reports?

Debits and Credits

Analyzing and Recording Business Transactions

Now that you are enrolled in college, your parents decided they wanted a home that was a little smaller, with less maintenance. They purchased a patio home in a new subdivision a few months ago.

Your parents went to a law office when they sold their home. An attorney who specializes in real estate law prepared the paperwork for your parents and conducted what is called a real estate closing. You remember seeing a thick legal-size file folder your parents brought home after the closing. The folder held numerous sheets of paper with estimate information, bank forms, a house appraisal, and a document called a settlement statement. The settlement statement struck you as pparticularly important because it listed all of the amounts that were part of the sale. The form had two long columns—one column listed amounts for the seller, and the other column listed amounts for the buyer. There were various numbers in each of the two columns, but you saw that the total amount in both columns was the same. In other words, the amounts listed in this document were in balance. The attorney used accounting in completing the sale of your parents' home.

It is important that the settlement statement achieve balance. In accounting, a key goal is keeping transactions in balance. In Chapter 1 we learned how to record business transactions using the accounting equation. In this chapter we will learn how to use the accounting equation to keep business transactions in balance. We will discuss the five steps in analyzing business transactions and a method accountants use to prove that recorded business transactions are in balance.

Your growing knowledge of accounting will make all the difference in your understanding of the world of business.

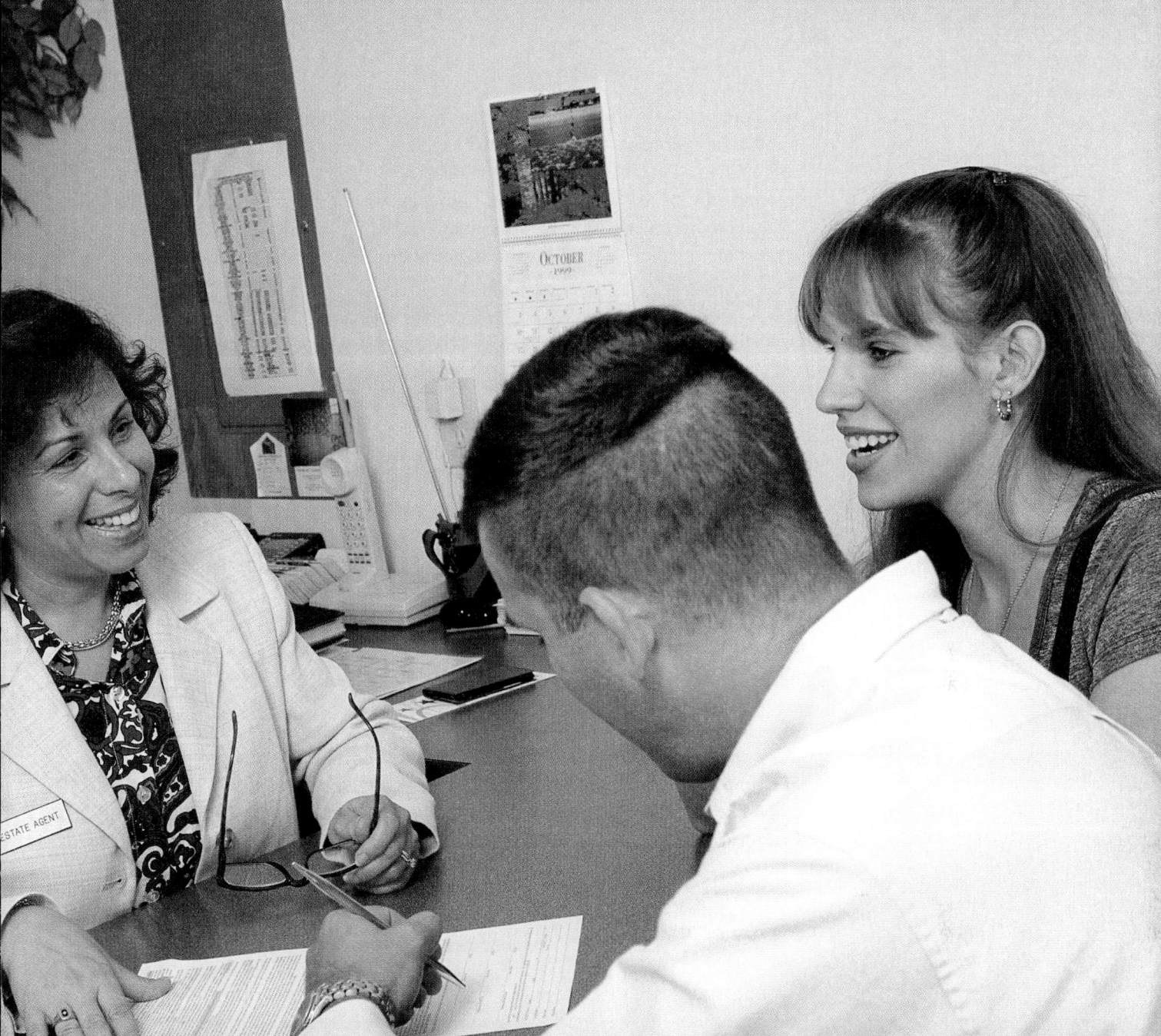

Learning Objectives

- Setting up and organizing a chart of accounts. (p. 42)
- Recording transactions in T accounts according to the rules of debit and credit. (p. 43)
- Preparing a trial balance. (p. 51)
- Preparing financial statements from a trial balance. (p. 53)

In Chapter 1 we used the expanded accounting equation to document the financial transactions performed by Cathy Hall's law firm. Remember how long it was: The cash column had a long list of pluses and minuses, and there was no quick system of recording and summarizing the increases and decreases of cash or other items. Can you imagine the problem Subway or Holiday Inn would have if they used the expanded accounting equation to track the thousands of business transactions they do each day?

Learning Unit 2-1   The T Account

Let's look at the problem a little more closely. Each business transaction is recorded in the accounting equation under a specific account. There are different accounts for each of the subdivisions of the accounting equation: asset accounts, liabilities accounts, expense accounts, revenue accounts, and so on. What is needed is a way to record the increases and decreases in specific account *categories* and yet keep them together in one place. The answer is the standard account form (see Fig. 2.1). A standard account is a formal account that includes columns for date, explanation, posting reference, debit, and credit. Each account has a separate form, and all transactions affecting that account are recorded on the form. All the business's account forms (which often are referred to as *ledger accounts*) are then placed in a ledger. Each page of the ledger contains one account. The ledger may be in the form of a bound or a loose-leaf book. If computers are used, the ledger may be part of a computer printout. For simplicity's sake, we use the T account form. This form got its name because it looks like the letter T. Generally, T accounts are used for demonstration purposes. Each T account contains three basic parts:

1

Title of Account	
2 Left side	Right side **3**

All T accounts have this structure.

In accounting, the left side of any T account is called the debit side.

Left side	
Dr. (debit)	

Just as the word *left* has many meanings, the word *debit* for now in accounting means a position, the left side of an account. Do not think of it as good (+) or bad (−).

> *Debit defined:*
> 1. The left side of any T account.
> 2. A number entered on the left side of any account is said to be debited to an account.

Figure 2-1 The Standard Account Form Is the Source of the T Account's Shape

Amounts entered on the left side of any account are said to be *debited* to an account. The abbreviation for debit, Dr., is from the Latin *debere*.

The right side of any T account is called the credit side.

	Right side
	Cr. (credit)

Amounts entered on the right side of an account are said to be *credited* to an account. The abbreviation for credit, Cr., is from the Latin *credere*.

At this point do not associate the definition of debit and credit with the words *increase* or *decrease*. Think of debit or credit as only indicating a *position* (left or right side) of a T account.

> Credit defined:
> 1. The right side of any T account.
> 2. A number entered on the right side of any account is said to be credited to an account.

BALANCING AN ACCOUNT

No matter which individual account is being balanced, the procedure used to balance it is the same.

	Dr.	Cr.
Entries	4,000	300
	500	400
Footings	4,500	700
Balance	3,800	

In the "real" world, the T account would also include the date of the transaction. The date would appear to the left of the entry:

		Dr.	Cr.
4/2		4,000	300
4/20		500	400
		4,500	700
Bal		3,800	

Note that on the debit (left) side the numbers add up to $4,500. On the credit (right) side the numbers add up to $700. The $4,500 and the $700 written in small type are called **footings**. Footing help in calculating the new (or ending) balance. The **ending balance** ($3,800) is placed on the debit or left side, because the balance of the debit side is greater than that of the credit side.

Remember that the ending balance does not tell us anything about increase or decrease. It only tells us that we have an ending balance of $3,800 on the debit side.

> Footings aid in balancing an account. The ending balance is the difference between the footings.

> If the balance is greater on the credit side, that is the side the ending balance would be on.

Learning Unit 2-1 Review

AT THIS POINT you should be able to

- Define ledger. (p. 38)
- State the purpose of a T account. (p. 38)
- Identify the three parts of a T account. (p. 38)
- Define debit. (p. 38)
- Define credit. (p. 39)
- Explain footings and calculate the balance of an account. (p. 39)

SELF-REVIEW QUIZ 2-1

(The blank forms you need are on page 25 of the *Study Guide and Working Papers*. See your DVD for worked-out solutions.)

Respond True or False to the following:

1.

Dr.	Cr.
3,000	200
200	600

The balance of the account is $2,400 Cr.

2. A credit always means increase.
3. A debit is the left side of any account.
4. A ledger can be prepared manually or by computer.
5. Footings replace the need for debits and credits.

Quiz Tip:
Dr. + Dr. → Add to get Dr. balance
Cr. + Cr. → Add to get Cr. balance
Dr. − Cr. → Subtract to get balance for the larger side.

SOLUTIONS TO SELF-REVIEW QUIZ 2-1

1. False   2. False   3. True   4. True   5. False

Learning Unit 2-2   Recording Business Transactions: Debits and Credits

Can you get a queen in checkers? In a baseball game does a runner rounding first base skip second base and run over the pitcher's mound to get to third? No; most of us don't do such things because we follow the rules of the game. Usually we learn the rules first and reflect on the reasons for them afterward. The same is true in accounting.

Instead of first trying to understand all the rules of debit and credit and how they were developed in accounting, it is easier to learn the rules by "playing the game."

Accounting in the Reel World

How Much Is That Dog Treat In the Window?

When their business is "going to the dogs" Dan Dye and Mark Beckloff have reason to cheer. The two business partners started Three Dog Bakery in 1989 to sell fresh, all-natural dog treats with names like "snickerpoodles" and "rollovers."

The idea of a bakery for dogs might seem far-fetched, yet people continue to spend ever more money on their pets. Now the partners have 30 stores in the United States, Canada, and Japan, national retail accounts with chains like PetsMart and even a "dogalogue" for direct-to-consumer sales.

As you watch the Three Dog Bakery on-location video on your DVD, pay attention to the relationship between what this company produces and how they sell their goods and the accounting process. After you have watched this brief segment, answer the questions below.

1. Why does Three Dog Bakery's VP of finance need to analyze accounting information to make business decisions?
2. What are at least three types of business decisions that the owners need to make?
3. On which item is the company losing money and why? What would you suggest to make this item more profitable?

T ACCOUNT ENTRIES FOR ACCOUNTING IN THE ACCOUNTING EQUATION

Have patience. Learning the rules of debit and credit is like learning to play any game: the more you play, the easier it becomes. Table 2-1 shows the rules for the side on which you enter an increase or a decrease for each of the separate accounts in the accounting equation. For example, an increase is entered on the debit side in the asset account but on the credit side for a liability account.

It might be easier to visualize these rules of debit and credit if we look at them in the T account form, using + to show increase and − to show decrease.

Assets		=	Liabilities		+		Owner's Equity									
							Capital		−	Withdrawals	+	Revenue		−	Expenses	
Dr.	Cr.	Dr.	Cr.	+			Dr.	Cr.		Dr.	Cr.	Dr.	Cr.		Dr.	Cr.
+	−	−	+				−	+		+	−	−	+		+	−

Rules for Assets Work in the Opposite Direction to Those for Liabilities   When you look at the equation you can see that the rules for assets work in the opposite direction to those for liabilities. That is, for assets the increases appear on the debit side and the decreases are shown on the credit side; the opposite is true for liabilities. As for the owner's equity, the rules for withdrawals and expenses, which *decrease* owner's equity, work in the opposite direction to the rules for capital and revenue, which *increase* owner's equity.

Assets		+	Withdrawals		+	Expenses		=	Liabilities		+	Capital		+	Revenue	
Dr.	Cr.		Dr.	Cr.		Dr.	Cr.		Dr.	Cr.		Dr.	Cr.		Dr.	Cr.
+	−		+	−		+	−		−	+		−	+		−	+

This setup may help you visualize how the rules for withdrawals and expenses are just the opposite of those for capital and revenue.

A **normal balance of an account** is the side that increases by the rules of debit and credit. For example, the balance of cash is a debit balance, because an asset is increased by a debit. We discuss normal balances further in Chapter 3.

Balancing the Equation   It is important to remember that any amount(s) entered on the debit side of a T account or accounts also must be on the credit side of another T account or accounts. This ensures that the total amount added to the debit side will equal the total amount added to the credit side, thereby keeping the accounting equation in balance.

Chart of Accounts   Our job is to analyze Cathy Hall's business transactions—the transactions we looked at in Chapter 1—using a system of accounts guided by the

Normal Balance	
Dr.	Cr.
Assets	Liabilities
Expenses	Capital
Withdrawals	Revenue

Be sure to follow the rules of debits and credits when recording accounts. They were designed to keep the accounting equation in balance.

TABLE 2-1 Rules of Debit and Credit

Account Category	Increase (Normal Balance)	Decrease
Assets	Debit	Credit
Liabilities	Credit	Debit
Owner's Equity		
Capital	Credit	Debit
Withdrawals	Debit	Credit
Revenue	Credit	Debit
Expenses	Debit	Credit

TABLE 2-2 Chart of Accounts for Cathy Hall, Attorney-at-Law

Balance Sheet Accounts

Assets		Liabilities	
111	Cash	211	Accounts Payable
112	Accounts Receivable	**Owner's Equity**	
121	Office Equipment	311	Cathy Hall, Capital
		312	Cathy Hall, Withdrawals

Income Statement Accounts

Revenue		Expenses	
411	Legal Fees	511	Salaries Expense
		512	Rent Expense
		513	Advertising Expense

> The chart of accounts aids in locating and identifying accounts quickly.

> Large companies may have up to four digits assigned to each title.

rules of debits and credits that will summarize increases and decreases of individual accounts in the ledger. The goal is to prepare an income statement, statement of owner's equity, and balance sheet for Cathy Hall. Sound familiar? If this system works, the rules of debits and credits and the use of accounts will give us the same answers as in Chapter 1, but with greater ease.

Cathy's accountant developed what is called a **chart of accounts.** The chart of accounts is a numbered list of all of the business's accounts. It allows accounts to be located quickly. In Cathy's business, for example, 100s are assets, 200s are liabilities, and so on. As you see in Table 2-2, each separate asset and liability has its own number. Note that the chart may be expanded as the business grows.

THE TRANSACTION ANALYSIS: FIVE STEPS

We will analyze the transactions in Cathy Hall's law firm using a teaching device called a *transaction analysis chart* to record these five steps. (Keep in mind that the transaction analysis chart is not a part of any formal accounting system.) There are five steps to analyzing each business transaction:

> Steps to analyze and record transactions. Steps 1 and 2 will come from the chart of accounts.

Step 1: Determine which accounts are affected. Example: Cash, Accounts Payable, Rent Expense. A transaction always affects at least two accounts.

Step 2: Determine which categories the accounts belong to: assets, liabilities, capital, withdrawals, revenue, or expenses. Example: Cash is an asset.

Step 3: Determine whether the accounts increase or decrease. Example: If you receive cash, that account is increasing.

Step 4: What do the rules of debits and credits say (Table 2-1)?

Step 5: What does the T account look like? Place amounts into accounts either on the left or right side depending on the rules in Table 2-1.

> Remember that the rules of debit and credit only tell us on which side to place information. Whether the debit or credit represents increases or decreases depends on the account category: assets, liabilities, capital, and so on. Think of a business transaction as an exchange: You get something and you give or part with something.

This is how the five-step analysis looks in chart form:

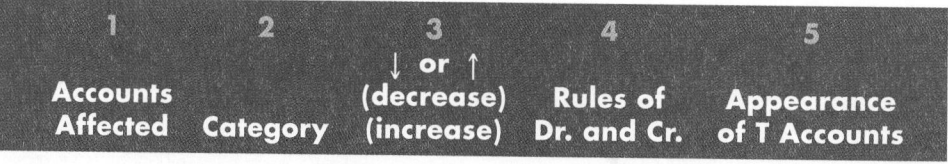

1	2	3	4	5
Accounts Affected	Category	↓ or ↑ (decrease) (increase)	Rules of Dr. and Cr.	Appearance of T Accounts

Let us emphasize a major point: *Do not try to debit or credit an account until you have gone through the first three steps of the transaction analysis.*

APPLYING THE TRANSACTION ANALYSIS TO CATHY HALL'S LAW PRACTICE

Transaction A   August 28: Cathy Hall invests $7,000 cash and $800 of office equipment in the business.

1 Accounts Affected	2 Category	3 ↓ ↑	4 Rules of Dr. and Cr.	5 Appearance of T Accounts
Cash	Asset	↑	Dr.	Cash 111 (A) 7,000 |
Office Equipment	Asset	↑	Dr.	Office Equipment 121 (A) 800 |
Cathy Hall, Capital	Capital	↑	Cr.	Cathy Hall, Capital 311 | 7,800 (A)

> Note in column 3 of the chart that it doesn't matter if both arrows go up, as long as the sum of the debits equals the sum of the credits in the T accounts in column 5.

Note again that every transaction affects at least two T accounts and that the total amount added to the debit side(s) must equal the total amount added to the credit side(s) of the T accounts of each transaction.

Analysis of Transaction A

Step 1: Which accounts are affected? The law firm receives its cash and office equipment, so three accounts are involved: Cash, Office Equipment, and Cathy Hall, Capital. These account titles come from the chart of accounts.

Step 2: Which categories do these accounts belong to? Cash and Office Equipment are assets. Cathy Hall, Capital, is capital.

Step 3: Are the accounts increasing or decreasing? The Cash and Office Equipment, both assets, are increasing in the business. The rights or claims of Cathy Hall, Capital, are also increasing, because she invested money and office equipment in the business.

Step 4: What do the rules say? According to the rules of debit and credit, an increase in assets (Cash and Office Equipment) is a debit. An increase in Capital is a credit. Note that the total dollar amount of debits will equal the total dollar amount of credits when the T accounts are updated in column 5.

Step 5: What does the T account look like? The amount for Cash and Office Equipment is entered on the debit side. The amount for Cathy Hall, Capital, goes on the credit side.

A transaction that involves more than one credit or more than one debit is called a compound entry. This first transaction of Cathy Hall's law firm is a compound entry; it involves a debit of $7,000 to Cash and a debit of $800 to Office Equipment (as well as a credit of $7,800 to Cathy Hall, Capital).

> **Double-entry bookkeeping system:** The total of all debits is equal to the total of all credits.

There is a name for this double-entry analysis of transactions, where two or more accounts are affected and the total of debits and credits is equal. It is called **double-entry bookkeeping.** This double-entry system helps in checking the recording of business transactions.

As we continue, the explanations will be brief, but do not forget to apply the five steps in analyzing and recording each business transaction.

Transaction B   Aug. 29: Law practice bought office equipment for cash, $900.

1 Accounts Affected	2 Category	3 ↓ ↑	4 Rules of Dr. and Cr.	5 T Account Update
Office Equipment	Asset	↑	Dr.	Office Equipment 121 (A) 800 / (B) 900
Cash	Asset	↓	Cr.	Cash 111 (A) 7,000 | 900 (B)

Analysis of Transaction B

Step 1: The law firm paid cash for the office equipment it received. The accounts involved in the transaction are Cash and Office Equipment.

Step 2: The accounts belong to these categories: Office Equipment is an asset; Cash is an asset.

Step 3: The asset Office Equipment is increasing. The asset Cash is decreasing; it is being reduced to buy the office equipment.

Step 4: An increase in the asset Office Equipment is a debit; a decrease in the asset Cash is a credit.

Step 5: When the amounts are placed in the T accounts, the amount for Office Equipment goes on the debit side and the amount for Cash on the credit side.

Transaction C   Aug. 30: Bought more office equipment on account, $400.

1 Accounts Affected	2 Category	3 ↓ ↑	4 Rules of Dr. and Cr.	5 T Account Update
Office Equipment	Asset	↑	Dr.	Office Equipment 121 (A) 800 / (B) 900 / (C) 400
Accounts Payable	Liability	↑	Cr.	Accounts Payable 211 | 400 (C)

Analysis of Transaction C

Step 1: The law firm receives office equipment by promising to pay in the future. An obligation or liability, Accounts Payable, is created.

Step 2: Office Equipment is an asset. Accounts Payable is a liability.

Step 3: The asset Office Equipment is increasing; the liability Accounts Payable is increasing because the law firm is increasing what it owes.

Step 4: An increase in the asset Office Equipment is a debit. An increase in the liability Accounts Payable is a credit.

Step 5: Enter the amount for Office Equipment on the debit side of the T account. The amount for the Accounts Payable goes on the credit side.

Transaction D   Sept. 1–30: Provided legal services for cash, $3,000.

1 Accounts Affected	2 Category ↓ ↑		3	4 Rules of Dr. and Cr.	5 T Account Update
Cash	Asset	↑		Dr.	Cash 111
					(A) 7,000 | 900 (B)
					(D) 3,000 |
Legal Fees	Revenue	↑		Cr.	Legal Fees 411
					| 3,000 (D)

Analysis of Transaction D

Step 1: The firm has earned revenue from legal services and receives $3,000 in cash.

Step 2: Cash is an asset. Legal Fees are revenue.

Step 3: Cash, an asset, is increasing. Legal Fees, or revenue, are also increasing.

Step 4: An increase in Cash, an asset, is debited. An increase in Legal Fees, or revenue, is credited.

Step 5: Enter the amount for Cash on the debit side of the T account. Enter the amount for Legal Fees on the credit side.

Transaction E   Sept. 1–30: Provided legal services on account, $4,000.

1 Accounts Affected	2 Category ↓ ↑		3	4 Rules of Dr. and Cr.	5 T Account Update
Accounts Receivable	Asset	↑		Dr.	Accounts Receivable 112
					(E) 4,000 |
Legal Fees	Revenue	↑		Cr.	Legal Fees 411
					| 3,000 (D)
					| 4,000 (E)

Analysis of Transaction E

Step 1:   The law practice has earned revenue but has not yet received payment (cash). The amounts owed by these clients are called Accounts Receivable. Revenue is earned at the time the legal services are provided, whether payment is received then or will be received some time in the future.

Step 2:   Accounts Receivable is an asset. Legal Fees are revenue.

Step 3:   Accounts Receivable is increasing because the law practice has increased the amount owed to it for legal fees that have been earned but not paid. Legal Fees, or revenue, are increasing.

Step 4:   An increase in the asset Accounts Receivable is a debit. An increase in Revenue is a credit.

Step 5:   Enter the amount for Accounts Receivable on the debit side of the T account. The amount for Legal Fees goes on the credit side.

> **Transaction F   Sept. 1–30: Received $700 cash from clients for services rendered previously on account.**

1 Accounts Affected	2 Category	3 ↓ ↑	4 Rules of Dr. and Cr.	5 T Account Update
Cash	Asset	↑	Dr.	Cash 111
				(A) 7,000 | 900 (B)
				(D) 3,000
				(F) 700
Accounts Receivable	Asset	↓	Cr.	Accounts Receivable 112
				(E) 4,000 | 700 (F)

Analysis of Transaction F

Step 1:   The law firm collects $700 in cash from previous revenue earned. Because the revenue is recorded at the time it is earned, and not when the payment is made, in this transaction we are concerned only with the payment, which affects the Cash and Accounts Receivable accounts.

Step 2:   Cash is an asset. Accounts Receivable is an asset.

Step 3:   Because clients are paying what is owed, Cash (asset) is increasing and the amount owed (Accounts Receivable) is decreasing (the total amount owed by clients to Hall is going down). This transaction results in a shift in assets, more Cash for less Accounts Receivable.

Step 4:   An increase in Cash, an asset, is a debit. A decrease in Accounts Receivable, an asset, is a credit.

Step 5:   Enter the amount for Cash on the debit side of the T account. The amount for Accounts Receivable goes on the credit side.

> **Transaction G   Sept. 1–30: Paid salaries expense, $600.**

1 Accounts Affected	2 Category ↓ ↑	3	4 Rules of Dr. and Cr.	5 T Account Update
Salaries Expense	Expense	↑	Dr.	Salaries Expense 511
Cash	Asset	↓	Cr.	Cash 111

Salaries Expense 511

| (G) | 600 | |

Cash 111

(A)	7,000	900	(B)
(D)	3,000	600	(G)
(F)	700		

Analysis of Transaction G

Step 1: The law firm pays $600 worth of salaries expense by cash.

Step 2: Salaries Expense is an expense. Cash is an asset.

Step 3: The Salaries Expense of the law firm is increasing, which results in a decrease in Cash.

Step 4: An increase in Salaries Expense, an expense, is a debit. A decrease in Cash, an asset, is a credit.

Step 5: Enter the amount for Salaries Expense on the debit side of the T account. The amount for Cash goes on the credit side.

Transaction H   Sept. 1–30: Paid rent expense, $700.

1 Accounts Affected	2 Category ↓ ↑	3	4 Rules of Dr. and Cr.	5 T Account Update
Rent Expense	Expense	↑	Dr.	Rent Expense 512
Cash	Asset	↓	Cr.	Cash 111

Rent Expense 512

| (H) | 700 | |

Cash 111

(A)	7,000	900	(B)
(D)	3,000	600	(G)
(F)	700	700	(H)

Analysis of Transaction H

Step 1: The law firm's rent expenses are paid in cash.

Step 2: Rent is an expense. Cash is an asset.

Step 3: The Rent Expense increases the expenses, and the payment for the Rent Expense decreases the cash.

Step 4: An increase in Rent Expense, an expense, is a debit. A decrease in Cash, an asset, is a credit.

Step 5: Enter the amount for Rent Expense on the debit side of the T account. Place the amount for Cash on the credit side.

**Transaction I   Sept. 1–30: Received a bill for Advertising Expense
(to be paid next month), $300.**

1 Accounts Affected	2 Category ↓ ↑	3	4 Rules of Dr. and Cr.	5 T Account Update
Advertising Expense	Expense	↑	Dr.	Advertising Expense 513
				(I) 300
Accounts Payable	Liability	↑	Cr.	Accounts Payable 211
				400 (C)
				300 (I)

Analysis of Transaction I

Step 1:   The advertising bill has come in and payment is due but has not yet been made. Therefore, the accounts involved here are Advertising Expense and Accounts Payable; the expense has created a liability.

Step 2:   Advertising Expense is an expense. Accounts Payable is a liability.

Step 3:   Both the expense and the liability are increasing.

Step 4:   An increase in an expense is a debit. An increase in a liability is a credit.

Step 5:   Enter the amount for Advertising Expense on the debit side of the T Account. Enter the amount for Accounts Payable on the credit side.

> **Transaction J   Sept. 1–30: Hall withdrew cash for personal use, $200.**

1 Accounts Affected	2 Category ↓ ↑	3	4 Rules of Dr. and Cr.	5 T Account Update
Cathy Hall, Withdrawals	Withdrawals	↑	Dr.	Cathy Hall, Withdrawals, 312
				(J) 200
Cash	Asset	↓	Cr.	Cash 111
				(A) 7,000 │ 900 (B)
				(D) 3,000 │ 600 (G)
				(F) 700 │ 700 (H)
				200 (J)

Analysis of Transaction J

Step 1:   Cathy Hall withdraws cash from business for *personal* use. This withdrawal is not a business expense.

Step 2:   This transaction affects the Withdrawals and Cash accounts.

Step 3:   Cathy has increased what she has withdrawn from the business for personal use. The business cash has been decreased.

Step 4:   An increase in Withdrawals is a debit. A decrease in Cash is a credit. (*Remember:* Withdrawals go on the statement of owner's equity; expenses go on the income statement.)

> Withdrawals are always increased by debits.

Step 5: Enter the amount for Cathy Hall, Withdrawals on the debit side of the T account. The amount for Cash goes on the credit side.

Summary of Transactions for Cathy Hall

Assets	=	Liabilities	+				Owner's Equity				

Cash 111		Accounts Payable 211		Capital Cathy Hall, Capital 311	−	Withdrawals Cathy Hall, Withdrawals 312	+	Revenue Legal Fees 411	−	Expenses Salaries Expense 511
(A) 7,000 | 900 (B)		400 (C)		7,800 (A)		(J) 200 |		3,000 (D)		(G) 600 |
(D) 3,000 | 600 (G)		300 (I)						4,000 (E)		
(F) 700 | 700 (H)										
| 200 (J)										

Accounts Receivable 112
(E) 4,000 | 700 (F)

Office Equipment 121
(A) 800 |
(B) 900 |
(C) 400 |

Rent Expense 512
(H) 700 |

Advertising Expense 513
(I) 300 |

Learning Unit 2-2 Review

AT THIS POINT you should be able to

- State the rules of debit and credit. (p. 41)
- List the five steps of a transaction analysis. (p. 42)
- Show how to fill out a transaction analysis chart. (p. 43)
- Explain double-entry bookkeeping. (p. 44)

SELF-REVIEW QUIZ 2-2

(The blank forms you need are on pages 25 and 26 of the *Study Guide and Working Papers*. See your DVD for worked-out solutions.)

King Company uses the following accounts from its chart of accounts: Cash (111), Accounts Receivable (112), Equipment (121), Accounts Payable (211), Jamie King, Capital (311), Jamie King, Withdrawals (312), Professional Fees (411), Utilities Expense (511), and Salaries Expense (512).

Record the following transactions into transaction analysis charts.

a. Jamie King invested in the business $1,000 cash and equipment worth $700 from his personal assets.

b. Billed clients for services rendered, $12,000.

c. Utilities bill due but unpaid, $150.

d. Withdrew cash for personal use, $120.

e. Paid salaries expense, $250.

SOLUTION TO SELF-REVIEW QUIZ 2-2

a.

1 Accounts Affected	2 Category	3 ↓ ↑	4 Rules of Dr. and Cr.	5 T Account Update
Cash	Asset	↑	Dr.	Cash 111
				(A) 1,000
Equipment	Asset	↑	Dr.	Equipment 121
				(A) 700
Jamie King, Capital	Capital	↑	Cr.	Jamie King, Capital 311
				1,700 (A)

b.

1 Accounts Affected	2 Category	3 ↓ ↑	4 Rules of Dr. and Cr.	5 T Account Update
Accounts Receivable	Asset	↑	Dr.	Accounts Receivable 112
				(B) 12,000
Professional Fees	Revenue	↑	Cr.	Professional Fees 411
				12,000 (B)

c.

1 Accounts Affected	2 Category	3 ↓ ↑	4 Rules of Dr. and Cr.	5 T Account Update
Utilities Expense	Expense	↑	Dr.	Utilities Expense 511
				(C) 150
Accounts Payable	Liability	↑	Cr.	Accounts Payable 211
				150 (C)

d.

1 Accounts Affected	2 Category	3 ↓ ↑	4 Rules of Dr. and Cr.	5 T Account Update
Jamie King, Withdrawls	Withdrawals	↑	Dr.	Jamie King, Withdrawals 312
				(D) 120
Cash	Asset	↓	Cr.	Cash 111
				(A) 1,000 | 120 (D)

e.

1 Accounts Affected	2 Category	3 ↓ ↑	4 Rules of Dr. and Cr.	5 T Account Update
Salaries Expense	Expense	↑	Dr.	Salaries Expense 512
				(E) 250
Cash	Asset	↓	Cr.	Cash 111
				(A) 1,000 | 120 (D)
				250 (E)

Learning Unit 2-3   The Trial Balance and Preparation of Financial Statements

Let us look at all the transactions we have discussed, arranged by T accounts and recorded using the rules of debit and credit. This grouping of accounts is much easier to use than the expanded accounting equation because all the transactions that affect a particular account are in one place.

As we saw in Learning Unit 2-2, when all the transactions are recorded in the accounts, the total of all the debits should be equal to the total of all the credits. (If they are not, the accountant must go back and find the error by checking the numbers and adding every column again.)

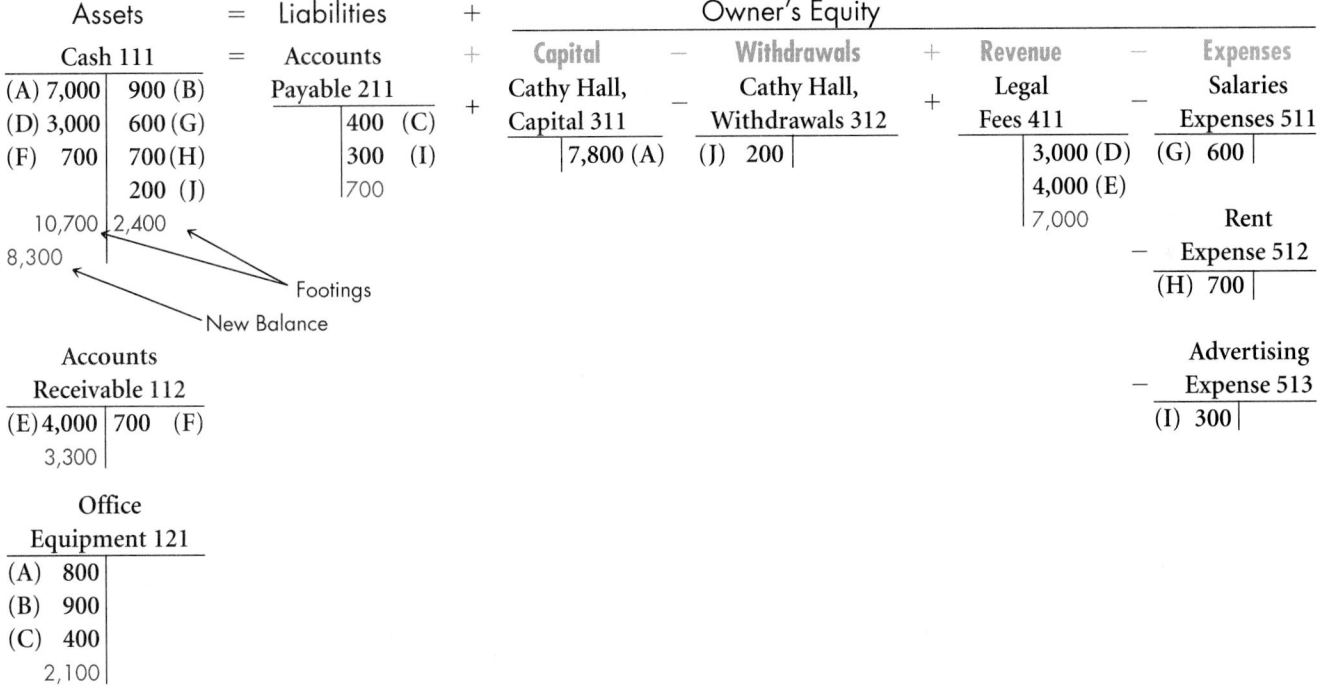

THE TRIAL BALANCE

Footings are used to obtain the balance of each side of every T account that has more than one entry. The footings are used to find the ending balance. The ending balances are used to prepare a **trial balance.** The trial balance is not a financial statement, although it is used to prepare financial statements. The trial balance lists all the accounts with their balances in the same order as they appear in the chart of accounts. It proves the accuracy of the ledger. For example, look at the preceding Cash account. The footing for the debit side is $10,700, and the footing for the credit side is $2,400. Because the debit side is larger, we subtract $2,400 from $10,700 to arrive at an *ending balance* of $8,300. Now look at the Rent Expense account. There is no need for a footing because there is only one entry. The amount itself is the ending balance. When the ending balance has been found for every account, we should be able to show that the total of all debits equals the total of all credits.

In the ideal situation, businesses would take a trial balance every day. The large number of transactions most businesses conduct each day makes this impractical. Instead, trial balances are prepared periodically.

> Footings are used to obtain the balance of each side of the T account. They are not needed if there is only one entry in the account.

> As mentioned earlier, the ending balance of Cash, $8,300, is a normal balance because it is on the side that increases the asset account.

Figure 2-2
Trial Balance for Cathy
Hall's Law Firm

CATHY HALL, ATTORNEY-AT-LAW TRIAL BALANCE SEPTEMBER 30, 200X		
	Dr.	Cr.
Cash	8 3 0 0 00	
Accounts Receivable	3 3 0 0 00	
Office Equipment	2 1 0 0 00	
Accounts Payable		7 0 0 00
Cathy Hall, Capital		7 8 0 0 00
Cathy Hall, Withdrawals	2 0 0 00	
Legal Fees		7 0 0 0 00
Salaries Expense	6 0 0 00	
Rent Expense	7 0 0 00	
Advertising Expense	3 0 0 00	
Totals	15 5 0 0 00	15 5 0 0 00

Because this is not a formal statement, there is no need to use dollar signs; the single and double lines under subtotals and final totals, however, are still used for clarity.

Only the ending balance of each account is listed.

Keep in mind that the figure for capital might not be the beginning figure if any additional investment has taken place during the period. You can tell this by looking at the capital account in the ledger.

A more detailed discussion of the trial balance is provided in the next chapter. For now, notice the heading, how the accounts are listed, the debits in the left column, the credits in the right, and that the total of debits is equal to the total of credits.

A trial balance of Cathy Hall's accounts is shown in Figure 2-2.

PREPARING FINANCIAL STATEMENTS

The trial balance is used to prepare the financial statements. The diagram in Figure 2-3 on page 53 shows how financial statements can be prepared from a trial balance. Statements do not have debit or credit columns. The left column is used only to subtotal numbers.

Learning Unit 2-3 Review

AT THIS POINT you should be able to

- Explain the role of footings. (p. 51)
- Prepare a trial balance from a set of accounts. (p. 52)
- Prepare financial statements from a trial balance. (p. 53)

SELF-REVIEW QUIZ 2-3

(The blank forms you need are on page 27 of the *Study Guide and Working Papers.* See your DVD for worked-out solutions.)

As the bookkeeper of Pam's Hair Salon, you are to prepare from the following accounts below Figure 2-3, p. 53 on June 30, 200X, (1) a trial balance as of June 30, (2) an income statement for the month ended June 30, (3) a statement of owner's equity for the month ended June 30, and (4) a balance sheet as of June 30, 200X.

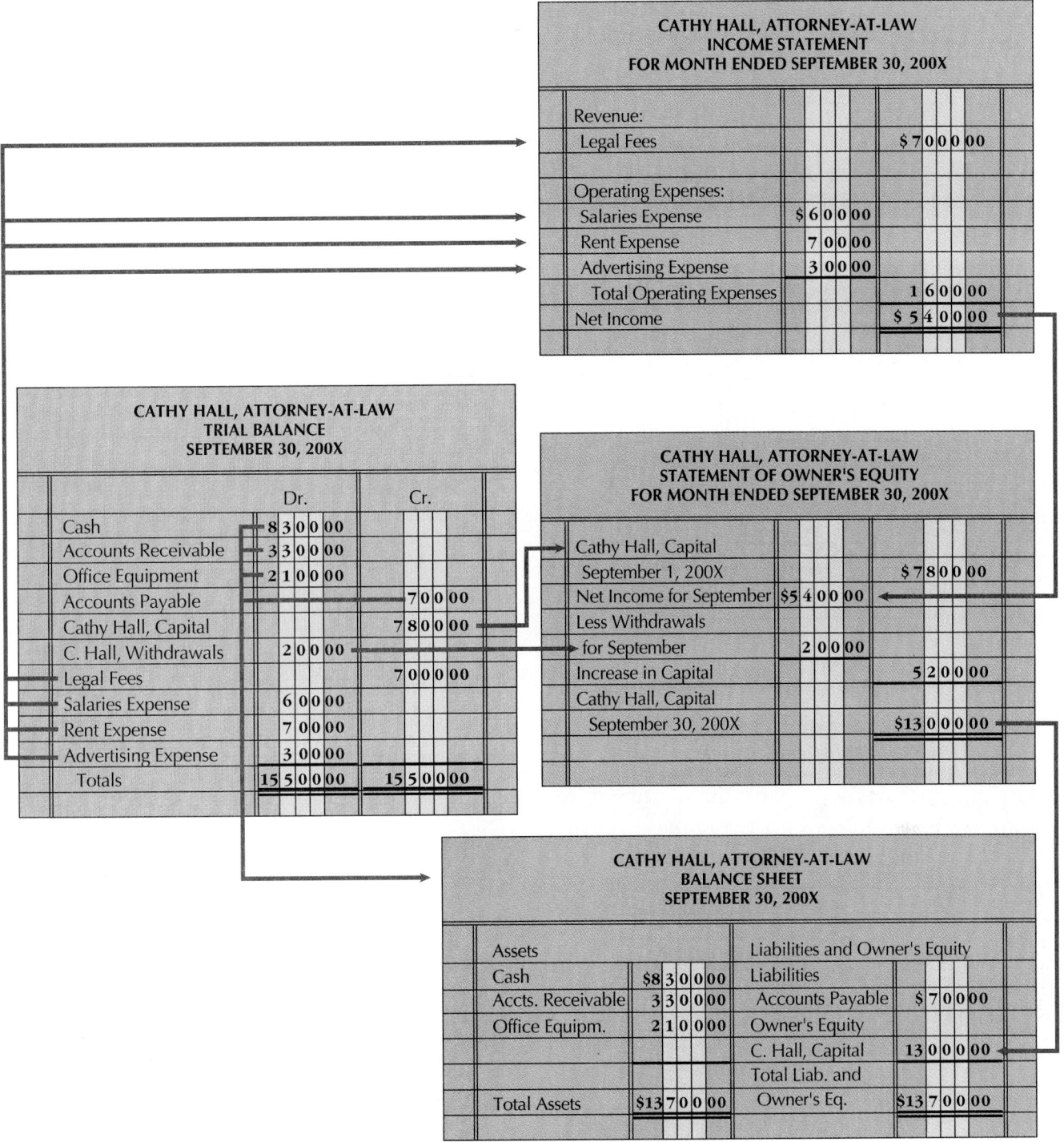

Figure 2-3 Steps in Preparing Financial Statements from a Trial Balance

Cash 111		Accounts Payable 211		Salon Fees 411	
4,500	300	300	700		3,500
2,000	100				1,000
1,000	1,200				
300	1,300				
	2,600				

Accounts Receivable 121		Pam Jay, Capital 311		Rent Expense 511	
1,000	300		4,000*	1,200	

(cont. on p. 54)

	Salon Equipment 131		Pam Jay, Withdrawals 321		Salon Supplies Expense 521
	700		100		1,300

		Salaries Expense 531
		2,600

*No additional investments.

SOLUTION TO SELF-REVIEW QUIZ 2-3

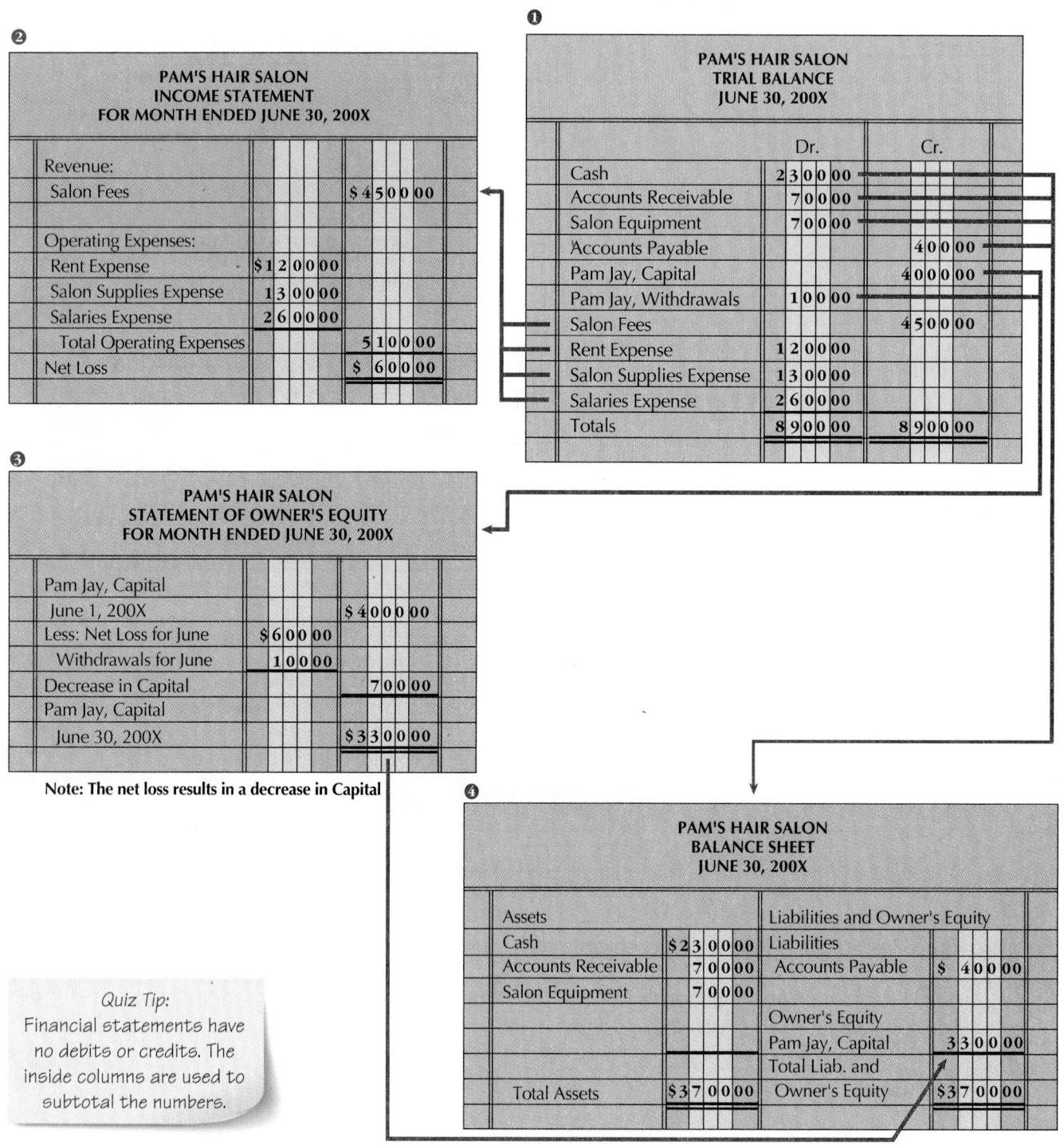

❷

PAM'S HAIR SALON
INCOME STATEMENT
FOR MONTH ENDED JUNE 30, 200X

Revenue:		
Salon Fees		$4 500 00
Operating Expenses:		
Rent Expense	$1 200 00	
Salon Supplies Expense	1 300 00	
Salaries Expense	2 600 00	
Total Operating Expenses		5 100 00
Net Loss		$ 600 00

❶

PAM'S HAIR SALON
TRIAL BALANCE
JUNE 30, 200X

	Dr.	Cr.
Cash	2 300 00	
Accounts Receivable	700 00	
Salon Equipment	700 00	
Accounts Payable		400 00
Pam Jay, Capital		4 000 00
Pam Jay, Withdrawals	100 00	
Salon Fees		4 500 00
Rent Expense	1 200 00	
Salon Supplies Expense	1 300 00	
Salaries Expense	2 600 00	
Totals	8 900 00	8 900 00

❸

PAM'S HAIR SALON
STATEMENT OF OWNER'S EQUITY
FOR MONTH ENDED JUNE 30, 200X

Pam Jay, Capital		
June 1, 200X		$4 000 00
Less: Net Loss for June	$600 00	
Withdrawals for June	100 00	
Decrease in Capital		700 00
Pam Jay, Capital		
June 30, 200X		$3 300 00

Note: The net loss results in a decrease in Capital

❹

PAM'S HAIR SALON
BALANCE SHEET
JUNE 30, 200X

Assets		Liabilities and Owner's Equity	
Cash	$2 300 00	Liabilities	
Accounts Receivable	700 00	Accounts Payable	$ 400 00
Salon Equipment	700 00		
		Owner's Equity	
		Pam Jay, Capital	3 300 00
		Total Liab. and	
Total Assets	$3 700 00	Owner's Equity	$3 700 00

Quiz Tip:
Financial statements have no debits or credits. The inside columns are used to subtotal the numbers.

Figure 2-4

If there were more than one liability we would have two columns, one to subtotal the liabilities (inside column) and one to total the liabilities (right column).

SOLUTION & TIPS TO COMPREHENSIVE PROBLEM: PUTTING THE PIECES TOGETHER

(The blank forms you need are on pages 30–32 of the *Study Guide and Working Papers.*)

The chart of accounts of Mel's Delivery Service includes the following: Cash, 111; Accounts Receivable, 112; Office Equipment, 121; Delivery Trucks, 122; Accounts Payable, 211; Mel Free, Capital, 311; Mel Free, Withdrawals, 312; Delivery Fees Earned, 411; Advertising Expense, 511; Gas Expense, 512; Salaries Expense, 513; and Telephone Expense, 514. The following transactions resulted for Mel's Delivery Service during the month of July:

Transaction A: Mel invested $10,000 in the business from his personal savings account.
Transaction B: Bought delivery trucks on account, $17,000.
Transaction C: Advertising bill received but unpaid, $700.
Transaction D: Bought office equipment for cash, $1,200.
Transaction E: Received cash for delivery services rendered, $15,000.
Transaction F: Paid salaries expense, $3,000.
Transaction G: Paid gas expense for company trucks, $1,250.
Transaction H: Billed customers for delivery services rendered, $4,000.
Transaction I: Paid telephone bill, $300.
Transaction J: Received $3,000 as partial payment of transaction H.
Transaction K: Mel paid home telephone bill from company checkbook, $150.

Assignment

As Mel's newly employed accountant, you must do the following:

1. Set up T accounts in a ledger.
2. Record transactions in the T accounts. (Place the letter of the transaction next to the entry.)
3. Foot the T accounts where appropriate.
4. Prepare a trial balance at the end of July.
5. Prepare from the trial balance, in proper form, (a) an income statement for the month of July, (b) a statement of owner's equity, and (c) a balance sheet as of July 31, 200X.

Solution to Comprehensive Problem

1,2,3.

GENERAL LEDGER

Cash 111			
(A) 10,000	1,200	(D)	
(E) 15,000	3,000	(F)	
(J) 3,000	1,250	(G)	
	300	(I)	
	150	(K)	
28,000	5,900		
22,100			

Acc. Payable 211		
	17,000	(B)
	700	(C)
	17,700	

Advertising Expense 511	
(C) 700	

Acc. Receivable 112		
(H) 4,000	3,000	(J)
1,000		

Mel Free, Capital 311	
	10,000 (A)

Gas Expense 512	
(G) 1,250	

Office Equipment 121	
(D) 1,200	

Mel Free, Withdrawals 312	
(K) 150	

Salaries Expense 513	
(F) 3,000	

Delivery Trucks 122		Delivery Fees Earned 411		Telephone Expense 514	
(B) 17,000			15,000 (E)	(I) 300	
			4,000 (H)		
			19,000		

Solution Tips to Recording Transactions

A.	Cash	A	↑	Dr.	G.	Gas Expense	Exp.	↑	Dr.
	Mel Free, Capital	Cap.	↑	Cr.		Cash	A	↓	Cr.
B.	Delivery Trucks	A	↑	Dr.	H.	Acc. Receivable	A	↑	Dr.
	Acc. Payable	L	↑	Cr.		Del. Fees Earned	Rev.	↑	Cr.
C.	Advertising Expense	Exp.	↑	Dr.	I.	Tel. Expense	Exp.	↑	Dr.
	Acc. Payable	L	↑	Cr.		Cash	A	↓	Cr.
D.	Office Equipment	A	↑	Dr.	J.	Cash	A	↑	Dr.
	Cash	A	↓	Cr.		Acc. Receivable	A	↓	Cr.
E.	Cash	A	↑	Dr.	K.	Mel Free, Withd.	Withd.	↑	Dr.
	Del. Fees Earned	Rev.	↑	Cr.		Cash	A	↓	Cr.
F.	Salaries Expense	Exp.	↑	Dr.					
	Cash	A	↓	Cr.					

MEL'S DELIVERY SERVICE
TRIAL BALANCE
JULY 31, 200X

	Dr.	Cr.
Cash	22,100	
Accounts Receivable	1,000	
Office Equipment	1,200	
Delivery Trucks	17,000	
Accounts Payable		17,700
Mel Free, Capital		10,000
Mel Free, Withdrawals	150	
Delivery Fees Earned		19,000
Advertising Expense	700	
Gas Expense	1,250	
Salaries Expense	3,000	
Telephone Expense	300	
TOTALS	46,700	46,700

Solution Tips to Footings and Preparation of a Trial Balance

3. Footings: Cash   Add left side, $28,000.

Add right side, $5,900.

Take difference, $22,100, and stay on side that is larger.

Accounts Payable   Add $17,000 + $700 and stay on same side. Total is $17,700.

4. Trial balance is a list of the ledger's ending balances. The list is in the same order as the chart of accounts. Each title has only one number listed either as a debit or credit balance.

5a.

Figure 2-5

MEL'S DELIVERY SERVICE INCOME STATEMENT FOR MONTH ENDED JULY 31, 200X		
Revenue:		
Delivery Fees Earned		$19 00 0 00
Operating Expenses:		
Advertising Expense	$ 7 00 00	
Gas Expense	1 25 0 00	
Salaries Expense	3 00 0 00	
Telephone Expense	3 00 00	
Total Operating Expenses		5 25 0 00
Net Income		$13 75 0 00

b.

MEL'S DELIVERY SERVICE STATEMENT OF OWNER'S EQUITY FOR MONTH ENDED JULY 31, 200X		
Mel Free, Capital		
July 1, 200X		$10 00 0 00
Net Income for July	$13 75 0 00	
Less Withdrawals for July	1 5 0 00	
Increase in Capital		$13 60 0 00
Mel Free, Capital		
July 31, 200X		$23 60 0 00

c.

MEL'S DELIVERY SERVICE BALANCE SHEET JULY 31, 200X				
Assets		Liabilities and Owner's Equity		
Cash	$22 10 0 00	Liabilities		
Accounts Receivable	1 00 0 00	Accounts Payable	$17 70 0 00	
Office Equipment	1 2 0 00			
Delivery Trucks	17 00 0 00			
		Owner's Equity		
		Mel Free, Capital	23 60 0 00	
		Total Liab. and		
Total Assets	$41 30 0 00	Owner's Equity	$41 30 0 00	

Solution Tips to Prepare Financial Statements from a Trial Balance

Trial Balance

		Dr.	Cr.
Balance Sheet	Assets	X	
	Liabilities		X
Statement of Equity	Capital		X
	Withdrawals	X	
Income Statement	Revenues		X
	Expenses	X	
		XX	XX

Net income of $13,750 on the income statement goes on the statement of owner's equity.

Ending capital of $23,600 on the statement of owner's equity goes on the balance sheet as the new figure for capital.

Note: There are no debits or credits on financial statements. The inside column is used for subtotaling.

Summary of Key Points

Learning Unit 2-1

1. A T account is a simplified version of a standard account.
2. A ledger is a group of accounts.
3. A debit is the left-hand position (side) of an account, and a credit is the right-hand position (side) of an account.
4. A footing is the total of one side of an account. The ending balance is the difference between the footings.

Learning Unit 2-2

1. A chart of accounts lists the account titles and their numbers for a company.
2. The transaction analysis chart is a teaching device, not to be confused with standard accounting procedures.
3. A compound entry is a transaction involving more than one debit or credit.

Learning Unit 2-3

1. In double-entry bookkeeping, the recording of each business transaction affects two or more accounts, and the total of debits equals the total of credits.
2. A trial balance is a list of the ending balances of all accounts, listed in the same order as on the chart of accounts.
3. Any additional investments during the period result in the Capital balance on the trial balance not being the beginning figure for the Capital account.
4. There are *no* debit or credit columns on the three financial statements.

Key Terms

Account   An accounting device used in bookkeeping to record increases and decreases of business transactions relating to individual assets, liabilities, capital, withdrawals, revenue, expenses, and so on.

Chart of accounts   A numbering system of accounts that lists the account titles and account numbers to be used by a company.

Compound entry   A transaction involving more than one debit or credit.

Credit   The right-hand side of any account. A number entered on the right side of any account is said to be credited to an account.

Debit   The left-hand side of any account. A number entered on the left side of any account is said to be debited to an account.

Double-entry bookkeeping   An accounting system in which the recording of each transaction affects two or more accounts and the total of the debits is equal to the total of the credits.

Ending balance   The difference between footings in a T account.

Footings   The totals of each side of a T account.

Ledger   A group of accounts that records data from business transactions.

Normal balance of an account   The side of an account that increases by the rules of debit and credit.

Standard account   A formal account that includes columns for date, explanation, posting reference, debit, and credit.

T account   A skeleton version of a standard account, used for demonstration purposes.

Trial balance   A list of the ending balances of all the accounts in a ledger. The total of the debits should equal the total of the credits.

Blueprint: Preparing Financial Statements from a Trial Balance

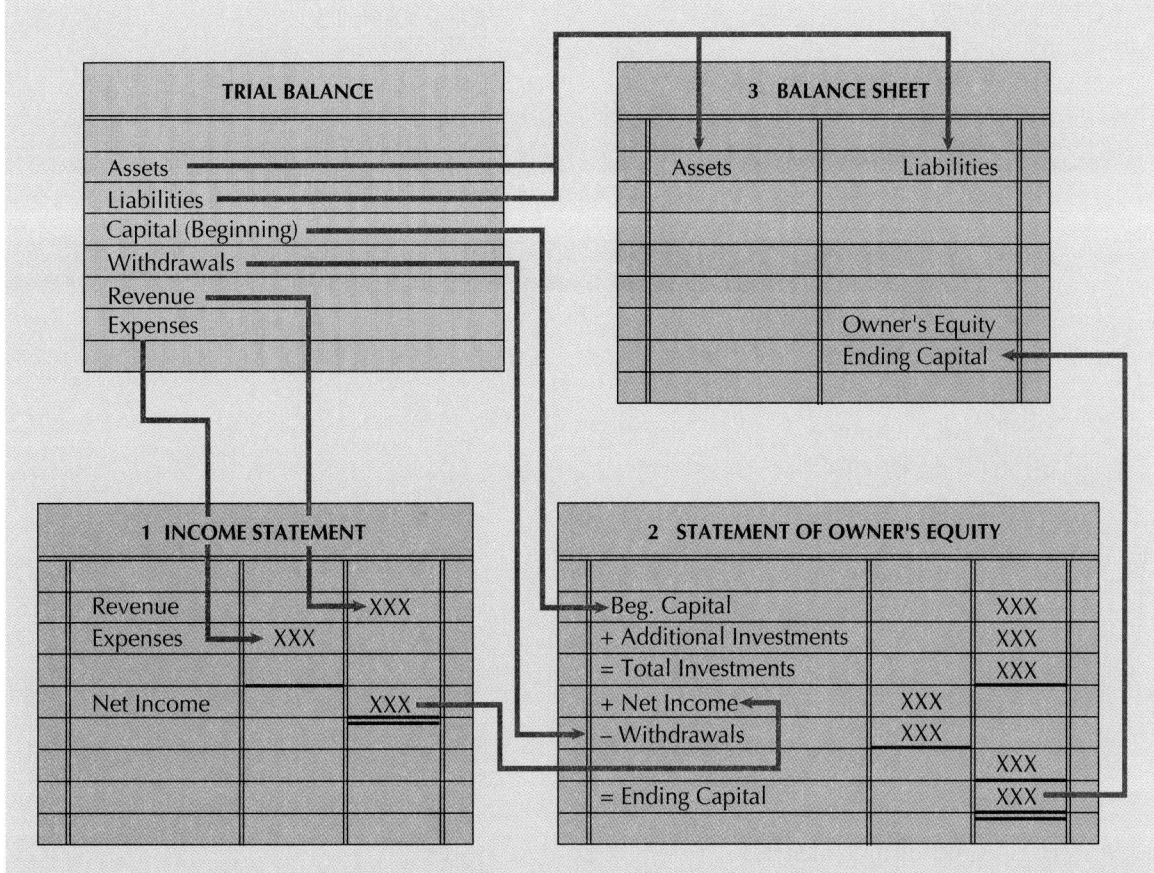

Questions, Mini Exercises, Exercises, and Problems

Discussion Questions

1. Define a ledger.
2. Why is the left-hand side of an account called a debit?
3. Footings are used in balancing all accounts. True or false? Please explain.
4. What is the end product of the accounting process?
5. What do we mean when we say that a transaction analysis chart is a teaching device?
6. What are the five steps of the transaction analysis chart?
7. Explain the concept of double-entry bookkeeping.
8. A trial balance is a formal statement. True or false? Please explain.
9. Why are there no debit or credit columns on financial statements?
10. Compare the financial statements prepared from the expanded accounting equation with those prepared from a trial balance.

Mini Exercises

(The blank forms you need are on page 34 in the *Study Guide and Working Papers*.)

The T Account

1. From the following, foot and balance each account.

Cash 110				C. Clark, Capital 311		
6/9	4,000	4/8	500		3/7	7,000
7/14	8,000				3/9	3,000
					4/12	6,000

Transaction Analysis

2. Complete the following:

Account	Category	↑	↓	Normal Balance
A. Digital Cameras				
B. Prepaid Rent				
C. Accounts Payable				
D. A. Sung, Capital				
E. A. Sung, Withdrawals				
F. Legal Fees				
G. Salary Expense				

Transaction Analysis

3. Record the following transaction into the transaction analysis chart: Provided legal services for $4,000, receiving $3,000 cash with the remainder to be paid next month.

Accounts Affected	Category	↓	↑	Rules of Dr. and Cr.	T Accounts

Trial Balance

4. Rearrange the following titles in the order they would appear on a trial balance:

Selling Expense	Legal Fees
Accounts Receivable	D. Cope, Withdrawals
Accounts Payable	Rent Expense
D. Cope, Capital	Advertising Expense
Computer Equipment	Cash

Trial Balance/Financial Statements

5. From the following trial balance, identify which statement each title will appear on:

- Income statement (IS)
- Statement of owner's equity (OE)
- Balance sheet (BS)

HEATH CO.
TRIAL BALANCE
SEPT. 30, 200X

		Dr.	Cr.
A. _____	Cash	390	
B. _____	Supplies	100	
C. _____	Office Equipment	200	
D. _____	Accounts Payable		100
E. _____	D. Heath, Capital		450
F. _____	D. Heath, Withdrawals	160	
G. _____	Fees Earned		290
H. _____	Hair Salon Fees		300
I. _____	Salaries Expense	130	
J. _____	Rent Expense	120	
K. _____	Advertising Expense	40	
	TOTALS	1,140	1,140

Exercises

(The blank forms you need are on page 35 in the *Study Guide and Working Papers.*)

2-1. From the following, prepare a chart of accounts, using the same numbering system used in this chapter.

Preparing a chart of accounts.

Digital Cameras	Professional Fees
Rent Expense	A. Sting, Capital
Accounts Payable	Cash
Accounts Receivable	Salaries Expense
Repair Expense	A. Sting, Withdrawals

2-2. Record the following transaction into the transaction analysis chart: Abe Reese bought a new piece of office equipment for $16,000, paying $4,000 down and charging the rest.

Preparing a transaction analysis chart.

2-3. Complete the following table. For each account listed on the left, fill in what category it belongs to, whether increases and decreases in the account are marked on the debit or credit sides, and which financial statement the account appears on. A sample is provided.

Accounts Affected	Category	↑	↓	Appears on which Financial Statements
Computer Supplies	Asset	Dr.	Cr.	Balance Sheet
Legal Fees Earned				
P. Rey, Withdrawals				
Accounts Payable				
Salaries Expense				
Auto				

Accounts categorizing, rules, and on which reports they appear.

2-4. Given the following accounts, complete the table by inserting appropriate numbers next to the individual transaction to indicate which account is debited and which account is credited.

Rules of debits and credits.

1.	Cash	6.	B. Baker, Withdrawals
2.	Accounts Receivable	7.	Plumbing Fees Earned
3.	Equipment	8.	Salaries Expense
4.	Accounts Payable	9.	Advertising Expense
5.	B. Baker, Capital	10.	Supplies Expenses

	Transaction	Rules	
		Dr.	Cr.
Example: **A.**	Paid salaries expense.	8	1
B.	Bob paid personal utilities bill from the company checkbook.		
C.	Advertising bill received but unpaid.		
D.	Received cash from plumbing fees.		
E.	Paid supplies expense.		
F.	Bob invested in additional equipment for the business.		
G.	Billed customers for plumbing services rendered.		
H.	Received one-half the balance from transaction G.		
I.	Bought equipment on account.		

Preparing financial statements.

2-5. From the following trial balance of Hall's Cleaners (Fig. 2-6), prepare the following:

- 🍃 Income statement
- 🍃 Statement of owner's equity
- 🍃 Balance sheet

Figure 2-6

HALL'S CLEANERS
TRIAL BALANCE
JULY 31, 200X

	Dr.	Cr.
Cash	5 5 0 00	
Equipment	6 9 2 00	
Accounts Payable		4 5 5 00
J. Hall, Capital		8 0 0 00
J. Hall, Withdrawals	1 9 8 00	
Cleaning Fees		4 5 8 00
Salaries Expense	1 6 0 00	
Utilities Expense	1 1 3 00	
Totals	1 7 1 3 00	1 7 1 3 00

Group A Problems

(The forms you need are on pages 38–45 of the *Study Guide and Working Papers.*)

Use of a transaction analysis chart.

2A-1. The following transactions occurred in the opening and operation of Melissa's Bookkeeping Service.

- **a.** Melissa Montgomery opened the bookkeeping service by investing $8,000 from her personal savings account.
- **b.** Purchased store equipment on account, $3,000.
- **c.** Rent expense due but unpaid, $600.
- **d.** Received cash for bookkeeping services rendered, $800.
- **e.** Billed a client on account, $500.
- **f.** Melissa withdrew cash for personal use, $200.

Check Figure:
After F:

Cash	
8,000	200
800	

Complete the transaction analysis chart in the *Study Guide and Working Papers.* The chart of accounts includes Cash; Accounts Receivable; Store Equipment; Accounts Payable; Melissa Montgomery, Capital; Melissa Montgomery, Withdrawals; Bookkeeping Fees Earned; and Rent Expense.

Recording transactions into ledger accounts.

2A-2. Matt Slater opened a travel agency, and the following transactions resulted:

- **a.** Matt invested $40,000 in the travel agency.
- **b.** Bought office equipment on account, $4,000.
- **c.** Agency received cash for travel arrangements that it completed for a client, $3,000.
- **d.** Matt paid a personal bill from the company checkbook, $50.

e. Paid advertising expense for the month, $700.
f. Rent expense for the month due but unpaid, $900.
g. Paid $800 as partial payment of what was owed from transaction B.

As Matt's accountant, analyze and record the transactions in T account form. Set up the T accounts and label each entry with the letter of the transaction.

Check Figure:
After G:
Cash
(A) 40,000 | 50 (D)
(C) 3,000 | 700 (E)
| 800 (G)

Chart of Accounts

Assets
Cash   111
Office Equipment   121

Liabilities
Accounts Payable   211

Owner's Equity
M. Slater, Capital   311
M. Slater, Withdrawals   312

Revenue
Travel Fees Earned   411

Expenses
Advertising Expense   511
Rent Expense   512

2A-3. From the following T accounts of Mike's Window Washing Service, (a) record and foot the balances in the *Study Guide and Working Papers* where appropriate, and (b) prepare a trial balance in proper form for May 31, 200X.

Preparing a trial balance from the T accounts.

Cash 111				Accounts Payable 211		Fees Earned 411	
5,000 (A)	100 (D)			100 (D)	1,300 (C)		6,500 (B)
3,500 (G)	200 (E)						
	400 (F)						
	200 (H)						
	900 (I)						

Accounts Receivable 112: 6,500 (B) | 3,500 (G)
Mike Frank, Capital 311: | 5,000 (A)
Rent Expense 511: 400 (F) |
Office Equipment 121: 1,300 (C) |; 200 (H) |
Mike Frank, Withdrawals 312: 900 (I) |
Utilities Expense 512: 200 (E) |

Check Figure:
Trial Balance Total $12,700

2A-4. From the trial balance of Gracie Lantz, Attorney-at-Law (Fig. 2-7), prepare (a) an income statement for the month of May, (b) a statement of owner's equity for the month ended May 31, and (c) a balance sheet as of May 31, 200X.

Preparing financial statements from the trial balance.

Figure 2-7

Check Figure:
Total Assets $6,400

GRACIE LANTZ, ATTORNEY-AT-LAW
TRIAL BALANCE
MAY 31, 200X

	Dr.	Cr.
Cash	5 0 0 0 00	
Accounts Receivable	6 5 0 00	
Office Equipment	7 5 0 00	
Accounts Payable		4 3 0 0 00
Salaries Payable		6 7 5 00
G. Lantz, Capital		1 2 7 5 00
G. Lantz, Withdrawals	3 0 0 00	
Revenue from Legal Fees		1 3 5 0 00
Utilities Expense	3 0 0 00	
Rent Expense	4 5 0 00	
Salaries Expense	1 5 0 00	
Totals	7 6 0 0 00	7 6 0 0 00

Comprehensive problem

2A-5. The chart of accounts for Angel's Delivery Service is as follows:

Chart of Accounts

Assets	Revenue
Cash 111	Delivery Fees Earned 411
Accounts Receivable 112	**Expenses**
Office Equipment 121	Advertising Expense 511
Delivery Trucks 122	Gas Expense 512
Liabilities	Salaries Expense 513
Accounts Payable 211	Telephone Expense 514
Owner's Equity	
Alice Angel, Capital 311	
Alice Angel, Withdrawals 312	

Check Figure:
Total Trial Balance
$38,100

Angel's Delivery Service completed the following transactions during the month of March:

Transaction A: Alice Angel invested $16,000 in the delivery service from her personal savings account.
Transaction B: Bought delivery trucks on account, $18,000.
Transaction C: Bought office equipment for cash, $600.
Transaction D: Paid advertising expense, $250.
Transaction E: Collected cash for delivery services rendered, $2,600.
Transaction F: Paid drivers' salaries, $900.
Transaction G: Paid gas expense for trucks, $1,200.
Transaction H: Performed delivery services for a customer on account, $800.
Transaction I: Telephone expense due but unpaid, $700.
Transaction J: Received $300 as partial payment of transaction H.
Transaction K: Alice withdrew cash for personal use, $300.

As Alice's newly employed accountant, you must:

1. Set up T accounts in a ledger.
2. Record transactions in the T accounts. (Place the letter of the transaction next to the entry.)
3. Foot the T accounts where appropriate.
4. Prepare a trial balance at the end of March.
5. Prepare from the trial balance, in proper form, (a) an income statement for the month of March, (b) a statement of owner's equity, and (c) a balance sheet as of March 31, 200X.

Use of a transaction analysis chart.

Group B Problems

(The forms you need are on pages 38–45 of the *Study Guide and Working Papers.*)

2B-1. Melissa Montgomery decided to open a bookkeeping service. Record the following transactions into the transaction analysis charts:

Check Figure:
After F:

	Cash		
(A)	2,500	275	(F)
(D)	1,200		

Transaction A: Melissa invested $2,500 in the bookkeeping service from her personal savings account.
Transaction B: Purchased store equipment on account, $900.
Transaction C: Rent expense due but unpaid, $250.
Transaction D: Performed bookkeeping services for cash, $1,200.
Transaction E: Billed clients for bookkeeping services rendered, $700.
Transaction F: Melissa paid her home heating bill from the company checkbook, $275.

Recording transactions into ledger accounts.

The chart of accounts for the shop includes Cash; Accounts Receivable; Store Equipment; Accounts Payable; Melissa Montgomery, Capital; Melissa Montgomery, Withdrawals; Bookkeeping Fees Earned; and Rent Expense.

2B-2. Matt Slater established a new travel agency. Record the following transactions for Matt in T account form. Label each entry with the letter of the transaction.

Transaction A: Matt invested $20,000 in the travel agency from his personal bank account.

Transaction B: Bought office equipment on account, $6,000.

Transaction C: Travel agency rendered service to Jensen Corp. and received cash, $1,200.

Transaction D: Matt withdrew cash for personal use, $200.

Transaction E: Paid advertising expense, $600.

Transaction F: Rent expense due but unpaid, $500.

Transaction G: Paid $400 in partial payment of transaction B.

The chart of accounts includes Cash, 111; Office Equipment, 121; Accounts Payable, 211; M. Slater, Capital, 311; M. Slater, Withdrawals, 312; Travel Fees Earned, 411; Advertising Expense, 511; and Rent Expense, 512.

Check Figure:
After G:
Cash

(A) 20,000	200 (D)
(C) 1,200	600 (E)
	400 (G)

2B-3. From the following T accounts of Mike's Window Washing Service, (a) record and foot the balances in the *Study Guide and Working Papers* where appropriate and (b) prepare a trial balance for May 31, 200X.

Preparing a trial balance from the T accounts.

Cash 111	
10,000 (A)	4,000 (C)
4,000 (F)	310 (D)
2,000 (G)	50 (E)
	600 (H)

Accounts Receivable 112	
2,000 (G)	

Office Equipment 121	
2,000 (B)	
4,000 (C)	

Accounts Payable 211	
	2,000 (B)

Mike Frank, Capital 311	
	10,000 (A)

Mike Frank, Withdrawals 312	
600 (H)	

Fees Earned 411	
	4,000 (F)
	4,000 (G)

Rent Expense 511	
310 (D)	

Utilities Expense 512	
50 (E)	

Check Figure:
Trial Balance Total
$20,000

2B-4. From the trial balance of Gracie Lantz, Attorney-at-Law (Fig. 2-8), prepare (a) an income statement for the month of May, (b) a statement of owner's equity for the month ended May 31, and (c) a balance sheet as of May 31, 200X.

Preparing financial statements from the trial balance.

Figure 2-8

GRACIE LANTZ, ATTORNEY-AT-LAW TRIAL BALANCE MAY 31, 200X	Debit	Credit
Cash	6 0 0 0 00	
Accounts Receivable	2 4 0 0 00	
Office Equipment	2 4 0 0 00	
Accounts Payable		2 0 0 00
Salaries Payable		6 0 0 00
G. Lantz, Capital		4 0 0 0 00
G. Lantz, Withdrawals	2 0 0 0 00	
Revenue from Legal Fees		8 8 0 0 00
Utilities Expense	1 0 0 00	
Rent Expense	3 0 0 00	
Salaries Expense	4 0 0 00	
Totals	13 6 0 0 00	13 6 0 0 00

Check Figure:
Total Assets $10,800

2B-5. The chart of accounts of Angel's Delivery Service includes the following: Cash, 111; Accounts Receivable, 112; Office Equipment, 121; Delivery Trucks, 122; Accounts Payable, 211; Alice Angel, Capital, 311; Alice Angel, Withdrawals, 312; Delivery Fees Earned, 411; Advertising Expense, 511; Gas Expense, 512; Salaries Expense, 513; and Telephone Expense, 514. The following transactions resulted for Angel's Delivery Service during the month of March:

Transaction A: Alice invested $40,000 in the business from her personal savings account.
Transaction B: Bought delivery trucks on account, $25,000.
Transaction C: Advertising bill received but unpaid, $800.
Transaction D: Bought office equipment for cash, $2,500.
Transaction E: Received cash for delivery services rendered, $13,000.
Transaction F: Paid salaries expense, $1,850.
Transaction G: Paid gas expense for company trucks, $750.
Transaction H: Billed customers for delivery services rendered, $5,500.
Transaction I: Paid telephone bill, $400.
Transaction J: Received $1,600 as partial payment of transaction H.
Transaction K: Alice paid her home telephone bill from company checkbook, $88.

As Alice's newly employed accountant, you must

1. Set up T accounts in a ledger.
2. Record transactions in the T accounts. (Place the letter of the transaction next to the entry.)
3. Foot the T accounts where appropriate.
4. Prepare a trial balance at the end of March.
5. Prepare from the trial balance, in proper form, (a) an income statement for the month of March, (b) a statement of owner's equity, and (c) a balance sheet as of March 31, 200X.

Real-World Applications

2R-1. Andy Leaf is a careless bookkeeper. He is having a terrible time getting his trial balance to balance. Andy has asked for your assistance in preparing a correct trial balance. The following is the incorrect trial balance:

Figure 2-9

RANCH COMPANY TRIAL BALANCE JUNE 30, 200X	Dr.	Cr.
Cash	5 1 0 00	
Accounts Receivable		6 3 5 00
Office Equipment	3 6 0 00	
Accounts Payable	1 1 0 00	
Wages Payable	1 0 00	
H. Clo, Capital	6 3 5 00	
H. Clo, Withdrawals	1 4 4 0 00	
Professional Fees		2 2 4 0 00
Rent Expense		2 4 0 00
Advertising Expense	2 5 00	
Totals	3 0 9 0 00	3 1 1 5 00

Facts you have discovered:

- Debits to the Cash account were $2,640; credits to the Cash account were $2,150.

- Amy Hall paid $15 but was not updated in Accounts Receivable.
- A purchase of office equipment for $5 on account was never recorded in the ledger.
- Revenue was understated in the ledger by $180.

Show how these errors affected the ending balances for the accounts involved and explain how the trial balance will indeed balance once they are corrected.

Tell Ranch Company how it can avoid this problem in the future. Write your recommendations.

2R-2. Cookie Mejias, owner of Mejias Company, asked her bookkeeper how each of the following situations will affect the totals of the trial balance and individual ledger accounts:

1. An $850 payment for a desk was recorded as a debit to Office Equipment, $85, and a credit to Cash, $85.

2. A payment of $300 to a creditor was recorded as a debit to Accounts Payable, $300, and a credit to Cash, $100.

3. The collection on an Accounts Receivable for $400 was recorded as a debit to Cash, $400, and a credit to C. Mejias, Capital, $400.

4. The payment of a liability for $400 was recorded as a debit to Accounts Payable, $40, and a credit to Supplies, $40.

5. A purchase of equipment of $800 was recorded as a debit to Supplies, $800, and a credit to Cash, $800.

6. A payment of $95 to a creditor was recorded as a debit to Accounts Payable, $95, and a credit to Cash, $59.

What did the bookkeeper tell her? Which accounts were overstated, and which were understated? Which were correct? Explain in writing how mistakes can be avoided in the future.

YOU make the call

Critical Thinking/Ethical Case

2R-3. Audrey Flet, the bookkeeper of ALN Co., was scheduled to leave on a three-week vacation at 5 o'clock on Friday. She couldn't get the company's trial balance to balance. At 4:30, she decided to put in fictitious figures to make it balance. Audrey told herself she would fix it when she got back from her vacation. Was Audrey right or wrong to do this? Why?

Internet Exercises: Priceline

EX-1. [www.priceline.com] In this chapter you have learned about debits and credits and their place in creating financial statements. Go to the Web site for Priceline, click on Investor Relations, and click on Financial Reports June 30, 2002. Print out the Condensed Financial Balance Sheet. How were debits and credits used to prepare the report?

EX-2. [www.priceline.com] Use your knowledge of debits and credits in this exercise. Look at the solution for exercise and answer these questions:

1. Calculate Total Assets, Total Liabilities, and Total Stockholders' Equity.

2. Use the accounting equation and calculate the balance of Stockholders' Equity (the Owner's Equity equivalent of a corporation), using the totals of Assets and Liabilities.

Continuing Problem

Eldorado Computer Center

The Eldorado Computer Center created its chart of accounts as follows:

Chart of Accounts
as of July 1, 200X

Assets		Revenue	
1000	Cash	4000	Service Revenue
1020	Accounts Receivable	**Expenses**	
1030	Supplies	5010	Advertising Expense
1080	Computer Shop Equipment	5020	Rent Expense
1090	Office Equipment	5030	Utilities Expense
Liabilities		5040	Phone Expense
2000	Accounts Payable	5050	Supplies Expense
Owner's Equity		5060	Insurance Expense
3000 Freedman, Capital		5070	Postage Expense
3010 Freedman, Withdrawals			

You will use this chart of accounts to complete the Continuing Problem.

The following problem continues from Chapter 1. The balances as of July 31 have been brought forward in your *Study Guide and Working Papers* on page 49.

Assignment for K – S

1. Set up T accounts in a ledger.
2. Record transactions k through s in the appropriate T accounts.
3. Foot the T accounts where appropriate.
4. Prepare a trial balance at the end of August.
5. Prepare from the trial balance an income statement, statement of owner's equity, and a balance sheet for the two months ending with August 31, 200X.

k. Received the phone bill for the month of July, $155.
l. Paid $150 (check #8099) for insurance for the month.
m. Paid $200 (check #8100) of the amount due from transaction d in Chapter 1.
n. Paid advertising expense for the month, $1,400 (check #8101).
o. Billed a client (Jeannine Sparks) for services rendered, $850.
p. Collected $900 for services rendered.
q. Paid the electric bill in full for the month of July (check #8102, transaction h, Chapter 1).
r. Paid cash (check #8103) for $50 in stamps.
s. Purchased $200 worth of supplies from Computer Connection on credit.

SUBWAY Case

DEBITS ON THE LEFT . . .

When Stan took the big leap from being an employee to a Subway owner, the thing that terrified him most was *not* the part about managing people—that was one of his strengths as a marketing manager. Why, at Xellent Media, 40 sales reps reported to him! No, Stan was terrified of having to manage the accounts. Subway restaurant owners have so many accounts to deal with—food costs, payroll, rent, utilities, supplies, advertising, promotion, and, biggest of all, cash. It's critical for them to keep debits and credits straight. If not, both they and Subway could lose a lot of money, quickly.

While Stan got some intense training in accounting and bookkeeping at Subway University, he still felt shaky about doing his own books. When he confided his fears to Mariah Washington, his field consultant, she suggested he hire an accountant. "You need to play to your strengths," said Mariah, and she told Stan, "More and more owners are using accountants, and almost all owners of multiple franchises do. In fact, some accountants actually specialize in handling Subway accounts for these multirestaurant owners."

Even though Stan decided to hire his cousin, Lila, to do his accounting, he still needs to feed her the right data so she can calculate his T accounts. Like many small business owners, Stan enters data into an accounting software program such as QuickBooks or Peachtree, which he then uploads to his accountant, who edits it and reviews it for accuracy. Several times in the beginning Stan mistakenly debited both cash and supplies when he paid for orders of paper cups, bread dough, and other supplies.

Lila urged Stan to review the rules for recording debits and credits. She even told him to practice for awhile using a paper ledger. "On the computer debits and credits are not as visible as they are with your paper system. Since you only enter the payables, the computer does the other side of the balance sheet. So you have to bone up on debits and credits to ensure that your Peachtree data is correct."

Discussion Questions

1. Why is the cash account so important in Stan's business?
2. Why do you think that most owners of the larger shops use accountants to do their books instead of doing them themselves?
3. Is the difference between debits and credits important to Subway restaurant owners who don't do their own books?

CHAPTER 3

Beginning the Accounting Cycle

Journalizing, Posting, and the Trial Balance

You stop by Hoffman's, a bagel shop just off campus. The owner, Stuart Hoffman, has been in the business of baking bagels for years. You wonder what makes Hoffman's bagels so good. You ask Mr. Hoffman how he does it. He replies simply, "Baking is nothing more than following several steps in order. You follow the same steps with every batch you bake—you don't change anything. It's just a cycle."

Accounting is also a cycle. You will recall in Chapters 1 and 2 we learned about the accounting equation and how it is used to record business transactions. We also learned about accounts, debits and credits, and how to prepare a trial balance. Now in Chapter 3 we will build upon this information and learn that recording business transactions is a set of steps that occur in a certain order and are then repeated. This series of steps is referred to as "the accounting cycle."

In a sense, the accounting cycle is similar to baking, since both accountants and bakers follow a set of steps in a certain order. In baking, once a batch of bagels has been baked, the baker begins another. And in accounting, once one accounting cycle is complete, the accountant begins another. Knowing about and understanding the accounting cycle won't turn you into a baker, but it will help you to succeed in gaining a better understanding of business and knowing how to speak its language, accounting.

Learning Objectives

- Journalizing: analyzing and recording business transactions into a journal. (p. 72)

- Posting: transferring information from a journal to a ledger. (p. 80)

- Preparing a trial balance. (p. 87)

The normal accounting procedures that are performed over a period of time are called the accounting cycle. The accounting cycle takes place in a period of time called an accounting period. An accounting period is the period of time covered by the income statement. Although it can be any time period up to one year (e.g., one month or three months), most businesses use a one-year accounting period. The year can be either a calendar year (January 1 through December 31) or a fiscal year.

A fiscal year is an accounting period that runs for any 12 consecutive months, so it can be the same as a calendar year. A business can choose any fiscal year that is convenient. For example, some retailers may decide to end their fiscal year when inventories and business activity are at a low point, such as after the Christmas season. This period is called a natural business year. Using a natural business year allows the business to count its year-end inventory when it is easiest to do so.

Businesses would not be able to operate successfully if they only prepared financial reports at the end of their calendar or fiscal year. That is why most businesses prepare interim reports on a monthly, quarterly, or semiannual basis.

In this chapter, as well as in Chapters 4 and 5, we follow Brenda Clark's new business, Clark's Word Processing Services. We follow the normal accounting procedures that the business performs over a period of time. Clark has chosen to use a fiscal period of January 1 to December 31, which also is the calendar year.

Take a moment to look at the four-color road map of the accounting cycle on the inside front cover. Use this map as a reference for Chapters 3, 4, and 5. It will help you to answer the question, When do I do what?

> This chapter covers Steps 1 to 4 of the accounting cycle. (See the road map on the inside front cover.)

Learning Unit 3-1	Analyzing and Recording Business Transactions into a Journal: Steps 1 and 2 of the Accounting Cycle

THE GENERAL JOURNAL

Chapter 2 taught us how to analyze and record business transactions into T accounts, or ledger accounts. Recording a debit in an account on one page of the ledger and recording the corresponding credit on a different page of the ledger, however, can make it difficult to find errors. It would be much easier if all the business's transactions were located in the same place. That is the function of the journal or general journal. Transactions are entered in the journal in chronological order (January 1, 8, 15, etc.), and then this recorded information is used to update the ledger accounts. In computerized accounting, a journal may be recorded on disk or tape.

> A business uses a journal to record transactions in chronological order. A ledger accumulates information from a journal. The journal and the ledger are in two different books.

We will use a general journal, the simplest form of a journal, to record the transactions of Clark's Word Processing Services. A transaction [debit(s) + credit(s)] that has been analyzed and recorded in a journal is called a journal entry. The process of recording the journal entry into the journal is called journalizing.

> Journal: book of original entry.

The journal is called the book of original entry, because it contains the first formal information about the business transactions. The ledger is known as the book of final entry, because the information the journal contains will be transferred to the ledger. Like the ledger, the journal may be a bound or loose-leaf book. Each of the journal pages looks like the one in Figure 3-1. The pages of the journal are numbered consecutively from page 1. Keep in mind that the journal and the ledger are separate books.

Figure 3-1
The General Journal

		CLARK'S WORD PROCESSING SERVICES GENERAL JOURNAL			
					Page 1
Date		Account Titles and Description	PR	Dr.	Cr.

Relationship Between the Journal and the Chart of Accounts

The accountant must refer to the business's chart of accounts for the account name that is to be used in the journal. Every company has its own "unique" chart of accounts.

The chart of accounts for Clark's Word Processing Services appears below. By the end of Chapter 5, we will have discussed each of these accounts.

Note that we will continue to use transaction analysis charts as a teaching aid in the journalizing process.

Clark's Word Processing Services
Chart of Accounts

Assets (100–199)
111   Cash
112   Accounts Receivable
114   Office Supplies
115   Prepaid Rent
121   Word Processing Equipment
122   Accumulated Depreciation,
        Word Processing Equipment

Liabilities (200–299)
211   Accounts Payable
212   Salaries Payable

Owner's Equity (300–399)
311   Brenda Clark, Capital
312   Brenda Clark, Withdrawals
313   Income Summary

Revenue (400–499)
411   Word Processing Fees

Expenses (500–599)
511   Office Salaries Expense
512   Advertising Expense
513   Telephone Expense
514   Office Supplies Expense
515   Rent Expense
516   Depreciation Expense,
        Word Processing Equipment

Journalizing the Transactions of Clark's Word Processing Services

Certain formalities must be followed in making journal entries:

- The debit portion of the transaction always is recorded first.
- The credit portion of a transaction is indented $\frac{1}{2}$ inch and placed below the debit portion.
- The explanation of the journal entry follows immediately after the credit and 1 inch from the date column.
- A one-line space follows each transaction and explanation. This makes the journal easier to read, and there is less chance of mixing transactions.
- Finally, as always, the total amount of debits must equal the total amount of credits. The same format is used for each of the entries in the journal.

MAY 1, 200X: BRENDA CLARK BEGAN THE BUSINESS BY INVESTING $10,000 IN CASH			
1 **Accounts Affected**	**2** **Category**	**3** ↓ ↑	**4** **Rules of Dr. and Cr.**
Cash	Asset	↑	Dr.
Brenda Clark, Capital	Capital	↑	Cr.

Figure 3-2
Owner Investment

For now the PR (posting reference) column is blank; we discuss it later.

CLARK'S WORD PROCESSING SERVICES
GENERAL JOURNAL

Page 1

Date			Account Titles and Description	PR	Dr.	Cr.
200X May	1		Cash		10 0 0 0 00	
			Brenda Clark, Capital			10 0 0 0 00
			Initial investment of cash by owner			

Let's now look at the structure of this journal entry (Fig. 3-2). The entry contains the following information:

1. Year of the journal entry   200X
2. Month of the journal entry   May
3. Day of journal entry   1
4. Name(s) of accounts debited   Cash
5. Name(s) of accounts credited   Brenda Clark, Capital
6. Explanation of transaction   Investment of cash
7. Amount of debit(s) $10,000
8. Amount of credit(s) $10,000

MAY 1: PURCHASED WORD PROCESSING EQUIPMENT FROM BEN CO. FOR $6,000, PAYING $1,000 AND PROMISING TO PAY THE BALANCE WITHIN 30 DAYS			
1 **Accounts Affected**	**2** **Category**	**3** ↓ ↑	**4** **Rules of Dr. and Cr.**
Word Processing Equipment	Asset	↑	Dr.
Cash	Asset	↓	Cr.
Accounts Payable	Liability	↑	Cr.

Note that in this compound entry we have one debit and two credits, but the total amount of debits equals the total amount of credits.

This transaction affects three accounts. When a journal entry has more than two accounts, it is called a compound journal entry.

In this entry, only the day is entered in the date column, because the year and month were entered at the top of the page from the first transaction. There is

Figure 3-3
Purchase of Equipment

	1	Word Processing Equipment		6 0 0 0 00			
		Cash			1 0 0 0 00		
		Accounts Payable			5 0 0 0 00		
		Purchase of equipment from Ben Co.					

Figure 3-3
Purchase of Equipment

A journal entry that requires three or more accounts is called a compound journal entry.

no need to repeat this information until a new page is needed or a change of months occurs.

MAY 1: RENTED OFFICE SPACE, PAYING $1,200 IN ADVANCE FOR THE FIRST THREE MONTHS

1 Accounts Affected	2 Category	3 ↓ ↑	4 Rules of Dr. and Cr.
Prepaid Rent	Asset	↑	Dr.
Cash	Asset	↓	Cr.

In this transaction Clark gains an asset called prepaid rent and gives up an asset, cash. The prepaid rent does not become an expense until it expires.

Rent paid in advance is an asset.

	1	Prepaid Rent		1 2 0 0 00			
		Cash			1 2 0 0 00		
		Rent paid in advance—3 mos.					

Figure 3-4
Rent Paid in Advance

MAY 3: PURCHASED OFFICE SUPPLIES FROM NORRIS CO. ON ACCOUNT, $600

1 Accounts Affected	2 Category	3 ↓ ↑	4 Rules of Dr. and Cr.
Office Supplies	Asset	↑	Dr.
Accounts Payable	Liability	↑	Cr.

Remember, supplies are an asset when they are purchased. Once they are used up or consumed in the operation of business, they become an expense.

Supplies become an expense when used up.

	3	Office Supplies		6 0 0 00			
		Accounts Payable			6 0 0 00		
		Purchase of supplies on account					
		from Norris					

Figure 3-5
Purchased Supplies on Account

MAY 7: COMPLETED SALES PROMOTION PIECES FOR A CLIENT AND IMMEDIATELY COLLECTED $3,000			
1 Accounts Affected	2 Category	3 ↓ ↑	4 Rules of Dr. and Cr.
Cash	Asset	↑	Dr.
Word Processing Fees	Revenue	↑	Cr.

Figure 3-6
Services Rendered

	7	Cash		3 0 0 0 00	
		Word Processing Fees			3 0 0 0 00
		Cash received for services rendered			

MAY 13: PAID OFFICE SALARIES, $650			
1 Accounts Affected	2 Category	3 ↓ ↑	4 Rules of Dr. and Cr.
Office Salaries Expense	Expense	↑	Dr.
Cash	Asset	↓	Cr.

Figure 3-7
Paid Salaries

	13	Office Salaries Expense		6 5 0 00	
		Cash			6 5 0 00
		Payment of office salaries			

Remember, expenses are recorded when they are incurred, no matter when they are paid.

MAY 18: ADVERTISING BILL FROM AL'S NEWS CO. COMES IN BUT IS NOT PAID, $250			
1 Accounts Affected	2 Category	3 ↓ ↑	4 Rules of Dr. and Cr.
Advertising Expense	Expense	↑	Dr.
Accounts Payable	Liability	↑	Cr.

Figure 3-8
Advertising Bill

	18	Advertising Expense		2 5 0 00	
		Accounts Payable			2 5 0 00
		Bill in but not paid from Al's News			

MAY 20: BRENDA CLARK WROTE A CHECK ON THE BANK ACCOUNT OF THE BUSINESS TO PAY HER HOME MORTGAGE PAYMENT OF $625

1 Accounts Affected	2 Category	3 ↓ ↑	4 Rules of Dr. and Cr.
Brenda Clark, Withdrawals	Withdrawals	↑	Dr.
Cash	Asset	↓	Cr.

Keep in mind that as withdrawals increase, owner's equity decreases.

					Dr.	Cr.
	20	Brenda Clark, Withdrawals			625 00	
		Cash				625 00
		Personal withdrawal of cash				

Figure 3-9
Personal Withdrawal

MAY 22: BILLED MORRIS COMPANY FOR A SOPHISTICATED WORD PROCESSING JOB, $5,000

1 Accounts Affected	2 Category	3 ↓ ↑	4 Rules of Dr. and Cr.
Accounts Receivable	Asset	↑	Dr.
Word Processing Fees	Revenue	↑	Cr.

Reminder: Revenue is recorded when it is earned, no matter when the cash is actually received.

					Dr.	Cr.
	22	Accounts Receivable			5000 00	
		Word Processing Fees				5000 00
		Billed Morris Co. for fees earned				

Figure 3-10
Fees Earned

MAY 27: PAID OFFICE SALARIES, $650

1 Accounts Affected	2 Category	3 ↓ ↑	4 Rules of Dr. and Cr.
Offices Salaries Expense	Expense	↑	Dr.
Cash	Asset	↓	Cr.

Figure 3-11
Paid Salaries

CLARK'S WORD PROCESSING SERVICES
GENERAL JOURNAL

Page 2

Date		Account Titles and Description	PR	Dr.	Cr.
200X May	27	Office Salaries Expense		650 00	
		Cash			650 00
		Payment of office salaries			

Note: Since we are on page 2 of the journal, the year and month are repeated.

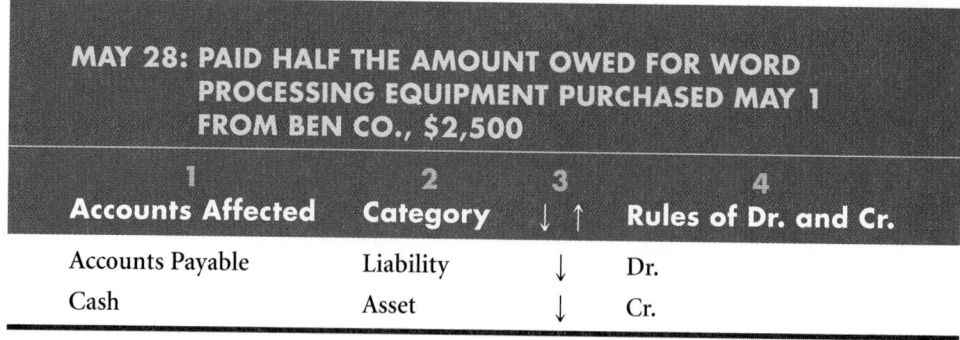

MAY 28: PAID HALF THE AMOUNT OWED FOR WORD PROCESSING EQUIPMENT PURCHASED MAY 1 FROM BEN CO., $2,500

1 Accounts Affected	2 Category	3 ↓ ↑	4 Rules of Dr. and Cr.
Accounts Payable	Liability	↓	Dr.
Cash	Asset	↓	Cr.

Figure 3-12
Partial Payment

	28	Accounts Payable		2 5 0 0 00	
		Cash			2 5 0 0 00
		Paid half the amount owed Ben Co.			

MAY 29: RECEIVED AND PAID TELEPHONE BILL, $220

1 Accounts Affected	2 Category	3 ↓ ↑	4 Rules of Dr. and Cr.
Telephone Expense	Expense	↑	Dr.
Cash	Asset	↓	Cr.

Figure 3-13
Paid Telephone

	29	Telephone Expense		2 2 0 00	
		Cash			2 2 0 00
		Paid telephone bill			

This concludes the journal transactions of Clark's Word Processing Services. (See page 83 for a summary of all the transactions.)

Learning Unit 3-1 Review

AT THIS POINT you should be able to

- Define an accounting cycle. (p. 72)
- Define and explain the relationship of the accounting period to the income statement. (p. 72)
- Compare and contrast a calendar year to a fiscal year. (p. 72)
- Explain the term *natural business year*. (p. 72)
- Explain the function of interim reports. (p. 72)
- Define and state the purpose of a journal. (p. 72)
- Compare and contrast a book of original entry to a book of final entry. (p. 72)

- Differentiate between a chart of accounts and a journal. (p. 73)
- Explain a compound entry. (p. 74)
- Journalize a business transaction. (p. 74)

SELF-REVIEW QUIZ 3-1

(The blank forms you need are on pages 52–53 of the *Study Guide and Working Papers.* See your DVD for worked-out solutions.)

The following are the transactions of Lowe's Repair Service. Journalize the transactions in proper form. The chart of accounts includes Cash; Accounts Receivable; Prepaid Rent; Repair Supplies; Repair Equipment; Accounts Payable; A. Lowe, Capital; A. Lowe, Withdrawals; Repair Fees Earned; Salaries Expense; Advertising Expense; and Supplies Expense.

200X

June 1 A. Lowe invested $7,000 cash and $5,000 of repair equipment in the business.

1 Paid two months' rent in advance, $1,200.

4 Bought repair supplies from Melvin Co. on account, $600. (These supplies have not yet been consumed or used up.)

15 Performed repair work, received $600 in cash, and had to bill Doe Co. for remaining balance of $300.

18 A. Lowe paid his home telephone bill, $50, with a check from the company.

20 Advertising bill for $400 from Jones Co. received but payment not due yet. (Advertising has already appeared in the newspaper.)

24 Paid salaries, $1,400.

SOLUTION TO SELF-REVIEW QUIZ 3-1

Figure 3-14
Transactions Journalized

	Date		Account Titles and Description	PR	Dr.	Cr.
200X June		1	Cash		7 0 0 0 00	
			Repair Equipment		5 0 0 0 00	
			A. Lowe, Capital			12 0 0 0 00
			Owner investment			
		1	Prepaid Rent		1 2 0 0 00	
			Cash			1 2 0 0 00
			Rent paid in advance—2mos.			
		4	Repair Supplies		6 0 0 00	
			Accounts Payable			6 0 0 00
			Purchase on account from Melvin Co.			
		15	Cash		6 0 0 00	
			Accounts Receivable		3 0 0 00	
			Repair Fees Earned			9 0 0 00
			Performed repairs for Doe Co.			
		18	A. Lowe, Withdrawals		5 0 00	
			Cash			5 0 00
			Personal withdrawal			
		20	Advertising Expense		4 0 0 00	
			Accounts Payable			4 0 0 00
			Advertising bill from Jones Co.			
		24	Salaries Expense		1 4 0 0 00	
			Cash			1 4 0 0 00
			Paid salaries			

LOWE'S REPAIR SERVICE
GENERAL JOURNAL

Page 1

Quiz Tip:
All titles for the debits and credits come from the chart of accounts, debits are entered next to the date column, and credits are indented. The PR column is left blank in the journalizing process.

Learning Unit 3-2   Posting to the Ledger: Step 3 of the Accounting Cycle

The general journal serves a particular purpose: It puts every transaction the business does in one place. There are things it cannot do, though. For example, if you were asked to find the balance of the cash account from the general journal, you would have to go through the entire journal and look for only the cash entries. Then you would have to add up the debits and credits for the Cash account and determine the difference between the two.

What we really need to do to find balances of accounts is to transfer the information from the journal to the ledger. This is called posting. In the ledger we will accumulate an ending balance for each account so that we can prepare financial statements.

Accounts Payable						Account No. 211		
			Post. Ref.	Debit	Credit	Balance		
Date	Explanation					Debit	Credit	
200X May 1			GJ1		5 0 0 0 00		5 0 0 0 00	
3			GJ1		6 0 0 00		5 6 0 0 00	
18			GJ1		2 5 0 00		5 8 5 0 00	
28			GJ2	2 5 0 0 00			3 3 5 0 00	

Figure 3-15
Four-Column Account

In Chapter 2 we used the T account form to make our ledger entries. T accounts are very simple, but they are not used in the real business world; they are only used for demonstration purposes. In practice, accountants often use a four-column account form that includes a column for the business's running balance. Figure 3-15 shows a standard four-column account. We use that format in the text from now on.

> Footings are not needed in four-column accounts.

POSTING

Now let's look at how to post the transactions of Clark's Word Processing Service from its journal. The diagram in Figure 3-16, p. 82 shows how to post the cash line from the journal to the ledger. The steps in the posting process are numbered and illustrated in the figure.

Step 1: In the Cash account in the ledger, record the date (May 1, 200X) and the amount of the entry ($10,000).

Step 2: Record the page number of the journal "GJ1" in the posting reference (PR) column of the Cash account.

Step 3: Calculate the new balance of the account. You keep a running balance in each account as you would in your checkbook. To do so, you take the present balance in the account on the previous line and add or subtract the transaction as necessary to arrive at your new balance.

Step 4: Record the account number of Cash (111) in the posting reference (PR) column of the journal. This is called cross-referencing.

The same sequence of steps occurs for each line in the journal. In a manual system like Clark's, the debits and credits in the journal may be posted in the order they were recorded, or all the debits may be posted first and then all the credits. If Clark used a computer system, the program menu would post at the press of a button.

Using Posting References

The posting references are very helpful. In the journal, the PR column tells us which transactions have or have not been posted and also to which accounts they were posted. In the ledger, the posting reference leads us back to the original transaction in its entirety, so we can see why the debit or credit was recorded and what other accounts were affected. (It leads us back to the original transaction by identifying the journal and the page in the journal from which the information came.)

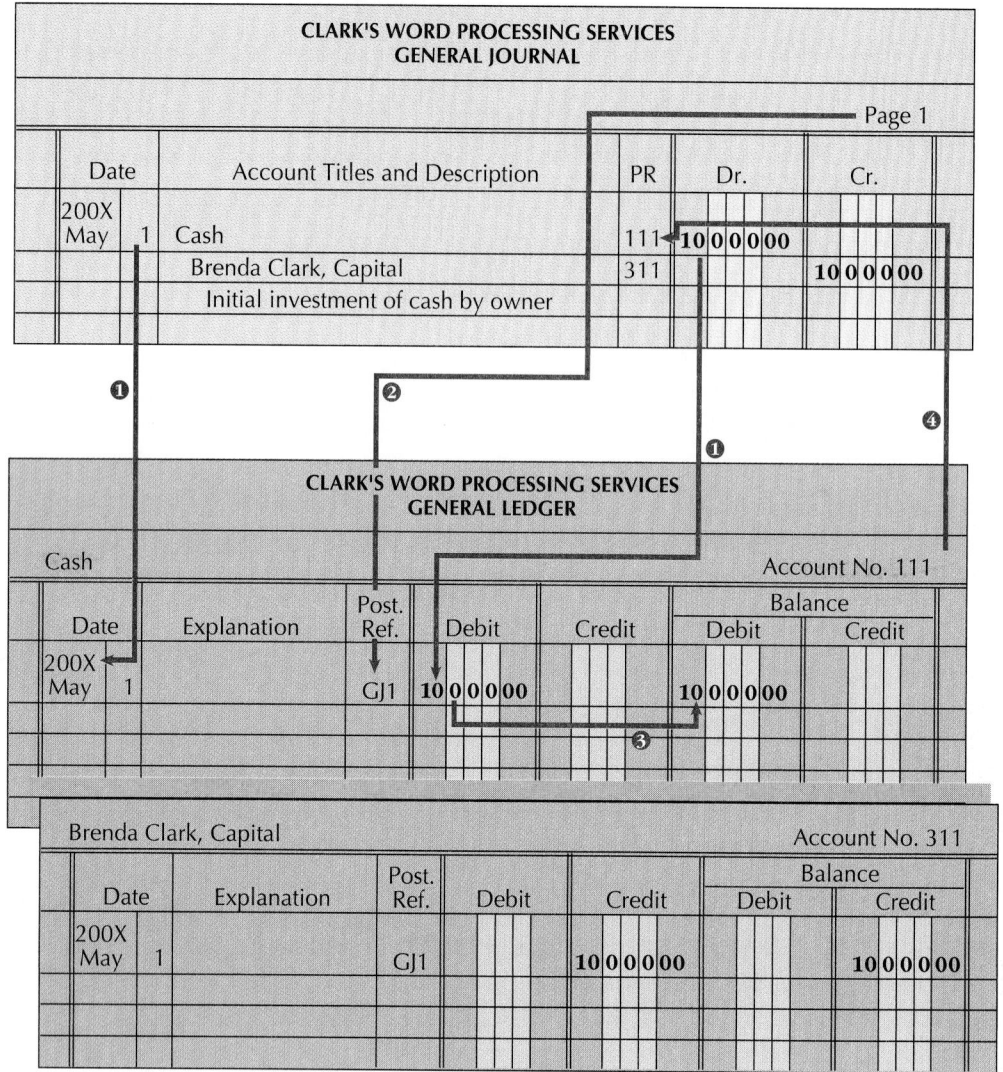

Figure 3-16 How to Post from Journal to Ledger

Learning Unit 3-2 Review

AT THIS POINT you should be able to

- State the purpose of posting. (p. 80)
- Discuss the advantages of the four-column account. (p. 81)
- Identify the elements to be posted. (p. 82)
- From journalized transactions, post to the general ledger. (p. 82)

SELF-REVIEW QUIZ 3-2

(The blank forms you need are on pages 54–59 of the *Study Guide and Working Papers*. See your DVD for worked-out solutions.)

Figure 3-17 shows the journalized transactions of Clark's Word Processing Services. Your task is to post information to the ledger. The ledger in your workbook has all the account titles and numbers that were used from the chart of accounts.

					CLARK'S WORD PROCESSING SERVICES GENERAL JOURNAL							

											Page 1	

Date			Account Titles and Description	PR	Dr.				Cr.			
200X May	1		Cash		10 0 0 0	00						
			Brenda Clark, Capital						10 0 0 0	00		
			Initial investment of cash by owner									
	1		Word Processing Equipment		6 0 0 0	00						
			Cash						1 0 0 0	00		
			Accounts Payable						5 0 0 0	00		
			Purchase of equip. from Ben Co.									
	1		Prepaid Rent		1 2 0 0	00						
			Cash						1 2 0 0	00		
			Rent paid in advance (3 months)									
	3		Office Supplies		6 0 0	00						
			Accounts Payable						6 0 0	00		
			Purchase of supplies on acct. from Norris									
	7		Cash		3 0 0 0	00						
			Word Processing Fees						3 0 0 0	00		
			Cash received for services rendered									
	13		Office Salaries Expense		6 5 0	00						
			Cash						6 5 0	00		
			Payment of office salaries									
	18		Advertising Expense		2 5 0	00						
			Accounts Payable						2 5 0	00		
			Bill received but not paid from Al's News									
	20		Brenda Clark, Withdrawals		6 2 5	00						
			Cash						6 2 5	00		
			Personal withdrawal of cash									
	22		Accounts Receivable		5 0 0 0	00						
			Word Processing Fees						5 0 0 0	00		
			Billed Morris Co. for fees earned									

Figure 3-17 Journalized Entries

Figure 3-17
(*continued*)

	Date		Account Titles and Description	PR	Dr.	Cr.
	200X					
	May	27	Office Salaries Expense		6 5 0 00	
			Cash			6 5 0 00
			Payment of office salaries			
		28	Accounts Payable		2 5 0 0 00	
			Cash			2 5 0 0 00
			Paid half the amount owed Ben Co.			
		29	Telephone Expense		2 2 0 00	
			Cash			2 2 0 00
			Paid telephone bill			

CLARK'S WORD PROCESSING SERVICES
GENERAL JOURNAL

Page 2

SOLUTION TO SELF-REVIEW QUIZ 3-2

Remember, the PR column remains empty until the entries have been posted.

CLARK'S WORD PROCESSING SERVICES
GENERAL JOURNAL

Page 1

	Date		Account Titles and Description	PR	Dr.	Cr.
	200X					
	May	1	Cash	111	10 0 0 0 00	
			Brenda Clark, Capital	311		10 0 0 0 00
			Initial investment of cash by owner			
		1	Word Processing Equipment	121	6 0 0 0 00	
			Cash	111		1 0 0 0 00
			Accounts Payable	211		5 0 0 0 00
			Purchase of equip. from Ben Co.			
		1	Prepaid Rent	115	1 2 0 0 00	
			Cash	111		1 2 0 0 00
			Rent paid in advance (3 months)			
		3	Office Supplies	114	6 0 0 00	
			Accounts Payable	211		6 0 0 00
			Purchase of supplies on acct. from Norris			
		7	Cash	111	3 0 0 0 00	
			Word Processing Fees	411		3 0 0 0 00
			Cash received from services rendered			
		13	Office Salaries Expense	511	6 5 0 00	
			Cash	111		6 5 0 00
			Payment of office salaries			

Figure 3-18 Postings

	18	Advertising Expense	512	2 5 0 00	
		Accounts Payable	211		2 5 0 00
		Bill received but not paid from Al's News			
	20	Brenda Clark, Withdrawals	312	6 2 5 00	
		Cash	111		6 2 5 00
		Personal withdrawal of cash			
	22	Accounts Receivable	112	5 0 0 0 00	
		Word Processing Fees	411		5 0 0 0 00
		Billed Morris Co. for fees earned			

CLARK'S WORD PROCESSING SERVICES
GENERAL JOURNAL

Page 2

Date		Account Titles and Description	PR	Dr.	Cr.
200X May	27	Office Salaries Expense	511	6 5 0 00	
		Cash	111		6 5 0 00
		Payment of office salaries			
	28	Accounts Payable	211	2 5 0 0 00	
		Cash	111		2 5 0 0 00
		Paid half the amount owed Ben Co.			
	29	Telephone Expense	513	2 2 0 00	
		Cash	111		2 2 0 00
		Paid telephone bill			

Figure 3-18 (continued)

CLARK'S WORD PROCESSING SERVICES
PARTIAL GENERAL LEDGER

Cash   Account No. 111

Date		Explanation	Post. Ref.	Debit	Credit	Balance Debit	Balance Credit
200X May	1		GJ1	10 0 0 0 00		10 0 0 0 00	
	1		GJ1		1 0 0 0 00	9 0 0 0 00	
	1		GJ1		1 2 0 0 00	7 8 0 0 00	
	7		GJ1	3 0 0 0 00		10 8 0 0 00	
	13		GJ1		6 5 0 00	10 1 5 0 00	
	20		GJ1		6 2 5 00	9 5 2 5 00	
	27		GJ2		6 5 0 00	8 8 7 5 00	
	28		GJ2		2 5 0 0 00	6 3 7 5 00	
	29		GJ2		2 2 0 00	6 1 5 5 00	

Figure 3-19 Partial General Ledger

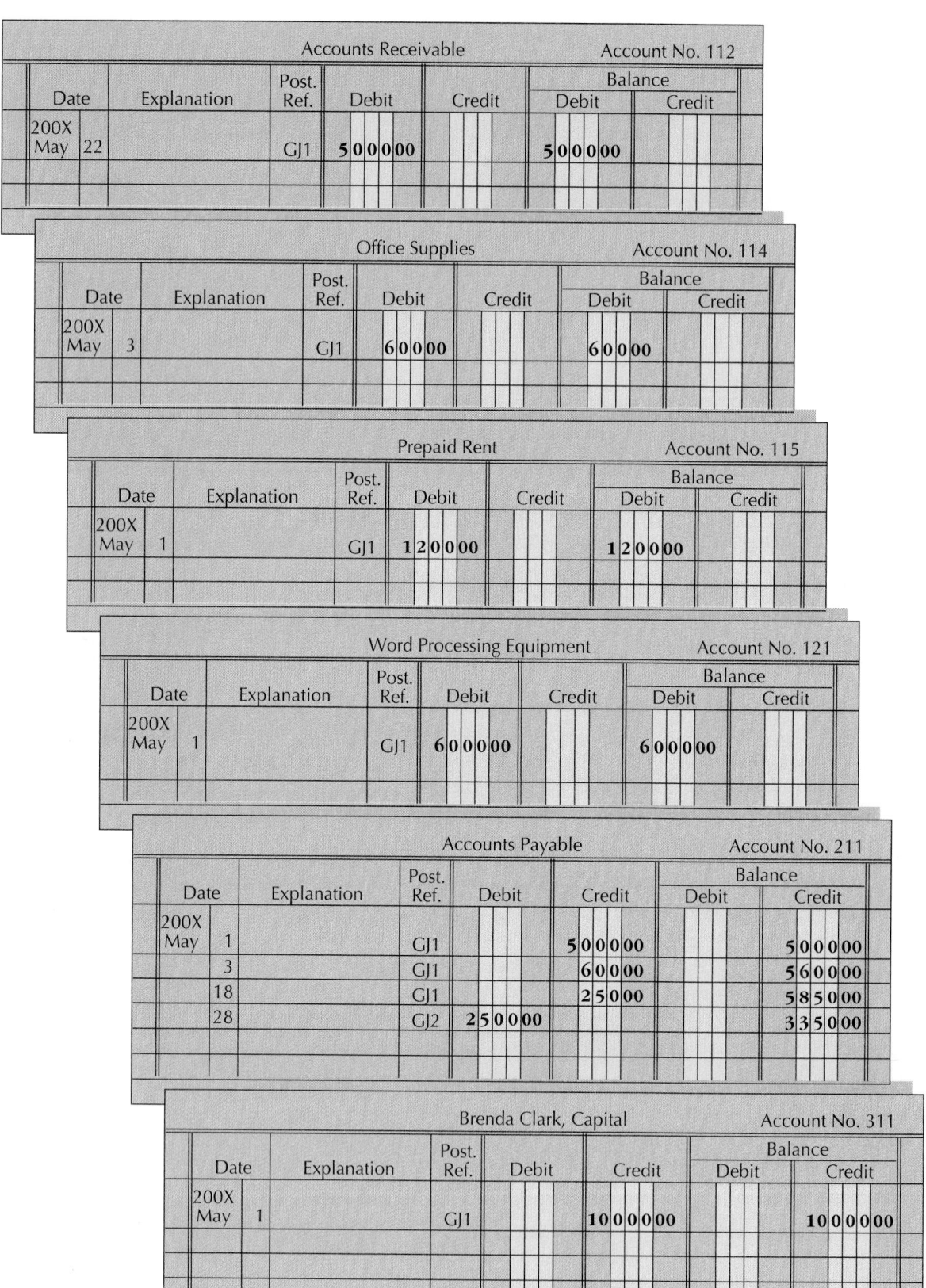

Figure 3-19 (continued)

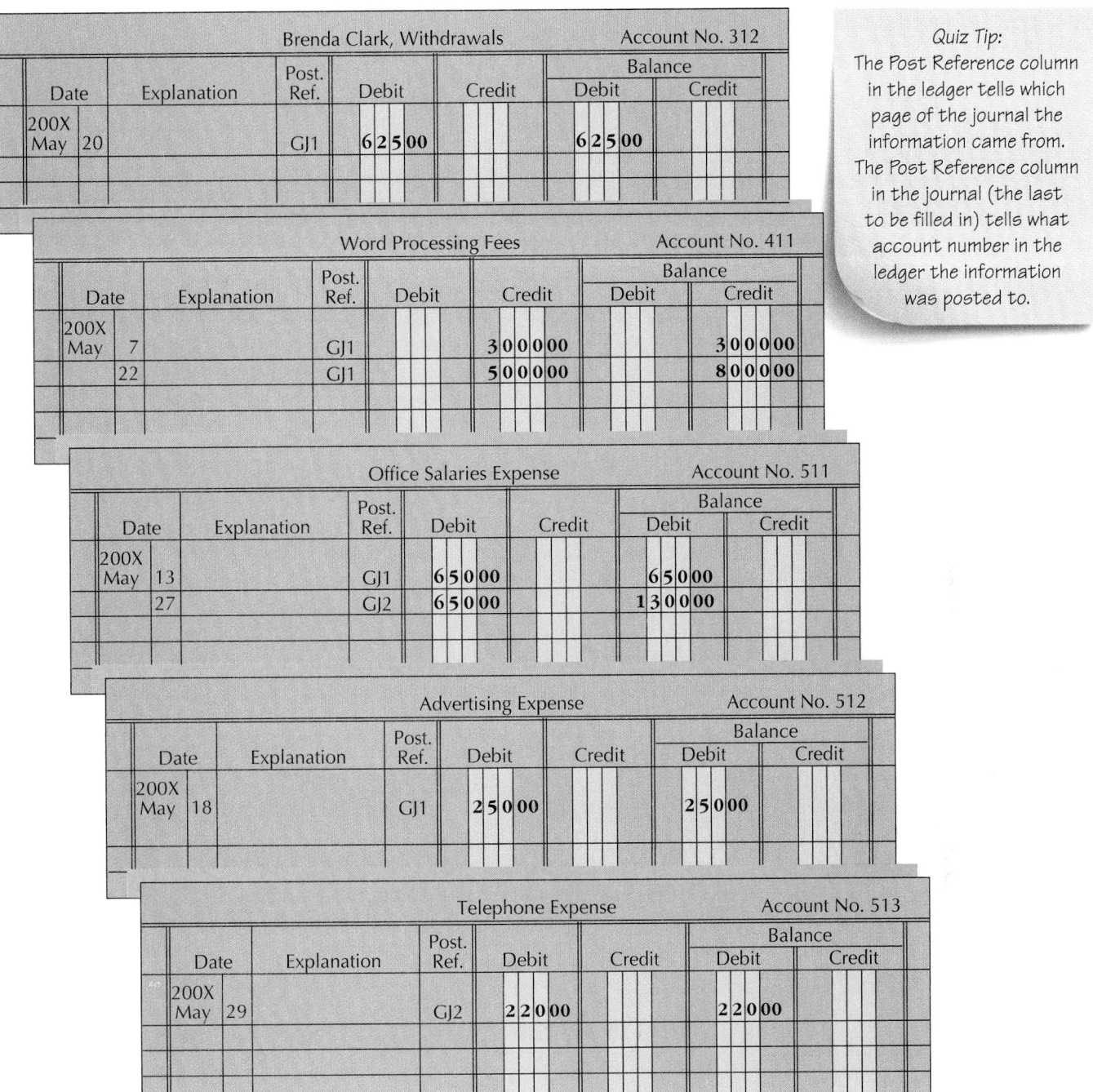

Figure 3-19 (*continued*)

Learning Unit 3-3   Preparing the Trial Balance: Step 4 of the Accounting Cycle

Did you note in Quiz 3-2 how each account had a running balance figure? Did you know the normal balance of each account in Clark's ledger? As we discussed in Chapter 2, the list of the individual accounts with their balances taken from the ledger is called a **trial balance.**

The trial balance shown in Figure 3-20, p. 88 was developed from the ledger accounts of Clark's Word Processing Services that were posted and balanced in Quiz 3-2. If the information is journalized or posted incorrectly, the trial balance will not be correct.

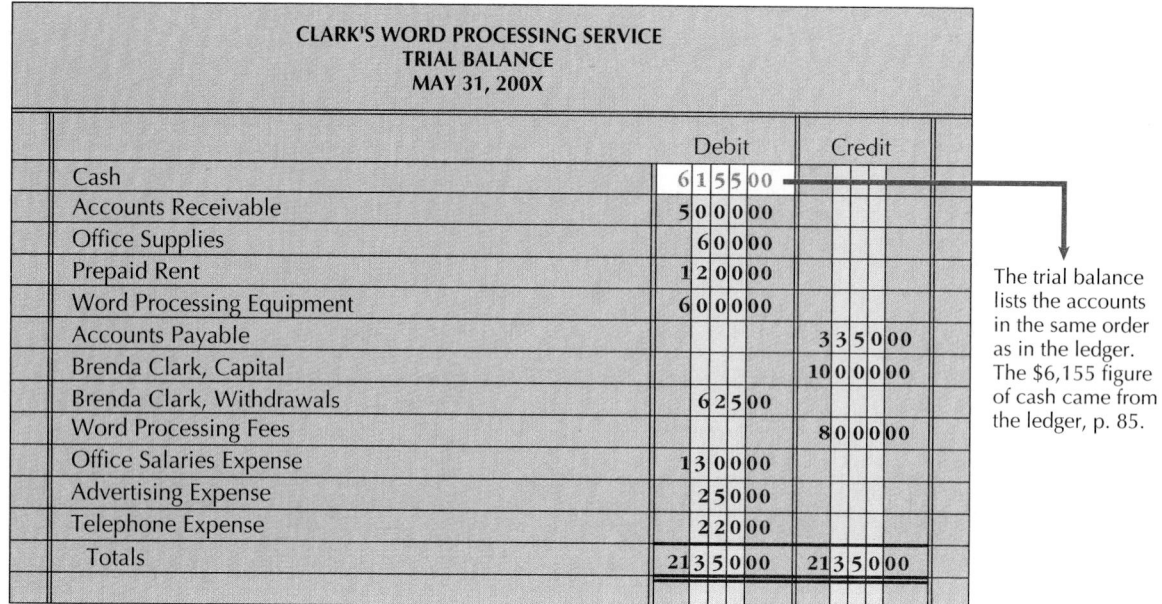

CLARK'S WORD PROCESSING SERVICE TRIAL BALANCE MAY 31, 200X	Debit	Credit
Cash	6 1 5 5 00	
Accounts Receivable	5 0 0 0 00	
Office Supplies	6 0 0 00	
Prepaid Rent	1 2 0 0 00	
Word Processing Equipment	6 0 0 0 00	
Accounts Payable		3 3 5 0 00
Brenda Clark, Capital		10 0 0 0 00
Brenda Clark, Withdrawals	6 2 5 00	
Word Processing Fees		8 0 0 0 00
Office Salaries Expense	1 3 0 0 00	
Advertising Expense	2 5 0 00	
Telephone Expense	2 2 0 00	
Totals	21 3 5 0 00	21 3 5 0 00

The trial balance lists the accounts in the same order as in the ledger. The $6,155 figure of cash came from the ledger, p. 85.

Figure 3-20 Trial Balance

There are some things the trial balance will not show:

- The capital figure on the trial balance may not be the beginning capital figure. For instance, if Brenda Clark had made additional investments during the period, the additional investment would have been journalized and posted to the Capital account. The only way to tell if the capital balance on the trial balance is the original balance is to check the ledger Capital account to see whether any additional investments were made. This will be important when we make financial reports.
- There is no guarantee that transactions have been properly recorded. For example, the following errors would remain undetected: (1) a transaction that may have been omitted in the journalizing process, (2) a transaction incorrectly analyzed and recorded in the journal, and (3) a journal entry journalized or posted twice.

> The totals of a trial balance can balance and yet be incorrect.

WHAT TO DO IF A TRIAL BALANCE DOESN'T BALANCE

The trial balance of Clark's Word Processing Services shows that the total of debits is equal to the total of credits. What happens, however, if the trial balance is in balance but the correct amount is not recorded in each ledger account? Accuracy in the journalizing and posting process will help ensure that no errors are made.

Even if there is an error, the first rule is "don't panic." Everyone makes mistakes, and there are accepted ways of correcting them. Once an entry has been made in ink, correcting an error in it must always show that the entry has been changed and who changed it. Sometimes the change has to be explained.

SOME COMMON MISTAKES

If the trial balance does not balance, the cause could be something relatively simple. Here are some common errors and how they can be fixed:

- If the difference (the amount you are off) is 10, 100, 1,000, and so forth, there is probably a mathematical error in addition.

- If the difference is equal to an individual account balance in the ledger, the amount could have been omitted. It is also possible the figure was not posted from the general journal.
- Divide the difference by 2, then check to see if a debit should have been a credit and vice versa in the ledger or trial balance. Example: $150 difference ÷ 2 = $75. This means you may have placed $75 as a debit to an account instead of a credit, or vice versa.
- If the difference is evenly divisible by 9, a **slide** or transposition may have occurred. A slide is an error resulting from adding or deleting zeros in writing numbers. For example, $4,175.00 may have been copied as $41.75. A **transposition** is the accidental rearrangement of digits of a number. For example, $4,175 might have been accidentally written as $4,157.
- Compare the balances in the trial balance with the ledger accounts to check for copying errors.
- Recompute balances in each ledger account.
- Trace all postings from journal to ledger.

If you cannot find the error after you have done all this, take a coffee break. Then start all over again.

Correcting the trial balance: What to do if your trial balance doesn't balance.

Did you clear your adding machine?

MAKING A CORRECTION BEFORE POSTING

Before posting, error correction is straightforward. Simply draw a line through the incorrect entry, write the correct information above the line, and write your initials near the change.

Correcting an Error in an Account Title   Figure 3-21 shows an error and its correction in an account title:

	1	Word Processing Equipment	6 0 0 0 00	
		Cash		1 0 0 0 00
		~~Accounts Receivable~~ Accounts Payable *amp*		5 0 0 0 00
		Purchase of equipment from Ben Co.		

Figure 3-21
Account Error

Correcting a Numerical Error   Numbers are handled the same way as account titles, as the next change from 520 to 250 in Figure 3-22 shows:

	18	Advertising Expense	2 5 0 00	
		Accounts Payable		*amp* ~~5 2 0 00~~ 2 5 0 00
		Bill from Al's News		

Figure 3-22
Number Error

Correcting an Entry Error   If a number has been entered in the wrong column, a straight line is drawn through it. The number is then written in the correct column, as shown in Figure 3-23:

	1	Word Processing Equipment	6 0 0 0 00	
		Cash		1 0 0 0 00
		Accounts Payable	*amp* ~~5 0 0 0 00~~	5 0 0 0 00
		Purchase of equip. from Ben Co.		

Figure 3-23
Correcting Entry

MAKING A CORRECTION AFTER POSTING

It is also possible to correct an amount that is correctly entered in the journal but posted incorrectly to the ledger of the proper account. The first step is to draw a line through the error and write the correct figure above it. The next step is changing the running balance to reflect the corrected posting. Here, too, a line is drawn through the balance and the corrected balance is written above it. Both changes must be initialed, as shown in Figure 3-24.

Figure 3-24
Correction After Posting

							Balance	
				Word Processing Fees			Account No. 411	
Date		Explanation	Post. Ref.	Debit	Credit	Debit	Credit	
200X May	7		GJ1		2 5 0 0|00		2 5 0 0|00
	22		GJ1		4 1 0 0|00 ~~250000~~ amp		6 6 0 0|00 ~~250000~~ amp

CORRECTING AN ENTRY POSTED TO THE WRONG ACCOUNT

Drawing a line through an error and writing the correction above it is possible when a mistake has occurred within the proper account, but when an error involves a posting to the wrong account, the journal must include a correction accompanied by an explanation. In addition, the correct information must be posted to the appropriate ledgers.

Suppose, for example, as a result of tracing postings from journal entries to ledgers you find that a $180 telephone bill was incorrectly debited as an advertising expense. The following illustration shows how this is done.

Step 1:   The journal entry is corrected and the correction is explained (Fig. 3-25):

Figure 3-25
Corrected Entry
for Telephone

		GENERAL JOURNAL					Page 3	
Date		Account Titles and Description	PR	Dr.		Cr.		
200X May	29	Telephone Expense	513	1 8 0	0 0			
		Advertising Expense	512			1 8 0	0 0	
		To correct error in which						
		Advertising Exp. was debited						
		for charges to Telephone Exp.						

Step 2:   The Advertising Expense ledger account is corrected (Fig. 3-26):

Figure 3-26
Ledger Update
for Advertising

				Advertising Expense			Account No. 512	
							Balance	
Date		Explanation	Post. Ref.	Debit	Credit	Debit	Credit	
200X May	18		GJ1	1 7 5|00		1 7 5|00	
	23		GJ1	1 8 0|00		3 5 5|00	
	29	Correcting entry	GJ3		1 8 0|00	1 7 5|00	

Step 3: The Telephone Expense ledger is corrected (Fig. 3-27):

				Telephone Expense			Account No. 513	
			Post.				Balance	
Date	Explanation		Ref.	Debit	Credit	Debit		Credit
200X May 29			GJ3	1 8 0 00		1 8 0 00		

Figure 3-27
Ledger Update
for Telephone

Learning Unit 3-3 Review

AT THIS POINT you should be able to

- Prepare a trial balance with a ledger, using four-column accounts. (p. 88)
- Analyze and correct a trial balance that doesn't balance. (p. 89)
- Correct journal and posting errors. (p. 90)

SELF-REVIEW QUIZ 3-3

(The blank forms you need are on page 60 of the *Study Guide and Working Papers.* See your DVD for worked-out solutions.)

1.

> **MEMO**
>
> To: Al Vincent
>
> From: Professor Jones
>
> Re: Trial Balance
>
> You have submitted to me an incorrect trial balance (Fig. 3-28). Could you please rework and turn in to me before next Friday?
>
> Note: Individual amounts look OK.

Figure 3-28
Incorrect Trial Balance

A. RICE TRIAL BALANCE OCTOBER 31, 200X	Dr.	Cr.
Cash		8 0 6 0 00
Operating Expenses		1 7 0 0 00
A. Rice, Withdrawals		4 0 0 00
Service Revenue		5 4 0 0 00
Equipment	5 0 0 0 00	
Accounts Receivable	3 5 4 0 00	
Accounts Payable	2 0 0 0 00	
Supplies	3 0 0 00	
A. Rice, Capital		11 6 0 0 00

2. An $8,000 debit to Office Equipment was mistakenly journalized and posted on June 9, 200X to Office Supplies. Prepare the appropriate journal entry to correct this error.

SOLUTION TO SELF-REVIEW QUIZ 3-3

1.

Figure 3-29
Correct Trial Balance

Quiz Tip:
Items in a trial balance
are listed in the same
order as in the ledger or
the chart of accounts.
Expect each account to
have its normal balance
(either debit or credit).

A. RICE TRIAL BALANCE OCTOBER 31, 200X	Dr.	Cr.
Cash	8 0 6 0 00	
Accounts Receivable	3 5 4 0 00	
Supplies	3 0 0 00	
Equipment	5 0 0 0 00	
Accounts Payable		2 0 0 0 00
A. Rice, Capital		11 6 0 0 00
A. Rice, Withdrawals	4 0 0 00	
Service Revenue		5 4 0 0 00
Operating Expenses	1 7 0 0 00	
Totals	19 0 0 0 00	19 0 0 0 00

2.

Figure 3-30
Correcting Entry

GENERAL JOURNAL					Page 4	
Date		Account Titles and Description	PR	Dr.	Cr.	
200X June	9	Office Equipment		8 0 0 0 00		
		Office Supplies			8 0 0 0 00	
		To correct error in which office supplies				
		had been debited for purchase of				
		office equipment				

Chapter Review

SOLUTIONS & TIPS TO COMPREHENSIVE PROBLEM: PUTTING THE PIECES TOGETHER

(The blank forms you need are on pages 61–65 in the *Study Guide and Working Papers*.)

In March, Abby's Employment Agency had the following transactions:

200X

Mar. 1 Abby Todd invested $5,000 in the new employment agency.

4 Bought equipment for cash, $200.

5 Earned employment fee commission, $200, but payment from Blue Co. will not be received until June.

6 Paid wages expense, $300.

7 Abby paid her home utility bill from the company checkbook, $75.

9 Placed Rick Wool at VCR Corporation, receiving $1,200 cash.

15 Paid cash for supplies, $200.

28 Telephone bill received but not paid, $180.

29 Advertising bill received but not paid, $400.

The chart of accounts includes Cash, 111; Accounts Receivable, 112; Supplies, 131; Equipment, 141; Accounts Payable, 211; A. Todd, Capital, 311; A. Todd, Withdrawals, 321; Employment Fees Earned, 411; Wage Expense, 511; Telephone Expense, 521; and Advertising Expense, 531.

Your task is to

a. Set up a ledger based on the chart of accounts.

b. Journalize (all page 1) and post transactions.

c. Prepare a trial balance for March 31.

Solution to Comprehensive Demonstration Problem

b.

	Date		Account Titles and Description	PR	Dr.	Cr.
			ABBY'S EMPLOYMENT AGENCY			Page 1
	200X Mar.	1	Cash	111	5 0 0 0 00	
			A. Todd, Capital	311		5 0 0 0 00
			Owner investment			
		4	Equipment	141	2 0 0 00	
			Cash	111		2 0 0 00
			Bought equipment for cash			
		5	Accounts Receivable	112	2 0 0 00	
			Employment Fees Earned	411		2 0 0 00
			Fees on account from Blue Co.			
		6	Wage Expense	511	3 0 0 00	
			Cash	111		3 0 0 00
			Paid wages			

Figure 3-31

Journal Entries and Post References

Figure 3-31
(*continued*)

Date	Account	PR	Dr.	Cr.
7	A. Todd, Withdrawals	321	75 00	
	Cash	111		75 00
	Personal withdrawals			
9	Cash	111	1 2 0 0 00	
	Employment Fees Earned	411		1 2 0 0 00
	Cash fees			
15	Supplies	131	2 0 0 00	
	Cash	111		2 0 0 00
	Bought supplies for cash			
28	Telephone Expense	521	1 8 0 00	
	Accounts Payable	211		1 8 0 00
	Telephone bill owed			
29	Advertising Expense	531	4 0 0 00	
	Accounts Payable	211		4 0 0 00
	Advertising bill received			

a.

GENERAL LEDGER

Cash 111

Date	PR	Dr.	Cr.	Balance Dr.	Balance Cr.
200X Mar. 1	GJ1	5,000		5,000	
4	GJ1		200	4,800	
6	GJ1		300	4,500	
7	GJ1		75	4,425	
9	GJ1	1,200		5,625	
15	GJ1		200	5,425	

Accounts Receivable 112

Date	PR	Dr.	Cr.	Balance Dr.	Balance Cr.
200X Mar. 5	GJ1	200		200	

Supplies 131

Date	PR	Dr.	Cr.	Balance Dr.	Balance Cr.
200X Mar. 15	GJ1	200		200	

A. Todd, Capital 311

Date	PR	Dr.	Cr.	Balance Dr.	Balance Cr.
200X Mar. 1	GJ1		5,000		5,000

A. Todd, Withdrawals 321

Date	PR	Dr.	Cr.	Balance Dr.	Balance Cr.
200X Mar. 7	GJ1	75		75	

Employment Fees Earned 411

Date	PR	Dr.	Cr.	Balance Dr.	Balance Cr.
200X Mar. 5	GJ1		200		200
9	GJ1		1,200		1,400

Wage Expense 511

Date	PR	Dr.	Cr.	Balance Dr.	Balance Cr.
200X Mar. 6	GJ1	300		300	

Figure 3-32 General Ledger (cont. on p. 95)

Equipment					141
				Balance	
Date	PR	Dr.	Cr.	Dr.	Cr.
200X Mar. 4	GJ1	200		200	

Telephone Expense					521
				Balance	
Date	PR	Dr.	Cr.	Dr.	Cr.
200X Mar. 28	GJ1	180		180	

Accounts Payable					211
				Balance	
Date	PR	Dr.	Cr.	Dr.	Cr.
200X Mar. 28	GJ1		180		180
29	GJ1		400		580

Advertising Expense					531
				Balance	
Date	PR	Dr.	Cr.	Dr.	Cr.
200X Mar. 29	GJ1	400		400	

Figure 3-32 *(continued)*

Solution Tips to Journalizing

1. When journalizing, the PR column is not filled in.
2. Write the name of the debit against the date column. Indent credits and list them below debits. Be sure total debits for each transaction equal total credits.
3. Skip a line between each transaction.

The Analysis of the Journal Entries

March 1	Cash	A	↑	Dr.	$5,000
	A. Todd, Capital	Capital	↑	Cr.	$5,000

4	Equipment	A	↑	Dr.	$ 200
	Cash	A	↓	Cr.	$ 200

5	Acc. Receivable	A	↑	Dr.	$ 200
	Empl. Fees Earned	Rev.	↑	Cr.	$ 200

6	Wage Expense	Exp.	↑	Dr.	$ 300
	Cash	A	↓	Cr.	$ 300

7	A. Todd, Withdrawals	Withd.	↑	Dr.	$ 75
	Cash	A	↓	Cr.	$ 75

9	Cash	A	↑	Dr.	$1,200
	Empl. Fees Earned	Rev.	↑	Cr.	$1,200

This analysis is what should be going through your head before determining debit or credit.

15	Supplies	A	↑	Dr.	$ 200
	Cash	A	↓	Cr.	$ 200

28	Telephone Expense	Exp.	↑	Dr.	$ 180
	Accounts Payable	L	↑	Cr.	$ 180

28	Advertising Expense	Exp.	↑	Dr.	$ 400
	Accounts Payable	L	↑	Cr.	$ 400

Solution Tips to Posting

The PR column in the ledger cash account tells you from which page journal information came (see page 94). After the ledger cash account is posted, Account Number 111 is put in the PR column of the journal. (This is called cross-referencing.)

Note how we keep a running balance in the cash account. A $5,000 debit balance and a $200 credit entry result in a new debit balance of $4,800 on page 94.

Figure 3-33

ABBY'S EMPLOYMENT AGENCY
TRIAL BALANCE
MARCH 31, 200X

	Dr.	Cr.
Cash	5 4 2 5 00	
Accounts Receivable	2 0 0 00	
Supplies	2 0 0 00	
Equipment	2 0 0 00	
Accounts Payable		5 8 0 00
A. Todd, Capital		5 0 0 0 00
A. Todd, Withdrawals	7 5 00	
Employment Fees Earned		1 4 0 0 00
Wage Expense	3 0 0 00	
Telephone Expense	1 8 0 00	
Advertising Expense	4 0 0 00	
Totals	6 9 8 0 00	6 9 8 0 00

Solution Tip to Trial Balance

The trial balance lists the ending balance of each title in the order in which they appear in the ledger. The total of $6,980 on the left equals $6,980 on the right.

Summary of Key Points

Learning Unit 3-1

1. The accounting cycle is a sequence of accounting procedures that are usually performed during an accounting period.
2. An accounting period is the time period for which the income statement is prepared. The time period can be any period up to one year.

3. A calendar year is from January 1 to December 31. The fiscal year is any 12-month period. A fiscal year could be a calendar year but does not have to be.

4. Interim statements are statements that are usually prepared for a portion of the business's calendar or fiscal year (e.g., a month or a quarter).

5. A general journal is a book that records transactions in chronological order. Here debits and credits are shown together on one page. It is the book of original entry.

6. The ledger is a collection of accounts where information is accumulated from the postings of the journal. The ledger is the book of final entry.

7. Journalizing is the process of recording journal entries.

8. The chart of accounts provides the specific titles of accounts to be entered in the journal.

9. When journalizing, the post reference (PR) column is left blank.

10. A compound journal entry occurs when more than two accounts are affected in the journalizing process of a business transaction.

Learning Unit 3-2

1. Posting is the process of transferring information from the journal to the ledger.

2. The journal and ledger contain the same information but in a different form.

3. The four-column account aids in keeping a running balance of an account.

4. The normal balance of an account will be located on the side that increases it according to the rules of debits and credits. For example, the normal balances of liabilities occur on the credit side.

5. The mechanical process of posting requires care in transferring to the appropriate account the dates, post references, and amounts.

Learning Unit 3-3

1. A trial balance can balance but be incorrect. For example, an entire journal entry may not have been posted.

2. If a trial balance doesn't balance, check for errors in addition, omission of postings, slides, transpositions, copying errors, and so on.

3. Specific procedures should be followed in making corrections in journals and ledgers.

Key Terms

Accounting cycle For each accounting period, the process that begins with the recording of business transactions or procedures into a journal and ends with the completion of a post-closing trial balance.

Accounting period The period of time for which an income statement is prepared.

Book of final entry Book that receives information about business transactions from a book of original entry (a journal). Example: a ledger.

Book of original entry Book that records the first formal information about business transactions. Example: a journal.

Calendar year January 1 to December 31.

Compound journal entry A journal entry that affects more than two accounts.

Cross-referencing Adding to the PR column of the journal the account number of the ledger account that was updated from the journal.

Fiscal year The 12-month period a business chooses for its accounting year.

Four-column account A running balance account that records debits and credits and has a column for an ending balance (debit or credit). Replaces the standard two-column account we used earlier.

General journal The simplest form of a journal, which records information from transactions in chronological order as they occur. This journal links the debit and credit parts of transactions together.

Interim reports Financial statements that are prepared for a month, quarter, or some other portion of the fiscal year.

Journal   A listing of business transactions in chronological order. The journal links on one page the debit and credit parts of transactions.

Journal entry   The transaction (debits and credits) that is recorded into a journal once it is analyzed.

Journalizing   The process of recording a transaction entry into the journal.

Natural business year   A business's fiscal year that ends at the same time as a slow seasonal period begins.

Posting   The transferring, copying, or recording of information from a journal to a ledger.

Slide   The error that results in adding or deleting zeros in the writing of a number. Example: 79,200 → 7,920.

Transposition   The accidental rearrangement of digits of a number. Example: 152 → 125.

Trial balance   An informal listing of the ledger accounts and their balances in the ledger that aids in proving the equality of debits and credits.

Blueprint of First Four Steps of Accounting Cycle

See the inside front cover for a road map of entire accounting cycle.

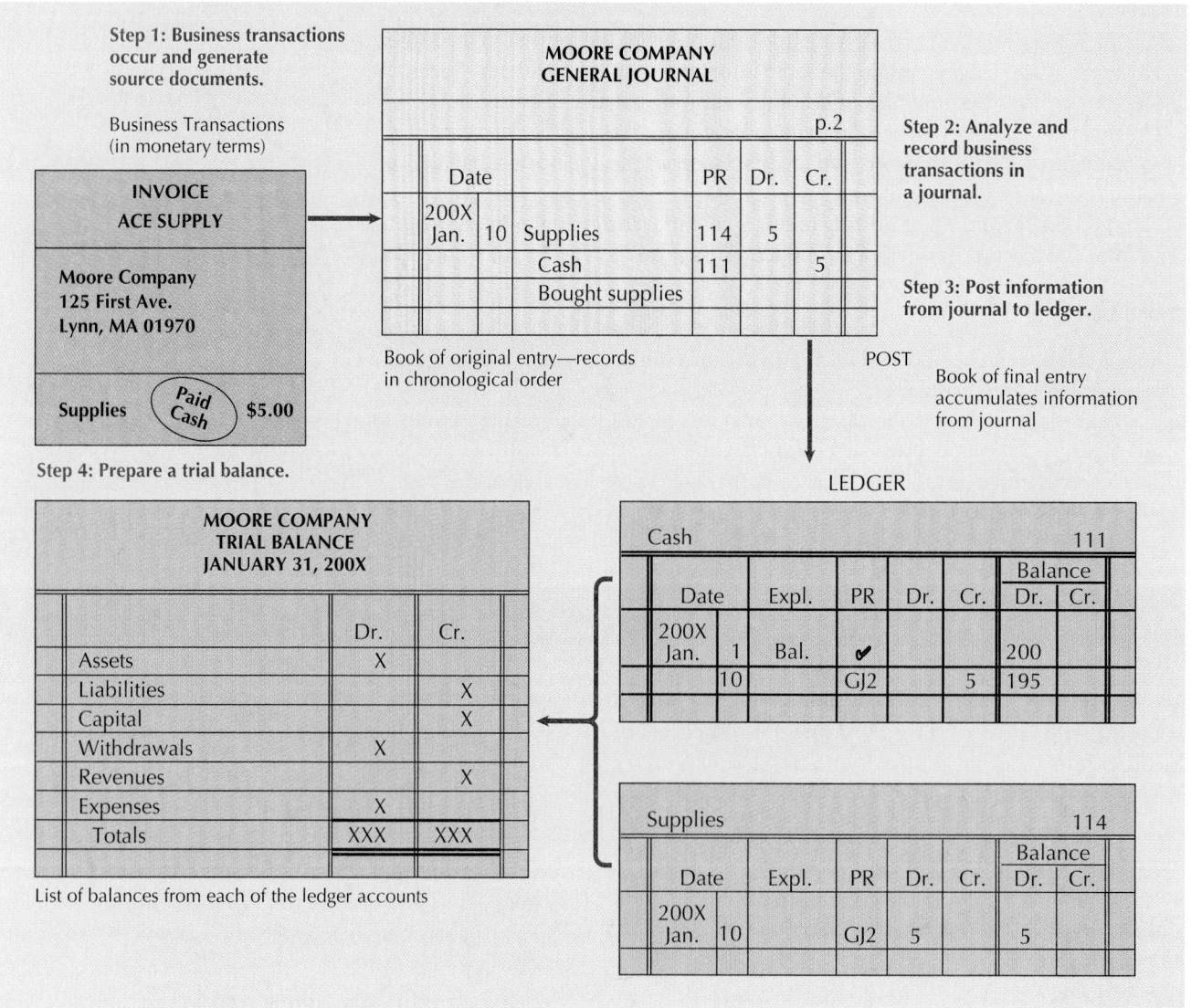

Questions, Mini Exercises, Exercises, and Problems

Discussion Questions

1. Explain the concept of the accounting cycle.
2. An accounting period is based on the balance sheet. Agree or disagree.
3. Compare and contrast a calendar year versus a fiscal year.
4. What are interim statements?
5. Why is the ledger called the book of final entry?
6. How do transactions get "linked" in a general journal?
7. What is the relationship of the chart of accounts to the general journal?
8. What is a compound journal entry?
9. Posting means updating the journal. Agree or disagree. Please comment.
10. The side that decreases an account is the normal balance. True or false?
11. The PR column of a general journal is the last item to be filled in during the posting process. Agree or disagree.
12. Discuss the concept of cross-referencing.
13. What is the difference between a transposition and a slide?

Mini Exercises

(The blank forms you need are on page 67 of the *Study Guide and Working Papers.*)

General Journal

1. Complete the following from the general journal of Ranger Co.:

Figure 3-34
General Journal

RANGER COMPANY
GENERAL JOURNAL — Page 1

Date	Account Titles and Descriptions	PR	Dr.	Cr.
200X Oct. 15	Cash		6 0 0 0 00	
	Equipment		4 0 0 00	
	L. Swan, Capital			6 4 0 0 00
	Initial Investment by Owner			

a. Year of journal entry _____
b. Month of journal entry _____
c. Day of journal entry _____
d. Name(s) of accounts debited _____
e. Name(s) of accounts credited _____
f. Explanation of transaction _____
g. Amount of debit(s) _____
h. Amount of credit(s) _____
i. Page of journal _____

Figure 3-35
Journal Entries

General Journal

2. Provide the explanation for each of the general journal entries in Figure 3-35:

	Date		Account Titles and Descriptions	PR	Debit	Credit
	200X July	9	Cash		8 0 0 0 00	
			Office Equipment		5 0 0 0 00	
			J. Walsh, Capital			13 0 0 0 00
			(A)			
		15	Cash		3 0 00	
			Accounts Receivable		6 0 00	
			Hair Fees Earned			9 0 00
			(B)			
		20	Advertising Expense		4 0 00	
			Accounts Payable			4 0 00
			(C)			

GENERAL JOURNAL — Page 4

Posting and Balancing

3. Balance this four-column account. What function does the PR column serve? When will Account 111 be used in the journalizing and posting process?

Cash   **Acct. 111**

Date	Explanation	PR	Dr.	Cr.	Balance Dr.	Cr.
200X						
June 4		GJ 1	15			
5		GJ 1	6			
9		GJ 2		4		
10		GJ 3	1			

The Trial Balance

4. The following trial balance (Figure 3-36) was prepared *incorrectly*.

    a. Rearrange the accounts in proper order.

Figure 3-36

LARKIN CO.
TRIAL BALANCE
OCTOBER 31, 200X

	Dr.	Cr.
B. Larkin, Capital	1 7 00	
Equipment	1 2 00	
Rent Expense		4 00
Advertising Expense		3 00
Accounts Payable		8 00
Taxi Fees	1 6 00	
Cash	1 7 00	
B. Larkin, Withdrawals	—	5 00
Totals	6 2 00	2 0 00

b. Calculate the total of the trial balance. (Small numbers are used intentionally so that you can do the calculations in your head.) Assume each account has a normal balance.

Correcting Entry

5. On May 1, 2001, a telephone expense for $180 was debited to Repair Expense. On June 12, 2002, this error was found. Prepare the corrected journal entry. When would a correcting entry *not* be needed?

Exercises

(The forms you need are on pages 68–73 of the *Study Guide and Working Papers*.)

3-1. Prepare journal entries for the following transactions that occurred during October:

Preparing journal entries.

200X
Oct.
- 1   Walter Lantz invested $40,000 cash and $2,000 of equipment into his new business.
- 3   Purchased building for $60,000 on account.
- 12   Purchased a truck from Lange Co. for $18,000 cash.
- 18   Bought supplies from Green Co. on account, $700.

3-2. Record the following into the general journal of Reggie's Auto Shop.

Preparing journal entries.

200X
Jan.
- 1   Reggie Long invested $16,000 cash in the auto shop.
- 5   Paid $7,000 for auto equipment.
- 8   Bought from Lowell Co. auto equipment for $6,000 on account.
- 14   Received $900 for repair fees earned.
- 18   Billed Sullivan Co. $900 for services rendered.
- 20   Reggie withdrew $300 for personal use.

3-3. Post the transactions in Figure 3-37 to the ledger of King Company. The partial ledger of King Company is Cash, 111; Equipment, 121; Accounts Payable, 211; and A. King, Capital, 311. Please use four-column accounts in the posting process.

Posting.

Figure 3-37
Journal Entries

Date 200X			PR	Dr.	Cr.	
						Page 4
April	6	Cash		15 0 0 0 00		
		A. King, Capital			15 0 0 0 00	
		Cash investment				
	14	Equipment		9 0 0 0 00		
		Cash			4 0 0 0 00	
		Accounts Payable			5 0 0 0 00	
		Purchase of equipment				

3-4. From the following transactions for Lowe Company for the month of July, (a) prepare journal entries (assume that it is page 1 of the journal), (b) post to the ledger (use a four-column account), and (c) prepare a trial balance.

Journalizing, posting, and preparing a trial balance.

200X

July
1   Joan Lowe invested $6,000 in the business.
4   Bought from Lax Co. equipment on account, $800.
15 Billed Friend Co. for services rendered, $4,000.
18 Received $5,000 cash for services rendered.
24 Paid salaries expense, $1,800.
28 Joan withdrew $400 for personal use.

A partial chart of accounts includes Cash, 111; Accounts Receivable, 112; Equipment, 121; Accounts Payable, 211; J. Lowe, Capital, 311; J. Lowe, Withdrawals, 312; Fees Earned, 411; and Salaries Expense, 511.

3-5. You have been hired to correct the trial balance in Figure 3-38 that has been recorded improperly from the ledger to the trial balance:

Figure 3-38
Incorrect Trial Balance

Correcting the trial balance.

SUNG CO. TRIAL BALANCE MARCH 31, 200X	Dr.	Cr.
Accounts Payable	2 0 0 0 0 0	
A. Sung, Capital		6 5 0 0 0 0
A. Sung, Withdrawals		3 0 0 0 0
Services Earned		4 7 0 0 0 0
Concessions Earned	2 5 0 0 0 0	
Rent Expense	4 0 0 0 0	
Salaries Expense	2 5 0 0 0 0	
Miscellaneous Expense		1 3 0 0 0 0
Cash	10 0 0 0 0 0	
Accounts Receivable		1 2 0 0 0 0
Totals	17 4 0 0 0 0	14 0 0 0 0 0

3-6. On February 6, 200X, Mike Sullivan made the journal entry in Figure 3-39 to record the purchase on account of office equipment priced at $1,400. This transaction had not yet been posted when the error was discovered. Make the appropriate correction.

Figure 3-39
Recording Error

Correcting an entry.

	GENERAL JOURNAL			
Date	Account Titles and Description	PR	Dr.	Cr.
200X Feb. 6	Office Equipment		9 0 0 00	
	Accounts Payable			9 0 0 00
	Purchase of office equip. on account			

Group A Problems

(The forms you need are on pages 74–85 of the *Working Papers and Study Guide.*)

Journalizing.

3A-1. Al Vincent operates Al's Fitness Center. As the bookkeeper, you have been requested to journalize the following transactions:

200X

Aug. 1 Paid rent for two months in advance, $6,000.

3 Purchased fitness equipment on account from Leek's Supply House, $4,200.

10 Purchased fitness supplies from Angel's Wholesale for $700 cash.

12 Received $1,400 cash from fitness fees earned.

20 Al withdrew $600 for his personal use.

21 Advertising bill received from *Daily Sun* but unpaid, $120.

25 Paid cleaning expense, $90.

28 Paid salaries expense, $500.

29 Performed fitness work for $1,700, but payment will not be received until May.

30 Paid Leek's Supply House half the amount owed from Aug. 3 transaction.

Check Figure:
July 21
Dr. Advertising
    expense $120
Cr. Accounts
    Payable $120

Your task is to journalize the preceding transactions. The chart of accounts for Al's Fitness Center is as follows:

Chart of Accounts

Assets	Owner's Equity
111 Cash	311 Al Vincent, Capital
112 Accounts Receivable	312 Al Vincent, Withdrawals
114 Prepaid Rent	**Revenue**
116 Fitness Supplies	411 Fitness Fees Earned
120 Office Equipment	**Expenses**
121 Fitness Equipment	511 Advertising Expense
Liabilities	512 Salaries Expense
211 Accounts Payable	514 Cleaning Expense

3A-2. On June 1, 200X, Molly Taylor opened Taylor's Dance Studio. The following transactions occurred in June:

Comprehensive problem:
Journalizing, posting, and
preparing a trial balance.

200X

June 1 Molly Taylor invested $9,000 in the dance studio.

1 Paid three months' rent in advance, $1,000.

3 Purchased $700 of equipment from Astor Co. on account.

5 Received $900 cash for fitness-training workshop for dancers.

8 Purchased $300 of supplies for cash.

9 Billed Lester Co. $2,100 for group dance lesson for its employees.

10 Paid salaries of assistants, $400.

15 Molly withdrew $150 from the business for her personal use.

28 Paid electrical bill, $125.

29 Paid telephone bill for June, $190.

Your task is to

a. Set up the ledger based on the following chart of accounts.

b. Journalize (journal is page 1) and post the June transactions.

c. Prepare a trial balance as of June 30, 200X.

Check Figure:
Trial Balance
    Total $12,700

The chart of accounts for Taylor's Dance Studio is as follows:

Chart of Accounts

Assets	Owner's Equity
111 Cash	311 Molly Taylor, Capital
112 Accounts Receivable	312 Molly Taylor, Withdrawals
114 Prepaid Rent	**Revenue**
121 Supplies	411 Fees Earned
131 Equipment	

Liabilities
211   Accounts Payable

Expenses
511   Electrical Expense
521   Salaries Expense
531   Telephone Expense

Comprehensive problem:
Journalizing, posting, and
preparing a trial balance.

3A-3. The following transactions occurred in June 200X for A. French's Placement Agency:

200X
June 1   A. French invested $9,000 cash in the placement agency.
1   Bought equipment on account from Hook Co., $2,000.
3   Earned placement fees of $1,600, but payment will not be received until July.
5   A. French withdrew $100 for his personal use.
7   Paid wages expense, $300.
9   Placed a client on a local TV show, receiving $600 cash.
15 Bought supplies on account from Lyon Co., $500.
28 Paid telephone bill for June, $160.
29 Advertising bill from Shale Co. received but not paid, $900.

Check Figure:
Trial Balance
   Total $14,600

The chart of accounts for A. French Placement Agency is as follows:

Chart of Accounts

Assets
111   Cash
112   Accounts Receivable
131   Supplies
141   Equipment

Liabilities
211   Accounts Payable

Owner's Equity
311   A. French, Capital
312   A. French, Withdrawals

Revenue
411   Placement Fees Earned

Expenses
511   Wage Expense
521   Telephone Expense
531   Advertising Expense

Your task is to

a. Set up the ledger based on the chart of accounts.
b. Journalize (page 1) and post the June transactions.
c. Prepare a trial balance as of June 30, 200X.

Group B Problems

(The forms you need are on pages 74–85 of the *Study Guide and Working Papers.*)

3B-1. In April Al Vincent opened a new Fitness Center. Please assist him by journalizing the following business transactions:

Journalizing.

200X
Apr. 1   Al Vincent invested $6,000 of fitness equipment as well as $3,000 cash in the new business.
3   Purchased fitness supplies on account from Rex Co., $500.
10 Purchased office equipment on account from Ross Stationery, $400.
12 Al paid his home telephone bill from the company checkbook, $60.
20 Received $600 cash for fitness services performed.
21 Advertising bill received but not paid, $75.
25 Cleaning bill received but not paid, $90.
28 Performed fitness work for $700, but payment will not be received until May.
29 Paid salaries expense, $400.
30 Paid Ross Stationery half the amount owed from April 10 transaction.

Check Figure:
April 21
Dr. Advertising
   expense $75
Cr. Accounts
   payable $75

The chart of accounts for Al's Fitness Center includes Cash, 111; Accounts Receivable, 112; Prepaid Rent, 114; Fitness Supplies, 116; Office Equipment, 120; Fitness Equipment, 121; Accounts Payable, 211; Al Vincent, Capital, 311; Al Vincent, Withdrawals, 312; Fitness Fees Earned, 411; Advertising Expense, 511; Salaries Expense, 512; and Cleaning Expense, 514.

3B-2. In June the following transactions occurred for Taylor's Dance Studio:

Comprehensive problem: Journalizing, posting, and preparing a trial balance.

200X

June
1   Molly Taylor invested $6,000 in the dance studio.
1   Paid four months rent in advance, $1,200.
3   Purchased supplies on account from A.J.K., $700.
5   Purchased equipment on account from Reese Company, $900.
8   Received $1,300 cash for dance-training program provided to Northwest Junior College.
9   Billed Long Co. for dance lessons provided, $600.
10 Molly withdrew $400 from the dance studio to buy a new chain saw for her home.
15 Paid salaries expense, $400.
28 Paid telephone bill, $118.
29 Electric bill received but unpaid, $120.

Check Figure:
Total Trial Balance $9,620

Your task is to

a. Set up a ledger.
b. Journalize (all page 1) and post the June transactions.
c. Prepare a trial balance as of June 30, 200X.

The chart of accounts includes Cash, 111; Accounts Receivable, 112; Prepaid Rent, 114; Supplies, 121; Equipment, 131; Accounts Payable, 211; M. Taylor, Capital, 311; M. Taylor, Withdrawals, 321; Fees Earned, 411; Electrical Expense, 511; Salaries Expense, 521; and Telephone Expense, 531.

3B-3. In June A. French's Placement Agency had the following transactions:

Comprehensive problem: Journalizing, posting, and preparing a trial balance.

200X

June
1   A. French invested $6,000 in the new placement agency.
2   Bought equipment for cash, $350.
3   Earned placement fee commission of $2,100, but payment from Avon Co. will not be received until July.
5   Paid wages expense, $400.
7   A. French paid his home utility bill from the company checkbook, $69.
9   Placed Jay Diamond on a national TV show, receiving $900 cash.
15 Paid cash for supplies, $350.
28 Telephone bill received but not paid, $185.
29 Advertising bill received but not paid, $200.

Check Figure:
Total Trial Balance $9,385

The chart of accounts includes Cash, 111; Accounts Receivable, 112; Supplies, 131; Equipment, 141; Accounts Payable, 211; A. French, Capital, 311; A. French, Withdrawals, 312; Placement Fees Earned, 411; Wage Expense, 511; Telephone Expense, 521; and Advertising Expense, 531.

Your task is to

a. Set up a ledger based on the chart of accounts.
b. Journalize (all page 1) and post transactions.
c. Prepare a trial balance for June 30, 200X.

Real-World Applications

3R-1. Paul Regan, bookkeeper of Hampton Co., has been up half the night trying to get his trial balance to balance. Figure 3-40 shows his results:

Figure 3-40
Incorrect Trial Balance

HAMPTON CO. TRIAL BALANCE JUNE 30, 200X	Dr.	Cr.
Office Sales		5 7 2 0 00
Cash in Bank	3 2 6 0 00	
Accounts Receivable	5 6 6 0 00	
Office Equipment	8 4 0 0 00	
Accounts Payable		4 1 6 0 00
D. Hole, Capital		11 5 6 0 00
D. Hole, Withdrawals		7 0 0 00
Wage Expense	2 6 0 0 00	
Rent Expense	9 4 0 00	
Utilities Expense	2 6 00	
Office Supplies	1 2 0 00	
Prepaid Rent	1 8 0 00	

Ken Small, the accountant, compared Paul's amounts in the trial balance with those in the ledger, recomputed each account balance, and compared postings. Ken found the following errors:

1. A $200 debit to D. Hole, Withdrawals, was posted as a credit.
2. D. Hole, Withdrawals, was listed on the trial balance as a credit.
3. A Note Payable account with a credit balance of $2,400 was not listed on the trial balance.
4. The pencil footings for Accounts Payable were debits of $5,320 and credits of $8,800.
5. A debit of $180 to Prepaid Rent was not posted.
6. Office Supplies bought for $60 was posted as a credit to Supplies.
7. A debit of $120 to Accounts Receivable was not posted.
8. A cash payment of $420 was credited to Cash for $240.
9. The pencil footing of the credits to Cash was overstated by $400.
10. The Utilities Expense of $260 was listed in the trial balance as $26.

Assist Paul Regan by preparing a correct trial balance. What advice could you give Ken about Paul? Can you explain the situation to Paul? Put your answers in writing.

3R-2. Lauren Oliver, an accountant lab tutor, is having a debate with some of her assistants. They are trying to find out how each of the following five unrelated situations would affect the trial balance:

1. A $5 debit to Cash in the ledger was not posted.
2. A $10 debit to Computer Supplies was debited to Computer Equipment.
3. An $8 debit to Wage Expense was debited twice to the account.
4. A $4 debit to Computer Supplies was debited to Computer Sales.
5. A $35 credit to Accounts Payable was posted as a $53 credit.

Could you indicate to Lauren the effect that each situation will have on the trial balance? If a situation will have no effect, indicate that fact. Put in writing how each of these situations could be avoided in the future.

YOU make the call

Critical Thinking/Ethical Case

3R-3. Jay Simons, the accountant of See Co., would like to buy a new software package for his general ledger. He couldn't do it because all funds were frozen for the rest of the fiscal period. Jay called his friend at Joor Industries and asked whether he could copy their software. Why should or shouldn't Jay have done that?

Internet Exercises: STAtravel — Student Travel, Discount Travel

EX-1. [www.statravel.com]   Travel agencies like STAtravel operate on the principle of buying travel packages, such as cruises, from cruise ship owners, then marking up the cost and selling it to STA customers. When they do this, the two transactions require two journal entries, just like the ones you learned in this chapter. Each customer sale generates two journal entries. The first represents STA's purchase of the cruise (an expense) from the cruise ship owner. The second represents the STA customer's buying the package from STA (a sale).

Suppose that you purchase a spring break cruise for $1,500 from STA and pay them with a check. They in turn will record the other transaction with the cruise ship owner for $1,200. The $300 difference is STA's profit.

1. Write the journal entry STA would make showing your booking the cruise for $1,500 with STA.

2. Write the journal entry showing, from STA's perspective, STA's purchase of your cruise for $1,200 from the cruise ship owner.

EX-2. [www.statravel.com]   Suppose STA has the following accounts in their accounting system:

Accounts Receivable
Airline Revenue
Airline Tickets Payable
Airline Ticket Purchase Expense
Cash
Cruise Ship Packages Payable
Cruise Ship Package Purchase Expense
Cruise Ship Revenue

1. List accounts in proper order with account numbers (you make them up).

2. Draw a table showing account name, account number, category, normal balance, and which financial statement these are found on.

Continuing Problem

Eldorado Computer Center

Tony's computer center is picking up in business, so he has decided to expand his bookkeeping system to a general journal/ledger system. The balances from August have been forwarded to the ledger accounts. (The forms are in the *Study Guide and Working Papers*, pages 89–99.)

Assignment

1. Use the chart of accounts provided in Chapter 2 to record the following transactions in Figures 3-41 to 3-51:

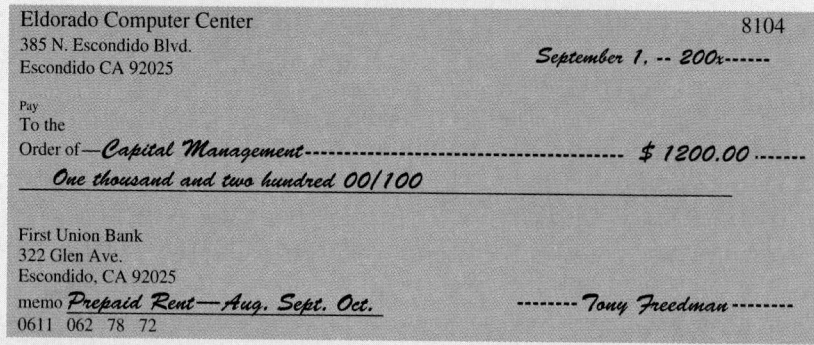

Figure 3-41 Prepaid Rent

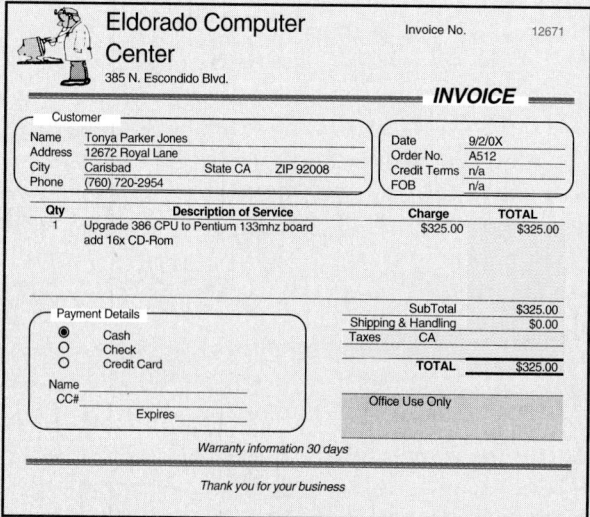

Figure 3-42 Service Revenue

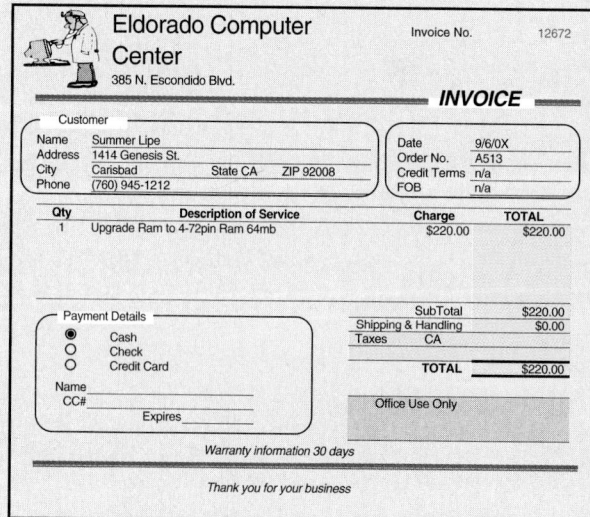

Figure 3-43 Service Revenue

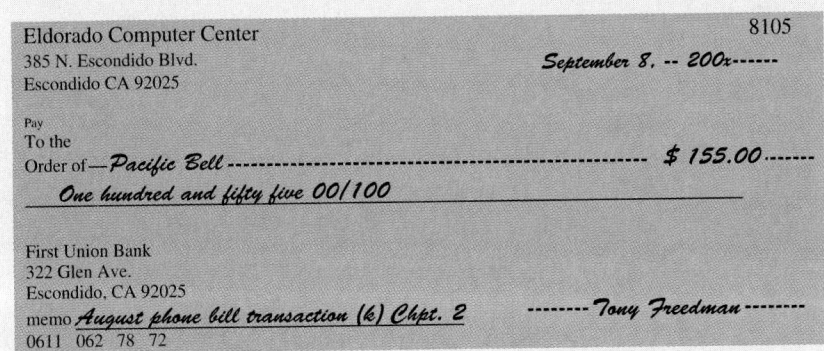

Figure 3-44 Phone Bill

Refer back to Chapter 2, transaction k.

Figure 3-45 Sparks Collection

Refer back to Chapter 2, transaction o.

Figure 3-46 Paid Computer Connection

Refer back to Chapter 2, transaction s.

Figure 3-47 Purchased Computer Equipment

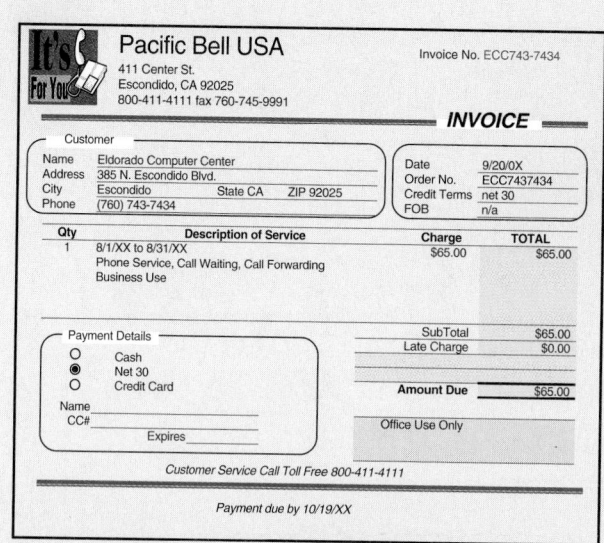

Figure 3-48 Received Phone Bill

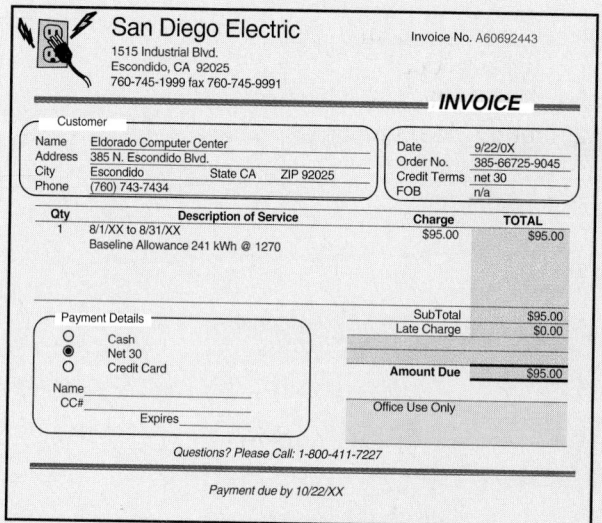

Figure 3-49 Received Electric Bill

Eldorado Computer Center
385 N. Escondido Blvd.

INVOICE

| | | Invoice No. | 12673 |

Customer

Name	Mike Hammer	Date	9/26/0X
Address	300 Carlsbad Dr.	Order No.	A514
City	Carlsbad State CA ZIP 92008	Credit Terms	n/a
Phone	(760) 720-2199	FOB	n/a

Qty	Description of Service	Charge	TOTAL
1	add video card 2mb dram 64 diamond stealth	$140.00	$140.00

Payment Details
- ● Cash
- ○ Check
- ○ Credit Card

Name _____
CC# _____
        Expires _____

	SubTotal	$140.00
	Shipping & Handling	$0.00
	Taxes CA	
	TOTAL	$140.00

Office Use Only

Warranty information 30 days

Thank you for your business

Figure 3-50 Service Revenue

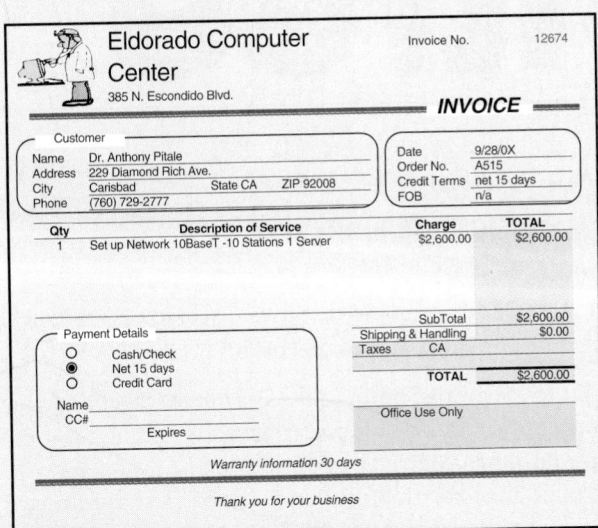

Figure 3-51 Service Revenue

2. Post all transactions to the general ledger accounts (the Prepaid Rent Account #1025 has been added to the chart of accounts).
3. Prepare a trial balance for September 30, 200X.
4. Prepare the financial statements for the three months ended September 30, 200X.

Peachtree® Computer Workshop

COMPUTERIZED ACCOUNTING APPLICATION FOR CHAPTER 3

JOURNALIZING, POSTING, GENERAL LEDGER, TRIAL BALANCE, AND CHART OF ACCOUNTS

Before starting on this assignment, read and complete the tasks discussed in Parts A, B, and F of the Computerized Accounting appendix at the back of this book.

How to Open the Company Data Files

1. Click on the Start button. Point to Programs; point to the Peachtree folder and select Peachtree Complete Accounting. Your desktop may have the Peachtree icon, allowing for a quicker entrance into the program by double clicking it.
2. Follow the "Open a File" instructions in Part A of the Computerized Accounting appendix at the back of this book to open **The Atlas Company.** You may be initially presented with the Peachtree Today window. If so, simply close it. Your screen should then look something like the screen capture below:

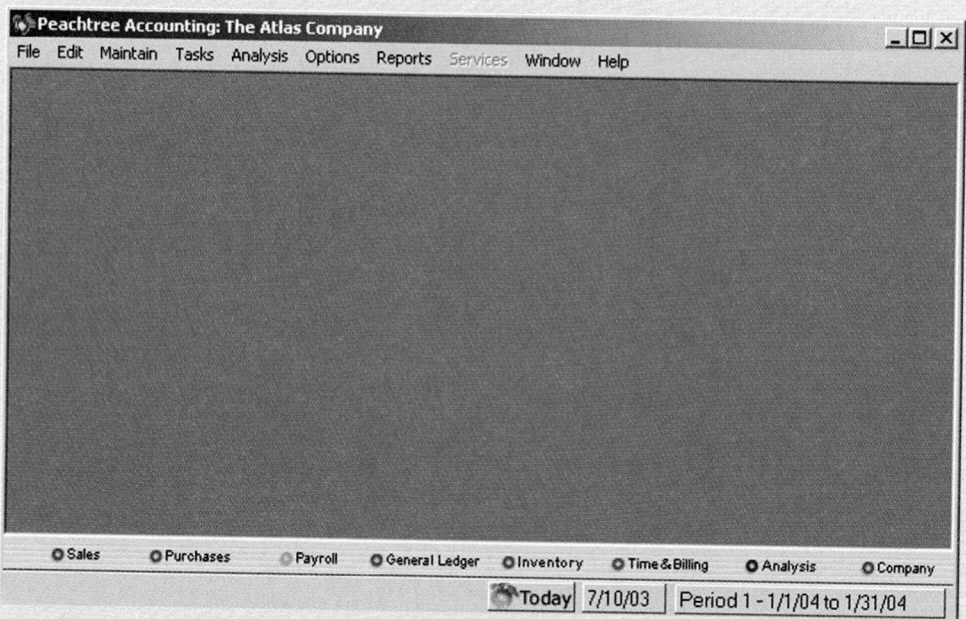

If you are missing the navigation aids at the bottom of the screen, you can activate them under the **Options** menu. Select **View Navigation Aid**. It will remain on until you turn it off. This feature offers an alternative way to access the different features of Peachtree.

How to Add Your Name to the Company Name

3. Click on the **Maintain** menu option. Then select **Company Information**. The program will respond by bringing up a dialogue box allowing the user to edit/add information about the company.
4. It is important for you to be able to identify the specific reports that you print for each assignment as your own, particularly if you are using a computer that shares a printer with other computers. Peachtree Complete Accounting 2003 prints the name of the company you are working with at the top of each report. To personalize your reports so that you can identify both the company and your printed reports, the company name needs to be modified to include your name:

   a. Click in the **Company Name** entry field at the end of **The Atlas Company**. If it is already highlighted, press the right arrow key.

b. Add a dash and your name **"-Student Name"** to the end of the company name. If your name is too long, you may abbreviate or use your initials. Your screen will look similar to the one shown below:

c. Click on the OK button to return to the Menu Window.

5. The owner of The Atlas Company has invested $10,000 in the business. Select **General Journal Entry** from the **Tasks** menu to open the General Journal dialog box. Enter the date 1/1/04 into the **Date** field; press the TAB key; enter "Memo" into the **Reference** field and press TAB. The **Date** text box is used to record the date the transaction occurred. The **Reference** text box can be used for any reference number or notation you wish to associate with a general journal entry and/or the source document that authorizes the entry. Pressing the TAB key will take you to the General Journal's **Account** field. Note that pressing ENTER will also move you from field to field.

6. With the flashing insertion point positioned in the **Account No.** field, click on the pull down menu (magnifying glass icon) and double click on "1110 Cash". Alternatively, you can highlight the account and click OK at the bottom. The program will enter the account number and name into the **Account No.** field and the flashing insertion point will move to the **Description** field. Enter "Initial investment of cash by owner" into this field and press TAB to move to the **Debit** field.

7. Enter "10000" into the **Debit** field. Dollar amounts can be entered in several ways. For example, to enter $10,000.00, type 10000, or 10,000.00 or 10,000. The comma separator is always optional while the decimal point is optional when dealing with whole dollar amounts. To enter an amount containing a decimal point, type the decimal point as part of the amount. For example, enter five dollars and twenty-five cents as 5.25. Press the TAB key three times to move through the **Credit** and **Job** fields.

8. With the flashing insertion point again positioned in the **Account No.** field, click on the pull down menu. Double click on "3110 Owner's Capital". Use the scroll bar if the account is not visible in the pull down menu. Press TAB to move to the **Description** field. This should repeat the information entered in step 6 by default. Although you can change the description for the credit, we will leave it the same.

How to Record a General Journal Entry

9. Press the TAB key twice to move to the **Credit** field. Enter "10000" as you did in step 7. Hit TAB twice to move the cursor back to the **Account No.** field. This completes the data you need to enter into the General Journal dialog box to record the journal entry for the initial investment of cash by the owner. Your screen should look like this:

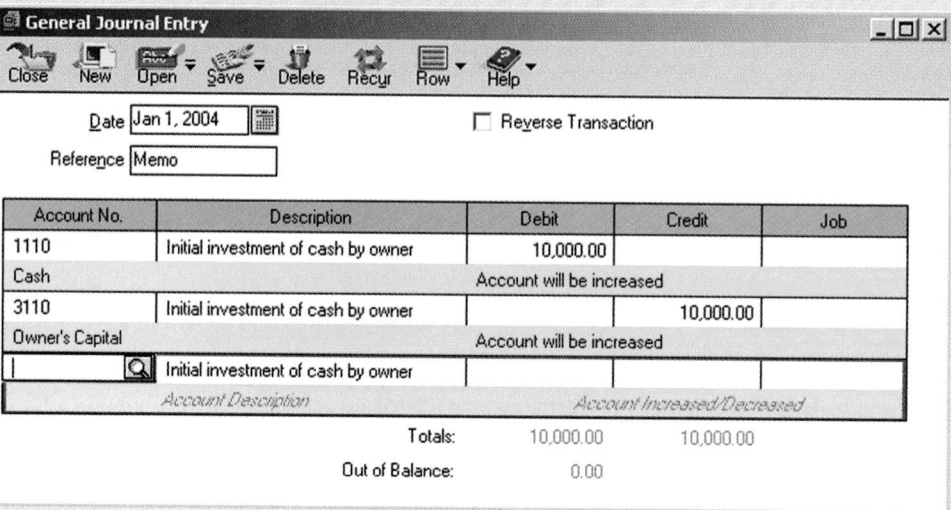

Review the Journal Entry Before Saving

10. Before saving this transaction, you should verify that the transaction data are correct by reviewing the journal entry. Review the journal entry for accuracy, noting any errors.
11. If you have made an error, use the following editing techniques to correct the error.

Editing a General Journal Entry

How to Edit an Entry Prior to Saving

- Using your mouse, click in the field that contains the error. This will highlight the selected text box information so that you can change it.
- Type the correct information; then press the TAB key to enter it. You may then either TAB to other fields needing corrections or again use the mouse to click in the proper field.
- If you have selected an incorrect account number, use the pull down menu to select the correct account. This will replace the incorrect account with the correct account.
- Note that even though the **Save** icon will be available if the entry is out of balance, Peachtree will not allow you to save the transaction until the entry is in balance.
- To discard an entry and start over, click on the **Delete** icon. You will not be given the opportunity to verify this step so be sure you want to delete the transaction before selecting this option.
- Review the journal entry for accuracy after any editing corrections.

How to Save an Entry

12. After verifying that the journal entry is correct, click on the **Save** icon to post this transaction. A blank General Journal dialog box is displayed, ready for additional General Journal transactions to be recorded. Peachtree has added a 1 to our memo in the **Reference** field and will do so as long as we remain in this input box and save as we go. Alternatively, we could have added more entries to the previous screen before saving. To keep the same reference for multiple entries on the same day, do not save between transactions.

Record Additional Transactions

13. Record the following additional journal entries Enter the **Date** listed for each transaction (you may use the "+" key to advance the date or use the calendar icon next to the field to select the date from a calendar). Enter "Memo" into the **Source** text

box for each transaction or accept Peachtree's additional number added to memo by pressing TAB:

2004

Jan. 1 Paid rent for two months in advance, $400.

      3 Purchased office supplies on account, $100.

      9 Billed a customer for fees earned, $1,500.

   13 Received and paid telephone bill, $180.

   20 Owner withdrew $500 from the business.

   27 Received $450 for fees earned.

   31 Paid salaries expense, $700.

14. After you have saved the additional journal entries, click on the close button to close the General Journal dialog box. This will restore the menu window.

15. Select **General Ledger** from the **Reports** menu to bring up reports associated with the general ledger such as the **General Journal** and the **Trial Balance.** Select **General Journal** from the report selection window to bring up the report. Your screen should display something similar to this:

How to Display and Print a General Journal

The Atlas Company- Student Name
General Journal
For the Period From Jan 1, 2004 to Jan 31, 2004

Filter Criteria includes: Report order is by Date. Report is printed with Accounts having Zero Amounts and with Truncated Transaction Descriptions and in Detail Format.

Date	Account ID	Reference	Trans Description	Debit Amt	Credit Amt
1/1/04	1110	Memo	Initial investment of cash by owner	10,000.00	
	3110		Initial investment of cash by owner		10,000.00
1/1/04	1140	Memo1	Prepaid rent	400.00	
	1110		Prepaid rent		400.00
1/3/04	1150	Memo2	Purchased office supplies on account	100.00	
	2110		Purchased office supplies on account		100.00
1/9/04	1120	Memo3	Performed services on account	1,500.00	
	4110		Performed services on account		1,500.00
1/13/04	5150	Memo4	Paid telephone bill	180.00	
	1110		Paid telephone bill		180.00
1/20/04	3120	Memo5	Owner withdrawal	500.00	
	1110		Owner withdrawal		500.00
1/27/04	1110	Memo6	Performed services for cash	450.00	
	4110		Performed services for cash		450.00
1/31/04	5120	Memo7	Paid salaries expense	700.00	
	1110		Paid salaries expense		700.00
		Total		13,830.00	13,830.00

16. The scroll bars can be used to advance the display to view other portions of the report if they are not visible. Note: You may display the entire General Journal Display window by clicking the maximize icon.

17. Click on the **Print** icon to print the General Journal. If you experience any difficulties with your printer (for example, the type size is too small), refer to Part F of the Computerized Accounting appendix for information on how to adjust the print and display settings.

18. Review your printed General Journal. If you note an error at this point, it can be easily fixed. With the General Journal report on your screen, place your cursor over the incorrect entry (it will resemble a magnifying glass with a "z" in the center). Double click on the entry you wish to correct and you will be taken to the **General Journal Entry** window that contains the entry. You may edit it using the same procedures as editing an unsaved entry in step 11. After making the necessary changes,

What to Do If You Saved an Incorrect Entry

How to Display and Print a General Ledger Report

click on the **Save** icon to save your changes. You will be returned to your report where you can view the changes made.

19. Click on the **Close** icon to close the General Journal report. You are taken back to the report selection window where you can select (double-click) **General Ledger.** Your screen will look something like this:

The Atlas Company- Student Name
General Ledger
For the Period From Jan 1, 2004 to Jan 31, 2004
Filter Criteria includes: Report order is by ID. Report is printed with Truncated Transaction Descriptions and in Detail Format.

Account ID Account Description	Date	Reference	Jrnl	Trans Description	Debit Amt	Credit Amt	Balance
1110	1/1/04			Beginning Balance			
Cash	1/1/04	Memo	GENJ	Initial investment of cash by	10,000.00		
	1/1/04	Memo1	GENJ	Prepaid rent		400.00	
	1/13/04	Memo4	GENJ	Paid telephone bill		180.00	
	1/20/04	Memo5	GENJ	Owner withdrawal		500.00	
	1/27/04	Memo6	GENJ	Performed services for cash	450.00		
	1/31/04	Memo7	GENJ	Paid salaries expense		700.00	
				Current Period Change	10,450.00	1,780.00	8,670.00
	1/31/04			Ending Balance			8,670.00
1120	1/1/04			Beginning Balance			
Accounts Receivable	1/9/04	Memo3	GENJ	Performed services on accou	1,500.00		
				Current Period Change	1,500.00		1,500.00
	1/31/04			Ending Balance			1,500.00

20. You will not see the entire report on the screen. The scroll bars can be used to advance the display to view other portions of the report. You may also double click your mouse on any transaction to bring up the entry window for that transaction.

21. Click on the **Print** icon to print the General Ledger report.

22. Click on the **Close** button to close the General Ledger report and return to the reports selection window. Double-click on the General Ledger Trial Balance option from this window. Your screen will look something like this:

How to Display and Print a Trial Balance

The Atlas Company- Student Name
General Ledger Trial Balance
As of Jan 31, 2004
Filter Criteria includes: Report order is by ID. Report is printed in Detail Format.

Account ID	Account Description	Debit Amt	Credit Amt
1110	Cash	8,670.00	
1120	Accounts Receivable	1,500.00	
1140	Prepaid Rent	400.00	
1150	Office Supplies	100.00	
2110	Accounts Payable		100.00
3110	Owner's Capital		10,000.00
3120	Owner's Withdrawals	500.00	
4110	Fees Earned		1,950.00
5120	Salaries Expense	700.00	
5150	Telephone Expense	180.00	
	Total:	12,050.00	12,050.00

23. The scroll bar can be used to advance the display to view other portions of the report. You may also display zero balance accounts by clicking on the **Options** icon and clicking the box next to **Include Accounts with Zero Amounts.** Clicking on **OK** will return you to the report. Click on the **Print** icon to print the Trial Balance.

24. Again click on the **Close** button to close the Trial Balance report. Select **Chart of Accounts** from the report selection window. Your screen will look something like this:

How to Display and Print a Chart of Accounts

The Atlas Company- Student Name
Chart of Accounts
As of Jan 31, 2004

Filter Criteria includes: Report order is by ID. Report is printed with Accounts having Zero Amounts and in Detail Format.

Account ID	Account Description	Active	Account Type
1110	Cash	Yes	Cash
1120	Accounts Receivable	Yes	Accounts Receivable
1140	Prepaid Rent	Yes	Other Current Assets
1150	Office Supplies	Yes	Other Current Assets
1210	Office Equipment	Yes	Fixed Assets
1221	Accum. Depr- Office Equipment	Yes	Accumulated Depreciation
1230	Automobile	Yes	Fixed Assets
1241	Accum. Depr- Automobile	Yes	Accumulated Depreciation
1250	Store Equipment	Yes	Fixed Assets
1261	Accum Depr- Store Equipment	Yes	Accumulated Depreciation
2110	Accounts Payable	Yes	Accounts Payable
3110	Owner's Capital	Yes	Equity-doesn't close
3120	Owner's Withdrawals	Yes	Equity-gets closed
3130	Retained Earnings	Yes	Equity-Retained Earnings
4110	Fees Earned	Yes	Income
5110	Rent Expense	Yes	Expenses
5120	Salaries Expense	Yes	Expenses
5150	Telephone Expense	Yes	Expenses

25. Click the **Print** icon to print the report. Click on the **Close** button to close the Chart of Accounts window and return to the Menu Window.

26. Click on the Menu Window **File** menu; then click on **Exit** to end the current work session and return to your Windows desktop. Your work will automatically be saved.

How to Exit from the Program

27. You can exit from Peachtree Complete Accounting 2003 at any time during a current work session from any window that offers the **File** menu. You may be asked if you wish to save any unsaved work.

28. Generally speaking, there is no need to save your work in Peachtree. Each time you make a change and click save, your work is automatically saved to your hard drive. You should back up your work after each session. This was discussed in Part A of the Appendix and will be discussed again in Chapter 4.

Saving Your Work During a Current Work Session

CHAPTER 4

The Accounting Cycle Continued

Preparing Worksheets and Financial Statements

Your roommate Sam is an art major. Sam is skilled at drawing and always has his sketchpad with him. Sam records all of his ideas for a picture by creating various drawings in his pad. Sam will begin a drawing and then make various changes and adjustments to it. Sam said that after he's completed the drawing he goes on to use it when completing a painting.

Sam and several other artists in the area have opened an art studio to display their works. You recently attended a show that featured several of Sam's paintings. While you were at the show, someone bought one of Sam's paintings. Sam was excited and happy. "Now I can pay my share of the rent and utilities for the studio. Everyone here loves art, but we have to run the studio like a business," Sam told you. Even an art studio needs to use accounting to record sales and expenses like other businesses.

Accounting is very different than art, but it does have its own "sketchpad," which is called a worksheet. In Chapter 3 we learned about the first four steps in the accounting cycle. In Chapter 4 we expand our understanding of the accounting cycle by focusing on the next step—preparing a worksheet. And similar to how Sam changes and revises his drawings, an accountant can use the worksheet to make changes and adjustments to numbers found in the trial balance.

In this chapter we also discuss the sixth step in the accounting cycle—using the worksheet to prepare financial statements. And like a sketchpad, the accounting worksheet is a tool that takes us from a trial balance to financial statements, or as Sam would say, from a sketch to a painting.

Learning Objectives

● Adjustments: prepaid rent, office supplies, depreciation on equipment, and accrued salaries. (p. 121)

● Preparation of adjusted trial balance on the worksheet. (p. 129)

● The income statement and balance sheet sections of the worksheet. (p. 130)

● Preparing financial statements from the worksheet. (p. 135)

In Figure 4-1, Steps 1–4 show the parts of the manual accounting cycle that were completed for Clark's Word Processing Services in the last chapter. This chapter continues the cycle with Steps 5–6: the preparation of a worksheet and the three financial statements. Be sure to check inside the front cover for a complete road map of the accounting cycle.

Learning Unit 4-1   Step 5 of the Accounting Cycle: Preparing a Worksheet

> The worksheet is not a formal report, so no dollar signs appear on it. Because it is a form, there are no commas, either.

An accountant uses a worksheet to organize and check data before preparing financial statements necessary to complete the accounting cycle. The most important function of the worksheet is to allow the accountant to find and correct errors before financial statements are prepared. In a way, a worksheet acts as the accountant's scratch pad. No one sees the worksheet once the formal reports are prepared. A sample worksheet is shown in Figure 4-2.

The accounts listed on the far left of the worksheet are taken from the ledger. The rest of the worksheet has five sections: the trial balance, adjustments, adjusted trial balance, income statement, and balance sheet. Each of these sections is divided into debit and credit columns.

> As is true for all accounting statements, the heading includes the name of the company, the name of the report, the date, and the length of the accounting period.

THE TRIAL BALANCE SECTION

We discussed how to prepare a trial balance in Chapter 2. Some companies prepare a separate trial balance; others, such as Clark's Word Processing Services, prepare the trial balance directly on the worksheet. A trial balance is taken on every account listed in the ledger that has a balance. Additional titles from the ledger are added as they are needed. (We will show this later.)

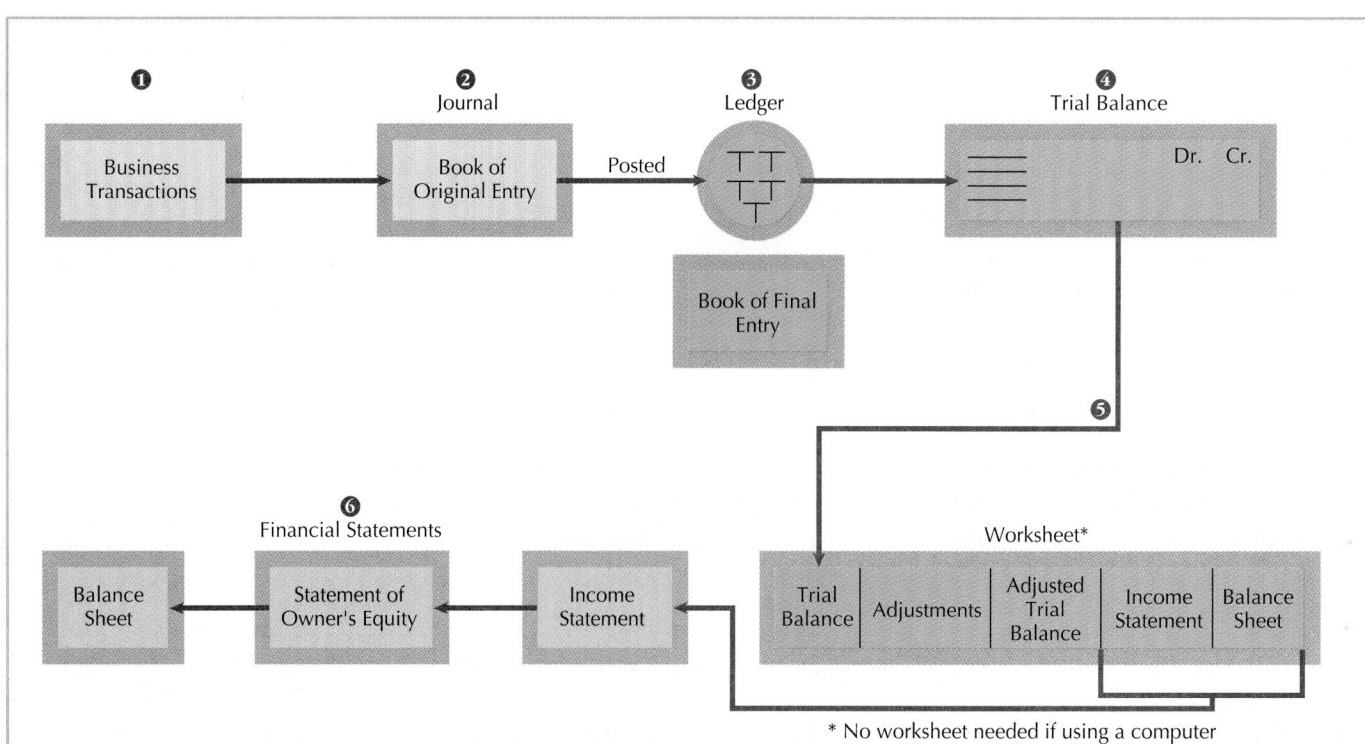

Figure 4-1

	Trial Balance		Adjustments		Adjusted Trial Balance		Income Statement	
Account Titles	Dr.	Cr.	Dr.	Cr.	Dr.	Cr.	Dr.	Cr.
Cash	6 1 5 5 00							
Accounts Receivable	5 0 0 0 00							
Office Supplies	6 0 0 00							
Prepaid Rent	1 2 0 0 00							
Word Processing Equipment	6 0 0 0 00							
Accounts Payable		3 3 5 0 00						
Brenda Clark, Capital		10 0 0 0 00						
Brenda Clark, Withdrawals	6 2 5 00							
Word Processing Fees		8 0 0 0 00						
Office Salaries Expense	1 3 0 0 00							
Advertising Expense	2 5 0 00							
Telephone Expense	2 2 0 00							
	21 3 5 0 00	21 3 5 0 00						

CLARK'S WORD PROCESSING SERVICES
WORKSHEET
FOR MONTH ENDING MAY 31, 200X

Figure 4-2 Sample Worksheet

THE ADJUSTMENTS SECTION

Chapters 1–3 discussed transactions that occurred with outside suppliers and companies. In a real business, though, inside transactions also occur during the accounting cycle. These transactions must be recorded, too. At the end of the worksheet process, the accountant will have all of the business's accounts up-to-date and ready to be used to prepare the formal financial reports. By analyzing each of Clark's accounts on the worksheet, the accountant will be able to identify specific accounts that must be adjusted, to bring them up-to-date. The accountant for Clark's Word Processing Services needs to adjust the following accounts:

A. Office Supplies   **C.** Word Processing Equipment
B. Prepaid Rent   **D.** Office Salaries Expense

Let's look at how to analyze and adjust each of these accounts.

A. Adjusting the Office Supplies Account

On May 31, the accountant found out that the company had only $100 worth of office supplies on hand. When the company had originally purchased the $600 of office supplies, they were considered an asset. But as the supplies were used up, they became an expense.

- Office supplies available, $600 on trial balance.
- Office supplies left or on hand as of May 31, $100 will end up on adjusted trial balance.
- Office supplies used up in the operation of the business for the month of May, $500 is shown in the adjustments column.

Worksheets can be completed on Excel spreadsheets

Adjusting is like fine-tuning your TV set.

The adjustment for supplies deals with the amount of supplies used up.

Adjustments affect both the income statement and balance sheet.

Office Supplies Exp. 514

500 |

This is supplies used up.

Office Supplies 114

600 | 500

100

↑

This is supplies on hand.

Note: All accounts listed below the trial balance will be increasing.

The Office Supplies Expense account indicates the amount of supplies used up. It is listed below other trial balance accounts, since it was not on the original trial balance.

Adjusting Prepaid Rent: On p. 88 the trial balance showed a figure for Prepaid Rent of $1,200. The amount of rent expired is the adjustment figure used to update Prepaid Rent and Rent Expense.

Rent Expense 515

400 |

Prepaid Rent 115

1200 | 400 Adj.

800 |

As a result, the asset Office Supplies is too high on the trial balance (it should be $100, not $600). At the same time, if we don't show the additional expense of supplies used, the company's *net income* will be too high.

If Clark's accountant does not adjust the trial balance to reflect the change, the company's net income would be too high on the income statement and both sides (Assets and Owner's Equity) of the balance sheet would be too high.

Now let's look at the adjustment for office supplies in terms of the transaction analysis chart.

Will go on income statement

Accounts Affected	Category	↓ ↑	Rules
Office Supplies Expense	Expense	↑	Dr.
Office Supplies	Asset	↓	Cr.

Will go on balance sheet

The Office Supplies Expense account comes from the chart of accounts on page 73. Since it is not listed in the account titles, it must be listed below the trial balance. Let's see how we enter this adjustment on the worksheet on the following page in Figure 4-3.

Place $500 in the debit column of the adjustments section on the same line as Office Supplies Expense. Place $500 in the credit column of the adjustments section on the same line as Office Supplies. The numbers in the adjustment column show what is used, *not* what is on hand.

B. Adjusting the Prepaid Rent Account

Back on May 1, Clark's Word Processing Services paid three months' rent in advance. The accountant realized that the rent expense would be $400 per month ($1,200 ÷ 3 months = $400).

Remember, when rent is paid in advance, it is considered an asset called *prepaid rent*. When the asset, prepaid rent, begins to expire or be used up, it becomes an expense. Now it is May 31, and one month's prepaid rent has become an expense.

How is this handled? Should the account be $1,200, or is there really only $800 of prepaid rent left as of May 31? What do we need to do to bring Prepaid Rent to the "true" balance? The answer is that we must increase Rent Expense by $400 and decrease Prepaid Rent by $400 (see Fig. 4-4).

Without this adjustment, the expenses for Clark's Word Processing Services for May will be too low, and the asset Prepaid Rent will be too high. If unadjusted amounts were used in the formal reports, the net income shown on the income statement would be too high, and both sides (Assets and Owner's Equity) would be too high on the balance sheet. In terms of our transaction analysis chart, the adjustment would look like this:

Will go on income statement

Accounts Affected	Category	↓ ↑	Rules
Rent Expense	Expense	↑	Dr.
Prepaid Rent	Asset	↓	Cr.

Will go on balance sheet

Like the Office Supplies Expense account, the Rent Expense account comes from the chart of accounts on page 73.

Figure 4-4 shows how to enter an adjustment to Prepaid Rent.

Note: Amount "used up" for supplies $500 goes in adjustments column.

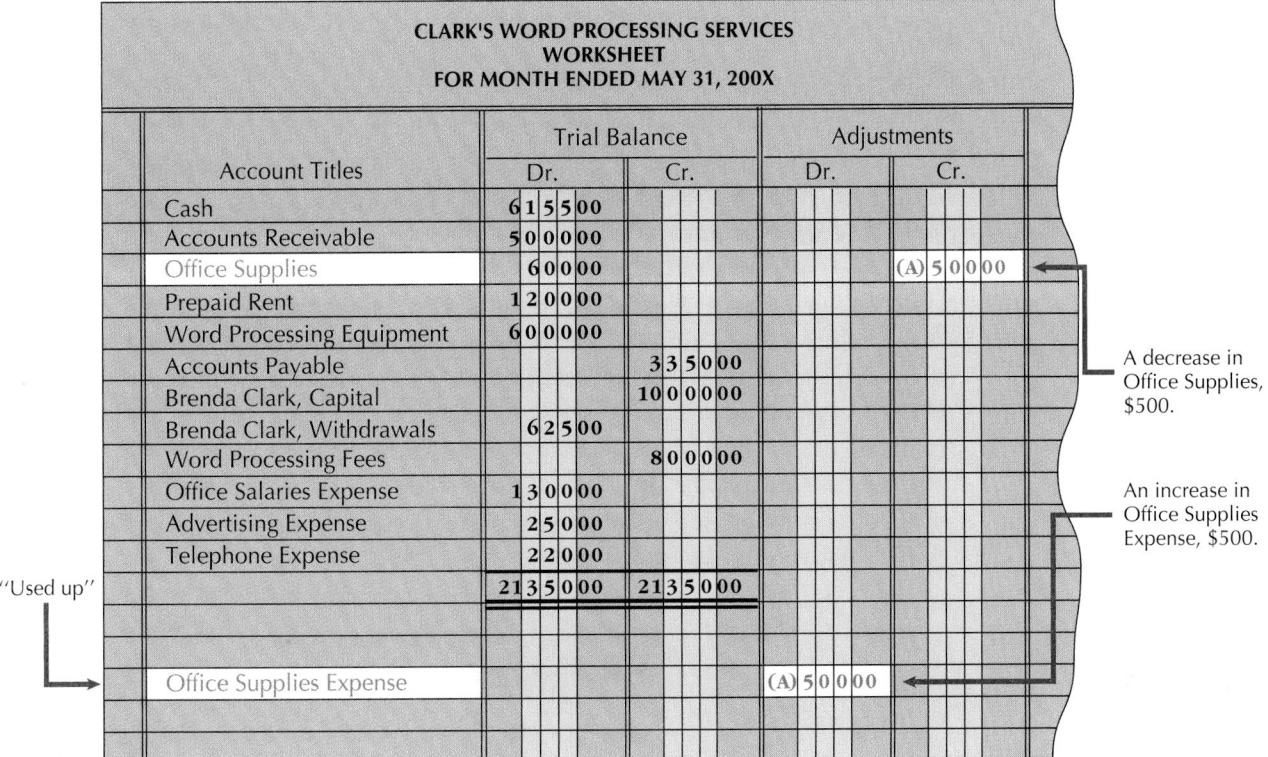

Figure 4-3

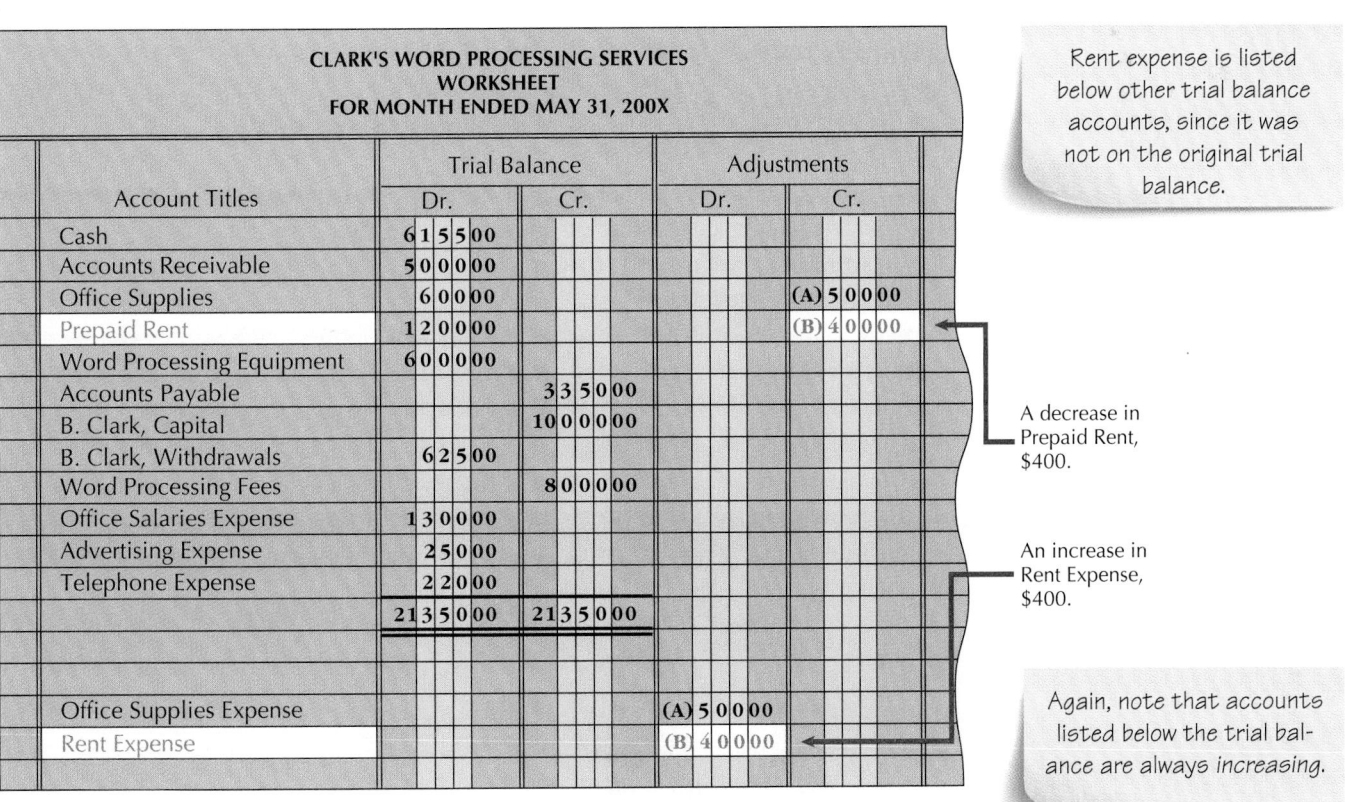

Figure 4-4

C. Adjusting the Word Processing Equipment Account for Depreciation

The life of the asset affects how it is adjusted. The two accounts we just discussed, Office Supplies and Prepaid Rent, involved things that are used up relatively quickly. Equipment—like word processing equipment—is expected to last much longer. Also, it is expected to help produce revenue over a longer period. That is why accountants treat it differently. The balance sheet reports the historical cost, or original cost, of the equipment. The original cost also is reflected in the ledger. The adjustment shows how the cost of the equipment is allocated (spread) over its expected useful life. This spreading is called depreciation. To depreciate the equipment, we have to figure out how much its cost goes down each month. Then we have to keep a running total of how that depreciation mounts up over time. The Internal Revenue Service (IRS) issues guidelines, tables, and formulas that must be used to estimate the amount of depreciation. Different methods can be used to calculate depreciation (see the Appendix at the end of the text). We will use the simplest method—straight-line depreciation—to calculate the depreciation of Clark's Word Processing Services' equipment. Under the straight-line method, equal amounts are taken over successive periods of time.

The calculation of depreciation for the year for Clark's Word Processing Services is as follows:

$$\frac{\text{Cost of Equipment} - \text{Residual Value}}{\text{Estimated Years of Usefulness}}$$

According to the IRS, word processing equipment has an expected life of five years. At the end of that time, the property's value is called its "residual value." Think of residual value as the estimated value of the equipment at the end of the fifth year. For Clark, the equipment has an estimated residual value of $1,200.

$$\frac{\$6,000 - \$1,200}{5 \text{ Years}} = \frac{\$4,800}{5} = \$960 \text{ Depreciation per Year}$$

Our trial balance is for one month, so we must determine the adjustment for that month:

$$\frac{\$960}{12 \text{ Months}} = \$80 \text{ Depreciation per Month}$$

This $80 is known as Depreciation Expense and will be shown on the income statement.

Next, we have to create a new account that can keep a running total of the depreciation amount apart from the original cost of the equipment. That account is called Accumulated Depreciation.

The Accumulated Depreciation account shows the relationship between the original cost of the equipment and the amount of depreciation that has been taken or accumulated over a period of time. This is a *contra-asset* account; it has the opposite balance of an asset such as equipment. Accumulated Depreciation will summarize, accumulate, or build up the amount of depreciation that is taken on the word processing equipment over its estimated useful life.

Figure 4-5 shows how this would look on a partial balance sheet of Clark's Word Processing Services.

Let's summarize the key points before going on to mark the adjustment on the worksheet:

1. Depreciation Expense goes on the income statement, which results in
   - An increase in total expenses.
   - A decrease in net income.
   - Therefore, less to be paid in taxes.

Margin notes (left column):

Original cost of $6,000 for word processing equipment remains unchanged after adjustments.

Assume equipment has a five-year life.

Clark will record $960 of depreciation each year.

Depreciation is an expense reported on the income statement.

Accumulated Depreciation	
Dr.	Cr.

is a contra-asset account found on the balance sheet.

At the end of June the accumulated depreciation will be $160, but historical cost will stay at $6,000.

Taking depreciation does not result in any new payment of cash. The result of depreciation provides some tax savings.

Figure 4-5

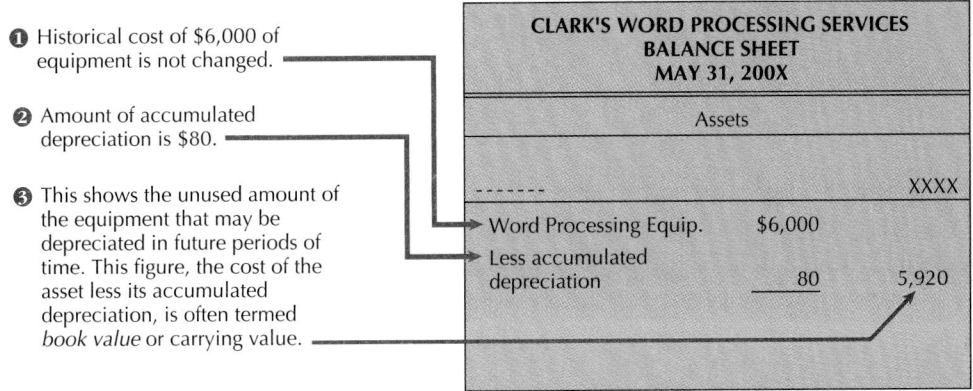

❶ Historical cost of $6,000 of equipment is not changed.

❷ Amount of accumulated depreciation is $80.

❸ This shows the unused amount of the equipment that may be depreciated in future periods of time. This figure, the cost of the asset less its accumulated depreciation, is often termed *book value* or carrying value.

CLARK'S WORD PROCESSING SERVICES
BALANCE SHEET
MAY 31, 200X

Assets

-------   XXXX

Word Processing Equip. $6,000
Less accumulated
depreciation   80   5,920

2. Accumulated depreciation is a contra-asset account found on the balance sheet next to its related equipment account.

3. The original cost of equipment is not reduced; it stays the same until the equipment is sold or removed.

4. Each month the amount in the Accumulated Depreciation account grows larger, while the cost of the equipment remains the same.

Now, let's analyze the adjustment on the transaction analysis chart:

Will go on income statement

Accounts Affected	Category	↓ ↑	Rules
Depreciation Expense, Word Processing Equipment	Expense	↑	Dr.
Accumulated Depreciation, Word Processing Equipment	Contra Asset	↑	Cr.

Will go on balance sheet

Remember, the original cost of the equipment never changes: (1) The Equipment account is not included among the affected accounts because the original cost of equipment remains the same, and (2) the original cost does not change. Even though the Accumulated Depreciation increases (as a credit), the equipment's book value decreases.

Figure 4-6 (p. 126) shows how we enter the adjustment for depreciation of word processing equipment.

Because this is a new business, neither account had a previous balance. Therefore, neither is listed in the account titles of the trial balance. We need to list both accounts below Rent Expense in the account titles section. On the worksheet, put $80 in the debit column of the adjustments section on the same line as Depreciation Expense, W. P. Equipment, and put $80 in the credit column of the adjustments section on the same line as Accumulated Depreciation, W. P. Equipment.

Next month, on June 30, $80 would be entered under Depreciation Expense, and Accumulated Depreciation would show a balance of $160. Remember, in May, Clark's was a new company, so no previous depreciation was taken.

Now let's look at the last adjustment for Clark's Word Processing Services.

D. Adjusting the Salaries Accrued Account

Clark's Word Processing Services paid $1,300 in Office Salaries Expense (see the trial balance of any previous worksheet in this chapter). The last salary checks for the

---

Remember, book value is not the same as market value.

Dep. Expense, W. P. 516

80 |

Accum. Dep., W. P. 122

| 80

Note that the original cost of the equipment on the worksheet has not been changed ($6,000).

Next month (June in our example), accumulated depreciation will appear listed in the original trial balance.

Accumulated Depreciation

Dr.	Cr.
	History of amount of depreciation taken to date

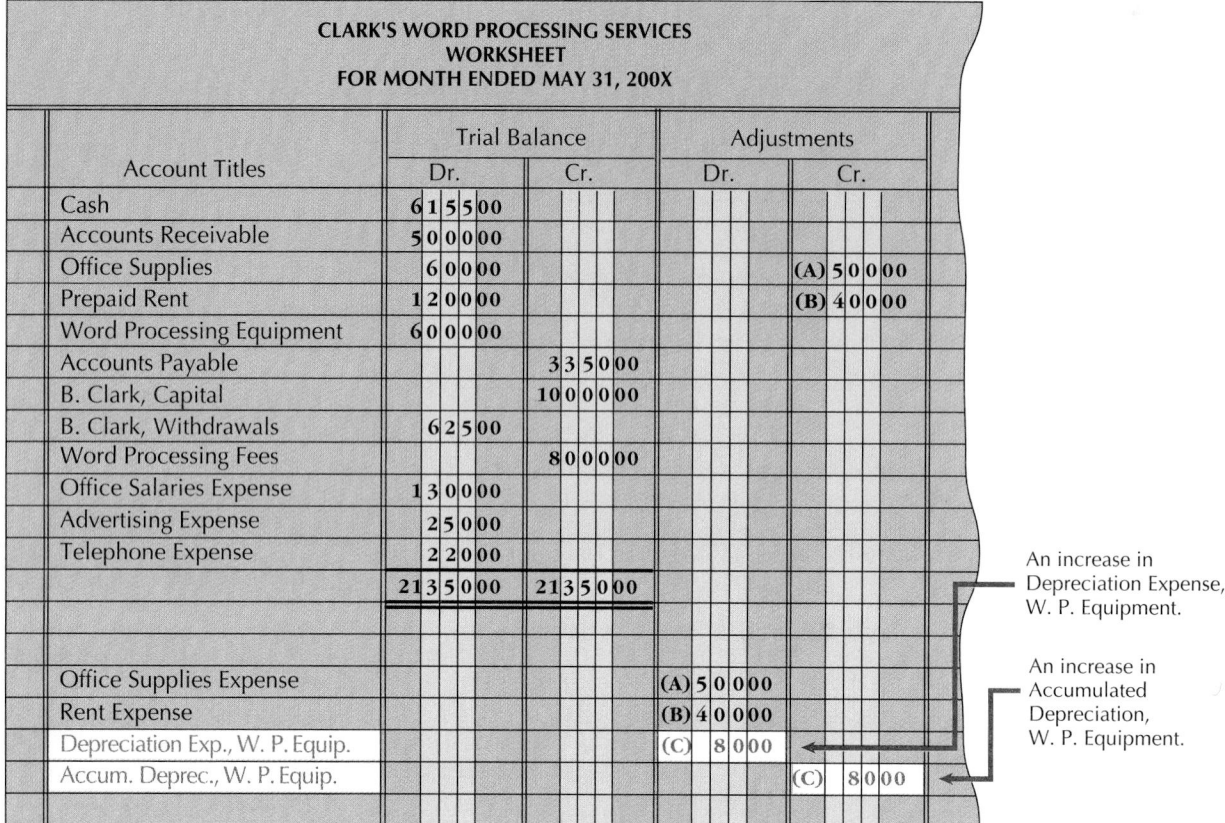

Figure 4-6

An increase in Depreciation Expense, W. P. Equipment.

An increase in Accumulated Depreciation, W. P. Equipment.

Adjusting Salaries

An expense can be incurred without being paid as long as it has helped in creating earned revenue for a period of time.

month were paid on May 27. How can we update this account to show the salary expense as of May 31?

John Murray worked for Clark on May 28, 29, 30, and 31 (see Fig. 4-7), but his next paycheck is not due until June 3. John earned $350 for these four days. Is the $350 an expense to Clark in May, when it was earned, or in June when it is due and is paid?

Think back to Chapter 1, when we first discussed revenue and expenses. We noted then that revenue is recorded when it is earned, and expenses are recorded when they are incurred, not when they are actually paid off. This principle will be discussed further in a later chapter; for now it is enough to remember that we record revenue and expenses when they occur, because we want to match earned revenue with the expenses that resulted in earning those revenues. In this case, by working those four days, John Murray created some revenue for Clark in May. Therefore, the office salaries expense must be shown in May—the month the revenue was earned.

Figure 4-7

May

Sunday	Monday	Tuesday	Wednesday	Thursday	Friday	Saturday
						1
2	3	4	5	6	7	8
9	10	11	12	13	14	15
16	17	18	19	20	21	22
23	24	25	26	27	28	29
30	31					

The results are:

Office Salaries Expense is increased by $350. This unpaid and unrecorded expense for salaries for which payment is not yet due is called accrued salaries. In effect, we now show the true expense for salaries ($1,650 instead of $1,300):

Office Salaries Expense

| 1,300 | |
| 350 | |

The second result is that Salaries Payable is increased by $350. Clark's has created a liability called Salaries Payable, meaning that the firm owes money for salaries. When the firm pays John Murray, it will reduce its liability, Salaries Payable, as well as decrease its cash.

In terms of the transaction analysis chart, the following would be done:

Accounts Affected	Category	↓ ↑	Rules
Office Salaries Expense,	Expense	↑	Dr.
Salaries Payable	Liability	↑	Cr.

Office Salaries Exp. 511

| 1,300 | |
| 350 | |

Salaries Payable 212

| | 350 |

How the adjustment for accrued salaries is entered is shown in Figure 4-8 below.

Remember, all accounts added below the trial balance are increasing.

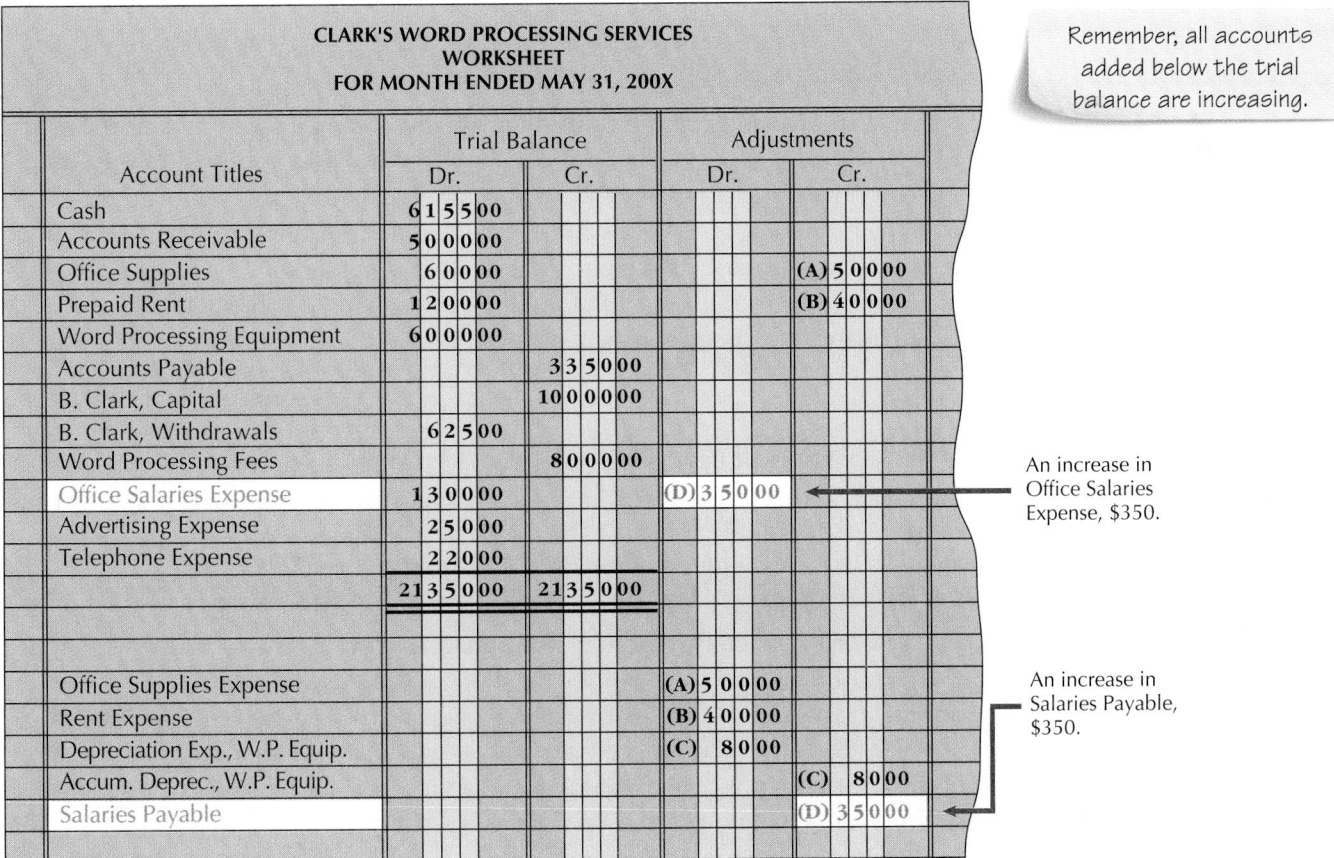

CLARK'S WORD PROCESSING SERVICES
WORKSHEET
FOR MONTH ENDED MAY 31, 200X

Account Titles	Trial Balance Dr.	Trial Balance Cr.	Adjustments Dr.	Adjustments Cr.
Cash	6 1 5 5 00			
Accounts Receivable	5 0 0 0 00			
Office Supplies	6 0 0 00			(A) 5 0 0 00
Prepaid Rent	1 2 0 0 00			(B) 4 0 0 00
Word Processing Equipment	6 0 0 0 00			
Accounts Payable		3 3 5 0 00		
B. Clark, Capital		1 0 0 0 0 00		
B. Clark, Withdrawals	6 2 5 00			
Word Processing Fees		8 0 0 0 00		
Office Salaries Expense	1 3 0 0 00		(D) 3 5 0 00	
Advertising Expense	2 5 0 00			
Telephone Expense	2 2 0 00			
	21 3 5 0 00	21 3 5 0 00		
Office Supplies Expense			(A) 5 0 0 00	
Rent Expense			(B) 4 0 0 00	
Deprec. Exp., W.P. Equip.			(C) 8 0 00	
Accum. Deprec., W.P. Equip.				(C) 8 0 00
Salaries Payable				(D) 3 5 0 00

An increase in Office Salaries Expense, $350.

An increase in Salaries Payable, $350.

Figure 4-8

Figure 4-9
The Adjustments Section
of the Worksheet

CLARK'S WORD PROCESSING SERVICES
WORKSHEET
FOR MONTH ENDED MAY 31, 200X

Account Titles	Trial Balance Dr.	Trial Balance Cr.	Adjustments Dr.	Adjustments Cr.
Cash	6 1 5 5 00			
Accounts Receivable	5 0 0 0 00			
Office Supplies	6 0 0 00			(A) 5 0 0 00
Prepaid Rent	1 2 0 0 00			(B) 4 0 0 00
Word Processing Equipment	6 0 0 0 00			
Accounts Payable		3 3 5 0 00		
B. Clark, Capital		10 0 0 0 00		
B. Clark, Withdrawals	6 2 5 00			
Word Processing Fees		8 0 0 0 00		
Office Salaries Expense	1 3 0 0 00		(D) 3 5 0 00	
Advertising Expense	2 5 0 00			
Telephone Expense	2 2 0 00			
	21 3 5 0 00	21 3 5 0 00		
Office Supplies Expense			(A) 5 0 0 00	
Rent Expense			(B) 4 0 0 00	
Depreciation Exp., W.P. Equip.			(C) 8 0 00	
Accum. Deprec., W.P. Equip.				(C) 8 0 00
Salaries Payable				(D) 3 5 0 00
			1 3 3 0 00	1 3 3 0 00

The account Office Salaries Expense is already listed in the account titles, so $350 is placed in the debit column of the adjustments section on the same line as Office Salaries Expense. However, because the Salaries Payable is not listed in the account titles, it is added below the trial balance after Accumulated Depreciation, W. P. Equipment. Also, $350 is placed in the credit column of the adjustments section on the same line as Salaries Payable.

Now that we have finished all the adjustments that we intended to make, we total the adjustments section, as shown in Figure 4-9.

THE ADJUSTED TRIAL BALANCE SECTION

The adjusted trial balance is the next section on the worksheet. To fill it out, we must summarize the information in the trial balance and adjustments sections, as shown in Figure 4-10 on page 129.

Note that when the numbers are brought across from the trial balance to the adjusted trial balance, two debits will be added together and two credits will be added together. If the numbers include a debit and a credit, take the difference between the two and place it on the side that is larger.

Now that we have completed the adjustments and adjusted trial balance sections of the worksheet, it is time to move on to the income statement and the balance sheet sections. Before we do that though, look at the chart shown in Table 4-1, p. 130. This table should be used as a reference to help you in filling out the next two sections of the worksheet.

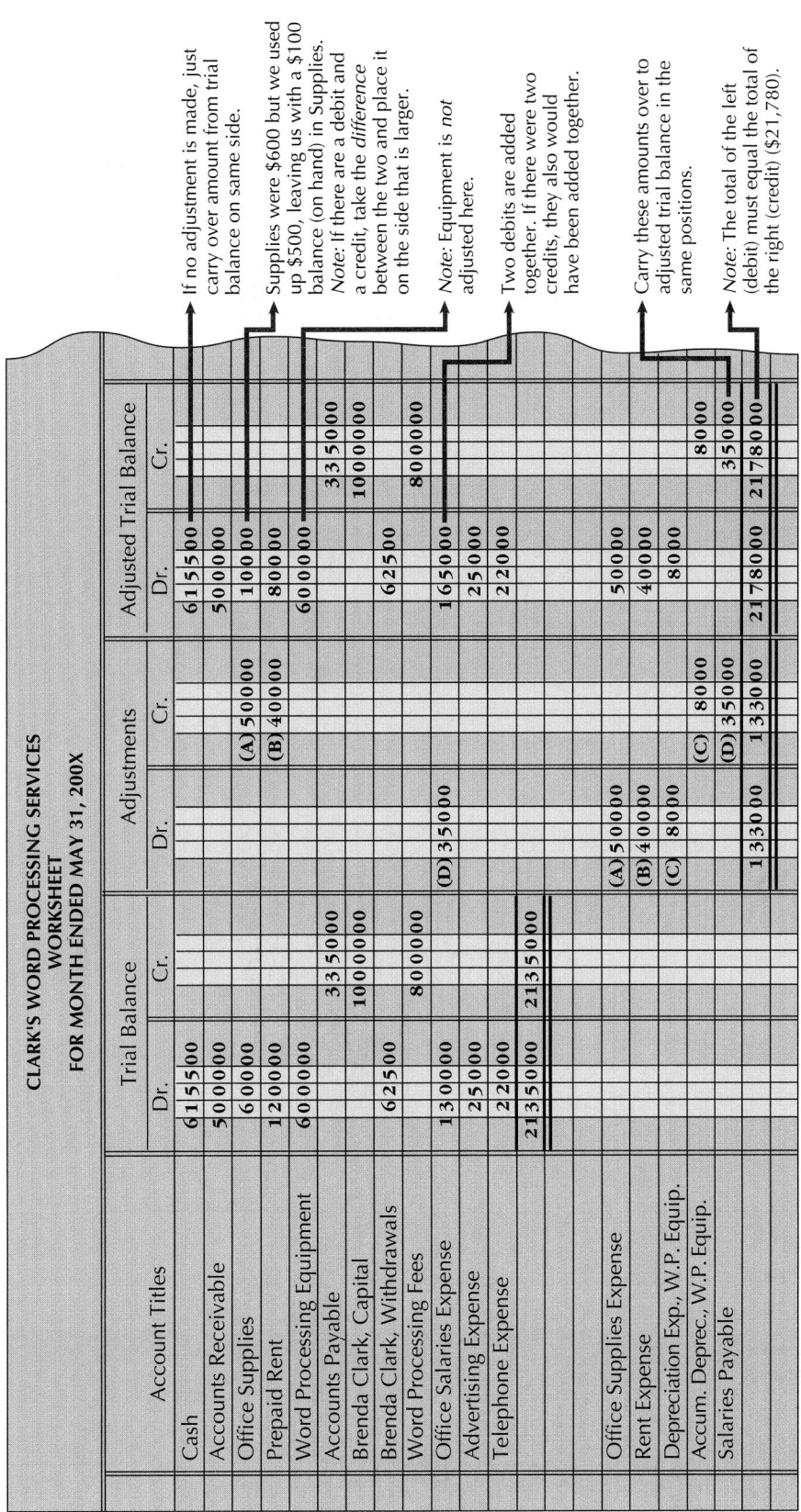

Figure 4-10 The Adjusted Trial Balance Section of the Worksheet

TABLE 4-1 Normal Balances and Account Categories

Account Titles	Category	Normal Balance on Adjusted Trial Balance	Income Statement Dr.	Income Statement Cr.	Balance Sheet Dr.	Balance Sheet Cr.
Cash	Asset	Dr.			X	
Accounts Receivable	Asset	Dr.			X	
Office Supplies	Asset	Dr.			X	
Prepaid Rent	Asset	Dr.			X	
Word Proc. Equip.	Asset	Dr.			X	
Accounts Payable	Liability	Cr.				X
Brenda Clark, Capital	Capital	Cr.				X
Brenda Clark, Withdrawals	Withdrawal	Dr.			X	
Word Proc. Fees	Revenue	Cr.		X		
Office Salaries Exp.	Expense	Dr.	X			
Advertising Expense	Expense	Dr.	X			
Telephone Expense	Expense	Dr.	X			
Office Supplies Exp.	Expense	Dr.	X			
Rent Expense	Expense	Dr.	X			
Dep. Exp., W. P. Equip.	Expense	Dr.	X			
Acc. Dep., W. P. Equip.	Contra Asset	Cr.				X
Salaries Payable	Liability	Cr.				X

Keep in mind that the numbers from the adjusted trial balance are carried over to one of the last four columns of the worksheet before the bottom section is completed.

THE INCOME STATEMENT SECTION

As shown in Figure 4-11 on page 131, the income statement section lists only revenue and expenses from the adjusted trial balance. Note that Accumulated Depreciation and Salaries Payable do not go on the income statement. Accumulated Depreciation is a contra-asset found on the balance sheet. Salaries Payable is a liability found on the balance sheet.

The revenue ($8,000) and all the individual expenses are listed in the income statement section. The revenue is placed in the credit column of the income statement section because it has a credit balance. The expenses have debit balances, so they are placed in the debit column of the income statement section. The following steps must be taken after the debits and credits are placed in the correct columns:

> In the worksheet, Net Income is placed in the debit column of the income statement. Net loss goes in the credit column.

Step 1: Total the debits and credits.

Step 2: Calculate the balance between the debit and credit columns and place the difference on the smaller side.

Step 3: Total the columns.

> The difference between $3,100 Dr. and $8,000 Cr. indicates a Net Income of $4,900. Do not think of the Net Income as a Dr. or Cr. The $4,900 is placed in the debit column to balance both columns to $8,000. Actually, the credit side is larger by $4,900.

The worksheet in Figure 4-11 shows that the label Net Income is added in the account title column on the same line as $4,900. When there is a net income, it will be placed in the debit column of the income statement section of the worksheet. If there is a net loss, it is placed in the credit column. The $8,000 total indicates that the two columns are in balance.

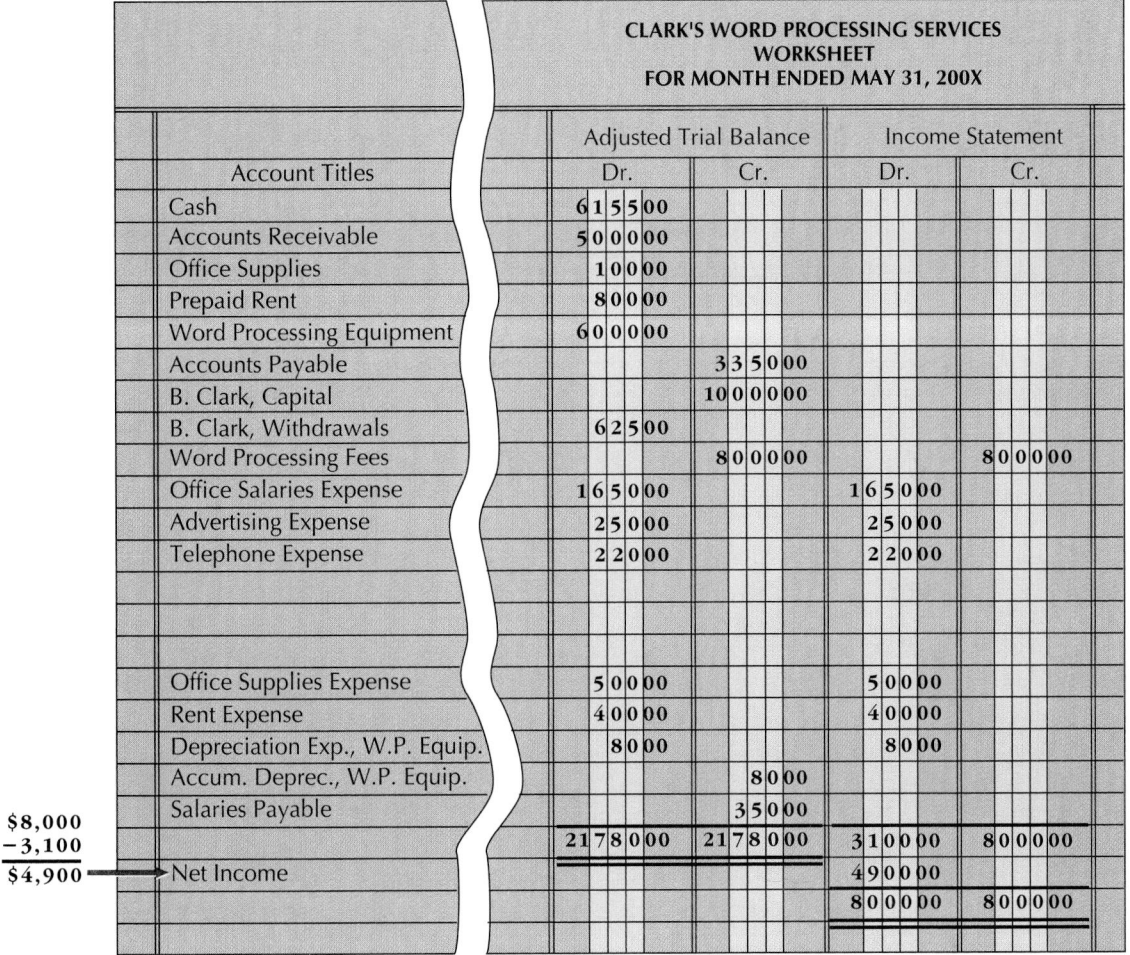

Figure 4-11 The Income Statement Section of the Worksheet

THE BALANCE SHEET SECTION

To fill out the balance sheet section of the worksheet, the following are carried over from the adjusted trial balance section: assets, contra-assets, liabilities, capital, and withdrawals. Because the beginning figure for Capital* is used on the worksheet, the Net Income is brought over to the credit column of the balance sheet so both columns balance.

Let's now look at the completed worksheet in Figure 4-12 (p. 132) to see how the balance sheet section is completed. Note how the Net Income of $4,900 is brought over to the Credit column of the worksheet. The figure for Capital is also in the credit column, while the figure for Withdrawals is in the debit column. By placing the net income in the credit column, both sides total $18,680. If a net loss were to occur, it would be placed in the debit column of the balance sheet column.

Now that we have completed the worksheet, we can go on to the three financial reports. But first let's summarize our progress.

> Remember: The ending figure for capital is not on the worksheet.

> To see whether additional investments occurred for the period you must check the Capital account in the ledger.

> The amounts come from the adjusted trial balance, except the $4,900, which was carried over from the income statement section.

*We assume no additional investments during the period.

Original cost of $6,000 is *not* adjusted

"used up"　"on hand"

CLARK'S WORD PROCESSING SERVICES
WORKSHEET
FOR MONTH ENDED MAY 31, 200X

Account Titles	Trial Balance Dr.	Trial Balance Cr.	Adjustments Dr.	Adjustments Cr.	Adjusted Trial Balance Dr.	Adjusted Trial Balance Cr.	Income Statement Dr.	Income Statement Cr.	Balance Sheet Dr.	Balance Sheet Cr.
Cash	6155 00				6155 00				6155 00	
Accounts Receivable	5000 00				5000 00				5000 00	
Office Supplies	600 00			(A) 500 00	100 00				100 00	
Prepaid Rent	1200 00			(B) 400 00	800 00				800 00	
Word Processing Equipment	6000 00				6000 00				6000 00	
Accounts Payable		3350 00				3350 00				3350 00
B. Clark, Capital		10000 00				10000 00				10000 00
B. Clark, Withdrawals	625 00				625 00				625 00	
Word Processing Fees		8000 00				8000 00		8000 00		
Office Salaries Expense	1300 00		(D) 350 00		1650 00		1650 00			
Advertising Expense	250 00				250 00		250 00			
Telephone Expense	220 00				220 00		220 00			
	21350 00	21350 00								
Office Supplies Expense			(A) 500 00		500 00		500 00			
Rent Expense			(B) 400 00		400 00		400 00			
Depreciation Exp., W. P. Equip.			(C) 80 00		80 00		80 00			
Accum. Deprec., W. P. Equip.				(C) 80 00		80 00				80 00
Salaries Payable				(D) 350 00		350 00				350 00
			1330 00	1330 00	21780 00	21780 00	3100 00	8000 00	18680 00	13780 00
Net Income							4900 00			4900 00
							8000 00	8000 00	18680 00	18680 00

contra-asset

Figure 4-12 The Completed Worksheet

Learning Unit 4-1 Review

AT THIS POINT you should be able to

- Define and explain the purpose of a worksheet. (p. 120)
- Explain the need as well as the process for adjustments. (p. 121)
- Explain the concept of depreciation. (p. 124)
- Explain the difference between depreciation expense and accumulated depreciation. (p. 124)
- Prepare a worksheet from a trial balance and adjustment data. (p. 132)

SELF-REVIEW QUIZ 4-1

From the accompanying trial balance and adjustment data in Figure 4-13, complete a worksheet for P. Logan Co. for the month ended Dec. 31, 200X. (You can use the blank fold-out worksheet located at the end of the *Study Guide and Working Papers.* See your DVD for worked-out solutions.)

Note: The numbers used on this quiz may seem impossibly small, but we have done that on purpose, so that at this point you don't have to worry about arithmetic, just about preparing the worksheet correctly.

ADJUSTMENT DATA

  a. Depreciation Expense, Store Equipment, $1.
  b. Insurance Expired, $2
  c. Supplies on hand, $1.
  d. Salaries owed but not paid to employees, $3.

Figure 4-13

P. LOGAN
TRIAL BALANCE
DECEMBER 31, 200X

	Dr.	Cr.
Cash	15 00	
Accounts Receivable	3 00	
Prepaid Insurance	3 00	
Store Supplies	5 00	
Store Equipment	6 00	
Accumulated Depreciation, Store Equipment		4 00
Accounts Payable		2 00
P. Logan, Capital		14 00
P. Logan, Withdrawals	3 00	
Revenue from Clients		25 00
Rent Expense	2 00	
Salaries Expense	8 00	
	45 00	45 00

SOLUTION TO SELF-REVIEW QUIZ 4-1

Don't adjust this line! Store Equipment always contains the historical cost.

Amount used up

Note that on hand ends up on the adjusted trial balance

P. LOGAN COMPANY
WORKSHEET
FOR MONTH ENDED DECEMBER 31, 200X

Account Titles	Trial Balance Dr.	Trial Balance Cr.	Adjustments Dr.	Adjustments Cr.	Adjusted Trial Balance Dr.	Adjusted Trial Balance Cr.	Income Statement Dr.	Income Statement Cr.	Balance Sheet Dr.	Balance Sheet Cr.
Cash	1500				1500				1500	
Accounts Receivable	300				300				300	
Prepaid Insurance	300			(B) 200	100				100	
Store Supplies	500			(C) 400	100				100	
Store Equipment	600				600				600	
Accum. Depr., Store Equipment		400		(A) 100		500				500
Accounts Payable		200				200				200
P. Logan, Capital		1400				1400				1400
P. Logan, Withdrawals	300				300				300	
Revenue from Clients		2500				2500		2500		
Rent Expense	200				200		200			
Salaries Expense	800		(D) 300		1100		1100			
	4500	4500								
Depr. Exp., Store Equipment			(A) 100		100		100			
Insurance Expense			(B) 200		200		200			
Supplies Expense			(C) 400		400		400			
Salaries Payable				(D) 300		300				300
			1000	1000	4900	4900	2000	2500	2900	2400
Net Income							500			500
							2500	2500	2900	2900

Note that Accumulated Depreciation is listed in trial balance, since this is not a new company. Store Equipment has already been depreciated $4.00 from an earlier period.

Figure 4-14

Accounting in the Reel World

Dating . . . and Accounting?

Everyone, at one point or another, has probably set up two friends on a blind date or been set up on one. Yet, not everyone sees this matchmaking activity as a business opportunity.

Jilted just five weeks before she was to walk down the aisle, Andrea McGinty turned her personal frustration at finding eligible singles into a lucrative matchmaking business. It's Just Lunch has over $2.5 million in revenues, over 20 locations across the country, and plans to open 1–2 units per month. As you watch the brief It's Just Lunch on-location video on your DVD, think about what it takes to set up a matchmaking business such as It's Just Lunch, and answer the following questions.

1. Can you name some account titles in the assets category? In the Liabilities category? In the Expenses category?
2. How often does It's Just Lunch generate financial statements and why does owner Andrea McGinty need them that often?
3. Is depreciation likely to show up on the It's Just Lunch balance sheet, and if so, for what types of things would Andrea McGinty make a depreciation adjustment?
4. What is the difference between It's Just Lunch's revenues and its income, and what could Andrea McGinty do to increase the company's income?

Learning Unit 4-2 — Step 6 of the Accounting Cycle: Preparing the Financial Statements from the Worksheet

The formal financial statements can be prepared from the worksheet completed in Learning Unit 4-1. Before beginning, we must check that the entries on the worksheet are correct and in balance. To do this, we have to be sure that (1) all entries are recorded in the appropriate column, (2) the correct amounts are entered in the proper places, (3) the addition is correct across the columns (i.e., from the trial balance to the adjusted trial balance to the financial statements), and (4) the columns are added correctly.

PREPARING THE INCOME STATEMENT

The first statement to be prepared for Clark's Word Processing Services is the income statement. When preparing the income statement, it is important to remember that

1. Every figure on the formal statement is on the worksheet. Figure 4-15 (p. 136) shows where each of these figures goes on the income statement.
2. There are no debit or credit columns on the formal statement.
3. The inside column on financial statements is used for subtotaling.
4. Withdrawals do not go on the income statement; they go on the statement of owner's equity.

Take a moment to look at the income statement in Figure 4-15. Note where items go from the income statement section of the worksheet onto the formal statement.

PREPARING THE STATEMENT OF OWNER'S EQUITY

Figure 4-16 (p. 136) is the statement of owner's equity for Clark's. The figure shows where the information comes from on the worksheet. It is important to remember that if there were additional investments, the figure on the worksheet for Capital would not be the beginning figure for Capital. Checking the ledger account for Capital will tell you whether the amount is correct. Note how Net Income and Withdrawals aid in calculating the new figure for Capital.

CLARK'S WORD PROCESSING SERVICES
INCOME STATEMENT
FOR MONTH ENDED MAY 31, 200X

Revenue:		
Word Processing Fees		$8 0 0 0 00
Operating Expenses:		
Office Salaries Expense	$1 6 5 0 00	
Advertising Expense	2 5 0 00	
Telephone Expense	2 2 0 00	
Office Supplies Expense	5 0 0 00	
Rent Expense	4 0 0 00	
Depreciation Expense, W.P. Equipment	8 0 00	
Total Operating Expenses		3 1 0 0 00
Net Income		$4 9 0 0 00

Income Statement

Account Titles	Dr.	Cr.
Cash		
Accounts Receivable		
Office Supplies		
Prepaid Rent		
Word Processing Equipment		
Accounts Payable		
Brenda Clark, Capital		
Brenda Clark, Withdrawals		
Word Processing Fees		8 0 0 0 00
Office Salaries Expense	1 6 5 0 00	
Advertising Expense	2 5 0 00	
Telephone Expense	2 2 0 00	
Office Supplies Expense	5 0 0 00	
Rent Expense	4 0 0 00	
Depreciation Expense, W.P. Equip.	8 0 00	
Accum. Deprec., W.P. Equip.		
Salaries Payable		
	3 1 0 0 00	8 0 0 0 00
Net Income	4 9 0 0 00	
	8 0 0 0 00	8 0 0 0 00

Figure 4-15 From Worksheet to Income Statement

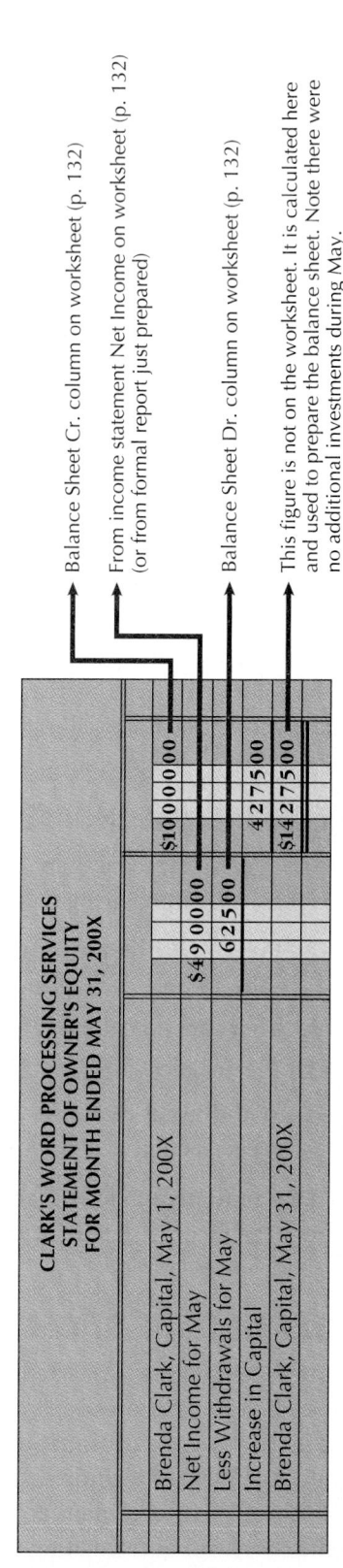

CLARK'S WORD PROCESSING SERVICES
STATEMENT OF OWNER'S EQUITY
FOR MONTH ENDED MAY 31, 200X

Brenda Clark, Capital, May 1, 200X		$10 0 0 0 00
Net Income for May	$4 9 0 0 00	
Less Withdrawals for May	6 2 5 00	
Increase in Capital		4 2 7 5 00
Brenda Clark, Capital, May 31, 200X		$14 2 7 5 00

→ Balance Sheet Cr. column on worksheet (p. 132)

→ From income statement Net Income on worksheet (p. 132) (or from formal report just prepared)

→ Balance Sheet Dr. column on worksheet (p. 132)

→ This figure is not on the worksheet. It is calculated here and used to prepare the balance sheet. Note there were no additional investments during May.

Figure 4-16 Completing a Statement of Owner's Equity

PREPARING THE BALANCE SHEET

In preparing the balance sheet (Fig. 4-17) remember that the balance sheet section totals on the worksheet ($18,680) do *not* match the totals on the formal balance sheet ($17,975). This is because information is grouped differently on the formal statement. First, in the formal report Accumulated Depreciation ($80) is subtracted from Word Processing Equipment, reducing the balance. Second, Withdrawals ($625) are subtracted from Owner's Equity, reducing the balance further. These two reductions (−$80 − $625 = −$705) represent the difference between the worksheet and the formal version of the balance sheet ($17,975 − $18,680 = −$705). Figure 4-17 shows how to prepare the balance sheet from the worksheet.

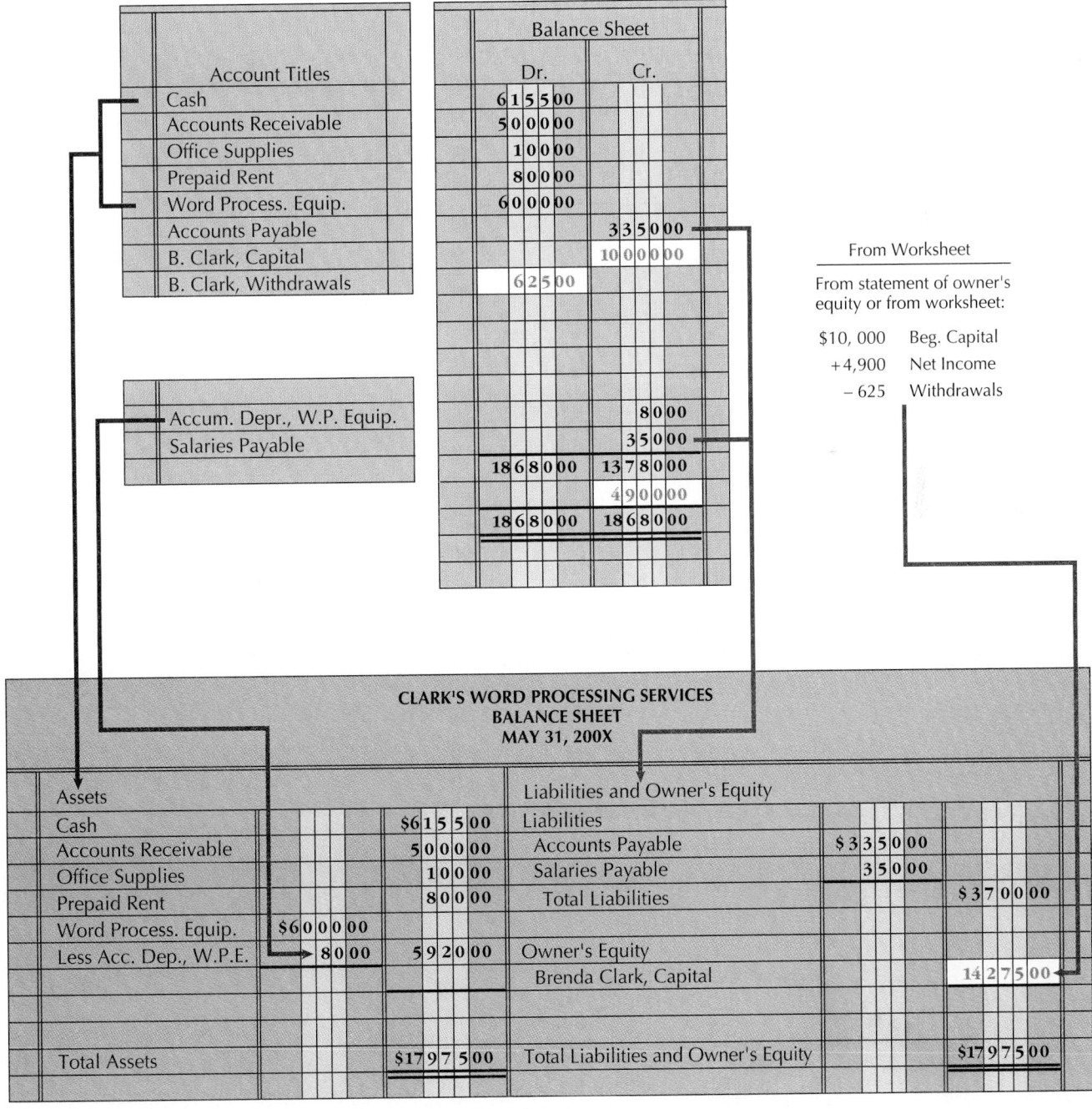

Figure 4-17 From Worksheet to Balance Sheet

Learning Unit 4-2 Review

AT THIS POINT you should be able to

- Prepare the three financial statements from a worksheet. (p. 136)
- Explain why totals of the formal balance sheet don't match totals of balance sheet columns on the worksheet. (p. 137)

SELF-REVIEW QUIZ 4-2

(The forms you need are located on pages 101 and 102 of the *Study Guide and Working Papers.* See your DVD for worked-out solutions.)

From the worksheet on page 134 for P. Logan, please prepare (1) an income statement for December, (2) a statement of owner's equity, and (3) a balance sheet for December 31, 200X. No additional investments took place during the period.

SOLUTION TO SELF-REVIEW QUIZ 4-2

Quiz Tips:
The income statement is made up of revenue and expenses. Use the inside column for subtotaling. The $5 on the income statement is used to update the statement of owner's equity.

P. LOGAN
INCOME STATEMENT
FOR THE MONTH ENDED DECEMBER 31, 200X

Revenue:			
Revenue from clients			$25 00
Operating Expenses:			
Rent Expense	$2 00		
Salaries Expense	11 00		
Depreciation Expense, Store Equipment	1 00		
Insurance Expense	2 00		
Supplies Expense	4 00		
Total Operating Expenses		20 00	
Net Income		$5 00	

P. LOGAN
STATEMENT OF OWNER'S EQUITY
FOR THE MONTH ENDED DECEMBER 31, 200X

P. Logan, Capital, December 1, 200X			$14 00
Net Income for December	$5 00		
Less Withdrawals for December	3 00		
Increase in Capital		2 00	
P. Logan, Capital, December 31, 200X		$16 00	

The ending Capital figure on the statement of owner's equity ($16) is used as the Capital figure on the balance sheet.

P. LOGAN
BALANCE SHEET
DECEMBER 31, 200X

Assets				Liabilities and Owner's Equity			
Cash			$15 00	Liabilities			
Accounts Receivable			3 00	Accounts Payable	$2 00		
Prepaid Insurance			1 00	Salaries Payable	3 00		
Store Supplies			1 00	Total Liabilities		$5 00	
Store Equipment	$6 00			Owner's Equity			
Less Acc. Dep., St. Eq.	5 00		1 00	P. Logan, Capital		16 00	
				Total Liabilities and			
Total Assets			$21 00	Owner's Equity		$21 00	

Figure 4-18

SOLUTIONS & TIPS TO COMPREHENSIVE PROBLEM: PUTTING THE PIECES TOGETHER

(The blank forms you need are on pages 103 and 104 of the *Study Guide and Working Papers.*)

From the following trial balance and additional data complete (1) a worksheet and (2) the three financial statements (numbers are intentionally small so you may concentrate on the theory).

FROST COMPANY
TRIAL BALANCE
DECEMBER 31, 200X

	Dr.	Cr.
Cash	14	
Accounts Receivable	4	
Prepaid Insurance	5	
Plumbing Supplies	3	
Plumbing Equipment	7	
Accumulated Depreciation, Plumbing Equipment		5
Accounts Payable		1
J. Frost, Capital		12
J. Frost, Withdrawals	3	
Plumbing Fees		27
Rent Expense	4	
Salaries Expense	5	
Totals	45	45

Adjustment Data

a. Insurance Expired		$3
b. Plumbing Supplies on Hand		$1
c. Depreciation Expense, Plumbing Equipment		$1
d. Salaries owed but not paid to employees		$2

Solution Tips to Building a Worksheet

1. Adjustments

a.

Insurance Expense	Expense	↑	Dr.	$3
Prepaid Insurance	Asset	↓	Cr.	$3

Expired means used up

b.

Plumbing Supplies Expense	Expense	↑	Dr.	$2
Plumbing Supplies	Asset	↓	Cr.	$2

$3 − 1 = $2 *used up* on hand

Solution to Worksheet

FROST COMPANY
WORKSHEET
FOR MONTH ENDED DECEMBER 31, 200X

Account Titles	Trial Balance Dr.	Trial Balance Cr.	Adjustments Dr.	Adjustments Cr.	Adjusted Trial Balance Dr.	Adjusted Trial Balance Cr.	Income Statement Dr.	Income Statement Cr.	Balance Sheet Dr.	Balance Sheet Cr.
Cash	1400				1400				1400	
Accounts Receivable	400				400				400	
Prepaid Insurance	500			(A) 300	200				200	
Plumbing Supplies	300			(B) 200	100				100	
Plumbing Equipment	700				700				700	
Accum. Depr., Plumb. Equip.		500		(C) 100		600				600
Accounts Payable		100				100				100
J. Frost, Capital		1200				1200				1200
J. Frost, Withdrawals	300				300				300	
Plumbing Fees		2700				2700		2700		
Rent Expense	400				400		400			
Salaries Expense	500		(D) 200		700		700			
	4500	4500								
Insurance Expense			(A) 300		300		300			
Plumbing Supplies Expense			(B) 200		200		200			
Depr. Exp. Plumb. Equip.			(C) 100		100		100			
Salaries Payable				(D) 200		200				200
			800	800	4800	4800	1700	2700	3100	2100
Net Income							1000			1000
							2700	2700	3100	3100

"used up"

"on hand"

Original cost not adjusted

Figure 4-19

c.

Depreciation Expense, Plumbing Equipment	Expense	↑	Dr.	$1
Contra Asset Accumulated Depreciation, Plumbing Equipment	Contra Asset	↑	Cr.	$1

The original cost of equipment of $7 is not "touched."

d.

Salaries Expense,	Expense	↑	Dr.	$2
Salaries Payable	Liability	↑	Cr.	$2

2. Last four columns of worksheet prepared from adjusted trial balance.
3. Capital of $12 is the old figure. Net income of $10 (revenue − expenses) is brought over to same side as capital on the balance sheet Cr. column to balance columns.

FROST COMPANY
INCOME STATEMENT
FOR MONTH ENDED DECEMBER 31, 200X

Revenue:		
Plumbing Fees		$27
Operating Expenses:		
Rent Expense	$4	
Salaries Expense	7	
Insurance Expense	3	
Plumbing Supplies Expense	2	
Depreciation Expense, Plumbing Equipment	1	
Total Operating Expenses		17
Net Income		$10

FROST COMPANY
STATEMENT OF OWNER'S EQUITY
FOR MONTH ENDED DECEMBER 31, 200X

J. Frost Capital, Dec. 1, 200X		$12
Net Income for December	$10	
Less Withdrawals for December	3	
Increase in Capital		7
J. Frost, Capital Dec. 31, 200X		$19

FROST COMPANY
BALANCE SHEET
DECEMBER 31, 200X

Assets			Liabilities and Owner's Equity		
Cash		$14	Liabilities		
Accounts Receivable		4	Accounts Payable	$1	
Prepaid Insurance		2	Salaries Payable	2	
Plumbing Supplies		1	Total Liabilities		$3
Original Cost					
Plumbing Equipment	$7				
Less Accumulated Dep.	6	1	Owner's Equity		
			J. Frost, Capital		19
			Total Liabilities and		
Total Assets		$22	Owner's Equity		$22

Solution Tips for Preparing Financial Statements from a Worksheet

Inside columns of the three financial statements are used for subtotaling. There are no debits or credits on the formal statements.

STATEMENTS

Income Statement	From Income Statement columns of worksheet for revenue and expenses.
Statement of Owner's Equity	From Balance Sheet Cr. column for old figure for Capital. Net Income from Income Statement. From Balance Sheet Dr. Column for Withdrawal figure.
Balance Sheet	From Balance Sheet Dr. column for Assets. From Balance Sheet Cr. Column for Liabilities and Accumulated Depreciation. New figure for Capital from statement of owner's equity.

Note how Plumbing Equipment $7 and Accumulated Depreciation $6 are rearranged on the formal balance sheet. The Total Assets of $22 is not on the worksheet. Remember there are no debits or credits on formal statements.

Summary of Key Points

Learning Unit 4-1

1. The worksheet is not a formal statement.
2. Adjustments update certain accounts so that they will be up to their latest balance before financial statements are prepared. Adjustments are the result of internal transactions.
3. Adjustments will affect both the income statement and the balance sheet.
4. Accounts listed *below* the account titles on the trial balance of the worksheet are *increasing*.
5. The original cost of a piece of equipment is not adjusted; historical cost is not lost.
6. Depreciation is the process of spreading the original cost of the asset over its expected useful life.
7. Accumulated depreciation is a contra-asset on the balance sheet that summarizes, accumulates, or builds up the amount of depreciation that an asset has accumulated.
8. Book value is the original cost less accumulated depreciation.
9. Accrued salaries are unpaid and unrecorded expenses that are accumulating but for which payment is not yet due.
10. Revenue and expenses go on income statement sections of the worksheet. Assets, contra-assets, liabilities, capital, and withdrawals go on balance sheet sections of the worksheet.

Learning Unit 4-2

1. The formal statements prepared from a worksheet do not have debit or credit columns.
2. Revenue and expenses go on the income statement. Beginning capital plus net income less withdrawals (or: beginning capital minus net loss less withdrawals) go on the statement of owner's equity. Be sure to check the capital account in the ledger to see if any additional investments took place. Assets, contra-assets, liabilities, and the new figure for capital go on the balance sheet.

Key Terms

Accrued salaries Salaries that are earned by employees but unpaid and unrecorded during the period (and thus need to be recorded by an adjustment) and will not come due for payment until the next accounting period.

Accumulated depreciation A contra-asset account that summarizes or accumulates the amount of depreciation that has been taken on an asset.

Adjusting   The process of calculating the latest up-to-date balance of each account at the end of an accounting period.

Book value   Cost of equipment less accumulated depreciation.

Depreciation   The allocation (spreading) of the cost of an asset (such as an auto or equipment) over its expected useful life.

Historical cost   The actual cost of an asset at time of purchase.

Residual value   Estimated value of an asset after all the allowable depreciation has been taken.

Worksheet   A columnar device used by accountants to aid them in completing the accounting cycle—often called a spreadsheet. It is not a formal report.

Blueprint of Steps 5 and 6 of the Accounting Cycle

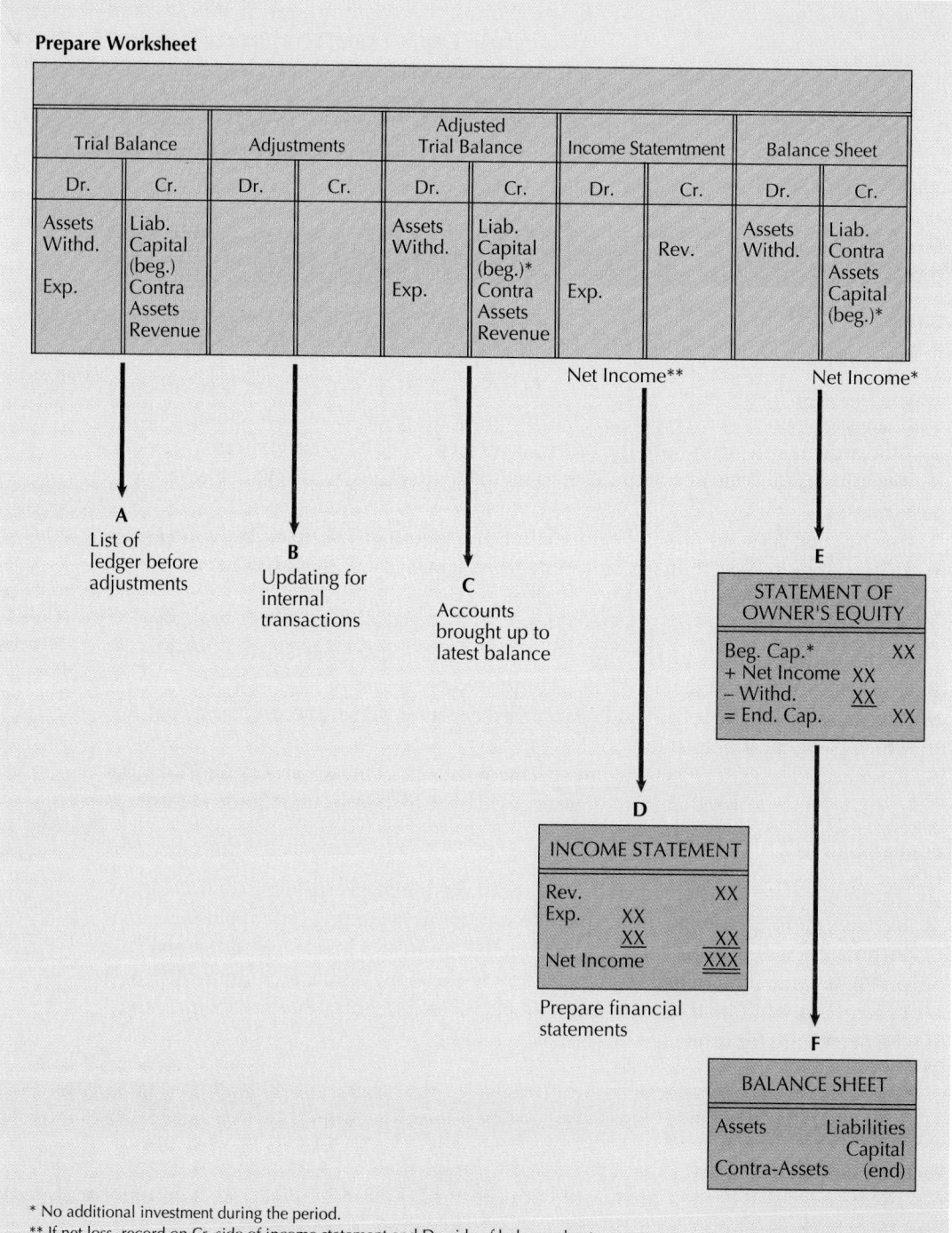

Prepare Worksheet

	Trial Balance		Adjustments		Adjusted Trial Balance		Income Statemtment		Balance Sheet	
	Dr.	Cr.	Dr.	Cr.	Dr.	Cr.	Dr.	Cr.	Dr.	Cr.
	Assets Withd. Exp.	Liab. Capital (beg.) Contra Assets Revenue			Assets Withd. Exp.	Liab. Capital (beg.)* Contra Assets Revenue	Exp.	Rev.	Assets Withd.	Liab. Contra Assets Capital (beg.)*

Net Income**   Net Income*

A
List of ledger before adjustments

B
Updating for internal transactions

C
Accounts brought up to latest balance

E

STATEMENT OF OWNER'S EQUITY
Beg. Cap.*   XX
+ Net Income   XX
− Withd.   XX
= End. Cap.   XX

D

INCOME STATEMENT
Rev.   XX
Exp.   XX
XX   XX
Net Income   XXX

Prepare financial statements

F

BALANCE SHEET
Assets   Liabilities
Capital
Contra-Assets   (end)

* No additional investment during the period.
** If net loss, record on Cr. side of income statement and Dr. side of balance sheet.

Questions, Mini Exercises, Exercises, and Problems

Discussion Questions

1. Worksheets are required in every company's accounting cycle. Please agree or disagree and explain why.
2. What is the purpose of adjusting accounts?
3. What is the relationship of internal transactions to the adjusting process?
4. Explain how an adjustment can affect both the income statement and balance sheet. Please give an example.
5. Why do we need the Accumulated Depreciation account?
6. Depreciation expense goes on the balance sheet. True or false. Why?
7. Each month Accumulated Depreciation grows while Equipment goes up. Agree or disagree. Defend your position.
8. Define the term *accrued salaries.*
9. Why don't the formal financial statements contain debit or credit columns?
10. Explain how the financial statements are prepared from the worksheet.

Mini Exercises

(The blank forms you need are on pages 106–107 of the *Study Guide and Working Papers.*)

Adjustment for Supplies

1. *Before Adjustment*

Computer Supplies	Computer Supplies Expense
700	

   Given: At year end an inventory of supplies showed $100.

   a. How much is the adjustment for Supplies?
   b. Draw a transaction analysis box for this adjustment.
   c. What will the balance of Supplies be on the adjusted trial balance?

Adjustment for Prepaid Rent

2. *Before Adjustment*

Prepaid Rent	Rent Expense
700	

   Given: At year end, rent expired is $300.

   a. How much is the adjustment for Prepaid Rent?
   b. Draw a transaction analysis box for this adjustment.
   c. What will be the balance of Prepaid Rent on the adjusted trial balance?

Adjustment for Depreciation

3. *Before Adjustment*

Equip.	Acc. Dep., Equip.	Dep. Exp., Equip.
6,000	1,000	

   Given: At year end depreciation on Equipment is $1,000.

   a. Which of the three T Accounts above is not affected?
   b. Which account is a contra-asset?

    c. Draw a transaction analysis box for this adjustment.

    d. What will be the balance of these three accounts on the adjusted trial balance?

Adjustment for Accrued Salaries

4. *Before Adjustment*

Salaries Expense	Salaries Payable
900	

Given: Accrued Salaries, $200.

    a. Draw a transaction analysis box for this adjustment.

    b. What will be the balance of these two accounts on the adjusted trial balance?

Worksheet

5. From the following adjusted trial balance titles of a worksheet, identify in which column each account will be listed on the last four columns of the worksheet:

    (ID) Income Statement Dr. Column

    (IC) Income Statement Cr. Column

    (BD) Balance Sheet Dr. Column

    (BC) Balance Sheet Cr. Column

	ATB	IS	BS
A. Ex: Supplies			BD
B. Acc. Receivable			
C. Cash			
D. Prepaid Rent			
E. Equipment			
F. Acc. Depreciation			
G. B., Capital			
H. B., Withdrawals			
I. Taxi Fees			
J. Advertising Expense			
K. Off. Supplies Expense			
L. Rent Expense			
M. Depreciation Expense			
N. Salaries Payable			

6. From the following balance sheet (which was made from the worksheet and other financial statements), explain why the lettered numbers were not found on the worksheet. *Hint:* There are no debits or credits on the formal financial statements.

H. WELLS BALANCE SHEET DECEMBER 31, 200X					
Assets			**Liabilities and Owner's Equity**		
Cash		$6	Liabilities		
Acc. Receivable		2	Accounts Payable	$2	
Supplies		2	Salaries, Payable	1	
Equipment	$10		Total Liabilities		$ 3 (B)
Less Acc. Dep.	4	6	Owner's Equity		
			H. Wells, Capital		13 (C)
			Total Liability and		
Total Assets		$16 (A)	**Owner's Equity**		$16 (D)

Exercises

(The blank forms you need are on pages 108–110 of the *Study Guide and Working Papers.*)

4-1. Complete the following table.

Account	Category	Normal Balance	Which Financial Statement(s) Found
Fax Machine			
Prepaid Insurance			
Digital Camera			
Accumulated Depreciation			
A. Jax, Capital			
A. Jax, Withdrawals			
Salaries Payable			
Depreciation Expense			

Categorizing accounts.

4-2. Use transaction analysis charts to analyze the following adjustments:

    a. Depreciation on equipment, $500.
    b. Rent expired, $200.

Reviewing adjustments and the transaction analysis charts.

4-3. From the following adjustment data, calculate the adjustment amount and record appropriate debits or credits:

    a. Supplies purchased, $600.
        Supplies on hand, $200.
    b. Store equipment, $10,000.
        Accumulated depreciation before adjustment, $900.
        Depreciation expense, $100.

Recording adjusting entries.

4-4. From the following trial balance (Fig. 4-20) and adjustment data, complete a worksheet for J. Trent as of December 31, 200X:

    a. Depreciation expense, equipment $2.00
    b. Insurance expired   1.00
    c. Store supplies on hand   4.00
    d. Wages owed, but not paid for
        (they are an expense in the old year)   5.00

Preparing a worksheet.

Figure 4-20

J. TRENT TRIAL BALANCE DECEMBER 31, 200X	Dr.	Cr.
Cash	9 00	
Accounts Receivable	2 00	
Prepaid Insurance	7 00	
Store Supplies	6 00	
Store Equipment	7 00	
Accumulated Depreciation, Equipment		2 00
Accounts Payable		4 00
J. Trent, Capital		17 00
J. Trent, Withdrawals	6 00	
Revenue from Clients		24 00
Rent Expense	4 00	
Wage Expense	6 00	
	47 00	47 00

Preparing financial statements from a worksheet.

4-5. From the completed worksheet in Exercise 4-4, prepare

  a. An income statement for December.
  b. A statement of owner's equity for December.
  c. A balance sheet as of December 31, 200X.

Group A Problems

(The blank forms you need are on pp. 111–114 of the *Study Guide and Working Papers.*)

4A-1.

Given the following adjustment data on December 31:

  a. Grooming supplies on hand, $800.
  b. Depreciation taken on grooming equipment, $500.

complete a partial worksheet (Fig. 4-21) up to the adjusted trial balance.

Figure 4-21

Completing a partial worksheet up to the adjusted trial balance.

Check Figure:
Total of adjusted trial balance $30,150

MATTY'S GROOMING SERVICE
TRIAL BALANCE
DECEMBER 31, 200X

	Debit	Credit
Cash in Bank	7 0 0 0 00	
Accounts Receivable	6 0 0 0 00	
Grooming Supplies	5 4 0 0 00	
Grooming Equipment	7 2 0 0 00	
Accumulated Depreciation, Grooming Equipment		6 0 0 0 00
M. Magee, Capital		12 3 5 0 00
M. Magee, Withdrawals	3 0 0 0 00	
Grooming Fees		11 3 0 0 00
Rent Expense	9 0 0 00	
Advertising Expense	1 5 0 00	
	29 6 5 0 00	29 6 5 0 00

4A-2. The trial balance for Fred's Plumbing Service (Fig. 4-22) for December 31, 200X.

Figure 4-22

Completing a worksheet.

Check Figure:
Net Income $804

FRED'S PLUMBING SERVICE
TRIAL BALANCE
DECEMBER 31, 200X

	Dr.	Cr.
Cash in Bank	3 6 0 6 00	
Accounts Receivable	7 0 0 00	
Prepaid Rent	8 0 0 00	
Plumbing Supplies	7 4 2 00	
Plumbing Equipment	1 4 0 0 00	
Accumulated Depreciation, Plumbing Equipment		1 0 6 0 00
Accounts Payable		4 4 2 00
Fred Jack, Capital		3 2 5 0 00
Plumbing Revenue		4 3 5 6 00
Heat Expense	4 0 0 00	
Advertising Expense	2 0 0 00	
Wage Expense	1 2 6 0 00	
	9 1 0 8 00	9 1 0 8 00

Adjustment Data to Update the Trial Balance

   a. Rent expired, $500.
   b. Plumbing supplies on hand (remaining), $100.
   c. Depreciation expense, plumbing equipment, $200.
   d. Wages earned by workers but not paid or due until January, $350.

     Your task is to prepare a worksheet for Fred's Plumbing Service for the month of December.

4A-3. The following is the trial balance (Fig. 4-23) for Kevin's Moving Co.

Figure 4-23

KEVIN'S MOVING CO.
TRIAL BALANCE
OCTOBER 31, 200X

	Dr.	Cr.
Cash	5 0 0 0 00	
Prepaid Insurance	2 5 0 0 00	
Moving Supplies	1 2 0 0 00	
Moving Truck	11 0 0 0 00	
Accumulated Depreciation, Moving Truck		9 0 0 00
Accounts Payable		2 7 6 8 00
K. Hoff, Capital		5 4 4 2 00
K. Hoff, Withdrawals	1 4 0 0 00	
Revenue from Moving		9 0 0 0 00
Wage Expense	3 7 1 2 00	
Rent Expense	1 0 8 0 00	
Advertising Expense	3 1 8 00	
	26 2 1 0 00	26 2 1 0 00

Comprehensive Problem

Check Figure:
Net Income $2,140

Adjustment Data to Update Trial Balance

   a. Insurance expired, $700.
   b. Moving supplies on hand, $900.   *– 300 has been used*
   c. Depreciation on moving truck, $500.
   d. Wages earned but unpaid, $250.

Your task is to

   1. Complete a worksheet for Kevin's Moving Co. for the month of October.
   2. Prepare an income statement for October, a statement of owner's equity for October, and a balance sheet as of October 31, 200X.

4A-4.

Adjustment Data to Update Trial Balance

   a. Insurance expired, $700.
   b. Repair supplies on hand, $3,000.
   c. Depreciation on repair equipment, $200.
   d. Wages earned but unpaid, $400.

Your task is to

   1. Complete a worksheet for Dick's Repair Service (Fig. 4-24) for the month of November.
   2. Prepare an income statement for November, a statement of owner's equity for November, and a balance sheet as of November 30, 200X.

Comprehensive Problem

Figure 4-24

Check Figure:
Net Income $1,830

DICK'S REPAIR SERVICE TRIAL BALANCE NOVEMBER 30, 200X	Dr.	Cr.
Cash	3 2 0 0 00	
Prepaid Insurance	4 0 0 0 00	
Repair Supplies	4 6 0 0 00	
Repair Equipment	3 0 0 0 00	
Accumulated Depreciation, Repair Equipment		7 0 0 00
Accounts Payable		5 5 7 0 00
D. Horn, Capital		3 8 0 0 00
Revenue from Repairs		7 0 0 0 00
Wages Expense	1 8 0 0 00	
Rent Expense	3 6 0 00	
Advertising Expense	1 1 0 00	
	17 0 7 0 00	17 0 7 0 00

Group B Problems

(The blank forms you need are on pages 111–114 of the *Study Guide and Working Papers.*)

4B-1. Please complete a partial worksheet (Fig. 4-25) up to the adjusted trial balance for Matty's Grooming Center using the following adjustment data:

Figure 4-25

Completing a partial worksheet up to adjusted trial balance.

Check Figure:
Total of Adjusted Trial Balance $22,600

MATTY'S GROOMING CENTER TRIAL BALANCE DECEMBER 31, 200X	Dr.	Cr.
Cash	6 0 0 0 00	
Accounts Receivable	2 0 0 0 00	
Grooming Supplies	4 2 0 0 00	
Grooming Equipment	8 0 0 0 00	
Accumulated Depreciation, Grooming Equipment		9 7 0 0 00
M. Magee, Capital		11 0 0 0 00
M. Magee, Withdrawals	1 0 0 0 00	
Grooming Fees		1 4 0 0 00
Rent Expense	8 0 0 00	
Advertising Expense	1 0 0 00	
	22 1 0 0 00	22 1 0 0 00

    a. Grooming supplies on hand, $3,000.
    b. Depreciation taken on grooming equipment, $500.

4B-2. Given the trial balance in Figure 4-26 and adjustment data of Fred's Plumbing Service, your task is to prepare a worksheet for the month of December.

Adjustment Data

    a. Plumbing supplies on hand, $60.
    b. Rent expired, $150.
    c. Depreciation on plumbing equipment, $200.
    d. Wages earned but unpaid, $115.

FRED'S PLUMBING SERVICE
TRIAL BALANCE
DECEMBER 31, 200X

	Dr.	Cr.
Cash in Bank	3 9 6 00	
Accounts Receivable	2 8 4 00	
Prepaid Rent	4 0 0 00	
Plumbing Supplies	3 1 0 00	
Plumbing Equipment	1 0 0 0 00	
Accumulated Depreciation, Plumbing Equipment		2 0 0 00
Accounts Payable		3 4 6 00
Fred Jack, Capital		4 5 6 00
Plumbing Revenue		4 6 8 0 00
Heat Expense	6 3 2 00	
Advertising Expense	1 2 0 0 00	
Wage Expense	1 4 6 0 00	
Total	5 6 8 2 00	5 6 8 2 00

Figure 4-26

Completing a worksheet.

Check Figure:
Net Income $673

4B-3. Using the trial balance in Figure 4-27 and adjustment data of Kevin's Moving Co., prepare

1. A worksheet for the month of October.
2. An income statement for October, a statement of owner's equity for October, and a balance sheet as of October 31, 200X.

Adjustment Data

a. Insurance expired	$600
b. Moving supplies on hand	$310
c. Depreciation on moving truck	$580
d. Wages earned but unpaid	$410

KEVIN'S MOVING CO.
TRIAL BALANCE
OCTOBER 31, 200X

	Dr.	Cr.
Cash	3 9 2 0 00	
Prepaid Insurance	3 2 8 8 00	
Moving Supplies	1 4 0 0 00	
Moving Truck	1 0 6 5 8 00	
Accumulated Depreciation, Moving Truck		3 6 6 0 00
Accounts Payable		1 3 1 2 00
K. Hoff, Capital		1 7 4 8 2 00
K. Hoff, Withdrawals	4 2 4 0 00	
Revenue from Moving		8 1 6 2 00
Wages Expense	5 7 1 2 00	
Rent Expense	1 0 8 0 00	
Advertising Expense	3 1 8 00	
	3 0 6 1 6 00	3 0 6 1 6 00

Figure 4-27

Comprehensive Problem

Check Figure:
Net Loss $1,628

Figure 4-28

DICK'S REPAIR SERVICE TRIAL BALANCE NOVEMBER 30, 200X	Dr.	Cr.
Cash	3 2 0 4 00	
Prepaid Insurance	4 0 0 0 00	
Repair Supplies	7 7 0 00	
Repair Equipment	3 1 0 6 00	
Accumulated Depreciation, Repair Equipment		6 5 0 00
Accounts Payable		1 9 0 4 00
D. Horn, Capital		6 2 5 8 00
Revenue from Repairs		5 6 3 4 00
Wages Expense	1 6 0 0 00	
Rent Expense	1 5 6 0 00	
Advertising Expense	2 0 6 00	
	14 4 4 6 00	14 4 4 6 00

4B-4. As the bookkeeper of Dick's Repair Service, use the information in Figure 4-28 to prepare

1. A worksheet for the month of November.
2. An income statement for November, a statement of owner's equity for November, and a balance sheet as of November 30, 200X.

Adjustment Data

    a. Insurance expired $300
    b. Repair supplies on hand $170
    c. Depreciation on repair equipment $250
    d. Wages earned but unpaid $106

Real-World Applications

4R-1

MEMO

To: Hal Hogan, Bookkeeper

From: Pete Tennant, V. P.

Re: Adjustments for year ended December 31, 200X

Hal, here is the information you requested. Please supply me with the adjustments needed ASAP. Also, please put in writing why we need to do these adjustments.

Thanks.

Attached to memo:

    a. Insurance data:

Policy No.	Date of Policy Purchase	Policy Length	Cost
100	November 1 of previous year	4 years	$480
200	May 1 of current year	2 years	600
300	September 1 of current year	1 year	240

b. Rent data: Prepaid rent had a $500 balance at the beginning of the year. An additional $400 of rent was paid in advance in June. At year end, $200 of rent had expired.

c. Revenue data: Accrued storage fees of $500 were earned but uncollected and unrecorded at year end.

4R-2.   Hint: Unearned Rent is a liability on the balance sheet.

On Friday, Harry Swag's boss asks him to prepare a special report, due on Monday at 8:00 A.M. Harry gathers the following material in his briefcase:

		Dec. 31	
		2004	**2005**
Prepaid Advertising		$300	$600
Interest Payable		150	350
Unearned Rent		500	300
Cash paid for: Advertising	$1,900		
Interest	1,500		
Cash received for: Rent	2,300		

As his best friend, could you help Harry show the amounts that are to be reported on the income statement for (a) Advertising Expense, (b) Interest Expense, and (c) Rent Fees Earned. Please explain in writing why Unearned Rent is considered a liability.

YOU make the call

Critical Thinking/Ethical Case

4R-3. Janet Fox, President of Angel Co., went to a tax seminar. One of the speakers at the seminar advised the audience to put off showing expenses until next year because doing so would allow them to take advantage of a new tax law. When Janet returned to the office, she called in her accountant, Frieda O'Riley. She told Frieda to forget about making any adjustments for salaries in the old year so more expenses could be shown in the new year. Frieda told her that putting off these expenses would not follow generally accepted accounting procedures. Janet said she should do it anyway. You make the call. Write your specific recommendations to Frieda.

Internet Exercises: Office Max

EX-1. [www.officemax.com]   On the Web site look for "General Information," then click on "Corporate Information." Under "Investor Information" look up Annual Reports and find the Consolidated Balance Sheet for 2001.

1. Under the caption "other current assets," what accounts do you think could be there that required end-of-period adjustments?

2. If Office Max rented the property where its stores are located and paid the rent in advance for 24 months, how would adjustments have been made in its financial statements?

3. What effect would these adjustments have on (a) Total Assets, and (b) Net Income?

4. Look at "current liabilities" in the balance sheet. Which accounts there seem most susceptible to the adjustment process, and why did you choose these accounts?

EX-2. [www.officemax.com]   Click on "CEO Sworn Statement." Why do you think the CEO is required to report this information?

Continuing Problem

Eldorado Computer Center

At the end of September, Tony took a complete inventory of his supplies and found the following:

5 dozen $\frac{1}{4}''$ screws at a cost of $8.00 a dozen

2 dozen $\frac{1}{2}''$ screws at a cost of $5.00 a dozen

2 cartons of computer inventory paper at a cost of $14 a carton

3 feet of coaxial cable at a cost of $4.00 per foot

After speaking to his accountant, he found that a reasonable depreciation amount for each of his long-term assets is as follows:

Computer purchased July 5, 200X	Depreciation $33 a month
Office equipment purchased July 17, 200X	Depreciation $10 a month
Computer workstations purchased Sept. 17, 200X	Depreciation $20 a month

Tony uses the straight-line method of depreciation and declares no salvage value for any of the assets. If any long-term asset is purchased in the first 15 days of the month, he will charge depreciation for the full month. If an asset is purchased on the 16th of the month, or later, he will not charge depreciation in the month it was purchased.

August and September's rent has now expired.

Assignment

Use your trial balance from the completed problem in Chapter 3 and the adjusting information given here to complete the worksheet for the three months ended September 30, 200X. From the worksheets prepare the financial statements. (See pp. 119–120 in your *Study Guide and Working Papers*.)

SUBWAY Case

WHERE THE DOUGH GOES . . .

No matter how harried Stan Hernandez feels as the owner of his own Subway restaurant, the aroma of his fresh-baked gourmet breads *always* perks him up. However, the sales generated by Subway's line of gourmet seasoned breads perks Stan up even more. Subway restaurants introduced freshly baked bread in 1983, a practice that made it stand out from other fast-food chains and helped build its reputation for made-to-order freshness. Since then Subway franchisees have introduced many types of gourmet seasoned breads—such as Hearty Italian or Monterey Cheddar—according to a schedule determined by headquarters.

Stan was one month into the "limited-time promotion" for the chain's new Roasted Garlic seasoned bread when his bake oven started faltering. "The temperature controls just don't seem quite right," said his employee and "sandwich artist," Rashid. "It's taking incrementally longer to bake the bread."

"This couldn't happen at a worse time," moaned Stan. "We're baking enough Roasted Garlic bread to keep a whole town of vampires away, but if we don't get it out of the oven fast enough, we'll keep our customers away!"

That very day Stan called his field consultant, Mariah, to discuss what to do about his bake oven. Mariah reminded Stan that his oven trouble illustrated the flip side of buying an existing store from a retired franchisee—having to repair or replace worn or old equipment. After receiving a rather expensive repair estimate and considering the age of the oven, Stan ultimately decided it would make sense for him to purchase a new one. Mariah concurred, "At the rate your sales are going, Stan, you're going to need that roomier new model."

"Wow, do you realize how much this new bake oven is going to cost me?— $3,000!" Stan exclaimed while meeting with his cousin-turned-Subway-accountant, Lila Hernandez. "Yes, it's a lot to lay out, Stan," said Lila, "but you'll be depreciating the cost over a period of 10 years, which will help you at tax time. Let's do the adjustment on your worksheet, so you can see it."

The two of them were sitting in Stan's small office, behind the Subway kitchen, and they pulled up this month's worksheet on Stan's Peachtree program. Lila laughed, "I'm sure glad you started entering your worksheets on Peachtree again! The figures on those old ones were so doodled over and crossed out that I could barely decipher them! We may need your worksheets at tax time."

"Anything for you, *mi prima*," Stan said, "I may depreciate my bake oven, but my gratitude for your accounting skills only appreciates with time!"

Discussion Questions

1. If you are using a straight-line method of depreciation and Stan's bake oven has a residual value of $1,000, how much depreciation will he account for each year and what would the adjustment be for each month?
2. Where does Lila get the information on the useful life of Stan's bake oven and the estimate for its residual value? Why do you think she gets her information from this particular source?
3. Why is a clear worksheet helpful even after that month's statements have been prepared?

COMPUTERIZED ACCOUNTING APPLICATION FOR CHAPTER 4

PART A: *Compound Journal Entries, Adjusting Entries, and Financial Reports*

PART B: *Backup Procedures*

Before starting on this assignment, read and complete the tasks discussed in Parts A, B, and F of the Computerized Accounting appendix at the back of this book and complete the Computerized Accounting Application assignment at the end of Chapter 3.

PART A: COMPOUND JOURNAL ENTRIES, ADJUSTING ENTRIES, AND FINANCIAL REPORTS

How to Open the Company Data Files

1. Click on the Start button. Point to Programs; point to the Peachtree folder and select Peachtree Complete Accounting. Your desktop may have the Peachtree icon allowing for a quicker entrance into the program.
2. Follow the "Open a File" instructions in Part A of the Computerized Accounting appendix at the back of this book to open **The Zell Company.** You may be initially presented with the Peachtree Today window. If so, simply close it. If you are missing the navigation aids at the bottom of the screen and want them, you can activate them under the **Options** menu. Select **View Navigation Aid.** It will remain on until you turn it off. This feature offers an alternative way to access the different features of Peachtree.
3. Click on the **Maintain** menu option. Then select **Company Information.** The program will respond by bringing up a dialogue box allowing the user to edit/add information about the company.

How to Add Your Name to the Company Name

4. Click in the **Company Name** entry field at the end of **The Zell Company.** If it is already highlighted, press the right arrow key. Add a dash and your name "**-Student Name**" to the end of the company name. Click on the OK button to return to the Menu Window.
5. In the computerized accounting application assignment in Chapter 3 you learned how to record journal entries in the General Journal dialog box. Compound journal entries can also be recorded in the General Journal dialog box. The owner of The Zell Company has made an investment in the business consisting of $5,000 in cash and an automobile valued at $12,000. Select **General Journal Entry** from the **Tasks** menu to open the General Journal dialog box. Enter the date 1/1/04 into the **Date** field; press the TAB key; enter "Memo" into the **Reference** field and press TAB.

How to Record a Compound Journal Entry

6. With the flashing insertion point positioned in the **Account No.** field, click on the pull down menu (magnifying glass icon) and double click on "1110 Cash". The program will enter the account number and name into the **Account No.** field and the flashing insertion point will move to the **Description** field. Enter "Initial investment by owner" into this field and press TAB to move to the **Debit** field. Enter "5000" and press TAB three times to move back to the **Account No.** field.
7. With the flashing insertion point positioned in the **Account No.** field, click on the pull down menu (magnifying glass icon) and double click on "1230 Automobile". Press TAB to move to the **Description** field. This should repeat the information entered in step 6 by default. Press the TAB key again to move to the **Debit** field. Enter "12000". Hit TAB three times to move the cursor back to the **Account No.** field. You should now have two debit entries.

8. With the flashing insertion point positioned in the **Account No.** field, click on the pull down menu and double click on "3110 Owner's Capital". Press TAB to move to the **Description** field. This should repeat the information entered in step 6 by default. Press the TAB key again twice to move to the **Credit** field. Enter 17000. Hit TAB twice to move the cursor back to the **Account No.** field. This completes the data you need to enter into the General Journal dialog box to record the compound journal entry for the initial investment by the owner. Your screen should look like this:

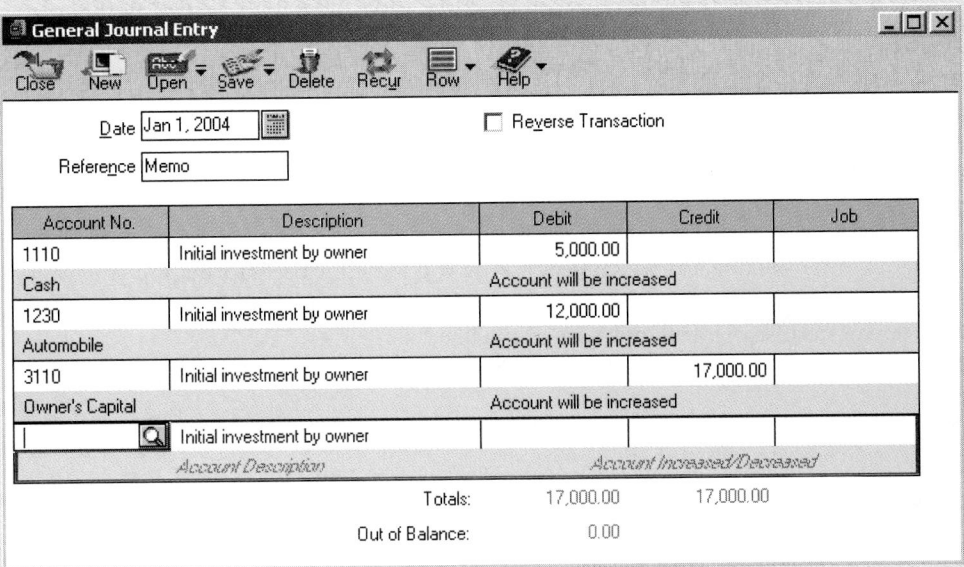

9. Review the compound journal entry for accuracy, noting any errors and making any editing corrections required.
10. After verifying that the compound journal entry is correct, click on the **Save** icon to post this transaction.
11. Record the following additional journal entries: Enter the **Date** listed for each transaction (you may use the "+" key to advance the date or use the calendar icon next to the field to select the date from a calendar). Enter "Memo" into the **Source** text box for each transaction or accept Peachtree's additional number added to memo by pressing TAB:

> Review the Compound Journal Entry

> Save the Entry

> Record Additional Transactions

2004

Jan.

1	Paid rent for two months in advance, $500.
3	Purchased office supplies ($200) and office equipment ($1,100) both on account.
9	Billed a customer for fees earned, $2,000.
13	Received and paid telephone bill, $150.
20	Owner withdrew $475 from the business for personal use.
27	Received $600 for fees earned.
31	Paid salaries expense, $800.

12. After you have saved the additional journal entries, close the General Journal dialogue box and print the following reports accepting all defaults:
    a. General Journal (Totals = $22,825.00)
    b. General Ledger Trial Balance (Totals = $20,900)

> Display and Print a General Journal and Trial Balance

How to Record Adjusting
Journal Entries

13. Review your printed reports. If you have made an error in a saved journal entry, see step 18 from the Chapter 3 assignment on page 115.

14. Open the General Journal dialogue box; then record adjusting journal entries based on the following adjustment data (*Date:* 1/31/04; *Reference:* Adjusting). You may enter all of the adjustments on the same page before saving:
    a. One month's rent has expired.
    b. An inventory shows $25 of office supplies remaining.
    c. Depreciation on office equipment, $50.
    d. Depreciation on automobile, $150.

Display and Print a
General Journal, General
Ledger, and Trial Balance

15. After you have saved the adjusting journal entries, close the General Journal dialogue box and print the following reports from the **General Ledger** option of the **Reports** menu:
    a. General Journal (Totals = $23,450)
    b. General Ledger Report (Cash Ending Balance = $3,675)
    c. General Ledger Trial Balance (Totals = $21,100)

16. Review your printed reports. If you have made an error in a saved journal entry, see step 18 from the Chapter 3 assignment.

How to Display and Print
an Income Statement

17. Select the **Financial Statements** option of the **Reports** menu. Select Income Stmnt. An Options dialog box will appear asking you to define the information you want displayed. Press the **OK** button to accept the defaults and display the report on your screen. Your screen will look something like this:

The Zell Company- Student Name
Income Statement
For the One Month Ending January 31, 2004

	Current Month		Year to Date	
Revenues				
Fees Earned	$ 2,600.00	100.00	$ 2,600.00	100.00
Total Revenues	2,600.00	100.00	2,600.00	100.00
Cost of Sales				
Total Cost of Sales	0.00	0.00	0.00	0.00
Gross Profit	2,600.00	100.00	2,600.00	100.00
Expenses				
Rent Expense	250.00	9.62	250.00	9.62
Salaries Expense	800.00	30.77	800.00	30.77
Telephone Expense	150.00	5.77	150.00	5.77
Supplies Expense	175.00	6.73	175.00	6.73
Depr Expense- Office Equipment	50.00	1.92	50.00	1.92
Depr Expense- Automobile	150.00	5.77	150.00	5.77
Total Expenses	1,575.00	60.58	1,575.00	60.58
Net Income	$ 1,025.00	39.42	$ 1,025.00	39.42

18. The scroll bars can be used to advance the display to view other portions of the report as needed.

19. Click on the **Print** icon to print the Income Statement.

How to Display and Print a
Balance Sheet

20. Close the Income Statement window. This should return you to the Select a Report dialogue box. Select Balance Sheet. An Options dialog box will appear asking you to define the information you want displayed. Press the **OK** button

to accept the defaults and display the report on your screen. Your screen will look something like this:

```
                        The Zell Company- Student Name
                                Balance Sheet
                               January 31, 2004

                                     ASSETS

Current Assets
  Cash                          $          3,675.00
  Accounts Receivable                      2,000.00
  Prepaid Rent                               250.00
  Office Supplies                             25.00
                                        _____

  Total Current Assets                                        5,950.00

Property and Equipment
  Office Equipment                         1,100.00
  Accum. Depr- Office Equipment            <50.00>
  Automobile                              12,000.00
  Accum. Depr- Automobile                  <150.00>
                                        _____

  Total Property and Equipment                              12,900.00

Other Assets
                                        _____

  Total Other Assets                                            0.00
                                                          _____

  Total Assets                          $                   18,850.00
                                                          ============
```

21. Use the scroll bars to advance the display to the Owner's Equity section of the Balance Sheet. Note that the program has included the Statement of Owner's Equity information directly in the Capital section of the Balance Sheet.
22. Click on **Print** to print the Balance Sheet and then close the Balance Sheet window.
23. Click on the Menu Window **File** menu; then click on **Exit** to end the current work session and return to your Windows desktop. Your work will automatically be saved.

Exit from the Program

PART B: BACKUP PROCEDURES

Companies that use computerized accounting systems make frequent backup copies of their accounting data for two major reasons:

1. To ensure that they have a copy of the accounting data in case the current data becomes damaged.
2. To permit the printing of historical reports after the period has been advanced to a new period.
3. In the event gross errors require restoring to an earlier time and the re-entering of data.

The methods used to make backup copies of company data files vary greatly. Large companies may backup daily using sophisticated high-speed tape backup devices while small companies may backup weekly on floppy disk using the backup program supplied with their operating system or applications software.

Normally all backup copies of a company's data files are stored on a secondary storage medium separate from the original data files in case the original storage medium becomes damaged. Your instructor will provide specific instructions on where you will store your backup files.

How to Make a Backup Copy of a Company's Data Files

1. If you are not still in Peachtree Complete Accounting 2003, start the program again and open The Zell Company.
2. While in the Menu Window, select **Back Up** from the **File** menu option. This will bring up the Back Up Company dialogue box as follows:

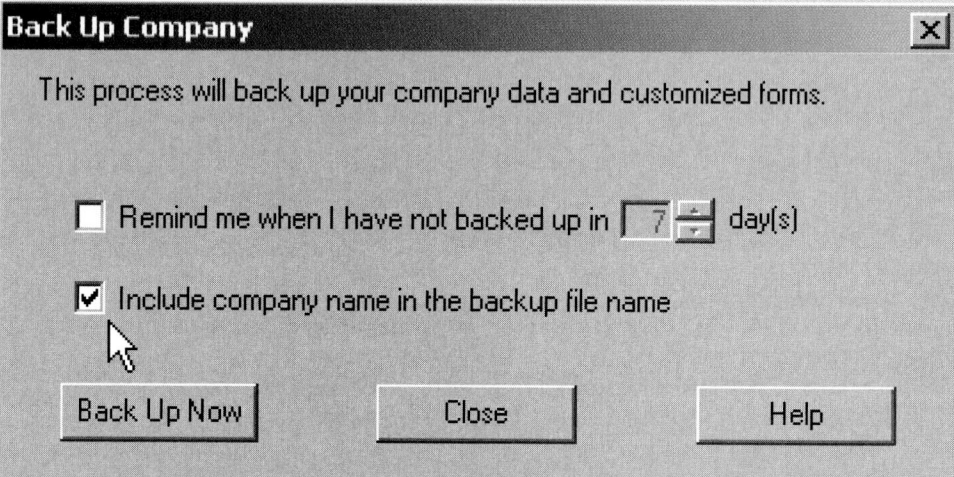

3. Click in the box next to **Include company name in the backup file name**. This will make Peachtree use Zell in the filename it selects for the backup. You could also use this dialogue box to have Peachtree provide a reminder at periodic intervals but we will leave this option alone for now. Press **Back Up Now** to continue.
4. You are now presented with a Save Backup for the Zell Company Student Name as: dialogue box as follows:

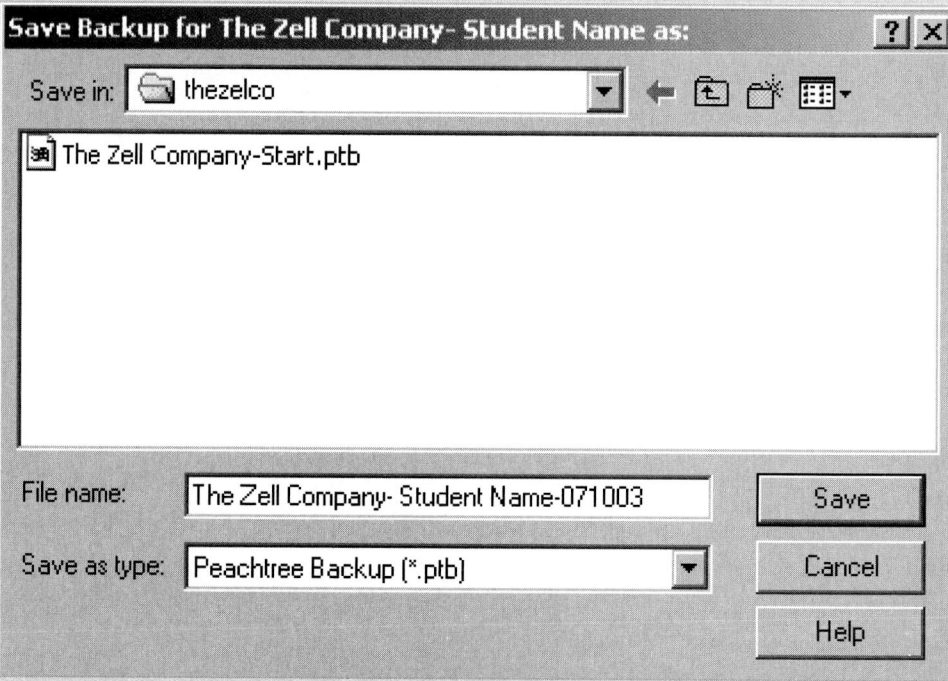

5. Peachtree will save your data files into one compressed .ptb file to any drive or path you specify. It defaults to the location where the program files are stored. Use the **Save in** pull down menu to save the files to a location specified by your instructor. Click **Save** and then **OK** to complete the process. You now have a back up of your data.

6. For more information on making and using backup copies of a company's data files, see Parts D & E of the Computerized Accounting appendix in the back of this book.

CHAPTER 5

The Accounting Cycle Completed

Adjusting, Closing, and Post-Closing Trial Balance

You are planning your school schedule for next term. Your goal is to take a full course load and find a part-time job to help pay your school expenses. You hear through your academic advisor that the school needs to hire someone to help process invoices in the business office a couple of afternoons each week.

You speak with Diane Lemke, the business office manager, about the job. Diane tells you that your work will consist of matching purchase orders with paid invoices and the checks issued for payment. Diane tells you that these last few steps in the process of paying bills is important for the proper operation of the school's business office. "It's essential that this work is done before we can close our books each month," Diane tells you. You believe you'll like the work, and you're happy you can work your school schedule around the hours you're needed at the business office.

In Chapter 4 we learned about using the worksheet as a tool in the accounting cycle to adjust various balances and prepare the financial statements. In this chapter we focus on journalizing and posting adjusting and closing entries. We will also discuss preparing a post-closing trial balance, which is the last step in the accounting cycle.

Like working in your school's business office, the last three steps in the accounting cycle are essential and must be done to prepare a company's books for the next accounting cycle. It's the only way an accountant can begin a new accounting cycle or the business office can prepare itself for a new month of expenses.

Learning Objectives

- Journalizing and posting adjusting entries. (p. 164)

- Journalizing and posting closing entries. (p. 167)

- Preparing a post-closing trial balance. (p. 178)

In Chapters 3 and 4 we completed these steps of the manual accounting cycle for Clark's Word Processing Services:

Step 1:   Business transactions occurred and generated source documents.

Step 2:   Business transactions were analyzed and recorded into a journal.

Step 3:   Information was posted or transferred from journal to ledger.

Step 4:   A trial balance was prepared.

Step 5:   A worksheet was completed.

Step 6:   Financial statements were prepared.

> Remember, for ease of presentation we are using a month as the accounting cycle for Clark. In the "real" world, the cycle can be any time period that does not exceed one year.

This chapter covers the following steps. This will complete Clark's accounting cycle for the month of May:

Step 7:   Journalizing and posting adjusting entries.

Step 8:   Journalizing and posting closing entries.

Step 9:   Preparing a post-closing trial balance.

Be sure to check the inside front cover of the text for the road map to the accounting cycle.

Learning Unit 5-1   Journalizing and Posting Adjusting Entries: Step 7 of the Accounting Cycle

RECORDING JOURNAL ENTRIES FROM THE WORKSHEET

> At this point, many ledger accounts are not up-to-date.

The information in the worksheet is up-to-date. The financial reports prepared from that information can give the business's management and other interested parties a good idea of where the business stands as of a particular date. The problem is that the worksheet is an informal report. The information concerning the adjustments has not been placed into the journal or posted to the ledger accounts. This means that the books are not up-to-date and ready for the next accounting cycle to begin. For example, the ledger shows $1,200 of Prepaid Rent (p. 86), but the balance sheet we prepared in Chapter 4 shows an $800 balance. Essentially, the worksheet is a tool for preparing financial statements. Now we must use the adjustment columns of the worksheet as a basis for bringing the ledger up-to-date. We do this by **adjusting journal entries** (see Figs. 5-1, 5-2). Again, the updating must be done before the next accounting period starts. For Clark's Word Processing Services, the next period begins on June 1.

> Purpose of adjusting entries.

Figure 5-2 shows the adjusting journal entries for Clark taken from the adjustments section of the worksheet. Once the adjusting journal entries are posted to the ledger, the accounts making up the financial statements that were prepared from the worksheet will equal the updated ledger. (Keep in mind that this is the same journal we have been using.) Let's look at some simplified T accounts to show how Clark's ledger looked before and after the adjustments were posted (see Adjustments A–D on pp. 164–166).

Adjustment (A)

	Office Supplies 114		Office Supplies Expense 514	
Before Posting:	600			
After Posting:	Office Supplies 114		Office Supplies Expense 514	
	600	500	500	

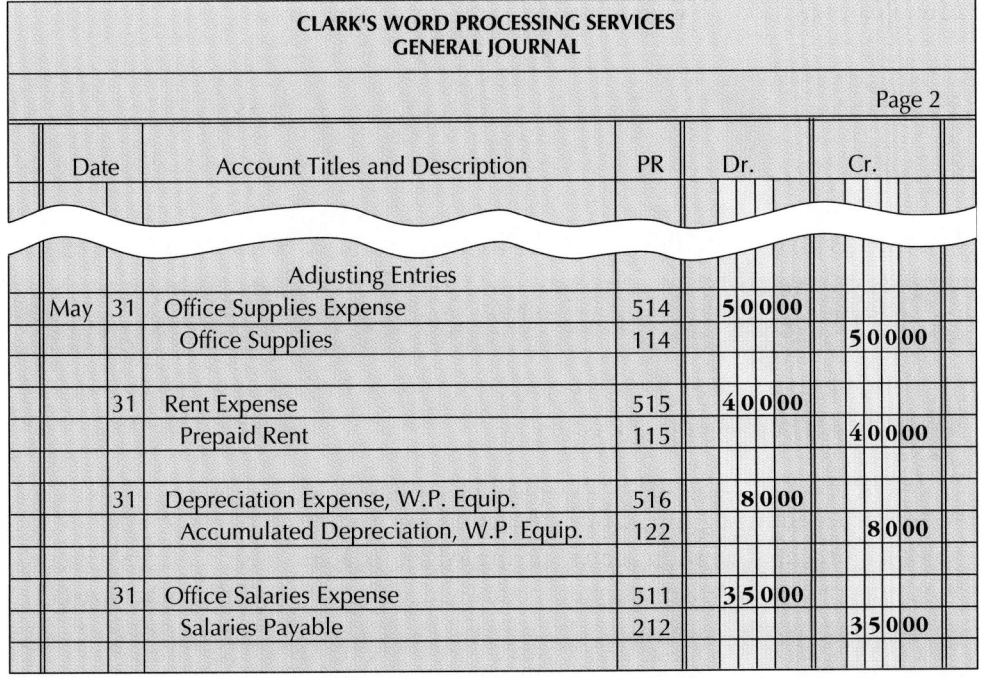

Figure 5-1
Journalizing and Posting Adjustments from the Adjustments Section of the Worksheet

Account Titles	Trial Balance Dr.	Trial Balance Cr.	Adjustments Dr.	Adjustments Cr.
Cash	6 1 5 5 00			
Accounts Receivable	5 0 0 0 00			
Office Supplies	6 0 0 00			(A) 5 0 0 00
Prepaid Rent	1 2 0 0 00			(B) 4 0 0 00
Word Processing Equipment	6 0 0 0 00			
Accounts Payable		3 3 5 0 00		
Brenda Clark, Capital		10 0 0 0 00		
Brenda Clark, Withdrawals	6 2 5 00			
Word Processing Fees		8 0 0 0 00		
Office Salaries Expense	1 3 0 0 00		(D) 3 5 0 00	
Advertising Expense	2 5 0 00			
Telephone Expense	2 2 0 00			
	21 3 5 0 00	21 3 5 0 00		
Office Supplies Expense			(A) 5 0 0 00	
Rent Expense			(B) 4 0 0 00	
Depreciation Exp., W.P. Equip.			(C) 8 0 00	
Accum. Deprec., W.P. Equip.				(C) 8 0 00
Salaries Payable				(D) 3 5 0 00
			1 3 3 0 00	1 3 3 0 00

Figure 5-2
Adjustments A–D in the Adjustments Section of the Worksheet Must Be Recorded in the Journal and Posted to the Ledger

CLARK'S WORD PROCESSING SERVICES
GENERAL JOURNAL

Page 2

Date		Account Titles and Description	PR	Dr.	Cr.
		Adjusting Entries			
May	31	Office Supplies Expense	514	5 0 0 00	
		Office Supplies	114		5 0 0 00
	31	Rent Expense	515	4 0 0 00	
		Prepaid Rent	115		4 0 0 00
	31	Depreciation Expense, W.P. Equip.	516	8 0 00	
		Accumulated Depreciation, W.P. Equip.	122		8 0 00
	31	Office Salaries Expense	511	3 5 0 00	
		Salaries Payable	212		3 5 0 00

Adjustment (B)

Before Posting:	Prepaid Rent 115	Rent Expense 515
	1,200	

After Posting:	Prepaid Rent 115	Rent Expense 515
	1,200 | 400	400 |

Adjustment (C)

Before Posting:

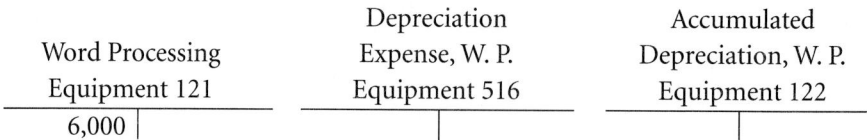

Word Processing Equipment 121	Depreciation Expense, W. P. Equipment 516	Accumulated Depreciation, W. P. Equipment 122
6,000		

After Posting:

Word Processing Equipment 121	Depreciation Expense, W. P. Equipment 516	Accumulated Depreciation, W. P. Equipment 122
6,000	80	80

The first adjustment in (C) shows the same balances for Depreciation Expense and Accumulated Depreciation. However, in subsequent adjustments the Accumulated Depreciation balance will keep getting larger, but the debit to Depreciation Expense and the credit to Accumulated Depreciation will be the same. We will see why in a moment.

Adjustment (D)

Before Posting:

Office Salaries Expense 511	Salaries Payable 212
650	
650	

After Posting:

Office Salaries Expense 511	Salaries Payable 212
650	350
650	
350	

Learning Unit 5-1 Review

AT THIS POINT you should be able to

- Define and state the purpose of adjusting entries. (p. 164)
- Journalize adjusting entries from the worksheet. (p. 165)
- Post journalized adjusting entries to the ledger. (p. 165)
- Compare specific ledger accounts before and after posting of the journalized adjusting entries. (p. 166)

SELF-REVIEW QUIZ 5-1

(The blank forms you need are on pages 121–122 of the *Study Guide and Working Papers*. See your DVD for worked-out solutions.)

Turn to the worksheet of P. Logan (p. 134) and (1) journalize and post the adjusting entries and (2) compare the adjusted ledger accounts before and after the adjustments are posted. T accounts are provided in your study guide with beginning balances.

SOLUTION TO SELF-REVIEW QUIZ 5-1

Figure 5-3
Journalized Adjusting
Entries

					Page 2	
Date		Account Titles and Description	PR	Dr.	Cr.	
		Adjusting Entries				
Dec.	31	Depreciation Expense, Store Equip.	511	1 00		
		Accumulated Depreciation, Store Equip.	122		1 00	
	31	Insurance Expense	516	2 00		
		Prepaid Insurance	116		2 00	
	31	Supplies Expense	514	4 00		
		Store Supplies	114		4 00	
	31	Salaries Expense	512	3 00		
		Salaries Payable	212		3 00	

Quiz Tip:
These journalized entries
come from the adjust-
ments column of the
worksheet.

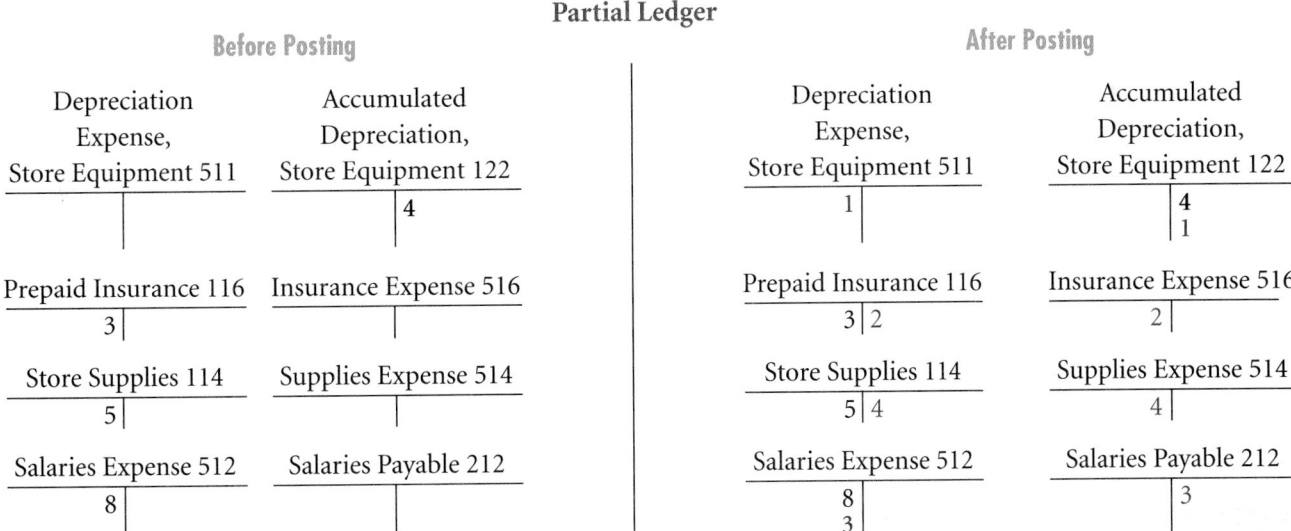

Partial Ledger

Before Posting

Depreciation Expense, Store Equipment 511

Accumulated Depreciation, Store Equipment 122
4

Prepaid Insurance 116
3

Insurance Expense 516

Store Supplies 114
5

Supplies Expense 514

Salaries Expense 512
8

Salaries Payable 212

After Posting

Depreciation Expense, Store Equipment 511
1

Accumulated Depreciation, Store Equipment 122
4
1

Prepaid Insurance 116
3 2

Insurance Expense 516
2

Store Supplies 114
5 4

Supplies Expense 514
4

Salaries Expense 512
8
3

Salaries Payable 212
3

Learning Unit 5-2   Journalizing and Posting Closing Entries: Step 8 of the Accounting Cycle

To make recording of the next period's transactions easier, a mechanical step, called *closing*, is taken by Clark's accountant. Closing is intended to end—or close off—the revenue, expense, and withdrawal accounts at the end of the accounting period. The information needed to complete closing entries will be found in the income statement and balance sheet sections of the worksheet.

To make it easier to understand this process, we will first look at the difference between temporary (nominal) accounts and permanent (real) accounts.

Here is the expanded accounting equation we used in an earlier chapter:

Assets = Liabilities + Capital − Withdrawals + Revenues − Expenses

Three of the items in that equation—Assets, Liabilities, and Capital—are known as real or **permanent accounts** because their balances are carried over from one accounting period to another. The other three items—Withdrawals, Revenues, and

Permanent accounts are found on the balance sheet.

Expenses—are called nominal or temporary accounts, because their balances are not carried over from one accounting period to another. Instead, their "balances" are set at zero at the beginning of each accounting period. This allows us to accumulate new data about revenue, expenses, and withdrawals in the new accounting period. The process of closing summarizes the effects of the temporary accounts on Capital for that period using closing journal entries. When the closing process is complete, the accounting equation will be reduced to

Assets = Liabilities + Ending Capital

If you look back to page 137 in Chapter 4, you will see that we already calculated the new capital on the balance sheet to be $14,275 for Clark's Word Processing Services. But before the mechanical closing procedures are journalized and posted, the Capital account of Clark in the ledger is only $10,000 (Chapter 3, p. 86). Let's look now at how to journalize and post closing entries.

> After all closing entries are journalized and posted to the ledger, all temporary accounts have a zero balance in the ledger. Closing is a step-by-step process.

HOW TO JOURNALIZE CLOSING ENTRIES

There are four steps to be performed in journalizing closing entries:

Step 1: Clear the revenue balance and transfer it to Income Summary. Income Summary is a temporary account in the ledger needed for closing. At the end of the closing process there will be no balance in Income Summary.

Revenue ⟶ Income Summary

Step 2: Clear the individual expense balances and transfer them to Income Summary.

Expenses ⟶ Income Summary

Step 3: Clear the balance in Income Summary and transfer it to Capital.

Income Summary ⟶ Capital

Step 4: Clear the balance in Withdrawals and transfer it to Capital.

Withdrawals ⟶ Capital

> An Income Summary is a temporary account located in the chart of accounts under Owner's Equity. It does not have a normal balance of a debit or a credit.

> Sometimes, closing the accounts is referred to as "clearing the accounts."

Figure 5-4 is a visual representation of these four steps. Keep in mind that this information must first be journalized and then posted to the appropriate ledger accounts. The worksheet presented in Figure 5-5 on page 169 contains all the figures we will need for the closing process.

Step 1: Clear Revenue Balance and Transfer to Income Summary

Here is what is in the ledger before closing entries are journalized and posted:

Word Processing Fees 411	Income Summary 313
8,000	

The income statement section on the worksheet in Figure 5-4 shows that Word Processing Fees has a credit balance of $8,000. To close or clear this to zero, a debit of $8,000 is needed. But if we add an amount to the debit side, we must also add a credit—so we add $8,000 on the credit side of the Income Summary.

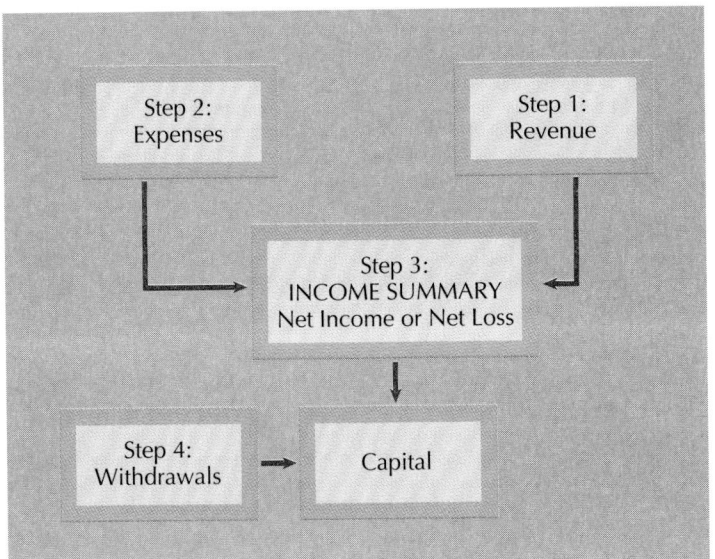

Figure 5-4
Four Steps in Journalizing Closing Entries. All numbers can be found on the worksheet in Figure 5-5.

Don't forget two goals of closing:
1. Clear all temporary accounts in ledger.
2. Update Capital to a new balance that reflects a summary of all the temporary accounts.

All numbers used in the closing process can be found on the worksheet. Note that the account Income Summary is not on the worksheet.

Account Titles	Income Statement		Balance Sheet	
	Dr.	Cr.	Dr.	Cr.
Cash			6 1 5 5 00	
Accounts Receivable			5 0 0 0 00	
Office Supplies			1 0 0 00	
Prepaid Rent			8 0 0 00	
Word Processing Equipment			6 0 0 0 00	
Accounts Payable				3 3 5 0 00
B. Clark, Capital		For Step 1		10 0 0 0 00
B. Clark, Withdrawals	For Step 2		6 2 5 00	
Word Processing Fees		8 0 0 0 00	For Step 4	
Office Salaries Expense	1 6 5 0 00			
Advertising Expense	2 5 0 00			
Telephone Expense	2 2 0 00			
Office Supplies Expense	5 0 0 00			
Rent Expense	4 0 0 00			
Depreciation Exp., W.P. Equip.	8 0 00			
Acc. Depreciation, W.P. Equip.		For Step 3		8 0 00
Salaries Payable				3 5 0 00
	3 1 0 0 00	8 0 0 0 00	18 6 8 0 00	13 7 8 0 00
Net Income	4 9 0 0 00			4 9 0 0 00
	8 0 0 0 00	8 0 0 0 00	18 6 8 0 00	18 6 8 0 00

Figure 5-5 Closing Figures on the Worksheet

Figure 5-6 is the journalized closing entry for Step 1:

May	31	Word Processing Fees	411	8 0 0 0 00		
		Income Summary	313		8 0 0 0 00	

Figure 5-6 Closing Revenue to Income Summary

This is what Word Processing Fees and Income Summary should look like in the ledger after the first step of closing entries is journalized and posted:

Word Processing Fees 411

8,000	8,000
Closing	Revenue

Income Summary 313

	8,000
	Revenue

Note that the revenue balance is cleared to zero and transferred to Income Summary, a temporary account also located in the ledger.

Step 2: Clear Individual Expense Balances and Transfer the Total to Income Summary

Here is what is in the ledger for each expense before Step 2 of closing entries is journalized and posted. Each expense is listed on the worksheet in the debit column of the income statement section on page 169.

Office Salaries Expense 511

650	
650	
350	

Advertising Expense 512

250	

Telephone Expense 513

220	

Office Supplies Expense 514

500	

Rent Expense 515

400	

Depreciation Expense, W. P. Equipment 516

80	

> Remember, the worksheet is a tool. The accountant realizes that the information about the total of the expenses will be transferred to the income Summary.

The income statement section of the worksheet lists all the expenses as debits. If we want to reduce each expense to zero, each one must be credited.

Figure 5-7 is the journalized closing entry for Step 2:

Figure 5-7
Closing Each Expense to Income Summary

		31	Income Summary	313	3 1 0 0 00	
			Office Salaries Expense	511		1 6 5 0 00
			Advertising Expense	512		2 5 0 00
			Telephone Expense	513		2 2 0 00
			Office Supplies Expense	514		5 0 0 00
			Rent Expense	515		4 0 0 00
			Depreciation Expense, W.P.Equip.	516		8 0 00

> The $3,100 is the total of the expenses on the worksheet.

The following is what individual expenses and Income Summary should look like in the ledger after Step 2 of closing entries is journalized and posted:

Office Salaries Expense 511

650	Closing	1,650
650		
350		

Advertising Expense 512

250	Closing	250

Telephone Expense 513

220	Closing	220

Office Supplies Expense 514

500	Closing	500

Rent Expense 515

400	Closing	400

Depreciation Expense, W. P. Equipment 516

80	Closing	80

Income Summary 313

	Expenses	Revenue	
Step 2	3,100	8,000	Step 1

Step 3: Clear Balance in Income Summary (Net Income) and Transfer It to Capital

This is how the Income Summary and B. Clark, Capital, accounts look before Step 3:

Income Summary 313		B. Clark, Capital 311	
3,100	8,000		10,000
	4,900		

Note that the balance of Income Summary (Revenues minus Expenses, or $8,000 − $3,100) is $4,900. That is the amount we must clear from the Income Summary account and transfer to the B. Clark, Capital, account.

In order to transfer the balance of $4,900 from Income Summary (check the bottom debit column of the income statement section on the worksheet in Fig. 5-5) to Capital, it will be necessary to debit Income Summary for $4,900 (the difference between the revenue and expenses) and credit or increase Capital of B. Clark for $4,900.

Figure 5-8 is the journalized closing entry for Step 3:

	31	Income Summary	313	4 9 0 0 00	
		B. Clark, Capital	311		4 9 0 0 00

Figure 5-8
Closing Net Income
to B. Clark, Capital

This is what the Income Summary and B. Clark, Capital, accounts will look like in the ledger after Step 3 of closing entries is journalized and posted:

Income Summary 313 — Total of Expenses → 3,100 | 8,000 ← Revenue; Debit to close account → 4,900 | 4,900 ← Net Income

B. Clark, Capital 311 — 10,000; 4,900 ← Net Income

> The opposite would take place if the business had a net loss.

Step 4: Clear the Withdrawals Balance and Transfer It to Capital

Next, we must close the Withdrawals account. The B. Clark, Withdrawals, and B. Clark, Capital, accounts now look like this:

B. Clark, Withdrawals 312		B. Clark, Capital 311	
625			10,000
			4,900

To bring the Withdrawals account to a zero balance and summarize its effect on Capital, we must credit Withdrawals and debit Capital.

Remember, withdrawals are a nonbusiness expense and thus not transferred to Income Summary. The closing entry is journalized as shown in Figure 5-9.

> At the end of these three steps, the Income Summary has a zero balance. If we had a net loss, the end result would be to decrease Capital. The entry would be debit Capital and credit Income Summary for the loss.

	31	B. Clark, Capital	311	6 2 5 00	
		B. Clark, Withdrawals	312		6 2 5 00

Figure 5-9
Close Withdrawal
to B. Clark, Capital

At this point the B. Clark, Withdrawals, and B. Clark, Capital, accounts would look like this in the ledger.

B. Clark, Withdrawals 312		B. Clark, Capital 311	
625	Closing 625	625 →	10,000 ←
		Withdrawals	Beg. Balance
			4,900 ←
			Net Income

> Note that the $10,000 is a beginning balance since no additional investments were made during the period.

Now let's look at a summary of the closing entries in Figure 5-10.

	Date		Account Titles and Description	PR	Dr.	Cr.	
			SUMMARY OF CLOSING ENTRIES				
			Closing Entries				
200X							
	May	31	Word Processing Fees	411	8 0 0 0 00		
			Income Summary	313		8 0 0 0 00	← Step 1
		31	Income Summary	313	3 1 0 0 00		
			Office Salaries Expense	511		1 6 5 0 00	
			Advertising Expense	512		2 5 0 00	
			Telephone Expense	513		2 2 0 00	← Step 2
			Office Supplies Expense	514		5 0 0 00	
			Rent Expense	515		4 0 0 00	
			Depreciation Expense, W.P. Equip.	516		8 0 00	
		31	Income Summary	313	4 9 0 0 00		
			B. Clark, Capital	311		4 9 0 0 00	← Step 3
		31	B. Clark, Capital	311	6 2 5 00		
			B. Clark, Withdrawals	312		6 2 5 00	← Step 4

Figure 5-10 Four Closing Entries

The following is the complete ledger for Clark's Word Processing Services (see Fig. 5-11). Note how "adjusting" or "closing" is written in the explanation column of individual ledgers, as for example in the one for Office Supplies. If the goals of closing have been achieved, only permanent accounts will have balances carried to the next accounting period. All temporary accounts should have zero balances.

CLARK'S WORD PROCESSING SERVICES
GENERAL LEDGER

Cash   Account No. 111

Date		Explanation	Post. Ref.	Debit	Credit	Balance Debit	Balance Credit
200X May	1		GJ1	10 000 00		10 000 00	
	1		GJ1		1 000 00	9 000 00	
	1		GJ1		1 200 00	7 800 00	
	7		GJ1	3 000 00		10 800 00	
	15		GJ1		650 00	10 150 00	
	20		GJ1		625 00	9 525 00	
	27		GJ2		650 00	8 875 00	
	28		GJ2		2 500 00	6 375 00	
	29		GJ2		220 00	6 155 00	

Accounts Receivable   Account No. 112

Date		Explanation	Post. Ref.	Debit	Credit	Balance Debit	Balance Credit
200X May	22		GJ1	5 000 00		5 000 00	

Office Supplies   Account No. 114

Date		Explanation	Post. Ref.	Debit	Credit	Balance Debit	Balance Credit
200X May	3		GJ1	600 00		600 00	
	31	Adjusting	GJ2		500 00	100 00	

Figure 5-11 Complete Ledger

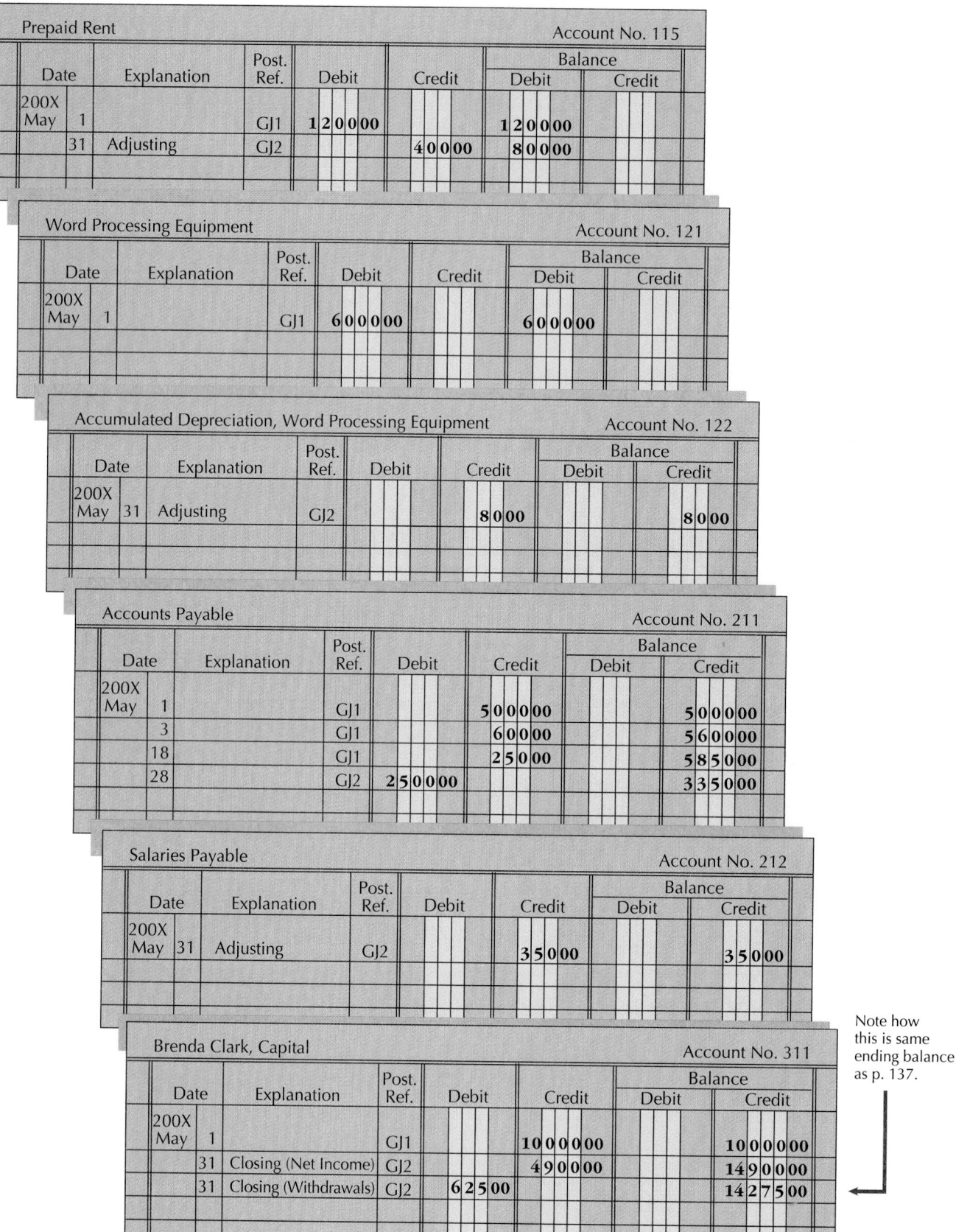

Prepaid Rent — Account No. 115

Date		Explanation	Post. Ref.	Debit	Credit	Balance Debit	Balance Credit
200X May	1		GJ1	1 2 0 0 00		1 2 0 0 00	
	31	Adjusting	GJ2		4 0 0 00	8 0 0 00	

Word Processing Equipment — Account No. 121

Date		Explanation	Post. Ref.	Debit	Credit	Balance Debit	Balance Credit
200X May	1		GJ1	6 0 0 0 00		6 0 0 0 00	

Accumulated Depreciation, Word Processing Equipment — Account No. 122

Date		Explanation	Post. Ref.	Debit	Credit	Balance Debit	Balance Credit
200X May	31	Adjusting	GJ2		8 0 00		8 0 00

Accounts Payable — Account No. 211

Date		Explanation	Post. Ref.	Debit	Credit	Balance Debit	Balance Credit
200X May	1		GJ1		5 0 0 0 00		5 0 0 0 00
	3		GJ1		6 0 0 00		5 6 0 0 00
	18		GJ1		2 5 00		5 8 5 0 00
	28		GJ2	2 5 0 0 00			3 3 5 0 00

Salaries Payable — Account No. 212

Date		Explanation	Post. Ref.	Debit	Credit	Balance Debit	Balance Credit
200X May	31	Adjusting	GJ2		3 5 0 00		3 5 0 00

Brenda Clark, Capital — Account No. 311

Date		Explanation	Post. Ref.	Debit	Credit	Balance Debit	Balance Credit
200X May	1		GJ1		1 0 0 0 0 00		1 0 0 0 0 00
	31	Closing (Net Income)	GJ2		4 9 0 0 00		1 4 9 0 0 00
	31	Closing (Withdrawals)	GJ2	6 2 5 00			1 4 2 7 5 00

Note how this is same ending balance as p. 137.

Figure 5-11 (*continued*)

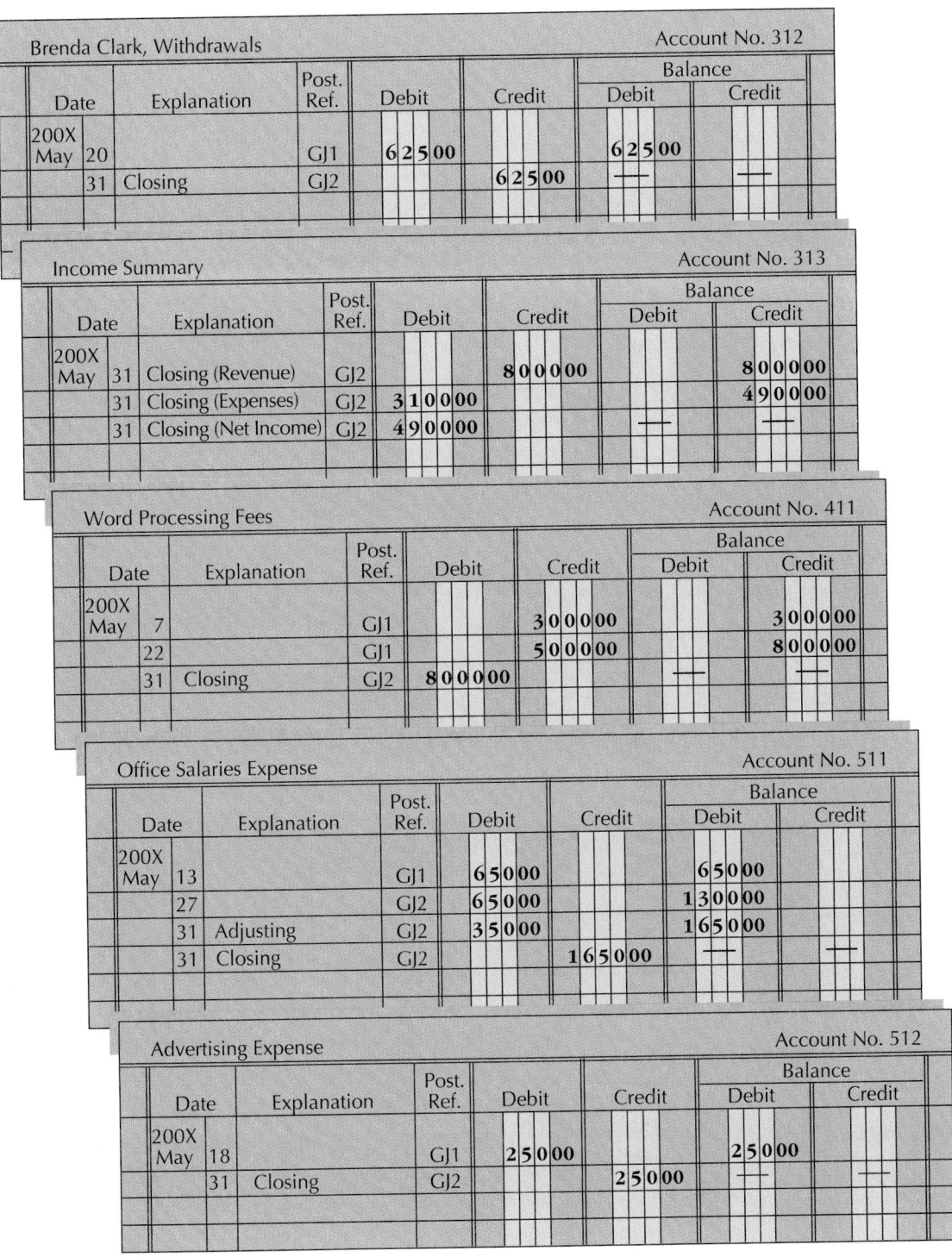

Brenda Clark, Withdrawals   Account No. 312

Date		Explanation	Post. Ref.	Debit	Credit	Balance Debit	Balance Credit
200X May	20		GJ1	6 2 5 00		6 2 5 00	
	31	Closing	GJ2		6 2 5 00	—	—

Income Summary   Account No. 313

Date		Explanation	Post. Ref.	Debit	Credit	Balance Debit	Balance Credit
200X May	31	Closing (Revenue)	GJ2		8 0 0 0 00		8 0 0 0 00
	31	Closing (Expenses)	GJ2	3 1 0 0 00			4 9 0 0 00
	31	Closing (Net Income)	GJ2	4 9 0 0 00		—	

Word Processing Fees   Account No. 411

Date		Explanation	Post. Ref.	Debit	Credit	Balance Debit	Balance Credit
200X May	7		GJ1		3 0 0 0 00		3 0 0 0 00
	22		GJ1		5 0 0 0 00		8 0 0 0 00
	31	Closing	GJ2	8 0 0 0 00		—	—

Office Salaries Expense   Account No. 511

Date		Explanation	Post. Ref.	Debit	Credit	Balance Debit	Balance Credit
200X May	13		GJ1	6 5 0 00		6 5 0 00	
	27		GJ2	6 5 0 00		1 3 0 0 00	
	31	Adjusting	GJ2	3 5 0 00		1 6 5 0 00	
	31	Closing	GJ2		1 6 5 0 00	—	—

Advertising Expense   Account No. 512

Date		Explanation	Post. Ref.	Debit	Credit	Balance Debit	Balance Credit
200X May	18		GJ1	2 5 0 00		2 5 0 00	
	31	Closing	GJ2		2 5 0 00	—	—

Figure 5-11 (*continued*)

Telephone Expense   Account No. 513

Date		Explanation	Post. Ref.	Debit	Credit	Balance Debit	Balance Credit
200X May	29		GJ2	2 2 0 00		2 2 0 00	
	31	Closing	GJ2		2 2 0 00	—	—

Office Supplies Expense   Account No. 514

Date		Explanation	Post. Ref.	Debit	Credit	Balance Debit	Balance Credit
200X May	31	Adjusting	GJ2	5 0 0 00		5 0 0 00	
	31	Closing	GJ2		5 0 0 00	—	—

Note: Accounts 312 to 516 are temporary and are closed to zero.

Rent Expense   Account No. 515

Date		Explanation	Post. Ref.	Debit	Credit	Balance Debit	Balance Credit
200X May	31	Adjusting	GJ2	4 0 0 00		4 0 0 00	
	31	Closing	GJ2		4 0 0 00	—	—

Depreciation Expense, Word Processing Equipment   Account No. 516

Date		Explanation	Post. Ref.	Debit	Credit	Balance Debit	Balance Credit
200X May	31	Adjusting	GJ2	8 0 00		8 0 00	
	31	Closing	GJ2		8 0 00	—	—

Figure 5-11 (*continued*)

Learning Unit 5-2 Review

AT THIS POINT you should be able to

- Define closing. (p. 168)
- Differentiate between temporary (nominal) and permanent (real) accounts. (p. 168)
- List the four mechanical steps of closing. (p. 168)
- Explain the role of the Income Summary account. (p. 168)
- Explain the role of the worksheet in the closing process. (p. 169)

SELF-REVIEW QUIZ 5-2

(The blank forms you need are on pages 123–124 of the *Study Guide and Working Papers*. See your DVD for worked-out solutions.)

Go to the worksheet for P. Logan on p. 134. Then (1) journalize and post the closing entries and (2) calculate the new balance for P. Logan, Capital.

SOLUTION TO SELF-REVIEW QUIZ 5-2

		Closing Entries			
Dec.	31	Revenue from Clients	410	25 00	
		Income Summary	312		25 00
	31	Income Summary	312	20 00	
		Rent Expense	518		2 00
		Salaries Expense	512		11 00
		Depreciation Expense, Store Equip.	510		1 00
		Insurance Expense	516		2 00
		Supplies Expense	514		4 00
	31	Income Summary	312	5 00	
		P. Logan, Capital	310		5 00
	31	P. Logan, Capital	310	3 00	
		P. Logan, Withdrawals	311		3 00

Quiz Tip:
Revenue closed to Income Summary

Each expense closed to Income Summary

Net Income closed to Capital

Withdrawals closed to Capital

Figure 5-12 Closing Entries for Logan

Partial Ledger

P. Logan, Capital 310

3	14
	5
	16

Revenue from Clients 410

25	25

Supplies Expense 514

4	4

P. Logan, Withdrawals 311

3	3

Dep. Exp., Store Equip. 510

1	1

Insurance Expense 516

2	2

Income Summary 312

20	25
5	5

Salaries Expense 512

11	11

Rent Expense 518

2	2

P. Logan, Capital		**$14**
Net Income	**$5**	
Less Withdrawals	**3**	
Increase in Capital		**2**
P. Logan, Capital (ending)		**$16**

Quiz Tip:
No calculations are needed in the closing process. ALL numbers come from the worksheet. Income Summary is a temporary account in the ledger.

Learning Unit 5-3
The Post-Closing Trial Balance: Step 9 of the Accounting Cycle and the Cycle Reviewed

> The post-closing trial balance helps prove the accuracy of the adjusting and closing process. It contains the true ending figure for Capital.

PREPARING A POST-CLOSING TRIAL BALANCE

The last step in the accounting cycle is the preparation of a post-closing trial balance, which lists only permanent accounts in the ledger and their balances after adjusting and closing entries have been posted. This post-closing trial balance aids in checking whether the ledger is in balance. This checking is important to do because so many new postings go to the ledger from the adjusting and closing process.

The procedure for taking a post-closing trial balance is the same as for a trial balance, except that, since closing entries have closed all temporary accounts, the post-closing trial balance will contain only permanent accounts (balance sheet). Keep in mind, however, that adjustments have occurred.

> Remember no worksheet is needed in a computerized cycle.

TABLE 5-1 Steps of the Manual Accounting Cycle

Steps	Explanation
1. Business transactions occur and generate source documents.	Cash register tape, sales tickets, bills, checks, payroll cards.
2. Analyze and record business transactions into a journal.	Called journalizing.
3. Post or transfer information from journal to ledger.	Copying the debits and credits of the journal entries into the ledger accounts.
4. Prepare a trial balance.	Summarizing each individual ledger account and listing those accounts to test for mathematical accuracy in recording transactions.
5. Prepare a worksheet.	A multicolumn form that summarizes accounting information to complete the accounting cycle.
6. Prepare financial statements.	Income statement, statement of owner's equity, and balance sheet.
7. Journalize and post adjusting entries.	Use figures in the Adjustment columns of worksheet.
8. Journalize and post closing entries.	Use figures in the income statement and balance sheet sections of worksheet.
9. Prepare a post-closing trial balance.	Prove the mathematical accuracy of the adjusting and closing process of the accounting cycle.

THE ACCOUNTING CYCLE REVIEWED

Table 5-1 lists the steps we completed in the manual accounting cycle for Clark's Word Processing Services for the month of May:

Insight   Most companies journalize and post adjusting and closing entries only at the end of their fiscal year. A company that prepares interim statements may complete only the first six steps of the cycle. Worksheets allow the preparation of interim reports without the formal adjusting and closing of the books. If this happens, foot-notes on the interim report will indicate the extent to which adjusting and closing were completed.

Insight   To prepare a financial statement for April, the data needed can be obtained by subtracting the worksheet accumulated totals from the end of March from the worksheet prepared at the end of April. In this chapter we chose a month that would show the completion of an entire cycle for Clark's Word Processing Services.

Learning Unit 5-3 Review

AT THIS POINT you should be able to

- Prepare a post-closing trial balance. (p. 178)
- Explain the relationship of interim statements to the accounting cycle. (p. 179)

SELF-REVIEW QUIZ 5-3

(The blank forms you need are on page 124 of the *Study Guide and Working Papers.* See your DVD for worked-out solutions.)

From the ledger on page 173, prepare a post-closing trial balance.

SOLUTION TO SELF-REVIEW QUIZ 5-3

CLARK'S WORD PROCESSING SERVICES POST-CLOSING TRIAL BALANCE MAY 31, 200X	Dr.	Cr.
Cash	6 1 5 5 00	
Accounts Receivable	5 0 0 0 00	
Office Supplies	1 0 0 00	
Prepaid Rent	8 0 0 00	
Word Processing Equipment	6 0 0 0 00	
Accumulated Depreciation, Word Processing Equip.		8 0 00
Accounts Payable		3 3 5 0 00
Salaries Payable		3 5 0 00
Brenda Clark, Capital		14 2 7 5 00
Totals	18 0 5 5 00	18 0 5 5 00

Figure 5-13
Post-Closing Trial Balance for Clark's Word Processing Services

Quiz Tip:
The post-closing trial balance contains only permanent accounts because all temporary accounts have been closed. All temporary accounts are summarized in the Capital account.

Chapter Review

SOLUTIONS & TIPS TO COMPREHENSIVE PROBLEMS: PUTTING THE PIECES TOGETHER

(The blank forms you need are on pages 125–133 of the *Study Guide and Working Papers.*)

From the following transactions for Rolo Co. complete the entire accounting cycle. The chart of accounts includes:

Assets
111 Cash
112 Accounts Receivable
114 Prepaid Rent
115 Office Supplies
121 Office Equipment
122 Accumulated Depreciation, Office Equipment

Liabilities
211 Accounts Payable
212 Salaries Payable

Owner's Equity
311 Rolo Kern, Capital
312 Rolo Kern, Withdrawals
313 Income Summary

Revenue
411 Fees Earned

Expenses
511 Salaries Expense
512 Advertising Expense
513 Rent Expense
514 Office Supplies Expense
515 Depreciation Expense, Office Equipment

Note: Accounts 312 to 515 are temporary accounts.

We will use unusually small numbers to simplify calculation and emphasize the theory.

200X
Jan.
1 Rolo Kern invested $1,200 cash and $100 of office equipment to open Rolo Co.
1 Paid rent for three months in advance, $300
4 Purchased office equipment on account, $50
6 Bought office supplies for cash, $40
8 Collected $400 for services rendered
12 Rolo paid his home electric bill from the company checkbook, $20
14 Provided $100 worth of services to clients who will not pay till next month
16 Paid salaries, $60
18 Advertising bill received for $70 but will not be paid until next month

Adjustment Data on January 31

a. Supplies on hand	$6
b. Rent Expired	$100
c. Depreciation, Office Equipment	$20
d. Salaries Accrued	$50

Solutions to Comprehensive Problem

Journalizing Transactions and Posting to Ledger, Rolo Company

Figure 5-14
Journal Entries for
Rolo Company

Date		Account Titles and Description	PR	Dr.	Cr.
200X Jan	1	Cash	111	1 2 0 0 00	
		Office Equipment	121	1 0 0 00	
		R. Kern, Capital	311		1 3 0 0 00
		Initial Investment			
	1	Prepaid Rent	114	3 0 0 00	
		Cash	111		3 0 0 00
		Rent Paid in Advance—3 mos.			
	4	Office Equipment	121	5 0 00	
		Accounts Payable	211		5 0 00
		Purchased Equipment on Account			
	6	Office Supplies	115	4 0 00	
		Cash	111		4 0 00
		Supplies purchased for cash			
	8	Cash	111	4 0 0 00	
		Fees Earned	411		4 0 0 00
		Services rendered			
	12	R. Kern, Withdrawals	312	2 0 00	
		Cash	111		2 0 00
		Personal payment of a bill			
	14	Accounts Receivable	112	1 0 0 00	
		Fees Earned	411		1 0 0 00
		Services rendered on account			
	16	Salaries Expense	511	6 0 00	
		Cash	111		6 0 00
		Paid salaries			
	18	Advertising Expense	512	7 0 00	
		Accounts Payable	211		7 0 00
		Advertising bill, but not paid			

General Journal — Page 1

Solution Tips to Journalizing and Posting Transactions

Jan 1	Cash	Asset	↑	Dr.	$1,200
	Office Equipment	Asset	↑	Dr.	$ 100
	R. Kern, Capital	Capital	↑	Cr.	$1,300

2	Prepaid Rent	Asset	↑	Dr.	$ 300
	Cash	Asset	↓	Cr.	$ 300

| 4 | Office Equipment | Asset | ↑ | Dr. | $ 50 |
| | Accounts Payable | Liability | ↑ | Cr. | $ 50 |

| 6 | Office Supplies | Asset | ↑ | Dr. | $ 40 |
| | Cash | Asset | ↓ | Cr. | $ 40 |

| 8 | Cash | Asset | ↑ | Dr. | $ 400 |
| | Fees Earned | Revenue | ↑ | Cr. | $ 400 |

| 12 | R. Kern, Withdrawals | Withdrawals | ↑ | Dr. | $ 20 |
| | Cash | Asset | ↓ | Cr. | $ 20 |

| 14 | Accounts Receivable | Asset | ↑ | Dr. | $ 100 |
| | Fees Earned | Revenue | ↑ | Cr. | $ 100 |

| 16 | Salaries Expense | Expense | ↑ | Dr. | $ 60 |
| | Cash | Asset | ↓ | Cr. | $ 60 |

| 18 | Advertising Expense | Expense | ↑ | Dr. | $ 70 |
| | Accounts Payable | Liability | ↑ | Cr. | $ 70 |

Note All account titles come from the chart of accounts. When journalizing, the PR column of the general journal is blank. It is in the posting process that we update the ledger. The PR column in the ledger accounts tells us from what journal page the information came. After the title in the ledger is posted to, we fill in the PR column of the journal, telling us to what account number the information was transferred.

Completing the Worksheet

See worksheet on page 183.

Solution Tips to the Trial Balance and Completion of the Worksheet

After the posting process is complete from the journal to the ledger, we take the ending balance in each account and prepare a trial balance on the worksheet (see Fig. 5-15). If a title has no balance, it is not listed on the trial balance. New titles on the worksheet will be added below as needed.

Adjustments

On hand of $6 is not the adjustment. Need to calculate amount used up.

| Office Supplies Expense | Expense | ↑ | Dr. | $ 34 | ($40–$6) |
| Office Supplies | Asset | ↓ | Cr. | $ 34 | |

Expired.

| Rent Expense | Expense | ↑ | Dr. | $100 |
| Prepaid Rent | Asset | ↓ | Cr. | $100 |

Do not touch original cost of equipment.

| Depr. Exp., Office Equip. | Expense | ↑ | Dr. | $ 20 |
| Accum. Dep., Office Equip. | Contra-Asset | ↑ | Cr. | $ 20 |

Owed but not paid.

| Salaries Expense | Expense | ↑ | Dr. | $ 50 |
| Salaries Payable | Liability | ↑ | Cr. | $ 50 |

ROLO CO
WORKSHEET
FOR MONTH ENDED JANUARY 31, 200X

Account Titles	Trial Balance Dr.	Trial Balance Cr.	Adjustments Dr.	Adjustments Cr.	Adjusted Trial Balance Dr.	Adjusted Trial Balance Cr.	Income Statement Dr.	Income Statement Cr.	Balance Sheet Dr.	Balance Sheet Cr.
Cash	118000				118000				118000	
Accounts Receivable	10000				10000				10000	
Prepaid Rent	30000			(B) 10000	20000				20000	
Office Supplies	4000			(A) 3400	600				600	
Office Equipment	15000				15000				15000	
Accounts Payable		12000				12000				12000
R. Kern, Capital		130000				130000				130000
R. Kern, Withdrawals	2000				2000				2000	
Fees Earned		50000				50000		50000		
Salaries Expense	6000		(D) 5000		11000		11000			
Advertising Expense	7000				7000		7000			
	192000	192000								
Office Supplies Expense			(A) 3400		3400		3400			
Rent Expense			(B) 10000		10000		10000			
Depr. Exp., Office Equip.			(C) 2000		2000		2000			
Acc. Dep., Office Equip.				(C) 2000		2000				2000
Salaries Payable				(D) 5000		5000				5000
			20400	20400	199000	199000	33400	50000	165600	149000
Net Income							16600			16600
							50000	50000	165600	165600

Supplies used up

Supplies on hand

Figure 5-15 Completed Worksheet for Rolo Company

Note   This information is on the worksheet but has *not* been updated in the ledger. (This will happen when we journalize and post adjustments at the end of the cycle.)

Note that the last four columns of the worksheet come from numbers on the adjusted trial balance.

We move the Net Income of $166 to the Balance Sheet credit column since the Capital figure is the old one on the worksheet.

PREPARING THE FORMAL FINANCIAL STATEMENTS

Figure 5-16
Income Statement for Rolo Company

ROLO CO.
INCOME STATEMENT
FOR MONTH ENDED JANUARY 31, 200X

Revenue:		
Fees Earned		$5 0 0 00
Operating Expenses		
Salaries Expense	$1 1 0 00	
Advertising Expense	7 0 00	
Office Supplies Expense	3 4 00	
Rent Expense	1 0 0 00	
Depreciation Expense, Office Equipment	2 0 00	
Total Operating Expenses		3 3 4 00
Net Income		$1 6 6 00

Figure 5-17
Statement of Owner's Equity for Rolo Company

ROLO CO.
STATEMENT OF OWNER'S EQUITY
FOR MONTH ENDED JANUARY 31, 200X

R. Kern, Capital, January 1, 200X		$13 0 0 00
Net Income for January	$1 6 6 00	
Less Withdrawals for January	2 0 00	
Increase in Capital		1 4 6 00
R. Kern, Capital, January 31, 200X		$14 4 6 00

ROLO CO.
BALANCE SHEET
JANUARY 31, 200X

Assets			Liabilities & Owner's Equity		
Cash		$1 1 8 0 00	Liabilities		
Accounts Receivable		1 0 0 00	Accounts Payable	$1 2 0 00	
Prepaid Rent		2 0 0 00	Salaries Payable	5 0 00	
Office Supplies		6 00	Total Liabilities		$1 7 0 00
Office Equipment	$1 5 0 00		Owner's Equity		
Less Accum. Depr.	2 0 00	1 3 0 00	R. Kern, Capital		1 4 4 6 00
			Total Liabilities &		
Total Assets		$1 6 1 6 00	Owner's Equity		$1 6 1 6 00

Figure 5-18 Balance Sheet for Rolo Company

Solution Tips to Preparing the Financial Statements

The statements are prepared from the worksheet. (Many of the ledger accounts are not up-to-date.) The income statement (Fig. 5-16) lists revenue and expenses. The Net Income figure of $166 is used to update the statement of owner's equity. The statement of owner's equity (Fig. 5-17) calculates a new figure for Capital, $1,446 (Beginning Capital + Net Income − Withdrawals). This new figure is then listed on the balance sheet (Fig. 5-18) (Assets, Liabilities, and a new figure for Capital).

Journalizing and Posting Adjusting and Closing Entries

See journal in Figure 5-19.

Solution Tips to Journalizing and Posting Adjusting and Closing Entries

Adjustments

The adjustments from the worksheet are journalized (same journal) and posted to the ledger. Now ledger accounts will be brought up-to-date. Remember, we have already prepared the financial statements from the worksheet. Our goal now is to get the ledger up-to-date.

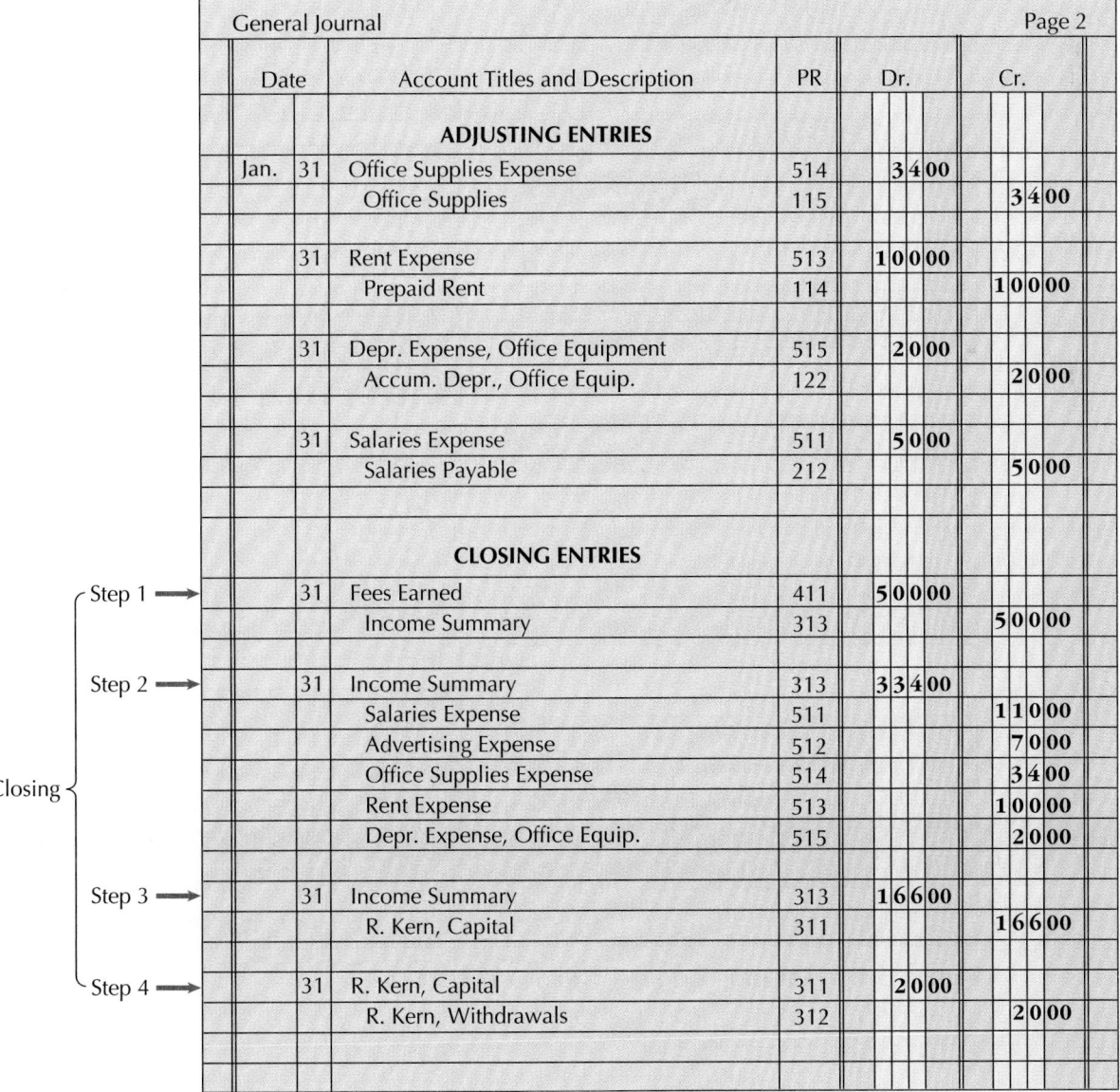

	Date		Account Titles and Description	PR	Dr.	Cr.
			General Journal Page 2			
			ADJUSTING ENTRIES			
	Jan.	31	Office Supplies Expense	514	3 4 00	
			Office Supplies	115		3 4 00
		31	Rent Expense	513	1 0 0 00	
			Prepaid Rent	114		1 0 0 00
		31	Depr. Expense, Office Equipment	515	2 0 00	
			Accum. Depr., Office Equip.	122		2 0 00
		31	Salaries Expense	511	5 0 00	
			Salaries Payable	212		5 0 00
			CLOSING ENTRIES			
Step 1 →		31	Fees Earned	411	5 0 0 00	
			Income Summary	313		5 0 0 00
Step 2 →		31	Income Summary	313	3 3 4 00	
			Salaries Expense	511		1 1 0 00
			Advertising Expense	512		7 0 00
			Office Supplies Expense	514		3 4 00
			Rent Expense	513		1 0 0 00
			Depr. Expense, Office Equip.	515		2 0 00
Step 3 →		31	Income Summary	313	1 6 6 00	
			R. Kern, Capital	311		1 6 6 00
Step 4 →		31	R. Kern, Capital	311	2 0 00	
			R. Kern, Withdrawals	312		2 0 00

Figure 5-19 Adjusting and Closing Entries Journalized and Posted

GENERAL LEDGER

Cash   111

Date	PR	Dr.	Cr.	Balance Dr.	Cr.
1/1	GJ1	1,200		1,200	
1/1	GJ1		300	900	
1/6	GJ1		40	860	
1/8	GJ1	400		1,260	
1/12	GJ1		20	1,240	
1/16	GJ1		60	1,180	

Accounts Receivable   112

Date	PR	Dr.	Cr.	Balance Dr.	Cr.
1/14	GJ1	100		100	

Prepaid Rent   114

Date	PR	Dr.	Cr.	Balance Dr.	Cr.
1/1	GJ1	300		300	
1/31Adj.	GJ2		100	200	

Office Supplies   115

Date	PR	Dr.	Cr.	Balance Dr.	Cr.
1/6	GJ1	40		40	
1/31Adj	GJ2		34	6	

Office Equipment   121

Date	PR	Dr.	Cr.	Balance Dr.	Cr.
1/1	GJ1	100		100	
1/4	GJ1	50		150	

Accumulated Depreciation, Equipment 122

Date	PR	Dr.	Cr.	Balance Dr.	Cr.
1/31Adj.	GJ2		20		20

Accounts Payable   211

Date	PR	Dr.	Cr.	Balance Dr.	Cr.
1/4	GJ1		50		50
1/18	GJ1		70		120

Salaries Payable   212

Date	PR	Dr.	Cr.	Balance Dr.	Cr.
1/31Adj.	GJ2		50		50

Rolo Kern, Capital   311

Date	PR	Dr.	Cr.	Balance Dr.	Cr.
1/1	GJ1		1,300		1,300
1/31Clos.	GJ2		166		1,466
1/31Clos.	GJ2	20			1,446

Rolo Kern, Withdrawals   312

Date	PR	Dr.	Cr.	Balance Dr.	Cr.
1/12	GJ1	20		20	
1/31Clos.	GJ2		20	—	

Income Summary   313

Date	PR	Dr.	Cr.	Balance Dr.	Cr.
1/31Clos.	GJ2		500		500
1/31Clos.	GJ2	334			166
1/31Clos.	GJ2	166		—	

Figure 5-20 General Ledger for Rolo Company

Fees Earned					411
				Balance	
Date	PR	Dr.	Cr.	Dr.	Cr.
1/8	GJ1		400		400
1/14	GJ1		100		500
1/31 Clos.	GJ2	500		———	

Rent Expense					513
				Balance	
Date	PR	Dr.	Cr.	Dr.	Cr.
1/31 Adj.	GJ2	100		100	
1/31 Clos.	GJ2		100	———	

Salaries Expense					511
				Balance	
Date	PR	Dr.	Cr.	Dr.	Cr.
1/16	GJ1	60		60	
1/31 Adj.	GJ2	50		110	
1/31 Clos.	GJ2		110	———	

Office Supplies Expense					514
				Balance	
Date	PR	Dr.	Cr.	Dr.	Cr.
1/31 Adj.	GJ2	34		34	
1/31 Clos.	GJ2		34	———	

Advertising Expense					512
				Balance	
Date	PR	Dr.	Cr.	Dr.	Cr.
1/18	GJ1	70		70	
1/31 Clos.	GJ2		70	———	

Depreciation Expenses Office Equipment 515					
				Balance	
Date	PR	Dr.	Cr.	Dr.	Cr.
1/31 Adj.	GJ2	20		20	
1/31 Clos.	GJ2		20	———	

Figure 5-20 (*continued*)

Closing

Note that Income Summary is a temporary account located in the ledger.

Goals:

1. Wipe out all temporary accounts in the ledger to zero balances.
2. Get a new figure for Capital in the ledger.

Steps in the Closing Process

Step 1: Close revenue to Income Summary.

Step 2: Close individual expenses to Income Summary.

Step 3: Close balance of Income Summary to Capital. (This really is the Net Income figure on the Worksheet.)

Step 4: Close balance of Withdrawals to Capital.

> Where do I get my information for closing?

All the journal closing entries (no new calculations are needed since all figures are on the worksheet) are posted. The result in the ledger is that all temporary accounts have a zero balance (Fig. 5-20).

Solution Tips for the Post-Closing Trial Balance

The post-closing trial balance is a list of the ledger *after* adjusting and closing entries have been completed. Note the figure for Capital, $1,446, is the new figure.

Figure 5-21
Post-Closing Trial Balance
for Rolo Company

These are all permanent accounts.

ROLO CO. POST-CLOSING TRIAL BALANCE JANUARY 31, 200X	Dr.	Cr.
Cash	1 1 8 0 00	
Accounts Receivable	1 0 0 00	
Prepaid Rent	2 0 0 00	
Office Supplies	6 00	
Office Equipment	1 5 0 00	
Accum. Dep., Office Equipment		2 0 00
Accounts Payable		1 2 0 00
Salaries Payable		5 0 00
R. Kern, Capital		1 4 4 6 00
TOTAL	1 6 3 6 00	1 6 3 6 00

Beginning Capital	$1,300
+ Net Income	166
– Withdrawals	20
= Ending Capital	$1,446

Next accounting period we will enter new amounts in the Revenues, Expenses, and Withdrawal accounts. For now, the post-closing trial balance is only made up of permanent accounts.

Summary of Key Points

Learning Unit 5-1

1. After formal financial statements have been prepared, the ledger has still not been brought up-to-date.
2. Information for journalizing adjusting entries comes from the Adjustments section of the worksheet.

Learning Unit 5-2

1. Closing is a mechanical process that aids the accountant in recording transactions for the next period.
2. Assets, Liabilities, and Capital are permanent (real) accounts; their balances are carried over from one accounting period to another. Withdrawals, Revenue, and Expenses are temporary (nominal) accounts; their balances are *not* carried over from one accounting period to another.
3. Income Summary is a temporary account in the general ledger and does not have a normal balance. It will summarize revenue and expenses and transfer the balance to Capital. Withdrawals do not go into Income Summary because they are *not* business expenses.
4. All information for closing can be obtained from the worksheet or ledger.
5. When closing is complete, all temporary accounts in the ledger will have a zero balance, and all this information will be updated in the Capital account.
6. Closing entries are usually done only at year end. Interim reports can be prepared from worksheets that are prepared monthly, quarterly, etc.

Learning Unit 5-3

1. The post-closing trial balance is prepared from the ledger accounts after the adjusting and closing entries have been posted.
2. The accounts on the post-closing trial balance are all permanent titles.

Key Terms

Adjusting journal entries   Journal entries that are needed in order to update specific ledger accounts to reflect correct balances at the end of an accounting period.

Closing journal entries   Journal entries that are prepared to (a) reduce or clear all temporary accounts to a zero balance or (b) update Capital to a new balance.

Income Summary   A temporary account in the ledger that summarizes revenue and expenses and transfers the balance (Net Income or Net Loss) to Capital. Does not have a normal balance.

Permanent accounts (real)   Accounts whose balances are carried over to the next accounting period. Examples: Assets, Liabilities, Capital.

Post-closing trial balance   The final step in the accounting cycle that lists only permanent accounts in the ledger and their balances after adjusting and closing entries have been posted.

Temporary accounts (nominal)   Accounts whose balances at the end of an accounting period are not carried over to the next accounting period. These accounts—Revenue, Expenses, Withdrawals—help summarize a new or ending figure for Capital to begin the next accounting period. Keep in mind that Income Summary is also a temporary account.

Blueprint of Closing Process from the Worksheet

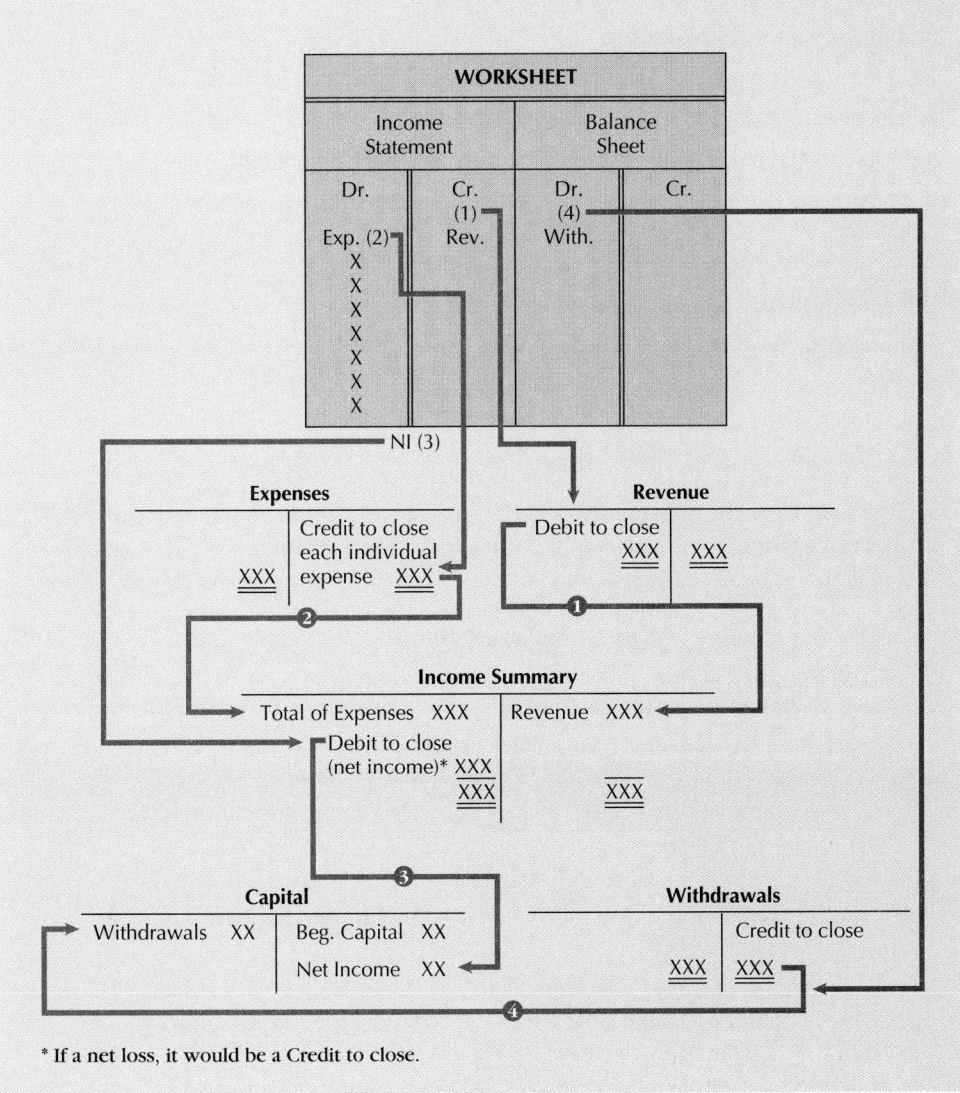

* If a net loss, it would be a Credit to close.

The Closing Steps

1. Close revenue balance to Income Summary.
2. Close each *individual* expense and transfer *total* of all expenses to Income Summary.
3. Transfer balance in Income Summary (Net Income or Net Loss) to Capital.
4. Close Withdrawals to Capital.

Questions, Mini Exercises, Exercises, and Problems

Discussion Questions

1. When a worksheet is completed, what balances are found in the general ledger?
2. Why must adjusting entries be journalized even though the formal statements have already been prepared?
3. "Closing slows down the recording of next year's transactions." Defend or reject this statement with supporting evidence.
4. What is the difference between temporary and permanent accounts?
5. What are the two major goals of the closing process?
6. List the four steps of closing.
7. What is the purpose of Income Summary and where is it located?
8. How can a worksheet aid the closing process?
9. What accounts are usually listed on a post-closing trial balance?
10. Closing entries are always prepared once a month. Agree or disagree. Why?

Mini Exercises

(The blank forms you need are on pages 135–136 of the *Study Guide and Working Papers*.)

Journalizing and Posting Adjusting Entries

1. Post the following adjusting entries (be sure to cross-reference back to the journal) that came from the Adjustment columns of the worksheet:

Ledger Accounts Before Adjusting Entries Posted

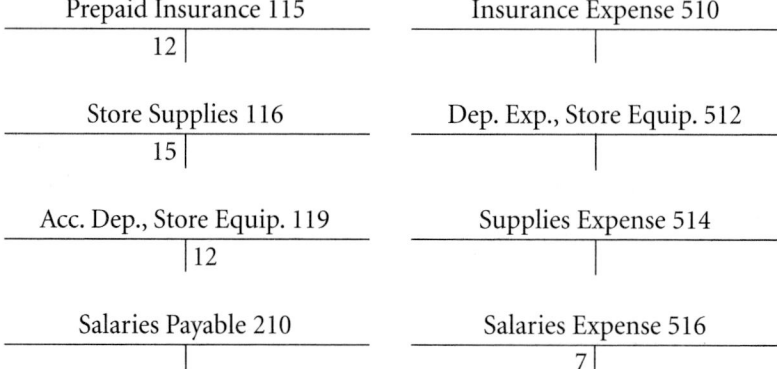

Prepaid Insurance 115	Insurance Expense 510
12	

Store Supplies 116	Dep. Exp., Store Equip. 512
15	

Acc. Dep., Store Equip. 119	Supplies Expense 514
12	

Salaries Payable 210	Salaries Expense 516
	7

General Journal				Page 3	
Date	Account Titles and Description	PR	Dr.	Cr.	
Dec. 31	Insurance Expense		4 00		
	Prepaid Insurance			4 00	
31	Supplies Expense		3 00		
	Store Supplies			3 00	
31	Depr. Exp., Store Equipment		7 00		
	Accum. Depr., Store Equipment			7 00	
31	Salaries Expense		4 00		
	Salaries Payable			4 00	

Figure 5-22
Journalized Adjusting Entries

Steps of Closing and Journalizing Closing Entries

2.

Figure 5-23

```
                Worksheet
        IS                      BS
   Dr.      Cr.           Dr.        Cr.
   (2)      Rev. (1)      Withd.     (4)
   E
   X
   P
   E
   N
   S
   E
   S
   ___      ___

   NI (3)
```

Goals of Closing

1. Temporary accounts in the ledger should have a zero balance.
2. New figure for Capital in closing.

Note   All closing can be done from the worksheet. Income Summary is a temporary account in the ledger.

From the preceding worksheet, Fig. 5-23, explain the four steps of closing. Keep in mind that each *individual* expense normally would be listed in the closing process.

Journalizing Closing Entries

3. From the following accounts, journalize the closing entries (assume December 31).

Mel Blanc, Capital 310	Gas Expense 510
30	5
Mel Blanc, Withdr. 312	Advertising Exp. 512
6	4

Income Summary 314   Dep. Exp., Taxi 516
                                       6 |

Taxi Fees 410
        | 18

Posting to Income Summary

4. Draw a T Account of Income Summary and post to it all entries from Question 3 that affect it. Is Income Summary a temporary or permanent account?

Posting to Capital

5. Draw a T Account for Mel Blanc, Capital, and post to it all entries from Question 3 that affect it. What is the final balance of the Capital account?

Exercises

(The blank forms you need are on pages 137–139 of the *Study Guide and Working Papers*.)

5-1. From the adjustments section of a worksheet presented in Figure 5-24, prepare adjusting journal entries for the end of December.

Figure 5-24
Adjustments on Worksheet

Journalize adjusting entries.

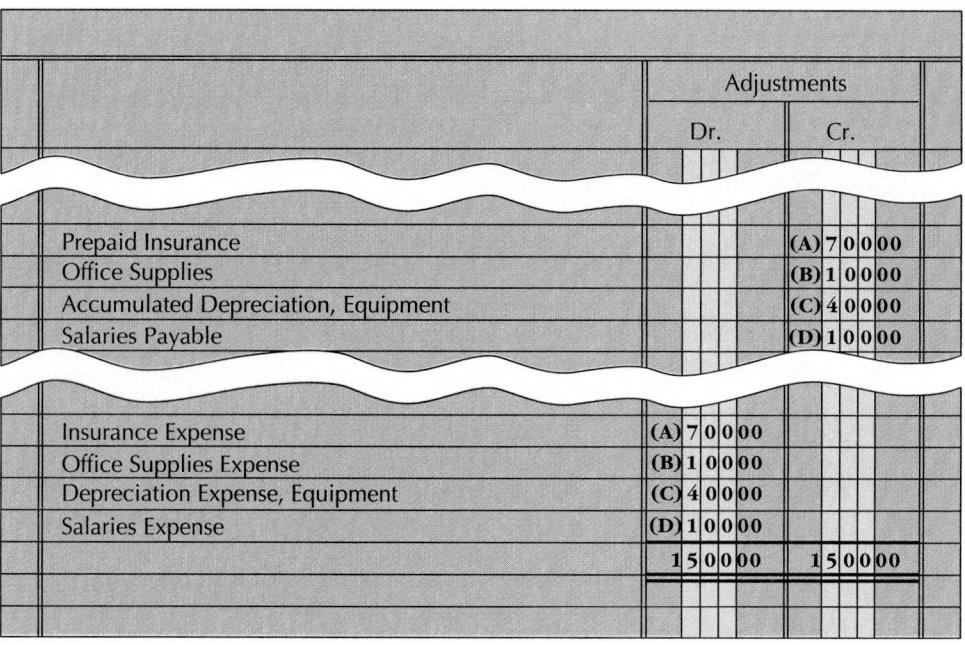

	Adjustments	
	Dr.	Cr.
Prepaid Insurance		(A) 7 0 0 00
Office Supplies		(B) 1 0 0 00
Accumulated Depreciation, Equipment		(C) 4 0 0 00
Salaries Payable		(D) 1 0 0 00
Insurance Expense	(A) 7 0 0 00	
Office Supplies Expense	(B) 1 0 0 00	
Depreciation Expense, Equipment	(C) 4 0 0 00	
Salaries Expense	(D) 1 0 0 00	
	1 5 0 0 00	1 5 0 0 00

5-2. Complete the following table by placing an X in the correct column.

Temporary vs. permanent accounts.

	Temporary	Permanent	Will Be Closed
Ex. Accounts Receivable		X	
1. Income Summary			
2. Melissa Bryant, Capital			
3. Salary Expense			
4. Melissa Bryant, Withdrawals			
5. Fees Earned			
6. Accounts Payable			
7. Cash			

Closing entries.

5-3. From the following T accounts, journalize the four closing entries on December 31, 200X.

J. King, Capital   Rent Expense
        | 14,000   5,000 |

J. King, Withdrawals		Wage Expense	
4,000		7,000	

Income Summary		Insurance Expense	
		1,200	

Fees Earned		Dep. Expense, Office Equipment	
	33,000	900	

Reconstructing closing entries.

5-4. From the following posted T accounts, reconstruct the closing journal entries for December 31, 200X.

M. Foster, Capital		Insurance Expense	
Withdrawals 100	2,000 (Dec. 1)	50	Closing 50
	700 Net income		

M. Foster, Withdrawals		Wage Expense	
	100 Closing 100	100	Closing 100

Income Summary		Rent Expense	
Expenses 600	Revenue 1,300	200	Closing 200
700	Net Income 700		

Salon Fees		Depreciation Expense, Equipment	
Closing 1,300	1,300	250	Closing 250

Post-closing trial balance.

5-5. From the following accounts (not in order), prepare a post-closing trial balance for Wey Co. on December 31, 200X. **Note:** These balances are **before** closing.

Accounts Receivable	$18,875	Salaries Expense	1,275
Legal Supplies	14,250	P. Wey, Capital	63,450
Office Equipment	59,700	P. Wey, Withdrawals	1,500
Repair Expense	2,850	Legal Fees Earned	12,000
		Accounts Payable	45,000
		Cash	22,000

Group A Problems

(The blank forms you need are on pages 140–157 of the *Study Guide and Working Papers.*)

5A-1. Given the data in Figure 5-25 for Lou's Consulting Service:

Figure 5-25
Trial Balance for Lou's Consulting Service

LOU'S CONSULTING SERVICE TRIAL BALANCE JUNE 30, 200X	Dr.	Cr.
Cash	20 00 00	
Accounts Receivable	6 50 00	
Prepaid Insurance	4 00 00	
Supplies	1 50 00	
Equipment	3 00 00	
Accumulated Depreciation, Equipment		1 90 00
Accounts Payable		11 00 00
Lou Dobbs, Capital		12 80 00
Lou Dobbs, Withdrawals	3 00 00	
Consulting Fees Earned		9 00 00
Salaries Expense	1 40 00	
Telephone Expense	1 00 00	
Advertising Expense	6 00 00	
	34 70 00	34 70 00

Review in preparing a worksheet and journalizing adjusting and closing entries.

Check Figure:
Net Income $4,600

Adjustment Data

a. Insurance expired	$300.
b. Supplies on hand	$700.
c. Depreciation on equipment	$100.
d. Salaries earned by employees but not to be paid until July	$200.

Your task is to

1. Prepare a worksheet.
2. Journalize adjusting and closing entries.

Journalizing and posting adjusting and closing entries. Preparing a post-closing trial balance.

5A-2. Enter the beginning balance in each account in your working papers from the Trial Balance columns of the worksheet (Fig. 5-26, p. 195). From the worksheet on page 195, (1) journalize and post adjusting and closing entries after entering the beginning balance in each account in the ledger, and (2) prepare from the ledger a post-closing trial balance for the month of March.

Check Figure:
Post-closing trial
balance $3,504

5A-3. As the bookkeeper of Pete's Plowing, you have been asked to complete the entire accounting cycle for Pete from the following information:

Comprehensive review of the entire accounting cycle, Chapters 1–5.

200X

Jan.	1	Pete invested $7,000 cash and $6,000 worth of snow equipment into the plowing company.
	1	Paid rent for three months in advance for garage space, $2,000.
	4	Purchased office equipment on account from Ling Corp., $7,200.
	6	Purchased snow supplies for $700 cash.
	8	Collected $15,000 from plowing local shopping centers.
	12	Pete Mack withdrew $1,000 from the business for his own personal use.
	20	Plowed North East Co. parking lots, payment not to be received until March, $5,000.
	26	Paid salaries to employees, $1,800.
	28	Paid Ling Corp. one-half amount owed for office equipment.
	29	Advertising bill received from Bush Co. but will not be paid until March, $900.
	30	Paid telephone bill, $210.

Check Figure:
Net income $15,780

Adjustment Data

a. Snow supplies on hand $400.
b. Rent expired $600.
c. Depreciation on office equipment $120. ($7,200 ÷ 5 yr. = $1,440/12 mo. = $120)
d. Depreciation on snow equipment $100. ($6,000 ÷ 5 yr. = $1,200/12 mo. = $100)
e. Accrued salaries $190.

POTTER CLEANING SERVICE
WORKSHEET
FOR MONTH ENDED MARCH 31, 200X

Account Titles	Trial Balance Dr.	Trial Balance Cr.	Adjustments Dr.	Adjustments Cr.	Adjusted Trial Balance Dr.	Adjusted Trial Balance Cr.	Income Statement Dr.	Income Statement Cr.	Balance Sheet Dr.	Balance Sheet Cr.
Cash	40000				40000				40000	
Prepaid Insurance	52000			(A) 18000	34000				34000	
Cleaning Supplies	14400			(B) 10000	4400				4400	
Auto	272000				272000				272000	
Accum. Depr. Auto		86000		(C) 15000		101000				101000
Accounts Payable		22400				22400				22400
B. Potter, Capital		54000				54000				54000
B. Potter, Withdrawals	46000				46000				46000	
Cleaning Fees		468000				468000		468000		
Salaries Expense	144000		(D) 16000		160000		160000			
Telephone Expense	26400				26400		26400			
Advertising Expense	19600				19600		19600			
Gas Expense	16000				16000		16000			
	630400	630400								
Insurance Expense			(A) 18000		18000		18000			
Cleaning Supplies Expense			(B) 10000		10000		10000			
Depr. Expense Auto			(C) 15000		15000		15000			
Salaries Payable				(D) 16000		16000				16000
			59000	59000	661400	661400	265000	468000	396400	193400
Net Income							203000			203000
							468000	468000	396400	396400

Figure 5-26 Worksheet for Potter Cleaning Service

Chart of Accounts	
Assets	**Owner's Equity**
111 Cash	311 Pete Mack, Capital
112 Accounts Receivable	312 Pete Mack, Withdrawals
114 Prepaid Rent	313 Income Summary
115 Snow Supplies	**Revenue**
121 Office Equipment	411 Plowing Fees
122 Accumulated Depreciation, Office Equipment	**Expenses**
123 Snow Equipment	511 Salaries Expense
124 Accumulated Depreciation Snow Equipment	512 Advertising Expense
	513 Telephone Expense
Liabilities	514 Rent Expense
211 Accounts Payable	515 Snow Supplies Expense
212 Salaries Payable	516 Depreciation Expense, Office Equipment
	517 Depreciation Expense, Snow Equipment

Group B Problems

(The blank forms you need are on pages 140–157 of the *Study Guide and Working Papers.*)

5B-1.

Review in preparing a worksheet and journalizing and closing entries.

> **MEMO**
>
> To: Matt Kaminsky
>
> From: Abby Ellen
>
> Re: Accounting Needs
>
> Please prepare ASAP from the following information (attached) (1) a worksheet along with (2) journalized adjusting and closing entries.

Figure 5-27
Trial Balance for Lou's Consulting Service

Check Figure:
Net income $3,530

LOU'S CONSULTING SERVICE
TRIAL BALANCE
JUNE 30, 200X

	Dr.	Cr.
Cash	10 15 0 00	
Accounts Receivable	5 00 0 00	
Prepaid Insurance	7 0 0 00	
Supplies	3 0 0 00	
Equipment	12 95 0 00	
Accumulated Depreciation, Equipment		4 00 0 00
Accounts Payable		5 75 0 00
L. Dobbs, Capital		15 15 0 00
L. Dobbs, Withdrawals	4 00 0 00	
Consulting Fees Earned		5 20 0 00
Salaries Expense	4 50 0 00	
Telephone Expense	7 0 0 00	
Advertising Expense	8 0 0 00	
	30 10 0 00	30 10 0 00

Adjustment Data

a. Insurance expired $100.
b. Supplies on hand $20.
c. Depreciation on equipment $200.
d. Salaries earned by employees but not due to be paid until July $490.

5B-2. Enter the beginning balance in each account in your working papers from the Trial Balance columns of the worksheet (Fig. 5-28, p. 198). From the worksheet on page 198, (1) journalize and post adjusting and closing entries after entering beginning balances in each account in the ledger, and (2) prepare from the ledger a post-closing trial balance at the end of March.

> Journalizing and posting adjusting and closing entries. Preparing a post-closing trial balance.

5B-3. From the following transactions as well as additional data, please complete the entire accounting cycle for Pete's Plowing (use the chart of accounts on page 196).

> Check Figure:
> Post-closing Trial Balance
> $3,294

200X

Jan.

1 To open the business, Pete invested $8,000 cash and $9,600 worth of snow equipment.
1 Paid rent for five months in advance, $3,000.
4 Purchased office equipment on account from Russell Co., $6,000.
6 Bought snow supplies, $350.
8 Collected $7,000 for plowing during winter storm emergency.
12 Pete paid his home telephone bill from the company checkbook, $70.
20 Billed Eastern Freight Co. for plowing fees earned but not to be received until March, $6,500.
24 Advertising bill received from Jones Co. but will not be paid until next month, $350.
26 Paid salaries to employees, $1,800.
28 Paid Russell Co. one-half of amount owed for office equipment.
29 Paid telephone bill of company, $165.

> Comprehensive review of entire accounting cycle. Review of Chapters 1–5.

> Check Figure:
> Net Income $9,610

Adjustment Data

a. Snow supplies on hand $200.
b. Rent expired $600.
c. Depreciation on office equipment $125.
   ($6,000/4 yr = $1,500 ÷ 12 = $125)
d. Depreciation on snow equipment $400.
   ($9,600 ÷ 2 = $4,800 ÷ 12 = $400)
e. Salaries accrued $300.

Real-World Applications

5R-1. Carol Miller needs a loan from the Charles Bank to help finance her business. She has submitted to the Charles Bank the following unadjusted trial balance. As the loan officer, you will be meeting with Carol tomorrow. Could you make some specific written suggestions to Carol regarding her loan report?

POTTER CLEANING SERVICE
WORKSHEET
FOR MONTH ENDED MARCH 31, 200X

Account Titles	Trial Balance Dr.	Trial Balance Cr.	Adjustments Dr.	Adjustments Cr.	Adjusted Trial Balance Dr.	Adjusted Trial Balance Cr.	Income Statement Dr.	Income Statement Cr.	Balance Sheet Dr.	Balance Sheet Cr.
Cash	172400				172400				172400	
Prepaid Insurance	35000			(A)20000	15000				15000	
Cleaning Supplies	80000			(B)60000	20000				20000	
Auto	122000				122000				122000	
Accumulated Depreciation, Auto		66000		(C)15000		81000				81000
Accounts Payable		67400				67400				67400
B. Potter, Capital		248000				248000				248000
B. Potter, Withdrawals	60000				60000				60000	
Cleaning Fees		370000				370000		370000		
Salaries Expense	200000		(D)17500		217500		217500			
Telephone Expense	28400				28400		28400			
Advertising Expense	27600				27600		27600			
Gas Expense	26000				26000		26000			
	751400	751400								
Insurance Expense			(A)20000		20000		20000			
Cleaning Supplies Expense			(B)60000		60000		60000			
Depreciation Expense, Auto			(C)15000		15000		15000			
Salaries Payable				(D)17500		17500				17500
			112500	112500	783900	783900	394500	370000	389400	413900
Net Loss								24500	24500	
							394500	394500	413900	413900

Figure 5-28 Worksheet for Potter Cleaning Service

Cash in Bank	770	
Accounts Receivable	1,480	
Office Supplies	3,310	
Equipment	7,606	
Accounts Payable		684
A. Humphrey, Capital		8,000
Service Fees		17,350
Salaries	11,240	
Utilities Expense	842	
Rent Expense	360	
Insurance Expense	280	
Advertising Expense	146	
Totals	26,034	26,034

5R-2 Janet Smother is the new bookkeeper who replaced Dick Burns, owing to his sudden illness. Janet finds on her desk a note requesting that she close the books and supply the ending Capital figure. Janet is upset, since she can only find the following:

a. Revenue and expense accounts all were zero balance.

b.   <u>   Income Summary   </u>
      14,360 | 19,300

c. Owner withdrew $8,000.

d. Owner beginning Capital was $34,400.

Could you help Janet accomplish her assignment? What written suggestions should Janet make to her supervisor so that this situation will not happen again?

YOU make the call

Critical Thinking/Ethical Case

5R-3. Todd Silver is the purchasing agent for Moore Co. One of his suppliers, Gem Co., offers Todd a free vacation to France if he buys at least 75% of Moore's supplies from Gem Co. Todd, who is angry because Moore Co. has not given him a raise in over a year, is considering the offer. Write your recommendation to Todd.

Internet Exercises: TADOnline; Peachtree; QuickBooks

EX-1. [www.tadonline.com]   At the beginning of your accounting education is a good time to begin formulating your philosophy of how to do accounting work. By studying and learning you are also learning good work habits. The TADOnline Web site presents a section on "Why Outsource Your Accounting." The discussion presents some good suggestions and may also cause you to reflect on how people choose an accounting or bookkeeping firm.

Use that discussion as a springboard and discuss what factors you believe affect a client's choice of someone to help with vital accounting records. TADOnline is not "just around the corner." Is location an important factor in deciding who will do a business's accounting?

EX-2. [www.peachtree.com]; [www.quickbookscom]   Most businesses today are employing some type of computerized accounting system. Some businesses' requirements are simple, and they use only a general ledger program. Others are much more complex and employ inventory modules and payroll modules, in addition to accounts receivable and accounts payable modules for tracking customer and vendor information.

1. Browse the two Web sites in this exercise. Compare and contrast the products by looking at information with these questions in mind:

   a. What kind of output is available?
   b. How are the input systems similar?
   c. Does the program have an inventory module?
   d. At each site are there different products for different complexities in accounting systems?
   e. What online help is available?

2. Set up a visit to a local accounting firm. Ask what programs are used in addition to the two sample programs in this exercise.

Continuing Problem

Eldorado Computer Center

Tony has decided to end the Eldorado Computer Center's first year as of September 30, 200X. Following is an updated chart of accounts.

Assets

1000	Cash
1020	Accounts Receivable
1025	Prepaid Rent
1030	Supplies
1080	Computer Shop Equip.
1081	Accum. Depr. CS Equip.
1090	Office Equipment
1091	Accum. Depr. Office Equip.

Liabilities

2000	Accounts Payable

Owner's Equity

3000	T. Freedman, Capital
3010	T. Freedman, Withdrawals
3020	Income Summary

Revenue

4000	Service Revenue

Expenses

5010	Advertising Expense
5030	Utilities Expense
5050	Supplies Expense
5070	Postage Expense
5090	Depr. Exp. Office Equip.
5020	Rent Expense
5040	Phone Expense
5060	Insurance Expense
5080	Depr. Exp. C.S. Equip.

Note: Accounts 3010 to 5080 are temporary accounts.

Assignment

(See pp. 162–169 in your *Study Guide and Working Papers.*)

1. Journalize the adjusting entries from Chapter 4.
2. Post the adjusting entries to the ledger.
3. Journalize the closing entries.
4. Post the closing entries to the ledger.
5. Prepare a post-closing trial balance.

SUBWAY Case

CLOSING TIME

"You wait and see," Stan told his new sandwich artist Wanda Kurtz, "everything will fall into place soon." Wanda had a tough time serving customers quickly enough, and Stan was in the middle of giving her a pep talk when the phone rang.

"I'll let the machine pick up," Stan reassured Wanda, as he proceeded to train her in some crucial POS touch-screen maneuvers.

"Stan!" an urgent voice came over the message machine, "I think you've forgotten something!" Stan picked up the phone and said, "Lila, can I get back to you tomorrow? I'm in the middle of an important talk with Wanda." One of Stan's strong points as an employer was his ability to focus 100% on his employees' concerns. Yet, Lila simply would not wait.

"Stan," Lila said impatiently, "you absolutely must get me your worksheet by 12 noon tomorrow so I can close your books," she insisted. "Tomorrow's the 31st of March and we close on the last day of the month!"

"*Ay caramba!*" Stan sighed, "Looks like I'm going to be up till the wee hours," he confided to Wanda when he put down the phone.

Although Subway company policy doesn't require a closing every month, closing the books is a key part of their accounting training for all new franchisees. By closing their books, business owners can clearly measure their net profit and loss for each period separate from all other periods. This makes activities like budgeting and comparing performance with similar businesses (or performance over time) possible.

At 9:00 A.M. the next morning, an exhausted Stan opened up the restaurant and e-mailed his worksheet to Lila. He was feeling quite pleased with himself—that is, until he heard Lila's urgent-sounding voice coming over the message machine 10 minutes later.

"I've been over and over this," said Lila after Stan picked up, "and I can't get it to balance. I know it's hard for you to do this during working hours, but I need you to go back over the figures."

Stan opened up Peachtree and pored over his worksheets. Errors are hard to find when closing the books and, unfortunately, there is no set way to detect errors and even no set place to start. Stan chose payroll because it is one of the largest expenses and because of the new hire.

At 11:45 he called Lila, who sounded both exasperated and relieved to hear from him. "I think I've got it! It looks like I messed up on adjusting the Salaries Expense account. I looked at the Payroll Register and compared the total to the Salaries Payable account. It didn't match! When I hired Wanda Kurtz on the 26th, I should have increased both the Salaries Expense and the Salaries Payable lines, because she has accrued wages."

"Yes," said Lila, "Salaries Expense is a debit and Salaries Payable is a credit, and you skipped the payable. Great! With this adjusting entry in the general journal, the worksheet will balance."

Stan's sigh of relief turned into a big yawn, and they both laughed. "I guess I just find it easier to hire people and train them than to account for them," said Stan.

Discussion Questions

1. How would the adjustment be made if Wanda Kurtz received $7.00 per hour and worked 25 additional hours? Where do you place her accrued wages?
2. Stan bought three new Subway aprons and hats for Wanda Smith for $20 each but forgot to post it to the Uniforms account. How much will the closing balance be off? In what way will it be off?
3. Put yourself in Stan's shoes: What is the value of doing a monthly closing, no matter how much—or little—business you do?

VALDEZ REALTY

Reviewing the Accounting Cycle TWICE

This comprehensive review problem requires you to complete the accounting cycle for Valdez Realty twice. This will allow you to review Chapters 1–5 while reinforcing the relationships between all parts of the accounting cycle. By completing two cycles, you will see how the ending June balances in the ledger are used to accumulate data in July. (The blank forms you need are on pages 170–190 of the *Study Guide and Working Papers*.)

Take a moment to review the road map of the accounting cycle on the inside front cover of the text.

First, look at the chart of accounts for Valdez Realty.

On June 1, 200X, Juan Valdez opened a real estate office called Valdez Realty. The following transactions were completed for the month of June:

Valdez Realty
Chart of Accounts

Assets
111 Cash
112 Accounts Receivable
114 Prepaid Rent
115 Office Supplies
121 Office Equipment
122 Accumulated Depreciation, Office Equipment
123 Automobile
124 Accumulated Depreciation, Automobile

Liabilities
211 Accounts Payable
212 Salaries Payable

Owner's Equity
311 Juan Valdez, Capital
312 Juan Valdez, Withdrawals
313 Income Summary

Revenue
411 Commissions Earned

Expenses
511 Rent Expense
512 Salaries Expense
513 Gas Expense
514 Repairs Expense
515 Telephone Expense
516 Advertising Expense
517 Office Supplies Expense
518 Depreciation Expense, Office Equipment
519 Depreciation Expense, Automobile
524 Miscellaneous Expense

200X

June 1 Juan Valdez invested $7,000 cash in the real estate agency along with $3,000 of office equipment.

```
──┤ DEPOSIT TICKET ├──

VALDEZ REALTY (213)478-3584
    8200 SUNSET BOULEVARD
    Los Angeles, CA 90028


DATE _____ June 1 ____ 200X _____

SIGN HERE IN PRESENCE OF TELLER FOR CASH RET'D FROM DEP.

    BAY BANK
    Box 1739 Terminal Annex
    Los Angeles, CA 90052

⑈ 1 2 2000 6 6 ⑈ 1 1 4 0 0 ⑈ 0 3 8 5 7 ⑈ 0 1 3 6 2 ⑈
```

CASH	CURRENCY	7,000	00
	COIN		
LIST CHECKS SINGLY			
TOTAL FROM OTHER SIDE			
TOTAL		7,000	00
LESS CASH RECEIVED			
NET DEPOSIT		7,000	00

16-66/1220

A hold for uncollected funds may be placed on funds deposited by check or similar instruments. This could delay your ability to withdraw such funds. The delay if any would not exceed the period of time permitted by law.

June 1 Rented and paid three months rent in advance to Miller Property Management $2,100.

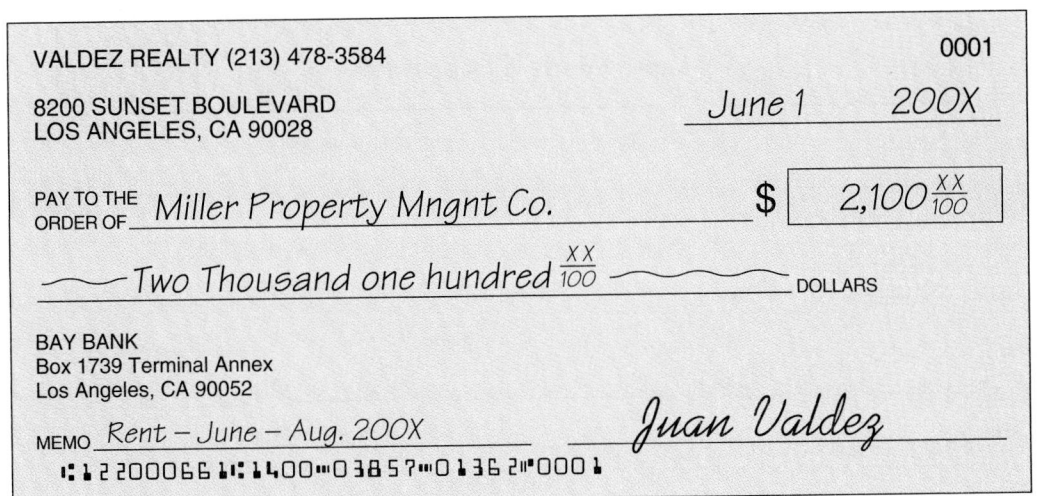

June 1 Bought an automobile on account from Volvo West, $12,000.

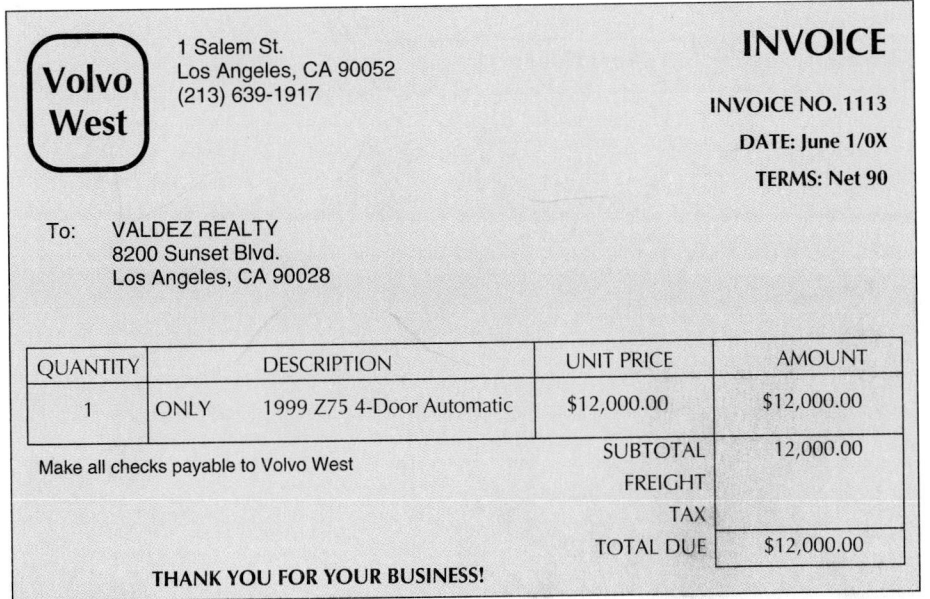

June 4 Purchased office supplies from Office Depot for cash, $300.

Office Depot   **INVOICE**

1 Ferncroft Rd.
Los Angeles, CA 90052
Phone (213) 631-0288

DATE:	June 4/0X
NUMBER:	D198795
TERMS:	Cash

SOLD TO:	SHIPPED TO:
Valdez Realty 8200 Sunset Blvd. Los Angeles, CA 90028	Valdez Realty 8200 Sunset Blvd. Los Angeles, CA 90028

DATE	DESCRIPTION	UNIT PRICE	AMOUNT
Jun 4/0X	Office supplies PAYMENT RECEIVED - - CHK #0002 - THANK YOU		$300.00
		Subtotal	300.00
		Total	$300.00

Business Number: 115555559

THANK YOU FOR YOUR BUSINESS

PLEASE PAY
THE ABOVE

VALDEZ REALTY (213) 478-3584   0002

8200 SUNSET BOULEVARD
LOS ANGELES, CA 90028   *June 4*   *200X*

PAY TO THE
ORDER OF *Office Depot* $ *300 $\frac{XX}{100}$*

Three Hundred and $\frac{XX}{100}$ DOLLARS

BAY BANK
Box 1739 Terminal Annex
Los Angeles, CA 90052

MEMO *Office supplies*   *Juan Valdez*

⑆ 1 2 2 0 0 0 6 6 ⑈ 1 4 0 0 ⑉ 0 3 8 5 7 ⑈ 0 1 3 6 2 ⑉ 0 0 0 2

June 5 Purchased additional office supplies from Office Depot on account, $150.

Office Depot

INVOICE

1 Ferncroft Rd.
Los Angeles, CA 90052
Phone (213) 631-0288

DATE: June 5/0X
NUMBER: D198825
TERMS: net 60

SOLD TO:	SHIPPED TO:
Valdez Realty 8200 Sunset Blvd. Los Angeles, CA 90028	Valdez Realty 8200 Sunset Blvd. Los Angeles, CA 90028

DATE	DESCRIPTION	UNIT PRICE	AMOUNT
Jun 5/0X	Office supplies		$150.00
		Subtotal	150.00
		Total	$150.00

Business Number: 115555559

THANK YOU FOR YOUR BUSINESS

PLEASE PAY
THE ABOVE

June 6 Sold a house to Bill Barnes and collected a $6,000 commission.

—| DEPOSIT TICKET |—

VALDEZ REALTY (213)478-3584
8200 SUNSET BOULEVARD
Los Angeles, CA 90028

DATE ____ June 6 ____ 200X ____

SIGN HERE IN PRESENCE OF TELLER FOR CASH RET'D FROM DEP.

BAY BANK
Box 1739 Terminal Annex
Los Angeles, CA 90052

CASH	CURRENCY		
	COIN		
LIST CHECKS SINGLY 250-99		6,000	00
TOTAL FROM OTHER SIDE			
TOTAL			
LESS CASH RECEIVED			
NET DEPOSIT		6,000	00

16-66/1220

A hold for uncollected funds may be placed on funds deposited by check or similar instruments. This could delay your ability to withdraw such funds. The delay if any would not exceed the period of time permitted by law.

⑆122000661⑆1400 03857 0136 2⑈

VALDEZ REALTY				
COMMISSION REPORT			**Date:**	June 6, 200X
Name:	Bill Barnes			
Date:	**Sales Description**	**Sales No.**	**Commission Amount**	
Jun 6/0X	Home at 66 Sullivan St.	A1001	$6,000.00	Paid in full.
C001		**Remarks:**		

June   8   Paid gas bill to Petro Petroleum, $22.

VALDEZ REALTY (213) 478-3584   0003

8200 SUNSET BOULEVARD
LOS ANGELES, CA 90028   *June 8*   *200X*

PAY TO THE
ORDER OF *Petro Petroleum* $ $22\frac{XX}{100}$

Twenty-two and $\frac{XX}{100}$ DOLLARS

BAY BANK
Box 1739 Terminal Annex
Los Angeles, CA 90052

MEMO *Gas Bill – June 6*   *Juan Valdez*

⑆12200066⑆ ⑆1400⑈03857⑈0136 2⑈0003

June   15   Paid Betty Long, office secretary, $350.

VALDEZ REALTY (213) 478-3584   0004

8200 SUNSET BOULEVARD
LOS ANGELES, CA 90028   *June 15*   *200X*

PAY TO THE
ORDER OF *Betty Long* $ $350\frac{XX}{100}$

Three Hundred fifty and $\frac{XX}{100}$ DOLLARS

BAY BANK
Box 1739 Terminal Annex
Los Angeles, CA 90052

MEMO *Salary – June 1–15*   *Juan Valdez*

⑆12200066⑆ ⑆1400⑈03857⑈0136 2⑈0004

June   17   Sold a building lot to West Land Developers and earned a commission, $6,500 payment to be received on July 8.

VALDEZ REALTY COMMISSION REPORT			Date: June 17, 200X	
Name: West Land Developers				
Date:	**Sales Description**	**Sales No.**	**Commission Amount**	
Jun 17/0X	Lot at 8 Ridge Rd.	A1002	$6,500.00	
C002		**Remarks:** Payment due July 8, 200X		

June 20   Juan Valdez withdrew $1,000 from the business to pay personal expenses.

```
VALDEZ REALTY (213) 478-3584                                    0005

8200 SUNSET BOULEVARD                          June 20      200X
LOS ANGELES, CA 90028


PAY TO THE    Juan Valdez                            $    1,000 XX/100
ORDER OF

One Thousand and XX/100                                      DOLLARS

BAY BANK
Box 1739 Terminal Annex
Los Angeles, CA 90052

MEMO  Withdrawal                              Juan Valdez

   122000661: 1400 03857 0136 2 0005
```

June 21   Sold a house to Ms. Laura Harrison and collected a $3,500 commission.

```
                DEPOSIT TICKET

                                          |        | CURRENCY |        |      |
     VALDEZ REALTY (213)478-3584          | CASH   |----------|        |      |
        8200 SUNSET BOULEVARD             |        |  COIN    |        |      |
        Los Angeles, CA 90028             | LIST CHECKS SINGLY| 3,500 | 00   |
                                          |     270-88       |        |      |
                                                                              16-66/1220
                                          |                  |        |      |
                                          | TOTAL FROM       |        |      |   A hold for uncollected
     DATE    June 21      200X            | OTHER SIDE       |        |      |   funds may be placed on
                                          |   TOTAL          |        |      |   funds deposited by
                                          |                  |        |      |   check or similar instru-
   SIGN HERE IN PRESENCE OF TELLER FOR    | LESS CASH RECEIVED|       |      |   ments. This could delay
   CASH RET'D FROM DEP.                   |                  |        |      |   your ability to withdraw
                                          | NET DEPOSIT      | 3,500 | 00   |   such funds. The delay if
        BAY BANK                                                              any would not exceed
        Box 1739 Terminal Annex                                              the period of time
        Los Angeles, CA 90052                                                permitted by law.

   122000661: 1400 03857 0136 2
```

VALDEZ REALTY				
COMMISSION REPORT			**Date:**	June 21, 200X
Name:	Ms. Laura Harrison			
Date:	**Sales Description**	**Sales No.**	**Commission Amount**	
Jun 21/0X	Home at 666 Jersey St.	A1003	$3,500.00	Paid in full.
C003			**Remarks:**	

June 22   Paid gas bill, $25, to Petro Petroleum.

VALDEZ REALTY (213) 478-3584   0006

8200 SUNSET BOULEVARD
LOS ANGELES, CA 90028   *June 22   200X*

PAY TO THE
ORDER OF *Petro Petroleum* $ 25 $\frac{XX}{100}$

Twenty-five and $\frac{XX}{100}$ —————————————————————— DOLLARS

BAY BANK
Box 1739 Terminal Annex
Los Angeles, CA 90052

MEMO *Gas Bill–June 22*   *Juan Valdez*

⑈⑆122000⑈66 1⑈: 1400⑈03857⑈0136 2⑈0006

June 24   Paid Volvo West $600 to repair automobile.

Volvo West	1 Salem St. Los Angeles, CA 90052 (213) 639-1917	**INVOICE**

INVOICE NO. 1184

DATE: June 24/0X

TERMS: Cash

To: VALDEZ REALTY   Ship To:
       8200 Sunset Blvd.
       Los Angeles, CA 90028   Pickup

QUANTITY	DESCRIPTION	UNIT PRICE	AMOUNT
1	ONLY Z75 Air conditioning repair		$ 600.00

Make all checks payable to Volvo West

PAYMENT RECEIVED - Check #0007

SUBTOTAL	600.00
FREIGHT	
TAX	
TOTAL DUE	$ 600.00

THANK YOU FOR YOUR BUSINESS!

VALDEZ REALTY (213) 478-3584   0007

8200 SUNSET BOULEVARD
LOS ANGELES, CA 90028   *June 24   200X*

PAY TO THE
ORDER OF *Volvo West* $ 600 $\frac{XX}{100}$

Six Hundred and $\frac{XX}{100}$ —————————————————————— DOLLARS

BAY BANK
Box 1739 Terminal Annex
Los Angeles, CA 90052

MEMO *Auto Repairs – Inv. 1184*   *Juan Valdez*

⑈⑆122000⑈66 1⑈: 1400⑈03857⑈0136 2⑈000 7

June 30   Paid Betty Long, office secretary, $350.

VALDEZ REALTY (213) 478-3584   0008

8200 SUNSET BOULEVARD
LOS ANGELES, CA 90028   June 30   200X

PAY TO THE   Betty Long $ 350 XX/100
ORDER OF

Three Hundred fifty and XX/100 ⸻⸻⸻ DOLLARS

BAY BANK
Box 1739 Terminal Annex
Los Angeles, CA 90052

MEMO Salary – June 16–30   Juan Valdez

⑈12 200066 1⑈ 1400 ⑈ 0 3857 ⑈ 0 136 2 ⑈ 0008

June 30   Paid Verizon June telephone bill, $510.

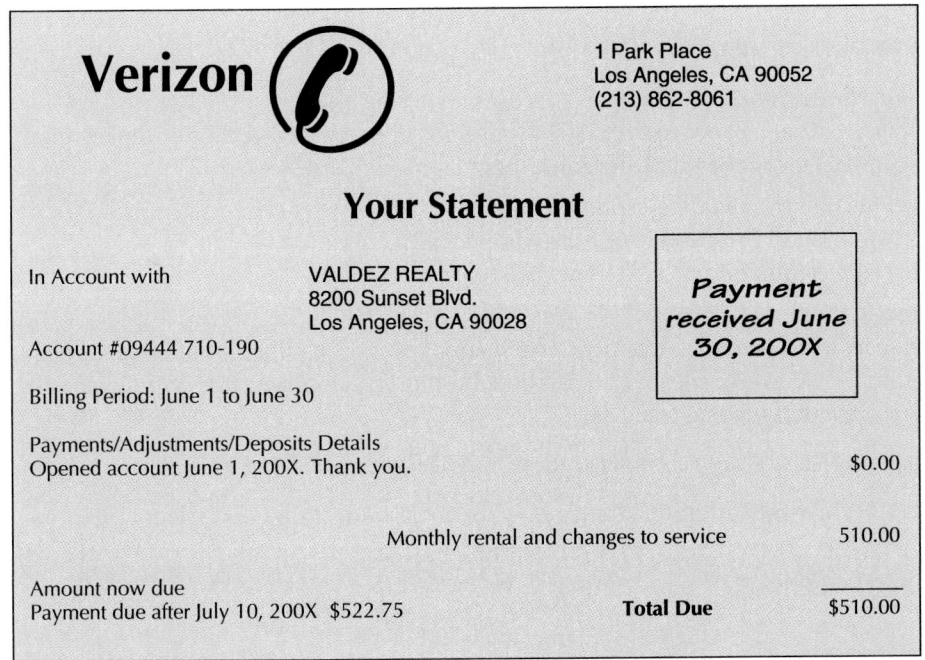

Verizon   1 Park Place
                                            Los Angeles, CA 90052
                                            (213) 862-8061

Your Statement

In Account with   VALDEZ REALTY
                         8200 Sunset Blvd.   *Payment*
                         Los Angeles, CA 90028   *received June*
Account #09444 710-190   *30, 200X*

Billing Period: June 1 to June 30

Payments/Adjustments/Deposits Details
Opened account June 1, 200X. Thank you. $0.00

                    Monthly rental and changes to service   510.00
                                                              ⸻
Amount now due
Payment due after July 10, 200X $522.75   **Total Due** $510.00

VALDEZ REALTY (213) 478-3584   0009

8200 SUNSET BOULEVARD
LOS ANGELES, CA 90028   June 30   200X

PAY TO THE   Verizon $ 510 XX/100
ORDER OF

Five Hundred Ten and XX/100 ⸻⸻⸻ DOLLARS

BAY BANK
Box 1739 Terminal Annex
Los Angeles, CA 90052

MEMO June Phone Bill   Juan Valdez

⑈12 200066 1⑈ 1400 ⑈ 0 3857 ⑈ 0 136 2 ⑈ 0009

June 30   Received advertising bill for June, $1,200, from *Salem News*. The bill is to be paid on July 2.

Salem News
1 Main St., Los Angeles, CA 90052
(213) 744-1000
I N V O I C E

SOLD TO:	Valdez Realty			
	8200 Sunset Blvd.	Invoice No.:	4879	
	Los Angeles, CA 90028	Date:	June 30, 200X	
		Due Date:	July 2, 200X	

DATE	DESCRIPTION		AMOUNT
June 26/0X	Advertising in Salem News during June 200X		$1,200.00
		SUBTOTAL	1,200.00
Business Number 944122338		TOTAL	$1,200.00

MAKE ALL CHECKS PAYABLE TO SALEM NEWS

Required Work for June

1. Journalize transactions and post to ledger accounts.
2. Prepare a trial balance in the first two columns of the worksheet and complete the worksheet using the following adjustment data:

   a. One month's rent had expired.
   b. An inventory shows $50 of office supplies remaining.
   c. Depreciation on office equipment, $100.
   d. Depreciation on automobile, $200.

3. Prepare a June income statement, statement of owner's equity, and balance sheet.
4. From the worksheet, journalize and post adjusting and closing entries (p. 3 of journal).
5. Prepare a post-closing trial balance.

During July, Valdez Realty completed these transactions:

July 1   Purchased additional office supplies on account from Office Depot, $700.

Office Depot   INVOICE

1 Ferncroft Rd.
Los Angeles, CA 90052   **DATE:** Jul 1/0X
Phone (213) 631-0288   **NUMBER:** D1996035
                               TERMS: Net 60

SOLD TO:	SHIPPED TO:
Valdez Realty	Valdez Realty
8200 Sunset Blvd.	8200 Sunset Blvd.
Los Angeles, CA 90028	Los Angeles, CA 90028

DATE	DESCRIPTION	UNIT PRICE	AMOUNT
Jul 2/0X	Office supplies		$700.00
		Subtotal	700.00
		Total	$700.00

Business Number: 115555559

THANK YOU FOR YOUR BUSINESS

PLEASE PAY THE ABOVE

July   2   Paid *Salem News* advertising bill for June.

VALDEZ REALTY (213) 478-3584		0010
8200 SUNSET BOULEVARD LOS ANGELES, CA 90028		*July 2 200X*

PAY TO THE ORDER OF *Salem News* $ *1,200 XX/100*

One Thousand Two Hundred and XX/100 ———————— DOLLARS

BAY BANK
Box 1739 Terminal Annex
Los Angeles, CA 90052

MEMO *Invoice # 4879*   *Juan Valdez*

⑈⑈12200066⑈⑈:1400⑈03857⑈0136 2⑈00 10

July   3   Sold a house to Melissa King and collected a commission of $6,600.

VALDEZ REALTY COMMISSION REPORT				*Date:*	July 3, 200X
Name:	Melissa King				
Date:	**Sales Description**	**Sales No.**	**Commission Amount**		
July 3/0X	Home at 800 Rose Ave.	A1004	$6,600.00	Paid in full.	
C004		**Remarks:**			

DEPOSIT TICKET

VALDEZ REALTY (213)478-3584
8200 SUNSET BOULEVARD
Los Angeles, CA 90028

DATE   *July 3   200X*

SIGN HERE IN PRESENCE OF TELLER FOR CASH RET'D FROM DEP.

BAY BANK
Box 1739 Terminal Annex
Los Angeles, CA 90052

⑈12200066⑈⑈:1400⑈03857⑈0136 2⑈

CASH	CURRENCY		
	COIN		
LIST CHECKS SINGLY 278-92		6,600	00
TOTAL FROM OTHER SIDE			
TOTAL			
LESS CASH RECEIVED			
NET DEPOSIT		6,600	00

16-66/1220

A hold for uncollected funds may be placed on funds deposited by check or similar instruments. This could delay your ability to withdraw such funds. The delay if any would not exceed the period of time permitted by law.

July   6   Paid gas bill to Petro Petroleum, $29.

VALDEZ REALTY (213) 478-3584   0011

8200 SUNSET BOULEVARD
LOS ANGELES, CA 90028   *July 6   200X*

PAY TO THE   *Petro Petroleum* $ 29 XX/100
ORDER OF

Twenty-nine and XX/100 ———————————————————— DOLLARS

BAY BANK
Box 1739 Terminal Annex
Los Angeles, CA 90052

MEMO *Gas Bill – July 6*   *Juan Valdez*

⑆122000661⑈1400⑈03857⑈01362⑈0011

July   8   Collected commission from West Land Developers for sale of building lot on June 17.

—| DEPOSIT TICKET |—

VALDEZ REALTY (213)478-3584
8200 SUNSET BOULEVARD
Los Angeles, CA 90028

CASH	CURRENCY		
	COIN		
LIST CHECKS SINGLY 228-114		6,500	00
TOTAL FROM OTHER SIDE			
TOTAL			
LESS CASH RECEIVED			
NET DEPOSIT		6,500	00

16-66/1220

A hold for uncollected funds may be placed on funds deposited by check or similar instruments. This could delay your ability to withdraw such funds. The delay if any would not exceed the period of time permitted by law.

DATE   *July 8   200X*

SIGN HERE IN PRESENCE OF TELLER FOR CASH RET'D FROM DEP. ⟶

BAY BANK
Box 1739 Terminal Annex
Los Angeles, CA 90052

⑆122000661⑈1400⑈03857⑈01362⑈

July   12   Paid $300 to Regan Realtors Assoc. to send employees to realtors' workshop.

VALDEZ REALTY (213) 478-3584   0012

8200 SUNSET BOULEVARD
LOS ANGELES, CA 90028   *July 12   200X*

PAY TO THE   *Regan Realtors Assoc.* $ 300 XX/100
ORDER OF

Three Hundred and XX/100 ——————————————————— DOLLARS

BAY BANK
Box 1739 Terminal Annex
Los Angeles, CA 90052

MEMO *Workshop Registration*   *Juan Valdez*

⑆122000661⑈1400⑈03857⑈01362⑈0012

July   15   Paid Betty Long, office secretary, $350.

```
VALDEZ REALTY (213) 478-3584                                      0013

8200 SUNSET BOULEVARD                       July 15      200X
LOS ANGELES, CA 90028


PAY TO THE   Betty Long                              $        350 XX/100
ORDER OF _____

Three Hundred fifty and XX/100 ~~~~~~~~~~~~~~~~~ DOLLARS

BAY BANK
Box 1739 Terminal Annex
Los Angeles, CA 90052
MEMO  Salary July 1–15                        Juan Valdez

⑆12200066⑆ 1400⑈03857⑈0136 2⑈0013
```

July   17   Sold a house to Matt Karminsky and earned a commission of $2,400.
Commission to be received on August 10.

VALDEZ REALTY COMMISSION REPORT			**Date:**	July 17, 200X
Name:	Matt Karminsky			
Date:	**Sales Description**	**Sales No.**	**Commission Amount**	
July 17/0X	Home at RR2, Site 3	A1010	$2,400.00	
C005		**Remarks:** Payment due August 10, 200X		

July   18   Sold a building lot to DiBiasi Builders and collected a commission of $7,000.

```
┤ DEPOSIT TICKET ├

VALDEZ REALTY (213)478-3584
   8200 SUNSET BOULEVARD
   Los Angeles, CA 90028
```

CASH	CURRENCY		
	COIN		
LIST CHECKS SINGLY 269-10		7,000	00
TOTAL FROM OTHER SIDE			
TOTAL			
LESS CASH RECEIVED			
NET DEPOSIT		7,000	00

```
DATE ____ July 18      200X

SIGN HERE IN PRESENCE OF TELLER FOR CASH RET'D FROM DEP.

   BAY BANK
   Box 1739 Terminal Annex
   Los Angeles, CA 90052

⑆12200066⑆ 1400⑈03857⑈0136 2⑈
```

16-66/1220

A hold for uncollected funds may be placed on funds deposited by check or similar instruments. This could delay your ability to withdraw such funds. The delay if any would not exceed the period of time permitted by law.

VALDEZ REALTY					
	COMMISSION REPORT			*Date:*	July 18, 200X
Name:	DiBiasi Builders				
Date:	*Sales Description*		*Sales No.*	*Commission Amount*	
July 18/0X	Building lot at 5004 King St. E		A1005	$7,000.00	Paid in full.
C006			*Remarks:*		

July 22 Sent a check to Catholic Charities for $40 to help sponsor a local road race to aid the poor. (This is not to be considered an advertising expense, but it is a business expense.)

VALDEZ REALTY (213) 478-3584	0014
8200 SUNSET BOULEVARD LOS ANGELES, CA 90028	*July 22 200X*

PAY TO THE ORDER OF _Catholic Charities_ $ 40 $\frac{XX}{100}$

Forty and $\frac{XX}{100}$ ———————————————————— DOLLARS

BAY BANK
Box 1739 Terminal Annex
Los Angeles, CA 90052

MEMO _Aid to Poor_   *Juan Valdez*

⑆ 1 2 2000 66 ⑆ 1400 ⑈ 0 38 5 7 ⑈ 0 136 2 ⑈ 00 14

July 24 Paid Volvo West $590 for repairs to automobile.

Volvo West
1 Salem St.
Los Angeles, CA 90052
(213) 639-1917

INVOICE

INVOICE NO. 2119
DATE: July 24/0X
TERMS: Cash

To: VALDEZ REALTY
8200 Sunset Blvd.
Los Angeles, CA 90028

QUANTITY	DESCRIPTION	UNIT PRICE	AMOUNT
	75,000 maintenance		$ 590.00
Make all checks payable to Volvo West		SUBTOTAL	590.00
		FREIGHT	
PAYMENT RECEIVED - Check #0015		TAX	
		TOTAL DUE	$ 590.00

THANK YOU FOR YOUR BUSINESS!

VALDEZ REALTY (213) 478-3584   0015

8200 SUNSET BOULEVARD   _July 24   200X_
LOS ANGELES, CA 90028

PAY TO THE   _Volvo West_ $ | _590 XX/100_ |
ORDER OF

Five Hundred Ninety and XX/100 ———————— DOLLARS

BAY BANK
Box 1739 Terminal Annex
Los Angeles, CA 90052

MEMO _Auto Repairs – Inv. 2119_   _Juan Valdez_

⑆12200066⑆ 1400‴03857‴0136 2‴0015

July   28   Juan Valdez withdrew $1,800 from the business to pay personal expenses.

VALDEZ REALTY (213) 478-3584   0016

8200 SUNSET BOULEVARD   _July 28   200X_
LOS ANGELES, CA 90028

PAY TO THE   _Juan Valdez_ $ | _1,800 XX/100_ |
ORDER OF

One Thousand Eight hundred and XX/100 ———— DOLLARS

BAY BANK
Box 1739 Terminal Annex
Los Angeles, CA 90052

MEMO _Withdrawal_   _Juan Valdez_

⑆12200066⑆ 1400‴03857‴0136 2‴0016

July   30   Paid Betty Long, office secretary, $350.

VALDEZ REALTY (213) 478-3584   0017

8200 SUNSET BOULEVARD   _July 30   200X_
LOS ANGELES, CA 90028

PAY TO THE   _Betty Long_ $ | _350 XX/100_ |
ORDER OF

Three Hundred fifty and XX/100 ———————— DOLLARS

BAY BANK
Box 1739 Terminal Annex
Los Angeles, CA 90052

MEMO _Salary – July 16–31_   _Juan Valdez_

⑆12200066⑆ 1400‴03857‴0136 2‴0017

July   30   Paid Verizon telephone bill, $590.

Your Statement

In Account with   VALDEZ REALTY
                       8200 Sunset Blvd.
                       Los Angeles, CA 90028

Account #09444 710-190

Billing Period: July 1 to July 31

Payments/Adjustments/Deposits Details
Payment Received July 2. Thank you.

	$590.00
	−590.00
Monthly rental and changes to service	590.00

Payment received July 30, 200X

Amount now due
Payment due after August 10, 200X $610.75   **Total Due** $590.00

VALDEZ REALTY (213) 478-3584   0018

8200 SUNSET BOULEVARD
LOS ANGELES, CA 90028   *July 30   200X*

PAY TO THE
ORDER OF   *Verizon* $ 590 XX/100

Five Hundred Ninety and XX/100 _____ DOLLARS

BAY BANK
Box 1739 Terminal Annex
Los Angeles, CA 90052

MEMO *July Phone Bill*   *Juan Valdez*

⑈ 1 2 2 0 0 0 6 6 ⑈ 1 4 0 0 ⑈ 0 3 8 5 7 ⑈ 0 1 3 6 2 ⑈ 0 0 1 8

July   30   Advertising bill from *Salem News* for July, $1,400. The bill is to be paid on August 2.

Salem News
1 Main St., Los Angeles, CA 90052
(213) 744-1000

I N V O I C E

SOLD TO: Valdez Realty   Invoice No.:   5400
            8200 Sunset Blvd.   Date: July 30, 200X
            Los Angeles, CA 90028   Due Date: August 2, 200X

DATE	DESCRIPTION		AMOUNT
July 30/0X	Advertising in Salem News during July 200X		$1,400.00
		SUBTOTAL	1,400.00
Business Number 944122338		TOTAL	$1,400.00
MAKE ALL CHECKS PAYABLE TO SALEM NEWS			

Required Work for July

1. Journalize transactions in a general journal (p. 4) and post to ledger accounts.
2. Prepare a trial balance in the first two columns of the worksheet and complete the worksheet using the following adjustment data:

   a. One month's rent had expired.
   b. An inventory shows $90 of office supplies remaining.
   c. Depreciation on office equipment, $100.
   d. Depreciation on automobile, $200.

3. Prepare a July income statement, statement of owner's equity, and balance sheet.
4. From the worksheet, journalize and post adjusting and closing entries (p. 6 of journal).
5. Prepare a post-closing trial balance.

COMPUTERIZED ACCOUNTING APPLICATION FOR VALDEZ REALTY MINI PRACTICE SET (CHAPTER 5)

Closing Process and Post-Closing Trial Balance

Before starting on this assignment, read and complete the tasks discussed in Parts A, B, and F of the Computerized Accounting appendix at the back of this book and complete the Computerized Accounting Application assignments for Chapters 3 and 4.

This comprehensive review problem requires you to complete the accounting cycle for Valdez Realty twice. This will allow you to review Chapters 1–5 while reinforcing the relationships between all parts of the accounting cycle. By completing two cycles, you will see how the ending June balances in the ledger are used when we accumulate data in July.

PART A: THE JUNE ACCOUNTING CYCLE

On June 1, 2004 Juan Valdez opened a real estate office called Valdez Realty.

Open the Company Data Files

1. Click on the Start button. Point to Programs; point to the Peachtree folder and select Peachtree Complete Accounting. Your desktop may have the Peachtree icon allowing for a quicker entrance into the program.
2. Follow the "Open a File" instructions in Part A of the Computerized Accounting appendix at the back of this book to open **Valdez Realty.**
3. Click on the **Maintain** menu option. Then select **Company Information.** The program will respond by bringing up a dialogue box allowing the user to edit/add information about the company.

How to Add Your Name to the Company Name

4. Click in the **Company Name** entry field at the end of **Valdez Realty.** If it is already highlighted, press the right arrow key. Add a dash and your name "-**Student Name**" to the end of the company name. Click on the **OK** button to return to the Menu Window.

Record June Transactions

5. Record the following journal entries. Enter the **Date** listed for each transaction (you may use the "+" key to advance the date or use the calendar icon next to the field to select the date from a calendar). Enter "Memo" into the **Source** text box for each transaction or accept Peachtree's additional number added to memo by pressing TAB:

2004

Jun.	1	Juan Valdez invested $7,000 cash in the real estate agency along with $3,000 in office equipment.
	1	Rented office space and paid three months' rent in advance, $2,100.
	1	Bought an automobile on account, $12,000.
	4	Purchased office supplies for cash, $300.
	5	Purchased office supplies on account, $150.
	6	Sold a house and collected a $6,000 commission.
	8	Received and paid gas bill, $22.
	15	Paid the salary of the office secretary, $350.
	17	Sold a building lot and earned a commission, $6,500. Expected receipt 7/8/04.
	20	Juan Valdez withdrew $1,000 from the business to pay personal expenses.
	21	Sold a house and collected a $3,500 commission.
	22	Received and paid gas bill, $25.
	24	Paid $600 to repair automobile.
	30	Paid the salary of the office secretary, $350.

    30   Received and paid the June telephone bill, $510.

    30   Received advertising bill for June, $1,200. The bill is to be paid on 7/2/04.

6. After you have saved the journal entries, close the General Journal; then print the following reports:

> *Print Working Reports*

  a. General Journal (check figure debit = $44,607)

  b. Trial Balance (check figure debit = $39,350)

Review your printed reports. If you have made an error in a saved journal entry, correct the error before proceeding.

7. Open the General Journal; then record adjusting journal entries based on the following adjustment data using "Adjusting" in the reference field:

> *Record June Adjusting Entries*

  a. One month's rent has expired

  b. An inventory shows $50 of office supplies remaining.

  c. Depreciation on office equipment, $100

  d. Depreciation on automobile, $200

8. After you have saved the adjusting journal entries, close the General Journal then print the following reports accepting all defaults offered by Peachtree:

> *Print Final Statements*

  a. General Journal (check figure debit = $46,007)

  b. Trial Balance (check figure debit = $39,650)

  c. General Ledger Report (check figure cash = $11,243)

  d. Income Statement (Net Income = $11,543)

  e. Balance Sheet (Total Capital = $20,543)

Review your printed reports. If you have made an error in a saved journal entry, use the procedures detailed in step 18 from Chapter 3 to make any necessary corrections. Reprint all reports if corrections are made.

9. Computerized Accounting systems maintain all of it's input in compartments called periods. Some systems identify these periods with the name of the month or with a simple numeric designation such as 1, 2, 3, et al. Peachtree currently has Valdez Realty in Period 6, the June period. You can see this in the status bar at the bottom of the screen. This is because Valdez has elected to use the calendar year for his Fiscal year. We will need to change the current period to the July period prior to inputting the July transactions in part B of this workshop. You must always tell Peachtree to move to the next accounting period when starting on the transactions for a new month. This process is the equivalent of "Closing" in a manual accounting system although the temporary accounts are not really closed until the end of the year.

> *Closing the Accounting Records*

10. It is always wise to backup accounting data at the end of each month, saving it into a file that will be saved until the end of the year. We will use Peachtree's Backup feature to do this. Click on the Company Window **File** menu; select **Backup,** use a filename such as "ValdezJune" to make sure you can recognize what the backup represents. Click on **OK.**

> *Make a Backup Copy of June Accounting Records*

11. We must now advance the period to prepare Peachtree for the July transactions.

> *Advancing the Period*

  ● Using your mouse, click on **System** from the **Tasks** menu. Select **Change Accounting Periods.** You are presented with the screen on p. 220.

  ● Using the menu, select period 7 - Jul 1, 2004 to Jul 31, 2004 and click on **OK.**

  ● You will be asked whether you wish to print reports before continuing. Since we have already printed our reports, we can answer "No".

  ● Note that the status bar at the bottom of the screen now reflects that you are in period 7.

Period 7 - 7/1/04 to 7/31/04

12. Click on the Company Window **File** menu; then click on Exit to end the current work session and return to your Windows desktop or continue with step 3 below.

> *Exit the Program*

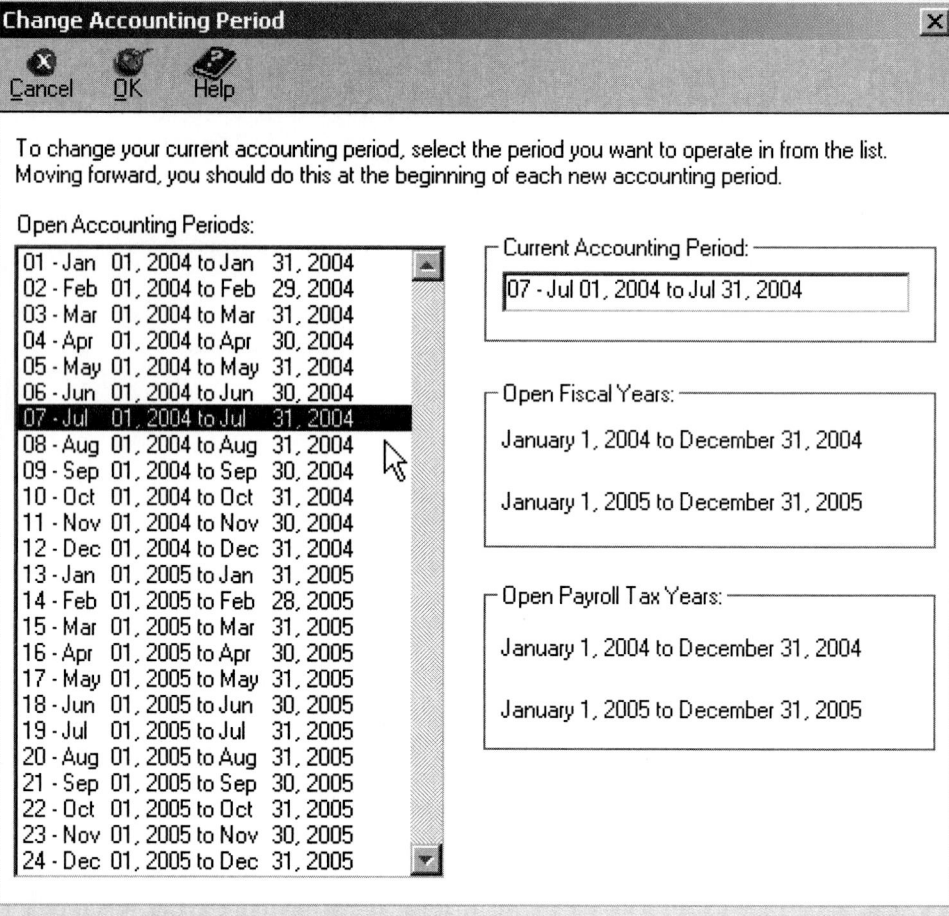

PART B: THE JULY ACCOUNTING CYCLE

1. Start Peachtree Complete Accounting.
2. Open **Valdez Realty.**

Open the Company Data Files

3. Record the following journal entries. Enter the **Date** listed for each transaction (you may use the "+" key to advance the date or use the calendar icon next to the field to select the date from a calendar). Enter "Memo" into the **Source** text box for each transaction or accept Peachtree's additional number added to memo by pressing TAB:

Record July Transactions

2004

Jul.

1   Purchased additional office supplies on account, $700.

2   Paid advertising bill for June, $1,200.

3   Sold a house and collected a commission, $6,600.

6   Received and paid gas bill, $29.

8   Collected commission from sale of building lot on 6/17/04 (collected our accounts receivable).

12   Paid $300 to send employees to realtor's workshop.

15   Paid the salary of the office secretary, $350.

17   Sold a house and earned a commission of $2,400. Expected receipt on 8/10/04.

18   Sold a building lot and collected a commission of $7,000.

22   Sent a check for $40 to help sponsor a local road race to aid the public. (This is not to be considered an advertising expense, but it is a business expense.)

24   Paid for repairs to automobile, $590.

28   Juan Valdez withdrew $1,800 from the business to pay personal expenses.

30   Paid the salary of the office secretary, $350.

30   Received and paid the July telephone bill, $590.

30   Received advertising bill for July, $1,400. The bill is to be paid on 8/2/04.

4. After you have saved the journal entries, close the General Journal; then print the following reports:

Print Working Reports

   a. General Journal (check figure debit = $29,849)
   b. Trial Balance (check figure debit = $56,550)

Review your printed reports. If you have made an error in a saved journal entry, correct the error before proceeding.

5. Open the General Journal; then record adjusting journal entries based on the following adjustment data using "Adjusting" in the reference field:

Record July Adjusting Entries

   a. One month's rent has expired.
   b. An inventory shows $90 of office supplies remaining.
   c. Depreciation on office equipment, $100.
   d. Depreciation on automobile, $200.

6. After you have saved the adjusting journal entries, close the General Journal then print the following reports accepting all defaults offered by Peachtree:

Print Final Statements

   a. General Journal (check figure debit = $31,509)
   b. Trial Balance (check figure debit = $56,850)
   c. General Ledger Report (check figure cash = $26,094)
   d. Income Statement (Net Income = $10,691)
   e. Balance Sheet (Total Capital = $29,434)

Review your printed reports. If you have made an error in a saved journal entry, use the procedures detailed in step 18 from Chapter 3 to make any necessary corrections. Reprint all reports if corrections are made. Note how the income statement shows both current month and year-to-date totals.

7. Computerized Accounting systems maintain all of it's input in compartments called periods. Some systems identify these periods with the name of the month or with a simple numeric designation such as 1, 2, 3, et al. Peachtree currently has Valdez Realty in Period 7, the July period. You can see this in the status bar at the bottom of the screen. This is because Valdez has elected to use the calendar year for his Fiscal year. We will need to change the current period to the August period prior to inputting the next month's transactions. You must always tell Peachtree to move to the next accounting period when starting on the transactions for a new month. This process is the equivalent of "Closing" in a manual accounting system although the temporary accounts are not really closed until the end of the year.

Closing the Accounting Records

8. It is always wise to backup accounting data at the end of each month, saving it into a file that will be saved until the end of the year. We will use Peachtree's Backup feature to do this. Click on the Company Window **File** menu; select **Backup**, use a filename such as "ValdezJuly" to make sure you can recognize what the backup represents.

Make a Backup Copy of July Accounting Records

9. We must now advance the period to prepare Peachtree for the August transactions.

Advancing the Period

   ● Using your mouse, click on **System** from the **Tasks** menu. Select **Change Accounting Periods.**
   ● Using the pull down menu, select period 8 - Aug 1, 2001 to Aug 31, 2001 and click on **OK.**
   ● You will be asked whether you wish to print reports before continuing. Since we have already printed our reports, we can answer "No".
   ● Note that the status bar at the bottom of the screen now reflects that you are in period 8.

10. Click on the Company Window **File** menu; then click on **Exit** to end the current work session and return to your Windows desktop.

Exit the Program

CHAPTER 6

Banking Procedures and Control of Cash

Last week you opened your first checking account at a local bank by depositing your first check from working at your school's sports arena. It feels good to be working and making money to help with school expenses. Today you received your first credit card bill in the mail, along with a check from your parents for monthly school expenses. You plan to deposit the check from your parents and then write a check to pay your credit card bill. You know that you will deposit more into your checking account than you will withdraw by writing the check, but exactly how much do you have left to spend? You won't know the answer until you have reconciled your checking account.

You share something in common with virtually every company in business today. Every company needs to know how much cash it has to spend at any point in time. The only way a company can answer this question is to reconcile its accounts.

In the last five chapters we have discussed the accounting equation and the nine steps in the accounting cycle. In this chapter we turn our attention to banking procedures and the control of cash. We will learn about bank statements and how to reconcile a bank account. We will also discuss how a company pays for small amounts such as postage and small supplies by using a petty cash fund. Knowing the basics of how a bank functions and a company maintains control over cash is important to your understanding of the world of business and the role accounting plays in it.

Learning Objectives

- Depositing, writing, and endorsing checks for a checking account. (p. 224)

- Reconciling a bank statement. (p. 230)

- Establishing and replenishing a petty cash fund; setting up an auxiliary petty cash record. (p. 235)

- Establishing and replenishing a change fund. (p. 239)

- Handling transactions involving cash short and over. (p. 240)

The internal control policies of a company will depend on things such as number of employees, company size, sources of cash, and usage of the Internet.

In the first five chapters of this book, we analyzed the accounting cycle for businesses that perform personal services (for example, word processing or legal services). In this chapter, we turn our attention to Debbie's Wholesale Stationery Company, a merchandising company that earns revenue by selling goods (or merchandise) to customers. When Debbie found that her business was increasing, she became concerned that she was not monitoring the business's cash closely enough. To remedy the situation, Debbie and her accountant decided to develop a system of internal controls.

After studying the situation carefully, Debbie began a series of procedures that were to be followed by all company employees. The new company policies that Debbie's Wholesale Stationery Company put into place are as follows:

1. Responsibilities and duties of employees will be divided. For example, the person receiving the cash, whether at the register or by opening the mail, will not record this information into the accounting records. The accountant will not be handling the cash receipts.

2. All cash receipts of Debbie's Wholesale will be deposited into the bank the same day they arrive.

3. All cash payments will be made by check (except petty cash, which is discussed later in this chapter).

4. Employees will be rotated. This change allows workers to become acquainted with the work of others as well as to prepare for a possible changeover of jobs.

5. Debbie Lawrence will sign all checks after receiving authorization to pay from the departments concerned.

6. At time of payment, all supporting invoices or documents will be stamped paid. The stamp will show when the invoice or document is paid as well as the number of the check used.

7. All checks will be prenumbered. This change will control the use of checks and make it difficult to use a check fraudulently without its being revealed at some point.

8. Use of Internet online banking will be continually evaluated.

Now let's look at how Debbie's Wholesale implemented these policies.

Learning Unit 6-1   Bank Procedures, Checking Accounts, and Bank Reconciliations

Before Debbie's Wholesale opened on April 1, 200X, Debbie had a meeting at Security National Bank to discuss the steps in opening up and using a checking account for the company.

OPENING A CHECKING ACCOUNT

Purpose of a signature card.

The bank manager gave Debbie a signature card to fill out. The signature card included space for signature(s), business and home addresses, references, type of account, and so forth. Because Debbie would be signing all the checks for her company, she was the only employee who had to sign the card. The bank keeps the signature card in its files. When checks are presented for payment, the bank checks it to validate Debbie's signature. Such checking helps avoid possible forgeries.

Once the account was opened, Debbie received a set of checks and **deposit tickets** that were preprinted with the business's name, address, and account number (see Fig. 6-1). Debbie's Wholesale was to use the deposit tickets when it received cash or checks from any source and deposited them into the checking account.

On a deposit ticket, check amounts are listed separately along with the code number of city and bank on which they are drawn. The code can be found in the upper right corner of a check (see Fig. 6-3 on p. 228). The top part of the fraction (53-393) is known as the *American Bankers' Association Transit Number*: 53 identifies the large city or state the bank is located in; 393 identifies the bank above the amount of the check.

The lower part of the fraction (113) is split in two: 1 represents the First Federal Reserve District; 13 is a routing number used by the Federal Reserve bank. This is the way the code number appears on a check.

Deposit tickets usually come in duplicate. The bank keeps one copy and the company keeps the other so it can verify that the items making up the deposit have

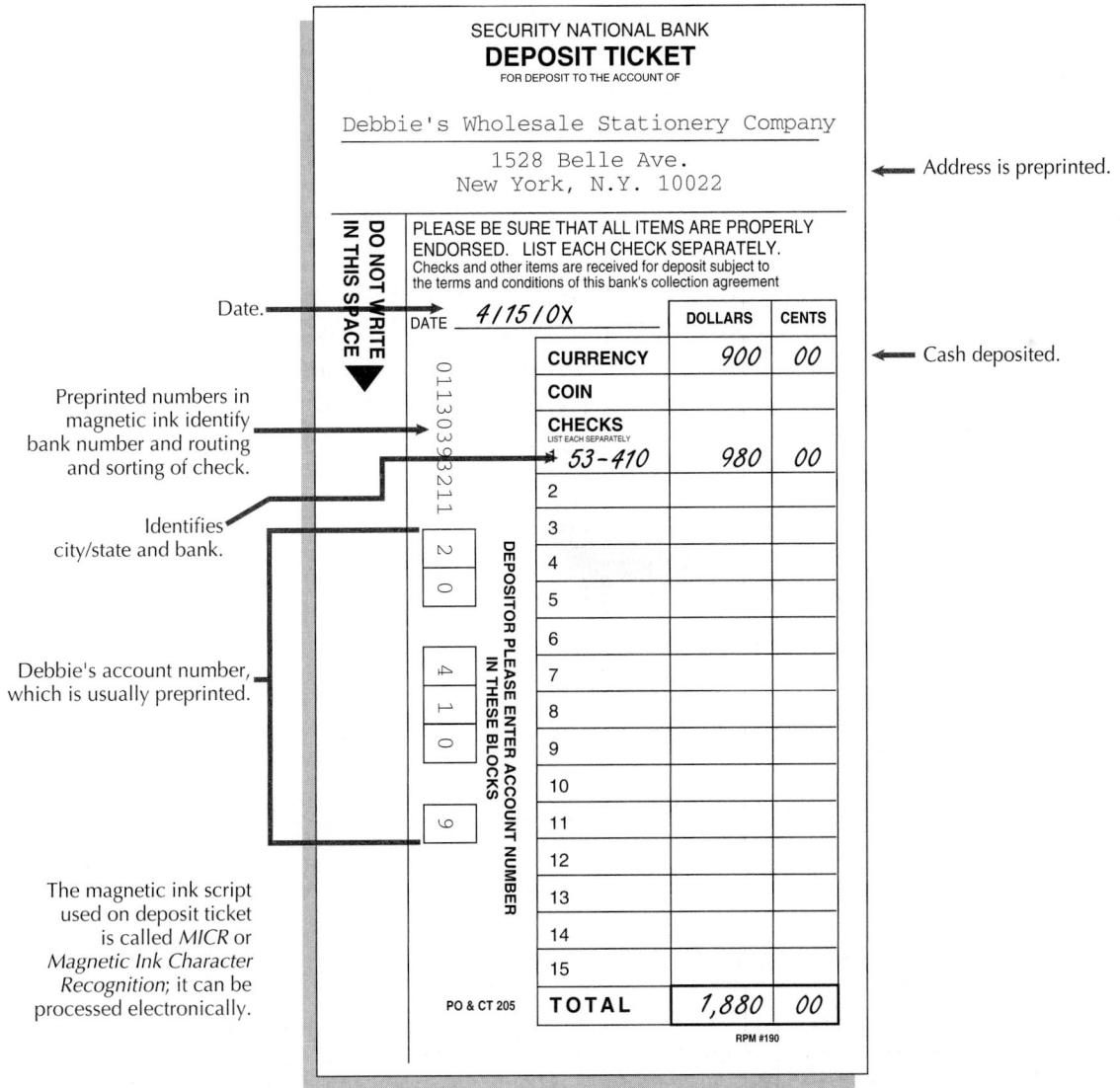

Figure 6-1 A Deposit Ticket

actually been deposited correctly. The bank manager told Debbie that she could give the deposits to a bank teller or she could use an automated teller machine (ATM). The ATM could also be used for withdrawing cash, transferring funds, or paying bills.

Often, Debbie makes her deposits after business hours, when the bank is closed. At those times, she puts the deposit into a locked bag (provided by the bank) and places the bag in the night depository. The bank will credit Debbie's account in the morning, when the deposit is processed. All payments of money are by written check (except petty cash), and all money (checks) received is deposited in the bank account.

Many checking accounts earn interest. For our purposes, however, we assume that the checking account for Debbie's Wholesale does not pay interest. Also assume that the checking account has a monthly service charge and that there is no individual charge for each check written.

> When a bank credits your account, it is increasing the balance.

CHECK ENDORSEMENT

Checks have to be *endorsed* (signed) by the person to whom the check is made out before they can be deposited or cashed. Endorsement is the signing or stamping of one's name on the back left-hand side of the check. This signature means that the payee has transferred the right to deposit or cash the check to someone else (the bank). The bank can then collect the money from the person or company that issued the check.

> Endorsements can be made by using a rubber stamp instead of a hand-written signature.

Three different types of endorsement can be used (see Fig. 6-2). The first is a *blank endorsement*. A blank endorsement does not specify that a particular person or firm must endorse it. It can be further endorsed by someone else. The bank will pay

Figure 6-2

Types of Check Endorsement

Types of Check Endorsement

Debbie Lawrence
204109

Blank Endorsement

A signature on the back left side of a check of the person or firm the check is payable to. This check can be *further* endorsed by someone else; the bank will give the money to the last person who signs the check. This type of endorsement is not very safe. If the check is lost, anyone who picks it up can sign it and get the money.

Pay to the order of
Security National Bank.

Debbie's Wholesale Stationery Co.
204109

Full Endorsement

This type of endorsement is safer than a simple signature, because the person or company signing (or stamping) the back of the check indicates the name of the company or person to whom the check is to be paid. Only the person or company named in the endorsement can transfer the check to someone else.

Payable to the order of
Security National Bank
for deposit only.

Debbie's Wholesale Stationery Co.
204109

Restrictive Endorsement

This endorsement is the safest for businesses. Debbie's Wholesale stamps the back of the check so that it must be deposited in the firm's account. This endorsement limits any further use of the check (it can only be deposited in the specified account).

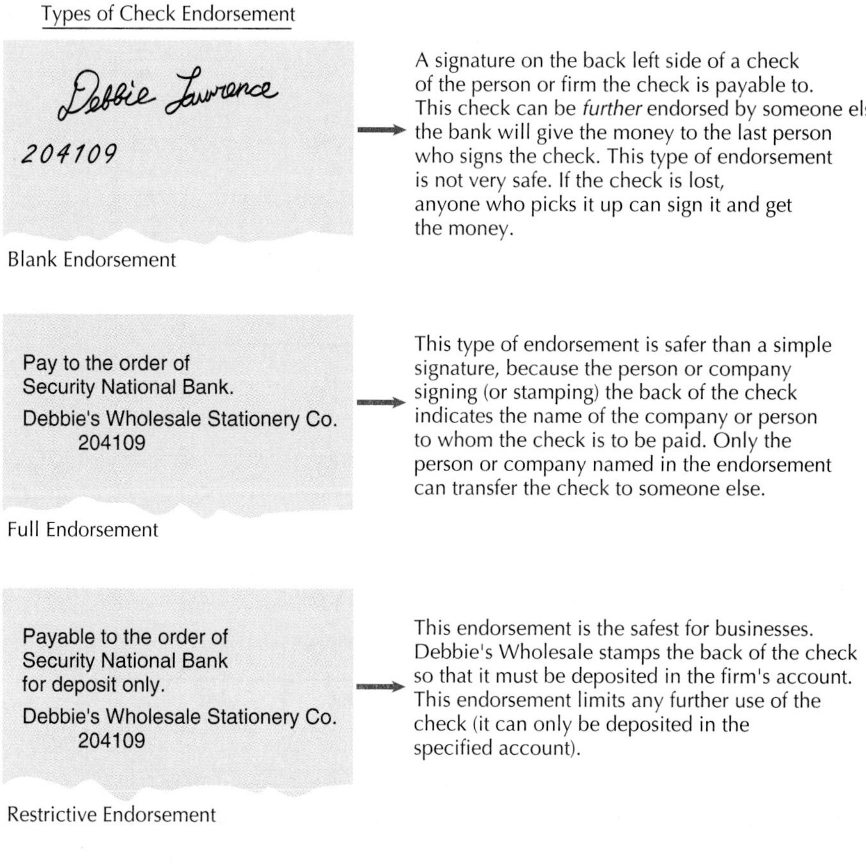

the last person who signs the check. This type of endorsement is not very safe. If the check is lost, the person who finds it can sign it and get the money.

The second type of endorsement is a *full endorsement*. The person or company signing (or stamping) the back of the check indicates the name of the company or the person to whom the check is to be paid. Only the person or company named in the endorsement can transfer the check to someone else.

Restrictive endorsements are the third type of endorsement. This endorsement is the safest one for businesses. Debbie's Wholesale stamps the back of the check so that it must be deposited in the firm's account. This stamp limits any further use of the check.

The regulations require the endorsement to be within the top 1½ inches to speed up the check clearing process.

THE CHECKBOOK

When Debbie opened her business's checking account, she received checks. These checks could be used to buy things for the business or to pay bills or salaries.

A **check** is a written order signed by a **drawer** (the person who writes the check) instructing a **drawee** (the person who pays the check) to pay a specific sum of money to the **payee** (the person to whom the check is payable). Figure 6-3 shows a check issued by Debbie's Wholesale Stationery Company. Debbie Lawrence is the drawer, Security National Bank is the drawee, and Joe Francis Company is the payee.

Drawer:
One who writes the check.

Drawee:
One who pays money to payee.

Payee:
One to whom the check is payable.

Look at the check in Figure 6-3. Notice that certain things, such as the company's name and address and the check number, are preprinted. Other things you should notice are (1) the line drawn after $\frac{XX}{100}$ which is to fill up the empty space and ensure that the amount cannot be changed, and (2) the word *and*, which should be used only to differentiate between dollars and cents.

Figure 6-3 includes a check stub. The check stub is used to record transactions, and it is kept for future reference. The information found on the stub includes the beginning balance ($7,100), the amount of any deposits ($784), the total amount in the account ($7,884), the amount of the check being written ($4,000), and the ending balance ($3,884). The check stub should be filled out before the check is written.

If the written amount on the check does not match the amount expressed in figures, Security National Bank may pay the amount written in words, return the check unpaid, or contact the drawer to see what was meant.

Many companies use checkwriting machines to type out the information on the check. These machines prevent people from making fraudulent changes on handwritten checks.

Banking on the Internet is expanding rapidly.

During the same time period, in-company records must be kept for all transactions affecting Debbie's Wholesale Stationery Company's checkbook balance. Figure 6-4 (p. 229) shows these records. Note that the bank deposits ($14,324) minus the checks written ($6,994) give an ending checkbook balance of $7,330.

MONTHLY RECORDKEEPING: THE BANK'S STATEMENT OF ACCOUNT AND IN-COMPANY RECORDS

Each month, Security National Bank will send Debbie's Wholesale Stationery Company a Statement of Account. This statement reflects all the activity in the account during that period. It begins with the beginning balance of the account at the start of the month, along with the checks the bank has paid and any deposits received (see Fig. 6-5, p. 229). Any other charges or additions to the bank balance are indicated by codes found on the statement. All checks that have been paid by the bank are sent back to Debbie's Wholesale. These are called **cancelled checks** because they have been processed by the bank and are no longer negotiable. The ending balance in Figure 6-5 is $6,919.

Figure 6.5 shows one format for a bank statement. Different banks use different formats.

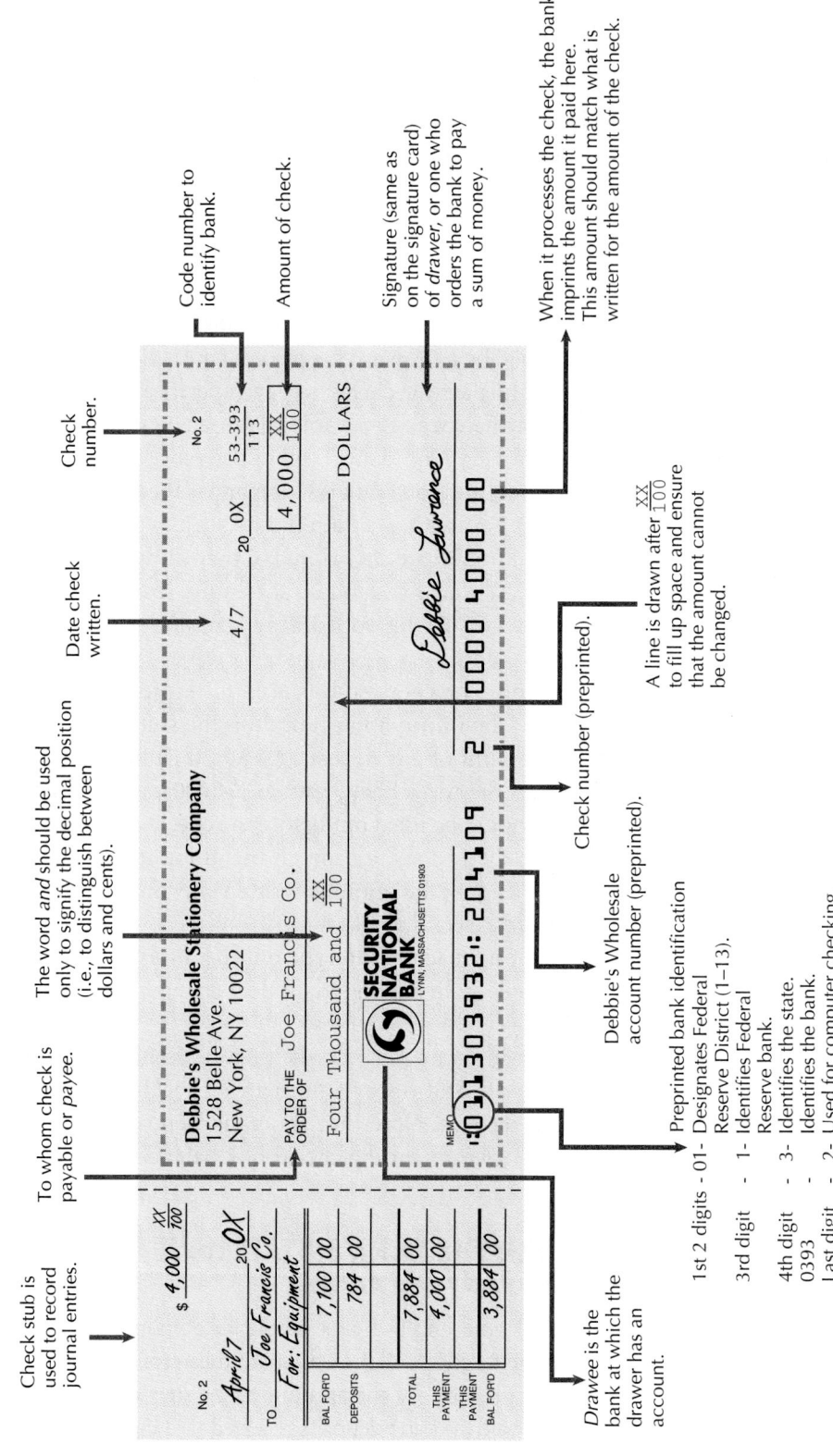

Code number to identify bank.

Amount of check.

Signature (same as on the signature card) of *drawer*, or one who orders the bank to pay a sum of money.

When it processes the check, the bank imprints the amount it paid here. This amount should match what is written for the amount of the check.

Check number.

Date check written.

A line is drawn after $\frac{XX}{100}$ to fill up space and ensure that the amount cannot be changed.

Check number (preprinted).

The word *and* should be used only to signify the decimal position (i.e., to distinguish between dollars and cents).

To whom check is payable or *payee*.

Check stub is used to record journal entries.

Debbie's Wholesale account number (preprinted).

Preprinted bank identification

1st 2 digits - 01- Designates Federal Reserve District (1–13).

3rd digit   -   1- Identifies Federal Reserve bank.

4th digit   -   3- Identifies the state.
0393   -   Identifies the bank.
Last digit -   2- Used for computer checking.

Drawee is the bank at which the drawer has an account.

Figure 6-3 A Company Check

Figure 6-4
Transactions Affecting
Checkbook Balance

Bank Deposits Made for April

Date of Deposit	Amount	Received From
Apr. 1	$ 8,000	Debbie Lawrence, Capital
4	784	Check — Hal's Clothing
16	1,880	Cash sales/Check — Bevans Company
22	1,960	Check — Roe Company
27	500	Sale of equipment
30	1,200	Cash sales
Total deposits for month:	$14,324	

Checks Written for Month of April

Date	Check No.	Payment To	Amount	Description
Apr. 2	1	Peter Blum	$ 900	Insurance paid in advance
7	2	Joe Francis Co.	4,000	Paid equipment
9	3	Rick Flo Co.	800	Cash purchases
12	4	Thorpe Co.	594	Paid purchases
28	5	Payroll	700	Salaries
		Total amount of checks written:	$ 6,994	

Cash/checks deposited	$14,324
Checks paid	−6,994
Balance in company checkbook	$ 7,330

In the next section we will show a more comprehensive bank statement.

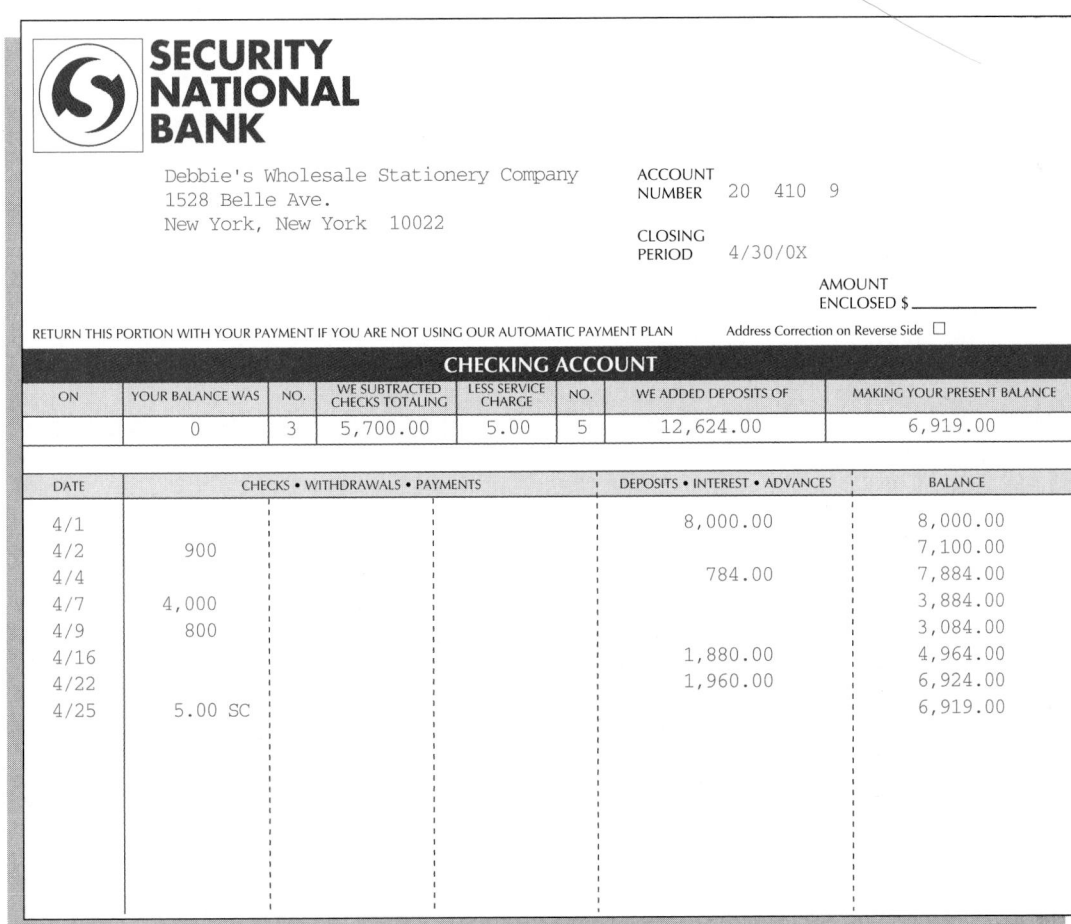

Figure 6-5 A Bank Statement

THE BANK RECONCILIATION PROCESS

The problem is that the ending bank balance of $6,919 does not agree with the amount in Debbie's checkbook, $7,330, or the balance in the cash amount in the ledger, $7,330. Such differences are caused partly by the time a bank takes to process a company's transactions. A company records a transaction when it occurs. A bank cannot record a deposit until it receives the funds, and it cannot pay a check until the check is presented by the payee. In addition, the bank statement will report fees and transactions that the company did not know about.

Debbie's accountant has to find out why there is a $411 difference between the balances and how the records can be brought into balance. The process of reconciling the bank balance on the bank statement versus the company's checkbook balance is called a **bank reconciliation.** Bank reconciliations involve several steps, including calculating the deposits in transit and the outstanding checks. The bank reconciliation usually is done on the back of the **bank statement** (see Fig. 6-6). It can also be done by computer software, however.

> Online banking and computer software has made the reconciliation process even easier.

Deposits in Transit

In comparing the list of deposits received by the bank with the checkbook, the accountant notices that the two deposits made on April 27 and 30 for $500 and $1,200 were not on the bank's statement. The accountant realizes that to prepare this statement, the bank only included information about Debbie's Wholesale Stationery up to April 25. These two deposits made by Debbie were not shown on the monthly bank statement because they arrived at the bank after the statement was printed. Thus, timing becomes a consideration in the reconciliation process. The deposits not yet added to the bank balance are called **deposits in transit**. These two deposits need to be added to the bank balance shown on the bank statement.

Figure 6-6
Bank Reconciliation Using the Back of the Bank Statement

> Keep in mind that both the bank and the depositor can make mistakes that will not be discovered until the reconciliation process.

CHECKS OUTSTANDING				
NUMBER	AMOUNT		1. Enter balance shown on this statement	6,919 | 00
4	594 | 00			
5	700 | 00		2. If you have made deposits since the date of this statement add them to the above balance.	1,700 | 00
			3. SUBTOTAL	8,619 | 00
			4. Deduct total of checks outstanding	1,294 | 00
			5. ADJUSTED BALANCE This should agree with your checkbook.	7,325 | 00
TOTAL OF CHECKS OUTSTANDING	1,294 | 00			

TO VERIFY YOUR CHECKING BALANCE
1. Sort checks by number or by date issued and compare with your check stubs and prior outstanding list. Make certain all checks paid have been recorded in your checkbook. If any of your checks were not included with this statement, list the numbers and amounts under "CHECKS OUTSTANDING."
2. Deduct the Service Charge as shown on the statement from your checkbook balance.
3. Review copies of charge advices included with this statement and check for proper entry in your checkbook.

IF THE ADJUSTED BALANCE DOES NOT AGREE WITH YOUR CHECKBOOK BALANCE, THE FOLLOWING SUGGESTIONS ARE OFFERED FOR YOUR ASSISTANCE.

- Recheck additions and subtractions in your checkbook and figures to the left.
- Make certain checkbook balances have been carried forward properly.
- Verify deposits recorded on statement against deposits entered in checkbook.
- Compare amount on each checkbook stub.

Debbie's checkbook is not affected, because the two deposits have already been added to its balance. The bank has no way of knowing that the deposits are coming until they are received.

Outstanding Checks

The first thing the accountant does when the bank statement is received is put the checks in numerical order (1, 2, 3, etc.). In doing so, the accountant notices that two payments were not made by the bank and two checks, no. 4 and no. 5, were not returned by the bank.

Debbie's books showed that these two checks had been deducted from the checkbook balance. These outstanding checks, however, had not yet been presented to the bank for payment or deducted from the bank balance. When these checks do reach the bank, the bank will reduce the amount of the balance.

Service Charges

Debbie's accountant also notices a bank service charge of $5. Thus, Debbie's checkbook balance should be lowered by $5.

Nonsufficient Funds

An NSF (nonsufficient funds) check is a check that has been returned because the drawer did not have enough money in its account to pay the check. Accountants are continually on the lookout for NSF (nonsufficient funds) checks. If there is an NSF check, it means that there is less money in the checking account than was thought. Debbie's Wholesale will have to (1) lower the checkbook balance and (2) try to collect the amount from the customer. The bank would notify Debbie's Wholesale of an NSF (or other deductions) check by a debit memorandum. Think of a debit memorandum as a deduction from the depositor's balance.

If the bank acts as a collecting agent for Debbie's Wholesale, say in collecting notes, it will charge Debbie a small fee and the net amount collected will be added to Debbie's bank balance. The bank will send to Debbie a credit memorandum verifying the increase in the depositor's balance.

A journal entry is also needed to bring the ledger accounts of Cash and Service Charge expense up-to-date. Any adjustment to the checkbook balance results in a journal entry. The entry in Figure 6-7 was made to accomplish this step:

Apr.	30	Service Charge Expense			5	00			
		Cash					5	00	
		Bank service charge for April							

Figure 6-7
Service Charge Journalized

Before we look at a more comprehensive bank statement, let's look at trends in banking.

TRENDS IN BANKING

Electronic Funds Transfer

Many financial institutions have developed or are developing ways to transfer funds electronically, without the use of paper checks. Such systems are called electronic funds transfers (EFT). Most EFTs are established to save money and avoid theft.

Deposits in transit: These unrecorded deposits could result if a deposit were placed in a night depository on the last day of the month.

Checks #4 and #5 are outstanding.

Checks outstanding are checks drawn by the depositor but not yet presented to the bank for payment by the payee.

(De)bit memorandum:
↓
Deducted from balance

Credit memorandum: Addition to balance.

Adjustments to the checkbook balance must be journalized and posted. These steps keep the depositor's ledger accounts (especially Cash) up-to-date. This charge could be recorded as a miscellaneous expense.

An automatic payroll deposit is an example of an EFT. It works as follows: The company asks its employees if they would like their paychecks deposited automatically into their checking accounts. Employees who agree to do so are asked to sign an authorization form. The bank, upon receiving computer-coded payroll data, adds each worker's payroll amount to his or her checking account. Employees who do not sign the authorization continue to get paper checks that they must cash themselves.

Another good example is the automatic teller machine (ATM). In some states, ATMs now issue postage stamps, railroad tickets, and grocery coupons. Debit cards are still another example of an EFT. If a customer buys a service or a product with a debit card, the amount of the purchase is deducted directly from the customer's bank account. The Internet continues to expand online banking.

Check Truncation (Safekeeping)

Some banks do not return cancelled checks to the depositor but use a procedure called check truncation or safekeeping. The bank holds a cancelled check for a specific period of time (usually 90 days) and then keeps a microfilm copy handy and destroys the original check. In Texas, for example, some credit unions and savings and loan institutions do not send back checks. Instead, the check date, number, and amount are listed on the bank statement. If the customer needs a copy of a check, the bank will provide the check or a photocopy for a small fee. (Photocopies are accepted as evidence in Internal Revenue Service tax returns and audits.)

Truncation cuts down on the amount of "paper" that is returned to customers and thus provides substantial cost savings. It is estimated that over 80 million checks are written each day in the United States.

Example of a More Comprehensive Bank Statement

The bank reconciliation of Debbie's Stationery was not as complicated as it is for many companies, even using today's computer technology. Let's look at a reconciliation for Matty's Supermarket (Figs. 6-8, 6-9), which is based on the following:

Matty's checkbook balance		$13,176.84
Bank balance		23,726.04
Leased space to Subway		8,456.00
Leased space to Dunkin Donuts		3,616.12
The rental payment is transferred by electronic transfer		
Matty pays a health insurance payment each month		1,444.00
by electronic transfer		
Deposits in transit 5/30		6,766.52
Checks outstanding		
ck # 738	$1,144.00	
739	1,277.88	
740	332.00	
741	812.56	
742	1,834.12	
Check # 734 was overstated		1,440.00

Note in Figure 6-9 (p. 234) that each adjustment to Matty's checkbook is the reconciliation process that would result in general journal entries.

Figure 6-8
Bank Statement for
Matty's Supermarket

Ranger Bank
1 Left St.
Marblehead, MA 01945

ACCOUNT STATEMENT

Matty's Supermarket
20 Sullivan St.
Lynn, MA 01917

Checking Account: 775800061

Checking Account Summary as of 6/30/0X

Beginning Balance	Total Deposits	Total Withdrawals	Service Charge	Ending Balance
$26,224.48	$17,410.56	$19,852.00	$57.00	$23,726.04

Checking Accounts Transactions

Deposits	Date	Amount
Deposit	6/05	4,000.00
Deposit	6/05	448.00
Deposit	6/09	778.40
EFT leasing: Dunkin Donuts	6/18	3,616.12
EFT leasing: Subway	6/27	8,456.00
Interest	6/30	112.04

Charges	Date	Amount
Service charge: Check printing	6/30	57.00
EFT: Blue Cross/Blue Shield	6/21	1,444.00
NSF	6/21	208.00

Checks

Number	Date	Amount
401	6/07	400.00
733	6/13	12,000.00
734	6/13	600.00
735	6/11	400.00
736	6/18	400.00
737	6/30	4,400.00

Daily Balance

Date	Balance	Date	Balance
5/28	26,224.48	6/18	21,059.00
6/05	30,464.48	6/21	19,615.00
6/07	29,664.48	6/28	28,071.00
6/09	30,442.88	6/30	23,726.04
6/11	30,042.88		
6/13	17,442.88		

Learning Unit 6-1 Review

AT THIS POINT you should be able to

- Define and explain the need for deposit tickets. (p. 225)
- Explain where the American Bankers' Association transit number is located on the check and what its purpose is. (p. 225)
- List as well as compare and contrast the three common types of check endorsement. (p. 226)
- Explain the structure of a check. (p. 228)
- Define and state the purpose of a bank statement. (p. 230)
- Explain deposits in transit, checks outstanding, service charge, and NSF. (p. 231)
- Explain the difference between a debit memorandum and a credit memorandum. (p. 232)

Figure 6-9
Bank Reconciliation for
Matty's Supermarket

MATTY'S SUPERMARKET Bank Reconciliation as of June 30, 2004					
Checkbook balance			**Bank balance**		
Matty's checkbook balance		$13,176.84	Bank balance		$23,726.04
Add:			Add:		
EFT leasing: Dunkin Donuts			Deposits in transit, 5/30		6,766.52
	$ 3,616.12				$30,492.56
EFT leasing: Subway					
	8,456.00				
Interest	112.04				
Error: Overstated					
check No. 734	1,440.00				
	$26,801.00				
Deduct:			Deduct:		
Service charge	$ 57.00		Outstanding checks:		
NSF check	208.00		No. 738	$1,144.00	
EFT health insurance			No. 739	1,277.88	
payment	1,444.00	1,709.00	No. 740	332.00	
			No. 741	812.56	
			No. 742	1,834.12	5,400.56
Reconciled balance		$25,092.00	Reconciled balance		$25,092.00

🖙 Explain how to do a bank reconciliation. (p. 230)
🖙 Explain electronic funds transfer and check truncation. (p. 231)

SELF-REVIEW QUIZ 6-1

(The blank forms you need are on page 191 of the *Study Guide and Working Papers*.)

Indicate, by placing an X under it, the heading that describes the appropriate action for each of the following situations:

Situation	Add to Bank Balance	Deduct from Bank Balance	Add to Checkbook Balance	Deduct from Checkbook Balance
1. Check printing charge				
2. Deposits in transit				
3. NSF check				
4. A $75 check was written and recorded by the company as $85				
5. Proceeds of a note collected by the bank				
6. Check outstanding				
7. Forgot to record ATM withdrawal				
8. Forgot to record direct depossit of a payroll check				

SOLUTION TO SELF-REVIEW QUIZ 6-1

Situation	Add to Bank Balance	Deduct from Bank Balance	Add to Checkbook Balance	Deduct from Checkbook Balance
1				X
2	X			
3				X
4			X	
5			X	
6		X		
7				X
8			X	

> *Quiz Tip:*
> Deposits in transit are added to the bank balance, whereas checks outstanding are subtracted from the bank balance.

Learning Unit 6-2   The Establishment of Petty Cash and Change Funds

Debbie realized how time-consuming and expensive it would be to write checks for small amounts to pay for postage, small supplies, and so forth, so she set up a **petty cash fund**. Similarly, she established a *change fund* to make cash transactions more convenient. This unit explains how to manage petty cash and change funds.

> Petty Cash is an asset on the balance sheet.

SETTING UP THE PETTY CASH FUND

The *petty cash fund* is an account dedicated to paying small day-to-day expenses. These petty cash expenses are recorded in an auxiliary record and later summarized, journalized, and posted. Debbie estimated that the company would need a fund of $60 to cover small expenditures during the month of May. This petty cash was not expected to last longer than one month. She gave one of her employees responsibility for overseeing the fund. This person is called the *custodian*.

Debbie named her office manager, John Sullivan, as custodian. In other companies, the cashier or secretary may be in charge of petty cash. Check no. 6 was drawn to the order of the custodian and cashed to establish the fund. John keeps the petty cash fund in a small tin box in the office safe.

Shown here is the transaction analysis chart for the establishment of a $60 petty cash fund, which would be journalized on May 1, 200X, as shown in Figure 6-10.

> The check for $60 is drawn to the order of the custodian and is cashed, and the proceeds are turned over to John Sullivan, the custodian.

> Petty Cash is an asset, which is established by writing a new check. The Petty Cash account is debited only once unless a greater or lesser amount of petty cash is needed on a regular basis.

Accounts Affected	Category	↑ ↓	Rules
Petty Cash	Asset	↑	Dr.
Cash (checks)	Asset	↓	Cr.

Note that the new asset called Petty Cash, which was created by writing check no. 6, reduced the asset Cash. In reality, the total assets stay the same; what has occurred is a shift from the asset Cash (check no. 6) to a new asset account called Petty Cash.

GENERAL JOURNAL						Page 1	
Date		Account Title and Description	PR	Dr.		Cr.	
200X May	1	Petty Cash		6 0 00			
		Cash				6 0 00	
		Establishment					

Figure 6-10 Establishing Petty Cash

The Petty Cash account is not debited or credited again if the size of the fund is not changed. If the $60 fund is used up quickly, the fund should be increased. If the fund is too large, the Petty Cash account should be reduced. We take a closer look at this when we discuss replenishment of petty cash.

MAKING PAYMENTS FROM THE PETTY CASH FUND

John Sullivan has the responsibility for filling out a petty cash voucher for each cash payment made from the petty cash fund. The petty cash vouchers are numbered in sequence.

Note that when the voucher (shown in Fig. 6-11) is completed, it will include

- The voucher number (which will be in sequence).
- The date.
- The person or organization to whom the payment was made.
- The amount of payment.
- The reason for payment: in this case, cleaning.
- The signature of the person who approved the payment.
- The signature of the person who received the payment from petty cash.
- The account to which the expense will be charged.

The completed vouchers are placed in the petty cash box. No matter how many vouchers John Sullivan fills out, *the total of (1) the vouchers in the box and (2) the cash on hand should equal the original amount of petty cash with which the fund was established ($60).*

Figure 6-11
Petty Cash Voucher

Petty Cash Voucher No. 1

Date: May 2, 200X   Amount: $3.00
Paid To: Al's Cleaning
For: Cleaning

                                   Approved By: *John Sullivan*

                        Payment Received By: *Debbie Lawrence*

Debit Account No.: 619

Date	Voucher No.	Description	Receipts	Payments	Postage Expense	Delivery Expense	Sundry Account	Sundry Amount
							Category of Payments	
200X May 1		Establishment	60 00					
2	1	Cleaning		3 00			Cleaning	3 00
5	2	Postage		9 00	9 00			
8	3	First Aid		15 00			Misc.	15 00
9	4	Delivery		6 00		6 00		
14	5	Delivery		15 00		15 00		
27	6	Postage		6 00	6 00			
		Total	60 00	54 00	15 00	21 00		18 00

Figure 6-12 Auxiliary Petty Cash Record

Assume that at the end of May the following items are documented by petty cash vouchers in the petty cash box as having been paid by John Sullivan:

200X
May 2 Cleaning package, $3.00.
  5 Postage stamps, $9.00.
  8 First-aid supplies, $15.00.
  9 Delivery expense, $6.00.
  14 Delivery expense, $15.00.
  27 Postage stamps, $6.00.

John records this information in the auxiliary petty cash record shown in Figure 6-12. It is not a required record but an aid to John, an auxiliary record that is not essential but is quite helpful as part of the petty cash system. You may want to think of the auxiliary petty cash record as an optional worksheet. Let's look at how to replenish the petty cash fund.

HOW TO REPLENISH THE PETTY CASH FUND

No postings are done from the auxiliary book because it is not a journal. At some point the summarized information found in the auxiliary petty cash record is used as a basis for a journal entry in the general journal and eventually posted to appropriate ledger accounts to reflect up-to-date balances.

This $54 of expenses (see Fig. 6-12) is recorded in the general journal (Fig. 6-13 on p. 238) and a new check, no. 17, for $54 is cashed and returned to John Sullivan. In replenishment, old expenses are updated in the journal and ledger to show where money has gone. The order is auxiliary before replenishment. The petty cash box now once again reflects $60 cash. The old vouchers that were used are stamped to indicate that they have been processed and the fund replenished.

Note that in the replenishment process the debits are a summary of the totals (except sundry, because individual items are different) of expenses or other items from the auxiliary petty cash record. Posting these specific expenses will ensure that the expenses will not be understated on the income statement. The credit to Cash allows us to draw a check for $54 to put money back in the petty cash box. The $60 in

A new check is written in the replenishment process, which is payable to the custodian, and is cashed by John, and the cash is placed in the petty cash box.

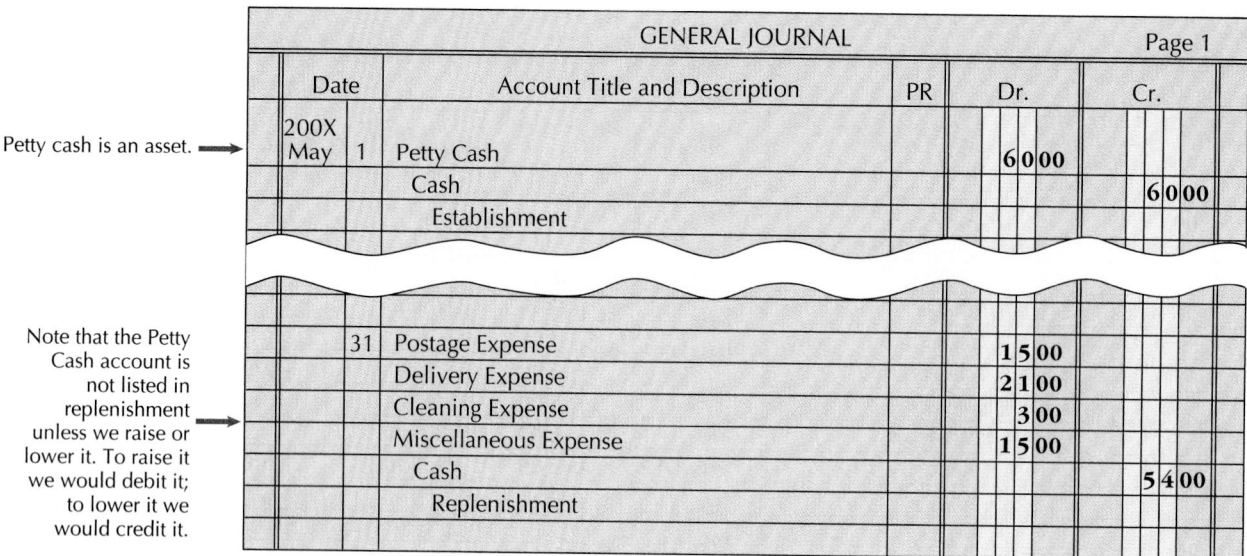

Petty cash is an asset. →

Note that the Petty Cash account is not listed in replenishment unless we raise or lower it. To raise it we would debit it; to lower it we would credit it. →

	Date		Account Title and Description	PR	Dr.	Cr.
GENERAL JOURNAL						Page 1
200X May	1		Petty Cash		6000	
			Cash			6000
			Establishment			
	31		Postage Expense		1500	
			Delivery Expense		2100	
			Cleaning Expense		300	
			Miscellaneous Expense		1500	
			Cash			5400
			Replenishment			

Figure 6-13 Establishment and Replenishment of Petty Cash Fund

the box now agrees with the Petty Cash account balance. The end result is that our petty cash box is filled, and we have justified for which accounts the petty cash money was spent. Think of replenishment as a single, summarizing entry.

Remember that if at some point the petty cash fund is to be greater than $60, a check can be written that will increase Petty Cash and decrease Cash. If the Petty Cash account balance is to be reduced, we can credit or reduce Petty Cash. For our present purpose, however, Petty Cash will remain at $60.

The auxiliary petty cash record after replenishment would look as shown in Figure 6-14 (keep in mind no postings are made from the auxiliary). Figure 6-15 may help you put the sequence together.

Before concluding this unit, let's look at how Debbie will handle setting up a change fund and problems with cash shortages and overages.

									Category of Payments			
											Sundry	
Date		Voucher No.	Description		Receipts		Payments	Postage Expense	Delivery Expense		Account	Amount
AUXILIARY PETTY CASH RECORD												
200X May	1		Establishment		6000							
	2	1	Cleaning				300				Cleaning	300
	5	2	Postage				900	900				
	8	3	First Aid				1500				Misc.	1500
	9	4	Delivery				600		600			
	14	5	Delivery				1500		1500			
	27	6	Postage				600	600				
			Total		6000		5400	1500	2100			1800
			Ending Balance				600					
					6000		6000					
			Ending Balance		600							
	31		Replenishment		5400							
	31		Balance (New)		6000							

Figure 6-14 Auxiliary Petty Cash Record with Replenishment

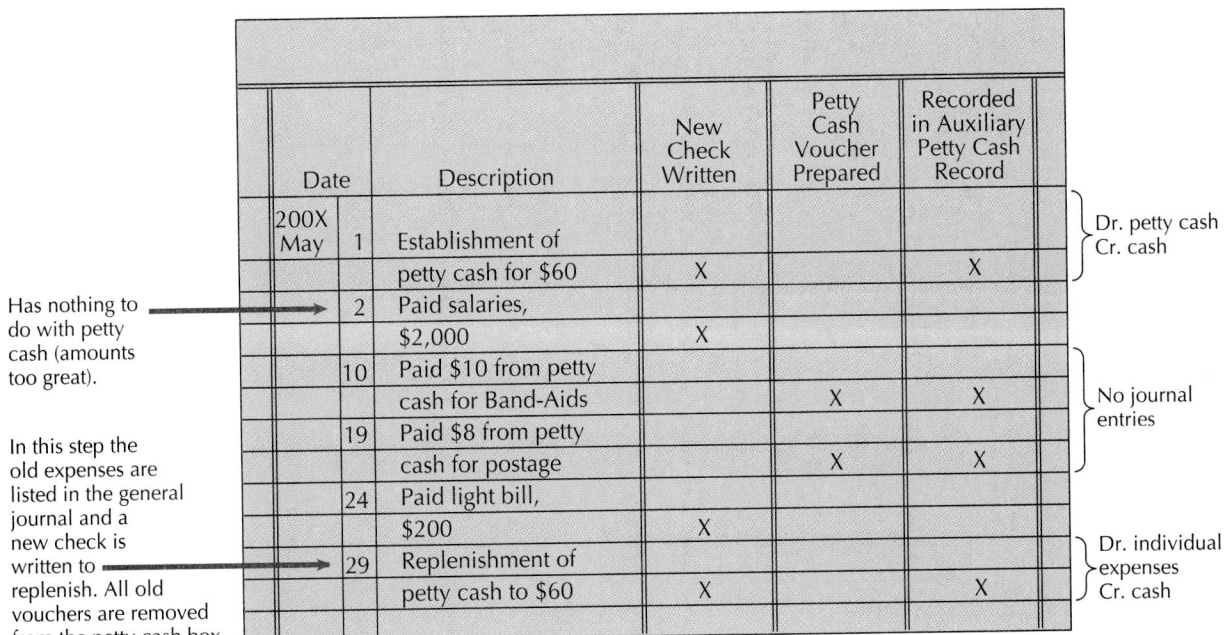

Date		Description	New Check Written	Petty Cash Voucher Prepared	Recorded in Auxiliary Petty Cash Record	
200X May	1	Establishment of				Dr. petty cash Cr. cash
		petty cash for $60	X		X	
	2	Paid salaries,				
		$2,000	X			
	10	Paid $10 from petty				
		cash for Band-Aids		X	X	No journal entries
	19	Paid $8 from petty				
		cash for postage		X	X	
	24	Paid light bill,				
		$200	X			
	29	Replenishment of				Dr. individual expenses Cr. cash
		petty cash to $60	X		X	

Has nothing to do with petty cash (amounts too great).

In this step the old expenses are listed in the general journal and a new check is written to replenish. All old vouchers are removed from the petty cash box.

Figure 6-15 Which Transactions Involve Petty Cash and How to Record Them

SETTING UP A CHANGE FUND AND INSIGHT INTO CASH SHORT AND OVER

If a company like Debbie's Stationery expects to have many cash transactions occurring, it may be a good idea to establish a change fund. This fund is placed in the cash register drawer and used to make change for customers who pay cash. Debbie decides to put $120 in the change fund, made up of various denominations of bills and coins. Let's look at a transaction analysis chart and the journal entry (Fig. 6-16) for this sort of procedure.

Accounts Affected	Category	↑↓	Dr./Cr.
Change Fund	Asset	↑	Dr.
Cash	Asset	↓	Cr.

Apr.	1	Change Fund		1 2 0 00	
		Cash			1 2 0 00
		Establish change fund			

Figure 6-16
Change Fund Established

At the close of the business day, Debbie will place the amount of the change fund back in the safe in the office. She will set up the change fund (the same $120) in the appropriate denominations for the next business day. She will deposit in the bank the *remainder* of the cash taken in for the day.

In the next section, we look at how to record errors that are made in making change, called cash short and over.

Cash Short and Over

In a local pizza shop the total sales for the day did not match the amount of cash on hand. Errors often happen in making change. To record and summarize the differences in cash, an account called *Cash Short and Over* is used. This account will record both overages (too much money) and shortages (not enough money). Lets first look at the account (in T account form).

Beg change fund
+ Cash register total
= Cash should have on hand
− Counted cash
= Shortage or overage of cash

Cash Short and Over	
Dr.	Cr.
shortage	overage

All shortages will be recorded as debits and all overages will be recorded as credits. This account is temporary. If the ending balance of the account is a debit (a shortage), it is considered a miscellaneous expense that would be reported on the income statement. If the balance of the account is a credit (an overage), it is considered as other income reported on the income statement. Let's look at how the Cash Short and Over account could be used to record shortages or overages in sales as well as in the petty cash process.

Example 1: Shortages and Overages in Sales

On December 5 a pizza shop rang up sales of $560 for the day but only had $530 in cash.

Accounts Affected	Category	↑ ↓	Dr./Cr.
Cash	Asset	↑	Debit $530
Cash Short and Over	Misc. Exp.	↑	Debit $30
Sales	Revenue	↑	Credit $560

The journal entry would be as shown in Figure 6-17.

Figure 6-17
Cash Shortage

Dec.	5	Cash		5 3 0 00		
		Cash Short and Over		3 0 00		
		Sales			5 6 0 00	
		Cash shortage				

Note that the shortage of $30 is a debit and would be recorded on the income statement as a miscellaneous expense.

What would the entry look like if the pizza shop showed a $50 overage?

Accounts Affected	Category	↑ ↓	Dr./Cr.
Cash	Asset	↑	Debit $610
Cash Short and Over	Other Income	↑	Credit $50
Sales	Revenue	↑	Credit $560

The journal entry would be as shown in Figure 6-18.

Figure 6-18
Cash Overage

Dec.	5	Cash		6 1 0 00		
		Cash Short and Over			5 0 00	
		Sales			5 6 0 00	
		Cash overage				

Note that the Cash Short and Over account would be reported as other income on the income statement. Now let's look at how to use this Cash Short and Over account to record petty cash transactions.

Example 2: Cash Short and Over in Petty Cash

A local computer company had established petty cash for $200. Today, November 30, the petty cash box had $160 in vouchers as well as $32 in coin and currency. What would be the journal entry to replenish petty cash? Assume the vouchers were made up of $90 for postage and $70 for supplies expense.

If you add up the vouchers and cash in the box, cash is short by $8.

Accounts Affected	Category	↑↓	Dr./Cr.
Postage Expense	Expense	↑	Debit $90
Supplies Expense	Expense	↑	Debit $70
Cash Short and Over	Misc. Expense	↑	Debit $8
Cash	Asset	↓	Credit $168

Note: The account Petty Cash is not used since the level in petty cash is not raised or lowered.

The journal entry is shown in Figure 6-19.

Nov.	8	Postage Expense		90 00		
		Supplies Expense		70 00		
		Cash Short and Over		8 00		
		Cash			168 00	

Figure 6-19
Petty Cash Replenished with Shortage

If there had been an overage, the Cash Short and Over would be a credit as other income. The solution to Self-Review Quiz 6-2 shows how a fund shortage would be recorded in the auxiliary record.

Learning Unit 6-2 Review

AT THIS POINT you should be able to

- State the purpose of a petty cash fund. (p. 235)
- Prepare a journal entry to establish a petty cash fund. (p. 235)
- Prepare a petty cash voucher. (p. 236)
- Explain the relationship of the auxiliary petty cash record to the petty cash process. (p. 237)
- Prepare a journal entry to replenish Petty Cash to its original amount. (p. 237)
- Explain why individual expenses are debited in the replenishment process. (p. 238)
- Explain how a change fund is established. (p. 239)
- Explain how Cash Short and Over could be a miscellaneous expense. (p. 239)

SELF-REVIEW QUIZ 6-2

(The blank forms you need are on pages 191–192 of the *Study Guide and Working Papers*.)

As the custodian of the petty cash fund, it is your task to prepare entries to establish the fund on October 1 as well as to replenish the fund on October 31. Please keep an auxiliary petty cash record.

200X
Oct.

1 Establish petty cash fund for $90, check no. 8.
5 Voucher 11, delivery expense, $21.
9 Voucher 12, delivery expense, $15.
10 Voucher 13, office repair expense, $24.
17 Voucher 14, general expense, $12.
30 Replenishment of petty cash fund, $78, check no. 108. (Check would be payable to the custodian.)

SOLUTION TO SELF-REVIEW QUIZ 6-2

	GENERAL JOURNAL				Page 6
Date	Account Title and Description	PR	Dr.	Cr.	
200X Oct. 1	Petty Cash		90 00		
	Cash			90 00	
	Establishment, Check 8				
31	Delivery Expense		36 00		
	General Expense		12 00		
	Office Repair Expense		24 00		
	Cash Short and Over		6 00		
	Cash			78 00	
	Replenishment, Check 108				

Figure 6-20 Establishment and Replenishment of Petty Cash

AUXILIARY PETTY CASH RECORD										
								Catagory of Payments		
									Sundry	
Date	Voucher No.	Description		Receipts	Payments	Delivery Expense	General Expense	Account	Amount	
200X Oct. 1		Establishment		90 00						
5	11	Delivery			21 00	21 00				
9	12	Delivery			15 00	15 00				
10	13	Repairs			24 00			Office Repair	24 00	
17	14	General			12 00		12 00			
25		Fund Shortage			6 00			Cash Short and Over	6 00	
		Totals		90 00	78 00	36 00	12 00		30 00	
		Ending Balance			12 00					
					90 00					
30		Ending Balance		12 00						
31		Replenishment		78 00						
Nov. 1		New Balance		90 00						

Figure 6-21 Auxiliary Petty Cash Record

Chapter Review

Summary of Key Points

Learning Unit 6-1

1. Restrictive endorsement limits any further negotiation of a check.
2. Check stubs are filled out before a check is written.
3. The payee is the person to whom the check is payable. The drawer is the one who orders the bank to pay a sum of money. The drawee is the bank with which the drawer has an account.
4. The process of reconciling the bank balance with the company's balance is called the bank reconciliation. The timing of deposits, when the bank statement was issued, and so forth, often result in differences between the bank balance and the checkbook balance.
5. Deposits in transit are added to the bank balance.
6. Checks outstanding are subtracted from the bank balance.
7. NSF means that a check has nonsufficient funds to be credited (deposited) to a checking account; therefore, the amount is not included in the bank balance and thus the checking account balance is lowered.
8. When a bank debits your account it is deducting an amount from your balance. A credit to the account is an increase to your balance.
9. All adjustments to the checkbook balance require journal entries.
10. The Internet has expanded online banking options.

Learning Unit 6-2

1. Petty Cash is an asset found on the balance sheet.
2. The auxiliary petty cash record is an auxiliary book; thus no postings are done from this book. Think of it as an optional worksheet.
3. When a petty cash fund is established, the amount is entered as a debit to Petty Cash and a credit to Cash.
4. At the time of replenishment of the petty cash fund, all expenses are debited (by category) and a credit to Cash (a new check) results. This replenishment, when journalized and posted, updates the ledger from the journal.
5. The only time the Petty Cash account is used is to establish the fund initially or to bring the fund to a higher or lower level. If the petty cash level is deemed sufficient, all replenishments will debit specific expenses and credit Cash (new check written). The asset Petty Cash account balance will remain unchanged.
6. A change fund is an asset that is used to make change for customers.
7. Cash Short and Over is an account that is either a miscellaneous expense or miscellaneous income, depending on whether the ending balance is a shortage or overage.

Key Terms

ATM   Automatic teller machine.

Auxiliary petty cash record   A supplementary record for summarizing petty cash information.

Bank reconciliation   The process of reconciling the checkbook balance with the bank balance given on the bank statement.

Bank statement   A report sent by a bank to a customer indicating the previous balance, individual checks processed, individual deposits received, service charges, and ending bank balance.

Cancelled check   A check that has been processed by a bank and is no longer negotiable.

Cash Short and Over   The account that records cash shortages and overages. If the ending balance is a debit, it is recorded on the income statement as a miscellaneous expense; if it is a credit, it is recorded as miscellaneous income.

Change fund   Fund made up of various denominations that are used to make change for customers.

Check   A form used to indicate a specific amount of money that is to be paid by the bank to a named person or company.

Check truncation (safekeeping)   Procedure whereby checks are not returned to the drawer with the bank statement but are instead kept at the bank for a certain amount of time before being first transferred to microfilm and then destroyed.

Credit memorandum   Increase in depositor's balance.

Debit card   A card similar to a credit card except that the amount of a purchase is deducted directly from the customer's bank account.

Debit memorandum   Decrease in depositor's balance.

Deposits in transit   Deposits that were made by customers of a bank but did not reach, or were not processed by, the bank before the preparation of the bank statement.

Deposit ticket   A form provided by a bank for use in depositing money or checks into a checking account.

Drawee   Bank that drawer has an account with.

Drawer   Person who writes a check.

Electronic funds transfer (EFT)   An electronic system that transfers funds without the use of paper checks.

Endorsement   *Blank:* Could be further endorsed. *Full:* Restricts further endorsement to only the person or company named. *Restrictive:* Restricts any further endorsement.

Internal control   A system of procedures and methods to control a firm's assets as well as monitor its operations.

NSF (nonsufficient funds)   Notation indicating that a check has been written on an account that lacks sufficient funds to back it up.

Outstanding checks   Checks written by a company or person that were not received or not processed by the bank before the preparation of the bank statement.

Payee   The person or company to whom the check is payable.

Petty cash fund   Fund (source) that allows payment of small amounts without the writing of checks.

Petty cash voucher   A petty cash form to be completed when money is taken out of petty cash.

Blueprint: A Bank Reconciliation

Checkbook Balance	Bank Balance
+ EFT (electronic funds transfer)	+ Deposits in transit
+ Interest earned	− Outstanding checks
+ Notes collected	± Bank errors
+ Direct deposits	
− ATM withdrawals	
− Check redeposits	
− NSF check	
− Online fees	
− Automatic withdrawals	
− Overdrafts	
− Service charges	
− Stop payments	
± Book errors*	
CM—adds to balance	
DM—deducts from balance	

*If a $60 check is recorded as $50, we must decrease checkbook balance by $10.

Questions, Mini Exercises, Exercises, and Problems

Discussion Questions

1. What is the purpose of internal control?
2. What is the advantage of having preprinted deposit tickets?
3. Explain the difference between a blank endorsement and a restrictive endorsement.
4. Explain the difference between payee, drawer, and drawee.

5. Why should check stubs be filled out first, before the check itself is written?

6. A bank statement is sent twice a month. True or false? Please explain.

7. Explain the end product of a bank reconciliation.

8. Why are checks outstanding subtracted from the bank balance?

9. An NSF check results in a bank issuing the depositor a credit memorandum. Agree or disagree. Please support your response.

10. Why do adjustments to the checkbook balance in the reconciliation process need to be journalized?

11. What is EFT?

12. What is meant by check truncation or safekeeping?

13. Petty cash is a liability. Accept or reject. Explain.

14. Explain the relationship of the auxiliary petty cash record to the recording of the cash payment.

15. At the time of replenishment, why are the totals of individual expenses debited?

16. Explain the purpose of a change fund.

17. Explain how Cash Short and Over can be a miscellaneous expense.

Mini Exercises

(The blank forms you need are on page 194 in the *Study Guide and Working Papers.*)

Bank Reconciliation

1. Indicate what effect each situation will have on the bank reconciliation process:

    1. Add to bank balance.
    2. Deduct from bank balance.
    3. Add to checkbook balance.
    4. Deduct from checkbook balance.

    _____ a. $12 bank service charge.
    _____ b. $300 deposit in transit.
    _____ c. $162 NSF check.
    _____ d. A $15 check was written and recorded as $25.
    _____ e. Bank collected a $1,000 note less $50 collection fee.
    _____ f. Check no. 111 was outstanding for $88.

Journal Entries in Reconciliation Process

2. Which of the transactions in Mini Exercise 1 would require a journal entry?

Bank Reconciliation

3. From the following, construct a bank reconciliation for June Co. as of May 31, 200X.

Checkbook balance	$20
Bank statement balance	30
Deposits in transit	10
Outstanding checks	30
Bank service charge	10

Petty Cash

4. Indicate what effect each situation will have:

    1. New check written.
    2. Recorded in general journal.
    3. Petty cash voucher prepared.
    4. Recorded in auxiliary petty cash record.

_____ **a.** Established petty cash.
_____ **b.** Paid $1,000 bill.
_____ **c.** Paid $2 for Band-Aids from petty cash.
_____ **d.** Paid $3.00 for stamps from petty cash.
_____ **e.** Paid electric bill, $250.
_____ **f.** Replenished petty cash.

Replenishment of Petty Cash

5. Petty cash was originally established for $20. During the month, $5 was paid out for Band-Aids and $6 for stamps. During replenishment, the custodian discovered that the balance in petty cash was $8. Record, using a general journal entry, the replenishment of petty cash back to $20.

Increasing Petty Cash

6. In Mini Exercise 5, if the custodian decided to raise the level of petty cash to $30, what would be the journal entry to replenish (use a general journal entry)?

Exercises

(The blank forms you need are on pages 195–196 of the *Study Guide and Working Papers*.)

6-1. From the following information, construct a bank reconciliation for Lang Co. as of July 31, 200X. Then prepare journal entries if needed.

Checkbook balance	$1,260	Outstanding checks	285
Bank statement balance	900	Bank service charge	45
Deposits (in transit)	600	(debit memo)	

6-2. In general journal form, prepare journal entries to establish a petty cash fund on July 1 and replenish it on July 31.

200X
July 1 A $40 petty cash fund is established.
          31 At end of month $12 cash plus the following paid vouchers exist: donations expense, $10; postage expense, $7; office supplies expense, $7; miscellaneous expense, $4.

6-3. If in Exercise 6-2 cash on hand is $11, prepare the entry to replenish the petty cash on July 31.

6-4. If in Exercise 6-2 cash on hand is $13, prepare the entry to replenish the petty cash on July 31.

6-5. At the end of the day the clerk for Pete's Variety Shop noticed an error in the amount of cash he should have. Total cash sales from the sales tape were $1,100, whereas the total cash in the register was $1,056. Pete keeps a $30 change fund in his shop. Prepare an appropriate general journal entry to record the cash sale as well as reveal the cash shortage.

Group A Problems

(The blank forms you need are on pages 197–204 of the *Study Guide and Working Papers*.)

6A-1. Able.com received a bank statement from Lee Bank indicating a bank balance of $8,000. Based on Able.com's check stubs, the ending checkbook balance was $6,600. Your task is to prepare a bank reconciliation for Able.com as of July 31, 200X, from the following information (journalize entries as needed):

   a. Checks outstanding: no. 122, $1,000; no. 130, $690.
   b. Deposits in transit $1,110.

Margin notes:

Bank reconciliation.

Establishing and replenishing petty cash.

Cash shortage in replenishment.

Cash overage in replenishment.

Calculate cash shortage with change fund.

Preparing a bank reconciliation including collection of a note.

Check Figure:
Reconciled
Balance $7,420

c. Bank service charges $83.
d. Lee Bank collected a note for Able.com, $910, less a $7 collection fee.

Preparing a bank reconciliation with NSF using the back side of a bank statement.

6A-2. From the following bank statement, please (1) complete the bank reconciliation for Rick's Deli found on the reverse of the bank statement and (2) journalize the appropriate entries as needed.

a. A deposit of $3,000 is in transit.
b. Rick's Deli has an ending checkbook balance of $6,600.
c. Checks outstanding: no. 111, $600; no. 119, $1,200; no. 121, $330.
d. Jim Rice's check for $300 bounced due to lack of sufficient funds.

Check Figure:
Reconciled
Balance $6,270

Lowell National Bank
Rio Mean Brand
Bugna, Texas

Rick's Deli
8811 2nd St,
Bugna, Texas

Old Balance	Checks in Order of Payment		Deposits	Date	New Balance
6,000				2/2	6,000
	90.00	210.00		2/3	5,700
	150.00		300.00	2/10	5,850
	600.00		600.00	2/15	5,850
	300.00	NSF	300.00	2/20	5,850
	1,200.00		1,200.00	2/24	5,850
	600.00	30.00 SC	180.00	2/28	5,400

Establishment and replenishment of petty cash.

6A-3. The following transactions occurred in April for Merry Co.:

200X
April
1 Issued check no. 14 for $80 to establish a petty cash fund.
5 Paid $5 from petty cash for postage, voucher no. 1.
8 Paid $10 from petty cash for office supplies, voucher no. 2.
15 Issued check no. 15 to Reliable Corp. for $200 from past purchases on account.
17 Paid $8 from petty cash for office supplies, voucher no. 3.
20 Issued check no. 16 to Roger Corp., $600 for past purchases on account.
24 Paid $4 from petty cash for postage, voucher no. 4.
26 Paid $9 from petty cash for local church donation, voucher no. 5 (a miscellaneous payment).
28 Issued check no. 17 to Roy Kloon to pay for office equipment, $700.
30 Replenish petty cash, check no. 18.

Check Figure:
Cash Replenishment $36

Your tasks are to

1. Record the appropriate entries in the general journal as well as the auxiliary petty cash record as needed.
2. Be sure to replenish the petty cash fund on April 30 (check no. 18).

6A-4. From the following, record the transactions into Logan's auxiliary petty cash record and general journal (p. 2) as needed:

Establishing and replenishing petty cash including a cash shortage.

200X
Oct.
1 A check was drawn (no. 444) payable to Roberta Floss, petty cashier, to establish a $100 petty cash fund.
5 Paid $14 for postage stamps, voucher no. 1.

9   Paid $12 for delivery charges on goods for resale, voucher no. 2.
12   Paid $8 for donation to a church (miscellaneous expense), voucher no. 3.
14   Paid $9 for postage stamps, voucher no. 4.
17   Paid $8 for delivery charges on goods for resale, voucher no. 5.
27   Purchased computer supplies from petty cash for $8, voucher no. 6.
28   Paid $4 for postage, voucher no. 7.
29   Drew check no. 618 to replenish petty cash and a $3 shortage.

Group B Problems

(The blank forms you need are on pages 197–204 of the *Study Guide and Working Papers.*)

6B-1. As the bookkeeper of Able.com, you received the bank statement from Lee Bank indicating a balance of $9,185. The ending checkbook balance was $8,215. Prepare the bank reconciliation for Able.com as of July 31, 200X, and prepare journal entries as needed based on the following:

  a. Deposits in transit, $3,600.
  b. Bank service charges, $29.
  c. Checks outstanding: no. 111, $590; no. 115, $1,255.
  d. Lee Bank collected a note for Able.com, $2,760, less a $6 collection fee.

6B-2. Based on the following, please (1) complete the bank reconciliation for Rick's Deli found on the reverse of the bank statement and (2) journalize the appropriate entries as needed.

  a. Checks outstanding: no. 110, $80; no. 116, $160; no. 118, $52.
  b. A deposit of $416 is in transit.
  c. The checkbook balance of Rick's Deli shows an ending balance of $798.
  d. Jim Rice's check for $40 bounced due to lack of sufficient funds.

Lowell National Bank
Rio Mean Brand
Bugna, Texas

Rick's Deli
8811 2nd St,
Bugna, Texas

Old Balance	Checks in Order of Payment		Deposits	Date	New Balance
718.00				4/2	718.00
	12.00	36.00		4/3	670.00
	20.00		40.00	4/10	690.00
	80.00		80.00	4/15	690.00
	40.00	NSF	40.00	4/20	690.00
	160.00		160.00	4/24	690.00
	80.00	2.00 SC	24.00	4/28	632.00

6B-3. From the following transactions, (1) record the entries as needed in the general journal of Merry Co. as well as the auxiliary petty cash record and (2) replenish the petty cash fund on April 30 (check no. 8).

200X
Apr.   1   Issued check no. 4 for $60 to establish a petty cash fund.
      5   Paid $9 from petty cash for postage, voucher no. 1.
      8   Paid $12 from petty cash for office supplies, voucher no. 2.
    15   Issued check no. 5 to Reliable Corp. for $400 for past purchases on account.
    17   Paid $7 from petty cash for office supplies, voucher no. 3.

20   Issued check no. 6 to Roger Corp. $300 for past purchases on account.

24   Paid $6 from petty cash for postage, voucher no. 4.

26   Paid $12 from petty cash for local church donation, voucher no. 5 (a miscellaneous payment).

28   Issued check no. 7 to Roy Kloon to pay for office equipment, $800.

30   Replenish petty cash, check no. 8.

6B-4. From the following, record the transactions into Logan's auxiliary petty cash record and general journal (p. 2) as needed:

200X

Oct. 1   Roberta Floss, the petty cashier, cashed a check, no. 444, to establish a $90 petty cash fund.

5   Paid $16 for postage stamps, voucher no. 1.

9   Paid $14 for delivery charges on goods for resale, voucher no. 2.

12   Paid $6 for donation to a church (miscellaneous expense), voucher no. 3.

14   Paid $10 for postage stamps, voucher no. 4.

17   Paid $7 for delivery charges on goods for resale, voucher no. 5.

27   Purchased computer supplies from petty cash for $9, voucher no. 6.

28   Paid $3 for postage, voucher no. 7.

29   Drew check no. 618 to replenish petty cash and a $4 shortage.

> *Check Figure:*
> Cash Replenishment $46

> Establishing and replenishing petty cash including a cash shortage.

> *Check Figure:*
> Cash Replenishment $69

Real-World Applications

6R-1. Claire Montgomery, the bookkeeper of Angel Co., has appointed Mike Kaminsky as the petty cash custodian. The following transactions occurred in November:

200X

Nov. 25   Check no. 441 was written and cashed to establish a $50 petty cash fund.

27   Paid $8.50 delivery charge for goods purchased for resale.

29   Purchased office supplies for $12 from petty cash.

30   Purchased postage stamps for $15 from petty cash.

On December 3, Mike received the following internal memo:

MEMO

TO: Mike Kaminsky

FROM: Claire Montgomery

RE: Petty Cash

Mike, I'll need $5 for postage stamps. By the way, I noticed that our petty cash account seems to be too low. Let's increase its size to $100.

Could you help Mike replenish petty cash on December 3 by providing him with a general journal entry? Support your answer and indicate in writing whether Claire was correct.

6R-2. Lee Company has the policy of depositing all receipts and making all payments by check. On receiving the bank statement, Bill Free, a new bookkeeper, is quite upset that the balance in Cash in the ledger is $4,209.50, whereas the ending bank balance is $4,440.50. Bill is convinced the bank has made an error. Based on the following facts, is Bill's concern warranted? What other written suggestions could you offer Bill in the bank reconciliation process?

a. The November 30 cash receipts, $611, had been placed in the bank's night depository after banking hours and consequently did not appear on the bank statement as a deposit.

b. Two debit memorandums and a credit memorandum were included with the returned check. None of the memorandums had been recorded at the time of the reconciliation. The first debit memorandum had a $130 NSF check written by Abby Ellen. The second was a $6.50 debit memorandum for service charges. The credit memorandum was for $494 and represented the proceeds less a $6 collection fee from a $500 non-interest-bearing note collected for Lee Company by the bank.

c. It was also found that checks no. 942 for $71.50 and no. 947 for $206.50, both written and recorded on November 28, were not among the cancelled checks returned.

d. Bill found that check no. 899 was correctly drawn for $1,094, in payment for a new cash register. This check, however, had been recorded as though it were for $1,148.

e. The October bank reconciliation showed two checks outstanding on September 30, no. 621 for $152.50 and no. 630 for $179.30. Check no. 630 was returned with the November bank statement, but check no. 621 was not.

YOU make the call

Critical Thinking/Ethical Case

6R-3. Sean Nah, the bookkeeper of Revell Co., received a bank statement from Lone Bank. Sean noticed a $250 mistake made by the bank in the company's favor. Sean called his supervisor, who said that as long as it benefits the company, he should not tell the bank about the error. You make the call. Write your specific recommendations to Sean.

Internet Exercises: Federal Reserve Bank of Dallas; Analytics.com

EX-1. [**www.dallasfed.org**]   This site will provide you details of the operation of the Federal Reserve Bank of Dallas, Texas. The Federal Reserve System, nicknamed "the Fed," has member banks in 13 cities. Each provides a wealth of economic information on the region it serves. The Dallas Fed Web site contains an article on "dot-com" banking.

1. Read that article and answer these questions:

    a. Do dot-com banks present a challenge to local banks in your city?

    b. What do you believe is the future of dot-com banks? Will they be scrutinized more closely than traditional banking institutions?

2. With a group of your fellow students compare paper money. Use the money you have to determine the location of other Federal Reserve banks. Look at the circular seal on the left side of the bills to determine these locations.

3. What services does the Fed offer to member banks?

EX-2. [**www.e-analytics.com/bonds/fed20.htm**]   Checks that you write on your bank eventually return to your bank and the amount of the check is deducted from your account. In between the time you write the check and it comes back, you have use of the funds because of a phenomenon called *float*. Individual checking accounts are handled much the same way the paragraph at this site describes. Float is the period of time that two banks have the funds on their books. Suppose you pay your bill for a magazine subscription. You write the check on your bank and mail it to the magazine company. When the company deposits it, it is then "float" because your bank has not yet paid the check.

The Federal Reserve System handles float for large commercial accounts in a method detailed in this article.

1. How does the Federal Reserve System handle checks from its member banks?
2. What is the impact of float on the monetary policy of the United States?

Continuing Problem

Eldorado Computer Center

The books have been closed for the first year of business for Eldorado Computer Center. The company ended up with a marginal profit for the first three months in operation. Tony expects faster growth as he enters into a busy season.

Following is a list of transactions for the month of October. Petty Cash account #1010 and Miscellaneous Expense account #5100 have been added to the chart of accounts.

Assignment

(See pages 208–218 in the *Study Guide and Working Papers.*)

1. Record the transactions in general journal or petty cash format.
2. Post the transactions to the general ledger accounts.
3. Prepare a trial balance.

Oct. 1 Paid rent for November, December, and January, $1,200 (check no. 8108).
2 Established a petty cash fund for $100.
4 Collected $3,600 from a cash customer for building five systems.
5 Collected $2,600, the amount due from A. Pitale's invoice no. 12674, customer on account.
6 Purchased $25 worth of stamps, using petty cash voucher no. 101.
7 Withdrew $2,000 (check no. 8109) for personal use.
8 Purchased $22 worth of supplies, using petty cash voucher no. 102.
12 Paid the newspaper carrier $10, using petty cash voucher no. 103.
16 Paid the amount due on the September phone bill, $65 (check no. 8110).
17 Paid the amount due on the September electric bill, $95 (check no. 8111).
22 Performed computer services for Taylor Golf; billed the client $4,200 (invoice no. 12675).
23 Paid $20 for computer paper, using petty cash voucher no. 104.
30 Took $15 out of petty cash for lunch, voucher no. 105.
31 Replenished the petty cash. Coin and currency in drawer total $8.00.

Because Tony was so busy trying to close his books, he forgot to reconcile his last three months of bank statements. What follows on pages 252 and 253 is a list of all deposits and checks written for the past three months (each entry is identified by chapter, transaction date, or transaction letter) and bank statements for July through September. The statement for October won't arrive until the first week of November.

Eldorado Computer Center Summary of Deposits and Checks

Chapter	Transaction	Payor/Payee	Amount
		Deposits	
1	a	Tony Freedman	$4,500
1	f	Cash customer	250
1	i	Taylor Golf	1,200
1	g	Cash customer	200
2	p	Cash customer	900
3	Sept. 2	Tonya Parker Jones	325
3	Sept. 6	Summer Lipe	220
3	Sept. 12	Jeannine Sparks	850
3	Sept. 26	Mike Hammer	140

Chapter	Transaction	Check #	Payor/Payee	Amount
			Checks	
1	b	8095	Multi Systems, Inc.	$1,200
1	c	8096	Office Furniture, Inc.	600
1	e	8097	Capital Management	400
1	j	8098	Tony Freedman	100
2	l	8099	Insurance Protection, Inc.	150
2	m	8100	Office Depot	200
2	n	8101	Computer Edge Magazine	1,400
2	q	8102	San Diego Electric	85
2	r	8103	U.S. Postmaster	50
3	Sept. 1	8104	Capital Management	1,200
3	Sept. 8	8105	Pacific Bell USA	155
3	Sept. 15	8106	Computer Connection	200
3	Sept. 16	8107	Multi Systems, Inc.	1,200

Bank Statement

First Union Bank 322 Glen Ave. Escondido, CA 92025

Eldorado Computer Center   Statement Date: July 22, 200X

Checks Paid:			Deposits and Credits:	
Date paid	Number	Amount	Date received	Amount
7–4	8085	1,200.00	7–1	4,500.00
7–7	8096	600.00	7–10	250.00
7–15	8097	400.00	7–20	1,200.00
			7–21	200.00
Total 3 checks paid for $2,200.00			Total Deposits	$6,150.00
Ending balance on July 22 — $3,950.00				

Received statement July 29, 200X.

Bank Statement

First Union Bank 322 Glen Ave. Escondido, CA 92025

Eldorado Computer Center   Statement Date: August 21, 200X

Checks Paid:

Date paid	Number	Amount
8–2	8098	100.00
8–3	8099	150.00
8–10	8100	200.00
8–15	8101	1,400.00
8–20	8102	85.00

Total 5 checks paid for $1,935.00
Beginning balance on July 22 —
$3,950.00

Deposits and Credits:

Date received	Amount
8–12	900.00

Total Deposits $900.00
Ending balance on August 21 —
$2,915.00

Received statement August 27, 200X.

Bank Statement

First Union Bank 322 Glen Ave. Escondido, CA 92025

Eldorado Computer Center   Statement Date: September 20, 200X

Checks Paid:

Date paid	Number	Amount
9–2	8103	50.00
9–6	8104	1,200.00
9–12	8105	155.00

Total 3 checks paid for $1,405.00
Beginning balance on August 21
$2,915.0

Deposits and Credits:

Date received	Amount
9–4	325.00
9–7	220.00
9–14	850.00

Total Deposits $1,395.00
Ending balance on September 20
$2,905.00

Received statement September 29, 200X.

Assignment

1. Compare the Computer Center's deposits and checks with the bank statements and complete a bank reconciliation as of September 30, 200X.

SUBWAY Case

COUNTING DOWN THE CASH

Subway now requires all of its franchisees to submit their weekly sales and inventory reports electronically using new point-of-sale (POS) touch-screen cash registers. With the new POS registers, clerks use a touch screen to punch in the number and type of items bought. Franchisees can quickly reconfigure prices and products to match new promotions. Not only is this POS method faster than using the old cash registers but it also allows franchisees to view every transaction as it occurs—from their own back office computers or even from home. Also, individual POS terminals within the restaurant are linked, so franchisees are able to see consolidated data quickly.

The transition to electronic reporting and networked POS terminals, however, has not been without bumps, as Stan can testify. About six months before the deadline for all Subway franchisees to "go electronic," Stan attended a heated meeting on the topic at his local chapter of the North American Association of Subway Franchisees (NAASF). The NAASF is an independent organization of franchisees that serves as an advisory council on Subway policies and issues of common concern. Everyone seemed to be talking at once.

"I just don't trust these machines. What am I supposed to do when the system crashes?" complained one man.

"Yeah, and I don't like the idea of a bunch of kids knowing more about how to run the software than I do," said one older franchisee.

"Don't be so quick to assume that our sandwich artists will love POS," said one woman. "I overheard one of my employees say to another, 'POS means **P**eeking **O**ver **S**houlders.' These young kids we hire have more reason to be resistant than we do!"

"I'll say they do!" rejoined Jay Harden, the president of Stan's local NAASF. "Employee theft is one of the largest problems we face as franchisees. I, for one, really welcome the cash control we get with POS."

Stan had to agree with Jay. Training staff to record every sale and record it correctly is a critical component of a cash business like Subway. In Stan's view, the POS machines would only make that training easier. Cash control is built into the new system, which also provides the owners with information that will help them spot problems—such as employee theft—and track trends. Of course, thought Stan, the chore of counting down the cash at the end of a shift remained. No matter what type of computer program you install, cash still must be counted down and rectified with the register tape at the end of each shift.

As the voices rung louder around him, Stan thought about what had happened that day, when Ellen closed out her cash register drawer. He had spent hours figuring out a discrepancy between the cash in the drawer and the register tape. Ellen had forgotten to void a mistaken entry for $99.99. Stan had first suspected that she had made a huge error in counting change.

Thinking of errors in counting brought him back to the topic of the meeting. Stan raised his hand to speak.

"One thing that concerns me is the potential for accounting errors. I still have to key in data from the POS into my Peachtree accounting software. Every time I have to re-enter data, the potential for error multiplies."

"That shows some foresight, Stan," said Jay Harden. "We're actually exploring computer programs that will feed the data directly from the POS into our accounting programs." Even some of the technophobes and POS skeptics in the group had to agree that would be a great idea.

Discussion Questions

1. What is an advisory council? Why do you think franchisees need one?
2. Why do you think some small business owners fear computerization?
3. How would Stan catch a discrepancy in the Cash account? How would he record a loss?
4. Why does Subway invest time, money, and effort in investigating new cash handling systems like its new POS terminals?

CHAPTER 7

Payroll Concepts and Procedures

You were happy when you received your first check from working at your school's business office. It feels good to be making money to help with school expenses and to save toward your spring break vacation. You had a good idea of how much you earned after working for two weeks at the business office. However, you were a little disappointed when you opened the envelope containing your check. The amount of your check wasn't nearly as much as you thought you would receive. You forgot about the taxes that were withheld from your paycheck. Perhaps you forgot about the taxes, but the payroll accountant at school remembered to withhold them from your check.

Any business that has employees must pay them for their time and services. An important part of preparing a payroll for a company is accurately calculating employee earnings and the proper amounts to withhold in Social Security, Medicare, as well as federal and state income taxes.

In this chapter we will discuss the steps necessary in calculating regular earnings, overtime earnings, and various withholding taxes. We will learn how to calculate federal, Social Security, and Medicare taxes on employee earnings. We will also introduce you to the payroll register and employee earnings records, which are used in recording a payroll for a business. After completing this chapter, you will know the difference between an employee's gross earnings and employee's net pay and the role taxes play when paying employees.

Learning Objectives

- Calculating overtime pay, FICA deductions for Social Security and Medicare, and federal income tax withholding. (p. 258)

- Preparing a payroll register. (p. 265)

- Journalizing and posting the payroll entry from the payroll register. (p. 266)

- Maintaining an individual employee earnings record. (p. 274)

An essential part of running a business is hiring and paying employees. Whether a business is a small mom-and-pop grocery store in your own town or a huge nation-wide corporation, the rules for payroll are really the same. That's why it's important to know how to calculate and record a payroll.

In this chapter we take a close look at the employees of Gradesoft.com, a company that programs and sells teacher grading software, to see how a payroll is figured and recorded. We look at how a payroll is affected by federal, state, and local taxes and how the accountant at Gradesoft.com handles a payroll for the company.

Learning Unit 7-1   Introduction to Payroll Accounting

Ernie Goldman is the accountant for Gradesoft.com. This new company creates software that allows teachers to track and calculate students' grades electronically using a personal computer. Ernie has the responsibility of calculating and recording each payroll for the company. Several key parts of Ernie's job in working with payroll need mention here. First, Ernie *must be accurate* in everything he does, because any mistake he makes in working with the payroll may affect both the employee and the company. Second, Ernie needs to be *on time* when working on the company's payroll so that the employees get their paychecks when they are due. Third, Ernie must at all times *comply with the appropriate federal, state, and local laws governing payroll matters.* Fourth, Ernie always needs to keep everything *confidential* when working on the payroll.

Ernie must first calculate the earnings for Gradesoft.com employees. For Ernie to make the correct calculations, he must know how each employee has been classified for payroll purposes. As a rule, a company will classify each employee as either "hourly" or "salaried" when it comes to paying earnings. If an employee is an *hourly employee,* that employee will only be paid for the hours he or she worked. If an employee is classified as a *salaried employee,* he or she will receive a set dollar amount for the hours worked.

Gradesoft.com has classified three of its six employees as hourly. For these employees, Ernie must compute the hours they have worked during a specific period of time known as a *pay period.* A pay period is important because Ernie uses it to determine how much each hourly employee has earned. For payroll purposes, **pay periods** are defined as daily, weekly, biweekly (every two weeks), semimonthly (twice each month), monthly, quarterly, or annual. A pay period can start on any day of the week and must end after the specified period of time has passed. Most companies use weekly, biweekly, semimonthly, or monthly pay periods when calculating their payrolls.

Gradesoft.com uses a biweekly pay period for its hourly employees and a monthly pay period for its three salaried employees. The biweekly pay period starts on Monday and ends 14 days (two weeks) later on a Sunday. The monthly pay period starts on the first day of the calendar month and ends on the last day.

Now that Ernie knows the pay period for Gradesoft.com's hourly employees, he must calculate their total or *gross earnings.* The **gross earnings** amount for an employee is composed of two amounts; regular earnings and overtime earnings (if any).

Overtime earnings must be figured according to federal (and in some cases, state) law. This federal law is known as the **Fair Labor Standards Act** (also known as Federal Wage and Hour Law). For most employers, the law states that an hourly employee must be paid more per hour for any hours worked over 40 during a period of time called a *workweek.* A **workweek** is a time period that can start at any time on any given day, but it must end 168 hours later (or seven calendar days of 24 hours each). One workweek follows another, and the starting time must be the same time each week.

For rules of the Fair Labor Standards Act to apply to an employer, the employer must be involved in interstate commerce.

For the hourly employees of Gradesoft.com, there are two workweeks in each biweekly pay period. Gradesoft.com's workweek starts on Monday morning at 12:01 A.M. and ends the following Sunday evening at 12:00 midnight (168 hours later). Thus, Ernie must figure any overtime pay if any employee has worked more than 40 hours during each week of the two-week (that is, biweekly) pay period.

The federal law also set the minimum standard for overtime pay. It is one and a half times the regular hourly rate of pay for an employee. Let's look at Lee Jackson, one of the hourly employees of Gradesoft.com who worked overtime hours during the biweekly pay period starting on August 7 and ending on August 20 (remember that there are 14 days in the biweekly pay period and two workweeks in the same pay period for figuring overtime earnings).

Lee worked 45 hours for the week of August 7 to August 13 and 39 for the week of August 14 to August 20. How many regular and overtime hours did Lee work for this biweekly pay period? First, Ernie must look at each workweek separately from the next. Thus, Lee worked 40 regular and 5 overtime hours for the first workweek and 39 regular and 0 overtime hours for the second workweek. Note that Ernie did not take any overtime hours from the first workweek and apply them to the second workweek to pay Lee for 40 hours. Remember that each workweek stands independently of another, even if during another workweek the employee worked fewer than 40 hours.

There are two ways of figuring the regular and overtime hours for Lee during this pay period. Ernie notes here that Lee makes $10.80 per hour. Now let's look at each way to figure the total hours Lee must be paid.

Method One

Total Hours × Regular Rate	= 84 hours × $10.80 / hour	=	$907.20
Worked of pay			
+ Overtime × $\frac{1}{2}$ Regular Rate	= 5 hours × $5.40 / hour	=	$ 27.00
Hours of pay			

Total Pay for Lee Jackson	**$934.20**

Method Two

Regular Hours × Regular Rate of Pay	= 79 hours × $10.80 / hour	=	$853.20
+ Overtime Hours × $1\frac{1}{2}$ Regular Rate of Pay	= 5 hours × $16.20	=	$ 81.00

Total Pay for Lee Jackson	**$934.20**

As you can see, Ernie can use either way to arrive at the total or gross earnings for Lee Jackson for the pay period. Method One clearly shows Ernie how much Lee is being paid in overtime. Because Method Two is more commonly used to figure gross earnings, we use it to figure gross earnings for Gradesoft.com employees in this chapter.

EMPLOYEE FEDERAL AND STATE INCOME TAX WITHHOLDING

After Ernie has figured Lee Jackson's gross earnings, he must now start figuring out how much Lee will receive in pay after several different taxes have been withheld. These taxes, known as payroll taxes or income tax withholding, must be paid by each employee based on how much was earned each pay period. Gradesoft.com is required to withhold payroll taxes for each employee and pay them to the government according to a special timetable. The amount paid by Gradesoft.com for payroll taxes is known as a **payroll tax deposit.** We discuss how payroll tax deposits work in Chapter 8.

For Ernie to determine how much to withhold from Lee's check in payroll taxes, Lee must complete a form known as a **Form W-4, Employee's Withholding Allowance Certificate.** This form contains information Ernie needs to calculate Lee's **federal income tax (FIT) withholding** for the pay period. Ernie will use the information from Form W-4, along with special tax withholding tables supplied by the Internal Revenue Service (IRS), to determine how much to withhold in FIT from Lee's check. Lee Jackson is actually paying the government the amount that he would owe in federal income taxes by having Gradesoft.com take it at the time he is paid. In this way Lee pays his taxes on a "pay-as-you-go" basis, which is based on how much he earns each pay period.

Notice in Figure 7-1 below that Lee's Form W-4 shows his marital status and total number of allowances he is claiming for federal income tax purposes. In general, an employee is granted one **allowance** (also known as an **exemption**) for himself or herself, one for a spouse (unless the spouse works and claims his or her own allowance), and one for each of his or her dependents (e.g., children) for whom the employee provides more than one-half support during a year. Employees who wish to have more withheld from their paychecks can elect to claim fewer allowances on Form W-4 than they actually have.

Ernie will use Lee's marital status and number of allowances claimed from his Form W-4 along with Lee's gross earnings for the pay period to look up the amount of federal tax to withhold using an IRS **wage bracket table** (see Fig. 7-2). These tables can be found in an IRS publication known as *Circular E, Employer's Tax Guide,* also known as Publication 15. Note in Figure 7-2 that the wage bracket table has been grouped according to pay period and marital status. *Circular E* contains tables for daily, weekly, biweekly, semimonthly, monthly, quarterly, and annual pay periods. For each pay period

---

- - - - - - - - - - - - - -   Cut here and give Form W-4 to your employer. Keep the top part for your records.   - - - - - - - - - - - - - -

Form **W-4** Department of the Treasury Internal Revenue Service	**Employee's Withholding Allowance Certificate** For Privacy Act and Paperwork Reduction Act Notice, see page 2.	OMB No. 1545-0010 **200X**

1 Type or print your first name and middle initial LEE	Last name JACKSON	**2** Your social security number 923 85 1316

Home address (number and street or rural route) 1225 HIGHTOWN STREET	**3** ☒ Single ☐ Married ☐ Married, but withhold at higher Single rate. **Note:** *If married, but legally separated, or spouse is a nonresident alien, check the Single box.*
City or town, state, and ZIP code SOUTHSIDE, MA 01945	**4** If your last name differs from that on your social security card, check here. **You must call 1-800-772-1213 for a new card** . . . ☐

5	Total number of allowances you are claiming (from line **H** above **OR** from the applicable worksheet on page 2)	**5**	1
6	Additional amount, if any, you want withheld from each paycheck	**6** $	
7	I claim exemption from withholding for 200X, and I certify that I meet **BOTH** of the following conditions for exemption: Last year I had a right to a refund of **ALL** Federal income tax withheld because I had **NO** tax liability **AND** This year I expect a refund of **ALL** Federal income tax withheld because I expect to have **NO** tax liability.		
	If you meet both conditions, write "EXEMPT" here	**7**	

Under penalties of perjury, I certify that I am entitled to the number of withholding allowances claimed on this certificate, or I am entitled to claim exempt status.

Employee's signature (Form is not valid unless you sign it) ▶ *Lee Jackson*   **Date** JANUARY 3, 200X

8 Employer's name and address (Employer: Complete lines 8 and 10 only if sending to the IRS.)	**9** Office code (optional)	**10** Employer identification number

Cat. No. 10220Q

Figure 7-1 Form W-4, Employee's Withholding Allowance Certificate

SINGLE Persons—BIWEEKLY Payroll Period

(For Wages Paid in 200X)

If the wages are—		And the number of withholding allowances claimed is—										
At least	But less than	0	1	2	3	4	5	6	7	8	9	10
		The amount of income tax to be withheld is—										
$800	$820	$95	$77	$60	$42	$24	$12	$0	$0	$0	$0	$0
820	840	98	80	63	45	27	14	2	0	0	0	0
840	860	101	83	66	48	30	16	4	0	0	0	0
860	880	104	86	69	51	33	18	6	0	0	0	0
880	900	107	89	72	54	36	20	8	0	0	0	0
900	920	110	92	75	57	39	22	10	0	0	0	0
920	940	113	95	78	60	42	25	12	1	0	0	0
940	960	116	98	81	63	45	28	14	3	0	0	0
960	980	119	101	84	66	48	31	16	5	0	0	0
980	1,000	122	104	87	69	51	34	18	7	0	0	0
1,000	1,020	125	107	90	72	54	37	20	9	0	0	0
1,020	1,040	128	110	93	75	57	40	22	11	0	0	0
1,040	1,060	131	113	96	78	60	43	25	13	1	0	0
1,060	1,080	134	116	99	81	63	46	28	15	3	0	0
1,080	1,100	137	119	102	84	66	49	31	17	5	0	0
1,100	1,120	140	122	105	87	69	52	34	19	7	0	0
1,120	1,140	143	125	108	90	72	55	37	21	9	0	0
1,140	1,160	146	128	111	93	75	58	40	23	11	0	0
1,160	1,180	150	131	114	96	78	61	43	26	13	1	0
1,180	1,200	156	134	117	99	81	64	46	29	15	3	0
1,200	1,220	161	137	120	102	84	67	49	32	17	5	0
1,220	1,240	167	140	123	105	87	70	52	35	19	7	0
1,240	1,260	172	143	126	108	90	73	55	38	21	9	0
1,260	1,280	177	146	129	111	93	76	58	41	23	11	0
1,280	1,300	183	151	132	114	96	79	61	44	26	13	2
1,300	1,320	188	156	135	117	99	82	64	47	29	15	4
1,320	1,340	194	162	138	120	102	85	67	50	32	17	6
1,340	1,360	199	167	141	123	105	88	70	53	35	19	8
1,360	1,380	204	173	144	126	108	91	73	56	38	21	10
1,380	1,400	210	178	147	129	111	94	76	59	41	24	12
1,400	1,420	215	183	152	132	114	97	79	62	44	27	14
1,420	1,440	221	189	157	135	117	100	82	65	47	30	16
1,440	1,460	226	194	163	138	120	103	85	68	50	33	18
1,460	1,480	231	200	168	141	123	106	88	71	53	36	20
1,480	1,500	237	205	173	144	126	109	91	74	56	39	22
1,500	1,520	242	210	179	147	129	112	94	77	59	42	24
1,520	1,540	248	216	184	153	132	115	97	80	62	45	27
1,540	1,560	253	221	190	158	135	118	100	83	65	48	30
1,560	1,580	258	227	195	163	138	121	103	86	68	51	33
1,580	1,600	264	232	200	169	141	124	106	89	71	54	36
1,600	1,620	269	237	206	174	144	127	109	92	74	57	39
1,620	1,640	275	243	211	180	148	130	112	95	77	60	42
1,640	1,660	280	248	217	185	153	133	115	98	80	63	45
1,660	1,680	285	254	222	190	159	136	118	101	83	66	48
1,680	1,700	291	259	227	196	164	139	121	104	86	69	51
1,700	1,720	296	264	233	201	169	142	124	107	89	72	54
1,720	1,740	302	270	238	207	175	145	127	110	92	75	57
1,740	1,760	307	275	244	212	180	149	130	113	95	78	60
1,760	1,780	312	281	249	217	186	154	133	116	98	81	63
1,780	1,800	318	286	254	223	191	159	136	119	101	84	66
1,800	1,820	323	291	260	228	196	165	139	122	104	87	69
1,820	1,840	329	297	265	234	202	170	142	125	107	90	72
1,840	1,860	334	302	271	239	207	176	145	128	110	93	75
1,860	1,880	339	308	276	244	213	181	149	131	113	96	78
1,880	1,900	345	313	281	250	218	186	155	134	116	99	81
1,900	1,920	350	318	287	255	223	192	160	137	119	102	84
1,920	1,940	356	324	292	261	229	197	166	140	122	105	87
1,940	1,960	361	329	298	266	234	203	171	143	125	108	90
1,960	1,980	366	335	303	271	240	208	176	146	128	111	93
1,980	2,000	372	340	308	277	245	213	182	150	131	114	96
2,000	2,020	377	345	314	282	250	219	187	155	134	117	99
2,020	2,040	383	351	319	288	256	224	193	161	137	120	102
2,040	2,060	388	356	325	293	261	230	198	166	140	123	105
2,060	2,080	393	362	330	298	267	235	203	172	143	126	108
2,080	2,100	399	367	335	304	272	240	209	177	146	129	111

$2,100 and over   Use Table 2(a) for a **SINGLE person** on page 34. Also see the instructions on page 32.

Figure 7-2 Wage Bracket Table—Single Persons

there are separate "single" and "married" tables. Finally, each individual table is organized according to the gross earnings of the employee for the pay period.

Let's look at how Ernie will use the Single Biweekly Payroll Period table in *Circular E* to see how he arrived at the amount of FIT to be withheld from Lee Jackson's check. First, Ernie knows that Lee is paid biweekly (once every two weeks). Ernie has also figured Lee's gross earnings for the last biweekly pay period Lee worked ($934.20). Ernie can then look at Lee's Form W-4 and see that Lee has claimed one allowance (for himself) and has indicated that he is single (look at Fig. 7-1 again). It is now easy for Ernie to look up the FIT amount from the table by going down the left-hand column labeled "If the wages are." Ernie will stop at the line "At least $920 But less than $940." Ernie stops at this line because Lee's earnings are $934.20, which is an amount within that range of earnings. Now Ernie will move to the right until he finds the amount in the column labeled "1," which indicates the number of withholding allowances per Lee's Form W-4. Where the row and the column meet, Ernie finds an amount of $95, the amount of FIT that Ernie will withhold from Lee's paycheck.

Now what would happen if Lee actually earned $940 for the pay period? Ernie would go to the next line below in the table because the first column reads "At least $940." The amount Lee would owe in FIT withholding would be $98; Lee would owe a little more in tax because he made a little more in gross earnings. Had Lee earned $939 instead of $940, his earnings would have still been "Less than $940." Ernie would use the same line of the table and would find that Lee would owe $95 in FIT.

Lee will probably owe state income tax (or SIT) as well as FIT. Many states allow payroll people to use the federal Form W-4 for state income tax withholding as well. Other states have their own versions of Form W-4 that employees must fill out. Many states have their own version of the IRS *Circular E* that can be used to look up SIT withholding. These states also require an employer to withhold and collect the state income taxes and then make state payroll tax deposits according to state rules. The majority of states currently tax an employee's gross earnings; several do not and do not require SIT withholding.

EMPLOYEE WITHHOLDING FOR SOCIAL SECURITY TAXES

Another tax that Ernie must compute and withhold from employee checks is known as Social Security Tax or FICA (FICA stands for Federal Insurance Contributions Act, a 1935 federal law that has required workers to pay this tax since 1937). The proceeds of this tax support federal payments for (1) monthly retirement benefits for those over 62 years old, (2) medical benefits for those over 65 years old, (3) benefits for workers who have become disabled, and (4) benefits for families of deceased workers who were covered by this law. Both employees of companies as well as self-employed individuals must pay FICA taxes.

There are two special things to know about Social Security (or FICA) tax. First, Social Security tax is really two taxes. One of these taxes is called Social Security (or OASDI, which stands for old age, survivors, and disability insurance), and the other is known as Medicare (or HI, which stands for health insurance). Usually, people group both taxes together and call them Social Security (or FICA) tax. Second, the rate of Social Security tax and the maximum dollar amount of earnings upon which the tax can be computed may change each year. The maximum dollar amount of earnings upon which the tax is computed is known as an earnings, or wage-base limit. Note that the wage-base limit applies only to the Social Security (or OASDI) part of the tax because there is no limit for Medicare (or HI) tax.

Let's look at how Ernie computes the Social Security tax on Lee's earnings to give you a better idea of how this tax is calculated. First, Ernie knows both the current year's tax rate and the wage-base limit for the Social Security portion of the tax. Here are the rates and limit he will use:

Current year's rate for Social Security (OASDI) tax = 6.20%

Current year's rate for Medicare (HI) tax = 1.45%

Current year's wage-base limit for Social Security (OASDI) tax = $87,000

Note again that these rates and the wage-base limit may change each year. In general, the wage-base limit will increase from year to year, as may the rate of taxes. Therefore, we use the term *current* when referring to these tax rates and the wage-base limit.

Once Ernie knows the rates and limit he is ready to begin making calculations. First, Ernie needs to look at how much Lee has earned for the year *prior* to his current pay-period earnings. He will use this information to determine whether Lee's earnings are under or over the current wage-base limit for Social Security tax. Ernie finds that Lee's year-to-date (abbreviated YTD) gross earnings before this pay period equal $20,872.65. This dollar amount is below the wage-base limit of $87,000 for the year, so Lee's total gross earnings of $934.20 will be taxed at a rate of 6.20% for Social Security purposes. Ernie will withhold $57.92 in Social Security taxes (or $934.20 × .062 = $57.92).

What if Lee had made close to or more than $87,000 for the year before his current pay-period earnings? Let's suppose that Lee's prior year-to-date earnings are $86,618.95. If we add $934.20 to this amount, Lee's new year-to-date earnings will be $87,553.15 ($86,618.95 + $934.20), which is more than the current $87,000 wage-base limit. In this situation Ernie must withhold Social Security tax *on only the portion of Lee's current gross earnings that will not exceed the $87,000 wage-base limit.* Ernie must make the following calculation to determine this amount by subtracting Lee's prior year-to-date earnings from the wage base-limit: $87,000 − $86,618.95 = $381.05. Thus, only $381.05 of Lee's $934.20 in current gross earnings will be subject to Social Security tax at a rate of 6.20%. The remaining $553.15 of Lee's current pay (or $934.20 − $381.05) will not be taxed for Social Security (OASDI) purposes. Therefore, whatever Lee earns for the rest of the current calendar year will not be subject to this tax because Lee has exceeded the wage-base limit for the year.

It is important to know that all these calculations apply only to each current calendar year. An employee's year-to-date earnings in one year will never be carried over and used in the next year for the purpose of looking at the Social Security wage-base limit. Every employee starts the new year on January 1 with $0.00 in year-to-date earnings for wage-base limit analysis.

It is easier to figure Medicare (or HI) tax because there is no wage-base limit connected with this tax. Ernie will simply figure Medicare tax at a rate of 1.45% of Lee's earnings no matter how much he earns during the year. Ernie will withhold $13.55 in Medicare (or HI) tax on Lee's gross earnings for the pay period ($934.20 × .0145 = $13.55).

Another important fact about Social Security tax is that the amount withheld and paid by each employee must be matched and paid by the employer, using the same rules we have discussed. In Chapter 8 we look at the employer's side of Social Security and Medicare taxes.

OTHER INCOME TAX WITHHOLDING

We pointed out previously that employees will have state income taxes withheld from their paychecks if they live in one of the states that tax income. In addition, many cities and counties tax employee earnings. Sometimes the tax will be a certain percentage of gross earnings, or it may be a flat dollar amount withheld every pay period. Such cities and counties will have their own rules regarding payroll tax deposits and tax reports for this type of withholding.

WORKERS' COMPENSATION INSURANCE

Workers' compensation insurance provides protection for employees from any loss they may incur due to injury or death while on the job. Each employer (working with an insurance agent or a state agency) must estimate the cost of this insurance. The premium must be paid in advance. In the majority of states, this tax is paid by the employer, not the employee. In Chapter 8 we look at how the premium is figured and what responsibility the employer has in paying this tax.

Learning Unit 7-1 Review

AT THIS POINT you should be able to

- Explain the purpose of the Federal Wage and Hour Law. (p. 258)
- Calculate overtime pay. (p. 259)
- Complete a W-4 form. (p. 260)
- Discuss the term *claiming an allowance*. (p. 260)
- Use a wage-bracket tax table to arrive at the withholding amount for federal income tax. (p. 262)
- Define the purposes of Social Security (FICA) tax. (p. 262)
- Calculate the deductions for Social Security and Medicare taxes. (p. 263)
- Understand the purpose of workers' compensation insurance. (p. 264)

SELF-REVIEW QUIZ 7-1

(The forms you need are found on page 219 of the *Study Guide and Working Papers*.)

John Small is a software engineer who is paid biweekly. He earned $2,064 in the current biweekly pay period. To date this year, *before* the current payroll, John has earned a total $85,800 in salary. Please calculate the amount of tax for Social Security and Medicare, federal income tax, and state income tax deducted for the pay period.

- Social security tax is 6.20% with a wage-base limit of $87,000 for the year.
- Medicare tax is 1.45% with no wage-base limit.
- John is single and claims two withholding allowances.
- The state income tax rate is 8%.
- No other deductions are taken out of John's paycheck by his employer.

SOLUTION TO SELF-REVIEW QUIZ 7-1

- Social Security tax: $74.40 ($1,200 × .062). The $1,200 was found by taking $87,000 − $85,800.
- Medicare tax: $29.93 ($2,064 × .0145). Remember that there is no wage-base limit for this tax.
- State income tax: $165.12 ($2,064 × .08).
- Federal income tax: $330, found by looking at where the "At least $2,060" line meets the "Two withholding allowance" column.

Learning Unit 7-2   The Payroll Process

Ernie Goldman will now enter the payroll information for the three hourly employees of Gradesoft.com into a worksheet known as a **payroll register.** Figure 7-3 (p. 266) shows a completed payroll register for the biweekly pay period from August 7 through August 20. We refer to this figure in both Chapters 7 and 8.

This multicolumn form is used specifically for the purpose of tracking the earnings of employees for any given pay period. Note that Gradesoft.com will have both biweekly and monthly payroll registers because it tracks its hourly employees on a biweekly basis and its salaried employees on a monthly basis. (We only show the biweekly register here.) Let's look closely at each column in the register to see how the numbers were generated.

(A) ALLOWANCES AND MARITAL STATUS

The information in column A comes from the Form W-4 that each employee has completed. You will recall that this form (see Fig. 7-1) indicates the employee's marital status and number of withholding allowances (or exemptions) that is used to arrive at the correct amount of federal income tax (column M) to be withheld for the pay period.

> **Example:** Sheila Stowe is single and provides total support for her 9-year-old daughter. Even though she can claim two withholding allowances, she claims zero allowances because she wants to have more taken out of her paycheck each pay period. If she has paid too much in FIT, she can claim a refund after the end of the year when filing her individual income tax return.

(B) CUMULATIVE (YTD) EARNINGS

Column B shows the employee's year-to-date (or cumulative) earnings for the year *before* the current pay period earnings have been added to it. Ernie will look at the amount in this column to determine if the employee is over or under the Social Security wage-base limit.

> **Example:** Lee Jackson has earned $20,872.65 before the current biweekly pay period.

(C) SALARY FOR PAY PERIOD, NUMBER OF HOURS WORKED, AND WAGES PER HOUR

Specific columns are used to record the amount any salaried employees have earned for the pay period, the hours worked by hourly employees, and the hourly rate of pay for nonsalaried employees.

GRADESOFT.COM INC.
PAYROLL REGISTER
AUGUST 7–20, 200X

Employee Name	Allowances and Marital Status	Cumulative Earnings (YTD)	Salary for Pay Period	No. of Hours Worked	Wages per Hour	Earnings			Cumulative Earnings (YTD)	Taxable Earnings		
						Regular	Overtime	Gross		Federal Unemploy-ment	Soc. Sec.	Medicare
Jackson, L.	S-1	2087265	—	8400	1080	85320	8100	93420	2180685	—	93420	93420
Stowe, S.	S-0	4850025	—	8000	2450	196000	—	196000	681025	196000	196000	196000
Regan, P.	S-2	4658705	—	8150	2175	174000	4894	178894	4837599	—	178894	178894
TOTALS		7230995	—			455320	12994	468314	7699309	196000	468314	468314
Discussions in this chapter are keyed to these letters	(A)	(B)	(C)	(C)	(C)	(D)	(E)	(F)	(G)	(H)	(I)	(J)

Figure 7-3 Payroll Register for Gradesoft.com

GRADESOFT.COM INC.
PAYROLL REGISTER
AUGUST 7–20, 200X

| | FICA | | Deductions | | | | | | Distribution of Expense Accounts | |
	Soc. Sec.	Medicare	Federal Income Tax	State Income Tax	Medical Insurance	Net Pay	Check No.		Business Analyst Expense	Program. Develop. Expense
	5792	1355	9500	7474	4400	64899	506		93420	
	12152	2842	36600	15680	2200	126526	507			196000
	11091	2594	25400	14312	2200	123297	508			178894
	29035	6791	71500	37466	8800	314722			93420	374894
	(K)	(L)	(M)	(N)	(O)	(P)	(Q)		(R)	(S)

Discussions in this chapter are keyed to these letters

Note: Sheila Stowe's medical insurance is $44.00 because she pays to cover both herself and her daughter.

Figure 7-3 (*continued*)

> **Example:** Because this payroll register is used only for hourly employees, no amounts are entered in the salary for pay period column. Please note that Lee Jackson is paid $10.80 per hour, and he worked 84 total hours for the pay period.

(D) "REGULAR" EARNINGS

To get an amount for column D, Ernie must multiply the total regular hours by the hourly rate of pay for each employee.

> **Example:** Sheila Stowe has earned $1,960.00 for the pay period.
>
> | Hours Worked | | Rate of Pay per Hour | | Regular Earnings |
> |:---:|:---:|:---:|:---:|:---:|
> | 80 | × | $24.50 | = | $1,960.00 |

(E) OVERTIME EARNINGS

After 40 hours each workweek, hourly employees are entitled to receive overtime pay at a rate of one and one-half times their regular hourly rate of pay.

> **Example:** Pat Regan worked 81.5 hours, of which 80 were regular and 1.5 hours were classified as overtime. Pat is paid overtime at a rate of $32.625 per hour.
>
> | Hourly Rate | | Time and a Half | | Overtime Rate of Pay |
> |:---:|:---:|:---:|:---:|:---:|
> | $21.75 | × | 1.5 | = | $32.625 |
>
> | Overtime Hours Worked | | Overtime Rate | | Overtime Earnings |
> |:---:|:---:|:---:|:---:|:---:|
> | 1.5 | × | $32.625 | = | $48.94 |

(F) GROSS EARNINGS

Gross earnings is the total amount that an employee has earned (regular earnings plus any overtime earnings). These amounts will be used to fill in columns R and S.

> **Example:** Pat Regan's gross earnings are $1,788.94.
>
> | Regular Earnings | | Overtime Earnings | | Gross Earnings |
> |:---:|:---:|:---:|:---:|:---:|
> | $1,740.00 | + | $48.94 | = | $1,788.94 |

(G) CUMULATIVE EARNINGS (YTD)

Column G shows the employee's year-to-date earnings after the current pay period earnings have been computed. This amount will be "carried over" to the next payroll register column B for the next pay period.

Example: Sheila Stowe has earned $6,810.25 as of August 20.

Cumulative Earnings Before the Pay Period		Gross Earnings for the Pay Period		Cumulative Earnings YTD as of August 20
$4,850.25	+	$1,960.00	=	$6,810.25

(H) TAXABLE EARNINGS: UNEMPLOYMENT INSURANCE

In Chapter 8 we talk about certain payroll taxes that are only paid by employers. Federal unemployment taxes (per the Federal Unemployment Tax Act, or FUTA) are paid according to a wage-base limit (like Social Security tax). The current wage-base limit for FUTA tax is the first $7,000 that each employee earns during a calendar year. Note that this column shows the FUTA wage-base limit for each employee, not the amount of FUTA tax that Gradesoft.com has paid.

Example: Before this pay period, Sheila Stowe's cumulative year-to-date earnings are $4,850.25. For the pay period ending on August 20, Sheila earned $1,960. Her new cumulative year-to-date earnings now amount to $6,810.25, which is under the $7,000 FUTA wage-base limit. Gradesoft.com will pay FUTA tax on the $1,960.00 that Sheila earned for the pay period.

During the next pay period, Gradesoft.com will pay FUTA tax only on $189.75 of Sheila's earnings (assuming Sheila earns at least this much during the next pay period) because Sheila's earnings will meet the FUTA wage-base limit of $7,000 in this pay period.

Example:

Total taxable earnings for FUTA tax	$7,000.00
Cumulative earnings for Sheila Stowe before the new pay period	6,810.25
Taxable earnings for FUTA tax	$ 189.75

(I) TAXABLE EARNINGS FOR SOCIAL SECURITY (OASDI) TAX

All employees pay Social Security tax until they reach each current year's wage-base limit. Our current limit for this example is $87,000. Column I shows the amount of earnings that will be taxed. It does not show that amount of Social Security tax the employee or employer pays. None of the three hourly employees has reached the wage-base limit as of the August 20 pay period. Keep in mind this column is *not* the tax, it is the amount subject to the tax.

(J) TAXABLE EARNINGS FOR MEDICARE TAX

Column J shows the amount of earnings subject to Medicare tax. Remember that there is no wage-base limit for Medicare tax, so this column will match the amount found in column F, cumulative year-to-date earnings. Keep in mind this column is *not* the tax, it is the amount subject to the tax.

(K) FICA DEDUCTION—SOCIAL SECURITY TAX

The current rate for Social Security tax is 6.20% up to $87,000. The amount in column I is multiplied by the 6.20% rate to arrive at the tax for each employee in this column.

> **Example:** Lee Jackson's Social Security tax for the pay period is $57.92.
>
> | Column I Amount | Current Social Security Rate | Column K Social Security Tax |
> |---|---|---|
> | $934.20 × | .062 = | $57.92 |

(L) FICA DEDUCTION—MEDICARE TAX

The current rate for Medicare tax is 1.45% on all employee earnings with no wage-base limit.

> **Example:** Sheila Stowe's gross earnings of $1,960.00 is multiplied by 1.45% to arrive at $28.42 in Medicare tax.
>
> | Gross Earnings | Medicare Tax Rate | Medicare Tax |
> |---|---|---|
> | $1,960.00 × | .0145 = | $28.42 |

(M) FEDERAL INCOME TAX (FIT)

Recall that federal income tax does not have any wage-base limit. Employees pay FIT on their gross earnings each pay period throughout the year. The amount of tax withheld depends on the employee's (1) income for the pay period, (2) marital status, and (3) number of withholding allowances claimed on Form W-4 (Fig. 7-1).

Ernie has used the IRS table found in *Circular E* (see Fig. 7-2) to find the amount of FIT to withhold from the three employees for the August 20 pay period. Look at Figure 7-2 again and use the information found in column A to verify the amounts Ernie has listed in column M of the payroll register.

(N) STATE INCOME TAX (SIT)

Ernie uses a rate of 8% to calculate and withhold state income tax for the August 20 pay period. Like federal income tax, there is no wage-base limit for state income tax, so all employee gross earnings for the pay period will be taxed.

> **Example:** Pat Regan's state income tax is $143.12.
>
> | Gross Earnings | Tax Rate | State Income Tax |
> |---|---|---|
> | $1,788.94 × | .08 = | $143.12 |

(O) MEDICAL INSURANCE

Gradesoft.com deducts an amount to pay for medical insurance coverage for its employees. The rate is $22.00 per pay period for coverage for an employee only and $44.00 per pay period for coverage of an employee and his or her dependents.

(P) NET PAY

Net pay, or take-home pay, is the employee's gross earnings minus taxes withheld and any other deductions, such as medical insurance. Gross pay is what all employees wish they had; net pay is what employees are left with!

Ernie will subtract all withholding taxes and medical insurance premiums from all employees' gross earnings to arrive at their net pay.

Example: Lee Jackson's net pay is $670.99, computed as follows:

Gross earnings		$934.20
Less: FICA — Social Security tax	$57.92	
FICA — Medicare tax	13.55	
Federal income tax	95.00	
State income tax	74.74	
Medical insurance	44.00	
Net pay		$648.99

(Q) CHECK NUMBER

When Ernie prepares the paychecks, he records each check number in column Q of the payroll register.

(R AND S) DISTRIBUTION OF EXPENSE ACCOUNTS

The gross earnings for each employee is an expense of Gradesoft.com. Ernie uses columns R and S to identify the specific expense account to which each employee's earnings will be posted. This identification will help him make the journal entry to record the August 20 payroll. Note that Lee Jackson's earnings will be posted to the Business Analyst Expense account, whereas Sheila's and Pat's earnings will be posted to the Programming Development Expense account.

Learning Unit 7-2 Review

AT THIS POINT you should be able to

- Explain and prepare a payroll register. (p. 265)
- Explain the purpose of the taxable earnings columns and how they relate to the cumulative earnings columns. (p. 269)

SELF-REVIEW QUIZ 7-2

(The forms you need are on page 219 of the *Study Guide and Working Papers.*)

Mike Chen is an hourly employee who is paid biweekly. He is paid overtime at a rate of 1.5 times his hourly rate of pay for any hours he works over 40 in a workweek. Mike has worked many overtime hours this year to develop a new software program, and as of December 10 he has cumulative earnings of $85,778.06. For the pay period ending on December 24, Mike's gross earnings are $1,940.85. Calculate Mike's net pay based on the following facts:

- The Social Security tax rate is 6.2% with a wage-base limit of $87,000 for the year; the Medicare rate is 1.45% with no wage-base limit.
- Mike is single and claims three withholding allowances per his Form W-4. Use the tax table in Figure 7-2 to find Mike's federal income tax withholding amount.
- The state income tax rate is 8% with no wage-base limit.
- Mike pays $44.00 for medical insurance for the pay period.

SOLUTION TO SELF-REVIEW QUIZ 7-2

Quiz Tip:
Only the first $1,221.94 of Mike's wages is subject to social security tax ($87,000 − $85,778.06).

1. FICA—Social Security tax is $75.76 ($1,221.94 × .062). Remember to subtract the cumulative year-to-date earnings from the wage-base limit when the employee's earnings approach the limit ($87,000 − $85,778.06). FICA—Medicare tax is $28.14 ($1,940.85 × .0145).
2. Federal income tax is $266 by the table (see Fig. 7-2).
3. State income tax is $155.27 ($1,940.85 × .08).

Mike Chen's net pay is $1,371.68 ($1,940.85 − $75.76 − $28.14 − $266.00 − $155.27 − $44.00).

Learning Unit 7-3   Recording and Paying the Payroll

After Ernie Goldman has completed the payroll register for the August 20 pay period, he must next take the summary total amounts (found at the bottom of the columns of the payroll register) and post them to specific accounts in the general ledger. Refer back to the payroll register in Figure 7-3.

For Gradesoft.com, the payroll for the biweekly pay period ending on August 20 is recorded in the general journal as shown in Figure 7-4.

Figure 7-4
Journalized Payroll Entry

General Journal								
	200X							
Aug.	20	Business Analyst expense		9 3 4 20				
		Programming Development expense		3 7 4 8 94				
		FICA—Social Security tax payable				2 9 0 35		
		FICA—Medicare tax payable				6 7 91		
		Federal income tax payable				7 1 5 00		
		State income tax payable				3 7 4 66		
		Medical insurance payable				8 8 00		
		Wages and salaries payable				3 1 4 7 22		
		To record payroll for August 20, 200X						

Note that the amounts recorded in the Gradesoft.com general journal come from the August 20 payroll register. Look back at Figure 7-3 and note that the two expense account amounts (Business Analyst and Programming Development Expense) are the same figures found in columns R and S. The credit amounts to the various tax payable and medical insurance accounts come from the totals found in columns K through O. The amount of the net pay comes from column P. The ledger (Figure 7-5) of Gradesoft.com will look as follows *after* the posting process has been completed.

Wages and Salaries Payable 202	FICA—Social Security Payable 203	FICA—Medicare Payable 204
	3,147.22		290.35		67.91
Liability on the balance sheet	Liability on the balance sheet	Liability on the balance sheet

Federal Income Tax Payable 205	State Income Tax Payable 206	Medical Insurance Payable 207
	715.00		374.66		88.00
Liability on the balance sheet	Liability on the balance sheet	Liability on the balance sheet

Business Analyst Expense 601	Programming Development Expense 602
934.20		3,748.94	
Expense on the income statement	Expense on the income statement

Figure 7-5 summarizes this process.

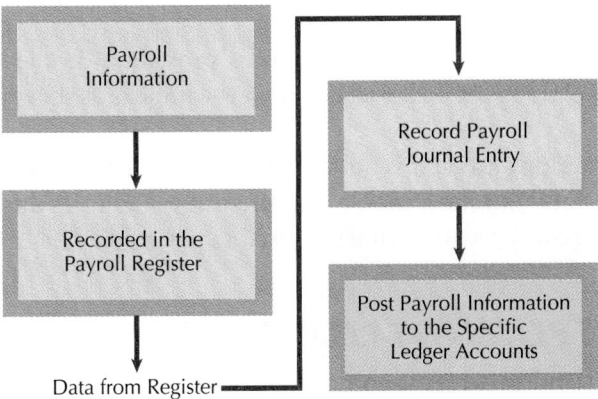

Figure 7-5
The Payroll Recording and Posting Process

PAYROLL CHECKING ACCOUNTS: PAYING THE PAYROLL

Gradesoft.com, like the vast majority of companies, uses a special checking account for paychecks. This account is called Payroll Checking Cash. A company with a medium to a large payroll will use this account to clear paychecks because (1) the company has much better internal control over the funds deposited to pay employees and (2) it is easier for the payroll person to reconcile the account each month and determine if someone has not cashed his or her paycheck for some reason.

A deposit for the total net amount of the payroll is placed in this separate checking account. When all the checks are written, the payroll checking account balance should be zero. The following journal entries would result in paying the payroll.

Figure 7-6
Check from
Gradesoft.com

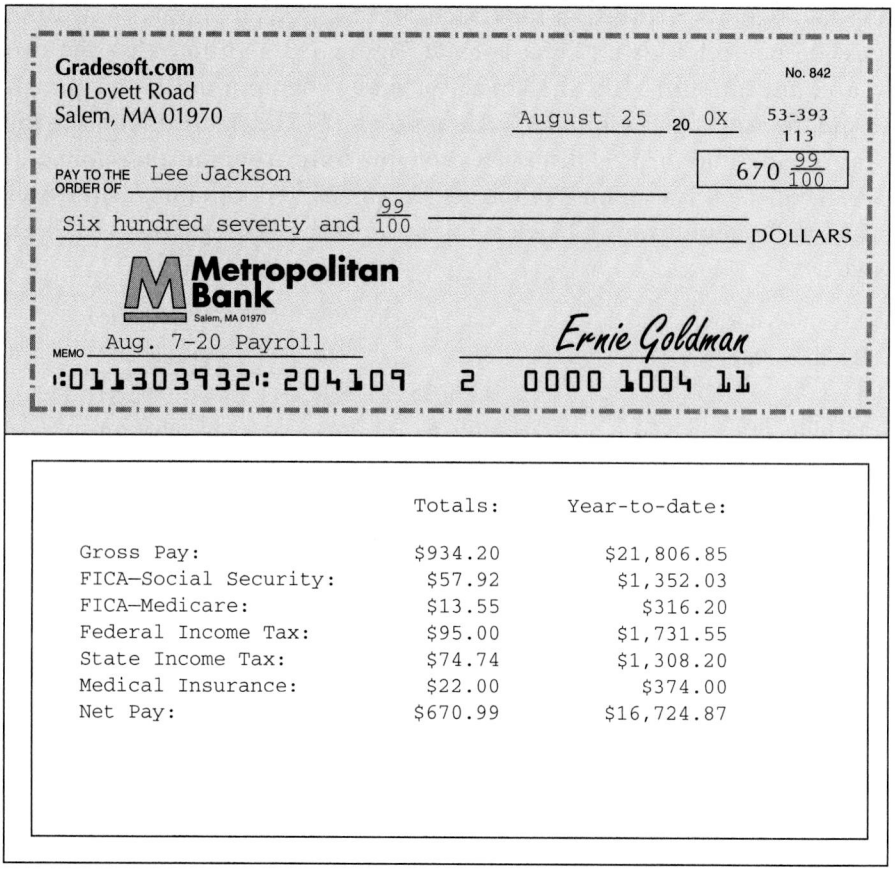

	Totals:	Year-to-date:
Gross Pay:	$934.20	$21,806.85
FICA—Social Security:	$57.92	$1,352.03
FICA—Medicare:	$13.55	$316.20
Federal Income Tax:	$95.00	$1,731.55
State Income Tax:	$74.74	$1,308.20
Medical Insurance:	$22.00	$374.00
Net Pay:	$670.99	$16,724.87

Payroll Checking Cash
   Cash
← Separate account for payroll setup.

Wages and Salaries Payable
   Payroll Checking Cash
← Payroll paid and balance in Payroll Checking is zero.

The checks that Gradesoft.com uses for payroll purposes provide a detailed accounting of an employee's gross earnings as well as all deductions withheld, as shown in Figure 7-6.

Remember that if a payroll checking account is not used by a business, its payroll can be paid by debiting Wages and Salaries Payable and crediting Cash. In this instance the company's regular checking account would be used to pay employees.

THE INDIVIDUAL EMPLOYEE EARNINGS RECORD

Ernie has yet another task to attend to when it comes to payroll recordkeeping. Individual employee earnings records must be maintained by Gradesoft.com to meet federal and state employment laws and regulations.

The employee earnings record (see Fig. 7-7) provides a summary of each employee's earnings, deductions, net pay, and cumulative earnings during each calendar year. The information summarized in this record will be used by Ernie to prepare quarterly and annual payroll tax reports (which we discuss in Chapter 8). Thus, the employee earnings record is broken into calendar quarters (each calendar quarter is 13 weeks in length).

Figure 7-8 on p. 276 shows the payroll function for Gradesoft.com. Note that the payroll function begins with recording the hours worked by employees each biweekly and monthly pay period. The flow of information is the same for each pay period during the calendar year.

INDIVIDUAL EMPLOYEE EARNINGS RECORD
FOR PAT REGAN
FOURTH QUARTER, 200X

Pay Period No. and Pay Dates	Hours Worked			Total Earnings	Deductions					Net Pay	Check No.	Cumulative Earnings
	Pay Period #	Regular	Overtime		Soc. Sec.	Medicare	Fed. Inc. Tax	State Inc. Tax	Med. Ins.‡			
10/02–10/15	20	80	4.5	1886 81	116 98	27 36	314 00	150 94	22 00	1255 53	511	55994 57
10/16–10/29	21	80	3.75	1862 34	115 46	27 00	309 00	148 99	22 00	1239 89	525	57856 91
10/30–11/12	22	80	5.25	1911 28	118 50	27 71	320 00	152 90	22 00	1270 17	530	59768 19
11/13–11/26	23	80	6	1935 75	120 02	28 08	326 00	154 86	22 00	1284 79	544	61703 94
11/27–12/10	24	80	8.75	2025 47	125 58	29 37	354 00	162 04	22 00	1332 48	565	63729 41
12/11–12/24	25	77	0	1674 75	103 83	24 28	253 00	133 98	22 00	1137 66	574	65404 16
12/25–12/31	26*	48	0	1044 00	64 73	15 14	110 00	83 52	22 00	748 61	590	66448 16
Total 4th Quarter				12340 40	765 10	178 94	1986 00	987 23	154 00	8269 13		
YTD Total				66448 16	4119 79	963 50	8265 00	5315 85	572 00	47212 02		

*Note the last biweekly pay period will end in the next calendar year (January 8); Ernie will only use Pat's hours worked this year to complete her employee earnings record for this year.

‡Note P. Regan decreased medical insurance to $22 from 44 in Fig. 7.3.

Figure 7-7 Individual Employee Earnings Record

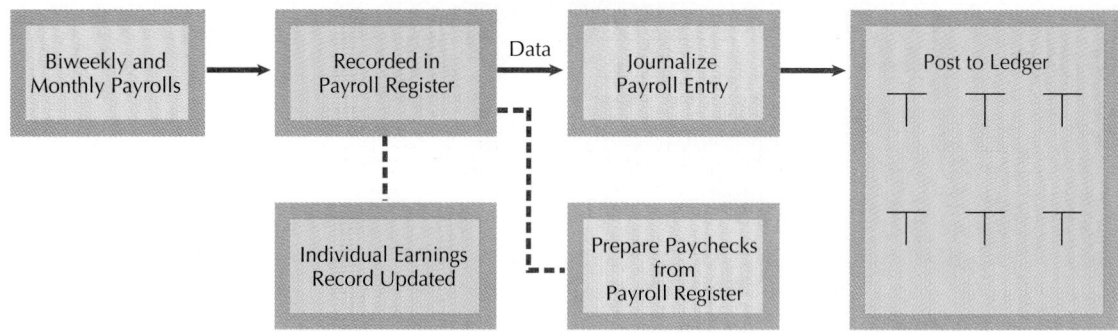

Figure 7-8 Payroll Function for Gradesoft.com

Learning Unit 7-3 Review

AT THIS POINT you should be able to

- Explain how to enter payroll information into the general journal from the payroll register. (p. 272)
- Journalize entries to pay a payroll. (p. 272)
- Update an individual employee earnings record. (p. 274)

SELF-REVIEW QUIZ 7-3

(The forms you need are on page 220 of the *Study Guide and Working Papers.*)
Indicate which of the following statements are false.

1. The use of a payroll register to record a company's payroll is optional.
2. FICA—Social Security Payable is a liability on the income statement.
3. Wages and Salaries Expense has a normal credit balance.
4. Individual employee earnings records are used by employees to keep track of their wages.
5. Every calendar quarter has 13 weeks.

Quiz Tip:
There are four quarters in a year.

SOLUTION TO SELF-REVIEW QUIZ 7-3

1. False   **2.** False   **3.** False   **4.** False   **5.** True

Chapter Review

Summary of Key Points

Learning Unit 7-1

1. The Fair Labor Standards Act states that a worker (1) will receive a minimum hourly rate of pay and (2) will work a maximum of 40 hours during a workweek at the regular rate of pay with time and a half after 40 hours.
2. For the rules of the Fair Labor Standards Act to apply to an employer, the employer must be involved in interstate commerce. Most companies today are involved in interstate commerce.
3. The employee and employer equally contribute to Social Security tax an amount that is based on a given yearly rate and wage base for a calendar year. Only Social Security tax has a wage-base limit of $87,000 as of this writing. Medicare has no wage-base limit, so an employee and employer will pay this tax on all the employee's earnings during the calendar year.
4. Tax tables for federal income tax withholding can be found in IRS *Circular E, Employer's Tax Guide* (also known as Publication 15).

Learning Unit 7-2

1. Gross pay less deductions equals net pay.
2. The taxable earnings columns do not show the tax. They show amount of earnings to be taxed for unemployment taxes, Social Security, and Medicare. Note that FICA is made up of two taxes, Social Security and Medicare.

Learning Unit 7-3

1. A payroll register provides the data for journalizing the payroll entry in the general journal.
2. Deductions for payroll represent liabilities for the employer until paid.
3. The account distribution columns of the payroll register indicate which accounts will be debited to record the total payroll wages and salaries expense when a journal entry is prepared.
4. The accounts FICA—Social Security Payable and FICA—Medicare Payable accumulate the tax liabilities of both the employer and the employee for Medicare and Social Security.
5. Paying a payroll results in debiting Wages and Salaries Payable and crediting Cash (or Payroll Checking Cash).
6. The individual employee earnings records are updated soon after the payroll register is prepared.

Key Terms

Allowance (also called exemption) A certain dollar amount of a person's income that will be considered nontaxable for income tax withholding purposes.

Calendar year A one-year period beginning on January 1 and ending on December 31. Employers must use a calendar year for payroll purposes, even if the employer uses a fiscal year for financial statements and for any other reasons.

Circular E An IRS tax publication of tax tables.

Fair Labor Standards Act (Federal Wage and Hour Law) A law the majority of employers must follow that contains rules stating the minimum hourly rate of pay and the maximum number of hours a worker will work before being paid time and a half for overtime hours worked. This law also has other rules and regulations that employers must follow for payroll purposes.

Federal income tax withholding   Amount of federal income tax withheld by the employer from the employee's gross pay; the amount withheld is determined by the employee's gross pay, the pay period, the number of allowances claimed by the employee on the W-4 form, and the marital status indicated on the W-4 form.

FICA (Federal Insurance Contributions Act)   Part of the Social Security Act of 1935, this law requires that a tax be levied on both the employer and employee up to a certain maximum rate and wage base for Social Security tax purposes. Furthermore, there is a tax for Medicare purposes with no employer or employee wage-base maximum.

FICA—Medicare Payable   A liability account that accumulates tax for Medicare.

FICA—Social Security Payable   A liability account that accumulates tax for Social Security.

Gross earnings   Amount of pay received before any deductions.

Individual employee earnings record   An accounting document that summarizes the total amount of wages paid and the deductions for the calendar year. It aids in preparing governmental reports. A new record is prepared for each employee each year.

Interstate commerce   A test that is applied to determine whether an employer must follow the rules of the Fair Labor Standards Act. If an employer communicates or does business with another business in some other state, it is usually considered to be involved in interstate commerce.

Market Wages Expense   An account that records from the payroll register gross wages earned by employees of a market (grocery) outlet.

Medical insurance   A deduction from employee's paycheck for health insurance.

Net pay   Gross pay less deductions. Net pay (or *take-home pay*) is what the worker actually takes home.

Office Salaries Expense   An account that records from the payroll gross salaries earned by employees of an office.

Pay (or payroll) period   A length of time used by an employer to calculate the amount of an employee's earnings. Pay periods can be weekly, biweekly (once every two weeks), semimonthly (twice each month), monthly, quarterly or annual.

Payroll register   A multicolumn form that can be used to record payroll data. The data in the payroll register are then used to prepare the general journal entry to record the paying of employees for a pay period.

Payroll tax   Amount of federal tax withheld from each employee's gross pay.

Payroll tax deposits   Amounts an employer pays to the government for payroll taxes. We discuss these deposits in more detail in Chapter 8.

State income tax withholding   Amount of state income tax withheld by the employer from the employee's gross pay.

Taxable earnings   Shows amount of earnings subject to a tax. The tax itself is not shown.

W-4 (Employee's Withholding Allowance Certificate)   A form filled out by employees and used by employers to supply needed information about the number of allowances claimed, marital status, and so forth. The form is used for payroll purposes to determine federal income tax withholding from an employee's paycheck.

Wage bracket tables   Various charts in IRS *Circular E* providing information about deductions for federal income tax based on earnings and data supplied on the W-4 form.

Wages and Salaries Payable   A liability account that shows net pay for payroll before employees are paid. Account zeros out after employees are paid.

Workers' compensation insurance   Insurance required by employers to protect their employees against losses due to injury or death incurred while on the job.

Workweek   A seven-day (168-hour) period used to determine overtime hours for employees. A workweek can begin on any given day, but must end seven days later.

Questions, Mini Exercises, Exercises, and Problems

Discussion Questions

1. What is the purpose of the Fair Labor Standards Act (also called the Federal Wage and Hour Law)?

2. Explain how to calculate overtime.

3. Define and state the purpose of completing a W-4 form (called the Employee's Withholding Allowance Certificate).

4. The more allowances an employee claims on a W-4 form, the more take-home pay the employee gets with each paycheck. True or false.

Blueprint: Recording, Posting, and Paying the Payroll

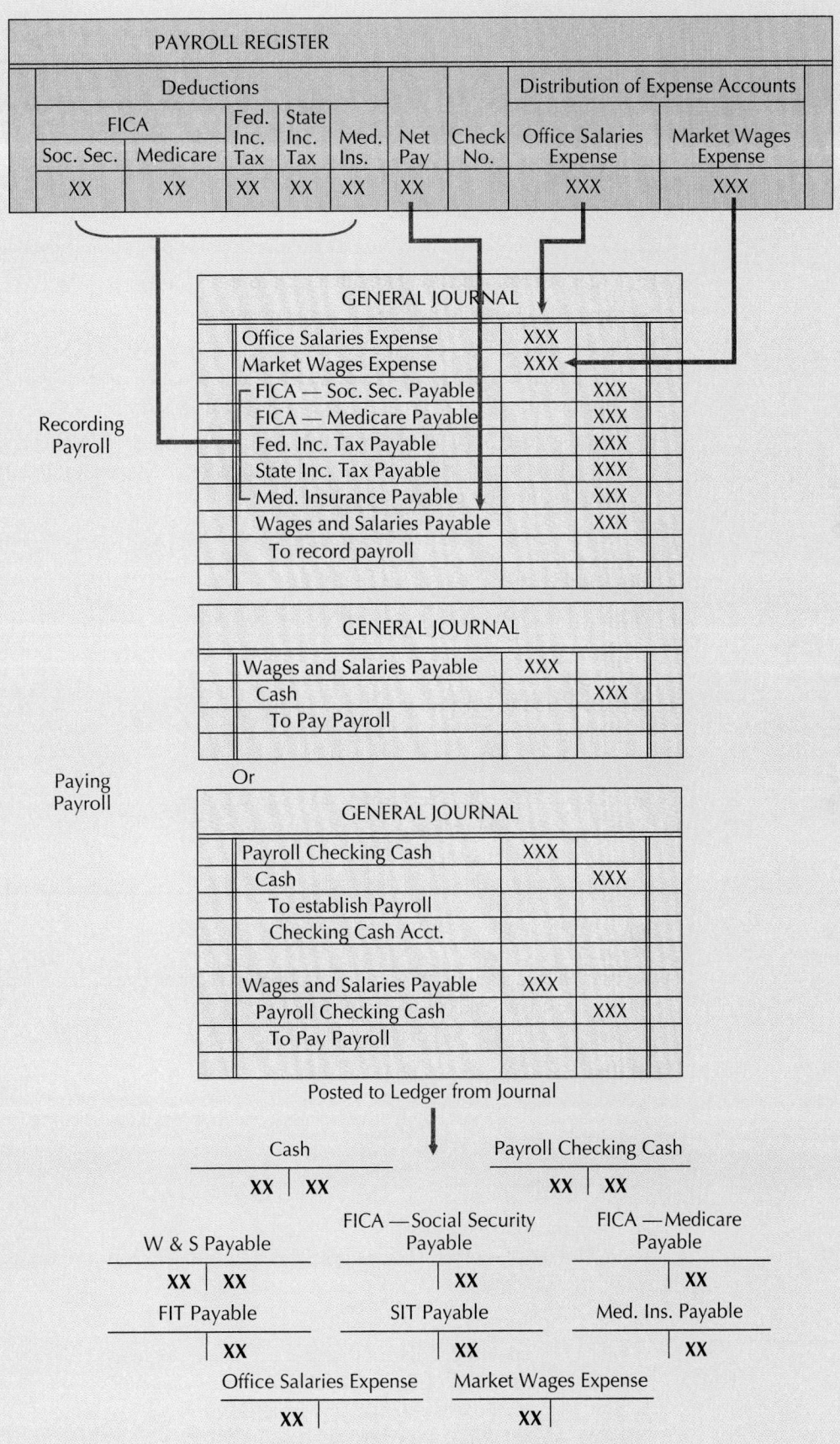

5. Why should a business prepare a payroll register before employees are paid? Please explain.

6. The taxable earnings column of a payroll register records the amount of tax due. True or false?

7. Define and state the purpose of FICA taxes.

8. Explain how to calculate Social Security and Medicare taxes.

9. The employer doesn't have to contribute to Social Security. Agree or disagree. Please explain.

10. Explain how federal and state income tax withholdings are determined.

11. What is a calendar year?

12. An employer must always use a calendar year for payroll purposes. True or false?

13. What purpose does the individual employee earnings record serve?

14. Why does payroll information center on 13-week quarters?

15. Please draw a diagram showing how the following items relate to each other: (a) a weekly payroll, (b) a payroll register, (c) individual employees' earnings, (d) general journal entries for payroll, (e) a payroll checking account.

16. If you earned $130,000 this year, you would pay more Social Security and Medicare taxes than your partner who earned $75,000. Do you agree or disagree? Please provide calculations to support your answer.

Mini Exercises

(The forms you need are on page 222 of the *Study Guide and Working Papers.*)

Calculating Gross Earnings

1. Calculate the total wages earned (assume an overtime rate of time and a half over 40 hours).

Employee	Hourly Rate	No. of Hours Worked
A. Dawn Slow	$10	39
B. Jill Jacobi	12	50

FICA

2. Pete Martin, single, claiming 1 exemption, has cumulative earnings before this biweekly pay period of $86,000. Assuming he is paid $2,000 this week, what will his deduction be for FIT and FICA (Medicare and Social Security)? Use tables and rates in the text.

Net Pay

3. Calculate Pete's net pay from Mini Exercise 2 above. State income tax is 5% and health insurance is $40.

Payroll Register

4. From the following identify
   1. Total of gross pay (comes from distribution of expense accounts).
   2. A deduction.
   3. Net pay.

   _____ **a.** Office Salaries Expense and Wages Expense
   _____ **b.** FICA—Social Security Payable
   _____ **c.** FICA—Medicare Payable
   _____ **d.** Federal Income Tax Payable

_____ e. Medical Insurance Payable
_____ f. Wages and Salaries Payable

Payroll Account

5. From the following, indicate if the title is

1. An asset.
2. A liability.
3. An expense.
4. Appears on the income statement.
5. Appears on the balance sheet.

_____ a. FICA—Social Security Payable
_____ b. Office Salaries Expense
_____ c. Federal Income Tax Payable
_____ d. FICA—Medicare Payable
_____ e. Wages and Salaries Payable

Exercises

(The forms you need are on pages 223–224 of the *Study Guide and Working Papers*.)

7-1. Calculate the total wages earned for each employee (assume an overtime rate of time and a half over 40 hours).

Calculating wages with overtime.

Employee	Hourly Rate	No. of Hours Worked
Joss Amando	$ 8	39
Jill West	12	44
Dale Aster	11	46

Tax table.

7-2. Compute the net pay for each employee using the federal income tax withholding tables in Figure 7-2. (Assume the following for FICA: Social Security tax is 6.2% on a wage-base limit of $87,000; Medicare is 1.45% on all earnings; the payroll is paid biweekly; there is no state income tax.)

Employee	Status	Claiming	Cumulative Pay	This Week's Pay
Alvin Cell	Single	1	$50,000	$1,190
Angel Lowe	Single	0	$64,300	$1,200

7-3. Complete the table.

	Category ↑	Normal Balance	Account Appears on Which Financial Statements
Medical Insurance Payable			
Wages and Salaries Payable			
Office Salaries Expense			
Market Wages Expense			
FICA—Social Security Payable			
Federal Income Tax Payable			
State Income Tax Payable			

Categorizing accounts.

7-4. The weekly payroll journal entry in Figure 7-9 was prepared by Landcaster Company from its payroll register. Which columns of the payroll register have the data come from? How does the *taxable earnings* column of the payroll register relate to this entry?

Figure 7-9
Payroll Journal Entry

Payroll register and the journal entry.

	Oct.	7	Shop Salaries Expense	4 0 0 0 00	
			Factory Wages Expense	2 0 0 0 00	
			FICA—Social Security Payable		3 7 2 00
			FICA—Medicare Payable		8 7 00
			Federal Income Tax Payable		1 2 0 0 00
			State Income Tax Payable		1 2 5 6 00
			Union Dues Payable		1 1 0 00
			Wages and Salaries Payable		2 9 7 5 00

7-5. The following amounts have been taken from the weekly payroll register for the Wu Lee Company on October 9, 200X. Using the same account title headings that we have used in this chapter, please prepare the general journal entry to record the payroll for Wu Lee Company for October 9.

Recording payroll by journal entry.

Factory Wages Expense	$3,579.00
Office Salaries Expense	1,597.00
Deduction for FICA—Social Security	296.15
Deduction for FICA—Medicare	75.05
Deduction for federal income tax	1,112.84
Deduction for state income tax	258.80
Deduction for union dues	480.00

Group A Problems

(The forms you need are on pages 225–229 of the *Study Guide and Working Papers.*)

7A-1. From the following information, please complete the chart for gross earnings for the week. (Assume an overtime rate of time and one-half over 40 hours.)

Calculating gross earnings with overtime.

		Hourly Rate	No. of Hours Worked	Gross Earnings
a.	Joe Vasquez	$ 9	40	
b.	Edna Kane	8	47	
c.	Dick Wall	10	42	
d.	Pat Green	13	50	

Check Figure:
d. $715   Gross Earnings

7A-2. March Company has five salaried employees. Your task is to record the following information into a payroll register:

Completing a payroll register.

Employee	Allowance and Marital Status	Cumulative Earnings Before This Payroll	Biweekly Salary	Department
Kool, Alice	S-1	$42,000	$1,200	Sales
Lose, Bob	S-1	30,000	800	Office
Moore, Linda	S-2	59,200	1,240	Office
Relt, Rusty	S-3	85,830	1,270	Sales
Veel, Larry	S-0	29,000	820	Sales

Assume the following:

1. FICA—Social Security: 6.2% on $87,000; FICA—Medicare: 1.45% on all earnings.
2. Each employee contributes $25 biweekly for union dues.
3. State income tax is 6% of gross pay.
4. FIT is calculated from Figure 7-2.

Check Figure:
Net Pay $3,938.99

7A-3. The bookkeeper of Pearl Co. gathered the following data from individual employee's earnings records and daily time cards. Your tasks are to (1) complete a payroll register on December 12 and (2) journalize the appropriate entry to record the payroll.

Completing a payroll register and journalizing the payroll entry.

Employee	Allowance and Marital Status	Cumulative Earnings Before This Payroll	M	T	W	T	F	Hourly Rate of Pay	FIT	Department
Boy, Pete	M-1	$64,100	5	11	9	8	8	$18	73	Sales
Heat, Donna	S-0	15,000	8	10	9	9	4	16	91	Office
Pyle, Ray	M-3	66,000	8	10	10	10	10	16	69	Sales
Vent, Joan	S-1	19,000	8	8	8	8	8	20	119	Office

Assume the following:

1. FICA—Social Security: 6.2% on $87,000; FICA—Medicare: 1.45% on all earnings.
2. Federal income tax has been calculated from a weekly table for you.
3. Each employee contributes $25 weekly for health insurance.
4. Overtime is paid at a rate of time and a half over 40 hours.

Check Figure:
Net pay $2,336.06

7A-4. Gary Nelson, Accountant, has gathered the following data from the time cards and individual employee earnings records. Your tasks are as follows:

Payroll register completed; journalizing and posting.

1. On December 5, 200X, prepare a payroll register for this biweekly payroll.
2. Journalize (p. 4) in the general journal and post to the general ledger accounts.

Check Figure:
Net Pay $3,450.67

Employee	Allowance and Marital Status	Cumulative Earnings Before This Payroll	Biweekly Salary	Check No.	Department
Aulson, Andy	S-3	$30,000	$ 950	30	Factory
Flynn, Jacki	S-1	50,000	1,000	31	Office
Moore, Jeff	S-2	60,000	1,200	32	Factory
Sullivan, Alison	S-1	65,000	1,300	33	Office

Assume the following:

1. FICA—Social Security: 6.2% on $87,000; FICA—Medicare: 1.45% on all earnings.
2. Federal income tax is calculated from Figure 7-2.
3. State income tax is 5% of gross pay.
4. Union dues are $10 biweekly.

Group B Problems

(The forms you need are on pages 225–229 in the *Study Guide and Working Papers*.)

7B-1. From the following information, please complete the chart for gross earnings for the week. (Assume an overtime rate of time and one-half over 40 hours.)

Calculating gross earnings with overtime.

	Hourly Rate	No. of Hours Worked	Gross Earnings
a. Joe Vasquez	$ 5	40	
b. Edna Kane	10	47	
c. Dick Wall	12	36	
d. Pat Green	14	55	

Check Figure:
d. Gross Pay. $875

7B-2. March Company has five salaried employees. Your task is to record the following information into a payroll register.

Employee	Allowance and Marital Status	Cumulative Earnings Before This Payroll	Biweekly Salary	Department
Kool, Alice	S-1	$45,150	$1,290	Sales
Lose, Bob	S-1	22,575	800	Office
Moore, Linda	S-2	59,300	1,240	Office
Relt, Rusty	S-3	86,100	1,300	Sales
Veel, Larry	S-0	21,875	860	Sales

Assume the following:

1. FICA—Social Security: 6.2% up to $87,000: FICA—Medicare: 1.45% on all earnings.
2. Each employee contributes $25 biweekly for union dues.
3. State income tax is 6% of gross pay.
4. FIT is calculated from Figure 7-2.

7B-3. The bookkeeper of Pearl Co. gathered the following data from individual employees' earnings records and daily time cards. Your tasks are to (1) complete a payroll register on December 12 and (2) journalize the appropriate entry to record the payroll.

Employee	Allowance and Marital Status	Cumulative Earnings Before This Payroll	M	T	W	T	F	Hourly Rate of Pay	FIT	Department
Boy, Pete	S-1	$64,900	12	11	7	7	7	$16	100	Sales
Heat, Donna	S-0	19,000	8	9	9	9	5	16	91	Office
Pyle, Ray	M-3	87,550	10	10	10	10	5	20	87	Sales
Vent, Joan	S-1	13,500	6	8	8	8	8	19	97	Office

Assume the following:

1. FICA—Social Security: 6.2% on $87,000; FICA—Medicare: 1.45% on all earnings.
2. Federal income tax has been calculated from a weekly table for you.
3. Each employee contributes $25 weekly for health insurance.
4. Overtime is paid at a rate of time and a half over 40 hours.

7B-4. Gary Nelson, accountant, has gathered the following data from the time cards and individual employee earnings records. Your task is to

1. On December 5, 200X, prepare a payroll register for this biweekly payroll.
2. Journalize (p. 4) in the general journal and post to the general ledger accounts.

Employee	Allowance and Marital Status	Cumulative Earnings Before This Payroll	Biweekly Salary	Check No.	Department
Aulson, Andy	S-3	$30,000	$ 800	30	Factory
Flynn, Jacki	S-1	50,000	1,100	31	Office
Moore, Jeff	S-2	60,000	1,050	32	Factory
Sullivan, Alison	S-1	65,000	1,200	33	Office

Assume the following:

1. FICA—Social Security: 6.2% on $87,000; FICA—Medicare: 1.45% on all earnings.
2. Federal income tax is calculated from Figure 7-2.
3. State income tax is 6% of gross pay.
4. Union dues are $15 biweekly.

Real-World Applications

7R-1. Small Company, a sole proprietorship, has two employees, Jim Roy and Janice Alter. The owner of Small Co. is Bert Ryan. During the current pay period, Jim worked 48 hours and Janice 56. The reason for these extra hours is that both Jim and Janice worked their regular 40-hour workweek, plus Jim worked 8 extra hours on Sunday and Janice worked 8 extra hours on Saturday and Sunday. Their contract with Small Co. is that they are each paid an hourly rate of $8 per hour with all hours over 40 to be time and a half and double time on Sunday. Bert, the owner, feels he is also entitled to a salary, because he works as many hours. He plans to pay himself $425.

    As the accountant for Small Co., (1) calculate the gross pay for Jim and Janice and (2) write a letter to Bert Ryan with your recommendations regarding his salary.

7R-2. Marcy Moore works for Moose Company during the day and GTA Company at night. Both her employers have deducted FICA taxes for Social Security and Medicare. At year end Marcy has earned $78,800 at her job at Moose Company and $12,000 at GTA.

    At a party she tells Bill Barnes, an accountant, who tells her she has paid too much Social Security tax and that she is entitled to a refund or credit on her tax return she files for the year. Bill suggests that she call the Internal Revenue Service's toll-free number and ask for taxpayer assistance. Assume Social Security of 6.2% on $87,000 and Medicare of 1.45% on all Marcy's earnings during the year.

    As Marcy's friend, (1) check to see if indeed she has overpaid any FICA tax and (2) write a brief note to her and show her your calculations to support your answer.

YOU make the call

Critical Thinking/Ethical Case

7R-3. Russ Todd works for a delicatessen. As the bookkeeper, Russ has been asked by the owner to keep two separate books for meals tax. The owner has asked Todd to hire someone on the weekends to punch in false tapes that can be submitted to the state. These tapes would show low sales and thus less liability for meals tax payments. You make the call. Write down your specific recommendations to Russ.

Internet Exercises: Starbucks; American Payroll Association

EX-1. [www.tei-employment.com]   Suppose that Starbucks decided to follow one of the great trends in American employment, that of "leasing" employees from a temporary agency. One such agency is Temporary Employees, Inc. in Houston, Texas. When a business employs temporary workers, they supervise the temps just like they do their own employees. What they do not have to do is the everyday administrative work that accompanies having employees.

1. Visit the Web site and describe how Starbucks, or any other employer, could save money by hiring temporary employees.
2. While there are advantages to hiring temporary workers, there are also disadvantages. List some of the disadvantages.

EX-2. [www.americanpayroll.org/mission.html]   The American Payroll Association (APA) is an organization of payroll professionals, and it provides a semiannual certification examination. APA provides an avenue for payroll professionals to support others and to assist in meeting common problems encountered in this important profession.

1. From your viewing of their Web site, discuss how this organization fills a niche in the field of human resources and payroll administration.
2. What would be the organization's advantage to you if you were to pursue a career in payroll administration?

Continuing Problem

In preparing for next year, Tony Freedman has hired two employees to work hourly, assisting with some troubleshooting and repair work.

Assignment

(See pages 232–241 in the *Study Guide and Working Papers.*)

1. Record the following transactions in general journal format and post to the general ledger.
2. Prepare a payroll register.
3. Prepare a trial balance as of November 30, 200X.

Assume the following transactions:

a. The following accounts have been added to the chart of accounts: Wage Expense #5110, FICA—Social Security Payable #2020, FICA—Medicare Payable #2030, FIT Payable #2040, State Income Tax Payable #2050, and Wages Payable #2010.
b. FICA—Social Security is taxed at 6.2% up to $76,200* in earnings, and Medicare at 1.45% on all earnings. Note that this is not the current wage-base limit for Social Security.
c. State income tax is 2% of gross pay.
d. Both employees have no federal income tax taken out of their pay.
e. Each employee earns $10 an hour and is paid $1\frac{1}{2}$ times salary for hours worked in excess of 40 weekly.

Nov. 1 Billed Vita Needle Company $6,800; invoice #12675 for services rendered.
3 Billed Accu Pac, Inc. $3,900; invoice #12676 for services rendered.
5 Purchased new shop benches, $1,400, on account from System Design Furniture.
7 Paid the two employee wages: Lance Kumm, 38 hours, and Anthony Hall, 42 hours.
9 Received the phone bill, $150.
12 Collected $500 of the amount due from Taylor Golf.
14 Paid the two employee wages: Lance Kumm, 25 hours, and Anthony Hall, 36 hours.
18 Collected $800 of the amount due from Taylor Golf.

*Note that this is not the current wage-base limit for Social Security.

20 Purchased a fax machine for the office from Multi Systems, Inc. on credit, $450.
21 Paid the two employee wages: Lance Kumm, 26 hours, and Anthony Hall, 35 hours.

SUBWAY Case

PAYROLL RECORDS: A FULL-TIME JOB

Like every Subway restaurant owner, Stan needs to keep a master file of important employee information. This file contains every employee's name, address, phone number, Social Security number, rate of pay, hours worked per week, and W-4 form.

Stan employs two part-time "sandwich artists" and no full-time managers—yet. If his sales continue to be high, he'll need to hire someone to manage operations so that he can spend more time analyzing the financials—with Lila's help—and growing his business. Most restaurants hire mostly part-timers with a core of full-time employees, but the numbers vary from restaurant to restaurant. Benefits vary too. Stan, for instance, plans to offer health and dental benefits when he hires a manager. He knows what a great incentive these benefits are, with health costs so high. He pays his sandwich artists, Rashid and Ellen, the minimum wage since they both have less than a year's experience. However, he's talking to Mariah Washington about creating some incentives to keep them motivated. If Rashid and Ellen are with him for a full year, they'll see a nice raise in their biweekly paychecks. The frequency of pay varies by state and sometimes by city or county. So, of course, do tax rates.

Stan must record all this vital information and report it to the various state, local, and federal authorities. In addition, Stan includes total payroll expenses on the weekly sales and inventory report, which he submits electronically to headquarters from his POS screen.

Scheduling workers and keeping payroll records are the bane of Stan's existence. These tasks are so incredibly time-consuming. He was pleased to hear, then, at the last meeting of his local North American Association of Subway Franchisees (NAASF) that the new point of sale (POS) terminals will soon offer an electronic scheduling package.

"Wow! That will really help," said Stan cheerfully to another franchisee. "No more different colors of ink just to keep track of who will work when! Now I can plan around Rashid and Ellen's exam schedules without a hassle. Scheduling might just become my favorite module in the new system."

"Sure," said Javier Gonzalez, another owner. "Now you can concentrate on payroll records. What fun!"

"Ay. Que lata," Stan groaned. *What a drag!*

Discussion Questions

1. What payroll records does Stan need to keep for his Subway restaurant?
2. What other information might Stan want so as to schedule working hours for each employee?
3. How does the payroll register help Stan prepare the payroll? Consult the process outlined on page 258.

CHAPTER 8

The Employer's Tax Responsibilities

Principles and Procedures

A favorite place for students to go after classes is the Green Earth Grocery and Coffee Shop. Students stop in and buy coffee, study, and socialize. Many students at school like the offbeat and off-campus atmosphere of the store, which specializes in organic groceries, coffees, teas, and a variety of gifts.

You stop in after school and see Martha Simpson, the owner of Green Earth Grocery, sitting in the corner of the coffee shop area. She appears to be wrestling with some paperwork. When you ask her how she's doing, she looks at you and snarls, "Reports, reports! It isn't enough that I pay everyone here each week and pay their withholding taxes on time, now I have to tell the government how much I paid my employees and how much tax I've paid to the government."

As we discussed in Chapter 7, businesses that employ workers must withhold certain payroll taxes on their earnings. In this chapter, we continue our discussion of payroll for businesses. We will learn that a business that employs workers must not only withhold taxes on earnings but also must summarize and report both the amount employees earn as well as the taxes withheld on those earnings. We will learn about several important federal payroll reports known as the Form 940-EZ, Form 941, and Forms W-2 and W-3. We will also discuss when and how a business must make payroll tax deposits.

Payroll taxes and reports seem to be inseparable when working with a company's payroll. After you finish studying this chapter and working through the problems and exercises, you will be able to help someone like Martha with the various federal payroll reports that must be prepared along with paying employees.

Learning Objectives

- Calculating and journalizing employer payroll tax expenses. (p. 290)
- Completing the Employer's Quarterly Federal Tax Return and Deposit Coupon (Forms 941 and 8109) and paying tax obligations for FICA tax (Social Security and Medicare) and federal income tax. (p. 295)
- Preparing Forms W-2, W-3, and 940-EZ and estimates of workers' compensation insurance premiums. (p. 303)

In Chapter 7 we looked at how Gradesoft.com computed and recorded payroll data about its employees. This chapter focuses on specific tax responsibilities of the employer.

Learning Unit 8-1   The Employer's Payroll Tax Expense

When opening a business, every employer must get a federal employer identification number (also known as an EIN) for purposes of reporting earnings, taxes, and so forth. When Gradesoft.com began, Ernie Goldman filled out Form SS-4 to obtain the company's EIN. The SS-4 form asks for the following information:

1. Name of applicant.
2. Trade name of business.
3. Address or place of business.
4. County in which business is located.
5. Name of the principal officer or owner of the business.
6. Type of business (sole proprietor, partnership, etc.).
7. The reason for applying for an EIN.
8. The date the business began.
9. The closing month of the accounting year.
10. First date that the business will pay its employees.
11. The potential number of employees in the coming year.
12. Main activity or nature of the business.

Gradesoft.com's payroll tax obligations are recorded in the general journal when the payroll is recorded. Gradesoft.com is responsible for (1) Social Security and Medicare tax (or FICA), (2) federal unemployment tax, and (3) state unemployment tax. The total of these taxes is recorded in the Payroll Tax Expense account in the general ledger.

Let's look at how Ernie calculates the amount of each tax.

CALCULATING THE EMPLOYER'S PAYROLL TAXES

FICA (Federal Insurance Contributions Act)

It is the responsibility of Gradesoft.com to match whatever its employees pay into the Federal Insurance Contributions Act (FICA) on a dollar-for-dollar basis each pay period. The accounts in the ledger, FICA—Social Security Payable and FICA—Medicare Payable, record the tax for *both* the employee and the employer. To determine the amount of FICA Gradesoft.com owes, we must use the FICA taxable earnings columns for Social Security and Medicare from the payroll register discussed in Chapter 7 and reproduced here for your convenience as Figure 8-1.

The payroll register shows that $4,683.14 (column I) of wages is subject to Social Security tax, and in column J we also see $4,683.14 of wages is subject to tax for Medicare.

$$\text{Social Security} \quad \$4{,}683.14 \times .062 \quad = \$290.36$$
$$\text{Medicare} \quad \$4{,}683.14 \times .0145 = \$\ 67.91$$

The employer must match the FICA contribution of the employee for Social Security *and* Medicare taxes.

GRADESOFT.COM INC.
PAYROLL REGISTER
AUGUST 7–20, 200X

Employee Name	Allowances and Marital Status	Cumulative Earnings (YTD)	Salary for Pay Period	No. of Hours Worked	Wages per Hour	Earnings			Cumulative Earnings (YTD)	Taxable Earnings		
						Regular	Overtime	Gross		Unemployment	Soc. Sec.	Medicare
Jackson, L.	s-1	2087265	—	84.00	1080	85320	8100	93420	2180685		93420	93420
Stowe, S.	s-0	485025	—	80.00	2450	196000	—	196000	681025	196000	196000	196000
Regan, P.	s-2	4658705	—	81.50	2175	174000	4894	178894	4837599	—	178894	178894
TOTALS		7230995	—			455320	12994	468314	7699309	196000	468314	468314
Discussions in this chapter are keyed to these letters	(A)	(B)	(C)			(D)	(E)	(F)	(G)	(H)	(I)	(J)

Figure 8-1 Partial Payroll for Gradesoft.com

FICA — Social Security Payable 203	FICA — Medicare Payable 204
290.36 (employee) 290.36 (employer)	67.91 (employee) 67.91 (employer)

FUTA (Federal Unemployment Tax Act)

Unemployment insurance is a joint effort on the part of the federal government, all 50 states, the District of Columbia, and U.S. territories. Each state is required to run its own unemployment program for its unemployed workers. The state programs are approved and monitored by the federal government.

To raise money for these unemployment programs, the federal government levies taxes on employers under a law called the Federal Unemployment Tax Act (FUTA). This law (1) induces states to create their own unemployment programs and (2) allows the federal government to monitor state programs. As mentioned in Chapter 7, the FUTA tax currently is 6.2% of wages paid during the year, and the wage-base limit is $7,000.

Usually, the federal government allows employers a credit against FUTA tax as long as the employer has paid all monies due to the state unemployment fund on time. This credit, called the normal FUTA tax credit, cannot exceed 5.4%. So, an employer who is entitled to the normal FUTA credit will pay a net amount of eight-tenths of 1%, as shown below:

6.2%	**FUTA tax**
−5.4%	**normal FUTA tax credit**
.8%	**net FUTA tax for federal purposes**

In effect, the federal law says to employers, "Comply with your state's unemployment tax laws and your total tax will not exceed a maximum of 6.2%: 0.8% to the federal government and a state rate that will vary up to a maximum of 5.4%." Remember that employers alone are responsible for paying FUTA tax; it is never deducted from employees' wages.

In Learning Unit 8-3, we look at how to complete the federal report and the deposit requirements for FUTA tax. For now, let's calculate the amount of accumulated federal unemployment tax for Gradesoft.com based on the unemployment column under taxable earnings in the payroll register. Remember that the $1,960.00 in column H represents the amount of earnings taxable for federal unemployment.

To calculate the FUTA tax, we multiply the FUTA taxable earnings times the net FUTA tax rate.

Taxable FUTA Earnings		FUTA Rate		FUTA Tax	FUTA Tax Payable 209
$1,960.00	×	**.008**	=	**$15.68**	15.68

FUTA tax is paid after the end of a calendar year if the total tax owed is less than $100 for the year. If the amount owed is more than $100, the tax is paid on a quarterly basis, no later than the end of the month following the end of the quarter.

SUTA (State Unemployment Tax Acts)

To support state unemployment programs, all states charge employers a certain percent in taxes under the State Unemployment Tax Act (SUTA). Usually, employers pay more in SUTA tax than FUTA tax.

Each state has its own state unemployment wage-base limit. Currently, these limits range from a low of $7,000 to a high of $28,400. The limits vary according to the needs of each state unemployment fund and are subject to change. For the current rate in your state, check with the state department of labor and employment.

The states vary the percentage rates charged to employers. The differences are based on the total amount of contributions the employer makes into the state fund and the dollar amount of unemployment claim money paid out of the fund to former employees of the employer. For example, employers who do not lay off employees during slack seasons (such as after the Christmas season or at the end of a ski resort season) owe a smaller percentage for state unemployment tax purposes. The variance, which is called an **experience** or **merit rating,** motivates employers to stabilize their workforce.

Gradesoft.com's current state unemployment tax rate is 5.4% of the first $7,000 paid to each of Fred's employees during the calendar year. From the taxable earnings column (column H) of the payroll register in Figure 8-1, we multiply $1,960.00 by the SUTA tax rate of 5.4%.

Taxable Earnings	×	SUTA Rate	=	SUTA Tax		SUTA Tax Payable 208
$1,960.00		.054		$105.84		105.84

SUTA taxes are paid after the end of each calendar quarter. Employers are required to complete a state unemployment tax report and pay any SUTA tax due at this time.

JOURNALIZING PAYROLL TAX EXPENSE

Before showing the general journal entry to record Gradesoft.com's payroll tax expense, let's review the categories and rules that affect the specific payroll ledger accounts used to record this expense.

Accounts Affected	Category	↑ ↓	Rules
Payroll Tax Expense	Expense	↑	Dr.
FICA — Social Security Payable	Liability	↑	Cr.
FICA — Medicare Payable	Liability	↑	Cr.
State Unemployment Tax Payable (SUTA)	Liability	↑	Cr.
Federal Unemployment Tax Payable (FUTA)	Liability	↑	Cr.

The total of the employer's portion of FICA for Social Security and Medicare tax, FUTA tax, and SUTA tax equals the total of Gradesoft.com's payroll tax expense.

The Journal Entry

Figure 8-2 is the general journal entry recording Gradesoft.com's payroll tax expense for the biweekly payroll ending August 20. (We look carefully at the general ledger entries in Learning Unit 8-2.)

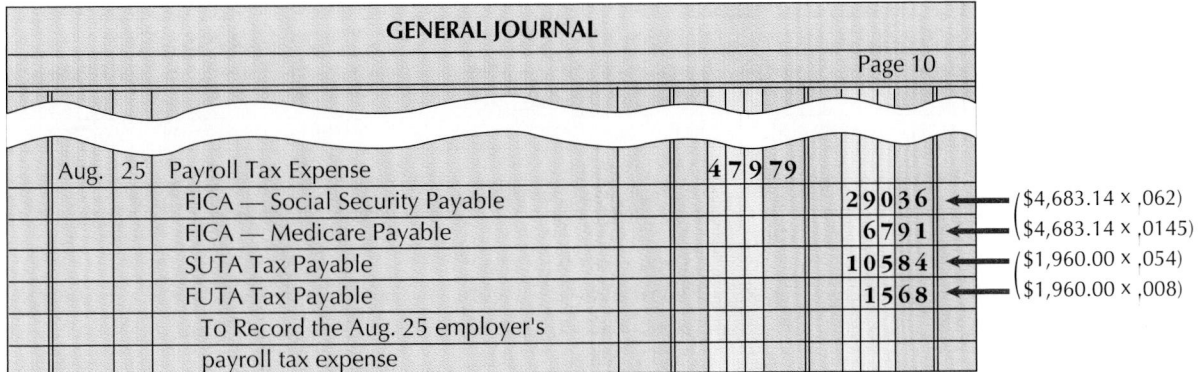

Figure 8-2 Journal Entry for Employer's Payroll Tax Expense

In Learning Unit 8-2 we see how to complete the form that goes with the payment of FICA tax (Social Security and Medicare) of the employee *and* the employer along with the amounts of federal income tax deducted from employees' paychecks. It is important to keep in mind that FUTA and SUTA taxes also have separate report forms to be completed, which we look at in Learning Unit 8-3.

Learning Unit 8-1 Review

AT THIS POINT you should be able to

- Explain the purpose of Form SS-4. (p. 290)
- Explain the use of the taxable earnings column in calculating the employer's payroll tax expense. (p. 290)
- Calculate the employer's payroll taxes. (p. 290)
- Explain the difference between FUTA and SUTA taxes. (p. 292)
- Explain when FUTA and SUTA taxes are paid. (p. 292)
- Journalize the employer's payroll tax expense. (p. 293)

SELF-REVIEW QUIZ 8-1

(The forms you need are on page 242 of the *Study Guide and Working Papers*.)

Given the following, prepare the general journal entry to record the payroll tax expense for Bill Co. for the weekly payroll of July 8. Assume the following: (a) SUTA tax is paid at a rate of 5.6% on the first $7,000 of earnings; (b) FUTA tax is paid at the net rate of .8% on the first $7,000 of earnings; (c) FICA tax rate for Social Security is 6.2% on $87,000, and Medicare is 1.45% on all earnings.

Employee	Cumulative Pay Before This Week's Payroll	Gross Pay for Week
Bill Jones	$6,000	$800
Julie Warner	6,600	400
Al Brooks	7,900	700

SOLUTION TO SELF-REVIEW QUIZ 8-1

Figure 8-3
Employer's Payroll Tax
Journal Entry

July	8	Payroll Tax Expense		2 2 2 15		
		FICA — Social Security Payable			1 1 7 80	
		FICA — Medicare Payable			2 7 55	
		SUTA Tax Payable			6 7 20	
		FUTA Tax Payable			9 60	
		Record employer's payroll tax				

FICA:
SS: $1,900 × .062 = $117.80
Med: 1,900 × .0145 =   27.55
SUTA: 1,200 × .056 =   67.20
FUTA: 1,200 × .008 =   9.60
                          $222.15

Quiz Tip:
Al Brooks earned more than $7,000; thus his employer takes no SUTA or FUTA tax on the $700 of Al's gross pay.

Learning Unit 8-2 — Form 941: Completing the Employer's Quarterly Federal Tax Return and Paying Tax Obligations for FICA Tax and Federal Income Tax

In this unit we look at Gradesoft.com's last calendar quarter (October, November, and December). Our goals are (1) determining the timing for paying FICA (for both the employees and the employer) and federal income tax (or FIT) and (2) completing Form 941, the Employer's Quarterly Federal Tax Return.

Before getting into specific deposit rules and form completions, let's look at Figure 8-4, a worksheet that Ernie prepared to monitor Gradesoft.com's deposit requirements for the taxes reported on Form 941: Social Security, Medicare, and federal income taxes. These so-called Form 941 taxes are discussed later in this Learning Unit. (The worksheet in Figure 8-2 has nothing to do with unemployment taxes, which follow different rules.)

Do note on the worksheet that the quarter is 13 weeks. Because Form 941 requires FICA information to be separated into Social Security and Medicare, you can see how helpful the worksheet can be. Note that for the December 31 monthly payroll some wages are not taxable for Social Security because the $87,000 wage-base limit was met. *All* wages are taxable for Medicare, however, because there is no wage-base limit for this tax. This worksheet can be built from the information in each individual's employee's earnings record and the weekly payroll registers.

Now let's look at the deposit rules Gradesoft.com must follow regarding Form 941 taxes (which are FICA and FIT).

DEPOSITING FORM 941 TAXES

The amount of tax due must be deposited in what is called an authorized depository in Gradesoft's area or a Federal Reserve bank. Authorized depositories are banks that have been authorized by the Federal Reserve System to accept payroll tax deposits

Payroll Period		Pay Check Date	Earnings	FIT	Taxable FICA Wages for		FICA		Total Tax	Cumulative Tax
					Soc. Sec.	Medicare	Soc. Sec. EE + ER	Medicare EE + ER		
October	2–15	Oct. 20	4892 75	778 00	4892 75	4892 75	606 70	141 89	1526 59	1526 59
October	16–29	Nov. 3	5013 25	810 00	5013 25	5013 25	621 64	145 38	1577 03	3103 62
October	31	Oct. 31	16231 84	3895 00	16231 84	16231 84	2012 75	470 72	6378 47	9482 09
Oct./Nov.	30–12	Nov. 17	5007 15	809 00	5007 15	5007 15	620 89	145 21	1575 09	11057 18
November	13–26	Dec. 1	5152 50	832 00	5152 50	5152 50	638 91	149 42	1620 33	12677 52
November	30	Nov. 30	16231 84	3895 00	16231 84	16231 84	2012 75	470 72	6378 47	19055 99
Nov./Dec.	27–10	Dec. 15	5629 00	909 00	5629 00	5629 00	698 00	163 24	1770 24	20826 22
December	11–24	Dec. 29	5700 75	921 00	5700 75	5700 75	706 89	165 32	1793 21	22619 44
December	25–31	Dec. 29	2105 68	367 00	2105 68	2105 68	261 10	61 06	689 17	23308 61
December	31	Dec. 29	16231 83	3895 00	11354 75	16231 83	1407 99	470 72	5773 71	29082 32
Totals for the Quarter			82196 59	17111 00	77319 51	82196 59	9587 62	2383 70	29082 32	29082 32
			(A)	(B)	(C)	(D)	(E)	(F)	(G)	(H)

Figure 8-4 Worksheet to Monitor Deposit Requirements

from their own checking account customers. A Federal Reserve bank can accept payroll tax deposits from any business, no matter where the business maintains its checking account.

Types of Payroll Tax Depositors

For payroll tax deposit purposes, employers are classified as either **monthly** or **semiweekly depositors.** A monthly depositor is an employer who only has to deposit Form 941 taxes on the fifteenth day of every month. Semiweekly depositors must deposit their Form 941 taxes once or twice each week.

The employer's classification depends on the dollar amount of the Form 941 taxes it has paid in the past. The IRS has developed a rule known as the **look-back period** rule to determine how to classify an employer for payroll tax deposits. Under this rule, the IRS will *look back* to a one-year time period that begins on July 1 and ends the following June 30. (For example, to determine the employer's status for 2004, the IRS will look at the period between July 1, 2002, and June 30, 2003.) If, during this look-back period, the employer has paid under $50,000 of Form 941 taxes, the IRS considers the employer to be a *monthly depositor.* If the employer has paid $50,000 or more during this period, it is considered to be a *semiweekly depositor.* Figure 8-5 shows how the look-back period works for payroll purposes.

Gradesoft.com is a semiweekly depositor because it made in excess of $50,000 in FICA and FIT deposits during the look-back period. If Gradesoft.com had made less than $50,000 in payroll tax deposits during the look-back period, it would have been classified as a monthly depositor.

New employers are automatically classified as monthly depositors until they have been in business long enough to have a look-back period for evaluation purposes. The employer's status is reevaluated every year.

Rules for Monthly Depositors   The rules for monthly depositors are fairly simple. They are

1. The employee and employer Social Security and Medicare taxes and the employees' FIT accumulated during any month must be deposited by the fifteenth of the next month.
2. If the fifteenth of the month is a Saturday, Sunday, or bank holiday, the employer must make the payroll tax deposit on the next **banking day**.

Rules for Semiweekly Depositors   Semiweekly depositors like Gradesoft.com may have to make up to two payroll tax deposits every week, depending on when employees are paid. For this purpose, each seven-day week begins on Wednesday and ends on the following Tuesday. The seven-day week is broken into two payday time periods:

The IRS examines the amount of Form 941 taxes paid during the period beginning July 1 and ending June 30 of the following year to determine whether the employer is a monthly depositor or a semiweekly depositor. This examination is called the look-back period rule.

Figure 8-5
The Level of Payroll Taxes Paid During the Look-Back Period Determines How Often the Employer Deposits Payroll Taxes

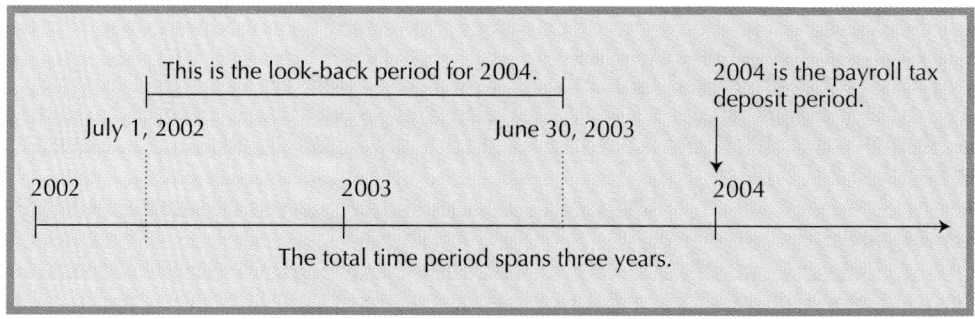

	Monday	Tuesday	Wednesday	Thursday	Friday	Saturday	Sunday
The payday occurs this week ⟶			■ If the payday occurs on one of these days, the deposit will be due Wednesday of the next week.			★ If the payday occurs on Saturday or Sunday, or...	
	★ ...Monday or Tuesday, then payroll tax deposit will be due and payable on Friday of this week.		■ Deposit day for Wednesday– Friday payday		★ Deposit day for Saturday– Tuesday payday		

Figure 8-6 The Payday Determines When the Tax Deposit Is Due

Wednesday through Friday and Saturday through Tuesday. In addition, the following rules apply:

1. If the company's payday occurs on Wednesday, Thursday, or Friday, the payroll tax deposit is due on the following Wednesday. If the company's payday occurs on Saturday, Sunday, Monday, or Tuesday, the payroll tax deposit is due on the following Friday. Thus, if an employer pays its employees on a Thursday and a Monday, it must make two payroll tax deposits—one on Wednesday for the Thursday payday, and one on Friday for the Monday payday.

2. If a bank holiday occurs after the end of the payday time period but before the day the payroll tax deposit is due, the employer gets one extra day in which to make the deposit. So, a deposit due on a Wednesday will be due on Thursday, and a Friday deposit will be due on the following Monday.

As a general rule, the depositor always has three banking days in which to make the payroll tax deposit. The diagram in Figure 8-6 shows how these rules are applied.

Here is how the rules apply to Gradesoft.com. First, look back at Figure 8-4 (p. 295) to locate the dates of each weekly payday. Next, look at Figure 8-7, which shows a calendar for the last quarter of the year.

Note that each payday falls on a Friday. Because Gradesoft.com is a semiweekly payroll tax depositor, its Form 941 payroll tax deposits are due on the following Wednesday. Gradesoft's first payday in October falls on October 6. Its first payroll tax deposit will be due on October 11. Another deposit will be due every Wednesday from that date until the end of the year. However, if we look at week 52 in Figure 8-7 (beginning Sunday, December 24), the payday for this week is Friday, December 29,

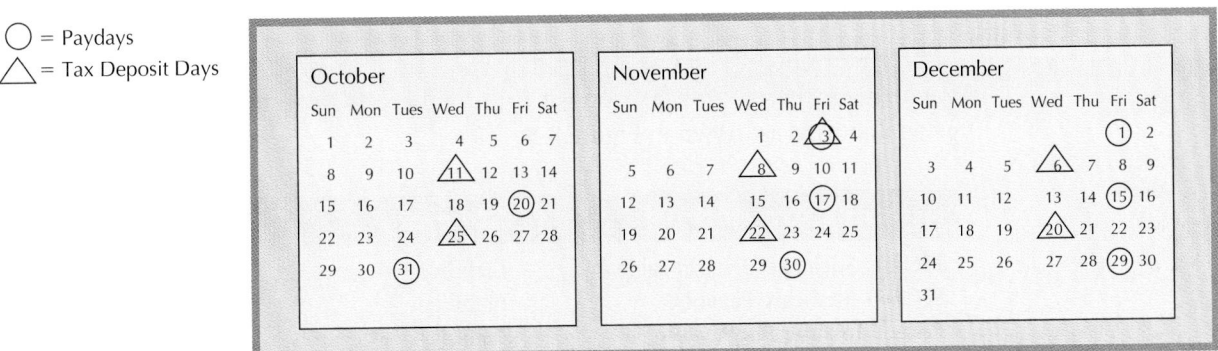

Figure 8-7 Last Calendar Quarter for Gradesoft.com Shows Paydays Falling on Fridays

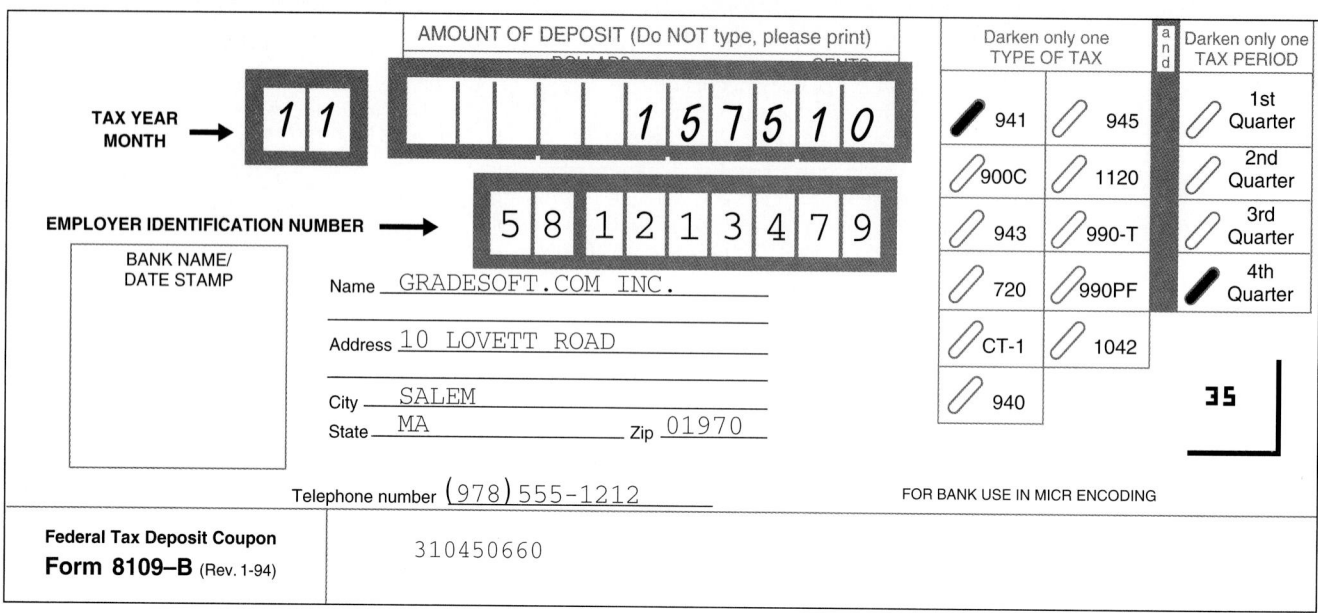

Figure 8-8 Form 8109

which is two days before New Year's Day. Under the law, January 1 is a federal holiday, so Ernie must apply the rule regarding a holiday that falls between a payday and a tax deposit day and will make the Form 941 tax deposit on Thursday, January 4, of the next year, rather than on Wednesday, January 3.

Completion of Form 8109 to Accompany Deposits

To make Gradesoft.com's payroll tax deposits properly, Ernie must write a check for the total amount of the Form 941 tax deposit after each pay period. The deposits must also be accompanied by IRS Form 8109, Federal Tax Deposit Coupon, as shown in Figure 8-8.

Ernie received a book of coupons when he got the EIN for Gradesoft.com. Figure 8-8 shows Form 8109 completed for the October 30/November 12 pay period Form 941 payroll tax deposit. Note that the dollar amount found at the top of the form ($1,575.10) is the same as the amount found in the total tax column for the pay period in Figure 8-2.

In Figure 8-8, in the upper-right-hand corner the "Type of Tax" and "Tax Period" must be indicated by darkening the appropriate oval using a No. 2 pencil. Ernie has darkened the "941" and "4th Quarter" ovals for the October 30/November 12 payday.

Journalizing and Posting Payroll Tax Deposits

Payment of the payroll tax deposit for October 30/November 12 is made in the general journal as shown in Figure 8-9.

Accounts Affected	Category	↑ ↓	Rules
FICA—Social Security Payable	Liability	↓	Dr.
FICA—Medicare Payable	Liability	↓	Dr.
Federal Income Tax Payable	Liability	↓	Dr.
Cash	Asset	↓	Cr.

		GRADESOFT.COM GENERAL JOURNAL				
Nov	22	FICA — Social Security Payable	203	6 2 0 89	
		FICA — Medicare Payable	204	1 4 5 21	
		Federal Income Tax Payable	205	8 0 9 00	
		Cash	111		1 5 7 5 10
		To record the Form 941 tax deposit for the			
		biweekly payroll on November 17, 200X			

Figure 8-9

Journal Entry to Record Payroll Tax Deposit

Now let's look at the partial general ledger of Gradesoft.com to get a better understanding of how specific payroll accounts in the ledger are updated regarding FICA (Social Security and Medicare) and FIT. Note in the FICA — Social Security and Medicare Payable accounts how the posting came from the general journal for the employees' and employer's share of FICA tax.* The general journal is also used when the payroll tax deposit is made, recording a debit to the FICA — Social Security and Medicare Payable accounts as well as the Federal Income Tax Payable account.

Under the Form 941 payroll tax deposit rules, the general journal entries to record the payroll are made biweekly on Friday, whereas the entries to record the payment of the payroll taxes are made the Wednesday after each biweekly payday. Check Figure 8-2 below to see how the Form 941 tax liability has been recorded and then paid in the partial general ledger accounts shown in Figure 8-10.

FORM 941: EMPLOYER'S QUARTERLY FEDERAL TAX RETURN

Ernie Goldman, the controller for Gradesoft.com, used the worksheet in Figure 8-2 in preparing Form 941 for the last quarter of the year (see Fig. 8-11). The top section of the form identifies the taxpayer (Gradesoft.com), its address, the date the quarter ended, and Gradesoft's EIN.

Ernie filled out Form 941 using the dollar amounts from Figure 8-2 as follows. Please refer back to the particular column identified by letter (A, B, C, etc.) to see where Ernie obtained the amounts used in preparing the form:

Line 1a: This line is only filled in for the first quarter of the year. It is left blank for the last quarter.
    2: Total gross pay: $82,196.59 (the total for the quarter). See column A.

FICA—Social Security Payable					203
Date	PR	Dr.	Cr.	Cr. Bal.	
200X					
Nov. 17	GJ28		6 2 0 89	6 2 0 89	
22	GJ28	6 2 0 89		0	
30	GJ28		2 0 1 2 75	2 0 1 2 75	
Dec. 1	GJ29		6 3 8 91	2 6 5 1 66	
6	GJ29	2 6 5 1 66		0	
15	GJ29		6 9 8 00	6 9 8 00	
20	GJ29	6 9 8 00		0	

FICA—Medicare Payable					204
Date	PR	Dr.	Cr.	Cr. Bal.	
200X					
Nov. 17	GJ28		1 4 5 21	1 4 5 21	
22	GJ28	1 4 5 21		0	
30	GJ28		4 7 0 42	4 7 0 42	
1	GJ29		1 4 9 42	6 1 9 84	
6	GJ29	6 1 9 84		0	
15	GJ29		1 6 3 24	1 6 3 24	
20	GJ29	1 6 3 24		0	

Figure 8-10 FICA for Social Security and Medicare

*Note: Each credit would actually be 2 credits: one from the employee and one from the employer.

Form **941**

Department of the Treasury
Internal Revenue Service (99)

Employer's Quarterly Federal Tax Return

▶ See separate instructions for information on completing this return.

Please type or print.

OMB No. 1545-0029

T
FF
FD
FP
I
T

Enter state code for state in which deposits were made **only** if different from state in address to the right ▶ (see page 2 of separate instructions).

Name (as distinguished from trade name)
Gradesoft.com

Trade name, if any

Address (number and street)
10 Lovett Road

Date quarter ended
Dec. 31, 200X

Employer identification number

City, state, and ZIP code
Salem, MA 01970

IRS Use

1 1 1 1 1 1 1 1 1 1   2   3 3 3 3 3 3 3 3   4 4 4   5 5 5

If address is different from prior return, check here ▶

6   7   8 8 8 8 8 8 8   9 9 9 9 9   10 10 10 10 10 10 10 10 10

A If you **do not have to file** returns in the future, check here ▶ ☐ and enter date final wages paid ▶

B If you are a seasonal employer, see **Seasonal employers** on page 1 of the instructions and check here ▶ ☐

1	Number of employees in the pay period that includes March 12th . ▶	**1**		
2	Total wages and tips, plus other compensation	**2**	82,196	59
3	Total income tax withheld from wages, tips, and sick pay . . .	**3**	17,111	00
4	Adjustment of withheld income tax for preceding quarters of **this calendar year**	**4**		
5	Adjusted total of income tax withheld (line 3 as adjusted by line 4)	**5**	17,111	00
6	Taxable social security wages . . . . **6a** 77,319 51 × 12.4% (.124) =	**6b**	9,587	62
	Taxable social security tips . . . . . **6c** × 12.4% (.124) =	**6d**		
7	Taxable Medicare wages and tips . . . **7a** 82,196 59 × 2.9% (.029) =	**7b**	2,383	70
8	Total social security and Medicare taxes (add lines 6b, 6d, and 7b). **Check here if wages are not subject to social security and/or Medicare tax** . . . . ▶ ☐	**8**	11,971	32
9	Adjustment of social security and Medicare taxes (see instructions for required explanation) Sick Pay $ _____ ± Fractions of Cents $ _____ ± Other $ _____ =	**9**		
10	Adjusted total of social security and Medicare taxes (line 8 as adjusted by line 9)	**10**	11,971	32
11	**Total taxes** (add lines 5 and 10)	**11**	29,082	32
12	Advance earned income credit (EIC) payments made to employees (see instructions) . . .	**12**		
13	Net taxes (subtract line 12 from line 11). **If $2,500 or more, this must equal line 17, column (d) below (or line D of Schedule B (Form 941))**	**13**	29,082	32
14	Total deposits for quarter, including overpayment applied from a prior quarter	**14**	29,082	32
15	**Balance due** (subtract line 14 from line 13). See instructions	**15**		
16	**Overpayment.** If line 14 is more than line 13, enter excess here ▶ $ _____ and check if to be: ☐ Applied to next return **or** ☐ Refunded.			

- **All filers:** If line 13 is less than $2,500, **do not** complete line 17 **or** Schedule B (Form 941).
- **Semiweekly schedule depositors:** Complete Schedule B (Form 941) and check here . . . . ▶ ☒
- **Monthly schedule depositors:** Complete line 17, columns (a) through (d), and check here. . . . . ▶ ☐

17	**Monthly Summary of Federal Tax Liability.** (Complete **Schedule B (Form 941)** instead, if you were a semiweekly schedule depositor.)		
(a) First month liability	**(b)** Second month liability	**(c)** Third month liability	**(d)** Total liability for quarter

Third Party Designee

Do you want to allow another person to discuss this return with the IRS (see separate instructions)? ☐ **Yes.** Complete the following. ☒ **No**

Designee's name ▶

Phone no. ▶ ( )

Personal identification number (PIN) ▶

Sign Here

Under penalties of perjury, I declare that I have examined this return, including accompanying schedules and statements, and to the best of my knowledge and belief, it is true, correct, and complete.

Signature ▶ *Ernie Goldman*

Print Your Name and Title ▶ Ernie Goldman, Controller

Date ▶ 1-31-200X

For Privacy Act and Paperwork Reduction Act Notice, see back of Payment Voucher.

Cat. No. 17001Z

Form **941**

Figure 8-11 Employer's Quarterly Federal Tax Return

3: Total income tax: $17,111.00. See column B.

4: No adjustment needed here: This line is used only for special situations.

5: Because there was no adjustment amount on line 4, this amount is the same as found on line 3: $17,111.00.

6a: The wages subject to Social Security tax are multiplied by 12.4% (6.2% for the employee and 6.2% for the employer). Total taxable wages are $77,319.51. Note that this line is different from line 2 because of the Social Security wage-base limit of $87,000 for the year. The tax is $9,587.62. See column E.

6b: Ernie multiplies the amount found on line 6a by 12.4% to arrive at the amount entered on line 6b.

6c: If Gradesoft.com had taxable tips for the quarter, the amount would be entered on line 6c.

6d: Since Gradesoft.com had no taxable tips for the quarter, this line is left blank on Form 941.

7a: The taxable wages for Medicare tax are $82,196.59 (see column D). Please note that this line will be the same as line 2 because there is no wage-base limit for Medicare tax. The tax amount is $2,383.70 (1.45% for the employee and 1.45% for the employer). See column F.

7b: Ernie multiplies the amount found on line 7a by 2.9% to arrive at the amount entered on line 7b.

8: The total of Social Security and Medicare taxes is $11,971.32 ($9,587.62 + $2,383.70).

9: Due to the rounding of individual FICA amounts calculated and pay period total FICA amounts paid, there may be a difference between the total taxes shown in a general ledger and the actual payroll tax deposits. Line 9 can be used to reconcile these differences (called *fractions of cents*) to account for rounding. Ernie's amounts do not need adjustment, so no amount is entered on line 9.

10: This line is the sum of lines 8 and 9.

11: This line is the sum of lines 5 and 10. See columns G and H.

12: If Gradesoft.com advanced any earned income credit to its employees, it would deduct the amount on this line.

13: This line is the net of line 11 as adjusted by any amount found on line 12. See columns G and H.

14: The total of the deposits made by Ernie for Gradesoft.com for the last quarter is $29,082.32. Remember that Gradesoft.com uses the semiweekly deposit rules. Note that the last Form 941 deposit is made after the year ends but is allowed to be taken as a last quarter deposit because it applies to the December 31 biweekly and monthly payrolls.

15: There is no balance due to Gradesoft.com.

16: There is no overpayment for Gradesoft.com. Note that directly below line 16 are two boxes that are checked only under certain circumstances. Ernie will check the box for semiweekly depositors and prepare Form 941 Schedule B. This schedule is an itemized listing of the semiweekly deposits made for the last quarter. It is not shown here.

17: This line is filled in only if the employer has been classified as a monthly depositor of employment taxes. Please note that the line is broken into four sections. The first three sections—(a), (b), and (c)—are the monthly Form 941 tax liabilities. The sum of sections (a), (b), (c) must equal the section (d) amount. Likewise, the section (d) amount on line 17 must equal the amount found on line 13 of the return. Ernie does not complete this line because Gradesoft.com has been classified as a semiweekly depositor.

Fraction of cents: If there is a difference between the total tax on line 8 and the total deducted from your employees' wages or tips because of fractions of cents added or dropped in collecting the tax, report the difference on line 9. Use the center column on line 9 with a + or − sign to show the amount of the adjustment.

Learning Unit 8-2 Review

AT THIS POINT you should be able to

- Explain which taxes are reported on Form 941. (p. 295)
- Understand how employers are classified as payroll tax depositors. (p. 296)
- Explain the summary of Form 941 payroll tax deposit rules for monthly depositors. (p. 296)
- Explain the summary of Form 941 payroll tax deposit rules for semiweekly depositors. (p. 296)
- Prepare and explain the purpose of Form 8109. (p. 298)
- Record the general journal entry to pay FICA (Social Security and Medicare) and federal income taxes when a payroll tax deposit is made. (p. 299)
- Review how the general journal entries are posted into the general ledger to record the paying of employees and the paying of payroll taxes. (p. 299)
- Complete an Employer's Quarterly Federal Tax Return from a worksheet. (p. 300)

SELF-REVIEW QUIZ 8-2

(The blank forms you need are on page 243 of the *Study Guide and Working Papers*.)

Carol Ann's Import Chalet is a business that employs five full-time employees and four part-time employees. The accountant for Carol Ann's has determined that the business is a monthly depositor. The accountant prepared a worksheet showing the following payroll tax liabilities for the month of October:

Date	Social Security (EE + ER)	Medicare (EE + ER)	FIT
10/7	$ 486.56	$169.05	$ 829.00
10/14	632.15	165.01	901.00
10/21	579.43	131.05	734.00
10/28	389.99	142.24	765.00
Totals	$2,088.13	$607.35	$3,229.00

1. What is the dollar amount of the Form 941 tax deposit and when must it be made under the monthly deposit rule? Use Figure 8-7 (p. 297) for the date.

2. Assume that Carol Ann's is classified as a semiweekly depositor. Please calculate the amount of each Form 941 tax deposit and when it would be made by completing the table on the next page (use Fig. 8-7 for the dates):

Payday Date	Date of Deposit	Amount of Deposit
10/7	?	?
10/14	?	?
10/21	?	?
10/28	?	?

SOLUTIONS TO SELF-REVIEW QUIZ 8-2

1. As a monthly depositor, Carol Ann's deposit date is Wednesday, November 14. The total amount of the deposit is $5,924.48 ($2,088.13 + $607.35 + $3,229.00).

2. As a semiweekly depositor, Carol Ann's deposit schedule is completed as follows:

Payday Date	Date of Deposit	Amount of Deposit
10/7	10/12	$1,484.61
10/14	10/19	1,698.16
10/21	10/26	1,444.48
10/28	11/2*	1,297.23*

Learning Unit 8-3   W-2, W-3, Form 940-EZ, and Workers' Compensation

W-2: WAGE AND TAX STATEMENT

Form W-2, Wage and Tax Statement is a multipart form that is prepared by the employer each year. Gradesoft.com is required to give (or mail) copies of Form W-2 to each person who was employed in the past year. These forms must be distributed by January 31 of the following year. Employees use the figures on Form W-2 to compute the amount of income tax they must pay. One copy of the form must be attached to the federal income tax return; other copies must be attached to state and local tax returns.

Anyone who stopped working for Gradesoft.com before the end of that year may be given a Form W-2 at any time after the employment ends. If the former employee asks for it, the employer must supply completed copies within 30 days of the request or the final wage payment, whichever is later.

Additional copies of Form W-2 are sent to the Social Security Administration and state and local governments. The employer retains a copy of the W-2 form for each employee for its records.

Figure 8-12 on page 304 shows the W-2 that James T. Zott received from Gradesoft.com. The information was obtained from his individual employee earnings record. Note that Social Security wages and taxes are shown separately from the amounts reported for Medicare wages and taxes because there is a wage-base limit for the Social Security tax, but not for the Medicare tax.

W-3: TRANSMITTAL OF INCOME AND TAX STATEMENTS

Form W-3, Transmittal of Income and Tax Statements, is prepared and sent by the employer to the Social Security Administration along with copies of each employees' Form W-2. Form W-3 reports the total amounts of wages, tips, and compensation paid to employees; the total federal income tax withheld; the total Social Security and Medicare taxes withheld; and some other information.

Employers are required to send Form W-3 and Form W-2 to the Social Security Administration for FICA tax purposes. The Social Security Administration, under

---

*Note that this deposit will be made in November given the calendar dates found in Figure 8-5.

a Control number	22222	Void ☐	For Official Use Only ▶ OMB No. 1545-0008		

b Employer identification number 58-12134791		**1** Wages, tips, other compensation $ 77,587.00	**2** Federal income tax withheld $ 19,818.00
c Employer's name, address, and ZIP code Gradesoft.com 10 Lovett Road Salem, MA 01970		**3** Social security wages $ 77,587.00	**4** Social security tax withheld $ 4,810.39
		5 Medicare wages and tips $ 77,587.00	**6** Medicare tax withheld $ 1,125.01
		7 Social security tips $	**8** Allocated tips $
d Employee's social security number 922-80-1250		**9** Advance EIC payment $	**10** Dependent care benefits $
e Employee's first name and initial James T.	Last name Zott	**11** Nonqualified plans $	**12a** See instructions for box 12 $
		13 Statutory employee ☐ Retirement plan ☐ Third-party sick pay ☐	**12b** $
80 Garfield Street Marblehead, MA 01945		**14** Other	**12c** $
			12d $
f Employee's address and ZIP code			

15 State MA	Employer's state ID number 621-8966-4	16 State wages, tips, etc. $ 77,587.00	17 State income tax $ 6,206.96	18 Local wages, tips, etc. $	19 Local income tax $	20 Locality name
		$	$	$	$	

Form **W-2** Wage and Tax Statement (99)   **200X**   Department of the Treasury—Internal Revenue Service

For Privacy Act and Paperwork Reduction Act Notice, see separate instructions.

Copy A For Social Security Administration—Send this entire page with Form W-3 to the Social Security Administration; photocopies are **not** acceptable.

Cat. No. 10134D

Do Not Cut, Fold, or Staple Forms on This Page — Do Not Cut, Fold, or Staple Forms on This Page

Figure 8-12 Completed Form W-2

a special agreement with the IRS, makes all information found on individual W-2 forms electronically available to the IRS so that it can check to verify the accuracy of the employer's 941 forms and individual employees' federal income tax returns.

The information used to complete Form W-3 in Figure 8-13 came from a summary of the individual employee earnings records that Ernie prepared after the end of the year (see Fig. 8-14 on p. 305).

FORM 940-EZ: EMPLOYER'S ANNUAL FEDERAL UNEMPLOYMENT TAX RETURN

There are two types of federal unemployment tax returns. **Form 940-EZ, Employer's Annual Federal Unemployment Tax Return,** is used by a business that only employs workers in one state. Businesses that employ workers in several states (multistate employers) must file a **Form 940, Employer's Annual Federal Unemployment Tax Return.** Form 940 asks for additional information that is not required on Form 940-EZ.

Gradesoft.com must file Form 940-EZ. After the first year it files this form, the IRS will send Ernie a preaddressed Form 940-EZ near the close of each calendar year. Form 940-EZ must be filed no later than January 31 unless all required FUTA deposits have been made during the year, in which case the return can be filed by February 10. The completed form is shown in Figure 8-15.

DO NOT STAPLE OR FOLD

a Control number	33333	For Official Use Only ► OMB No. 1545-0008		

b Kind of Payer ►	941 ☒ CT-1 ☐	Military ☐ Hshld. emp. ☐	943 ☐ Medicare govt. emp. ☐	Third-party sick pay ☐

1 Wages, tips, other compensation	2 Federal income tax withheld
$ 316,994.82	$ 61,996.00
3 Social security wages	4 Social security tax withheld
$ 316,994.82	$ 19,653.68
5 Medicare wages and tips	6 Medicare tax withheld
$ 316,994.82	$ 4,596.43
7 Social security tips	8 Allocated tips
$	$
9 Advance EIC payments	10 Dependent care benefits
$	$
11 Nonqualified plans	12 Deferred compensation
$	$

c Total number of Forms W-2 **6**   d Establishment number

e Employer identification number **58-12134791**

f Employer's name **Gradesoft.com Inc.**

10 Lovett Road
Salem, MA 01970

g Employer's address and ZIP code

h Other EIN used this year

13 For third-party sick pay use only

14 Income tax withheld by payer of third-party sick pay
$

15 State **MA**	Employer's state ID number **621-8966-4**

16 State wages, tips, etc.	17 State income tax
$ 316,994.82	$ 25,359.59
18 Local wages, tips, etc.	19 Local income tax
$	$

Contact person **E. Goldman**

Telephone number **(617) 555-1212**

For Official Use Only

E-mail address **egoldman@gradesoft.com**

Fax number **(617) 555-1213**

Under penalties of perjury, I declare that I have examined this return and accompanying documents, and, to the best of my knowledge and belief, they are true, correct, and complete.

Signature ► *Ernie Goldman*   Title ► **Controller**   Date ► **1-31-200X**

Form **W-3** Transmittal of Wage and Tax Statements   **200X**   Department of the Treasury Internal Revenue Service

Send this entire page with the entire Copy A page of Form(s) W-2 to the Social Security Administration. Photocopies are not acceptable.

Do not send any payment (cash, checks, money orders, etc.) with Forms W-2 and W-3.

Figure 8-13 Completed Form W-3

Employee	Total Earnings	FICA Taxable Earnings Soc. Sec.	Medicare	FICA Tax Soc. Sec.	Medicare	FIT
Jackson, Lee	34,812.55	34,812.55	34,812.55	2,158.38	504.78	3,984.00
Sheila Stowe	19,872.11	19,872.11	19,872.11	1,232.07	288.15	2,290.00
Regan, Pat	66,448.16	66,448.16	66,448.16	4,119.79	963.50	8,265.00
Goldman, Ernie	38,500.00	38,500.00	38,500.00	2,387.00	558.25	5,989.00
Zott, Jim	77,587.00	77,587.00	77,587.00	4,810.39	1,125.01	19,818.00
Nguyen, Vince	79,775.00	79,775.00	79,775.00	4,946.05	1,156.74	21,650.00
	316,994.82	316,994.82	316,994.82	19,653.68	4,596.43	61,996.00

Figure 8-14 Employee Earnings Record Summary

Form 940-EZ

Department of the Treasury
Internal Revenue Service   (99)

**Employer's Annual Federal
Unemployment (FUTA) Tax Return**

► **See separate Instructions for Form 940-EZ for information on completing this form.**

OMB No. 1545-1110

200X

T	
FF	
FD	
FP	
I	
T	

You must complete this section. ►

Name (as distinguished from trade name)
Gradesoft.com Inc.

Trade name, if any

Address and ZIP code
10 Lovett Road, Salem, MA 01970

Calendar year
200X

Employer identification number
58:12134791

*Answer the questions under **Who May Use Form 940-EZ** on page 2. If you cannot use Form 940-EZ, you must use Form 940.*

A   Enter the amount of contributions paid to your state unemployment fund. (see separate instructions) . . . ► $ .... 1,890|00

B   (1) Enter the name of the state where you have to pay contributions . . . . ► ....Massachusetts..........
     (2) Enter your state reporting number as shown on your state unemployment tax return ► 281-615

If you will not have to file returns in the future, check here (see **Who Must File** in separate instructions) **and complete and sign the return.** ► ☐

If this is an Amended Return, check here (see **Amended Returns** on page 2 of the separate instructions) . . . . ► ☐

Part I   Taxable Wages and FUTA Tax

1	Total payments (including payments shown on lines 2 and 3) during the calendar year for services of employees	**1**	316,994	82
2	Exempt payments. (Explain all exempt payments, attaching additional sheets if necessary.) ►	**2**		
3	Payments of more than $7,000 for services. Enter only amounts over the first $7,000 paid to each employee. **(see separate instructions)**	**3**	274,994 82	
4	Add lines 2 and 3	**4**	274,994	82
5	**Total taxable wages** (subtract line 4 from line 1) . . . . ►	**5**	42,000	00
6	**FUTA tax.** Multiply the wages on line 5 by .008 and enter here. **(If the result is over $100, also complete Part II.)**	**6**	336	00
7	Total FUTA tax deposited for the year, including any overpayment applied from a prior year	**7**	336	00
8	**Balance due** (subtract line 7 from line 6). Pay to the "United States Treasury." . . . . ►	**8**	–0–	
	If you owe more than $100, see **Depositing FUTA tax** in separate instructions.			
9	**Overpayment** (subtract line 6 from line 7). Check if it is to be: ☐ **Applied to next return** or ☐ **Refunded** ►	**9**		

Part II   Record of Quarterly Federal Unemployment Tax Liability (Do not include state liability.) **Complete only if line 6 is over $100.**

Quarter	First (Jan. 1 – Mar. 31)	Second (Apr. 1 – June 30)	Third (July 1 – Sept. 30)	Fourth (Oct. 1 – Dec. 31)	Total for year
Liability for quarter	198.00	–0–	114.00	24.00	336.00

Third Party Designee

Do you want to allow another person to discuss this return with the IRS (see instructions page 5)? ☐ **Yes.** Complete the following. ☐ **No**

Designee's name ►   Phone no. ► (   )   Personal identification number (PIN) ►

Under penalties of perjury, I declare that I have examined this return, including accompanying schedules and statements, and, to the best of my knowledge and belief, it is true, correct, and complete, and that no part of any payment made to a state unemployment fund claimed as a credit was, or is to be, deducted from the payments to employees.

Signature ► *Ernie Goldman*   Title (Owner, etc.) ► Controller   Date ► 2-10-200X

For Privacy Act and Paperwork Reduction Act Notice, see separate instructions.   ▼ **DETACH HERE** ▼   Cat. No. 10983G   Form **940-EZ**

Figure 8-15 Completed Form 940-EZ

FUTA   As we saw earlier, the FUTA tax rate is .8% (or eight tenths of 1%) on the first $7,000 of each employee's gross pay. If Gradesoft.com's accumulated FUTA tax liability is $100 or more during the calendar year, Ernie must make a FUTA tax deposit with a Federal Reserve bank or a bank authorized to take payroll tax deposits. The FUTA tax deposit rule is quite simple: If the amount of FUTA tax owed is $100 or more during any calendar quarter, the employer must deposit the amount due no later than one month after the quarter ends.

At the end of the first quarter Gradesoft.com owes $198 for FUTA taxes. Ernie has prepared a schedule showing how the tax was computed. (See Table 8-1 for the calculations.) If an employee earned over the $7,000 FUTA wage-base limit, only the first $7,000 will be taxable for FUTA purposes. Note that only one of Gradesoft.com's

TABLE 8-1 Computation of FUTA Tax for the First Quarter of 200X

Employee	Amount Earned in First Quarter	Amount Taxable for FUTA
Lee, Jackson	$ 4,703.56	$ 4,703.56
Stowe, Sheila*	0	0
Regan, Pat	$ 4,512.14	$ 4,512.14
Goldman, Ernie†	$ 3,208.33	$ 3,208.33
Zott, James T.†	$ 5,325.59	$ 5,325.59
Nguyen, Vince	$19,943.75	$ 7,000.00
		$24,749.62 × .008 = $198.00

*Sheila Stowe was not hired until the third quarter of the year.

†Ernie Goldman and James T. Zott were hired in March of the year (one month's earnings for quarter).

employees earned over the $7,000 FUTA limit during the first quarter of the year. Please see Part II of Form 940-EZ in Figure 8-15.

Because Gradesoft.com owes $198 in FUTA taxes, Ernie will make the FUTA tax deposit on April 30 to comply with the FUTA deposit rule. The general journal entry is prepared as shown in Figure 8-16.

SUTA   Gradesoft.com must also pay state unemployment tax to Massachusetts. The SUTA tax is also due one month after the quarter ends, on April 30. Ernie will pay out $1,336.48 in tax, based on a SUTA percentage rate of 5.4% on the first $7,000 that each of the employees has earned ($24,749.62 × .054 = $1,336.48). The amount of SUTA Ernie pays is shown on lines A and B of Form 940-EZ.

WORKERS' COMPENSATION INSURANCE

Gradesoft.com is required to have workers' compensation insurance to insure its employees against losses due to accidental injury or death incurred while on the job. Ernie is required to estimate the cost of this insurance and pay the premium in advance.

The premium for workers' compensation insurance is based on the total estimated gross payroll, and the rate is calculated per $100 of weekly payroll. At year end, the actual payroll is compared with the estimated payroll, and Fred will either receive credit for overpayment or be responsible for paying additional premiums.

These are the facts on which Gradesoft.com's insurance cost was calculated:

1. Estimated payroll: $320,000.

2. Two grades of workers: Developers and Managers.

			GRADESOFT.COM GENERAL JOURNAL										
*	April	30	FUTA Payable	212		1	9	8	00			
			SUTA Payable	213	1	3	3	6	48			
			Cash	111						1	5	3	4	48
			To record the FUTA and SUTA tax									
			deposits for the first quarter of the year.									

*Note: This entry could be two separate entries.

Figure 8-16 Recording FUTA and SUTA Deposit

3. Rate per $100 of payroll: Developers, $1.90; Managers $.14.
4. Estimated payroll: Developers, $120,000; Managers, $200,000.

The estimated premium was calculated as follows:

$$
\begin{array}{lll}
\textbf{Developers:} & \$120,000/\$100 = 1,200 \times \$1.90 = & \$2,280 \\
\textbf{Managers:} & \$200,000/\$100 = 2,000 \times \$.14 \;\; = & \underline{280} \\
& \textbf{\textit{Total Estimated Premium:}} & \underline{\underline{\$2,560}}
\end{array}
$$

Accounts Affected	Category	↑ ↓	Dr./Cr.
Prepaid Insurance, Worker's Compensation	Asset	↑	Dr.
Cash	Asset	↓	Cr.

Gradesoft.com would have to pay $2,560 in advance. At the end of the year, records show that the Developer payroll was $121,114 and the Manager payroll was $195,881.

Given those amounts, Gradesoft.com's actual premium should be $2,575.16, calculated as follows:

$$
\begin{array}{lll}
\textbf{Developers:} & \$121,114/\$100 = 1,211 \times \$1.90 = & \$2,300.90 \\
\textbf{Managers:} & \$195,881/\$100 = 1,959 \times \$.14 \;\; = & \underline{274.26} \\
& \textbf{\textit{Total Estimated Premium:}} & \underline{\underline{\$2,575.16}}
\end{array}
$$

Because the actual premium is $15.16 higher than the estimate, Ernie must pay this amount in January together with the estimated premium for the next year.

The $15.16 adjustment takes place on December 31 by debiting Workers' Compensation Insurance Expense and crediting Workers' Compensation Insurance Payable.

Accounts Affected	Category	↑ ↓	Dr./Cr.
Workers' Compensation Insurance Expense	Expense	↑	Dr.
Workers' Compensation Insurance Payable	Liability	↑	Cr.

Learning Unit 8-3 Review

AT THIS POINT you should be able to

- Prepare a W-2 form. (p. 303)
- Explain the difference between a W-2 form and a W-3 form. (p. 303)
- Prepare a 940-EZ form. (p. 306)
- Explain the difference between a Form 940-EZ and a Form 940. (p. 306)
- Calculate estimated premium for workers' compensation insurance. (p. 307)
- Prepare journal entries to record as well as adjust the premiums for workers' compensation insurance. (p. 307)

SELF-REVIEW QUIZ 8-3

(The forms you need are on page 243 of the *Study Guide and Working Papers*.)
Are the following questions true or false?

1. W-4s must be received by employees by January 31 of the following year.
2. Form W-3 is sent to the Social Security Administration yearly.
3. A Form 940 is prepared by a business that employs workers in only one state.
4. The Employer's Annual Federal Unemployment Tax Return records the employer's FICA and FIT tax liabilities.
5. A FUTA tax liability of $100 must be paid 10 days after the quarter ends.
6. Premiums for workers' compensation insurance may be adjusted based on actual payroll figures.

SOLUTIONS TO SELF-REVIEW QUIZ 8-3

1. False. W-2 forms must be sent to each employee by January 31 of the next year. The W-4 form is filled out by a new employee and is used for calculating federal and state income taxes.
2. True.
3. False. Form 940 will be prepared by a business that employs workers in more than one state. Form 940-EZ will be prepared by an employer with workers in only one state.
4. False. The Employer's Annual Federal Unemployment Tax Return records and reports the FUTA tax liability. Form 941 records and reports the FICA and FIT tax liabilities.
5. False. A FUTA tax liability of $100 must be paid one month after the quarter ends.
6. True.

Quiz Tip:
If you are getting refunds for FIT, you may want to change your withholding.

Chapter Review

Summary of Key Points

Learning Unit 8-1

1. The Payroll Tax Expense for the employer is made up of FICA tax (Social Security and Medicare) and the state and federal unemployment insurance taxes.
2. The maximum amount of credit given for state unemployment taxes paid against the FUTA tax is 5.4%. This figure is known as the normal FUTA tax credit.
3. The Payroll Tax Expense is recorded at the time the payroll is recorded.

Learning Unit 8-2

1. Federal Form 941 is prepared and filed no later than one month after the calendar quarter ends. It reports the amount of Social Security, Medicare, and federal income taxes withheld from employees and the Social Security and Medicare taxes due from the employer during the quarter.
2. Social Security, Medicare, and federal income taxes are known as Form 941 taxes.
3. The total amount of Form 941 taxes paid by a business during a specific period of time determines how often the business will have to make its payroll tax deposits. This time period is called a look-back period.
4. Businesses will make their payroll tax deposits either monthly or semiweekly when paying Form 941 taxes.
5. Different deposit rules apply to monthly and semiweekly depositors.
6. Form 941 payroll tax deposits must be made using Form 8109, known as the Federal Tax Deposit Coupon.

Learning Unit 8-3

1. Information to prepare W-2 forms can be obtained from the individual employee earnings records.
2. Form W-3 is used by the Social Security Administration in verifying that taxes have been withheld as reported on individual employee W-2 forms.
3. 940-EZ is prepared by January 31, after the end of the previous calendar year. This form can be filed by February 10 if all required deposits have been made by January 31.
4. If the amount of FUTA taxes is equal to or more than $100 during any calendar quarter, the deposit must be made no later than one month after the quarter ends. If the amount is less than $100, no deposit is required until the liability reaches the $100 point.
5. Workers' compensation insurance (the estimated premium) is paid at the beginning of the year by the employer to protect against potential losses to its employees due to accidental death or injury incurred while on the job.

Key Terms

Banking day A banking day is an established time each business day before which bank transactions are considered to be completed on that day. Generally, a banking day will end a 2 or 3 P.M. local time. Banking business transacted after this time is usually considered to be the next day's business. Saturdays, Sundays, and federal holidays are usually not considered banking days.

Calendar quarter A three-month time period. There are four calendar quarters in a calendar year (January 1 through December 31). The first quarter is January through March, the second is April through June, the third is July through September, and the fourth is October through December.

Employer identification number (EIN) This number assigned by the IRS is used by an employer when recording and paying payroll and income taxes.

Experience/merit rating A percentage rate that is assigned to a business by the state in calculating state unemployment taxes. The rate is based on the employment record and amount of contributions paid into the state unemployment fund. The lower the rating, the less tax that must be paid.

Federal Insurance Contributions Act (FICA) Part of the Social Security law that requires employees and employers to pay Social Security taxes and Medicare taxes.

Federal Unemployment Tax Act (FUTA) A tax paid by employers to the federal government. The current rate is .8% after applying the normal FUTA tax credit on the first $7,000 of earnings of each employee.

Form 940, Employer's Annual Federal Unemployment Tax Return One version of the form used by employers at the end of the year to report the amount of unemployment tax due for the calendar year. This version of the form is used by an employer with workers in more than one state. If more than $100 is cumulatively owed in a quarter, it should be paid quarterly, one month after the end of the quarter. Normally, payment is due January 31 after the calendar year, or February 10 if deposits have already been made by an employer.

Form 940-EZ, Employer's Annual Federal Unemployment Tax Return The other version of the form used by employers at the end of the year to report the amount of unemployment tax due for the calendar year. The "EZ" version of this form is used by an employer with workers in only one state.

Form 941, Employer's Quarterly Federal Tax Return A tax report that a business will complete after the end of each calendar quarter indicating the total FICA (Social Security and Medicare) owed plus the amount of federal income tax withheld from employees' pay for the quarter. If federal tax deposits have been made on time, the total amount deposited should equal the amount due on Form 941. If there is a difference, a payment may be due.

Form 941 taxes Another term used to describe Social Security, Medicare, and federal income taxes. This name comes from the form used to report these taxes.

Form 8109, Federal Tax Deposit Coupon A coupon that is completed and sent along with payments of tax deposits relating to either Forms 940-EZ or 941. This form can also be used to deposit other types of taxes a business may owe the federal government.

Form SS-4 The form filled out by an employer to get an employer identification number. The form is sent to the IRS, which assigns the number to the business.

Form W-2, Wage and Tax Statement A form completed by the employer at the end of the calendar year to provide a summary of gross earnings and deductions to each employee. At least two copies go to the employee, one copy to the IRS, one copy to any state where employees' income taxes have been withheld, one copy to the Social Security Administration, and one copy into the records of the business.

Form W-3, Transmittal of Income and Tax Statements A form completed by the employer to verify the number of W-2s and amounts withheld as shown on them. This form is sent to a Social Security Administration data processing center along with copies of each employee's W-2 forms.

Look-back period A period of time used to determine if a business will make its Form 941 tax deposits on a monthly or semiweekly basis. The IRS has defined this period as July 1 through June 30 of the year prior to the year in which Form 941 tax deposits will be made.

Monthly depositor A business classified as a monthly depositor will make its payroll tax deposits only once each month for the amount of Form 941 due from the prior month.

Normal FUTA Tax Credit A credit given to employers who pay their state unemployment taxes on time. The credit is usually 5.4%, which is applied against a 6.2% rate. The result is a net FUTA tax of .8%.

Payroll Tax Expense The general ledger account that records the total of the employer's FICA (Social Security and Medicare), SUTA, and FUTA tax responsibilities.

Semiweekly depositor A business classified as a semiweekly depositor may make its payroll tax deposits up to twice in one week. Semiweekly depositors will make a minimum of one Form 941 payroll tax deposit each week.

State Unemployment Tax Act (SUTA) A tax usually paid only by employers to the state for employee unemployment insurance.

Workers' compensation insurance Insurance paid for, in advance, by an employer to protect its employees against loss due to injury or death incurred during employment.

Blueprint: Form 941 Tax Deposit Rules

10 Frequently Asked Questions and Answers About Depositing Social Security, Medicare, and Federal Income Taxes to the Government

Here is a summary of questions and answers to help you understand the payroll tax deposit rules for Form 941 taxes.

1. **What are Form 941 taxes?** The term *Form 941 taxes* is used to describe the amount of Social Security, Medicare, and federal income tax paid by employees and the amount of Social Security and Medicare taxes that are

matched and paid by an employer. The total of these taxes are known as Form 941 taxes because they are reported on Form 941 each quarter.

2. **When does an employer deposit Form 941 taxes?** How often an employer deposits Form 941 taxes depends on how the employer is classified for this purpose. The IRS classifies an employer as either a *monthly* or *semiweekly depositor* based on the amount of Form 941 taxes paid during a time period known as a *look-back period.*

3. **When is a look-back period?** A look-back period is a fiscal year that begins on July 1 and ends on June 30 of the year before the calendar year when the deposits will be made. For example, for the 2004 calendar year, an employer's look-back period will begin on July 1, 2002, and end June 30, 2003.

4. **What is the dollar amount used to classify an employer for Form 941 tax deposits?** The key dollar amount used to determine if an employer is a monthly or semiweekly depositor is $50,000 in Form 941 taxes. Two rules apply here:

   a. If the total amount deposited in Form 941 taxes is less than $50,000 during the look-back period, the employer is considered a *monthly tax depositor.*
   b. If the total amount deposited in Form 941 taxes is $50,000 or more during the look-back period, the employer is considered a *semiweekly tax depositor.*

5. **How do employers deposit Form 941 taxes?** An employer fills out a Form 8109 (Federal Tax Deposit Coupon) and gives this form with a check to a bank authorized to receive payroll tax deposits or to a Federal Reserve bank. Usually, authorized banks will only take checks written from an account maintained at that same bank. Therefore, an employer usually cannot make a Form 941 deposit at Bank A using a check written from an account maintained at Bank B. A Federal Reserve bank will accept a check from any U.S. bank for payroll tax deposit purposes.

6. **When do monthly depositors make their deposits?** A monthly depositor will figure the total amount of Form 941 taxes owed in a calendar month and then pay this amount by the fifteenth of the next month. If an employer owes $3,125 in Form 941 taxes for the month of June, it will deposit this same amount no later than July 15 of the same year.

7. **When do semiweekly depositors make their deposits?** The rules for making deposits are a little more complicated for a semiweekly depositor. The depositor may have to make up to two Form 941 deposits each week. When a tax deposit is due depends on when the employees are paid. To keep the rules consistent, the IRS has taken a calendar week and divided it into two payday time periods. It is easiest to think of a two-week period of time when discussing these time periods: *Wednesday, Thursday*, and *Friday* of week one, *Saturday* of week one, and *Sunday, Monday*, and *Tuesday* of week two.

   Two deposit rules apply to these two time periods. We can call these rules the Wednesday and Friday rules.

   a. **Wednesday rule:** If employees are paid during the week one Wednesday–Friday period, the tax deposit will be due on Wednesday of week two.
   b. **Friday rule:** If employees are paid anytime from Saturday of week one or Sunday, Monday, or Tuesday of week two, the tax deposit will be due on Friday of week two.

These rules mean that the payroll tax deposit will be due three banking days after the payday time period ends. For the Wednesday rule, the deposit is due three banking days after Friday of week one, on the following Wednesday (in week two). For the Friday rule, the deposit is due three banking days after Tuesday of week two, on Friday of week two.

8. **What is a banking day?** The term *banking day* refers to any day that a bank is open to the public for business. Saturdays, Sundays, and legal holidays are not banking days.

9. **How do legal holidays affect payroll tax deposits?** If a legal holiday occurs after the last day of a payday time period, the employer will get one extra day to make its Form 941 tax deposit as follows:

   a. **For monthly depositors:** If the fifteenth of the month is a Saturday, Sunday, or legal holiday, the deposit will be due and payable on the next banking day.

   b. **For semiweekly depositors:** A deposit due on Wednesday will be due on Thursday of the same week, and a Friday deposit will be due on Monday of the following week. Remember that the employer will always have three banking days after the last day of either payday time period to make its payroll tax deposit.

10. **What happens if an employer is late with its Form 941 tax deposit?** If a Form 941 tax deposit is not made the day it should be deposited, the employer may be assessed a fine for lateness and may even be charged interest, depending on how late the deposit is.

Questions, Mini Exercises, Exercises, and Problems

Discussion Questions

1. What taxes make up Payroll Tax Expense?
2. Explain how an employer can receive a credit against the FUTA tax due.
3. Explain what an experience or merit rating is and how it affects the amount paid by an employer for state unemployment insurance.
4. How is an employer classified as a monthly or semiweekly depositor for Form 941 tax purposes?
5. What is the purpose of Form 8109?
6. How often is Form 941 completed?
7. Please comment on the following statement: The amount found on line 17(d) of Form 941 must always be the same amount found on line 13 of the form.
8. Bill Smith leaves his job on July 9. He requests a copy of his W-2 form when he leaves. His boss tells him to wait until January of next year. Please discuss whether Bill's boss is correct in making this statement.
9. Why would one employer prepare a Form 940 but another would prepare a 940-EZ?
10. Employer A has a FUTA tax liability of $67.49 on March 31 of the current year. When does the employer have to make the deposit for this liability?
11. Employer B has a FUTA tax liability of $553.24 on January 31 of the current year. When does the employer have to make the deposit for this liability?
12. Why is the year-end adjusting entry needed for workers' compensation insurance?

Mini Exercises

(The forms you need are on page 245 of the *Study Guide and Working Papers*.)

Account Classifications

1. Complete the following table:

Accounts Affected	Category	↑	Rules
a. Payroll Tax Expense			
b. FICA — Social Security Payable			
c. FICA — Medicare Payable			
d. State Unemployment Tax Payable			
e. Federal Unemployment Tax Payable			

Exempt Wages

2. Pete Bole's cumulative earnings before this pay period were $6,800; his gross pay for this week is $500. How much of *this* week's pay will be subject to taxes for: FICA — Medicare, FICA — Social Security, and FUTA. Assume the wage base and rates in the text.

Look-Back Periods

3. Label the following look-back periods for 200C by months.

A	B	C	D
200A		200B	

Monthly Versus Semiweekly Depositor

4. In November 200B, Pete is trying to find out if he is a monthly or semiweekly depositor for FICA (Social Security and Medicare) and federal income tax for 200C. Please advise based on the following taxes owed:

200A	Quarter 3	$28,000
	Quarter 4	12,000
200B	Quarter 1	3,000
	Quarter 2	10,000

Paying the Tax

5. Complete the following table:

Depositor	Four-Quarter Look-Back Period Tax Liability	Payroll Paid	Tax Paid by
Monthly	$28,000	Nov.	A
Semiweekly	$66,000	On Wednesday	B
		On Thursday	C
		On Friday	D
		On Saturday	E
		On Sunday	F
		On Monday	G

Exercises

(The forms you need are on pages 246–248 of the *Study Guide and Working Papers.*)

8-1. From the following information, prepare a general journal entry to record the payroll tax expense for Baker Company for the payroll of August 9:

EMPLOYEE	CUMULATIVE EARNINGS BEFORE WEEKLY PAYROLL	GROSS PAY FOR WEEK
J. Kline	$3,500	$900
A. Met	6,600	750
D. Ring	7,900	300

The FICA tax rate for Social Security is 6.2% on $87,000, and Medicare is 1.45% on all earnings. Federal unemployment tax is .8% (.008 when expressed as a decimal) on the first $7,000 earned by each employee. The experience or merit rating for Baker is 5.6% on the first $7,000 of employee earnings for state unemployment purposes.

Journalizing the payroll tax.

8-2. Using Exercise 8-1, the state changed Baker's experience/merit rating to 4.9%. What effect would this change have on the total payroll tax expense?

Change in merit rating.

8-3. Using Exercise 8-1, if D. Ring earned $2,000 for the week instead of $300, what effect would this change have on the total payroll tax expense?

Change in payroll tax expense.

8-4. At the end of January 200X, the total amount of Social Security, $610, and Medicare, $200, was withheld as tax deductions from the employees of Wheat Fields Inc. Federal income tax of $3,000 was also deducted from their paychecks. Wheat Fields has been classified as a monthly depositor of Form 941 taxes. Indicate when this payroll tax deposit is due and provide a general journal entry to record the payment.

Journalizing payment of deposit.

8-5. The total wage expense for Howell Co. was $160,000. Of this total, $30,000 was beyond the Social Security wage-base limit and not subject to this tax. All earnings are subject to Medicare tax, and $60,000 was beyond the federal and state unemployment wage-base limits and not subject to unemployment taxes. Please calculate the total payroll tax expense for Howell Co. given the following rates and wage-base limits:

Calculating total payroll tax expense.

   a. FICA tax rate: Social Security, 6.2%; Medicare, 1.45%.
   b. State unemployment tax rate: 5.9%.
   c. Federal unemployment tax rate (after credit): .8%.

8-6. Carol's Grocery Store made the following Form 941 payroll tax deposits during the look-back period of July 1, 200A, through June 30, 200B:

Determining when tax deposits are due.

QUARTER ENDED	AMOUNT PAID IN 941 TAXES
September 30, 200A	$13,783.26
December 31, 200A	14,893.22
March 31, 200B	14,601.94
June 30, 200B	15,021.01

Should Carol's Grocery Store make Form 941 tax deposits monthly or semiweekly for 200C?

8-7. If Carol's Grocery Store downsized its operation during the second quarter of 200B and as a result paid only $6,121.93 in Form 941 taxes for the quarter that ended on June 30, 200B, should Carol's Grocery make its Form 941 payroll tax deposits monthly or semiweekly for 200C?

Determining when tax deposits are due.

8-8. From the following accounts, record the payment of (a) the July 3 payment for FICA (Social Security and Medicare) and federal income taxes, (b) the July 30 payment of state unemployment tax, and (c) the July 30 deposit of FUTA tax that may be required. Please prepare general journal entries from the following T accounts:

Journal entry to record payment of taxes.

FICA — Social Security Payable 203		FICA — Medicare Payable 204	
	June 30 400 (EE)		June 30 100 (EE)
	400 (ER)		100 (ER)

FIT Payable 205		FUTA Tax Payable 206	
	June 30 3,005		June 30 143

SUTA Tax Payable 207	
	June 30 612

8-9. At the end of the first quarter of 200X, you have been asked to determine the FUTA tax liability for Oscar Company as well as to record any payment of tax liability. The following information has been supplied to you; the FUTA tax rate is .8% on the first $7,000 each employee earns during the year.

FUTA.
Recall there are 13 weeks in a calender quarter.

EMPLOYEE	GROSS PAY PER WEEK
J. King	$500
A. Lane	500
B. Move	600
C. Slade	900

Workers' compensation.

8-10. From the following data, estimate the annual premium and record it by preparing a general journal entry:

TYPE OF WORK	ESTIMATED PAYROLL	RATE PER $100
Office	$15,000	$ .21
Sales	42,000	1.90

Group A Problems

(The forms you need are on pages 249–255 of the *Study Guide and Working Papers.*)

8A-1. For the biweekly pay period ending on April 8 at Kane's Hardware, the partial payroll summary shown below is taken from the individual employee earnings records.

Your tasks are to

1. Complete the table. Use the federal income tax withholding table in Figure 7-2 (p. 261) to figure the amount of income tax withheld.
2. Prepare a journal entry to record the payroll tax expense for Kane's. Please show the calculations for FICA taxes.

Journal entry to record payroll tax expense.

Check Figure:
Payroll Tax Expense
$593.58

EMPLOYEE	ALLOWANCE AND MARITAL STATUS	GROSS	FICA SOCIAL SECURITY	MEDICARE	FEDERAL INCOME TAX
Al Jones	S-1	$ 850			
Janice King	S-0	900			
Alice Long	S-2	800			
Jill Reese	S-0	1,060			
Jeff Vatack	S-2	1,365			

Assume the FICA tax rate for Social Security is 6.2% up to $87,000 in earnings (no one has earned this much as of April 8) and Medicare is 1.45% on all earnings. The state unemployment tax rate is 5.1% on the first $7,000 of earnings, and the federal unemployment tax rate is .8% of the first $7,000 of earnings. (Only Jeff Vatack has earned more than $7,000 as of April 8.) In cases where the amount of FICA tax calculates to one-half cent, round up to the next cent.

8A-2. The following is the monthly payroll of Hogan Company, owned by Dean Hogan. Employees are paid on the last day of each month.

Employer's tax responsibilities.

January

EMPLOYEE	MONTHLY EARNINGS	YEAR-TO-DATE EARNINGS	FICA SOCIAL SECURITY	MEDICARE	FEDERAL INCOME TAX
Sam Koy	$1,900	$1,900	$117.80	$ 27.55	$ 258
Joy Lane	3,150	3,150	195.30	45.68	361
Amy Hess	4,100	4,100	254.20	59.45	500
	$9,150	$9,150	$567.30	$132.68	$1,119

February

EMPLOYEE	MONTHLY EARNINGS	YEAR-TO-DATE EARNINGS	FICA SOCIAL SECURITY	MEDICARE	FEDERAL INCOME TAX
Sam Koy	$2,100	$ 4,000	$130.20	$ 30.45	$ 302
Joy Lane	2,900	6,050	179.80	42.05	325
Amy Hess	3,775	7,875	234.05	54.74	426
	$8,775	$17,925	$544.05	$127.24	$1,053

March

EMPLOYEE	MONTHLY EARNINGS	YEAR-TO-DATE EARNINGS	FICA SOCIAL SECURITY	MEDICARE	FEDERAL INCOME TAX
Sam Koy	$ 2,975	$ 6,975	$184.45	$ 43.14	$ 586
Joy Lane	4,080	10,130	252.96	59.16	558
Amy Hess	4,250	12,125	263.50	61.63	545
	$11,305	$29,230	$700.91	$163.93	$1,689

Check Figure: Deposit of SUTA Tax $ 1,195.58

Hogan Company is located at 2 Roundy Road, Marblehead, MA 01945. Its employer identification number is 29-3458821. The FICA tax rate for Social Security is 6.2% up to $87,000 in earnings during the year and Medicare is 1.45% on all earnings. The SUTA tax rate is 5.7% on the first $7,000. The FUTA tax rate is .8% on the first $7,000 of earnings. Hogan Company is classified as a monthly depositor for Form 941 taxes.

Your tasks are to

1. Journalize entries to record the employer's payroll tax expense for each pay period in the general journal.
2. Journalize entries for the payment of each tax liability including SUTA tax in the general journal.

Journal entries and Form 941.

8A-3. Ed Ward, accountant of Hogan Company, has been requested to complete Form 941 for the first quarter of the current year. Using Problem 8A-2, Ed gathers the needed data. Ed has suddenly been called away to an urgent budget meeting and has requested you to assist him by preparing the Form 941 for the first quarter. Please note that the difference in the tax liability, a few cents, should be adjusted in the middle column of line 9; this difference is due to the rounding of FICA tax amounts.

Check Figure: Total Liability for Quarter $ 8,333.22

8A-4. The following is the monthly payroll for the last three months of the year for Henson's Sporting Goods Shop, 1 Roe Road, Lynn, MA 01945. The shop is a sole proprietorship owned and operated by Bill Henson. The employer ID number for Henson's Sporting Goods is 28-93118921.

Journal entries and Form 941.

Check Figure:
Dec. 31 Payroll Tax Expense
$736.67

The employees at Henson's are paid once each month on the last day of the month. Pete Avery is the only employee who has contributed the maximum into Social Security. None of the other employees will reach the Social Security wage-base limit by the end of the year. Assume the rate for Social Security to be 6.2% with a wage-base maximum of $87,000, and the rate for Medicare to be 1.45% on all earnings. Henson's is classified as a monthly depositor for Form 941 payroll tax deposit purposes.

October

EMPLOYEE	MONTHLY EARNINGS	YEAR-TO-DATE EARNINGS	FICA SOCIAL SECURITY	MEDICARE	FEDERAL INCOME TAX
Pete Avery	$ 2,950	$ 83,050	$182.90	$ 42.78	$ 530
Janet Lee	3,590	40,150	222.58	52.06	427
Sue Lyons	3,800	43,900	235.60	55.10	536
	$10,340	$167,100	$641.08	$149.94	$1,493

November

EMPLOYEE	MONTHLY EARNINGS	YEAR-TO-DATE EARNINGS	FICA SOCIAL SECURITY	MEDICARE	FEDERAL INCOME TAX
Pete Avery	$ 3,180	$ 86,230	$197.16	$ 46.11	$ 597
Janet Lee	3,772	43,922	233.86	54.69	468
Sue Lyons	3,891	47,791	241.24	56.42	559
	$10,843	$177,943	$672.26	$157.22	$1,624

December

EMPLOYEE	MONTHLY EARNINGS	YEAR-TO-DATE EARNINGS	FICA SOCIAL SECURITY	MEDICARE	FEDERAL INCOME TAX
Pete Avery	$ 4,250	$ 90,480	$ 47.74	$ 61.63	$ 867
Janet Lee	3,800	47,722	235.60	55.10	479
Sue Lyons	4,400	52,191	272.80	63.80	704
	$12,450	$190,393	$556.14	$180.53	$2,050

Your tasks are to

1. Journalize entries to record the employer's payroll tax expense for each pay period in the general journal.
2. Journalize entries for the payment of each tax for FICA tax (Social Security and Medicare) and federal income tax, given that Henson's is a monthly Form 941 tax depositor.
3. Complete Form 941 for the fourth quarter of the current year.

Form 940-EZ

8A-5. Using the information from Problem 8A-4, please complete a Form 940-EZ for Henson's Sporting Goods for the current year. Additional information needed to complete the form is as follows:

Check Figure:
Total Exempt Payments
$169,393

     a. FUTA tax deposit for first quarter: $168.00.
     b. SUTA rate: 5.7%.
     c. State reporting number: 025-319-2.

Please note that there were no FUTA tax deposits for the second, third, or fourth quarters of the year. Henson's had three employees for the year who all earned over $7,000.

Group B Problems

(The forms you need are on pages 249–255 of the *Study Guide and Working Papers*.)

8B-1. For the biweekly pay period ending on April 8 at Kane's Hardware, the following partial payroll summary is taken from the individual employee earnings records. Both Jill Reese and Jeff Vatack have earned more than $7,000 before this payroll.

Your tasks are to

1. Complete the table.
2. Prepare a journal entry to record the payroll tax expense for Kane's. Use the federal income tax withholding tables in Figures 7-2 and 7-3 to figure the amount of income tax withheld. Please show the calculations for FICA taxes.

EMPLOYEE	ALLOWANCE AND MARITAL STATUS	GROSS	FICA SOCIAL SECURITY	MEDICARE	FEDERAL INCOME TAX
Al Jones	S-1	$ 820			
Janice King	S-2	890			
Alice Long	S-0	850			
Jill Reese	S-1	1,100			
Jeff Vatack	S-2	1,340			

Assume the FICA tax rate for Social Security is 6.2% up to $87,000 in earnings (no one has earned this much as of April 8) and Medicare is 1.45% on all earnings. The state unemployment tax rate is 5.2% on the first $7,000 of earnings, and the federal unemployment tax rate is .8% of the first $7,000 of earnings. In cases where the FICA tax calculates to one-half cent, round up to the next cent.

8B-2. The following is the monthly payroll of Hogan Company owned by Dean Hogan. Employees are paid on the last day of each month.

January

EMPLOYEE	MONTHLY EARNINGS	YEAR-TO-DATE EARNINGS	FICA SOCIAL SECURITY	MEDICARE	FEDERAL INCOME TAX
Sam Koy	$1,850	$1,850	$114.70	$ 26.83	$222
Joy Lane	3,000	3,000	186.00	43.50	343
Amy Hess	3,590	3,590	222.58	52.06	396
	$8,440	$8,440	$523.28	$122.39	$961

February

EMPLOYEE	MONTHLY EARNINGS	YEAR-TO-DATE EARNINGS	FICA SOCIAL SECURITY	MEDICARE	FEDERAL INCOME TAX
Sam Koy	$2,200	$ 4,050	$136.40	$ 31.90	$ 293
Joy Lane	2,900	5,900	179.80	42.05	325
Amy Hess	3,775	7,365	234.05	54.74	426
	$8,875	$17,315	$550.25	$128.69	$1,044

Journal entry to record payroll tax expense.

Check Figure:
Payroll Tax Expense
$536.11

Employer's tax responsibilities.

March

EMPLOYEE	MONTHLY EARNINGS	YEAR-TO-DATE EARNINGS	FICA SOCIAL SECURITY	MEDICARE	FEDERAL INCOME TAX
Sam Koy	$ 2,820	$ 6,870	$174.84	$ 40.89	$ 405
Joy Lane	4,000	9,900	248.00	58.00	535
Amy Hess	4,300	11,665	266.60	62.35	556
	$11,120	$28,435	$689.44	$161.24	$1,496

Hogan Company is located at 2 Roundy Road, Marblehead, MA 01945. Its employer identification number is 29-3458821. The FICA tax rate for Social Security is 6.2% up to $87,000 in earnings during the year, and Medicare is 1.45% on all earnings. The SUTA tax rate is 5.7% on the first $7,000. The FUTA tax rate is .8% on the first $7,000 of earnings. Hogan Company is classified as a monthly depositor for Form 941 taxes.

Your tasks are to

1. Journalize entries to record the employer's payroll tax expense for each pay period in the general journal.
2. Journalize entries for the payment of each tax liability, including SUTA tax, in the general journal.

Journal entries and Form 941.

Check Figure:
Liability for Quarter
$7,851.58

8B-3. Ed Ward, accountant of Hogan Company, has been requested to complete Form 941 for the first quarter of the current year. Using Problem 8B-2, Ed gathers the needed data. Ed has suddenly been called away to an urgent budget meeting and has requested you to assist him by preparing the Form 941 for the first quarter. Please note that the difference in the tax liability, a few cents, should be adjusted in the middle column of line 9; this difference is due to the rounding of FICA tax amounts.

Journal entries and Form 941.

8B-4. The following is the monthly payroll for the last three months of the year for Henson's Sporting Goods Shop, 1 Roe Road, Lynn, MA 01945. The shop is a sole proprietorship owned and operated by Bill Henson. The employer ID number for Henson's Sporting Goods is 28-93118921.

The employees at Henson's are paid once each month on the last day of the month. Pete Avery is the only employee who has contributed the maximum into Social Security. None of the other employees will reach the Social Security wage-base limit by the end of the year. Assume the rate for Social Security to be 6.2% with a wage-base maximum of $87,000 and the rate for Medicare to be 1.45% on all earnings. Henson's is classified as a monthly depositor for Form 941 payroll taxes.

October

EMPLOYEE	MONTHLY EARNINGS	YEAR-TO-DATE EARNINGS	FICA SOCIAL SECURITY	MEDICARE	FEDERAL INCOME TAX
Pete Avery	$ 2,950	$ 84,200	$182.90	$ 42.78	$ 530
Janet Lee	3,590	41,075	222.58	52.06	427
Sue Lyons	3,800	44,000	235.60	55.10	536
	$10,340	$169,275	$641.08	$149.94	$1,493

November

EMPLOYEE	MONTHLY EARNINGS	YEAR-TO-DATE EARNINGS	FICA SOCIAL SECURITY	MEDICARE	FEDERAL INCOME TAX
Pete Avery	$ 3,000	$ 87,200	$173.60	$ 43.50	$ 552
Janet Lee	3,650	44,725	226.30	52.93	439
Sue Lyons	3,710	47,710	230.02	53.80	503
	$10,360	$179,635	$629.92	$150.23	$1,494

Check Figure:
Dec 31 Payroll Tax
Expense $654.51

December

EMPLOYEE	MONTHLY EARNINGS	YEAR-TO-DATE EARNINGS	FICA SOCIAL SECURITY	MEDICARE	FEDERAL INCOME TAX
Pete Avery	$ 4,250	$ 91,450	—	$ 61.63	$ 857
Janet Lee	3,850	48,575	$238.70	55.83	490
Sue Lyons	3,900	51,610	241.80	56.55	559
	$12,000	$191,635	$480.50	$174.01	$1,906

Your tasks are to

1. Journalize entries to record the employer's payroll tax expense for each pay period in the general journal.
2. Journalize entries for the payment of each tax for FICA tax (Social Security and Medicare) and federal income tax.
3. Complete Form 941 for the fourth quarter of the current year.

8B-5. Using the information from Problem 8B-4, please complete a form 940-EZ for Henson's Sporting Goods for the current year. Additional information needed to complete the form is as follows:

Form 940-EZ.

Check Figure:
Line 4 Total Exempt
Payments $170,635.00

    a. FUTA tax deposit for first quarter: $168.
    b. SUTA tax rate: 5.7%.
    c. State reporting number: 025-319-2.

Please note that there were no FUTA tax deposits for the third or fourth quarters of the year. Henson's had three employees for the year who all earned over $7,000.

Real-World Applications

8R-1. Sunshine School Supplies is a leading manufacturer of back-to-school kits and other items used by students in elementary and middle schools. Each summer Sunshine needs additional help to assemble, pack, and ship school items sold in stores around the country. Sunshine's company policy has been to hire 30 additional workers for 12 weeks during the summer. Each employee works 40 hours per week and earns $6.50 per hour. At the end of August these additional workers are laid off.

    Sunshine's state unemployment rate has risen to 5.4% with no experience/merit rating allowed due to these layoffs in the last few years.

Miriam Holtz, who is the president of Sunshine, asks for your help to find a way to reduce Sunshine's 5.4 state unemployment rate. When Miriam called the state department of labor and employment, she was told that Sunshine's unemployment rate could drop to 4.1% if it stopped laying off workers.

Miriam has thought about using temporary employment agency workers during the summer months as a way to obtain the help the company needs and at the same time stop the seasonal layoffs.

Miriam asks you if this is a good idea. She gives you the following facts to use in analyzing this idea:

1. Five hundred workers who are permanent employees of Sunshine earn in excess of $7,000 each by September of each year.
2. A temporary employment agency told Miriam it would charge Sunshine $7.00 per hour for each worker it supplied during the summer.
3. The current federal unemployment tax rate is .8% up to the first $7,000 each employee earns during a year.
4. The current SUTA wage-base limit is the first $7,000 each employee earns during a year.
5. Sunshine pays a FICA tax rate of 6.2% for Social Security and 1.45% for Medicare. The Social Security wage-base limit is $87,000; there is no wage-base limit for Medicare.

Please write a short memo to Miriam Holtz that shows your analysis of two options: (1) continue to hire 30 additional workers for the summer and then lay them off or (2) have the temporary employment agency provide 30 additional workers for the summer.

In your memo be sure to show the financial effect of both options in terms of the tax calculations on employee earnings for SUTA, FUTA, and FICA. For option 1 be sure to include the SUTA and FUTA tax effects for *both* the permanent and temporary workers. At the end of your memo please provide Miriam with your conclusion so she can make a good decision for her company.

8R-2. Cathy Johnson has just been hired as a bookkeeper for The Pet World Dog Toy Company. She recently graduated from the local community college with an associate degree in business. She took several accounting courses at school but was unable to take the school's payroll accounting course.

Cathy is confused about payroll tax forms and their purpose. She wants to learn more about the forms the business must prepare and send in to the government.

You are the accountant for Pet World. Your boss has asked you to help teach Cathy about the forms and why they are used. The boss feels it is best to give Cathy a brief written summary about the following forms:

1. Form 941.
2. Form 940-EZ.
3. Form 8109.
4. Form W-2.
5. Form W-3.

Please write a brief report to Cathy to help her to understand the following points about these payroll tax forms:

a. The purpose of each form.
b. What is reported on each form.
c. When each form is sent to the government.
d. Where the amounts found on each form come from in the accounting system.

YOU make the call

Critical Thinking/Ethical Case

8R-3. Abby Ross works in the Payroll Department for Lange Co. as a junior accountant. Abby is also going to school for an advanced degree in accounting. After work each day she uses the company's photocopy machine to make extra copies of her assignments. Should she be photocopying personal material on a company machine? You make the call. Write down your specific recommendations to Abby.

Internet Exercises: Microsoft; Automatic Data Processing

EX-1. [www.microsoft.com] Microsoft is one of the growing number of American companies who hires temporary workers who are independent contractors to fill permanent spots in its labor force. These "permatemps" do not have the status of employees who enjoy full benefits with Microsoft.

In this exercise, let us say that Microsoft hires a temporary worker and pays her $20 per hour. Assuming this employee does not go over the statutory FICA limits described by the chapter, nor goes over the FUTA $7,000 ceiling, how much does the company save by having an "independent contractor" perform the work over the cost of having an "employee" do the same work?

EX-2. [http://ebs.adp.com/prod/index.html] Automatic Data Processing, Inc. (ADP) is a long-recognized leader in payroll preparation for businesses of all sizes. ADP does provide other services to businesses, but much of its professional reputation stems from being one of the early "outsourcing" companies for payroll.

Services it provides in addition to strictly payroll calculation include benefits administration, staffing, time and attendance reporting, and assisting businesses in retaining high-quality employees.

1. From information you obtain from this Web site, explain why ADP has an important niche in human relations and payroll preparation.
2. What advantage can a company of any size obtain by outsourcing its payroll preparation and tax reporting activities?

Continuing Problem

Eldorado Computer Center

As December comes to an end, Tony Freedman wants to take care of his payroll obligations. He will complete Form 941 for the first quarter of the current year and Form 940-EZ for federal unemployment taxes. Tony will make the necessary deposits and payments associated with his payroll.

Assignment

(See pages 260–262 in your *Study Guide and Working Papers.*)

1. Record the payroll tax expense entry in general journal format for the quarter, using the information in the Chapter 7 problem.

2. Journalize entries for the payment of each tax liability, including SUTA tax, in the general journal. Eldorado Computer Center is classified as a quarterly depositor.
3. Prepare Form 941 for the first quarter. Eldorado Computer Center's employer identification number is 35-41325881.
4. Complete Form 940 for Eldorado Computer Center. The FUTA tax ceiling is $7,000, and the SUTA tax ceiling is $10,000 in cumulative wages for each employee. The Eldorado Computer Center's FUTA rate is .8%, and the SUTA rate is 2.7%. No deposits have been made.

Hint: Sometimes the amount of Social Security taxes paid by the employee for the quarter will not equal the employee's tax liability because of rounding. Any overage or difference should be reported on line 9 of Form 941.

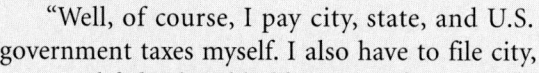

HOLD THE LETTUCE, WITHHOLD THE TAXES

"As an employer, Stan, what are your tax responsibilities?" asked Angel Tavarez, president of the Los Palmos Kiwanis club. They were at one of the luncheons sponsored by the club every month, and Stan had been asked to join a discussion on the Role of Small Business in Our Local Economy. Fortunately, Angel had told the panelists the questions in advance, so Stan had his answers ready.

"Well, of course, I pay city, state, and U.S. government taxes myself. I also have to file city, state, and federal withholding taxes for each of my two employees. I have to withhold state unemployment taxes, as well as FICA, which is another name for Social Security and Medicare taxes, for each of them. I pay workers' compensation, too," said Stan.

"That's strange," said a voice from the audience. "My brother-in-law has a Subway restaurant in the southern part of the state, and he doesn't pay any city taxes. What's going on here?"

"Naturally, the situation is slightly different for Subway owners in different cities in our state—and across the country," said Stan confidently. "Not all cities have city income taxes. Different states have different regulations about worker's comp, as well."

"Oh, right," said the voice, sounding embarrassed.

"So, Stan, how often do you have to pay taxes," asked Angel Tavarez, shifting the topic diplomatically.

Stan picked up a piece of chalk and drew four large circles on the blackboard. Then he wrote the word "ASPIRIN" in each of the circles. A murmur of "Huhs" and "Whats" went around the room.

"The average employee working for a company pays tax once a year on April 15 and has one big tax headache. As an employer," Stan said, "I file tax returns on a quarterly basis, so I have four big tax headaches a year! Rather than filling out the 1040-EZ, I complete Form 941, the Employers Quarterly Federal Return to report and pay payroll taxes to the IRS. Yet, while the form is due quarterly, I need to actually deposit the tax money into a Federal Reserve Bank once a month. In addition, I have to file the 940-EZ at the end of each year to pay my federal and state unemployment taxes. Then, for each employee . . ."

"Stan," Angel interrupted, "I'm afraid time is running out for your segment of the panel discussion. We'll move on to Pamela Pudelle, who is going to tell us about advertising her new pet-grooming parlor." Stan suppressed a chuckle as a woman who looked amazingly like a poodle took the microphone from Stan.

Later, during the reception, Stan tapped Angel on the shoulder, "Sorry I went over my time limit," he said. "You didn't really go over," said Angel, "but you were getting a little too technical for the audience." While Stan was sorry to have let the discussion veer off course, he felt a little burst of pride: who would have thought a year ago that he would be willing—and able—to expound about the tax burden of a small business owner!

Discussion Questions

1. What are the taxes called "Form 941 taxes"?
2. Why is Stan classified as a monthly depositor of Form 941 taxes?
3. Assume Stan owed $2,069.90 in Form 941 taxes for March. When would it be due? What would happen if that day were Sunday?

PETE'S MARKET

Completing Payroll Requirements for First Quarter and Preparing Form 941

This Mini Practice Set aids in putting the pieces of payroll together. In this project you are the bookkeeper and have the responsibility of recording payroll in the payroll register, paying the payroll, recording the employer's tax responsibilities, and paying tax deposits as well as completing the quarterly report. (The forms you need are on pages 263–268 of the *Study Guide and Working Papers.*)

Pete's Market, owned by Pete Reel, is located at 4 Sun Avenue, Swampscott, MA 01970. His employer identification number is 42-4583312. Please assume the following:

1. FICA: Social Security, 6.2% on $87,000; Medicare, 1.45% on all earnings.
2. SUTA: 4.9% (due to favorable merit rating) on $7,000.
3. FUTA: .8% on first $7,000.
4. Employees are paid monthly. The payroll is recorded the last day of each month and is paid on the first day of the next month.
5. FIT table from IRS Circular E, *Employer's Tax Guide* (see p. 328).
6. State income tax is 8%.

The following are the employees of Pete's Market along with their monthly salary exemptions and other information:

SALARY PER MONTH

		January	February	March	
Fred Flynn	S-0	$2,500	$2,590	$2,575	(Sales Salaries)
Mary Jones	S-2	3,000	3,000	4,000	(Market Salaries)
Lilly Vron	S-1	3,000	3,000	4,260	(Sales Salaries)

Partial Ledger Accounts
as of December 31, 200X

FICA—Social Security Payable 210		FICA—Medicare Payable 212		FIT Payable 220
	410.90 (EE)		100 (EE)	600
	410.90 (ER)		100 (ER)	

SIT Payable 225	FUTA Payable 230	SUTA Payable 240
150	88	155

Using the general journal and payroll register provided, please complete the following:

200X

Jan. 15 Record the entry for the deposit of Social Security, Medicare, and FIT from last month's payroll. (For simplicity, we will not record the payment of state income tax in this problem.)

31 Pay state unemployment tax due from last quarter.

31 Pay federal unemployment tax owed.

31 Complete payroll register for January payroll, journalize payroll entry, and journalize entry for employer's payroll tax expense.

Feb.   1   Transfer cash for the January Net Pay from Cash to Payroll Checking Cash.
         1   Pay payroll.
        15   Pay taxes due for Social Security, Medicare, and FIT.
        28   Complete payroll register for February payroll. Journalize payroll entry as well as journalize entry for employer's payroll tax expense.

Mar.   1   Transfer cash for the February Net Pay from Cash to Payroll Checking Cash.
         1   Pay payroll.
        15   Pay taxes due for Social Security, Medicare, and FIT.
        31   Complete payroll register for March payroll. Journalize payroll entry as well as journalize entry for employer's payroll tax expense.

Apr.   1   Transfer cash for the March Net Pay from Cash to Payroll Checking Cash.
         1   Pay payroll.
        15   Pay taxes due for Social Security, Medicare, and FIT.
        30   Pay federal unemployment tax due for quarter 1.
        30   Pay state unemployment tax due for quarter 1.
        30   Complete Form 941 for the first quarter.

SINGLE Persons—MONTHLY Payroll Period
(For Wages Paid in 200X)

If the wages are—		And the number of withholding allowances claimed is—										
At least	But less than	0	1	2	3	4	5	6	7	8	9	10
		The amount of income tax to be withheld is—										
$2,480	$2,520	$317	$279	$241	$203	$165	$127	$89	$50	$25	$0	$0
2,520	2,560	327	285	247	209	171	133	95	56	29	3	0
2,560	2,600	338	291	253	215	177	139	101	62	33	7	0
2,600	2,640	349	297	259	221	183	145	107	68	37	11	0
2,640	2,680	359	303	265	227	189	151	113	74	41	15	0
2,680	2,720	370	309	271	233	195	157	119	80	45	19	0
2,720	2,760	381	315	277	239	201	163	125	86	49	23	0
2,760	2,800	392	323	283	245	207	169	131	92	54	27	2
2,800	2,840	403	334	289	251	213	175	137	98	60	31	6
2,840	2,880	413	345	295	257	219	181	143	104	66	35	10
2,880	2,920	424	356	301	263	225	187	149	110	72	39	14
2,920	2,960	435	366	307	269	231	193	155	116	78	43	18
2,960	3,000	446	377	313	275	237	199	161	122	84	47	22
3,000	3,040	457	388	319	281	243	205	167	128	90	52	26
3,040	3,080	467	399	330	287	249	211	173	134	96	58	30
3,080	3,120	478	410	341	293	255	217	179	140	102	64	34
3,120	3,160	489	420	352	299	261	223	185	146	108	70	38
3,160	3,200	500	431	363	305	267	229	191	152	114	76	42
3,200	3,240	511	442	373	311	273	235	197	158	120	82	46
3,240	3,280	521	453	384	317	279	241	203	164	126	88	50
3,280	3,320	532	464	395	326	285	247	209	170	132	94	56
3,320	3,360	543	474	406	337	291	253	215	176	138	100	62
3,360	3,400	554	485	417	348	297	259	221	182	144	106	68
3,400	3,440	565	496	427	359	303	265	227	188	150	112	74
3,440	3,480	575	507	438	370	309	271	233	194	156	118	80
3,480	3,520	586	518	449	380	315	277	239	200	162	124	86
3,520	3,560	597	528	460	391	323	283	245	206	168	130	92
3,560	3,600	608	539	471	402	333	289	251	212	174	136	98
3,600	3,640	619	550	481	413	344	295	257	218	180	142	104
3,640	3,680	629	561	492	424	355	301	263	224	186	148	110
3,680	3,720	640	572	503	434	366	307	269	230	192	154	116
3,720	3,760	651	582	514	445	377	313	275	236	198	160	122
3,760	3,800	662	593	525	456	387	319	281	242	204	166	128
3,800	3,840	673	604	535	467	398	330	287	248	210	172	134
3,840	3,880	683	615	546	478	409	340	293	254	216	178	140
3,880	3,920	694	626	557	488	420	351	299	260	222	184	146
3,920	3,960	705	636	568	499	431	362	305	266	228	190	152
3,960	4,000	716	647	579	510	441	373	311	272	234	196	158
4,000	4,040	727	658	589	521	452	384	317	278	240	202	164
4,040	4,080	737	669	600	532	463	394	326	284	246	208	170
4,080	4,120	748	680	611	542	474	405	337	290	252	214	176
4,120	4,160	759	690	622	553	485	416	347	296	258	220	182
4,160	4,200	770	701	633	564	495	427	358	302	264	226	188
4,200	4,240	781	712	643	575	506	438	369	308	270	232	194
4,240	4,280	791	723	654	586	517	448	380	314	276	238	200
4,280	4,320	802	734	665	596	528	459	391	322	282	244	206
4,320	4,360	813	744	676	607	539	470	401	333	288	250	212
4,360	4,400	824	755	687	618	549	481	412	344	294	256	218
4,400	4,440	835	766	697	629	560	492	423	354	300	262	224
4,440	4,480	845	777	708	640	571	502	434	365	306	268	230
4,480	4,520	856	788	719	650	582	513	445	376	312	274	236
4,520	4,560	867	798	730	661	593	524	455	387	318	280	242
4,560	4,600	878	809	741	672	603	535	466	398	329	286	248
4,600	4,640	889	820	751	683	614	546	477	408	340	292	254
4,640	4,680	899	831	762	694	625	556	488	419	350	298	260
4,680	4,720	910	842	773	704	636	567	499	430	361	304	266
4,720	4,760	921	852	784	715	647	578	509	441	372	310	272
4,760	4,800	932	863	795	726	657	589	520	452	383	316	278
4,800	4,840	943	874	805	737	668	600	531	462	394	325	284
4,840	4,880	953	885	816	748	679	610	542	473	404	336	290
4,880	4,920	964	896	827	758	690	621	553	484	415	347	296
4,920	4,960	975	906	838	769	701	632	563	495	426	357	302
4,960	5,000	986	917	849	780	711	643	574	506	437	368	308
5,000	5,040	997	928	859	791	722	654	585	516	448	379	314
5,040	5,080	1,007	939	870	802	733	664	596	527	458	390	321

$5,080 and over   Use Table 4(a) for a **SINGLE person** on page 34. Also see the instructions on page 32.

COMPUTERIZED ACCOUNTING APPLICATION FOR PETE'S MARKET MINI PRACTICE SET FOR CHAPTER 8

Completing Payroll Requirements for First Quarter and Preparing Form 941

Before starting on this assignment, read and complete the tasks discussed in Parts A, B, and F of the Computerized Accounting appendix at the back of this book and complete the Computerized Accounting Application assignments for Chapter 3, Chapter 4, and the Valdez Realty Mini Practice Set (Chapter 5).

Pete's Market, owned by Pete Reel, is located at 4 Sun Avenue, Swampscott, Massachusetts, 01970. His employer identification number is 42-4583312. The version of Peachtree Complete Accounting used with this text (2003) uses the state and federal tax laws in effect for calendar year 2003. Federal Income Tax (FIT), State Income Tax (SIT), Social Security, Medicare, FUTA, and SUTA are all calculated automatically by the program based on the following assumptions and built-in tax rates:

1. FICA: Social Security, 6.2 percent on $84,900; Medicare, 1.45 percent on all earnings.
2. SUTA: 4.9 percent on the first $10,800 in earnings.
3. FUTA: .8 percent on the first $7,000 in earnings.
4. Employees are paid monthly. The payroll is recorded and paid on the last day of each month. The company uses a payroll checking account and the net pay must be transferred to that account as part of the payroll process.
5. FIT is calculated automatically by the program based on the marital status and number of exemptions claimed by each employee. These have been set up already.
6. SIT for Massachusetts is calculated automatically by the program based on the marital status and number of exemptions claimed by each employee.

The Payroll module in Peachtree Complete Accounting is designed to work with the General Ledger module in an integrated fashion. When transactions are recorded in the Payroll Journal, the program automatically updates the employee records, records the journal entry, and posts all accounts affected in the general ledger.

The following are the employees of Pete's Market and their monthly wages (note the changes) they will earn for the first payroll quarter:

	JANUARY	FEBRUARY	MARCH
Fred Flynn	$2,500	$2,590	$2,475
Mary Jones	3,000	3,000	4,000
Lilly Vron	3,000	3,000	4,260

The trial balance for Pete's Market as of 1/1/04 appears below:

		Debits	Credits
1010	Cash	$84,964.04	$ —
1020	Payroll Checking Cash	—	—
2310	FIT Payable	—	1,415.94
2320	SIT Payable	—	535.50
2330	Social Security Tax Payable	—	1,116.00
2335	Medicare Tax Payable	—	261.00
2340	FUTA Payable	—	48.00
2350	SUTA Payable	—	1,587.60
3560	Pete Reel, Capital	$ —	$80,000.00
		$84,964.04	$84,964.04

Open the Company Data
Files

1. Click on the Start button. Point to Programs; point to the Peachtree folder and select Peachtree Complete Accounting. Your desktop may have the Peachtree icon allowing for a quicker entrance into the program.

2. Follow the "Open a File" instructions in Part A of the Computerized Accounting appendix at the back of this book to open **Pete's Market.**

3. Click on the **Maintain** menu option. Then select **Company Information.** The program will respond by bringing up a dialogue box allowing the user to edit/add information about the company.

Add Your Name to the
Company Name

4. Click in the **Company Name** entry field at the end of **Pete's Market.** If it is already highlighted, press the right arrow key. Add a dash and your name "**-Student Name**" to the end of the company name. Click on the **OK** button to return to the Menu Window.

Record Payment of
December Payroll Liabilities
and Taxes

5. Record the payment of last month's payroll liabilities using the General Journal Entry window. Enter the **Date** listed for each transaction (you may use the "+" key to advance the date or use the calendar icon next to the field to select the date from a calendar). Enter "Memo" into the **Source** text box for each transaction or accept Peachtree's additional number added to memo by pressing TAB:

2004

Jan.   15   Record the compound journal entry for the deposit of Social Security, Medicare, and FIT from last month's payroll. (We will not record the payment of state income tax.) This is a 941 Deposit

        31   Record the payment of SUTA taxes owed from last quarter.

        31   Record the payment of FUTA tax owed from last quarter. This is a 940 Deposit

How to Record the Payroll

6. Close the General Journal. Peachtree has two options for paying your employees. Both are available under the **Tasks** menu. The first option is **Select for Payroll Entry** that selects all employees who meet a selected criteria while the second, **Payroll Entry,** allows you to select the employees one by one. Since we wish to pay all of our salaried employees, we will select the first option, **Select for Payroll Entry.** This will bring up a dialogue box from which we can filter which employees to pay this period:

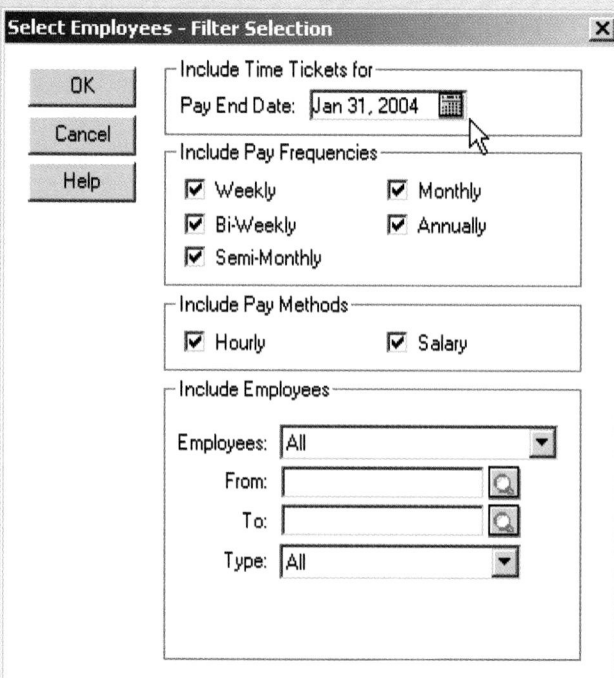

7. Since ours is a monthly payroll paid on the last day of the month, we will change the **Pay End Date:** to reflect January 31 using the small calendar to the right of the field. Click on the small calendar and then select the 31st from the calendar presented. The other filters allow us to pay only a certain frequency type employee, hourly and/or salary, or a range of employees by employee number. You can explore these options but leave them set at the default values shown in the illustration on page 330.

8. Click on the **OK** button when you are ready to continue. This will bring up a Select Employees to Pay dialogue box:

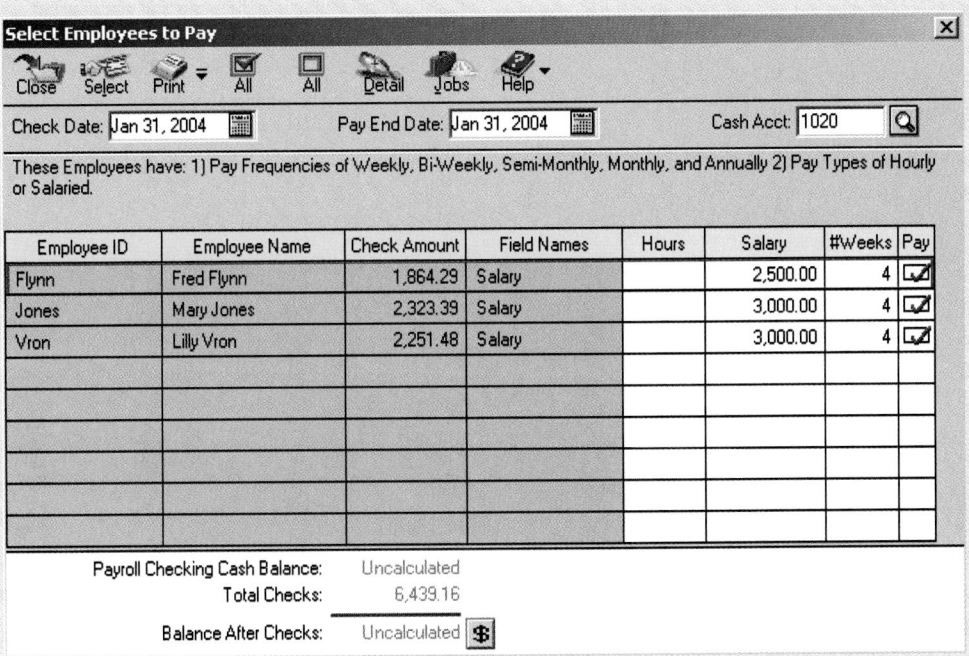

9. Notice how Peachtree has selected all three of our employees and has automatically flagged them for payment with a red check mark. It has also calculated all of the required withholdings and payroll taxes for each employee. Since we are paying the employees on the last day of the month, we should change the **Check Date** to reflect January 31, 2004. Also, verify and/or change the **Cash Acct** to 1020 Payroll Checking Cash using the pull down menu. Any employee can be deselected by clicking in the Pay column.

10. If you want to see the detail on any of the employees, simply double click on that employee's entry to bring up a Detail dialogue box. Try selecting Fred Flynn. If necessary, you can change any of the numbers presented in the white fields of this dialogue box by double clicking on the number you wish to change. We will accept all the information as shown. Leave this dialogue box by clicking on **OK** or **Cancel** since we made no changes:

Review the Payroll

How to Edit a Payroll
Journal Entry Prior to
Posting

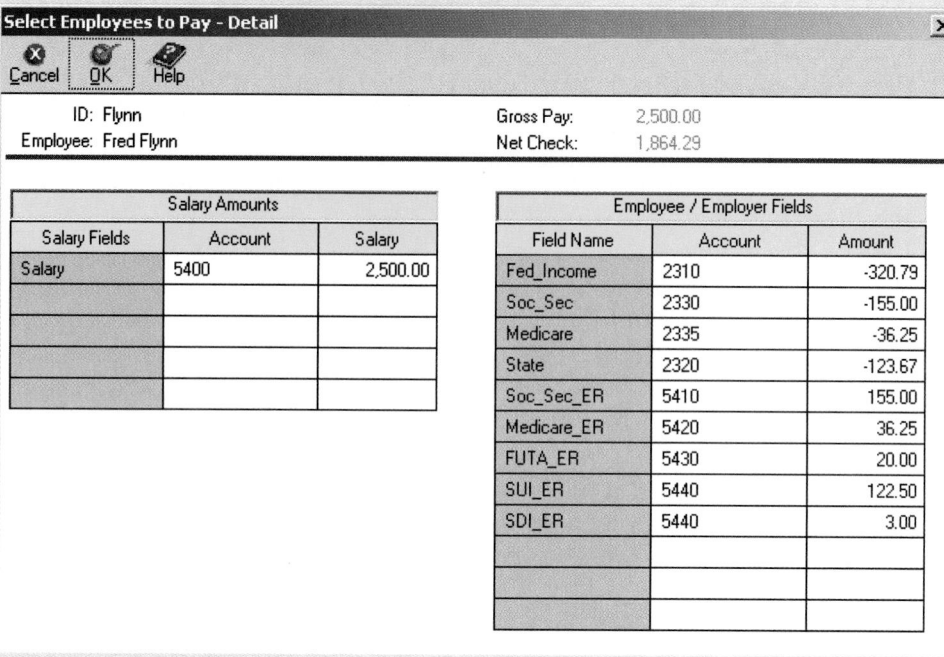

11. After verifying that the payroll entries are correct, click on the **Print** icon to print checks and post this transaction. A Print Forms: Payroll Checks dialogue box is presented for the user to select the proper check format and the starting check number. Accept the default form and use check #100 for the starting check number. Your screen should appear as shown below:

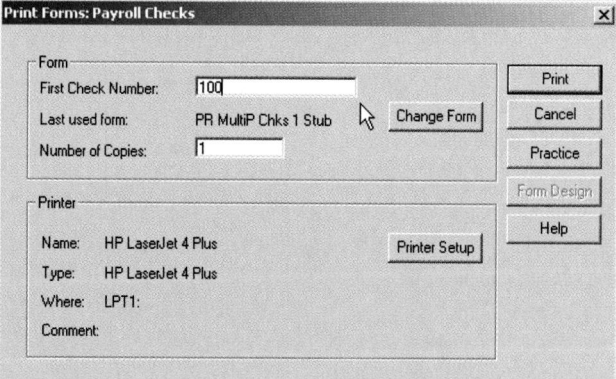

12. You are now presented with a dialogue box to select **Print** or **Practice.** Practice would be used to make sure the checks are aligned in the printer. This is particularly important with dot matrix type printers. Select **Print** since we are not printing on real forms and do not have to worry about alignment. You would normally load blank checks into your printer at this time so it may prompt you to do so. Just tell it to Continue.

13. When the checks have finished, you will be asked to confirm the printing process. This feature allows you to print them a second time if something interfered with the printing process the first time through. Upon confirming a successful run, you will be taken back to the Menu Screen of Peachtree and Peachtree will create and post all the necessary journal entries internally.

14. From the **Reports** menu, select **Payroll**. This will bring up a Select a Report dialogue box containing a list of several payroll reports available to us. Select **Payroll Register** to bring up a payroll register for the checks we just issued. We will use this report to determine the net pay for the payroll period. This amount must be transferred to our Payroll Checking account since our paychecks are drawn on that account. It must be funded prior to issuing the checks to our employees. Accept all defaults provided by Peachtree and we are presented with:

Pete's Market- Student Name
Payroll Register
For the Period From Jan 1, 2004 to Jan 31, 2004

Filter Criteria includes: Report order is by Check Date. Report is printed in Detail Format.

Employee ID Employee SS No Reference Date	Pay Type	Pay Hrs	Pay Amt	Amount	Gross State SUI_ER	Fed_Income Soc_Sec_ER SDI_ER	Soc_Sec Medicare_ER	Medicare FUTA_ER
Flynn Fred Flynn 100 1/1/04	Salary		2,500.00	1,864.29	2,500.00 -123.67 -122.50	-320.79 -155.00	-155.00 -36.25	-36.25 -20.00
Jones Mary Jones 101 1/1/04	Salary		3,000.00	2,323.39	3,000.00 -126.32 -147.00	-320.79 -186.00	-186.00 -43.50	-43.50 -24.00
Vron Lilly Vron 102 1/1/04	Salary		3,000.00	2,251.48	3,000.00 -130.73 -147.00	-388.29 -186.00	-186.00 -43.50	-43.50 -24.00
Summary Total 1/1/04 thru 1/31/04	Salary		8,500.00	6,439.16	8,500.00 -380.72 -416.50	-1,029.87 -527.00	-527.00 -123.25	-123.25 -68.00
Report Date Final Total 1/1/04 thru 1/31/04	Salary		8,500.00	(6,439.16)	8,500.00 -380.72 -416.50	-1,029.87 -527.00	-527.00 -123.25	-123.25 -68.00

15. We will now transfer cash from our regular Cash account into our Payroll Checking account in order to cover the checks we have just written. Note from the register totals, we have a total of $ 6,439.16 in net pay.

- Select **General Journal Entry** from the **Tasks** menu to open the General Journal dialog box. Enter the date 1/31/04 into the **Date** field; press the TAB key; enter "Memo" into the **Reference** field and press TAB.
- Select account number "1020 Payroll Checking Cash".
- Enter "Transfer net payroll" in the **Description** field.
- Enter "6439.16" in the **Debit** field.
- Tab to **Account No.** and select "1010 Cash".
- Tab to the **Credit** field and enter "6439.16" again.
- Click **Save** to complete the transfer.

Print Reports

16. After you have posted the journal entry, close the General Journal Entry window and print the following reports accepting all defaults offered by Peachtree:

    a. General Journal (check figure debit = $10,867.70)
    b. Trial Balance (check figure debit = $83,731.09)

    Review your printed reports. If you have made an error in a posted journal entry, use the procedures detailed in step 18 from Chapter 3 to make any necessary corrections. Reprint all reports if corrections are made.

Make a January Backup Copy

17. It is always wise to backup accounting data at the end of each month, saving it into a file that will be saved until the end of the year. We will use Peachtree's Backup feature to do this. Click on the Company Window **File** menu; select **Backup,** use a filename such as "PeteJan" to make sure you can recognize what the backup represents. Click on **OK.**

Advancing the Period

18. We must now advance the period to prepare Peachtree for the February transactions.

    🔹 Using your mouse, click on **System** from the **Tasks** menu. Select **Change Accounting Periods.**

    🔹 Using the pull down menu, select period 2—Feb 1, 2004 to Feb 29, 2004 and click on **OK.**

    🔹 You will be asked whether you wish to print reports before continuing. Since we have already printed our reports, we can answer **No.**

    🔹 Note that the status bar at the bottom of the screen now reflects that you are in period 2.

Record Payment of January Payroll Liabilities and Taxes

19. Record the following general journal entry:

2004
Feb.   15   Record the compound journal entry for the deposit of Social Security, Medicare, and FIT from last month's payroll. Use the trial balance created in #16 above to determine the amounts owed.

Record February Payroll

20. Record the February payroll journal entries for Fred Flynn, Mary Jones, and Lilly Vron. Remember that Fred Flynn is making more than his usual amount this month. He will earn $2,590 instead of his usual $2,500. After selecting employees to pay (See "How to Record the Payroll" above except use February 29), double click on Fred's Salary field and change his salary to the new amount. Everything will automatically recalculate using the new gross. Follow the same procedure for printing checks as you used in January except use the date February 29. Peachtree should select check #103 as the starting check number automatically. Change this if necessary. Be sure to transfer the net pay into the Payroll Checking Cash account.

Print Reports

21. Print the following reports accepting all defaults:

    a. Payroll Register (check figure net = $6,493.20)
    b. General Journal (check figure debit = $8,823.57)
    c. Trial Balance (check figure debit = $84,644.29)

Make a February Backup Copy

22. Click on the Company Window **File** menu; select **Backup,** use a filename such as "PeteFeb" to make sure you can recognize what the backup represents. Click on **OK.**

Advance Dates

23. We must now advance the period to prepare Peachtree for the March transactions.

    🔹 Using your mouse, click on **System** from the **Tasks** menu. Select **Change Accounting Periods.**

- Using the pull down menu, select period 3—Mar 1, 2004 to Mar 31, 2004 and click on **OK.**
- You will be asked whether you wish to print reports before continuing. Since we have already printed our reports, we can answer **No.**
- Note that the status bar at the bottom of the screen now reflects that you are in period 3.

24. Record the following general journal entry:

2004

Mar. 15 Record the compound journal entry for the deposit of Social Security, Medicare, and FIT from last month's payroll. (941 Deposit)

Record Payment of February Payroll Liabilities and Taxes

25. Record the March payroll journal entries for Fred Flynn, Mary Jones, and Lilly Vron. Note from the table at the start of the workshop that all three will receive other than their normal salary for this pay period. Be sure to transfer the net pay into the Payroll Checking Cash account after generating the paychecks. Check numbers should begin with #106.

Record March Payroll

26. Print the following reports accepting all defaults:

   a. Payroll Register (check figure net = $7,781.28)
   b. General Journal (check figure debit = $10,149.73)
   c. Trial Balance (check figure debit = $86,608.09)

Print Reports

27. From the **Reports** menu, select **Payroll.** This will bring up a Select a Report dialogue box containing a list of several payroll reports available to us. Select the **941** folder near the bottom to open up our 941 options. Peachtree will print both pages needed for a semi-weekly depositor (941 and 941B). If you have access to the blank 941 forms, you may print the report directly on the form. If not, you can still print the report on plain paper. You could also select the worksheet option if you wish to fill out the 941 manually using Peachtree's data. With the **941** folder open, select **FedForm 941 2002.** Accept all defaults by clicking on **OK.** Peachtree will automatically print the report. Note that in a real working situation, you would subscribe to Peachtree's Payroll Tax Service which would bring not only the tax tables up to date, but also the forms.

How to Print 941 Summary Reports

28. Peachtree has placed the numbers where they would go on a blank 941. Close the Select a Report Window when you are finished.

29. Click on the Company Window **File** menu; select **Backup,** use a filename such as "PeteMar" to make sure you can recognize what the backup represents. Click on **OK.**

Make a March Backup Copy

30. We must now advance the period to prepare Peachtree for the April transactions.

Advance Dates

- Using your mouse, click on **System** from the **Tasks** menu. Select **Change Accounting Periods.**
- Using the pull down menu, select period 4—Apr 1, 2000 to Apr 30, 2000 and click on **OK.**
- You will be asked whether you wish to print reports before continuing. Since we have already printed our reports, we can answer **No.**
- Note that the status bar at the bottom of the screen now reflects that you are in period 4.

31. Record the following general journal entries using your last trial balance to obtain the amounts owed:

Record Payment of March Payroll Liabilities and Taxes

2004

Apr.   15   Record the compound journal entry for the deposit of Social Security, Medicare, and FIT from last month's payroll. (941 Deposit)

        30   Record the payment of SUTA from last quarter.

        30   Record the payment of FUTA tax owed. (940 Deposit)

Print Reports

32. Print the following reports accepting all defaults:

    a. General Journal (check figure debit = $4,807.21)
    b. Trial Balance (check figure debit = $81,800.88)

CHAPTER 9

Special Journals

With Special Appendix for Merchandise Company Using a General Journal for a Perpetual Inventory System

You need some bookshelf space in your dorm room and decide to buy a couple of wood boards and concrete blocks to make a temporary bookshelf. You drive over to the James Hardware and Lumber Company to buy the materials you'll need. You have heard that Mr. and Mrs. James have owned the business for 35 years and they tend to go about running it in "the old-fashioned way."

Mr. James cuts the boards you need to length and gets the blocks from another section of the lumberyard. He writes down what you are buying on a sales slip and asks you to go into the store and pay for your purchase. Once inside, you see Mrs. James helping a contractor who is making a large purchase. After totaling the invoice, the contractor signs for the building materials. Mrs. James then pulls out a folder from a file cabinet with the contractor's name on it. She files the signed invoice and then makes a notation in a book labeled "Sales Journal."

When you hand Mrs. James your sales slip, she adds the amounts, which total $18.21. After you've paid for your purchase, you notice on your way out that Mrs. James writes the amount of your purchase down in a book labeled "Cash Receipts."

Whether the business is a mom-and-pop hardware store and lumberyard or a gigantic multinational corporation, special journals are used to group and accurately account for specific recurring transactions. In this chapter we discuss two special journals — the sales and cash receipts journals. We will learn that these two special journals are designed to quickly and accurately track sales and cash receipts transactions. After studying this chapter, you will realize that James Lumber and Hardware Company and General Motors, although very different in many ways, still speak the same language of business — accounting.

Learning Objectives

- Journalizing sales on account in a sales journal. (p. 346)

- Posting from a sales journal to the general ledger. (p. 347)

- Recording to the accounts receivable subsidiary ledger from a sales journal. (p. 347)

- Preparing, journalizing, recording, and posting a credit memorandum. (p. 350)

- Journalizing and posting transactions using a cash receipts journal as well as recording to the accounts receivable subsidiary ledger. (p. 355)

In Chapters 9 and 10 we look at how merchandise companies operate. Chapter 9 focuses on sellers of goods; Chapter 10 discusses buyers. In both chapters companies do not keep continual track of their inventory. This is called a **periodic inventory system**. A company simply takes an inventory at the end of its accounting period of what is left. In this edition is appendix material at the end of Chapters 9 and 10 that looks at how a company keeps continual track of its inventory. This system is called a **perpetual inventory system**.

Let's first look at Chou's Toy Shop to get an overview of merchandise terms and journal entries. After that, we take an in-depth look at how Art's Wholesale Clothing Company keeps its books. Remember that we will first look at the periodic system (no continual track of inventory).

Learning Unit 9-1   Chou's Toy Shop: Seller's View of a Merchandise Company

Chou's Toy Shop, owned by Chou Li, is a **retailer**. It buys toys, games, bikes, and so forth from manufacturers and **wholesalers** and resells these goods (or **merchandise**) to its customers. The shelving, display cases, and so forth are called "fixtures" or "equipment." These items are not for resale.

GROSS SALES

> Gross sales:
> Revenue earned from sale of merchandise to customers.

Each cash or charge sale made at Chou's Toy Shop is rung up at the register. Suppose the shop had $3,000 in sales on July 18. Of that amount, $1,800 was cash sales and $1,200 was charges. The account that recorded those sales would be

```
        Sales (Gross)
        Dr. | Cr.
            | 3,000     ◄——— Revenue account with a credit balance
```

This account is a revenue account with a credit balance and will be found on the income statement. Figure 9-1 shows the journal entry for the day. *Note:* We talk about sales tax later.

Accounts Affected	Category	↑ ↓	Rules	T Account Update
Cash	Asset	↑	Dr.	Cash
				1,800 |
Accounts Receivable	Asset	↑	Dr.	Accounts Receivable
				1,200 |
Sales	Revenue	↑	Cr.	Sales
				| 3,000

Figure 9-1
Recording Cash and Charge Sales for the Day

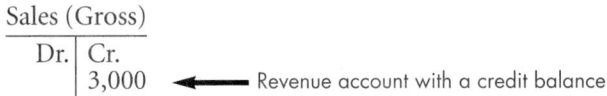

	July	18	Cash		1 8 0 0 00		
			Accounts Receivable		1 2 0 0 00		
			Sales				3 0 0 0 00
			Sales for July 18				

SALES RETURNS AND ALLOWANCES

It would be great for Chou if all the customers were completely satisfied, but that rarely is the case. On July 19, Michelle Reese brought back a doll she bought on account for $50. She told Chou that the doll was defective and that she wanted either a price reduction or a new doll. They agreed on a $10 price reduction. Michelle now owes Chou $40. The account called Sales Returns and Allowances (SRA) would record this information.

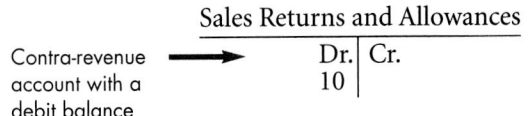

Sales Returns and Allowances

Contra-revenue account with a debit balance → Dr. | Cr.
10 |

This account is a contra-revenue account with a debit balance. It will be recorded on the income statement. Figure 9-2 shows how the journal entry would look:

Accounts Affected	Category	↑ ↓	Rules	T Account Update
Sales Returns and Allowances	Contra-revenue	↑	Dr.	Sales Ret. & Allow Dr. | Cr. 10 |
Accounts Receivable, Michelle Reese	Asset	↓	Cr.	Accounts Receivable Dr. | Cr. 1,200 | 10

Look at how the sales returns and allowances increase.

July	19	Sales Returns and Allowances		1000		
		Accounts Receivable, Michelle Reese			1000	
		Issued credit memorandum				

Figure 9-2
Issuing a Credit Memorandum in the General Journal

SALES DISCOUNT

Chou gives a 2% sales discount to customers who pay their bills early. He wants his customers to know about this policy, so he posted the following sign at the cash register:

Sales Discount Policy

2/10, n/30	2% discount is allowed off price of bill if paid within the first 10 days or full amount is due within 30 days
n/10, EOM	No discount. Full amount of bill is due within 10 days after the end of the month.

Note that the discount period is the time when a discount is granted. The discount period is less time than the credit period, which is the length of time allowed to pay back the amount owed on the bill.

If Michelle pays her $40 bill early, she will get an $.80 discount. This information is recorded as follows:

Sales Discount

Contra-revenue account with a debit balance → Dr. | Cr.
.80 |

Michelle's discount is calculated as follows:

$$.02 \times \$40 = \$.80$$

Michelle pays her bill on July 24. She is entitled to the discount because she paid her bill within 10 days. Figure 9-3 shows how Chou would record this payment on his books.

Gross Sales
— Sales discount
— SRA
= Net sales

Accounts Affected	Category	↑ ↓	Rules	T Account Update
Cash	Asset	↑	Dr.	**Cash** Dr. | Cr. 39.20 |
Sales Discount	Contra-revenue	↑	Dr.	**Sales Discount** Dr. | Cr. .80 |
Accounts Receivable	Asset	↓	Cr.	**Accounts Receivable** Dr. | Cr. 1,200 | 40

Figure 9-3
Recording Sales Discount

	July	24	Cash			3 9 20		
			Sales Discount			80		
			Accounts Receivable, Michelle Reese					4 0 00
			Payment from Sale on Account					

Although Michelle pays $39.20, her Accounts Receivable is credited for the full amount, $40.

In the examples so far we have not shown any transactions with sales tax. Note that the actual or **net sales** for Chou would be **gross sales** less sales returns and allowances less any sales discounts. Let's look at how Chou would record his monthly sales if sales tax were charged.

SALES TAX PAYABLE

None of the preceding examples shows state sales tax. Still, like it or not, Chou must collect that tax from his customers and send it to the state. Sales tax represents a liability to Chou.

Assume the state Chou's is located in charges a 5% sales tax. Remember that Chou's sales on July 18 were $3,000. Chou must figure out the sales tax on the purchases. For this purpose, let's assume there were only two sales on that date: the cash sale ($1,800) and the charge sale ($1,200).

The sales tax on the cash purchase is calculated as follows:

$$\$1,800 \times .05 = \$90 \text{ Tax}$$
$$\$1,800 + \$90 \text{ tax} = \$1,890 \text{ Cash}$$

Here is how the sales tax on the charge sale is computed:

$$\$1,200 \times .05 = \$60 \text{ Tax} + \$1,200 \text{ Charge} = \$1,260 \text{ Accounts Receivable}$$

It would be recorded as shown in Figure 9-4.

Accounts Affected	Category	↑ ↓	Rules	T Account Update
Cash	Asset	↑	Dr.	Cash Dr. | Cr. 1,890 |
Accounts Receivable	Asset	↑	Dr.	Accounts Receivable Dr. | Cr. 1,260 |
Sales Tax Payable	Liability	↑	Cr.	Sales Tax Payable Dr. | Cr. | 90 | 60
Sales	Revenue	↑	Cr.	Sales Dr. | Cr. | 3,000

	July	18	Cash			1	8	9	0	00					
			Accounts Receivable			1	2	6	0	00					
			Sales Tax Payable									1	5	0	00
			Sales								3	0	0	0	00
			July 18 Sales												

Figure 9-4
Credit Memorandum
with Sales Tax

In Learning Unit 9-3 we show you how to record a credit memorandum with sales tax.

Accounting in the Reel World

Show me the Merchandise!

Have you ever shopped in Express? Lord and Taylor's? Robinson May? Hecht's or Kaufmann's? These are just five of the 300 stores owned by St. Louis department store giant, The May Department Stores Company. While Express may cater to younger shoppers than Hecht's and Lord & Taylor's may have a different market than Kaufmann's, all May's stores need to earn income for the owner.

In the May Department Stores on-location video segment on your DVD, you'll learn about the different types of earnings that appear on May Department Stores' income statement.

1. How is The May Department Stores Company's "gross sales" different than its "earnings from continuous operations."
2. Suppose you buy a tank top for your cousin at an Express store and find a small hole in the side seam. Into what account would Express record the information about the return and where would it be recorded?
3. Any one of the stores owned and operated by May Department Stores has hundreds of thousands of customers. Can each store keep its books in a general ledger and, if not, what type of journals might they need to record account receivables?

Learning Unit 9-1 Review

AT THIS POINT you should be able to

● Explain the purpose of a contra-revenue account. (p. 340)
● Explain how to calculate net sales. (p. 340)

- Define, journalize, and explain gross sales, sales returns and allowances, and sales discounts. (p. 341)
- Journalize an entry for sales tax payable. (p. 343)

SELF-REVIEW QUIZ 9-1

(The forms you need can be found on page 269 of the *Study Guide and Working Papers.*)

Respond true or false to the following:

1. Sales Returns and Allowances is a contra-asset account.
2. Sales Discount has a normal balance of a debit.
3. Sales Tax Payable is a liability.
4. Sales Discount is a contra-asset.
5. A periodic system of inventory keeps continual track of the merchandise.

Quiz Tip:
Sales: Revenue   ↑ Cr.
SRA: Contra-revenue ↑ Dr.
SD: Contra-revenue ↑ Dr.

SOLUTIONS TO SELF-REVIEW QUIZ 9-1

1. False   2. True   3. True   4. False   5. False

Learning Unit 9-2   The Sales Journal and Accounts Receivable Subsidiary Ledger

SPECIAL JOURNALS*

Now let's examine how Art's Wholesale Clothing Company keeps its books. Art's business conducts many transactions. The partial general journal in Figure 9-5 shows the journal entries Art's must make for these sales on account transactions.

Figure 9-5
Recording Sales on Account in General Journal

ART'S WHOLESALE CLOTHING COMPANY GENERAL JOURNAL				
Apr.	3	Accounts Receivable, Hal's	80000	
		Sales		80000
		Sales on Account		
	6	Accounts Receivable, Bevans	160000	
		Sales		160000
		Sales on Account		
	18	Accounts Receivable, Roe	200000	
		Sales		200000
		Sales on Account		

*Special journals for a perpetual system are shown at the end of Chapter 10.

This method is not very efficient. If Art's Wholesale Clothing Company kept a **special journal** for each type of transaction he conducts, however, the number of postings and recordings required for each transaction would be reduced. After carefully looking at the situation with his accountant, Art Newner, the owner, decided to use the following special journals:

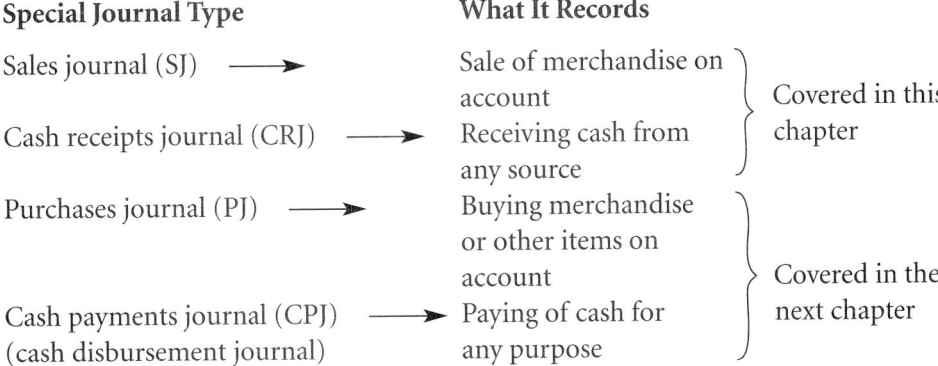

Special Journal Type	What It Records	
Sales journal (SJ) →	Sale of merchandise on account	Covered in this chapter
Cash receipts journal (CRJ) →	Receiving cash from any source	
Purchases journal (PJ) →	Buying merchandise or other items on account	Covered in the next chapter
Cash payments journal (CPJ) (cash disbursement journal) →	Paying of cash for any purpose	

SUBSIDIARY LEDGERS

In the same way Art's Wholesale Clothing Company needs more than just a general journal, the business needs more than just a general ledger. For example, so far in this text, the only title we have used for recording amounts owed to the seller has been Accounts Receivable. Art could have replaced the Accounts Receivable title in the general ledger with the following list of customers who owe him money:

- Accounts Receivable, Bevans Company.
- Accounts Receivable, Hal's Clothing.
- Accounts Receivable, Mel's Department Store.
- Accounts Receivable, Roe Company.

As you can see, this system would not be manageable if Art had 1,000 credit customers. To solve this problem, Art sets up a separate **accounts receivable subsidiary ledger.** Such a special ledger, often simply called a **subsidiary ledger,** contains a single type of account, such as credit customers. An account is opened for each customer, and the accounts are arranged alphabetically.

The diagram in Figure 9-6 on p. 346 shows how the accounts receivable subsidiary ledger fits in with the general ledger. To clarify the difference in updating the general ledger versus the subsidiary ledger, we will *post* to the general ledger and *record* to the subsidiary ledger. The word *post* refers to information that is moved from the journal to the general ledger; the word *record* refers to information that is transferred from the journal into the individual customer's account in the subsidiary ledger.

The accounts receivable subsidiary ledger, or any other subsidiary ledger, can be in the form of a card file, a binder notebook, or computer tapes or disks. It will not have page numbers. The accounts receivable subsidiary ledger is organized alphabetically based on customers' names and addresses; new customers can be added and inactive customers deleted.

When using an accounts receivable subsidiary ledger, the title Accounts Receivable in the general ledger is called the **controlling account**—Accounts Receivable because it summarizes or controls the accounts receivable subsidiary ledger. At the end of the month the total of the individual accounts in the accounts receivable ledger will equal the ending balance in Accounts Receivable in the general ledger.

> The general ledger is not in the same book as the accounts receivable subsidiary ledger.

Figure 9-6

Partial General Ledger of Art's Wholesale Clothing Company and Accounts Receivable Subsidiary Ledger

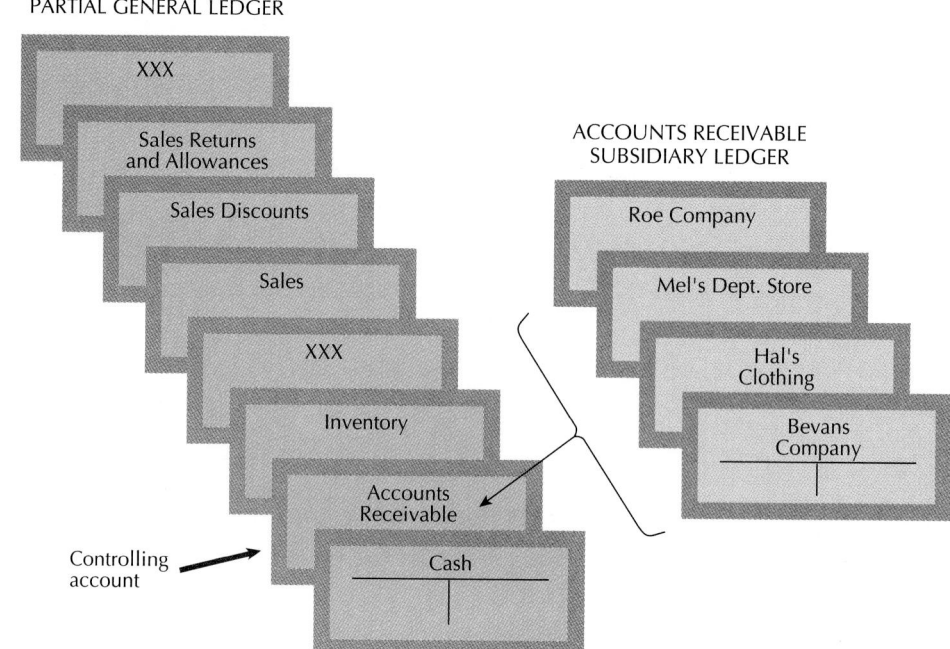

PARTIAL GENERAL LEDGER

ACCOUNTS RECEIVABLE SUBSIDIARY LEDGER

Proving:
At the end of the month, the sum of the accounts receivable subsidiary ledger will equal the ending balance in accounts receivable, the controlling account in the general ledger.

Art's Wholesale Clothing Company will use the following subsidiary ledgers:

Accounts receivable subsidiary ledger (debit balance)	Records money owed by credit customers	Covered in this chapter
Accounts payable subsidiary ledger (credit balance)	Records money owed by Art to creditors	Covered in next chapter

Let's now look closer at the sales journal, general ledger, and subsidiary ledger for Art's to see how transactions are updated in the special journal as well as posted and recorded to specific titles.

THE SALES JOURNAL

The **sales journal** for Art's Wholesale Clothing Company records all sales made on account to customers. Figure 9-7 shows the sales journal at the end of the first month in operation along with the recordings to the accounts receivable ledger and posting to the general ledger. Keep in mind that the reason the balances in the accounts receivable subsidiary ledger are *debit* balances is that the customers listed *owe* Art's Wholesale money. For some other companies, a sales journal might have multiple revenue account columns.

Look at the first transaction listed in the sales journal. It shows that on April 3, Art's Wholesale Clothing Company sold merchandise on account to Hal's Clothing for $800. The bill or **sales invoice** for this sale is shown in Figure 9-8 on p. 348.

Recording from the Sales Journal to the Accounts Receivable Subsidiary Ledger

As shown on the first line of the sales journal in Figure 9-2, the information on the invoice is recorded in the sales journal. The *PR column is left blank,* however. As soon as possible we now update the accounts receivable subsidiary ledger. To do so, we pull out the Hal's Clothing file card and update it: The debit side must show the

Recording to the accounts receivable subsidiary ledger occurs daily.

Hal's Clothing

Dr.	Cr.
4/3 SJ1	
800	

A ✓ means that the accounts receivable ledger has been updated.

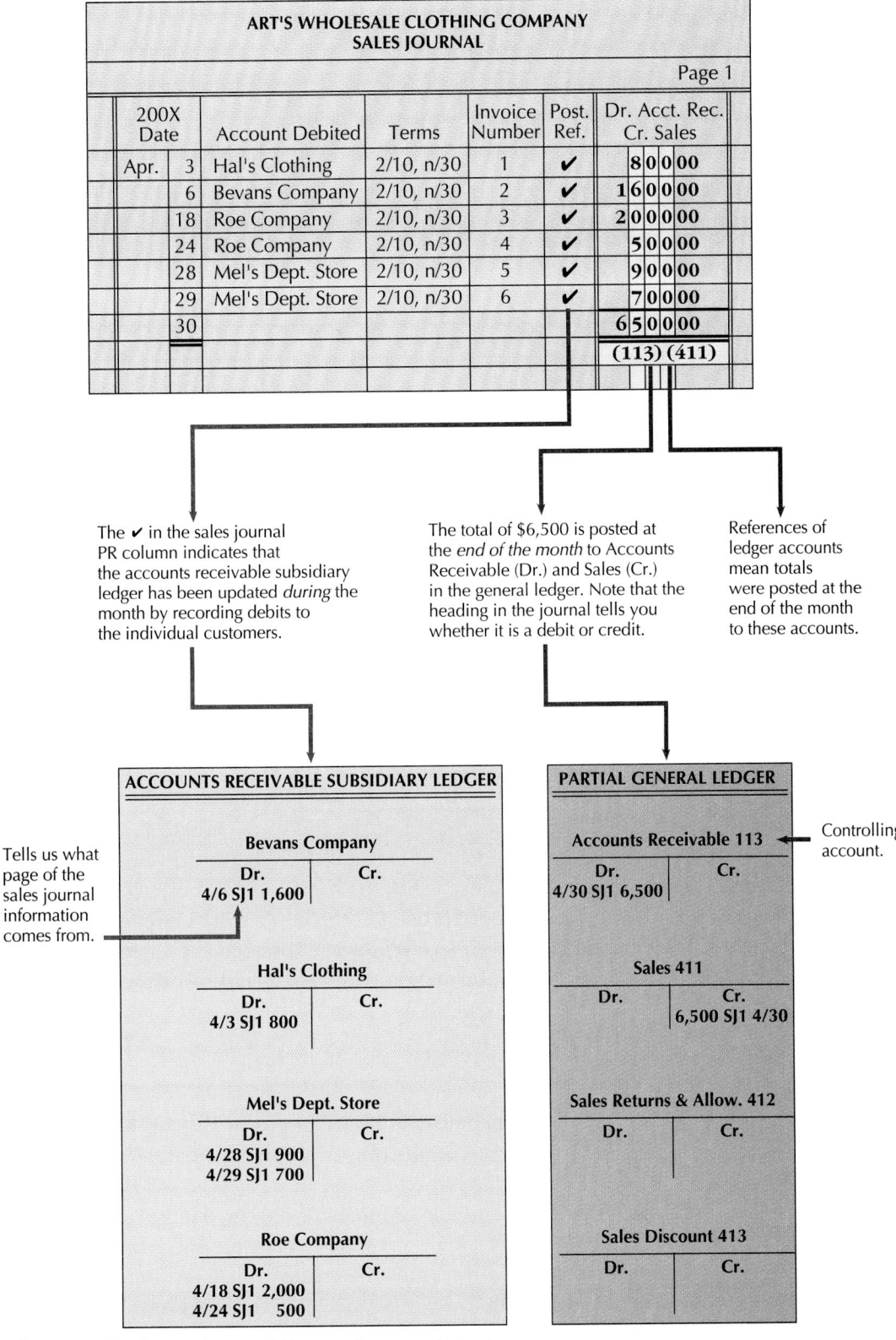

Figure 9-7 Sales Journal Recording and Postings

$800 he owes Art along with the date (April 3) and page of the sales journal (p. 1). Once that is done, place a ✓ in the post-reference column of the sales journal. The accounts receivable subsidiary ledger shows us Hal's outstanding balance at any moment in time. We do not have to go through all the invoices. Note how the sales

Figure 9-8
Sales Invoice

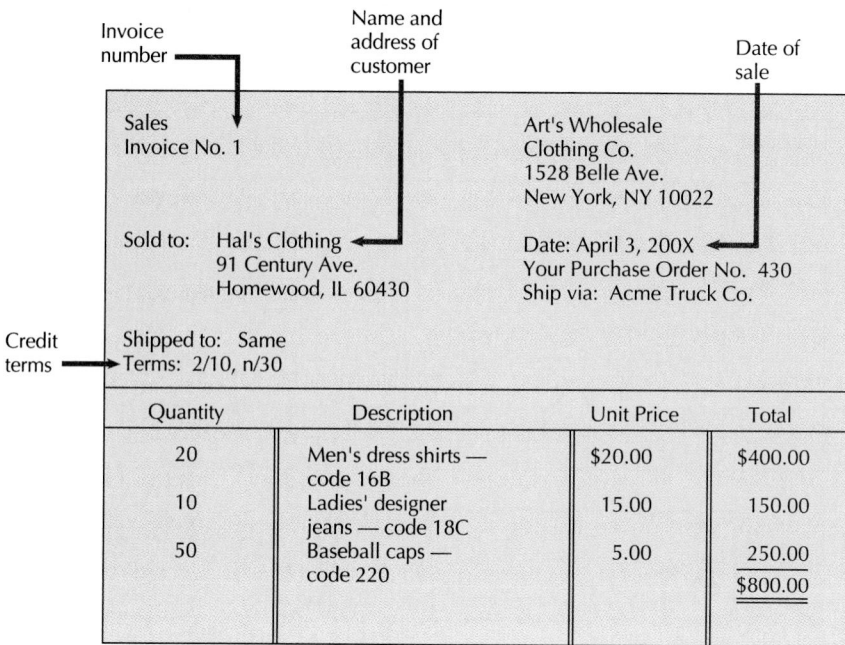

journal only needs one line instead of the three lines that would have been required in a general journal.

Posting at End of Month from the Sales Journal to the General Ledger

The sales journal is totaled ($6,500) at the end of the month. Looking back at page 347, you can see that the heading of Art's sales journal is a debit to Accounts Receivable and a credit to Sales. Therefore, at the end of the month the $6,500 total is posted to Accounts Receivable (debit) *and* to Sales (credit) in the general ledger. In the general ledger we record the date (4/30), the initials of the journal (SJ), the page of the sales journal (1), and appropriate debit or credit ($6,500). Once the account in the general ledger is updated, we place below the totals in the sales journal the account numbers to which the information was posted (in this case, accounts 113 and 411).

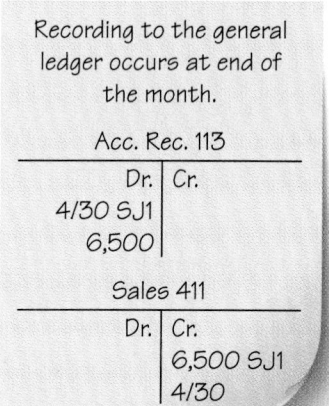

Recording to the general ledger occurs at end of the month.

Acc. Rec. 113

Dr.	Cr.
4/30 SJ1	
6,500	

Sales 411

Dr.	Cr.
	6,500 SJ1
	4/30

Sales Tax

Art's Wholesale Clothing Company does not have to deal with sales tax because it sells goods wholesale. If Art's were a retail company, however, it would have to pay sales tax.

Let's look at how Munroe Menswear Company, a retailer, handles sales tax on a purchase made by Jones Company. Figure 9-9 shows Munroe's sales journal.

A new account, Sales Tax Payable, must be created. That account is a liability account in the general ledger with a credit balance. The customer owes Munroe the sale amount plus the tax.

Keep in mind that if sales discounts are available, they are not calculated on the sales tax. The discount is on the selling price less any returns before the tax. For example, if Jones receives a 2% discount, he pays the following:

Sales Tax Payable

	Cr.
	XXX

A liability in general ledger.

$5,000 × .02 = $100 savings ⟶

$5,250	Total owed (tax is $250)
−100	Savings (discount)
$5,150	Amount paid

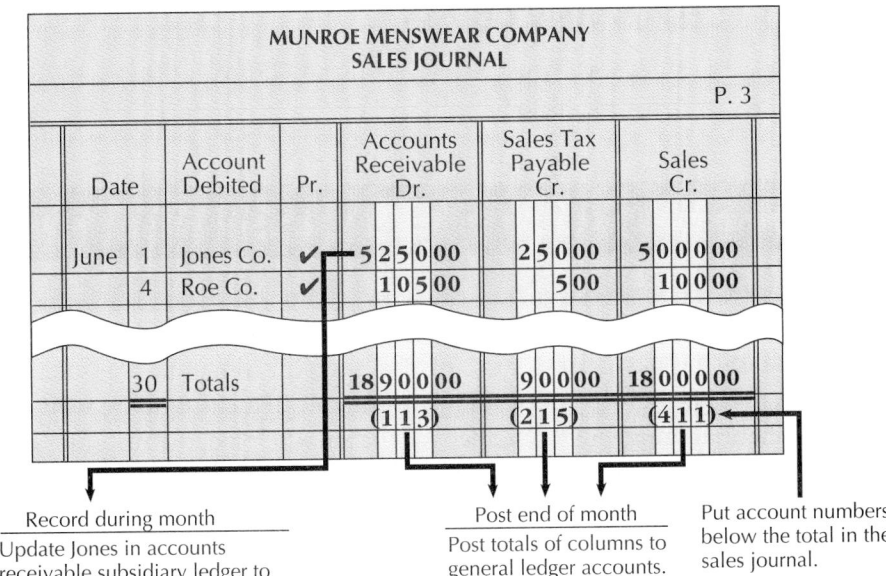

Figure 9-9
Munroe Sales Journal

Record during month
Update Jones in accounts receivable subsidiary ledger to indicate that he owes $5,250 to Munroe.

Post end of month
Post totals of columns to general ledger accounts.

Put account numbers below the total in the sales journal.

Learning Unit 9-2 Review

AT THIS POINT you should be able to

- Define and state the purposes of special journals. (p. 345)
- Define and state the purposes of the accounts receivable subsidiary ledger. (p. 345)
- Define and state the purpose of the controlling account, Accounts Receivable. (p. 346)
- Journalize, record, or post sales on account to a sales journal and its related accounts receivable and general ledgers. (p. 347)

SELF-REVIEW QUIZ 9-2

(The forms you need are on page 269 of the *Study Guide and Working Papers*.)
Respond true or false to the following:

1. Special journals completely replace the general journal.
2. Special journals aid the division of labor.
3. The subsidiary ledger makes the general ledger less manageable.
4. The subsidiary ledger is separate from the general ledger.
5. The controlling account is located in the accounts receivable subsidiary ledger.
6. The totals of a sales journal are posted to the general ledger at the end of the month.
7. The accounts receivable subsidiary ledger is arranged in alphabetical order.
8. Transactions recorded into a sales journal are recorded only weekly to the accounts receivable subsidiary ledger.

Quiz Tip:
The normal balance of the accounts receivable subsidiary ledger is a debit.

SOLUTIONS TO SELF-REVIEW QUIZ 9-2

1. False   **2.** True   **3.** False   **4.** True
5. False   **6.** True   **7.** True   **8.** False

Learning Unit 9-3   The Credit Memorandum

At the beginning of this chapter we introduced the Sales Returns and Allowances account. Merchandising businesses often use this account to handle transactions involving goods that have already been sold. For example, if a customer returns the goods purchased, the account will be credited for the amount paid; if a customer gets an allowance because the goods purchased were damaged, the account will be credited for the amount of the allowance. In both these examples, the company's sales revenue decreases. Hence, the account is called a contra-revenue account: The sales revenue decreases and the normal balance is a debit.

Companies usually handle sales returns and allowances by means of a **credit memorandum.** Credit memoranda inform customers that the amount of the goods returned or the amount allowed for damaged goods has been subtracted (credited) from the customer's ongoing account with the company.

A sample credit memorandum from Art's Wholesale Clothing Company appears in Figure 9-10. It shows that on April 12 credit memo no. 1 was issued to Bevans Company for defective merchandise that had been returned. (Figure 9-7 shows that Art's Wholesale Clothing Company sold Bevans Company $1,600 of merchandise on April 6.)

Let's assume that Art's Clothing has high-quality goods and does not expect many sales returns and allowances. Based on this assumption, no special journal for sales returns and allowances will be needed. Instead, any returns and allowances will be recorded in the general journal, and all postings and recordings will be done when journalized. Let's look at a transaction analysis chart before we journalize, record, and post this transaction.

> A credit memorandum reduces accounts receivable.

> Remember:
> No sales tax was involved because Art's is a wholesale company.

> **Sales Returns and Allowances**
>
> | Dr. | Cr. |
> |-----|-----|
> | + | − |
>
> A contra-revenue account.

> Note that the Sales Returns and Allowances account is increasing, which in turn reduces sales revenue and reduces the amount owed by the customer (Accounts Receivable).

Accounts Affected	Category	↑ ↓	Rules
Sales Returns and Allowances	Contra-revenue account	↑	Dr.
Accounts Receivable, Bevans Co.	Asset	↓	Cr.

Figure 9-10
Credit Memorandum

> The end result is that Bevan owes Art's Wholesale less money.

Art's Wholesale
Clothing Co.
1528 Belle Ave.
New York, NY 10022

Credit
Memorandum No. _1_
Date: _April 12, 200X_
Credit to Bevans Company
         110 Aster Rd.
         Cincinnati, Ohio 45227
We credit your account as follows:
Merchandise returned 60 model 8 B men's dress gloves—$600

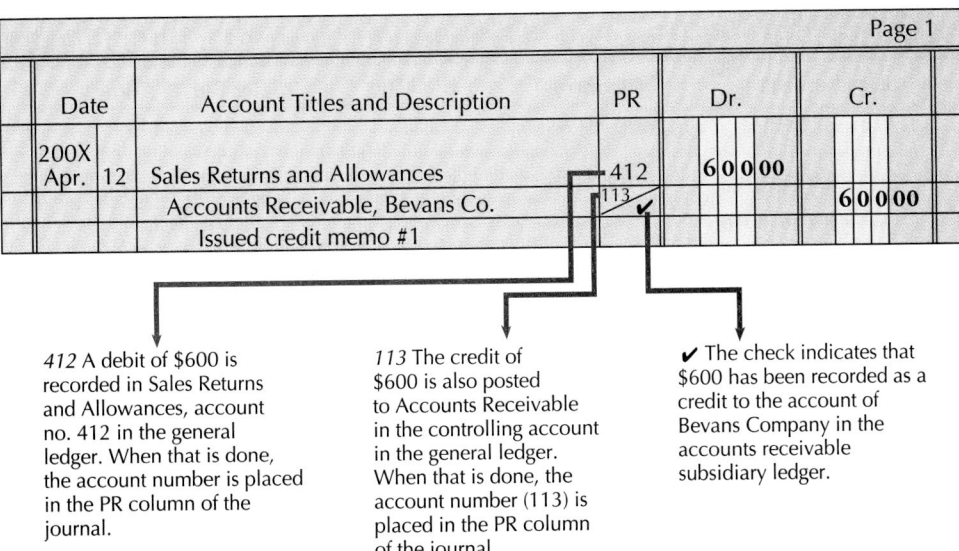

Figure 9-11
Postings and Recordings for the Credit Memorandum into the Subsidiary and General Ledger

412 A debit of $600 is recorded in Sales Returns and Allowances, account no. 412 in the general ledger. When that is done, the account number is placed in the PR column of the journal.

113 The credit of $600 is also posted to Accounts Receivable in the controlling account in the general ledger. When that is done, the account number (113) is placed in the PR column of the journal.

✔ The check indicates that $600 has been recorded as a credit to the account of Bevans Company in the accounts receivable subsidiary ledger.

JOURNALIZING, RECORDING, AND POSTING THE CREDIT MEMORANDUM

The credit memorandum results in two postings to the general ledger and one recording to the accounts receivable subsidiary ledger (see Fig. 9-11).

Note in the PR column next to Accounts Receivable, Bevans Co., that there is a diagonal line with the account number 113 above and a ✔ below. This notation is to show that the amount of $600 has been credited to Accounts Receivable in the controlling account in the general ledger *and* credited to the account of Bevans Company in the accounts receivable subsidiary ledger.

If the accountant for Art's Wholesale Clothing Company decided to develop a special journal for Sales Returns and Allowances, the entry for a credit memorandum such as the one we've been discussing would be as shown in Figure 9-12.

THE CREDIT MEMORANDUM WITH SALES TAX

Figure 9-9 (p. 349) shows the sales journal for Munroe Menswear Company. Remember that because Munroe is a retail company, its customers must pay sales tax. Let's assume that on June 8 Roe returns $50 worth of the $100 of merchandise he bought earlier in the month. Let's analyze and journalize the credit memo that Munroe issued. Keep in mind that the customer is no longer responsible for paying for either the returned merchandise or the tax on it.

> *Remember:*
> *Sales discounts are not taken on returns.*

Figure 9-12
Special Journal for Recording Sales Returns and Allowances

			SALES RETURNS AND ALLOWANCES JOURNAL			
	Date		Credit Memo No.	Account Credited	PR	Sales Ret. and Allow. – Dr. Accts. Rec. – Cr.
	200X April	12	1	Bevans Company	✔	6 0 0 00

During the month the subsidiary ledger is updated

Accounts Affected	Category	↑ ↓	Rules	T Account Update			
Sales Returns and Allowances	Contra-revenue	↑	Dr.	Sales Ret. & Allow.			
				Dr.	Cr.		
				50			
Sales Tax Payable ($5 tax on $100) ($2.50 tax on $50)	Liability	↓	Dr.	Sales Tax Payable			
				Dr.	Cr.		
				2.50			
Accounts Receivable, Roe	Asset	↓	Cr.	Acc. Rec.		Roe Co.	
				Dr.	Cr.	Dr.	Cr.
					52.50	105	52.50

Figure 9-13
Credit Memorandum with Sales Tax

	June	8	Sales Returns and Allowances				5	0	00							
			Sales Tax Payable				2	50								
			Accounts Receivable, Roe Co.									5	2	50		
			Received credit memo													

The journal entry in Figure 9-13 requires three postings to the general ledger and one recording to Roe in the accounts receivable subsidiary ledger. Note that because Roe returned half of his merchandise he was able to reduce what he pays for sales tax by half (from $5 to $2.50).

Learning Unit 9-3 Review

AT THIS POINT you should be able to

- Explain Sales Tax Payable in relation to Sales Discount. (p. 351)
- Explain, journalize, post, and record a credit memorandum with or without sales tax. (p. 351)

SELF-REVIEW QUIZ 9-3

(The forms you need are on pages 269–271 of the *Study Guide and Working Papers*.)

Journalize the following transactions into the sales journal or general journal for Shoes.com. Record to the accounts receivable subsidiary ledger and post to general ledger accounts as appropriate. Use the same journal headings that we used for Art's Wholesale Clothing Company. (All sales carry credit terms of 2/10, n/30.) There is no tax.

200X

May 1   Sold merchandise on account to Jane Company, invoice no. 1, $600.

5   Sold merchandise on account to Ralph Company, invoice no. 2, $2,500.

20   Issued credit memo no. 1 to Jane Company for $200 due to defective merchandise returned.

SOLUTION TO SELF-REVIEW QUIZ 9-3

SHOES.COM
SALES JOURNAL

Page 1

Date		Account Debited	Terms	Invoice No.	Post Ref.	Dr. Acct. Rec. Cr. Sales
200X May	1	Jane Company	2/10, n/30	1	✔	600 00
	5	Ralph Company	2/10, n/30	2	✔	2500 00
	31					3100 00
						(112) (411)

Figure 9-14
Sales on Account

Quiz Tip:
The total of accounts receivable subsidiary ledger $400 + $2,500 does indeed equal the balance in the controlling account, Accounts Receivable $2,900 at end of month, in the general ledger.

SHOES.COM
GENERAL JOURNAL

Page 1

Date		Account Titles and Description	PR	Dr.	Cr.
200X May	20	Sales Ret. and Allowances	412	200 00	
		Acct. Rec., Jane Company	112 ✔		200 00
		Issued credit memo #1			

Figure 9-15
Credit Memo Issued

Controlling Account

PARTIAL GENERAL LEDGER

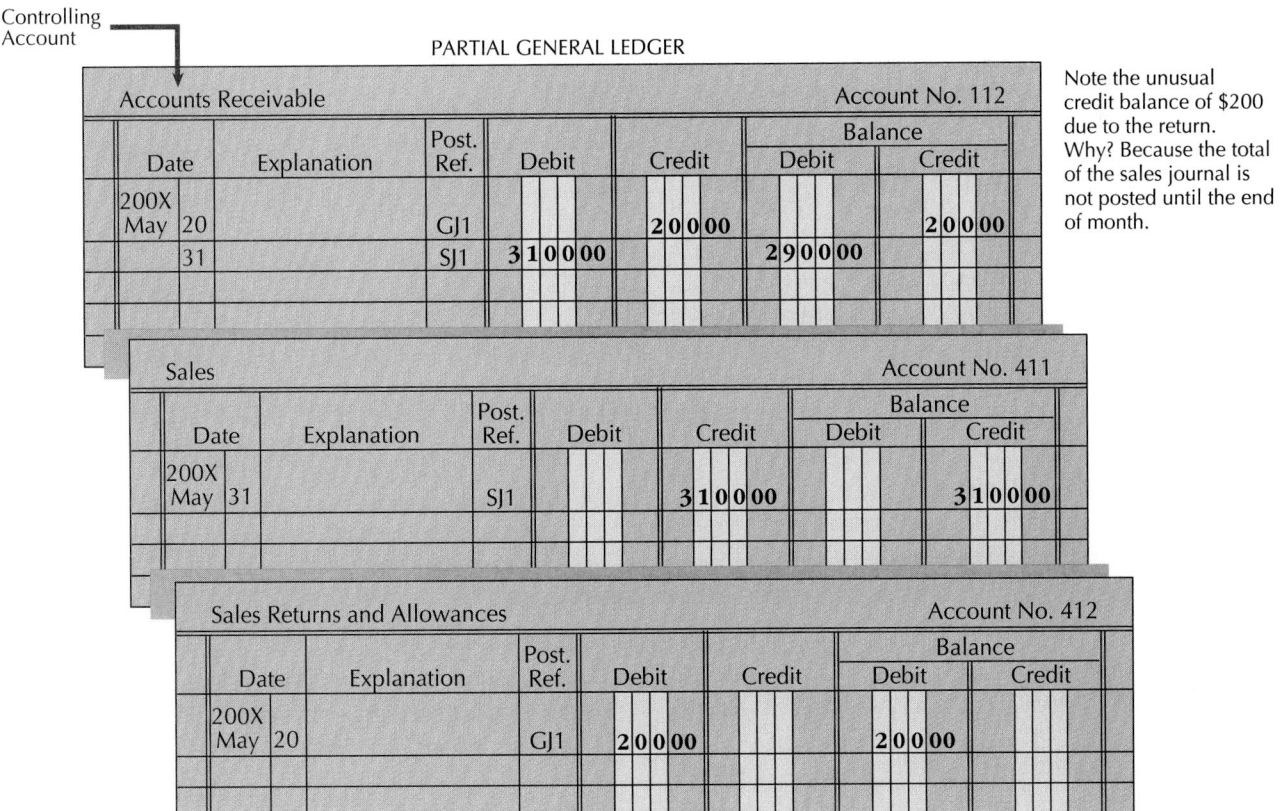

Note the unusual credit balance of $200 due to the return. Why? Because the total of the sales journal is not posted until the end of month.

Figure 9-16 Partial General Ledger

ACCOUNTS RECEIVABLE SUBSIDIARY LEDGER

			Post.				Dr.	
Date		Explanation	Ref.	Debit	Credit		Balance	
200X May	1		SJ1	6 0 0 00			6 0 0 00	
	20		GJ1		2 0 0 00		4 0 0 00	

NAME Jane Company
ADDRESS 118 Morris Rd., Boston, MA 01935

Customers owe Shoes.com money and thus have a debit balance.

NAME Ralph Company
ADDRESS 31 Norris Rd., Boston, MA 01935

			Post.				Dr.	
Date		Explanation	Ref.	Debit	Credit		Balance	
200X May	5		SJ1	2 5 0 0 00			2 5 0 0 00	

Figure 9-17 Accounts Receivable Subsidiary Ledger

Learning Unit 9-4   Cash Receipts Journal and Schedule of Accounts Receivable

A cash receipts journal is another special journal often used in a merchandising operation. The cash receipts journal records the receipt of cash (or checks) from any source. The number of columns in the cash receipts journal depends on how frequently certain types of transactions occur. Figure 9-18 shows the headings in the cash receipts journal for Art's Wholesale, describes the purpose of each column, and tells when to update the accounts receivable ledger as well as the general ledger.

The following transactions occurred and affected the cash receipts journal for Art's Clothing in April:

200X
Apr. 1 Art Newner invested $8,000 in the business.
       4 Received check from Hal's Clothing for payment of invoice no. 1 less discount.
      15 Cash sales for first half of April, $900.
      16 Received check from Bevans Company in settlement of invoice no. 2 less returns and discount.
      22 Received check from Roe Company for payment of invoice no. 3 less discount.
      27 Sold store equipment, $500.
      30 Cash sales for second half of April, $1,200.

Benefits of a Cash Receipts Journal

Before we look at how these transactions will look in the cash receipts journal, let's see how the April 4 transaction would look if it were put into a general journal (Fig. 9-19). This step illustrates the benefits of using a cash receipts journal.

200X
Apr. 4 Received check from Hal's Clothing for payment of invoice no. 1 less discount. (Keep in mind the sales journal showed the invoice at $800 on April 3.)

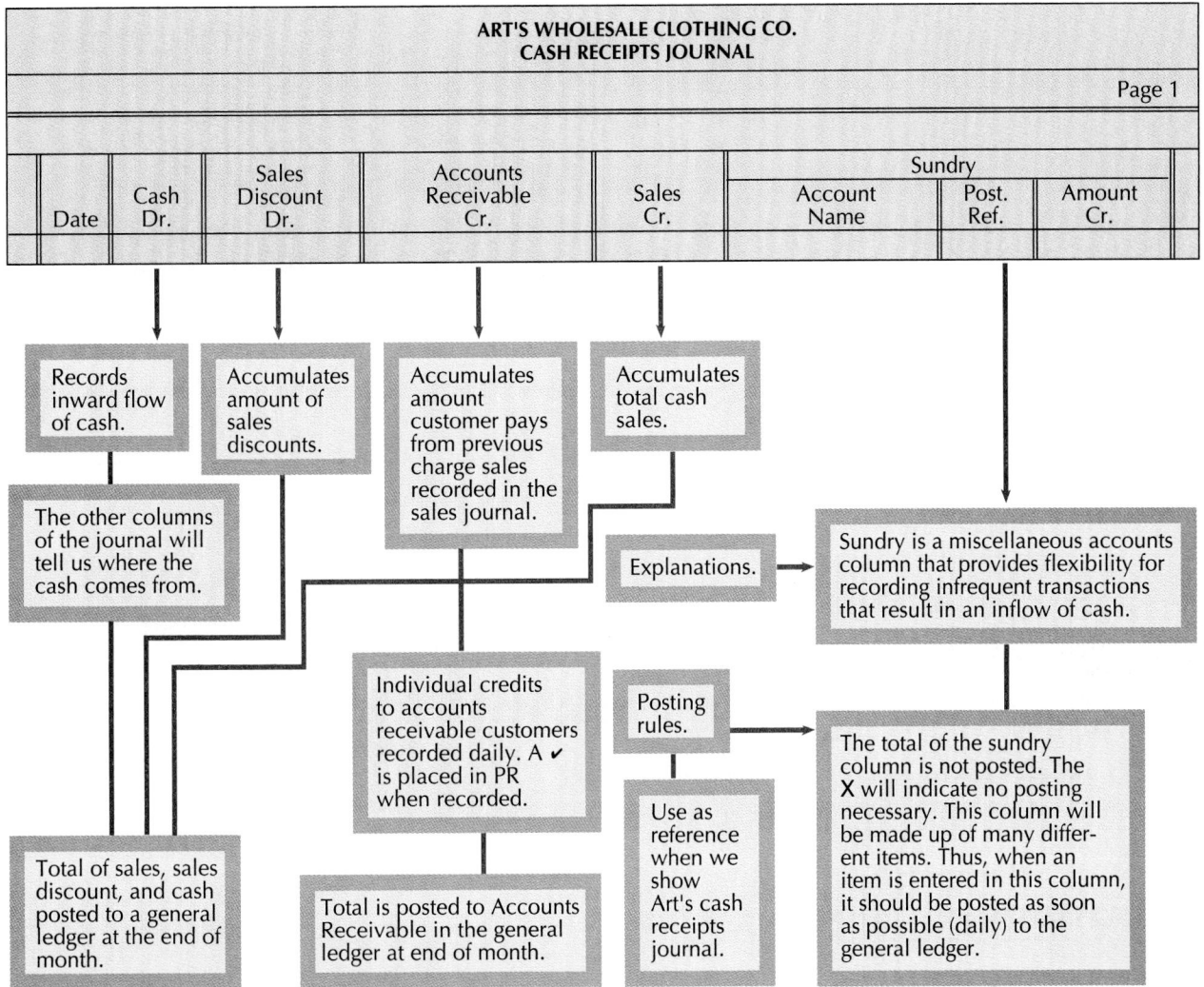

Figure 9-18 Cash Receipts Journal

Accounts Affected	Category	↓ ↑	Rules	T Account Update	
Cash	Asset	↑	Dr.	**Cash** Dr. 784 / Cr.	
Sales Discount	Contra-revenue	↑	Dr.	**Sales Discount** Dr. 16 / Cr.	
Accounts Receivable, Hal's Clothing	Asset	↓	Cr.	**Acc. Rec.** Dr. 800 / Cr. 800	**Hal's Clothing** Dr. 800 / Cr. 800

> Hal's Clothing is located in the accounts receivable subsidiary ledger.

Apr.	4	Cash		784 00		
		Sales Discount		16 00		
		Accounts Receivable, Hal's Clothing			800 00	

Figure 9-19
Recording Sales Discount
in General Journal

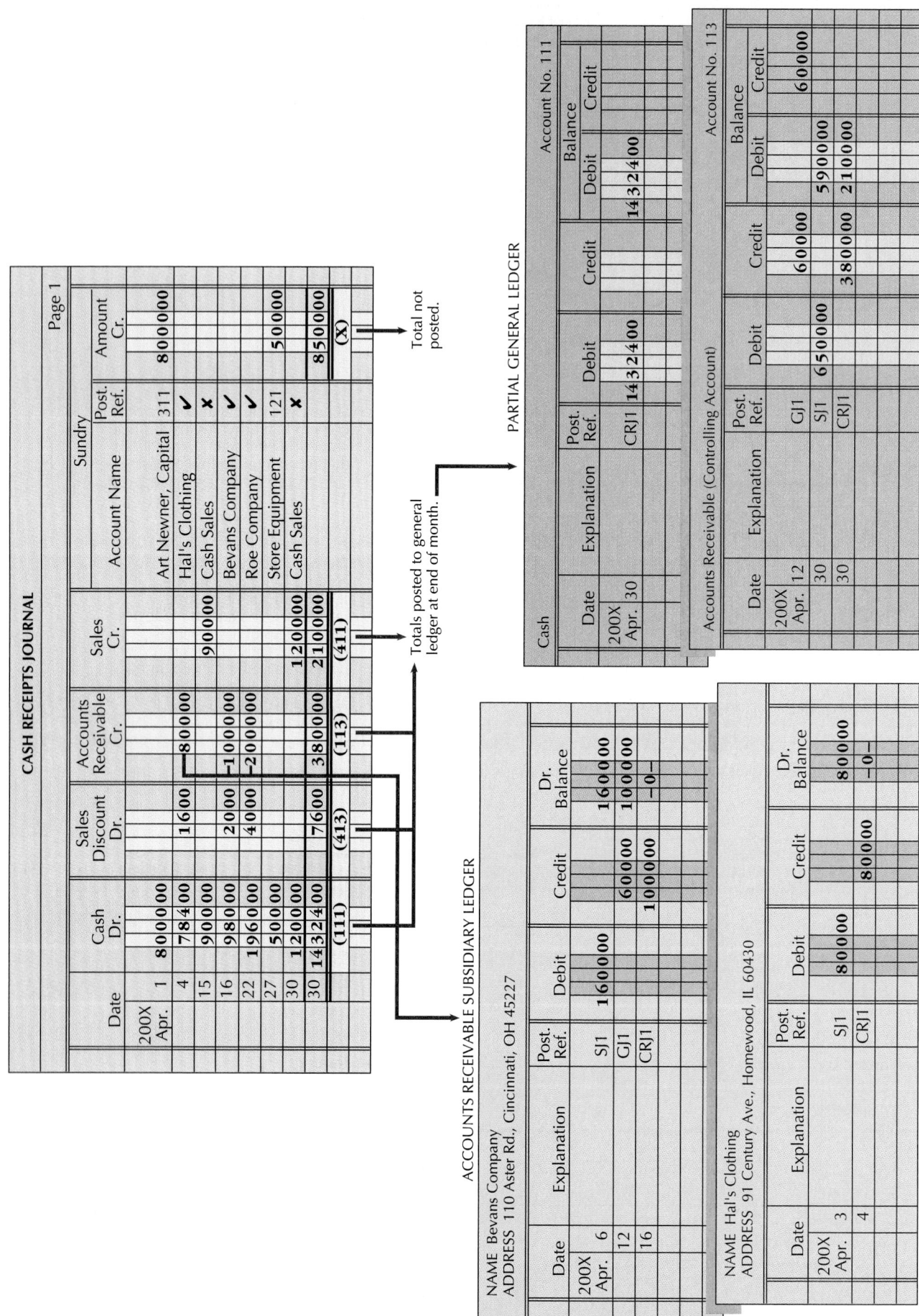

Figure 9-20 Cash Receipts Journal and Posting

PARTIAL GENERAL LEDGER

Store Equipment — Account No. 121

Date	Explanation	Post. Ref.	Debit	Credit	Balance Debit	Balance Credit
200X Apr. 1	Balance	✔			4 0 0 0 00	
27		CRJ1		5 0 0 00	3 5 0 0 00	

Art Newner, Capital — Account No. 311

Date	Explanation	Post. Ref.	Debit	Credit	Balance Debit	Balance Credit
200X Apr. 1		CRJ1		8 0 0 0 00		8 0 0 0 00

Sales — Account No. 411

Date	Explanation	Post. Ref.	Debit	Credit	Balance Debit	Balance Credit
200X Apr. 30		SJ1		6 5 0 0 00		6 5 0 0 00
30		CRJ1		2 1 0 0 00		8 6 0 0 00

Sales Discount — Account No. 413

Date	Explanation	Post. Ref.	Debit	Credit	Balance Debit	Balance Credit
200X Apr. 30		CRJ1	7 6 00		7 6 00	

ACCOUNTS RECEIVABLE SUBSIDIARY LEDGER

NAME Mel's Dept. Store
ADDRESS 181 Foss Rd., Swampscott, MA 01907

Date	Explanation	Post. Ref.	Debit	Credit	Dr. Balance
200X Apr. 28		SJ1	9 0 0 00		9 0 0 00
29		SJ1	7 0 0 00		1 6 0 0 00

NAME Roe Company
ADDRESS 18 Rantool St., Beverly, MA 01915

Date	Explanation	Post. Ref.	Debit	Credit	Dr. Balance
200X Apr. 18		SJ1	2 0 0 0 00		2 0 0 0 00
22		CRJ1		2 0 0 0 00	– 0 –
24		SJ1	5 0 0 00		5 0 0 00

Figure 9-20 (continued)

If a general journal had been used, there would have been three postings and one recording. Using a cash receipts journal (see Fig. 9-18 on p. 355), the totals of cash sales discount and accounts receivable are not posted till the end of the month.

The diagram in Figure 9-20 shows the cash receipts journal for the end of April along with the recordings in the accounts receivable subsidiary ledger and posting to the general ledger.

JOURNALIZING, RECORDING, AND POSTING FROM THE CASH RECEIPTS JOURNAL

Now let's look at how the April 4 transaction is recorded in the cash receipts journal.

When payment is received, Art's Wholesale updates the cash receipts journal (see Fig. 9-20 on p. 356) by entering the date (April 4), Cash debit of $784, Sales Discount debit of $16, credit to Accounts Receivable of $800, and which account name (Hal's Clothing) is to be credited. The terms of sale indicate that Hal's Clothing is entitled to the discount and no longer owes Art's Wholesale the $800 balance. As soon as this line is entered into the cash receipts journal, Art's Wholesale will update the card file of Hal's Clothing. Note in the accounts receivable subsidiary ledger of Hal's Clothing how the date (April 4), post reference (CRJ1), and credit amount ($800) are recorded. The balance in the accounts receivable ledger is zero. The last step of this transaction is to go back to the cash receipts journal and put a ✓ in the post-reference column.

In looking back at this cash receipts journal, note the following:

- All totals of the cash receipts journal *except* **sundry** were posted to the general ledger at the end of the month.
- Art Newner, Capital, and Store Equipment were posted to the general ledger when entered in the sundry column. For now in the general ledger it was assumed that the equipment account had a beginning balance of $4,000.
- The cash sales were not posted when entered (thus the X to show no posting is needed). The Sales and Cash totals are posted at the *end* of the month.
- A ✓ means information was recorded daily to the accounts receivable subsidiary ledger.
- The Account Name column was used to describe each transaction.

We can prove the accuracy of recording transactions of the cash receipts journal by totaling the columns with debit balances and credit balances. This process, called **crossfooting,** is done before the totals are posted.

If a bookkeeper were using more than one page for the cash receipts journal, the balances on the bottom of one page would be brought forward to the next page. Let's crossfoot the cash receipts journal of Art's Wholesale (Fig. 9-20, p. 356).

Debit Columns		Credit Columns		
Cash + **Sales Discount** =		**Accounts Receivable** +	**Sales** +	**Sundry**
$14,324 + $76		= $3,800	+ $2,100 +	$8,500
	$14,400 = $14,400			

Recording Sales Tax

Consider the following situation. It involves Ryan Stationery, a retail stationer that must charge 5% sales tax to its customers. On July 1 Hope Co. bought $600 of equipment for cash from Ryan.

Remember:
Subsidiary ledgers can be in the form of a card file, a binder note-book, or computer tapes or disks.

Sundry:
Miscellaneous accounts column(s) in a special journal that record transactions that seldom occur.

The last step is to put a ✓ back in the PR of the cash receipts journal to show the accounts receivable ledger is up-to-date.

Crossfooting special journals makes it easier to look for journalizing or posting errors.

The total of Sales Tax Payable would be posted to Sales Tax Payable in the general ledger at the end of the month.

Figure 9-21 shows how the transaction would be recorded in the general journal:

Accounts Affected	Category	↑ ↓	Rules	T Account Update
Cash	Asset	↑	Dr.	Cash 630 |
Sales Tax Payable	Liability	↑	Cr.	Sales Tax Payable | 30
Sales	Revenue	↑	Cr.	Sales | 600

July	1	Cash		6 3 0 00			
		Sales Tax Payable				3 0 00	
		Sales				6 0 0 00	
		Cash Sale					

Figure 9-21
Recording Receipt of Sales
Tax in General Journal

The transaction would be recorded in a cash receipts journal as shown in Figure 9-22.

	CASH RECEIPTS JOURNAL							
Date	Cash Dr.	Sales Discount Dr.	Accounts Receivable Cr.	Sales Tax Payable Cr.	Sales Cr.	Sundry		
						Acct.	Post Ref.	Amt.
July 1	6 3 0 00			3 0 00	6 0 0 00		✗	

Figure 9-22 Sales Tax in Cash Receipts Journal

The total of the sales tax as a result of cash sales would be posted to Sales Tax Payable in the general ledger at the end of the month. It represents a liability of the merchant to forward the tax to the government. Remember that no cash discounts are taken on the sales tax.

Now let's prove the accounts receivable subsidiary ledger to the controlling account—Accounts Receivable—at the end of April for Art's Wholesale Clothing Company.

SCHEDULE OF ACCOUNTS RECEIVABLE

The schedule of accounts receivable is an alphabetical list of the companies that have an outstanding balance in the accounts receivable subsidiary ledger. This total should be equal to the balance of the Accounts Receivable controlling account in the general ledger at the end of the month.

Let's examine the schedule of accounts receivable for Art's Wholesale Clothing Company in Figure 9-23.

ART'S WHOLESALE CLOTHING COMPANY SCHEDULE OF ACCOUNTS RECEIVABLE APRIL 30, 200X	
Mel's Dept. Store	$1 6 0 0 00
Roe Company	5 0 0 00
Total Accounts Receivable	$ 2 1 0 0 00

Figure 9-23
Schedule of Accounts
Receivable

Schedule is listed in alphabetical order.

The balance of the controlling account, Accounts Receivable ($2,100), in the general ledger (p. 356) does indeed equal the sum of the individual customer balances in the accounts receivable ledger ($2,100) as shown in the schedule of accounts receivable. The schedule of accounts receivable can help forecast potential cash inflows as well as possible credit and collection decisions.

Learning Unit 9-4 Review

AT THIS POINT you should be able to

- Journalize, record, and post transactions using a cash receipts journal with or without sales tax. (p. 354)
- Prepare a schedule of accounts receivable. (p. 359)

SELF-REVIEW QUIZ 9-4

(The forms you need are on pages 272–274 of the *Study Guide and Working Papers.*)

Journalize, crossfoot, record, and post when appropriate the following transactions into the cash receipts journal of Moore Co. Use the same headings as for Art's Wholesale Clothing.

ACCOUNTS RECEIVABLE SUBSIDIARY LEDGER

Name	Balance	Invoice No.
Irene Welch	$500	1
Janis Fross	200	2

Partial General Ledger

	Acct. No.	Balance
Cash	110	$600
Accounts Receivable	120	700
Store Equipment	130	600
Sales	410	700
Sales Discount	420	

200X

May 1 Received check from Irene Welch for invoice no. 1 less 2% discount.
  8 Cash sales collected, $200.
  15 Received check from Janis Fross for invoice no. 2 less 2% discount.
  19 Sold store equipment at cost, $300.

SOLUTION TO SELF-REVIEW QUIZ 9-4

		Cash Dr.	Sales Discount Dr.	Accounts Receivable Cr.	Sales Cr.	Sundry Account Name	Post. Ref.	Amount Cr.
MOORE COMPANY								
CASH RECEIPTS JOURNAL								Page 2
Date								
200X May	1	490 00	10 00	500 00		Irene Welch	✔	
	8	200 00			200 00	Cash Sales	✗	
	15	196 00	4 00	200 00		Janis Fross	✔	
	19	300 00				Store Equipment	130	300 00
	31	1186 00	14 00	700 00	200 00			300 00
		(110)	(420)	(120)	(410)			(X)

Crossfooting: $1,200 = $1,200

Figure 9-24 Cash Receipts Journal

PARTIAL GENERAL LEDGER

Cash   Account No. 110

Date		Explanation	Post. Ref.	Debit	Credit	Balance Debit	Balance Credit
200X May	1	Balance	✔			6 0 0 00	
	31		CRJ2	1 1 8 6 00		1 7 8 6 00	

Accounts Receivable   Account No. 120

Date		Explanation	Post. Ref.	Debit	Credit	Balance Debit	Balance Credit
200X May	1	Balance	✔			7 0 0 00	
	31		CRJ2		7 0 0 00	—	—

Store Equipment   Account No. 130

Date		Explanation	Post. Ref.	Debit	Credit	Balance Debit	Balance Credit
200X May	1	Balance	✔			6 0 0 00	
	19		CRJ2		3 0 0 00	3 0 0 00	

Sales   Account No. 410

Date		Explanation	Post. Ref.	Debit	Credit	Balance Debit	Balance Credit
200X May	1	Balance	✔				7 0 0 00
	31		CRJ2		2 0 0 00		9 0 0 00

Sales Discount   Account No. 420

Date		Explanation	Post. Ref.	Debit	Credit	Balance Debit	Balance Credit
200X May	31		CRJ2	1 4 00		1 4 00	

Figure 9-25 Partial General Ledger

Quiz Tip:
Sum of all debits equals sum of all credits.

Quiz Tip:
The total of the sundry column, $300, is not posted. Only individual amounts are posted to the general ledger during the month.

Figure 9-26
Accounts Receivable
Subsidiary Ledger

ACCOUNTS RECEIVABLE SUBSIDIARY LEDGER

NAME Irene Welch
ADDRESS 10 Rong Rd., Beverly, MA 01915

Date		Explanation	Post. Ref.	Debit	Credit	Dr. Balance
200X May	1	Balance	✔			5 0 0 00
	1		CRJ2		5 0 0 00	—

NAME Janis Fross
ADDRESS 81 Foster Rd., Beverly, MA 01915

Date		Explanation	Post. Ref.	Debit	Credit	Dr. Balance
200X May	1	Balance	✔			2 0 0 00
	15		CRJ2		2 0 0 00	—

SOLUTION & TIPS TO COMPREHENSIVE PROBLEM: PUTTING THE PIECES TOGETHER

(The forms you need are on pages 275–278 of the *Study Guide and Working Papers.*)

a. Journalize, record, and post, as needed, the following transactions to the sales, cash receipts, and general journal. All terms are 2/10, n/30.

b. Prepare a schedule of accounts receivable.

Solution Tips to Journalizing

200X

CRJ July	1	Walter Lantze invested $2,000 into the business.
SJ	1	Sold merchandise on account to Panda Co., invoice no. 1 for $300.
SJ	2	Sold merchandise on account to Buzzard Co., invoice no. 2 for $600.
CRJ	3	Cash sale, $400.
GJ	9	Issued credit memorandum no. 1 to Panda Co. for defective merchandise, $100.
CRJ	10	Received check from Panda Co. for invoice no. 1 less returns and discount.
CRJ	16	Cash sale, $500.
SJ	19	Sold merchandise on account to Panda Co., $550, invoice no. 3.

Record immediately to subsidiary ledger.

**WALTER LANTZE CO.
SALES JOURNAL**

Page 1

Date		Account Debited	Terms	Invoice No.	Post Ref.	Dr. Acct. Rec. Cr. Sales
200X July	1	Panda Co.	2/10, n/30	1	✔	3 0 0 00
	2	Buzzard Co.	2/10, n/30	2	✔	6 0 0 00
	19	Panda Co.	2/10, n/30	3	✔	5 5 0 00
	31					1 4 5 0 00
						(112) (411)

Total posted at end of month to general ledger accounts.

Figure 9-27 Sales on Account

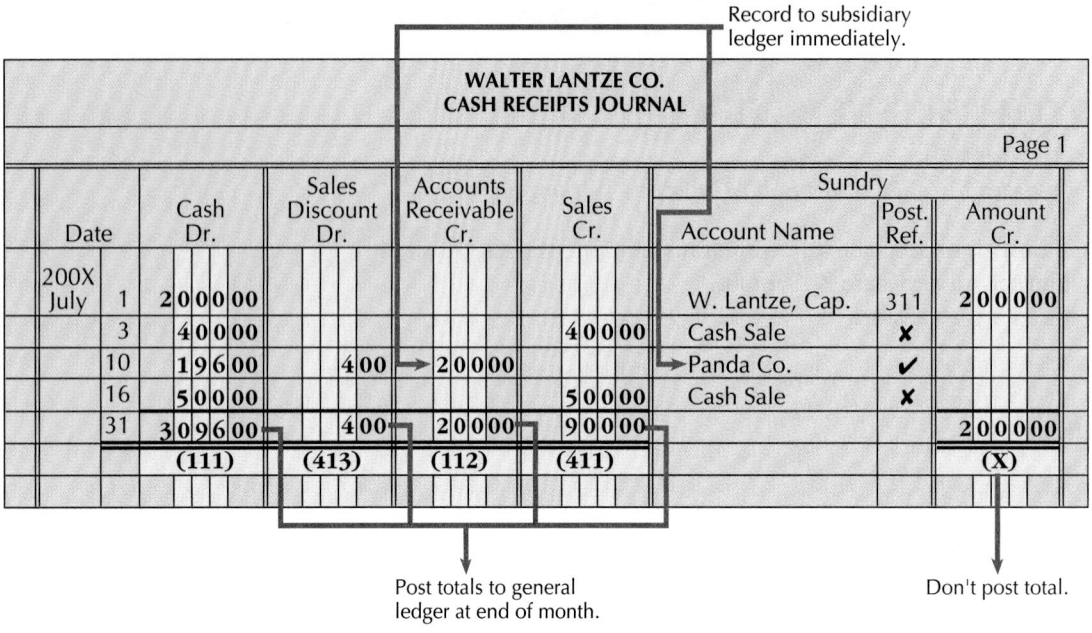

Record to subsidiary ledger immediately.

WALTER LANTZE CO.
CASH RECEIPTS JOURNAL

Page 1

Date		Cash Dr.	Sales Discount Dr.	Accounts Receivable Cr.	Sales Cr.	Sundry		
						Account Name	Post. Ref.	Amount Cr.
200X July	1	2 000 00				W. Lantze, Cap.	311	2 000 00
	3	4 00 00			4 00 00	Cash Sale	✗	
	10	1 96 00	4 00	2 00 00		Panda Co.	✔	
	16	5 00 00			5 00 00	Cash Sale	✗	
	31	30 96 00	4 00	2 00 00	9 00 00			2 000 00
		(111)	(413)	(112)	(411)			(X)

Post totals to general ledger at end of month.

Don't post total.

	GENERAL JOURNAL			Page 1
Date	Account Title and Description	PR	Dr.	Cr.
200X July 9	Sales Returns and Allowances	412	1 00 00	
	Accounts Receivable, Panda Co.	112 ✔		1 00 00
	Issued credit memo #1			

Post immediately to general ledger.

Record immediately to subsidiary ledger.

Figure 9-28 Cash Received—Cash Receipts Journal

Accounts receivable subsidiary ledger is usually a debit balance.

Accounts Receivable Subsidiary Ledger

Buzzard Co.

Date	PR	Debit	Credit	Dr. Balance
200X July 2	SJ1	6 00 00		6 00 00

Panda Co.

Date	PR	Debit	Credit	Dr. Balance
200X July 1	SJ1	3 00 00		3 00 00
9	GJ1		1 00 00	2 00 00
10	CRJ1		2 00 00	—
19	SJ1	5 50 00		5 50 00

Figure 9-29 Accounts Receivable Subsidiary Ledger

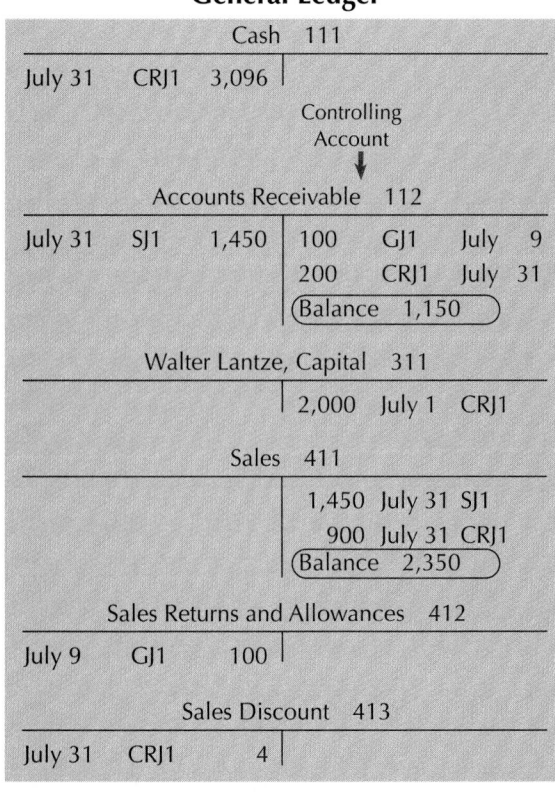

General Ledger

Cash　111

July 31	CRJ1	3,096	

Controlling Account

Accounts Receivable　112

July 31	SJ1	1,450	100	GJ1	July 9
			200	CRJ1	July 31
			Balance 1,150		

Walter Lantze, Capital　311

			2,000	July 1	CRJ1

Sales　411

			1,450	July 31	SJ1
			900	July 31	CRJ1
			Balance 2,350		

Sales Returns and Allowances　412

July 9	GJ1	100	

Sales Discount　413

July 31	CRJ1	4	

Figure 9-30 General Ledger

The controlling account at end of the month (Fig. 9-31) equals the sum of the accounts receivable subsidiary ledger.

WALTER LANTZE CO. SCHEDULE OF ACCOUNTS RECEIVABLE JULY 31, 200X		
Buzzard Co.	$ 600	00
Panda Co.	550	00
Total Accounts Receivable	$1 150	00

Figure 9-31 Schedule of Accounts Receivable

Summary of Key Points

Learning Unit 9-1

1. A periodic inventory system records the cost of ending inventory at the end of each accounting period.
2. A perpetual inventory system keeps a continual update of inventory.
3. Sales Returns and Allowances and Sales Discount are contra-revenue accounts.
4. Net Sales = Gross Sales − Sales Returns and Allowances − Sales Discounts.
5. Discounts are not taken on sales tax, freight, or goods returned. The discount period is shorter than the credit period.

Learning Unit 9-2

1. A general journal is still used with special journals.
2. A sales journal records sales on account.
3. The accounts receivable subsidiary ledger, organized in alphabetical order, is not in the same book as Accounts Receivable, the controlling account in the general ledger.
4. At the end of the month the total of all customers' ending balances in the accounts receivable subsidiary ledger should be equal to the ending balance in Accounts Receivable, the controlling account in the general ledger.

Learning Unit 9-3

1. The ✓ in the PR column of the sales journal means a customer's account in the accounts receivable ledger (or the accounts receivable subsidiary ledger) (on the debit side) has been updated (or recorded) during the month.
2. At the end of the month the totals of the sales journal are posted to general ledger accounts.
3. Sales Tax Payable is a liability found in the general ledger.
4. When a credit memorandum is issued, the result is that Sales Returns and Allowances is increasing and Accounts Receivable is decreasing. When we record this entry into a general journal, we assume all parts of the transaction will be posted to the general ledger and recorded in the subsidiary ledger when the entry is journalized.

Learning Unit 9-4

1. The cash receipts journal records receipt of cash from any source.
2. The sundry column records the credit part of a transaction that does not occur frequently. Never post the *total* of sundry. Post items in the sundry column to the general ledger when entered.

3. A ✔ in the PR column of the cash receipts journal means that the accounts receivable ledger (or the accounts receivable subsidiary ledger) has been updated (recorded) with a credit.
4. An X in the cash receipts journal PR column means no posting was necessary, because the totals of these columns will be posted at the end of the month.
5. Crossfooting means proving that the total of debits and the total of credits are equal in the special journal, thus verifying the accuracy of recording.
6. A schedule of accounts receivable is a listing of the ending balances of customers in the accounts receivable subsidiary ledger. This total should be the same balance as found in the controlling account, Accounts Receivable, in the general ledger.

Key Terms

Accounts receivable subsidiary ledger   A book or file that contains, in alphabetical order, the individual records of amounts owed by various credit customers.

Cash receipts journal   A special journal that records all transactions involving the receipt of cash from any source.

Controlling account—Accounts Receivable   The Accounts Receivable account in the general ledger, after postings are complete, shows a firm the total amount of money owed to it. This figure is broken down in the accounts receivable ledger, where it indicates specifically who owes the money.

Credit memorandum   A piece of paper sent by the seller to a customer who has returned merchandise previously purchased on credit. The credit memorandum indicates to the customer that the seller is reducing the amount owed by the customer.

Credit period   Length of time allowed for payment of goods sold on account.

Crossfooting   The process of proving that the total debit columns of a special journal are equal to the total credit columns of a special journal.

Discount period   A period shorter than the credit period when a discount is available to encourage early payment of bills.

Gross sales   The revenue earned from sale of merchandise to customers.

Merchandise   Goods brought into a store for resale to customers.

Net sales   Gross sales less sales returns and allowances less sales discounts.

Periodic inventory system   An inventory system that, at the *end* of each accounting period, calculates the cost of the unsold goods on hand by taking the cost of each unit times the number of units of each product on hand.

Perpetual inventory system   An inventory system that keeps *continual track* of each type of inventory by recording units on hand at beginning, units sold, and the current balance after each sale or purchase.

Retailers   Merchants who buy goods from wholesalers for resale to customers.

Sales Discount account   A contra-revenue account that records cash discounts granted to customers for payments made within a specific period of time.

Sales invoice   A bill sent to customer(s) reflecting a sale on credit.

Sales journal   A special journal used to record only sales made on account.

Sales Returns and Allowances (SRA) account   A contra-revenue account that records price adjustments and allowances granted on merchandise that is defective and has been returned.

Sales Tax Payable account   An account in the general ledger that accumulates the amount of sales tax owed. It has a credit balance.

Schedule of accounts receivable   A list of the customers, in alphabetical order, that have an outstanding balance in the accounts receivable ledger (or the accounts receivable subsidiary ledger). This total should be equal to the balance of the Accounts Receivable controlling account in the general ledger at the end of the month.

Special journal   A journal used to record similar groups of transactions. Example: The sales journal records all sales on account.

Subsidiary ledger   A ledger that contains accounts of a single type. Example: The accounts receivable subsidiary ledger records all credit customers.

Sundry   Miscellaneous accounts column(s) in a special journal, which records part of transactions that do not occur too often.

Wholesalers   Merchants who buy goods from suppliers and manufacturers for sale to retailers.

Questions, Mini Exercises, Exercises, and Problems

Discussion Questions

1. What is the difference between a perpetual inventory system and a periodic inventory system?
2. Explain the purpose of a contra-revenue account.
3. What is the normal balance of sales discount?
4. Give two examples of contra-revenue accounts.
5. What is the difference between a discount period and a credit period?
6. Explain the terms:
   a. 2/10, n/30.
   b. n/10, EOM.
7. If special journals are used, what purpose will a general journal serve?
8. Compare and contrast the controlling account Accounts Receivable to the accounts receivable subsidiary ledger.
9. Why is the accounts receivable subsidiary ledger organized in alphabetical order?
10. When is a sales journal used?
11. What is an invoice? What purpose does it serve?
12. Why is sales tax a liability to the business?
13. Sales discounts are taken on sales tax. Agree or disagree and tell why.
14. When a seller issues a credit memorandum (assume no sales tax), what accounts will be affected?
15. Explain the function of a cash receipts journal.
16. When is the sundry column of the cash receipts journal posted?
17. Explain the purpose of a schedule of accounts receivable.

Mini Exercises

(The forms you need are on pages 280–281 of the *Study Guide and Working Papers*.)

Overview

1. Complete the table below for Sales, Sales Returns and Allowances, and Sales Discounts.

Accounts Affected	Category	↓ ↑	Temporary or Permanent

Calculating Net Sales

2. Given the following, calculate net sales:

Gross sales	$30
Sales Returns and Allowances	8
Sales Discounts	2

Sales Journal and General Journal

3. Match the following to the three journal entries (more than one number can be used).

   1. Journalized into sales journal.
   2. Record immediately to subsidiary ledger.

3. Post totals from sales journal at end of month to general ledger.
4. Journalized in general journal.
5. Record and post immediately to subsidiary and general ledgers.

a. _____ Sold merchandise on account to Ree Co., invoice no. 1, $50.
b. _____ Sold merchandise on account to Flynn Co., invoice no. 2, $100.
c. _____ Issued credit memorandum no. 1 to Flynn Co. for defective merchandise, $25.

Credit Memorandum

4. Draw a transactional analysis box for the following credit memorandum: Issued credit memorandum to Met.com for defective merchandise, $200.

Sales and Cash Receipts Journal

5. Match the following to the four journal entries (a number can be used more than once).

1. Journalized into sales journal.
2. Journalized into cash receipts journal.
3. Record immediately to subsidiary ledger.
4. Totals of special journals will be posted at end of month (except sundry column).
5. Post to general ledger immediately.
6. Journalize into general journal.

a. _____ Sold merchandise on account to Ally Co., invoice no. 10, $40.
b. _____ Received check from Moore Co., $100 less 2% discount.
c. _____ Cash Sales, $100.
d. _____ Issued credit memorandum no. 2 to Ally Co. for defective merchandise, $20.

6. From the following, prepare a schedule of accounts receivable for Blue Co. for May 31, 200X.

Accounts Receivable Subsidiary Ledger

General Ledger

Bon Co.

| 5/6 SJ1 | 100 | |

Accounts Receivable

| 5/31 SJ1 | 140 | 5/31 CRJ1 | 10 |

Peke Co.

| 5/20 SJ1 | 30 | 5/27 CRJ1 | 10 |

Green Co.

| 5/9 SJ1 | 10 | |

Blueprint: Sales and Cash Receipts Journals

SUMMARY OF HOW TO POST AND RECORD
Single-Column Sales Journal

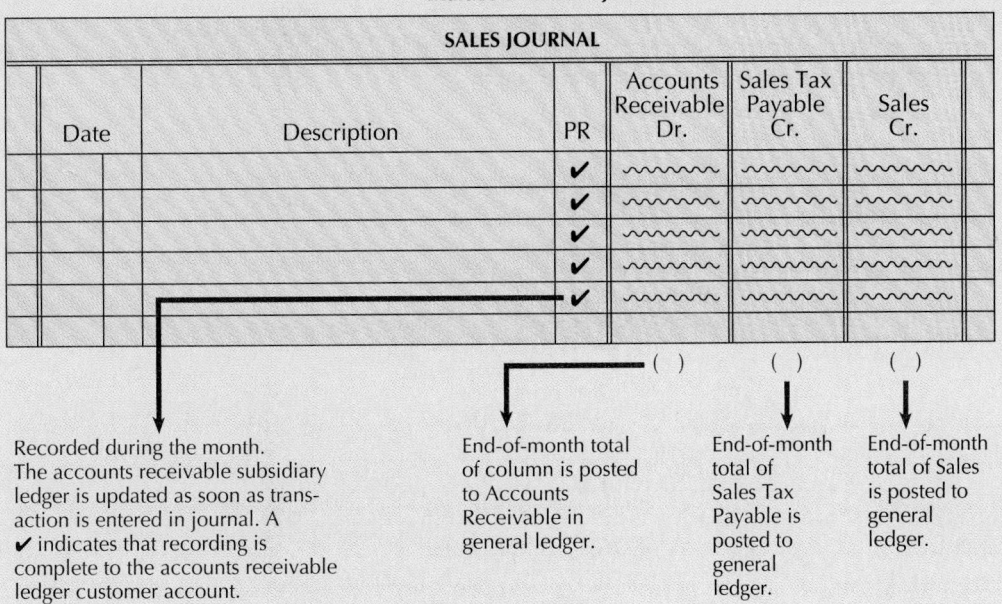

SALES JOURNAL

Date	Description	PR	Accounts Rec.: Dr. Sales: Cr.
		✔	. . .
		✔	. . .
		✔	. . .
		✔	. . .
		✔	. . .

Posted End of Month
Total of column is posted to general ledger accounts Accounts Receivable and Sales.

Recorded During the Month
Accounts receivable subsidiary ledger is updated as soon as transaction is entered in sales journal.
A ✔ indicates that recording is complete to the accounts receivable ledger customer account.

Multicolumn Sales Journal

SALES JOURNAL

Date	Description	PR	Accounts Receivable Dr.	Sales Tax Payable Cr.	Sales Cr.
		✔			
		✔			
		✔			
		✔			
		✔			

Recorded during the month. The accounts receivable subsidiary ledger is updated as soon as transaction is entered in journal. A ✔ indicates that recording is complete to the accounts receivable ledger customer account.

End-of-month total of column is posted to Accounts Receivable in general ledger.

End-of-month total of Sales Tax Payable is posted to general ledger.

End-of-month total of Sales is posted to general ledger.

Issuing a Credit Memo without Sales Tax Recorded in a General Journal

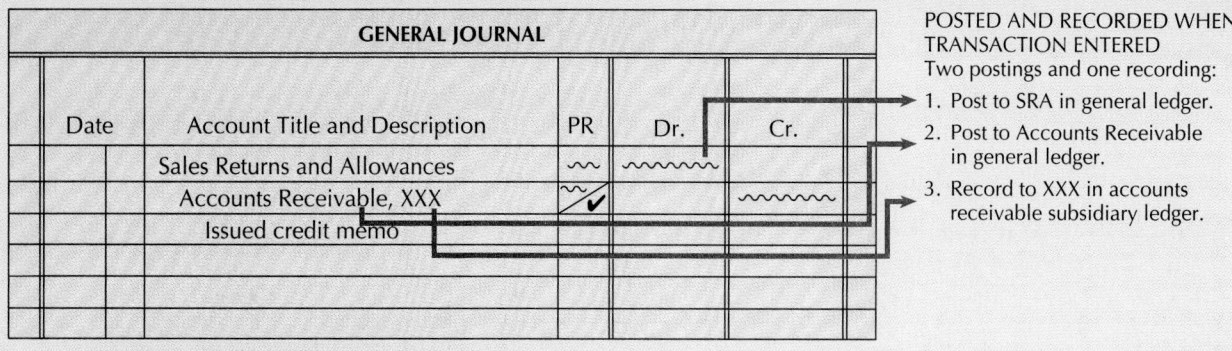

GENERAL JOURNAL

Date	Account Title and Description	PR	Dr.	Cr.
	Sales Returns and Allowances			
	Accounts Receivable, XXX	✔		
	Issued credit memo			

POSTED AND RECORDED WHEN TRANSACTION ENTERED
Two postings and one recording:

1. Post to SRA in general ledger.
2. Post to Accounts Receivable in general ledger.
3. Record to XXX in accounts receivable subsidiary ledger.

Issuing a Credit Memo with Sales Tax Recorded in a General Journal

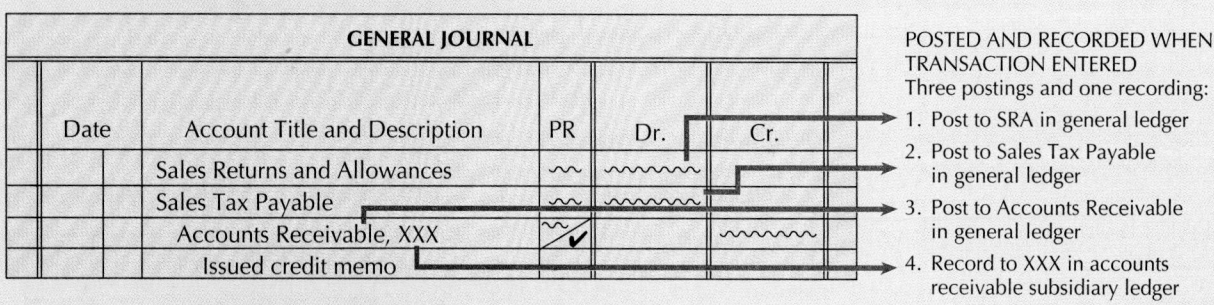

GENERAL JOURNAL

Date	Account Title and Description	PR	Dr.	Cr.
	Sales Returns and Allowances			
	Sales Tax Payable			
	Accounts Receivable, XXX	✔		
	Issued credit memo			

POSTED AND RECORDED WHEN TRANSACTION ENTERED
Three postings and one recording:

1. Post to SRA in general ledger
2. Post to Sales Tax Payable in general ledger
3. Post to Accounts Receivable in general ledger
4. Record to XXX in accounts receivable subsidiary ledger

The Cash Receipts Journal

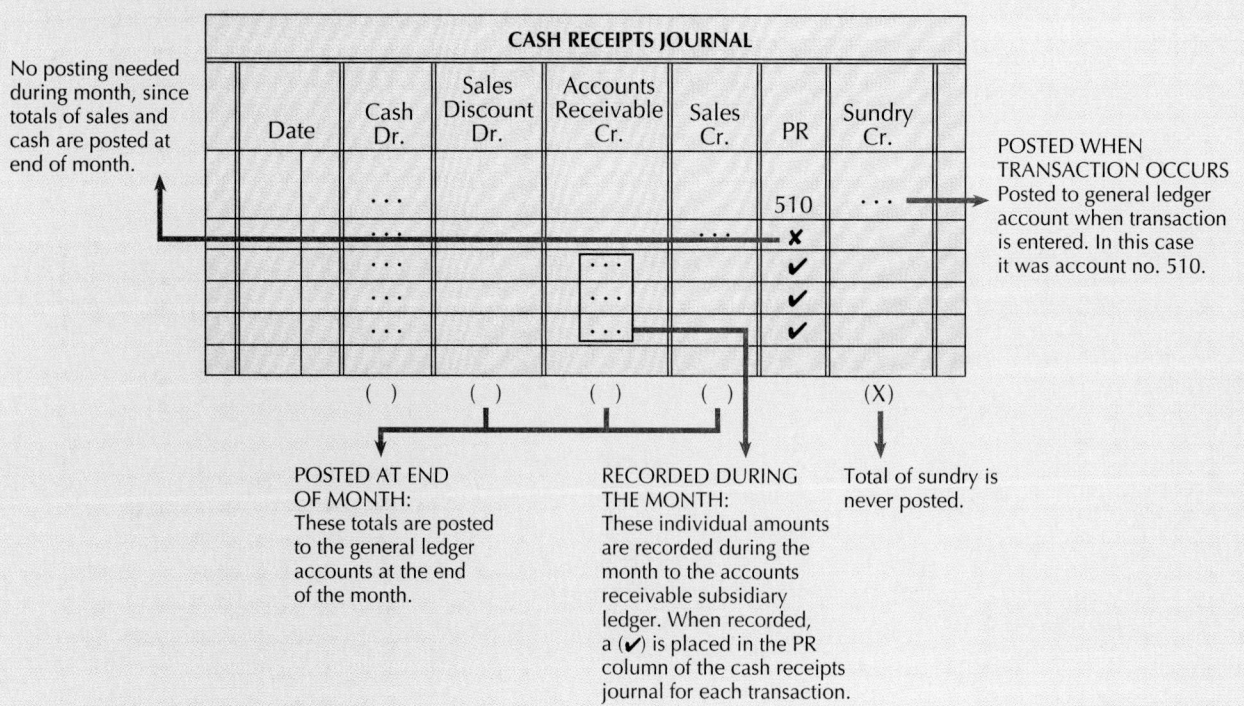

No posting needed during month, since totals of sales and cash are posted at end of month.

CASH RECEIPTS JOURNAL

Date	Cash Dr.	Sales Discount Dr.	Accounts Receivable Cr.	Sales Cr.	PR	Sundry Cr.
	. . .				510	. . .
	. . .			. . .	✗	
	. . .		. . .		✔	
	. . .		. . .		✔	
	. . .		. . .		✔	
	( )	( )	( )	( )		(X)

POSTED WHEN TRANSACTION OCCURS
Posted to general ledger account when transaction is entered. In this case it was account no. 510.

POSTED AT END OF MONTH:
These totals are posted to the general ledger accounts at the end of the month.

RECORDED DURING THE MONTH:
These individual amounts are recorded during the month to the accounts receivable subsidiary ledger. When recorded, a (✔) is placed in the PR column of the cash receipts journal for each transaction.

Total of sundry is never posted.

Note: If a Sales Tax Payable column were added, total of column would be posted at end of month.

Exercises

(The forms you need are on pages 282–284 of the *Study Guide and Working Papers*.)

9-1. From the sales journal in Figure 9-32 record to the accounts receivable subsidiary ledger and post to the general ledger accounts as appropriate.

Recording to accounts receivable ledger and posting to general ledger.

9-2. Journalize, record, and post when appropriate the following transactions into the sales journal (same heading as Exercise 9-1) and general journal (p. 1) (all sales carry terms of 2/10, n/30):

200X

May   16   Sold merchandise on account to Ronald Co., invoice no. 1, $1,000.
      18   Sold merchandise on account to Bass Co., invoice no. 2, $1,700.
      20   Issued credit memorandum no. 1 to Bass Co. for defective merchandise, $700.

Journalizing, recording, and posting that includes credit memorandum.

Use the following account numbers: Accounts Receivable, 112; Sales, 411; Sales Returns and Allowances, 412.

9-3. From Exercise 9-2, journalize in the cash receipts journal the receipt of a check from Ronald Co. for payment of invoice no. 1 on May 24. Use the same headings as for Art's Wholesale Clothing (on p. 356).

Journalizing transaction into cash receipts journal.

9-4. From the following transactions for Edna Co., journalize, record, post, and prepare a schedule of accounts receivable when appropriate. Use the same journal headings (all p. 1) and chart of accounts (use Edna Cares, Capital) that Art's Wholesale Clothing used in the text. You will have to set up your own accounts receivable subsidiary ledger and partial general ledger as needed. All sales terms are 2/10, n/30.

Journalizing, recording, and posting sales and cash receipts journal schedule of accounts receivable.

200X

June   1   Edna Cares invested $3,000 in the business.
       1   Sold merchandise on account to Boston Co., invoice no. 1, $700.
       2   Sold merchandise on account to Gary Co., invoice no. 2, $900.
       3   Cash sale, $200.
       8   Issued credit memorandum no. 1 to Boston for defective merchandise, $200.
      10   Received check from Boston for invoice no. 1 less returns and discount.
      15   Cash sale, $400.
      18   Sold merchandise on account to Boston Co., invoice no. 3, $600.

SALES JOURNAL				
				P. 1
Date	Account Debited	Invoice No.	PR	Dr. Accts. Receivable Cr. Sales
200X Apr. 18	Amazon.com	1		5 0 0 00
19	Bill Valley Co.	2		6 0 0 00

Figure 9-32
Sales Journal, Subsidiary Ledger; Partial General Ledger

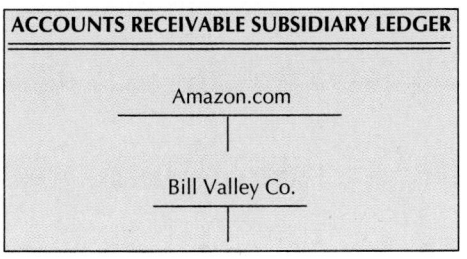

ACCOUNTS RECEIVABLE SUBSIDIARY LEDGER

Amazon.com

Bill Valley Co.

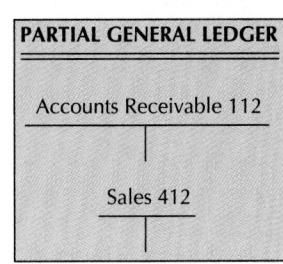

PARTIAL GENERAL LEDGER

Accounts Receivable 112

Sales 412

Sales tax and cash
discount calculation.

9-5. From the following facts calculate what Ann Frost paid Blue Co. for the purchase of a dining room set. Sale terms are 2/10, n/30.

    a. Sales ticket price before tax, $4,000, dated April 5.
    b. Sales tax, 7%.
    c. Returned one defective chair for credit of $400 on April 8.
    d. Paid bill on April 13.

Multicolumn journal:
Journalizing and posting
to general ledger, recording
to accounts receivable
subsidiary ledger, and
preparing a schedule of
accounts receivable.

Group A Problems

(The forms you need are on pages 285–304 of the *Study Guide and Working Papers.*)

9A-1. Jill Blue has opened Food.com, a wholesale grocery and pizza company. The following transactions occurred in June:

200X

June	1	Sold grocery merchandise to Duncan Co. on account, $500, invoice no. 1.
	4	Sold pizza merchandise to Sue Moore Co. on account, $600, invoice no. 2.
	8	Sold grocery merchandise to Long Co. on account, $700, invoice no. 3.
	10	Issued credit memorandum no. 1 to Duncan Co. for $150 of grocery merchandise returned due to spoilage.
	15	Sold pizza merchandise to Sue Moore Co. on account, $160, invoice no. 4.
	19	Sold grocery merchandise to Long Co. on account, $300, invoice no. 5.
	25	Sold pizza merchandise to Duncan Co. on account, $1,200, invoice no. 6.

Check Figure:
Schedule of accounts
receivable $3,310

Required

1. Journalize the transactions in the appropriate journals.
2. Record to the accounts receivable subsidiary ledger and post to the general ledger as appropriate.
3. Prepare a schedule of accounts receivable.

9A-2. The following transactions of Ted's Auto Supply occurred in November (your working papers have balances as of November 1 for certain general ledger and accounts receivable ledger accounts):

200X

Nov.	1	Sold auto parts merchandise to R. Volan on account, $1,000, invoice no. 60, plus 5% sales tax.
	5	Sold auto parts merchandise to J. Seth on account, $800, invoice no. 61, plus 5% sales tax.
	8	Sold auto parts merchandise to Lance Corner on account, $9,000, invoice no. 62, plus 5% sales tax.
	10	Issued credit memorandum no. 12 to R. Volan for $500 for defective auto parts merchandise returned from Nov. 1 transaction. (Be careful to record the reduction in Sales Tax Payable as well.)
	12	Sold auto parts merchandise to J. Seth on account, $600, invoice no. 63, plus 5% sales tax.

Multicolumn sales journal:
Use of sales tax, journalizing and posting to general
ledger and recording to
accounts receivable ledger,
and preparing a schedule
of accounts receivable.

Check Figure:
Schedule of accounts
receivable $13,045

Required

1. Journalize the transactions in the appropriate journals.
2. Record to the accounts receivable subsidiary ledger and post to the general ledger as appropriate.
3. Prepare a schedule of accounts receivable.

9A-3. Mark Peaker owns Peaker's Sneaker Shop. (In your working papers balances as of May 1 are provided for the accounts receivable and general ledger accounts.) The following transactions occurred in May:

200X

May

1   Mark Peaker invested an additional $12,000 in the sneaker store.

3   Sold $700 of merchandise on account to B. Dale, sales ticket no. 60, terms 1/10, n/30.

4   Sold $500 of merchandise on account to Ron Lester, sales ticket no. 61, terms 1/10, n/30.

9   Sold $200 of merchandise on account to Jim Zon, sales ticket no. 62, terms 1/10, n/30.

10 Received cash from B. Dale in payment of May 3 transaction, sales ticket no. 60, less discount.

20 Sold $3,000 of merchandise on account to Pam Pry, sales ticket no. 63, terms 1/10, n/30.

22 Received cash payment from Ron Lester in payment of May 4 transaction, sales ticket no. 61.

23 Collected cash sales, $3,000.

24 Issued credit memorandum no. 1 to Pam Pry for $2,000 of merchandise returned from May 20 sales on account.

26 Received cash from Pam Pry in payment of May 20, sales ticket no. 63. (Don't forget about the credit memo and discount.)

28 Collected cash sales, $7,000.

30 Sold sneaker rack equipment for $300 cash. (Beware.)

30 Sold merchandise priced at $4,000, on account to Ron Lester, sales ticket no. 64, terms 1/10, n/30.

31 Issued credit memorandum no. 2 to Ron Lester for $700 of merchandise returned from May 30 transaction, sales ticket no. 64.

> *Comprehensive Problem:*
> Recording transactions into sales, cash receipts, and general journals. Recording to accounts receivable subsidiary ledger and posting to general ledger. Preparing a schedule of accounts receivable.

> *Check Figure:*
> Schedule of Accounts Receivable $5,700

Required

1. Journalize the transactions.
2. Record to the accounts receivable subsidiary ledger and post to the general ledger as needed.
3. Prepare a schedule of accounts receivable.

9A-4. Bill Murray opened Bill's Cosmetic Market on April 1. There is a 6% sales tax on all cosmetic sales. Bill offers no sales discounts. The following transactions occurred in April:

200X

Apr.

1   Bill Murray invested $8,000 in the Cosmetic Market from his personal savings account.

5   From the cash register tapes, lipstick cash sales were $5,000 plus sales tax.

5   From the cash register tapes, eye shadow cash sales were $2,000 plus sales tax.

8   Sold lipstick on account to Alice Koy Co., $300, sales ticket no. 1, plus sales tax.

9   Sold eye shadow on account to Marika Sanchez Co., $1,000, sales ticket no. 2, plus sales tax.

15 Issued credit memorandum no. 1 to Alice Koy Co. for $150 for lipstick returned. (Be sure to reduce Sales Tax Payable for Bill.)

19 Marika Sanchez Co. paid half the amount owed from sales ticket no. 2, dated April 9.

21 Sold lipstick on account to Jeff Tong Co., $300, sales ticket no. 3, plus sales tax.

> *Comprehensive Problem:*
> Using sales tax in recording transactions into sales, cash receipts, and general journals. Recording to accounts receivable subsidiary ledger and posting to general ledger. Crossfooting and preparing a schedule of accounts receivable.

24   Sold eye shadow on account to Rusty Neal Co., $800, sales ticket no. 4, plus sales tax.

25   Issued credit memorandum no. 2 to Jeff Tong Co. for $200 for lipstick returned from sales ticket no. 3, dated April 21.

29   Cash sales taken from the cash register tape showed:
   1. Lipstick: $1,000 + $60 sales tax collected.
   2. Eye shadow: $3,000 + $180 sales tax collected.

29   Sold lipstick on account to Marika Sanchez Co., $400, sales ticket no. 5, plus sales tax.

30   Received payment from Marika Sanchez Co. of sales ticket no. 5, dated April 29.

Required

1. Journalize the preceeding in the sales journal, cash receipts journal, or general journal.
2. Record to the accounts receivable subsidiary ledger and post to the general ledger when appropriate.
3. Prepare a schedule of accounts receivable for the end of April.

Group B Problems

(The forms you need are on pages 285–304 of the *Study Guide and Working Papers*.)

9B-1. The following transactions occurred for Food.com for the month of June:

200X

June	1	Sold grocery merchandise to Duncan Co. on account, $800, invoice no. 1.
	4	Sold pizza merchandise to Sue Moore Co. on account, $550, invoice no. 2.
	8	Sold grocery merchandise to Long Co. on account, $900, invoice no. 3.
	10	Issued credit memorandum no. 1 to Duncan Co. for $160 of grocery merchandise returned due to spoilage.
	15	Sold pizza merchandise to Sue Moore Co. on account, $700, invoice no. 4.
	19	Sold grocery merchandise to Long Co. on account, $250, invoice no. 5.

Required

1. Journalize the transactions in the appropriate journals.
2. Record to the accounts receivable subsidiary ledger and post to the general ledger as appropriate.
3. Prepare a schedule of accounts receivable.

9B-2. In November the following transactions occurred for Ted's Auto Supply (your working papers have balances as of November 1 for certain general ledger and accounts receivable ledger accounts):

200X

Nov.	1	Sold merchandise to R. Volan on account, $4,000, invoice no. 70, plus 5% sales tax.
	5	Sold merchandise to J. Seth on account, $1,600, invoice no. 71, plus 5% sales tax.
	8	Sold merchandise to Lance Corner on account, $15,000, invoice no. 72, plus 5% sales tax.
	10	Issued credit memorandum no. 14 to R. Volan for $2,000 for defective merchandise returned from Nov. 1 transaction. (Be sure to record the reduction in Sales Tax Payable as well.)
	12	Sold merchandise to J. Seth on account, $1,400, invoice no. 73, plus 5% sales tax.

Required

1. Journalize the transactions in the appropriate journals.
2. Record to the accounts receivable subsidiary ledger and post to the general ledger as appropriate.
3. Prepare a schedule of accounts receivable.

9B-3. (In your working papers all the beginning balances needed are provided for the accounts receivable subsidiary and general ledgers.) The following transactions occurred for Peaker's Sneaker Shop:

200X

May
- 1   Mark Peaker invested an additional $14,000 in the sneaker store.
- 3   Sold $2,000 of merchandise on account to B. Dale, sales ticket no. 60, terms 1/10, n/30.
- 4   Sold $900 of merchandise on account to Ron Lester, sales ticket no. 61, terms 1/10, n/30.
- 9   Sold $600 of merchandise on account to Jim Zon, sales ticket no. 62, terms 1/10, n/30.
- 10   Received cash from B. Dale in payment of May 3 transaction, sales ticket no. 60, less discount.
- 20   Sold $4,000 of merchandise on account to Pam Pry, sales ticket no. 63, terms 1/10, n/30.
- 22   Received cash payment from Ron Lester in payment of May 4 transaction, sales ticket no. 61.
- 23   Collected cash sales, $6,000.
- 24   Issued credit memorandum no. 1 to Pam Pry for $500 of merchandise returned from May 20 sales on account.
- 26   Received cash from Pam Pry in payment of May 20 sales ticket no. 63. (Don't forget about the credit memo and discount.)
- 28   Collected cash sales, $12,000.
- 30   Sold sneaker rack equipment for $200 cash.
- 30   Sold $6,000 of merchandise on account to Ron Lester, sales ticket no. 64, terms 1/10, n/30.
- 31   Issued credit memorandum no. 2 to Ron Lester for $800 of merchandise returned from May 30 transaction, sales ticket no. 64.

Required

1. Journalize the transactions in the appropriate journals.
2. Record and post as appropriate.
3. Prepare a schedule of accounts receivable.

9B-4. Bill's Cosmetic Market began operating in April. There is a 6% sales tax on all cosmetic sales. Bill offers no discounts. The following transactions occurred in April:

200X

Apr.
- 1   Bill Murray invested $10,000 in the Cosmetic Market from his personal account.
- 5   From the cash register tapes, lipstick cash sales were $5,000 plus sales tax.
- 5   From the cash register tapes, eye shadow cash sales were $3,000 plus sales tax.
- 8   Sold lipstick on account to Alice Koy Co., $400, sales ticket no. 1, plus sales tax.
- 9   Sold eye shadow on account to Marika Sanchez Co., $900, sales ticket no. 2, plus sales tax.

Check Figure:
Schedule of accounts
receivable $22,600

Check Figure:
Schedule of accounts
receivable $8,000

Comprehensive Problem:
Recording transactions into sales, cash receipts, and general journals. Recording to accounts receivable subsidiary ledger and posting to general ledger. Preparing a schedule of accounts receivable.

15 Issued credit memorandum no. 1 to Alice Koy Co. for lipstick returned, $200. (Be sure to reduce Sales Tax Payable for Bill.)

19 Marika Sanchez Co. paid half the amount owed from sales ticket no. 2, dated April 9.

21 Sold lipstick on account to Jeff Tong Co., $600, sales ticket no. 3, plus sales tax.

24 Sold eye shadow on account to Rusty Neal Co., $1,000, sales ticket no. 4, plus sales tax.

25 Issued credit memorandum no. 2 to Jeff Tong Co. for $300, for lipstick returned from sales ticket no. 3, dated April 21.

29 Cash sales taken from the cash register tape showed:
   1. Lipstick: $4,000 + $240 sales tax collected.
   2. Eye shadow: $2,000 + $120 sales tax collected.

29 Sold lipstick on account to Marika Sanchez Co., $700, sales ticket no. 5 plus sales tax.

30 Received payment from Marika Sanchez Co. of sales ticket no. 5, dated April 29.

Required

1. Journalize, record, and post as appropriate.
2. Prepare a schedule of accounts receivable for the end of April.

Real-World Applications

9R-1. Ronald Howard has been hired by Green Company to help reconstruct the sales journal, general journal, and cash receipts journal, which were recently destroyed in a fire. The owner of Green Company has supplied him with the following data. Please ignore dates, invoice numbers, and so forth and enter the entries into the reconstructed sales journal, general journal, and cash receipts journal. What written recommendation should Ron make so reconstruction will not be needed in the future?

Accounts Receivable Subsidiary Ledger

P. Bond		
Bal.	100	150 CRJ
SJ	150	Entitled to 2% discount

M. Raff		
Bal.	200	
SJ	100	

J. Smooth		
Bal.	300	1,000 GJ
SJ	2,000	1,000 CRJ
SJ	1,000	500 GJ
		Entitled to 1% discount

R. Venner		
Bal.	200	400 CRJ
SJ	400	

Partial General Ledger

Cash	
Bal. 12,737	

Accounts Receivable			
Bal.	800	1,000	GJ
SJ	3,650	500	GJ
		1,550	CRJ

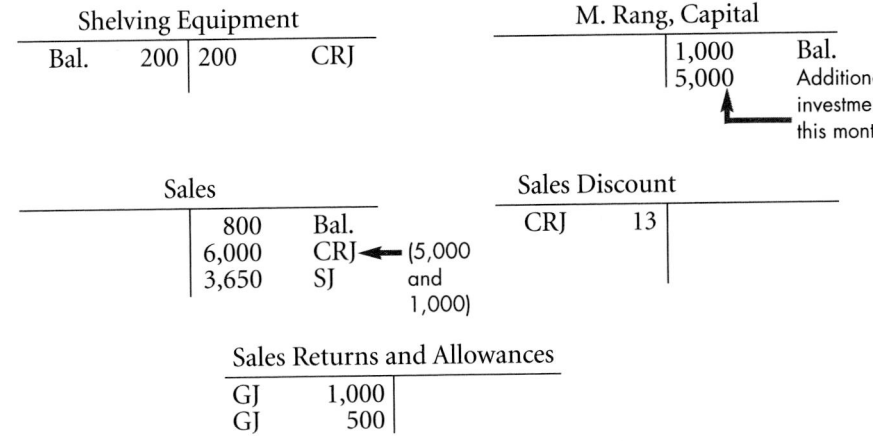

Shelving Equipment			
Bal.	200	200	CRJ

M. Rang, Capital		
	1,000	Bal.
	5,000	Additional investment this month

Sales		
	800	Bal.
	6,000	CRJ ← (5,000 and
	3,650	SJ 1,000)

Sales Discount		
CRJ	13	

Sales Returns and Allowances		
GJ	1,000	
GJ	500	

9R-2. The bookkeeper of Floore Company records credit sales in a sales journal and returns in a general journal. The bookkeeper did the following:

1. Recorded an $18 credit sale as $180 in the sales journal.
2. Correctly recorded a $40 sale in the sales journal but posted it to B. Blue's account as $400 in the accounts receivable ledger.
3. Made an additional error in determining the balance of J. B. Window Co. in the accounts receivable ledger.
4. Posted a sales return that was recorded in the general journal to the Sales Returns and Allowance account and the Accounts Receivable account but forgot to record it to the B. Katz Co.
5. Added the total of the sales column incorrectly.
6. Posted a sales return to the Accounts Receivable account but not to the Sales Returns and Allowances account. The Accounts Receivable ledger was recorded correctly.

Could you inform the bookkeeper in writing as to when each error will be discovered?

YOU make the call

Critical Thinking/Ethical Case

9R-3. Amy Jak is the National Sales Manager of Land.com. To get sales up to the projection for the old year, Amy asked the accountant to put the first two weeks of sales in January back into December. Amy told the accountant that this secret would only be between them. Should Amy move the new sales into the old sales year? You make the call. Write down your specific recommendations to Amy.

Internet Exercises: Dillard's

EX-1. [www.dillards.com] Special journals are designed to be excellent labor savers. Now that you have been shown the basics of the sales journal and the cash receipts journal, you will recognize them next time you visit any large retailer. The labor saved by these journals is that transactions in them are posted monthly, rather than as they occur. Briefly explain the advantages of using them instead of merely posting transactions in a general journal. In your explanation discuss posting differences between special journals and the general journal.

EX-2. [www.dillards.com] Compare the process of entering transactions from source documents into a manual sales journal or cash receipts journal with the "automatic" creation of the entries from a "point-of-sale terminal" you would see in a department store. Mention in your answer what different types of accounting records would be posted at the "point of sale."

Continuing Problem

Eldorado Computer Center

Tony will use two specialized journals for recording business transactions in the month of January. To assist you in recording the transactions, at the end of this problem is the schedule of accounts receivable as of December 31 and an updated chart of accounts with the current balance listed for each account.

Assignment

(See p. 309 in the *Study Guide and Working Papers*.)

1. Journalize the transactions in the appropriate journals (cash receipts, sales journal, or general journal).
2. Record in the accounts receivable subsidiary ledger and post to the general ledger as appropriate. A partial general ledger is included in the *Working Papers*.
3. Prepare a schedule of accounts receivable as of January 31, 200X.

The January transactions are as follows:

Jan.	1	Sold $700 worth of merchandise to Taylor Golf on credit, sales invoice no. 5000; terms are 2/10, n/30.
	10	Sold $3,000 worth of merchandise on account to Anthony Pitale, sales invoice no. 5001; terms are 2/10, n/30.
	11	Received $3,000 from Accu Pac, Inc. toward payment of its balance; no discount allowed.
	12	Collected $2,000 cash sales.
	19	Sold $4,000 worth of merchandise on account to Vita Needle, sales invoice no. 5002; terms are 4/10, n/30.
	20	Collected balance in full from invoice no. 5001, Anthony Pitale.
	29	Issued credit memorandum to Taylor Golf for $400 worth of merchandise returned, invoice no. 5000.
	29	Collected full payment from Vita Needle, invoice no. 5002.

Schedule of Accounts Receivable
Eldorado Computer Center
December 31, 200X

Taylor Golf	$ 2,900.00
Vita Needle	6,800.00
Accu Pac	$ 3,900.00
Total Amount Due	$13,600.00

Chart of Accounts and Current Balances as of 12/31/0X

Account #	Account Name	Debit Balance	Credit Balance
1000	Cash	$ 3,336.65	
1010	Petty Cash	100	
1020	Accounts Receivable	13,600	
1025	Prepaid Rent	1,600	
1030	Supplies	132	
1040	Merchandise Inventory	0	
1080	Computer Shop Equipment	3,800	
1081	Accumulated Dep., CS Equip.		$ 99
1090	Office Equipment	1,050	
1091	Accumulated Dep., Office Equip.		20
2000	Accounts Payable		2,050
2010	Wages Payable		0
2020	FICA—Social Security Payable		0
2030	FICA—Medicare Payable		0
2040	FIT Payable		0
2050	SIT Payable		0
2060	FUTA Payable		0
2070	SUTA Payable		0
3000	Freedman Capital		7,406
3010	Freedman Withdrawals	2,015	
3020	Income Summary		0
4000	Service Revenue		18,500
4010	Sales		0
4020	Sales Returns and Allowances	0	
4030	Sales Discounts	0	
5010	Advertising Expense	0	
5020	Rent Expense	0	
5030	Utilities Expense	0	
5040	Phone Expense	150	
5050	Supplies Expense	0	
5060	Insurance Expense	0	
5070	Postage Expense	25	
5080	Dep. Exp., C.S. Equipment	0	
5090	Dep. Exp., Office Equipment	0	
5100	Miscellaneous Expense	10	
5110	Wage Expense	2,030	
5120	Payroll Tax Expense	226.35	
5130	Interest Expense	0	
5140	Bad Debt Expense	0	
6000	Purchases	0	
6010	Purchases Returns and Allowances		0
6020	Purchases Discounts		0
6030	Freight In	0	

INTRODUCTION TO A MERCHANDISE COMPANY USING A GENERAL JOURNAL FOR A PERPETUAL INVENTORY SYSTEM

Introduction to the Merchandise Cycle

Let's use Wal-Mart as an example. We know that Wal-Mart must buy inventory from suppliers to sell to you, the customer. This inventory is called *merchandise inventory*. It is an asset sold to you for cash and/or accounts receivable and represents *sales revenue* or sales for Wal-Mart.

What did it cost Wal-Mart to bring the inventory into the store? The *cost of goods sold* is the total cost of merchandise inventory brought into the store and sold. These costs do not include any operating expenses such as heat, advertising, and salaries. To find Wal-Mart's profit before operating expenses, we take the sales revenue less cost of goods sold. Figure A-1 is called *gross profit on sales*.

Figure A-1
Calculating Gross Profit on Sales

| Wal-Mart Sales Revenue | − | Cost of Goods Sold | = | Gross Profit on Sales |

For example, if Wal-Mart sells a TV for $500 that cost it $300 to bring into the store, its gross profit is $200. To find its net income or net loss, Wal-Mart would subtract its operating expenses. Figure A-2 shows how a merchandiser calculates its net income or net loss.

Figure A-2
Introduction to Perpetual Inventory for a Merchandise Company

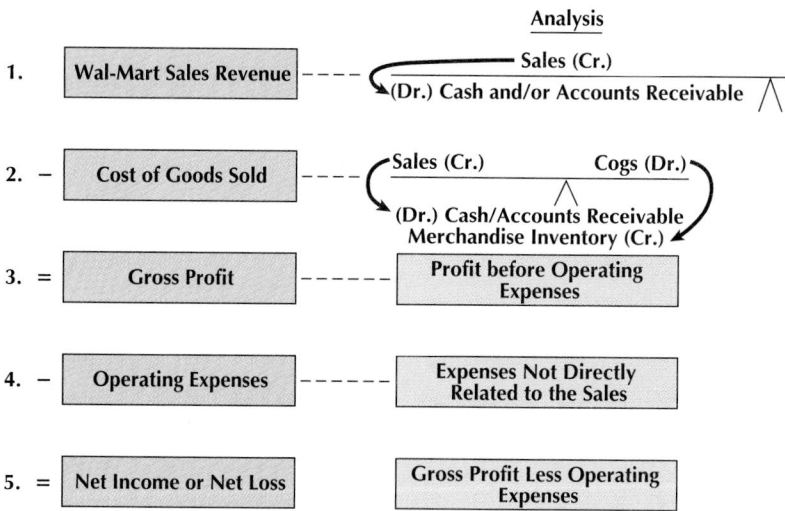

Note In Step 1 the sales provide an inflow of cash and/or accounts receivable. Step 2 shows that when the inventory is sold, it is recognized as a cost (cost of goods sold). By subtracting sales less cost of goods sold, we arrive at the gross profit in Step 3. Step 4 shows that operating expenses subtracted from gross profit result in a net income or net loss in Step 5.

What Inventory System Wal-Mart Uses

When you pay at Wal-Mart you see the use of bar codes and optical scanners. Wal-Mart keeps detailed records of the inventory it brings into the store and what inventory is sold. This continuous updating of inventory is called a *perpetual inventory system*. With this method, Wal-Mart keeps track of what it costs to make the sale (cost of goods sold).

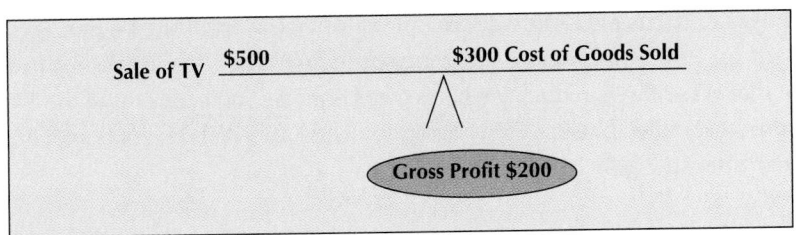

Figure A-3
Matchings Revenues and Costs

More and more companies large or small are using the perpetual inventory system due to increasing computerization. Wal-Mart knows that using the perpetual inventory system will help control stocks of inventory as well as lost or stolen goods.

Recording Merchandise Transactions

Now let's look at Wal-Mart as both a buyer and seller. Let's first focus on Wal-Mart the buyer.

Wal-Mart: The Buyer

When Wal-Mart brings merchandise inventory into the stores from suppliers it is recorded in the *Merchandise Inventory account*. Think of this account as purchases of merchandise for cash or on account that is for resale to customers. Each order is documented by an invoice for Wal-Mart. Keep in mind Merchandise Inventory is the cost of bringing the merchandise into the store, not the price at which the merchandise will be sold to customers. Let's assume on *July 9 that Wal-Mart bought flat-screen TVs from Sony Corp. for $7,000 with terms 2/10, n/30*. Wal-Mart would record the purchase as shown in Figure A-4.

Figure A-4
Purchase Inventory on Account

Analysis:

Merchandise Inventory	A	↑	Dr.	$7,000	
Accounts Payable	L	↑	Cr.	$7,000	

Journal Entry:

July	9	Merchandise Inventory	7 0 0 0 00		
		Accounts Payable		7 0 0 0 00	
		Purchased Inventory on account			
		from Sony 2/10, n/30			

Keep in mind not all purchases will go to Merchandise Inventory. Wal-Mart will buy supplies, equipment and so forth that are not for resale to customers. These amounts will be debited to the specific account. For example, if Wal-Mart bought $5,000 of shelving equipment on account for its store on November 9, the transaction would be recorded as in Figure A-5.

Figure A-5
Purchasing of Equipment on Account

Analysis:

Shelving Equipment	A	↑	Dr.	$5,000	
Accounts Payable	L	↑	Cr.	$5,000	

Journal Entry:

Nov.	9	Shelving Equipment	5 0 0 0 00		
		Accounts Payable		5 0 0 0 00	
		Bought equipment on account			

What happens if Wal-Mart finds a TV to be defective from its purchase from Sony?

Figure A-6
Recording a Debit
Memorandum

Recording Purchases Returns and Allowances   Because Wal-Mart noticed a damaged TV in the shipment on July 14, it issues a *debit memorandum.* This document notified Sony, the supplier, that Wal-Mart is reducing what is owed Sony by $600, the cost of the TV (to bring it into the store) and that the TV is being returned. On Wal-Mart's books the analysis and journal entry in Figure A-6 resulted.

Analysis:					
Accounts Payable	L	↓	Dr.	$600
Merchandise Inventory	A	↓	Cr.	$600

Journal Entry:	July	14	Accounts Payable		6 0 0 00		
			Merchandise Inventory			6 0 0 00
			To record Debit Memo #10			

Note that the cost of Merchandise Inventory has been reduced by $600 due to the return. In the perpetual inventory system there is no purchases, returns, and allowances title. The savings from the return are recorded *directly* into the Merchandise Inventory account. Let's now look at how Wal-Mart would record any cash discounts it would receive due to payment of the Sony bill within the discount period.

Recording Purchase Discounts   Let's assume Wal-Mart pays Sony within the first 10 days. Keep in mind that we take no discounts on returned goods (the $600 return). The amount of purchase discount will be recorded as a reduction to the cost of Merchandise Inventory. Figure A-7 shows the analysis and journal entry on July 16. A discount lowers the cost of inventory.

Figure A-7
Recording a Purchase
Discount

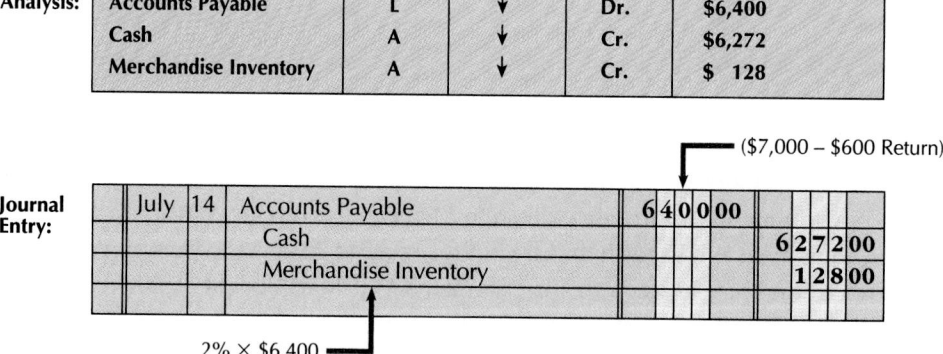

Analysis:					
Accounts Payable	L	↓	Dr.	$6,400
Cash	A	↓	Cr.	$6,272
Merchandise Inventory	A	↓	Cr.	$ 128

($7,000 – $600 Return)

Journal Entry:	July	14	Accounts Payable		6 4 0 0 00		
			Cash			6 2 7 2 00
			Merchandise Inventory			1 2 8 00

2% × $6,400

Keep in mind that had Wal-Mart missed the discount period it would have debited Accounts Payable $6,400 and credited Cash for $6,400. Merchandise Inventory would not be reduced.

Recording Cost of Freight   The cost of freight ($300) is to be paid by Wal-Mart. When the purchaser is responsible for cost of freight, it is added to the cost of Merchandise Inventory. If the cost of freight is paid by the seller, it could be recorded in an operating expense account called Freight-out. Figure A-8 is the analysis and journal entry for freight on July 10.

Wal-Mart: The Seller

Now let's look at Wal-Mart as the *seller* of merchandise.

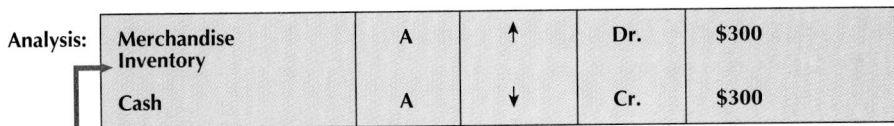

Analysis:	Merchandise Inventory	A	↑	Dr.	$300
	Cash	A	↓	Cr.	$300

Freight Cost added to Merchandise Inventory

Journal Entry:		July	10	Merchandise Inventory		3 0 0 00		
				Cash			3 0 0 00
				Payment of Freight			

Recording Sales at Wal-Mart   Sales revenues are earned at Wal-Mart when the goods are transferred to the buyer. The earned revenue can be for cash and or credit. Let's look at the following example of the sale of a TV at Wal-Mart for $950 on credit on August 10 that cost Wal-Mart $600. Keep in mind when using the perpetual inventory system that at the time of the earned sale Wal-Mart will:

At selling price →   1. **Record the sales (cash and/or credit).**
At cost →   2. **Record the cost of the inventory sold and the reduction in inventory.**

First, let's analyze the transaction in Figure A-9. Note that we will have two entries, one to record the sale and one to show a new cost and less inventory on hand.

Be sure to go back to Steps 1 and 2 of Figure A-2. These two steps reinforce the preceding journal entries. Remember that if the sale were a cash sale, we would have debited Cash instead of Accounts Receivable. Note also that the Sales account only records sales of goods held for resale.

Selling < Price	Accounts Receivable	Asset	↑	Dr.	$950
	Sales	Revenue	↑	Cr.	$950
Cost to < Make sale	Cost of Goods Sold	Cost	↑	Dr.	$600
	Merchandise Inventory	Asset	↓	Cr.	$600

Figure A-9
Recording Sales and Cost of Goods Sold

Journal Entries:		Aug.	10	Accounts Receivable		9 5 0 00		
				Sales			9 5 0 00
				Charge sales			
			10	Cost of Goods Sold		6 0 0 00	
				Merchandise Inventory			6 0 0 00
				To record cost of			
				merchandise sold on account			

How Wal-Mart Records Sales Returns Allowances and Sales Discounts   Keep in mind that we are now looking at how the *seller* of merchandise records a transaction giving the customer a credit due to an allowance or a return of goods from a previous sale. Usually, the seller will issue a *credit memorandum*, a document informing the customer of the adjustment due to the return or allowance. For example, on August 15, let's look at a customer who returned a $950 TV that had been purchased at Wal-Mart. On Wal-Mart's books, the analysis and journal entry in Figure A-10 resulted.

The first entry records the return at the original selling price using the contra-revenue account Sales Returns and Allowances. The second entry records putting the inventory back in Wal-Mart's books at cost and reducing its Cost of Goods Sold because the inventory was

Figure A-10
Return of Goods

The Analysis: at Selling Price	Sales Returns and Allowances	Contra-Revenue	↑	Dr.	$950
	Accounts Receivable	Asset	↓	Cr.	$950
At Cost	Merchandise Inventory	Asset	↑	Dr.	$600
	Costs of Goods Sold	Cost	↓	Cr.	$600

Journal Entries:

Aug.	15	Sales Returns and Allowances	9 5 0 00		
		Accounts Receivable		9 5 0 00
		Returned Goods		
	15	Merchandise Inventory	6 0 0 00	
		Cost of Goods Sold		6 0 0 00

not sold. Remember that we only record the Cost of Goods Sold when the sale has been earned. Keep in mind that if the customer kept the TV but at a reduced price, no entry affecting Merchandise Inventory and Cost of Goods Sold would be needed. Let's assume a customer on August 25 gets a 2% discount for paying for a $950 TV early. The analysis and entry in Figure A-11 would result on the seller's book:

Figure A-11
Recording Sales Discount

The Analysis:	Cash	Asset	↑	Dr.	$931
	Sales Discount	Contra-Revenue	↑	Dr.	$ 19
	Accounts Receivable	Asset	↓	Cr.	$950

Journal Entry:

Aug.	25	Cash	9 3 1 00	
		Sales Discount	1 9 00	
		Accounts Receivable		9 5 0 00

Now let's summarize (Fig. A-12) all the entries for both the buyer and the seller (in this case, Wal-Mart).

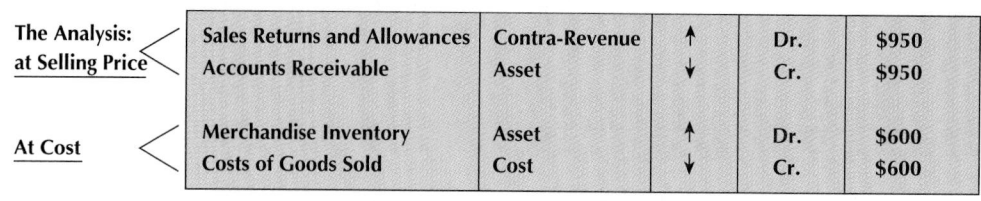

Wal-Mart the Buyer			Wal-Mart the Seller	
Bought Inventory for Resale on Account	Merchandise Inventory → At Accounts Payable Cost	Sold Inventory on Account	Accounts Receivable → At Sales Selling Price Cost of Goods Sold → At Merchandise Inventory Cost
Issued a Debit Memo for Merchandise Returned	Accounts Payable → At Merchandise Inventory Cost	Issued a Credit Memo for Returned Merchandise	Sales Returns and Allowances → At Accounts Receivable Selling Price Merchandise Inventory → At Cost of Goods Sold Cost
Recorded a Purchase Discount	Accounts Payable Cash Merchandise Inventory	Recorded a Sales Discount	Cash Sales Discount Accounts Receivable

Amount of discount ⎯

Figure A-12

PROBLEM FOR APPENDIX

(The blank forms you need are on page 314 of the *Study Guide and Working Papers.*)

Pete's Clock Shops completed the following merchandise transactions in the month of June:

200X

June

1   Purchased merchandise on account from Clock Suppliers, $4,000; terms 2/10, n/30.

3   Sold merchandise on account, $2,000; terms 2/10, n/30. The cost of the merchandise sold was $1,200.

4   Received credit from Clock Suppliers for merchandise returned, $400.

10   Received collections in full, less discounts, from June 3 sales.

11   Paid Clock Suppliers in full, less discount.

14   Purchased office equipment for cash, $500.

15   Purchased $2,800 of merchandise from Abe's Distribution for cash.

16   Received a refund due to defective merchandise from supplier on cash puchase of $400.

17   Purchased merchandise from Rose Corp., $6,000 free on board shipping point (buyer pays freight); terms 2/10, n/30. Freight to be paid on June 20.

18   Sold merchandise for $3,000 cash; the cost of the merchandise sold was $1,600.

20   Paid freight on June 17 purchase, $180.

25   Purchased merchandise from Lee Co., $1,400, free on board destination (seller pays freight); terms 2/10, n/30.

26   Paid Rose Corp. in full, less discount.

27   Made refunds to cash customers for defective clocks, $300. The cost of the defective clocks was $120.

Pete's Clock Shop accounts included the following:

No. 101 Cash, No. 112 Accounts Receivable

No. 120 Merchandise Inventory, No. 124 Office Equipment, No. 201 Accounts Payable

No. 301 P. Rings Capital, No. 401 Sales

No. 412 Sales Discounts, No. 501 Cost of Goods Sold

Assignment

Journalize the transactions using a perpetual inventory system.

CHAPTER 10

Special Journals

With Appendix on What Special Journals Would Look Like in a Perpetual Inventory System

Purchases and Cash Payments

One sport that you love is golf. Now that you're in school you don't have much time to play, but you do your best to keep up with your hero, Tiger Woods, and pro circuit tournaments. On Saturday afternoon, you decide to take a break from your studies and go to the town's municipal golf course and pro shop.

After getting a slot and shooting nine holes, you go into the pro shop to look at all the clubs you wish you owned. Frank Smith, who is the manager of the shop, tells you that he just made a terrific purchase on selected irons, drivers, and putters. Frank told you that he had to really deal to get these prices; in fact, he said he was lucky enough to take advantage of a large cash discount by paying cash to the distributor. After looking at the prices, you definitely agree that Mr. Smith made an excellent purchase on some fine golf clubs.

Driving back to the campus you think about what Frank Smith told you. The pro shop got a special purchase price for the clubs because it took advantage of a cash discount by paying cash. It makes sense and it sounds like a good business practice. You never thought about the purchase side of running a retail business—it's both a buyer as well as a seller.

In Chapter 9 we learned about the use of special journals such as the sales and cash receipts journal and their role in the sales cycle of a merchandising business. In this chapter we discuss two other special journals—the purchases and cash payment journals. The purchases and cash payments journals are essential in the purchasing cycle for a merchandising business. After completing Chapter 10, you'll know about the accounting behind the purchasing side of a merchandising business and have a complete picture of the business as both buyer and seller.

Learning Objectives

- Calculating net purchases. (p. 390)
- Journalizing transactions in a purchases journal. (p. 393)
- Posting from a purchases journal to the accounts payable subsidiary ledger and the general ledger. (p. 393)
- Preparing, journalizing, recording, and posting a debit memorandum. (p. 395)
- Journalizing and posting from a cash payments journal. (p. 398)
- Preparing a schedule of accounts payable. (p. 400)

Chapter 9 focused on the sellers in merchandise companies. This chapter looks at the buyers. Many of the concepts and rules related to special journals carry over to this chapter. At the end of this chapter is an appendix showing how all the special journals in Chapters 9 and 10 would look like in a perpetual inventory system.

Learning Unit 10-1   Chou's Toy Shop: Buyer's View of a Merchandise Company

PURCHASES

Chou brings merchandise into his toy store for resale to customers. The account that records the cost of this merchandise is called Purchases. Suppose Chou buys $4,000 worth of Barbie dolls on account from Mattel Manufacturing on July 6. The Purchases account records all merchandise bought for resale. Here's how this purchase would be recorded if special journals were not used.

	Purchases	
Purchases is a cost.	Dr.	Cr.
The rules work just like they were an expense.	4,000	

This account has a debit balance and is classified as a cost. Purchases represent costs that are directly related to bringing merchandise into the store for resale to customers. The July 6 entry would be analyzed and journalized as in Figure 10-1.

If Chou's purchased a new display case for the store, it would not show up in the Purchases account. The case is considered equipment that is not for resale to customers.

Accounts Affected	Category	↑ ↓	Rules	T Account Update	
Purchases	Cost	↑	Dr.	Purchases	
				Dr. 4,000	Cr.
Accounts Payable, Mattel	Liability	↑	Cr.	Acc. Payable Dr. Cr. 4,000	Mattel 4,000

Figure 10-1
Purchased Merchandise on Account

	July	6	Purchases	4 0 0 0 00	
			Accounts Payable, Mattel		4 0 0 0 00
			Purchases on account		

Keep in mind we would have to record to Mattel in the accounts payable subsidiary ledger. We talk about the subsidiary ledger in Learning Unit 10-2.

PURCHASES RETURNS AND ALLOWANCES

Chou noticed that some of the dolls he received were defective, and he notified the manufacturer of the defects. On July 9, Mattel issued a debit memorandum indicating that Chou would get a $500 reduction from the original selling price. Chou then agreed to keep the dolls. The account that records a decrease to a buyer's cost is a contra-cost account called Purchases Returns and Allowances. The account lowers the cost of purchases.

Purchases Returns and Allowances

Dr.	Cr.
	500

← Normal balance is a credit.

Let's analyze this reduction to cost and prepare a general journal entry (Fig 10-2).

Accounts Affected	Category	↑ ↓	Rules	T Account Update	
Accounts Payable Mattel	Liability	↓	Dr.	Acc. Payable Dr. | Cr. 500 | 4,000	Mattel 500 | 4,000
Purchases Returns and Allowances	Contra-cost	↑	Cr.	Purchases Ret. & Allow. Dr. | Cr. | 500	

	July	9	Accounts Payable, Mattel				5 0 0 00				
			Purchases Returns and Allowances						5 0 0 00		
			Received debit memorandum								

Figure 10-2
Debit Memorandum Received

When posted to general ledger accounts as well as recorded to Mattel in the accounts payable subsidiary ledger, Chou owes $500 less.

Purchases Discount

Now let's look at the analysis and journal entry when Chou pays Mattel. Mattel offers a 2% cash discount if the invoice is paid within 10 days. To take advantage of this cash discount, Chou sent a check to Mattel on July 15. The discount is taken after the allowance.

$4,000
− 500 allowance
$3,500 × .02 = $70 purchases discount

The account that records this discount is called Purchases Discount. It, too, is a contra-cost account because it lowers the cost of purchases.

Purchases Discount

Dr.	Cr.
	70

← Normal balance is a credit

Let's analyze and prepare a general journal entry (Fig. 10-3).

Accounts Affected	Category	↑ ↓	Rules	T Account Update	
Accounts Payable Mattel	Liability	↓	Dr.	Acc. Payable Dr. | Cr. 500 | 4,000 3,500 |	Mattel 500 | 4,000 3,500 |
Purchases Discount	Contra-cost	↑	Cr.	Purchases Discount Dr. | Cr. | 70	
Cash	Asset	↓	Cr.	Cash Dr. | Cr. | 3,430	

Remember:
For Mattel, it is a sales discount, whereas for Chou it is a purchases discount.

Remember:
Purchases were a debit; purchases discounts are credits.

Figure 10-3
Purchase Discount
Journalized

	July	15	Accounts Payable, Mattel					3	5	0	0	00								
			Purchases Discount													7	0	00		
			Cash												3	4	3	0	00	
			Paid Mattel balance owed																	

After the journal entry is posted and recorded to Mattel, the result will show that Chou saved $70 and totally reduced what he owed to Mattel. The actual—or net—cost of his purchase is $3,430, calculated as follows:

Purchases	$4,000
− Purchases Returns and Allowances	500
− Purchases Discounts	70
= Net Purchases	$3,430

Freight charges are not taken into consideration in calculating net purchases. Still, they are very important. If the seller is responsible for paying the shipping cost until the goods reach their destination, the freight charges are F.O.B. destination. (F.O.B. stands for "free on board" the carrier.) For example, if a seller located in Boston sold goods F.O.B. destination to a buyer in New York, the seller would have to pay the cost of shipping the goods to the buyer.

> *F.O.B. Destination:*
> *Seller pays freight to point*
> *of destination.*

If the buyer is responsible for paying the shipping costs, the freight charges are F.O.B. shipping point. In this situation, the seller will sometimes prepay the freight charges as a matter of convenience and will add it to the invoice of the purchaser.

> *F.O.B. Shipping Point:*
> *Buyer pays freight from*
> *seller's shipping point.*

Example:

Bill amount ($800 + $80 prepaid freight)	$880
Less 5% cash discount (.05 × $800)	40
Amount to be paid by buyer	$840

Purchases discounts are not taken on freight. The discount is based on the purchase price.

> *When does title change to*
> *goods shipped?*

If the seller ships goods F.O.B. shipping point, legal ownership (title) passes to the buyer *when the goods are shipped.* If goods are shipped by the seller F.O.B. destination, title will change *when goods have reached their destination.*

Learning Unit 10-1 Review

AT THIS POINT you should be able to

- Explain and calculate purchases, purchases returns and allowances, and purchases discounts. (p. 388)
- Calculate net purchases. (p. 390)
- Explain why purchase discounts are not taken on freight. (p. 390)
- Compare and contrast F.O.B. destination with F.O.B. shipping point. (p. 390)

SELF-REVIEW QUIZ 10-1

(The forms you need can be found on page 316 of the *Study Guide and Working Papers.*)
    Respond true or false to the following:

1. Net purchases = Purchases − Purchases Returns and Allowances − Purchases Discount.

2. Purchases is a contra-cost.

3. F.O.B. destination means the seller covers shipping cost and retains title till goods reach their destination.

4. Purchases discounts are not taken on freight.

5. Purchases Discount is a contra-cost account.

SOLUTIONS TO SELF-REVIEW QUIZ 10-1

1. True   **2.** False   **3.** True   **4.** True   **5.** True

Quiz Tip:

	Buyer				Seller
Purchase	Dr.	Cost	Sale	Cr	Revenue
PRA	Cr.	Contra-cost	SRA	Dr.	Contra-revenue
PD	Cr.	Contra-cost	SD	Dr.	Contra-revenue

Learning Unit 10-2   Steps Taken in Purchasing Merchandise and Recording Purchases

Merchandising companies must take specific steps when they purchase goods for resale. Let's look at the steps Art's Wholesale Clothing Company took when it ordered goods from Abby Blake Company on April 3.

Step 1: Prepare a Purchase Requisition at Art's Wholesale Clothing Company

The inventory clerk notes a low inventory level of ladies' jackets for resale, so the clerk sends a **purchase requisition** to the purchasing department. A duplicate copy is sent to the accounting department. A third copy remains with the department that initiated the request, to be used as a check on the purchasing department.

> Authorized personnel initiate purchase requisition.

Step 2: Purchasing Department of Art's Wholesale Clothing Company Prepares a Purchase Order

After checking various price lists and suppliers' catalogs, the purchasing department fills out a form called a **purchase order**. This form gives Abby Blake Company the authority to ship the ladies' jackets ordered by Art's Wholesale Clothing Company (see Fig. 10-4).

> Four copies of purchase order: (1) (original) to supplier, (2) to accounting department, (3) to department that initiated purchase requisition, and (4) to file of purchasing department.

Step 3: Sales Invoice Prepared by Abby Blake Company

Abby Blake Company receives the purchase order and prepares a sales invoice. The sales invoice for the seller is the **purchase invoice** for the buyer. A sales invoice is shown in Figure 10-5.

The invoice shows that the goods will be shipped F.O.B. Englewood Cliffs. Thus, Art's Wholesale Clothing Company is responsible for paying the shipping costs.

The sales invoice also shows a freight charge. Thus, Abby Blake prepaid the shipping costs as a matter of convenience. Art's will repay the freight charges when it pays the invoice.

Figure 10-4
Purchase Order

```
                    PURCHASE ORDER NO. 1
              ART'S WHOLESALE CLOTHING COMPANY
                     1528 BELLE AVE.
                     NEW YORK, NY 10022

Purchased From:  Abby Blake Company        Date: April 1, 200X
                 12 Foster Road            Shipped VIA: Freight Truck
                 Englewood Cliffs, NJ 07632 Terms: 2/10, n/60
                                           FOB: Englewood Cliffs
```

Quantity	Description	Unit Price	Total
100	Ladies' Jackets Code 14-0	$50	$5,000

```
                                           Art's Wholesale
                                           By: Bill Joy
Purchase order number must appear on all invoices.
```

Figure 10-5
Sales Invoice

```
                    SALES INVOICE NO. 228
                    ABBY BLAKE COMPANY
                      12 FOSTER ROAD
               ENGLEWOOD, CLIFFS, NJ 07632

Sold To:  Art's Wholesale          Date: April 3, 200X
          Clothing Co.             Shipped VIA: Freight Truck
          1528 Belle Ave.          Terms: 2/10, n/60
          New York, NY 10022       Your Order No: 1
                                   FOB: Englewood Cliffs
```

Quantity	Description	Unit Price	Total
100	Ladies' Jackets Code 14-0	$50	$5,000
	Freight		50
			$5,050

Step 4: Receiving the Goods

When goods are received, Art's Wholesale inspects the shipment and completes a receiving report. The receiving report verifies that the exact merchandise that was ordered was received in good condition.

Step 5: Verifying the Numbers

Before the invoice is approved for recording and payment, the accounting department must check the purchase order, invoice, and receiving report to make sure that all are in agreement and that no steps have been omitted. The form used for checking and approval is an invoice approval form (see Fig. 10-6).

Figure 10-6
Invoice Approval Form

```
                  INVOICE APPROVAL FORM
                  Art's Wholesale Clothing Co.

Purchase Order #                        _____
Requisition check                       _____
Purchase Order check                    _____
Receiving Report check                  _____
Invoice check                           _____
Approved for Payment                    _____
```

Keep in mind that Art's Wholesale Clothing Company does not record this purchase until the *invoice is approved for recording and payment.* Abby Blake Company records this transaction in its records when the sales invoice is prepared, however.

THE PURCHASES JOURNAL AND ACCOUNTS PAYABLE SUBSIDIARY LEDGER

Let's look at how Art's Wholesale Clothing Company journalizes, posts, and records to the accounts payable subsidiary ledger (Fig. 10-7). We also look at the purchases

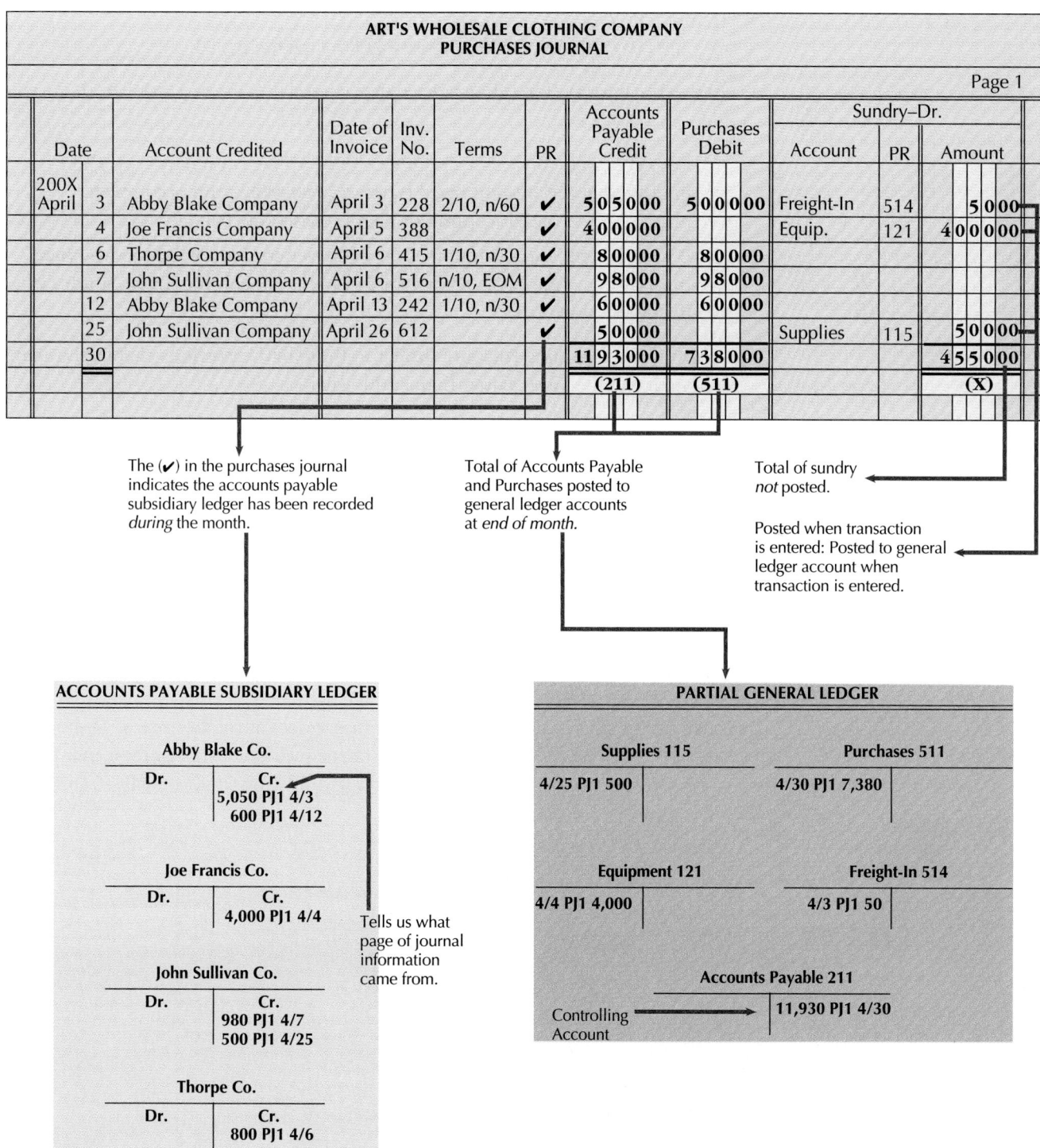

Figure 10-7 Purchases Journal

journal, a multicolumn special journal Art's uses to record the buying of merchandise or other items on account, and the accounts payable subsidiary ledger, an alphabetical list of the amounts owed to creditors from purchases on account.

For example, on April 3 Art's Wholesale Clothing Company records in its purchases journal the following:

- Date: April 3, 200X.
- Account Credited: Abby Blake Company.
- Date of Invoice: April 3.
- Invoice Number: 228.
- Terms: 2/10, n/60.
- Accounts Payable: $5,050; Purchases: $5,000; Freight-In, $50.

As soon as the information is journalized in the purchases journal (see Fig. 10-7), you should:

See Figure 10-7 for a complete purchases journal.

1. Record to Abby Blake Co. in the accounts payable subsidiary ledger to indicate that the amount owed is now $5,050. When this is complete, place a "✓" in the PR column of the purchases journal.

Note that the normal balance in the accounts payable subsidiary ledger is a credit.

2. Post to Freight-In, account no. 514, in the general ledger right away. When this posting is complete, record the 514 in the PR column under Sundry in the purchases journal.

The posting and recording rules are similar to those in the previous chapter, but here we are looking at the buyer rather than at the seller.

THE DEBIT MEMORANDUM

In Chapter 9, Art's Wholesale Clothing Company had to handle returned goods as a seller. It did so by issuing credit memoranda to customers who returned or received an allowance on the price. In this chapter, Art's must handle returns as a buyer. It does so by using debit memoranda. A debit memorandum is a piece of paper issued by a customer to a seller. It indicates that a return or allowance has occurred.

Suppose Art's Wholesale had purchased men's hats for $800 from Thorpe Company on April 6 (p. 393). On April 9, 20 hats valued at $200 were found to have defective brims. Art's issued a debit memorandum to Thorpe Company, as shown in Figure 10-8. At some point in the future, Thorpe will issue Art's a credit memorandum. Let's look at how Art's Wholesale Clothing Company handles such a transaction in its accounting records.

Figure 10-8
Debit Memorandum

A debit memo shows that Art's does not owe as much money as was indicated in the company's purchases journal.

DEBIT MEMORANDUM		No. 1
Art's Wholesale Clothing Company 1528 Belle Ave. New York, NY 10022		
TO: Thorpe Company 3 Access Road Beverly, MA 01915		April 9, 200X
WE DEBIT your account as follows:		
Quantity	Unit Cost	Total
20 Men's Hats Code 827 – defective brims	$10	$200

Journalizing and Posting the Debit Memo

First, let's look at a transactional analysis chart.

Accounts Affected	Category	↑ ↓	Rules
Accounts Payable	Liability	↓	Dr.
Purchases Returns and Allowances	Contra-cost	↑	Cr.

Next, let's examine the journal entry for the debit memorandum (Fig. 10-9).

GENERAL JOURNAL

Page 1

Date	Account Titles and Description	PR	Dr.	Cr.
April 9	Accounts Payable, Thorpe Company	211 ✓	2 0 0 00	
	Purchases Returns and Allowances	513		2 0 0 00
	Debit memo #1			

> Result of debit memo: debits or reduces Accounts Payable. On seller's books, accounts affected would include Sales Returns and Allowances and Accounts Receivable.

Figure 10-9
Debit Memorandum Journalized and Posted

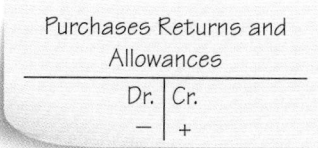

> Purchases Returns and Allowances
> Dr. | Cr.
> − | +

> A contra-cost-of-goods-sold account.

The two postings and one recording are

1. **211:** Post to Accounts Payable as a debit in the general ledger account no. 211. When done, place in the PR column the account number, 211, above the diagonal on the same line as Accounts Payable in the journal.

2. **✓:** Record to Thorpe Co. in the accounts payable subsidiary ledger to show that Art's doesn't owe Thorpe as much money. When done, place a ✓ in the journal in the PR column below the diagonal line on the same line as Accounts Payable in the journal.

3. **513:** Post to Purchases Returns and Allowances as a credit in the general ledger (account no. 513). When done, place the account number, 513, in the PR column of the journal on the same line as Purchases Returns and Allowances. (If equipment was returned that was not merchandise for resale, we would credit Equipment and not Purchases Returns and Allowances.)

Learning Unit 10-2 Review

AT THIS POINT you should be able to

- Explain the relationship between a purchase requisition, a purchase order, and a purchase invoice. (p. 391)
- Explain why a typical invoice approval form may be used. (p. 392)
- Journalize transactions into a purchases journal. (p. 393)
- Explain how to record the accounts payable subsidiary ledger and post to the general ledger from a purchases journal. (p. 393)
- Explain a debit memorandum and be able to journalize an entry resulting from its issuance. (p. 394)

SELF-REVIEW QUIZ 10-2

(The forms you need are on pages 317 of the *Study Guide and Working Papers*.)

Journalize the following transactions into the purchases journal or general journal for Munroe Co. Record accounts as appropriate to the accounts payable subsidiary ledger and post to the general ledger. Use the same journal headings we used for Art's Wholesale Clothing Company.

200X

May 5 Bought merchandise on account from Flynn Co., invoice no. 512, dated May 6, $900, terms 1/10, n/30.

7 Bought merchandise from John Butler Company, invoice no. 403, dated May 7, $1,000, terms n/10 EOM.

13 Issued debit memo no. 1 to Flynn Co. for merchandise returned, $300, from invoice no. 512.

17 Purchased $400 of equipment on account from John Butler Company, invoice no. 413, dated May 18.

SOLUTION TO SELF-REVIEW QUIZ 10-2

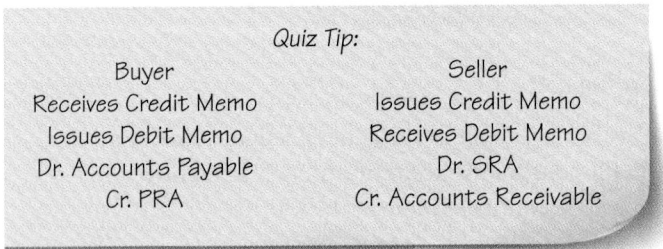

Quiz Tip:

Buyer	Seller
Receives Credit Memo	Issues Credit Memo
Issues Debit Memo	Receives Debit Memo
Dr. Accounts Payable	Dr. SRA
Cr. PRA	Cr. Accounts Receivable

							Accounts Payable Credit	Purchases Debit	Sundry–Dr.			Page 2
Date		Account Credited	Date of Invoice	Inv. No.	Terms	PR			Account	PR	Amount	
200X May	5	Flynn Co.	May 6	512	1/10, n/30	✔	900 00	900 00				
	7	John Butler	May 7	403	n/10, EOM	✔	100 0 00	100 0 00				
	17	John Butler	May 18	413		✔	400 00		Equip.	121	400 00	
	31						230 0 00	190 0 00			400 00	
							(212)	(512)			(X)	

Figure 10-10 Purchases Journal

Figure 10-11
General Journal

			MUNROE CO. GENERAL JOURNAL						
							Page 1		
	Date		Account Titles and Description	PR	Dr.		Cr.		
200X May	13		Accounts Payable, Flynn Co.	212/ ✔	300 00				
			Purchases Returns and Allowances	513			300 00		
			Issued Debit Memo						

ACCOUNTS PAYABLE SUBSIDIARY LEDGER

Figure 10-12
Accounts Payable
Subsidiary Ledger

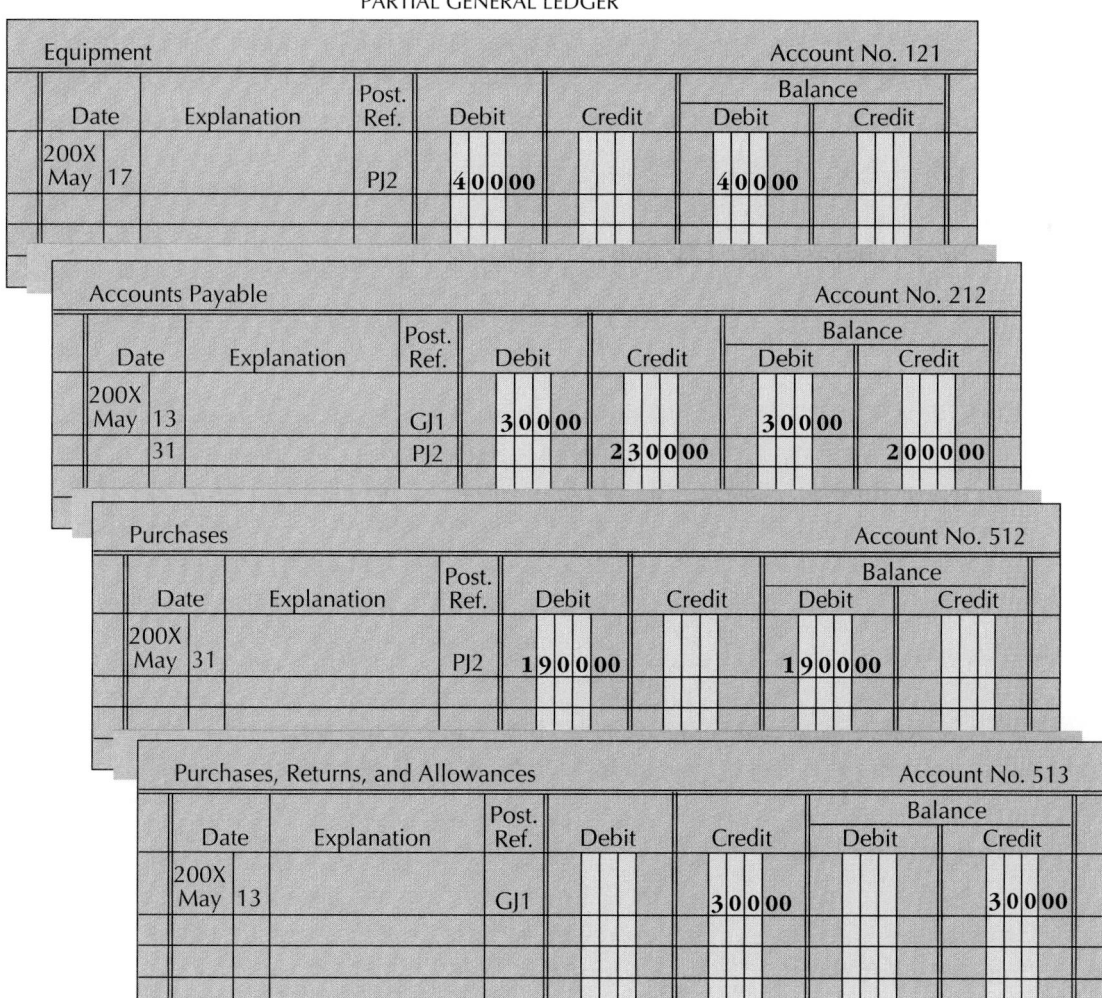

JOHN BUTLER COMPANY
18 REED RD.
HOMEWOOD, ILLINOIS 60430

Date		Explanation	Post. Ref.	Debit	Credit	Cr. Balance
200X May	7		PJ2		1 0 0 0 00	1 0 0 0 00
	17		PJ2		4 0 0 00	1 4 0 0 00

FLYNN COMPANY
15 FOSS AVE.
ENGLEWOOD CLIFFS, NEW JERSEY 07632

Date		Explanation	Post. Ref.	Debit	Credit	Cr. Balance
200X May	5		PJ2		9 0 0 00	9 0 0 00
	13		GJ1	3 0 0 00		6 0 0 00

PARTIAL GENERAL LEDGER

Equipment   Account No. 121

Date		Explanation	Post. Ref.	Debit	Credit	Balance Debit	Balance Credit
200X May	17		PJ2	4 0 0 00		4 0 0 00	

Accounts Payable   Account No. 212

Date		Explanation	Post. Ref.	Debit	Credit	Balance Debit	Balance Credit
200X May	13		GJ1	3 0 0 00		3 0 0 00	
	31		PJ2		2 3 0 0 00		2 0 0 0 00

Purchases   Account No. 512

Date		Explanation	Post. Ref.	Debit	Credit	Balance Debit	Balance Credit
200X May	31		PJ2	1 9 0 0 00		1 9 0 0 00	

Purchases, Returns, and Allowances   Account No. 513

Date		Explanation	Post. Ref.	Debit	Credit	Balance Debit	Balance Credit
200X May	13		GJ1		3 0 0 00		3 0 0 00

Figure 10-13 Partial General Ledger

Learning Unit 10-3   The Cash Payments Journal and Schedule of Accounts Payable

Art's Wholesale Clothing Company will record all payments made in cash (or by check) in a cash payments journal (also called a cash disbursements journal). In many ways the structure of this journal resembles that of the cash receipts journal discussed in Chapter 9. Now, however, we are looking at the outward flow of cash instead of the inward flow.

Art's conducted the following cash transactions in April:

200X

Apr.   2   Issued check no. 1 to Pete Blum for insurance paid in advance, $900.

7   Issued check no. 2 to Joe Francis Company in payment of its April 5 invoice no. 388.

9   Issued check no. 3 to Rick Flo Co. for merchandise purchased for cash, $800.

12   Issued check no. 4 to Thorpe Company in payment of its April 6 invoice no. 414 less the return and discount.

28   Issued check no. 5, $700, for salaries paid.

Figure 10-14 on pages 399–400 shows the cash payments journal for the end of April along with the recordings to the accounts payable subsidiary ledger and postings to the general ledger. Study the diagram; we review it in a moment.

JOURNALIZING, POSTING, AND RECORDING FROM THE CASH PAYMENTS JOURNAL TO THE ACCOUNTS PAYABLE SUBSIDIARY LEDGER AND THE GENERAL LEDGER

Figure 10-14 shows how Art's Wholesale Clothing Company recorded the payment of cash on April 12 to Thorpe Company. The purchases journal shows that Art's purchased $800 of merchandise from Thorpe on account on April 6. The amount Art's owes is discounted 1%. The amount owed ($800–$200 returns) is recorded in the accounts payable subsidiary ledger as soon as the entry is made in the cash payments journal. The payment reduces the balance to Thorpe to zero. Art's Wholesale Clothing Company receives a $6 purchases discount.

At the end of the month, the totals of the Cash, Purchases Discount, and Accounts Payable accounts are posted to the general ledger. The total of Sundry is *not* posted. The accounts Prepaid Insurance, Purchases, and Salaries Expense are posted to the general ledger at the time the entry is put in the journal.

The cash payments journal of Art's Wholesale Clothing Company can be cross-footed as follows:

$$\text{Debit} = \text{Credit Columns}$$
$$\text{Sundry} + \text{Accounts Payable} = \text{Purchases Discounts} + \text{Cash}$$
$$\$2,400 + \$4,600 \qquad = \$6 \qquad\qquad + \$6,994$$
$$\underline{\underline{\$7,000}} = \underline{\underline{\$7,000}}$$

Schedule of Accounts Payable

Now let's prove that the sum of the accounts payable subsidiary ledger at the end of the month is equal to the controlling account, Accounts Payable, at the end of April for Art's Wholesale Clothing Company. To do so, creditors with an ending balance in Art's accounts payable subsidiary ledger must be listed in the schedule of accounts payable (see Fig. 10-15). At the end of the month, the total owed ($7,130) in Accounts

Posting and recording rules for this journal are similar to those for the cash receipts journal in Chapter 9.

As explained in Chapter 9, Sundry is a miscellaneous accounts column that provides flexibility for reporting infrequent transactions that result in an inflow of cash.

Remember: There is no discount on sales tax or freight.

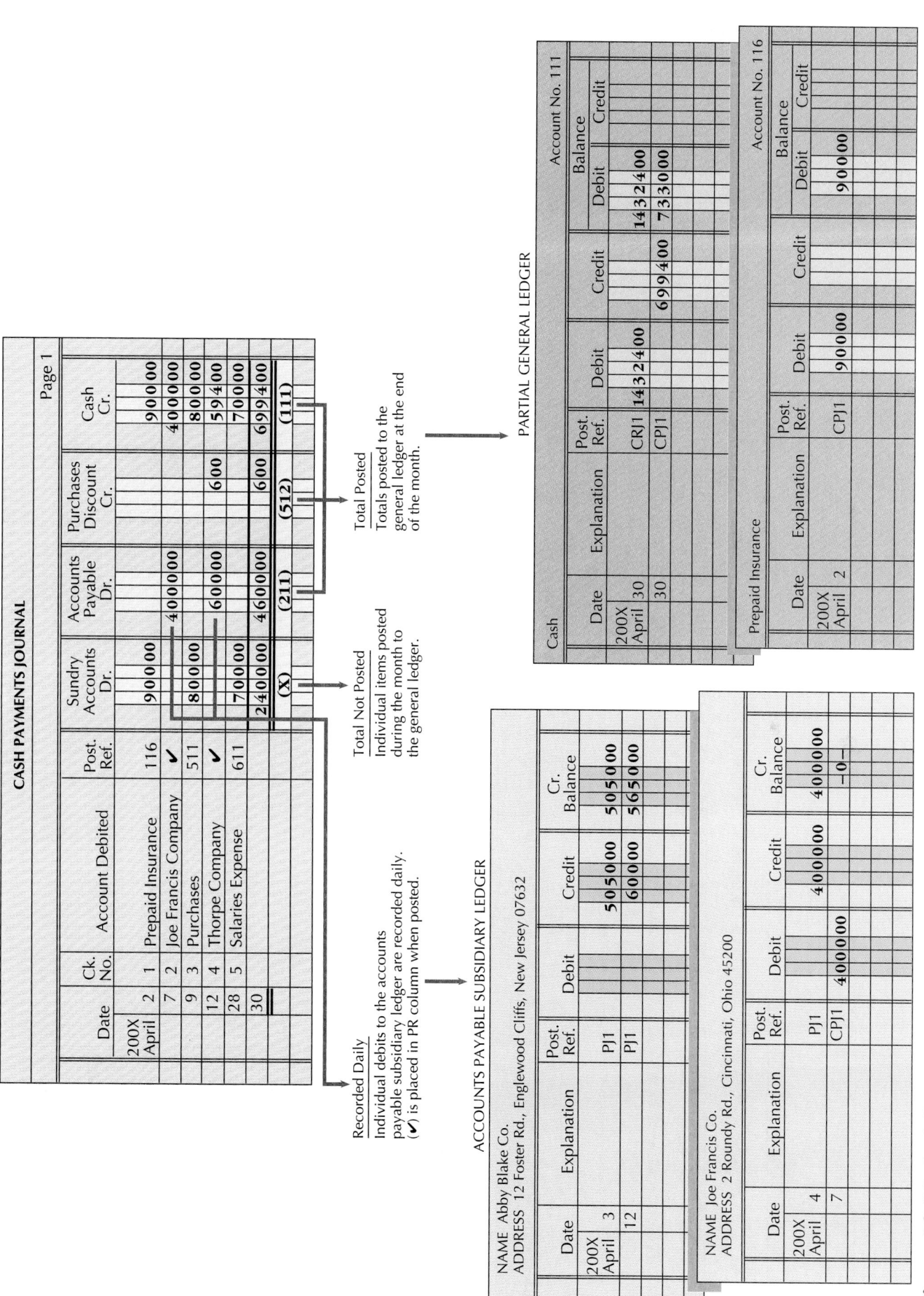

Figure 10-14 Cash Payments Journal Recording and Posting

Controlling Account

Accounts Payable   Account No. 211

Date	Explanation	Post. Ref.	Debit	Credit	Balance Debit	Balance Credit
200X April 9		GJ1	2 00 00		2 00 00	
30		PJ1		11 93 0 00		11 73 0 00
30		CPJ1	4 60 0 00			7 13 0 00

Purchases   Account No. 511

Date	Explanation	Post. Ref.	Debit	Credit	Balance Debit	Balance Credit
200X April 9		CPJ1	8 00 00		8 00 00	
30		PJ1	7 38 0 00		8 18 0 00	

Purchases Discount   Account No. 512

Date	Explanation	Post. Ref.	Debit	Credit	Balance Debit	Balance Credit
200X April 30		CPJ1		6 00		6 00

Salaries Expense   Account No. 611

Date	Explanation	Post. Ref.	Debit	Credit	Balance Debit	Balance Credit
200X April 28		CPJ1	7 00 00		7 00 00	

NAME John Sullivan Co.
ADDRESS 18 Print St., Wellesley, Mass. 01980

Date	Explanation	Post. Ref.	Debit	Credit	Cr. Balance
200X April 7		PJ1		9 80 00	9 80 00
25		PJ1		5 00 00	14 80 00

NAME Thorpe Co.
ADDRESS 3 Access Rd., Chicago, Illinois 60430

Date	Explanation	Post. Ref.	Debit	Credit	Cr. Balance
200X April 6		PJ1		8 00 00	8 00 00
9		GJ1	2 00 00		6 00 00
12		CPJ1	6 00 00		-0-

Figure 10-14 (continued)

ART'S WHOLESALE CLOTHING COMPANY SCHEDULE OF ACCOUNTS PAYABLE APRIL 30, 200X		
Abby Blake Co.		$5 6 5 0 00
John Sullivan Co.		1 4 8 0 00
Total Accounts Payable		$7 1 3 0 00

Figure 10-15
Schedule of Accounts
Payable

Payable, the **controlling account** in the general ledger, should equal the sum owed the individual creditors that are listed on the schedule of accounts payable. If it doesn't, the journalizing, posting, and recording must be checked to ensure that they are complete. Also, the balances of each title should be checked.

Trade Discounts

Trade discounts are reductions from the purchase price. Usually, they are given to customers who buy items to resell or to use to produce other salable goods.

Amount of Trade Discount = List Price − Net Price

Different trade discounts are available to different classes of customers. Often, trade discounts are listed in catalogs that contain the list price and the amount of trade discount available. Such catalogs usually are updated by discount sheets.

Trade discounts have *no relationship* to whether a customer is paying a bill early. Trade discounts and list prices are not shown in the accounts of either the purchaser or the seller. Cash discounts are not taken on the amount of trade discount.

For example, look at the following:

Trade discounts are not reflected on the books.

- List price, $800.
- 30% trade discount.
- 5% cash discount.
- Thus: Invoice cost of $560 ($800 − $240) less the cash discount of $28 ($560 × .05) results in a final cost of $532 if the cash discount is taken.

The purchaser as well as the seller would record the invoice amount at $560.

Learning Unit 10-3 Review

AT THIS POINT you should be able to

- Journalize, post, and record transactions utilizing a cash payments journal. (p. 398)
- Prepare a schedule of accounts payable. (p. 401)
- Compare and contrast a cash discount to a trade discount. (p. 401)

SELF-REVIEW QUIZ 10-3

(The forms you need are on pages 319–322 of the *Study Guide and Working Papers*.)

Given the following information, journalize, crossfoot, and, when appropriate, record and post the transactions of Melissa Company. Use the same headings as used for Art's Clothing. All purchases discounts are 2/12, n/30. The cash payments journal is page 2.

Accounts Payable Subsidiary Ledger

Name	Balance	Invoice No.
Bob Finkelstein	$300	488
Al Jeep	200	410

Partial General Ledger

Account No.	Balance
Cash 110	$700
Accounts Payable 210	500
Purchases Discount 511	—
Advertising Expense 610	—

200X

June 1 Issued check no. 15 to Al Jeep in payment of its May 25 invoice no. 410 less purchases discount.

8 Issued check no. 16 to Moss Advertising Co. to pay advertising bill due, $75, no discount.

9 Issued check no. 17 to Bob Finkelstein in payment of its May 28 invoice no. 488 less purchases discount.

SOLUTION TO SELF-REVIEW QUIZ 10-3

MELISSA COMPANY
CASH PAYMENTS JOURNAL

Page 2

Date	Ck. No.	Account Debited	Post. Ref.	Sundry Accounts Dr.	Accounts Payable Dr.	Purchases Discount Cr.	Cash Cr.
200X June 1	15	Al Jeep	✔		200 00	4 00	196 00
8	16	Advertising Expense	610	75 00			75 00
9	17	Bob Finkelstein	✔		300 00	6 00	294 00
30				75 00	500 00	10 00	565 00
				(X)	(210)	(511)	(110)

$75 + $500 = $10 + $565
$575 = $575

Figure 10-16 Cash Payments Journal

Figure 10-17
Accounts Payable
Subsidiary Ledger

ACCOUNTS PAYABLE SUBSIDIARY LEDGER

NAME Bob Finkelstein
ADDRESS 112 Flying Highway, Trenton, New Jersey 08611

Date		Explanation	Post. Ref.	Debit	Credit	Cr. Balance
200X June	1	Balance	✔			3 0 0 00
	9		CPJ2	3 0 0 00		-0-

NAME Al Jeep
ADDRESS 118 Wang Rd., Saugus, Mass. 01432

Date		Explanation	Post. Ref.	Debit	Credit	Cr. Balance
200X June	1	Balance	✔			2 0 0 00
	1		CPJ2	2 0 0 00		-0-

Figure 10-17
Accounts Payable
Subsidiary Ledger

Quiz Tip:
The normal balance of
the accounts payable
subsidiary ledger is
a credit.

PARTIAL GENERAL LEDGER

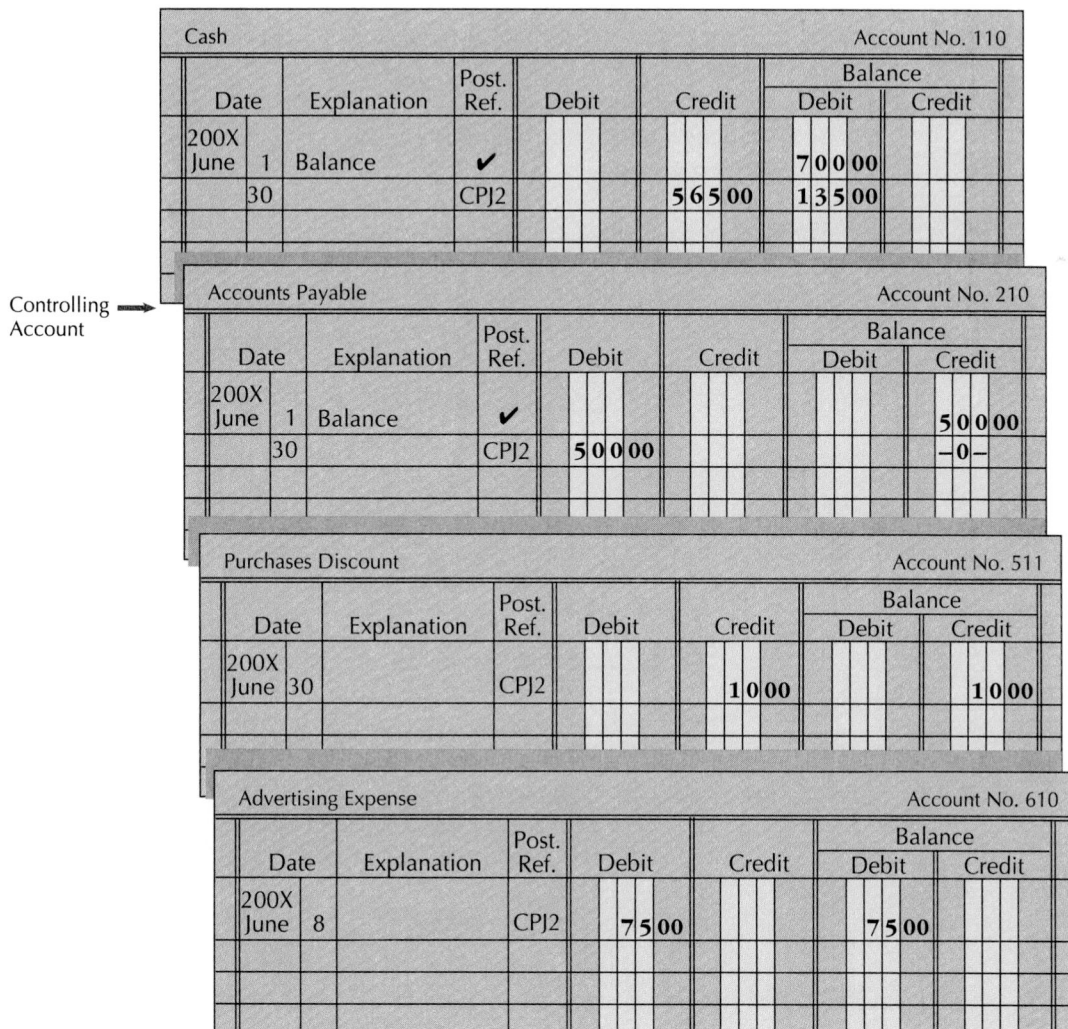

Cash   Account No. 110

Date		Explanation	Post. Ref.	Debit	Credit	Balance Debit	Balance Credit
200X June	1	Balance	✔			7 0 0 00	
	30		CPJ2		5 6 5 00	1 3 5 00	

Accounts Payable   Account No. 210

Date		Explanation	Post. Ref.	Debit	Credit	Balance Debit	Balance Credit
200X June	1	Balance	✔				5 0 0 00
	30		CPJ2	5 0 0 00			-0-

Controlling Account →

Purchases Discount   Account No. 511

Date		Explanation	Post. Ref.	Debit	Credit	Balance Debit	Balance Credit
200X June	30		CPJ2		1 0 00		1 0 00

Advertising Expense   Account No. 610

Date		Explanation	Post. Ref.	Debit	Credit	Balance Debit	Balance Credit
200X June	8		CPJ2	7 5 00		7 5 00	

Figure 10-18 Partial General Ledger

SOLUTION & TIPS TO COMPREHENSIVE PROBLEM: PUTTING THE PIECES TOGETHER

(The forms you need are on pages 322–324 of the *Study Guide and Working Papers.*)

Record the following transactions into special or general journals. Record and post as appropriate.

Note: All credit sales are 2/10, n/30. All merchandise purchased on account has 3/10, n/30 credit terms.

Solution Tips to Journalizing

200X

Mar.			
	1	J. Ling invested $2,000 into the business.	CRJ
	1	Sold merchandise on account to Balder Co., $500, invoice no. 1.	SJ
	2	Purchased merchandise on account from Case Co., $500.	PJ
	4	Sold $2,000 of merchandise for cash.	CRJ
	6	Paid Case Co. from previous purchases on account, check no. 1.	CPJ
	8	Sold merchandise on account to Lewis Co., $1,000, invoice no. 2.	SJ
	10	Received payment from Balder for invoice no. 1.	CRJ
	12	Issued a credit memorandum to Lewis Co. for $200 for faulty merchandise.	GJ
	14	Received payment from Lewis Co.	CRJ
	16	Purchased merchandise on account from Noone Co., $1,000.	PJ
	17	Purchased equipment on account from Case Co., $300.	PJ
	18	Issued a debit memorandum to Noone Co. for $500 for defective merchandise.	GJ
	20	Paid salaries, $300, check no. 2.	CPJ
	24	Paid Noone balance owed, check no. 3.	CPJ

Figure 10-19
Sales Journal

Record accounts receivable subsidiary ledger immediately.

**J. LING, CO.
SALES JOURNAL**

Page 1

Date		Account Debited	Terms	Invoice No.	PR	Dr. Acc. Rec Cr. Sales
200X Mar.	1	Balder Co.	2/10, N/30	1	✔	5 0 0 00
	8	Lewis Co.	2/10, N/30	2	✔	1 0 0 0 00
	31					1 5 0 0 00
						(112) (410)

Total posted at end of month to these accounts.

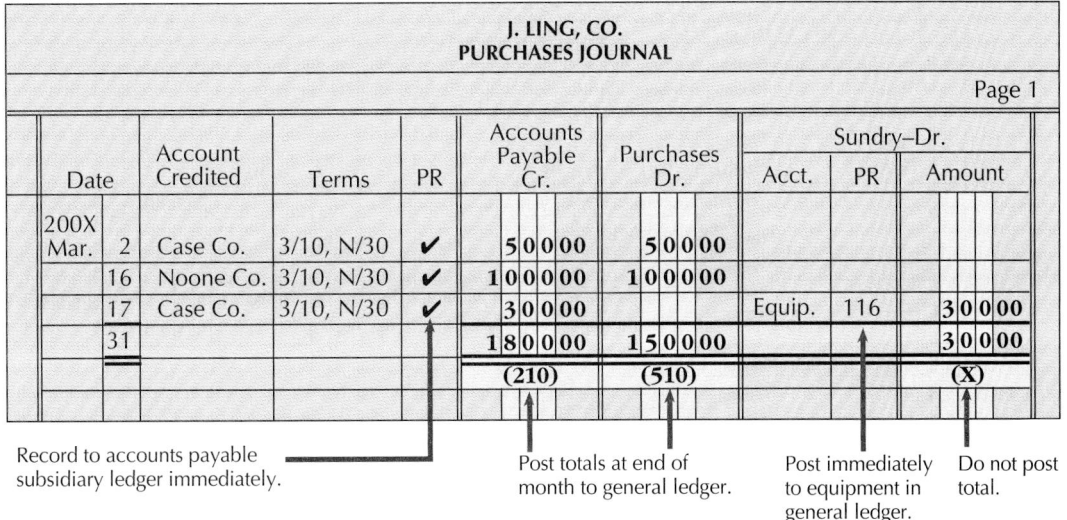

Figure 10-20 Purchases Journal

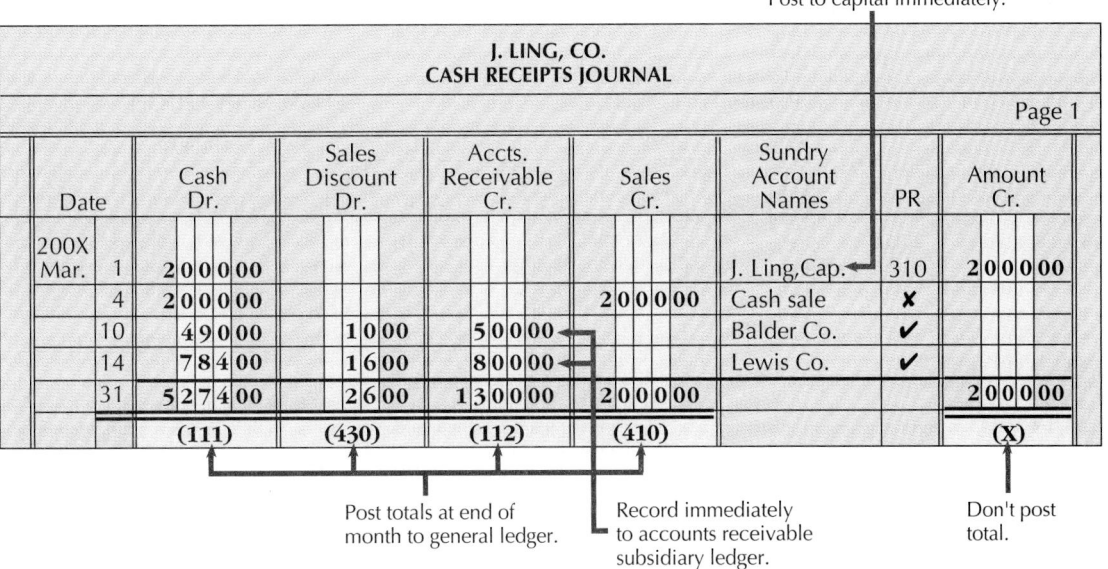

Figure 10-21 Cash Receipts Journal

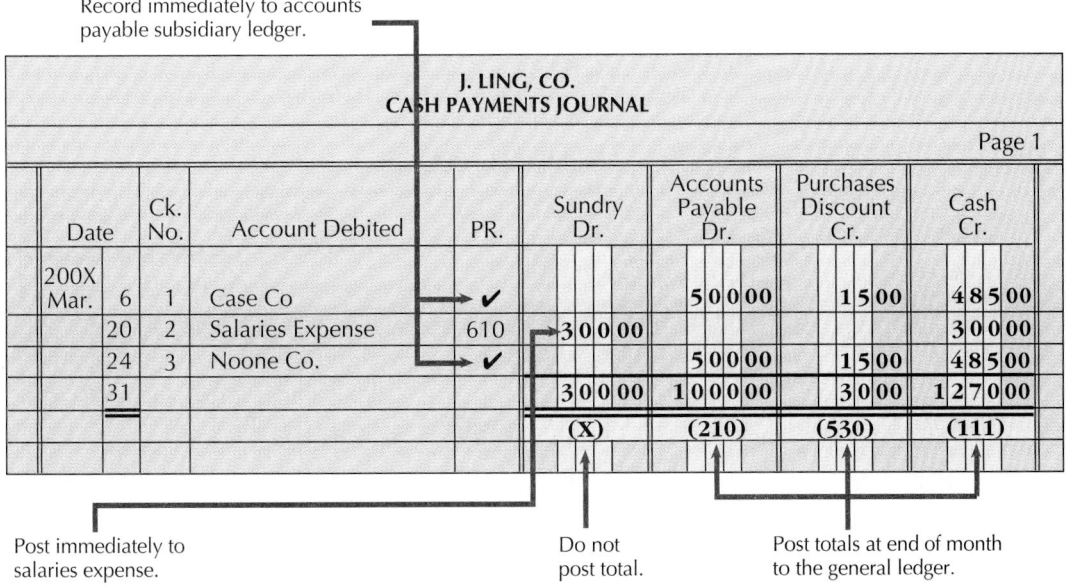

Figure 10-22 Cash Payments Journal

Figure 10-23
General Journal

		GENERAL JOURNAL						Page 1	
	Date	Account Titles and Description	PR	Dr.			Cr.		
200X Mar.	12	Sales Returns and Allowances	420	2 0 0 00					
		Accounts Receivable, Lewis Co.	112 ✓				2 0 0 00		
		Issued Credit Memo							
	18	Accounts Payable, Noone Co.	210 ✓	5 0 0 00					
		Purchases Returns and Allowances	520				5 0 0 00		
		Issued Debit Memo							

Record and post immediately to subsidiary and general ledgers.

Figure 10-24
Subsidiary and General Ledgers

ACCOUNTS RECEIVABLE SUBSIDIARY LEDGER

Balder Company

Date	PR	Dr.	Cr.	Dr. Bal.
200X 3/1	SJ1	500		500
3/10	CRJ1		500	—

Lewis Company

Date	PR	Dr.	Cr.	Dr. Bal.
200X 3/8	SJ1	1,000		1,000
3/12	GJ1		200	800
3/14	CPJ1		800	—

ACCOUNTS PAYABLE SUBSIDIARY LEDGER

Case Company

Date	PR	Dr.	Cr.	Cr. Bal.
200X 3/2	PJ1		500	500
3/6	CPJ1	500		—
3/17	PJ1		300	300

Noone Company

Date	PR	Dr.	Cr.	Cr. Bal.
200X 3/16	PJ1		1,000	1,000
3/18	GJ1	500		500
3/24	CPJ1	500		—

GENERAL LEDGER

Cash 111

3/31 CRJ1 5,274	1,270 3/31 CPJ1
Balance 4,004	

Sales 410

	1,500 3/31 SJ1
	2,000 3/31 CRJ1
	3,500 Balance

Accounts Receivable 112

3/31 SJ1 1,500	200 3/12 GJ1
Balance 0	1,300 3/31 CRJ1

Sales Returns + Allowances 420

3/12 GJ1 200	

Equipment 116

3/17 PJ1 300	

Sales Discount 430

3/31 CRJ1 26	

Accounts Payable 210				Purchases 510	
3/18 GJ1	500	1,800 3/31 PJ1	3/31 PJ1	1,500	
3/31 CPJ1	1,000	300 Balance			

J. Ling, Capital 310		Purchase Ret. + Allow. 520	
	2,000 3/1 CRJ1		500 3/18 GJ1

Purchase Discount 530	
	30 3/31 CPJ1

Salaries Expense 610	
3/20 CPJ1 300	

Summary of Solution Tips

Chapter 9: Seller	**Chapter 10: Buyer**
Sales journal	Purchases journal
Cash receipts journal	Cash payments journal
Accounts receivable subsidiary ledger	Accounts payable subsidiary ledger
Sales (Cr.)	Purchases (Dr.)
Sales Returns + Allowances (Dr.)	Purchase Returns + Allowances (Cr.)
Sales Discounts (Dr.)	Purchase Discounts (Cr.)
Accounts Receivable (Dr.)	Accounts Payable (Cr.)
Issue a credit memo	Receive a credit memo
or	or
Receive a debit memo	Issue a debit memo
Schedule of accounts receivable	Schedule of accounts payable

When Do I Do What? A Step-by-Step Walk-Through of This Comprehensive Problem

Transaction   What to Do Step-by-Step

200X

Mar.

1   *Money Received:* Record in cash receipts journal. Post immediately to J. Ling, Capital, because it is in Sundry.

1   *Sale on Account:* Record in sales journal. Record immediately to Balder Co. in accounts receivable subsidiary ledger. Place a ✓ in PR column of sales journal when subsidiary is updated.

2   *Buy Merchandise on Account:* Record in purchases journal. Record to Case Co. immediately in the accounts payable subsidiary ledger.

4   *Money In:* Record in cash receipts journal. No posting needed (put an × in PR column).

6   *Money Out:* Record in cash payments journal. Save $15, which is a Purchases Discount. Record immediately to Case Co. in accounts payable subsidiary ledger (the full amount of $500).

8   *Sales on Account:* Record in sales journal. Update immediately to Lewis in accounts receivable subsidiary ledger.

10 *Money In:* Record in cash receipts journal. Because Balder pays within 10 days, it gets a $10 discount. Record the full amount immediately to Balder in the accounts receivable subsidiary ledger.

Transaction   What to Do Step-by-Step

12   *Returns:* Record in general journal. Seller issues credit memo resulting in higher sales returns and customers owing less. All postings and recordings are done immediately.

14   *Money In:* Record in cash receipts journal:

$$\$1,000 - \$200 \text{ returns} = \$800$$
$$\underline{\times .02}$$
$$\$\ 16 \text{ discount}$$

Record immediately the $800 to Lewis in the accounts receivable subsidiary ledger.

16   *Buy Now, Pay Later:* Record in purchases journal. Record immediately to Noone Co. in the accounts payable subsidiary ledger.

17   *Buy Now, Pay Later:* Record in purchases journal in Sundry. This item is not merchandise for resale. Record and post immediately.

18   *Returns:* Record in general ledger. Buyer issues a debit memo reducing the Accounts Payable due to Purchases Return and Allowances. Post and record immediately.

20   *Salaries:* Record in cash payments journal, sundry column. Post immediately to Salaries Expense.

24   *Money Out:* Record in cash payments journal. Save 3% ($15), a Purchases Discount. Record immediately to accounts payable subsidiary ledger that you reduce Noone by $500.

End of Month:

Post totals (except Sundry) of special journal to the general ledger.

Note: In this problem at the end of the month, (1) Accounts Receivable in the general ledger, the controlling account, has a zero balance, as does each title in the accounts receivable subsidiary ledger; and (2) the balance in Accounts Payable (the controlling account) is $300. In the accounts payable subsidiary ledger, we owe Case $300. The sum of the accounts payable subsidiary ledger does equal the balance in the controlling account at the end of the month.

Summary of Key Points

Learning Unit 10-1

1. Purchases are merchandise for resale. It is a cost.
2. Purchases Returns and Allowances and Purchases Discount are contra-costs.
3. *F.O.B. shipping point* means that the purchaser of the goods is responsible for covering the shipping costs. If the terms were *F.O.B. destination,* the seller would be responsible for covering the shipping costs until the goods reached their destination.
4. Purchases discounts are not taken on freight.

Learning Unit 10-2

1. The steps for buying merchandise from a company may include the following:
   a. The requesting department prepares a purchase requisition.
   b. The purchasing department prepares a purchase order.
   c. Seller receives the order and prepares a sales invoice (a purchase invoice for the buyer).

    d. Buyer receives the goods and prepares a receiving report.

    e. Accounting department verifies and approves the invoice for payment.

2. The purchases journal records the buying of merchandise or other items on account.
3. The accounts payable subsidiary ledger, organized in alphabetical order, is not in the same book as Accounts Payable, the controlling account in the general ledger.
4. At the end of the month the total of all creditors' ending balances in the accounts payable subsidiary ledger should equal the ending balance in Accounts Payable, the controlling account in the general ledger.
5. A debit memorandum (issued by the buyer) indicates that the amount owed from a previous purchase is being reduced because some goods were defective or not up to a specific standard and thus were returned or an allowance requested. On receiving the debit memorandum, the seller will issue a credit memorandum.

Learning Unit 10-3

1. All payments of cash (check) are recorded in the cash payments journal.
2. At the end of the month, the schedule of accounts payable, a list of ending amounts owed individual creditors, should equal the ending balance in Accounts Payable, the controlling account in the general ledger.
3. Trade discounts are deductions off the list price that have nothing to do with early payments (cash discounts). Invoice amounts are recorded *after* the trade discount is deducted. Cash discounts are not taken on trade discounts.

Key Terms

Accounts payable subsidiary ledger A book or file that contains in alphabetical order the name of the creditor and amount owed from purchases on account.

Cash payments journal (cash disbursements journal) A special journal that records all transactions involving the payment of cash.

Controlling account The account in the general ledger that summarizes or controls a subsidiary ledger. Example: The Accounts Payable account in the general ledger is the controlling account for the accounts payable subsidiary ledger. After postings are complete, it shows the total amount owed from purchases made on account.

Debit memorandum A memo issued by a purchaser to a seller, indicating that some Purchases Returns and Allowances have occurred and therefore the purchaser now owes less money on account.

F.O.B. Free on board, which means without shipping charge either to the buyer or seller up to or from a specified location. In the view of one or the other, the shipment is *free* on board the carrier.

F.O.B. destination *Seller* pays or is responsible for the cost of freight to purchaser's location or destination.

F.O.B. shipping point *Purchaser* pays or is responsible for the shipping costs from seller's shipping point to purchaser's location.

Invoice approval form Used by the accounting department in checking the invoice and finally approving it for recording and payment.

Purchase invoice The seller's sales invoice, which is sent to the purchaser.

Purchase order A form used in business to place an order for the buying of goods from a seller.

Purchase requisition A form used within a business by the requesting department asking the purchasing department of the business to buy specific goods.

Purchases Merchandise for resale. It is a cost.

Purchases Discount A contra-cost account in the general ledger that records discounts offered by suppliers of merchandise for prompt payment of purchases by buyers.

Purchases journal A multicolumn special journal that records the buying of merchandise or other items on account.

Purchases Returns and Allowances A contra-cost account in the ledger that records the amount of defective or unacceptable merchandise returned to suppliers and/or price reductions given for defective items.

Receiving report A business form used to notify the appropriate people of the ordered goods received along with the quantities and specific condition of the goods.

Questions, Mini Exercises, Exercises, and Problems

Discussion Questions

1. Explain how net purchases is calculated.
2. What is the normal balance of Purchases Discount?
3. What is a contra-cost?
4. Explain the difference between F.O.B. shipping point and F.O.B. destination.
5. F.O.B. destination means that title to the goods will switch to the buyer when goods are shipped. Agree or disagree. Why?
6. What is the normal balance of each creditor in the accounts payable subsidiary ledger?
7. Why doesn't the balance of the controlling account, Accounts Payable, equal the sum of the accounts payable subsidiary ledger during the month?
8. What is the relationship between a purchase requisition and a purchase order?
9. What purpose could a typical invoice approval form serve?
10. Explain the difference between merchandise and equipment.
11. Why would the purchaser issue a debit memorandum?
12. Explain the relationship between a purchases journal and a cash payments journal.
13. Explain why a trade discount is not a cash discount.

Mini Exercises

(The forms you need are on page 326 of the *Study Guide and Working Papers.*)

Overview

1. Complete the following table:

To the Seller		To the Buyer
Sales	↔	a. _____
Sales Returns and Allowances	↔	b. _____
Sales discount	↔	c. _____
Sales journal	↔	d. _____
Cash receipts journal	↔	e. _____
Credit memorandum	↔	f. _____
Schedule of accounts receivable	↔	g. _____
Accounts receivable subsidiary ledger	↔	h. _____

Blueprint: Purchases and Cash Payments Journals

Purchase of Merchandise or Other Items on Account

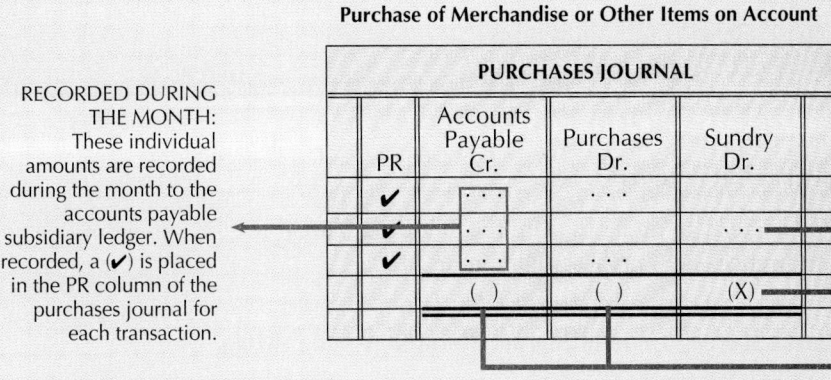

RECORDED DURING THE MONTH: These individual amounts are recorded during the month to the accounts payable subsidiary ledger. When recorded, a (✔) is placed in the PR column of the purchases journal for each transaction.

POSTED WHEN TRANSACTION IS ENTERED: Posted to general ledger account when transaction is entered.

The total of sundry is never posted.

END OF MONTH: These totals are posted to the general ledger accounts at the end of the month. Examples: Accounts Payable, Purchases.

Issuing a Debit Memo (or Receiving a Credit Memo)

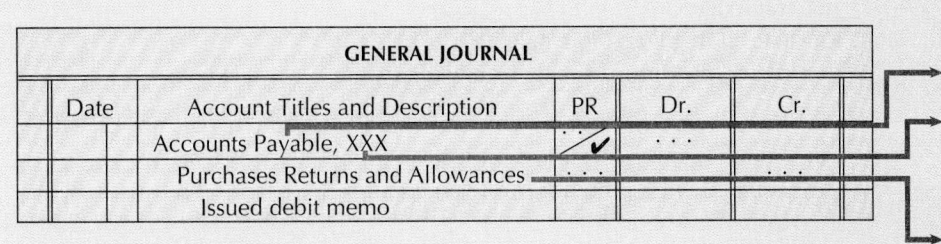

POSTED AND RECORDED WHEN TRANSACTION IS ENTERED: Two postings and one recording:
1. Posted to Accounts Payable in the general ledger.
2. Recorded to XXX in the accounts payable subsidiary ledger. A (✔) indicates recording to the accounts payable subsidiary ledger is complete.
3. Posted to Purchases Returns and Allowances in general ledger.

Outward Flow of Cash

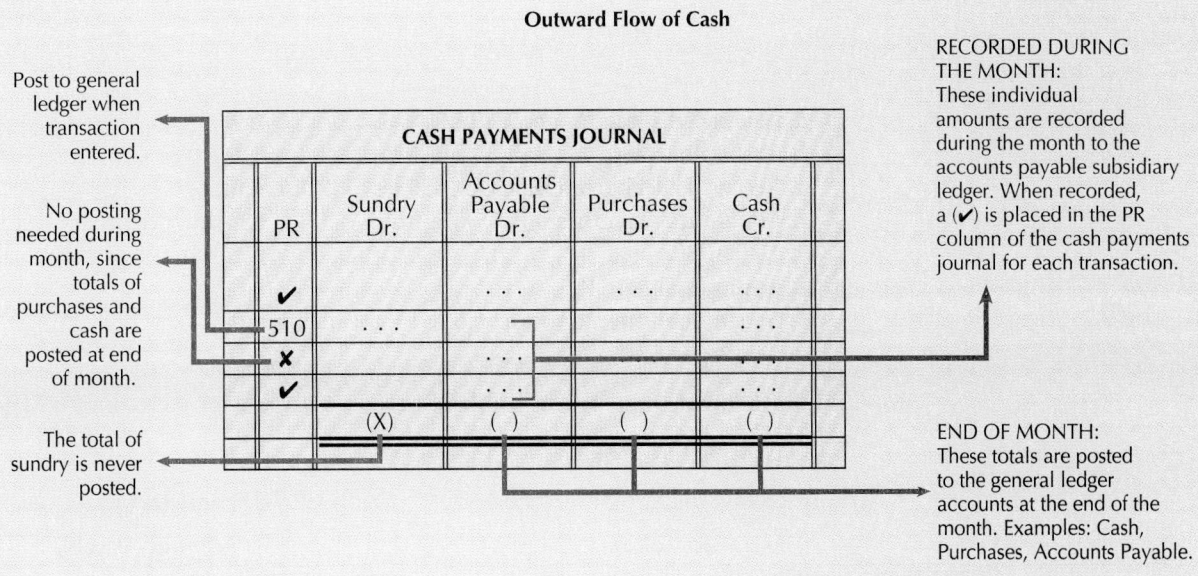

Post to general ledger when transaction entered.

No posting needed during month, since totals of purchases and cash are posted at end of month.

The total of sundry is never posted.

RECORDED DURING THE MONTH: These individual amounts are recorded during the month to the accounts payable subsidiary ledger. When recorded, a (✔) is placed in the PR column of the cash payments journal for each transaction.

END OF MONTH: These totals are posted to the general ledger accounts at the end of the month. Examples: Cash, Purchases, Accounts Payable.

2. Complete the following table:

	Category	↑	↓	Temporary or Permanent
Purchases				
Purchases Returns and Allowances				
Purchases Discount				

Calculating Net Purchases

3. Calculate Net Purchases from the following: Purchases, $8; Purchases Returns and Allowances, $3; Purchases Discounts, $1.

Purchases Journal, General Journal, Recording, and Posting

4. Match the following to the three journal entries (more than one number can be used).

  1. Journalized into purchases journal.
  2. Record immediately to subsidiary ledger.
  3. Post totals from purchases journal (except sundry total) at end of month to general ledger.
  4. Journalized in general journal.
  5. Record and post immediately to subsidiary and general ledgers.

   a. Bought merchandise on account from Ryan.com, invoice no. 12, $40.
   b. Bought equipment on account from Jone Co., invoice no. 13, $75.
   c. Issued debit memo no. 1 to Ryan.com for merchandise returned, $7, from invoice no. 12.

Recording Transactions in Special Journals

5. Indicate in which journal each transaction will be journalized:

1. SJ	**4.** CPJ
2. PJ	**5.** GJ
3. CRJ	

_____ **a.** Issued credit memo no. 2, $29.
_____ **b.** Cash sales, $180.
_____ **c.** Received check from Blue Co., $50 less 3% discount.
_____ **d.** Bought merchandise on account from Mel Co., $35, invoice no. 20, terms 1/10, n/30.
_____ **e.** Cash purchase, $15.
_____ **f.** Issued debit memo to Mel Co., $15, for merchandise returned from invoice no. 20.

6. From the following prepare a schedule of Accounts Payable for Web.com for May 31, 200X:

Accounts Payable Subsidiary Ledger

Rowe Co.

			5/7	PJ1	60

Bloss Co

5/25	CPJ1	10	5/20	PJ1	50

General Ledger

Accounts Payable

5/31	CPJ	10	5/31	PJ1	110

Exercises

(The forms you need are on pages 327–329 of the *Study Guide and Working Papers*.)

10-1. From the purchases journal in Figure 10-25, record to the accounts payable subsidiary ledger and post to general ledger accounts as appropriate.

Recording to the accounts payable subsidiary ledger and posting to the general ledger from a purchases journal.

PURCHASES JOURNAL

			Date of Invoice	Terms	Post Ref.	Accounts Payable Credit	Purchases Debit	Sundry-Dr.		
Date		Account Credited						Account	PR	Amount
200X June	3	Rey.com	May 3	1/10, n/30		8 0 0 00	8 0 0 00			
	4	Lane.com	May 4	n/10, EOM		9 0 0 00	9 0 0 00			
	8	Sail.com	May 8			4 0 0 00		Equipment		4 0 0 00

Page 1

Figure 10-25 Purchases Journal

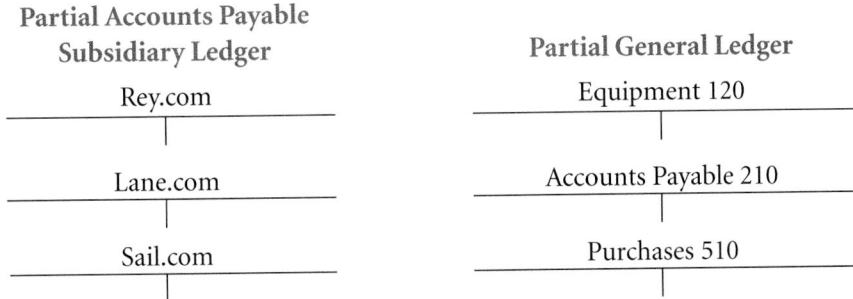

Partial Accounts Payable Subsidiary Ledger

Rey.com

Lane.com

Sail.com

Partial General Ledger

Equipment 120

Accounts Payable 210

Purchases 510

10-2. On July 10, 200X, Aster Co. issued debit memorandum no. 1 for $400 to Reel Co. for merchandise returned from invoice no. 312. Your task is to journalize, record, and post this transaction as appropriate. Use the same account numbers as found in the text for Art's Wholesale Clothing Company. The general journal is page 1.

Journalizing, recording, and posting a debit memorandum.

10-3. Journalize, record, and post when appropriate the following transactions into the cash payments journal (p. 2) for Morgan's Clothing. Use the same headings as found in the text (p. 398). All purchases discounts are 2/10, n/30.

Journalizing, recording, and posting a cash payments journal.

Accounts Payable Subsidiary Ledger

Name	Balance	Invoice No.
A. James	$1,000	522
B. Foss	400	488
J. Ranch	900	562
B. Swanson	100	821

Partial General Ledger

Account	Balance
Cash 110	$3,000
Accounts Payable 210	2,400
Purchases Discount 511	
Advertising Expense 610	

200X

Apr. 1 Issued check no. 20 to A. James Company in payment of its March 28 invoice no. 522.

      8 Issued check no. 21 to Flott Advertising in payment of its advertising bill, $100, no discount.

      15 Issued check no. 22 to B. Foss in payment of its March 25 invoice no. 488.

10-4. From Exercise 10-3, prepare a schedule of accounts payable and verify that the total of the schedule equals the amount in the controlling account.

10-5. Record the following transaction in a transaction analysis chart for the buyer: Bought merchandise for $9,000 on account. Shipping terms were F.O.B. destination. The cost of shipping was $500.

10-6. Angie Rase bought merchandise with a list price of $4,000. Angie was entitled to a 30% trade discount as well as a 3% cash discount. What was Angie's actual cost of buying this merchandise after the cash discount?

Group A Problems

(The forms you need are on pages 330–351 of the *Study Guide and Working Papers*.)

10A-1. Abby Kim recently opened Skates.com. As the bookkeeper of her company, please journalize, record, and post when appropriate the following transactions (account numbers are Store Supplies, 115; Store Equipment, 121; Accounts Payable, 210; Purchases, 510):

200X

June 4 Bought $700 of merchandise on account from Mail.com, invoice no. 442, dated June 5, terms 2/10, n/30.

      5 Bought $4,000 of store equipment from Norton Co., invoice no. 502, dated June 6.

      8 Bought $1,400 of merchandise on account from Rolo Co., invoice no. 401, dated June 9, terms 2/10, n/30.

      14 Bought $900 of store supplies on account from Mail.com, invoice no. 419, dated June 14.

10A-2. Mabel's Natural Food Store uses a purchases journal (p. 10) and a general journal (p. 2) to record the following transactions (continued from April):

200X

May 8 Purchased $600 of merchandise on account from Aton Co., invoice no. 400, dated May 9, terms 2/10, n/60.

      10 Purchased $1,200 of merchandise on account from Broward Co., invoice no. 420, dated May 11, terms 2/10, n/60.

      12 Purchased $500 of store supplies on account from Midden Co., invoice no. 510, dated May 13.

      14 Issued debit memo no. 8 to Aton Co. for merchandise returned, $400, from invoice no. 400.

      17 Purchased $560 of office equipment on account from Relar Co., invoice no. 810, dated May 18.

      24 Purchased $650 of additional store supplies on account from Midden Co., invoice no. 516, dated May 25, terms 2/10, n/30.

The food store has decided to keep a separate column for the purchases of supplies in the purchases journal. Your tasks are to

1. Journalize the transactions.
2. Post and record as appropriate.
3. Prepare a schedule of accounts payable.

Accounts Payable
Subsidiary Ledger

Name	Balance
Aton Co.	$400
Broward Co.	600
Midden Co.	1,200
Relar Co.	500

Partial General Ledger

Account	Number	Balance
Store Supplies	110	$ —
Office Equipment	120	—
Accounts Payable	210	2,700
Purchases	510	16,000
Purchases Returns and Allowances	512	—

10A-3. Wendy Jones operates a wholesale computer center. All transactions requiring the payment of cash are recorded in the cash payments journal (p. 5). The account balances as of May 1, 200X, are as follows:

Journalizing, recording, and posting a cash payments journal. Preparing a schedule of accounts payable.

Accounts Payable
Subsidiary Ledger

Name	Balance
Alvin Co.	$1,200
Henry Co.	600
Soy Co.	800
Xon Co.	1,400

Partial General Ledger

Account	Number	Balance
Cash	110	$17,000
Delivery Truck	150	—
Accounts Payable	210	4,000
Computer Purchases	510	—
Computer Purchases Discount	511	—
Rent Expense	610	—
Utilities Expense	620	—

*Check Figure:
Total of Schedule of
Accounts Payable $1,900*

Your tasks are to

1. Journalize the following transactions.
2. Record to the accounts payable subsidiary ledger and post to the general ledger as appropriate.
3. Prepare a schedule of accounts payable.

200X

May 1 Paid half the amount owed Henry Co. from previous purchases of appliances on account, less a 2% purchases discount, check no. 21.

3 Bought a delivery truck for $8,000 cash, check no. 22, payable to Bill Ring Co.

6   Bought computer merchandise from Lectro Co.,
check no. 23, $2,900.

18   Bought additional computer merchandise from Pulse Co.,
check no. 24, $800.

24   Paid Xon Co. the amount owed less a 2% purchases discount,
check no. 25.

28   Paid rent expense to King's Realty Trust, check no. 26, $2,000.

29   Paid utilities expense to Stone Utility Co., check no. 27, $300.

30   Paid half the amount owed Soy Co., no discount, check no. 28.

Comprehensive Problem: All special journals and the general journal. Schedule of accounts payable and accounts receivable.

10A-4. Abby Ellen opened Abby's Toy House. As her newly hired accountant, your tasks are to

1. Journalize the transactions for the month of March.
2. Record to subsidiary ledgers and post to the general ledger as appropriate.
3. Total and rule the journals.
4. Prepare a schedule of accounts receivable and a schedule of accounts payable.

The following is the partial chart of accounts for Abby's Toy House:

Abby's Toy House Chart of Accounts

Assets		Revenue	
110	Cash	410	Toy Sales
112	Accounts Receivable	412	Sales Returns and Allowances
114	Prepaid Rent	414	Sales Discounts
121	Delivery Truck	**Cost of Goods**	
Liabilities		510	Toy Purchases
210	Accounts Payable	512	Purchases Returns and Allowances
Owner's Equity		514	Purchases Discount
310	A. Ellen, Capital	**Expenses**	
		610	Salaries Expense
		612	Cleaning Expense

Check Figures:
Total of Schedule of accounts receivable $7,600
Total of schedule of accounts payable $9,000

200X

Mar.

1   Abby Ellen invested $8,000 in the toy store.

1   Paid three months' rent in advance, check no. 1, $3,000.

1   Purchased merchandise from Earl Miller Company on account, $4,000, invoice no. 410, dated March 2, terms 2/10, n/30.

3   Sold merchandise to Bill Burton on account, $1,000, invoice no. 1, terms 2/10, n/30.

6   Sold merchandise to Jim Rex on account, $700, invoice no. 2, terms 2/10, n/30.

8   Purchased merchandise from Earl Miller Co. on account, $1,200, invoice no. 415, dated March 9, terms 2/10, n/30.

9   Sold merchandise to Bill Burton on account, $600, invoice no. 3, terms 2/10, n/30.

9   Paid cleaning service, check no. 2, $300.

10   Jim Rex returned merchandise that cost $300 to Abby's Toy House. Abby issued credit memorandum no. 1 to Jim Rex for $300.

10   Purchased merchandise from Minnie Katz on account, $4,000, invoice no. 311, dated March 11, terms 1/15, n/60.

12   Paid Earl Miller Co. invoice no. 410, dated March 2, check no. 3.

13   Sold $1,300 of toy merchandise for cash.

13   Paid salaries, $600, check no. 4.

14   Returned merchandise to Minnie Katz in the amount of $1,000. Abby's Toy House issued debit memorandum no. 1 to Minnie Katz.

15   Sold merchandise for $4,000 cash.

16 Received payment from Jim Rex, invoice no. 2 (less returned merchandise) less discount.

16 Bill Burton paid invoice no. 1.

16 Sold toy merchandise to Amy Rose on account, $4,000, invoice no. 4, terms 2/10, n/30.

20 Purchased delivery truck on account from Sam Katz Garage, $3,000, invoice no. 111, dated March 21 (no discount).

22 Sold to Bill Burton merchandise on account, $900, invoice no. 5, terms 2/10, n/30.

23 Paid Minnie Katz balance owed, check no. 5.

24 Sold toy merchandise on account to Amy Rose, $1,100, invoice no. 6, terms 2/10, n/30.

25 Purchased toy merchandise, $600, check no. 6.

26 Purchased toy merchandise from Woody Smith on account, $4,800, invoice no. 211, dated March 27, terms 2/10, n/30.

28 Bill Burton paid invoice no. 5, dated March 22.

28 Amy Rose paid invoice no. 6, dated March 24.

28 Abby invested an additional $5,000 in the business.

28 Purchased merchandise from Earl Miller Co., $1,400, invoice no. 436, dated March 29, terms 2/10, n/30.

30 Paid Earl Miller Co. invoice no. 436, check no. 7.

30 Sold merchandise to Bonnie Flow Company on account, $3,000, invoice no. 7, terms 2/10, n/30.

Group B Problems

(The forms you need are on pages 330–351 of the *Study Guide and Working Papers*.)

Journalizing, recording, and posting a purchases journal.

10B-1. From the following transactions of Abby Kim's Skate.com, journalize in the purchases journal and record and post as appropriate:

200X

June 4 Bought merchandise on account from Rolo Co., invoice no. 400, dated June 5, $1,800, terms 2/10, n/30.

5 Bought store equipment from Norton Co., invoice no. 518, dated June 6, $6,000.

8 Bought merchandise on account from Mail.com, invoice no. 411, dated June 5, $400, terms 2/10, n/30.

14 Bought store supplies on account from Mail.com, invoice no. 415, dated June 13, $1,200.

Check Figure:
Total of purchases column $2,200

10B-2. As the accountant of Mabel's Natural Food Store (1) journalize the following transactions into the purchases (p. 10) or general journal (p. 2), (2) record and post as appropriate, and (3) prepare a schedule of accounts payable. Beginning balances are in the *Study Guide and Working Papers.*

Journalizing, recording, and posting a purchases journal as well as recording the issuing of a debit memorandum and preparing a schedule of accounts payable.

200X

May 8 Purchased merchandise on account from Broward Co., invoice no. 420, dated May 9, $500, terms 2/10, n/60.

10 Purchased merchandise on account from Aton Co., invoice no. 400, dated May 11, $900, terms 2/10, n/60.

12 Purchased store supplies on account from Midden Co., invoice no. 510, dated May 13, $700.

14 Issued debit memo no. 7 to Aton Co. for merchandise returned, $400, from invoice no. 400.

Check Figure:
Total of schedule of accounts payable $6,000

    17   Purchased office equipment on account from Relar Co., invoice no. 810, dated May 18, $750.

    24   Purchased additional store supplies on account from Midden Co., invoice no. 516, dated May 25, $850.

Journalizing, recording, and posting a cash payments journal. Preparing a schedule of accounts payable.

10B-3. Wendy Jones has hired you as her bookkeeper to record the following transactions in the cash payments journal. She would like you to record and post as appropriate and supply her with a schedule of accounts payable. (Beginning balances are in your workbook or Problem 10A-3, p. 415 in the text.)

Check Figure:
Total of schedule of accounts payable $1,900

200X
May   1   Bought a delivery truck for $8,000 cash, check no. 21, payable to Randy Rosse Co.

    3   Paid half the amount owed Henry Co. from previous purchases of computer merchandise on account, less a 5% purchases discount, check no. 22.

    6   Bought computer merchandise from Jane Co. for $900 cash, check no. 23.

    18   Bought additional computer merchandise from Jane Co., check no. 24, $1,000.

    24   Paid Xon Co. the amount owed less a 5% purchases discount, check no. 25.

    28   Paid rent expense to Regan Realty Trust, check no. 26, $3,000.

    29   Paid half the amount owed Soy Co., no discount, check no. 27.

    30   Paid utilities expense to French Utility, check no. 28, $425.

10B-4. As the new accountant for Abby's Toy House, your tasks are to

  1. Journalize the transactions for the month of March.

  2. Record to subsidiary ledgers and post to the general ledger as appropriate.

  3. Total and rule the journals.

  4. Prepare a schedule of accounts receivable and a schedule of accounts payable.

(Use the same chart of accounts as in Problem 10A-4, p. 416. Your *Study Guide and Working Papers* has all the forms you need to complete this problem.)

Check Figures:
Total of schedule of accounts receivable $9,900
Total of schedule of accounts payable $9,200

200X
Mar.   1   Abby invested $4,000 in the new toy store.

    1   Paid two months' rent in advance, check no. 1, $1,000.

    1   Purchased merchandise from Earl Miller Company, invoice no. 410, dated March 2, $6,000, terms 2/10, n/30.

    3   Sold merchandise to Bill Burton on account, $1,600, invoice no. 1, terms 2/10, n/30.

    6   Sold merchandise to Jim Rex on account, $800, invoice no. 2, terms 2/10, n/30.

    8   Purchased merchandise from Earl Miller Company, $800, invoice no. 415, dated March 9, terms 2/10, n/30.

    9   Sold merchandise to Bill Burton on account, $700, invoice no. 3, terms 2/10, n/30.

    9   Paid cleaning service, $400, check no. 2.

    10   Jim Rex returned merchandise that cost $200 to Abby. Abby issued credit memorandum no. 1 to Jim Rex for $200.

    10   Purchased merchandise from Minnie Katz, $7,000, invoice no. 311, dated March 11, terms 1/15, n/60.

    12   Paid Earl Miller Co. invoice no. 410, dated March 2, check no. 3.

    13   Sold $1,500 of toy merchandise for cash.

    13   Paid salaries, $700, check no. 4.

    14   Returned merchandise to Minnie Katz in the amount of $500. Abby issued debit memorandum no. 1 to Minnie Katz.

    15   Sold merchandise for cash, $4,800.

    16   Received payment from Jim Rex for invoice no. 2 (less returned merchandise) less discount.

16   Bill Burton paid invoice no. 1.

16   Sold toy merchandise to Amy Rose on account, $6,000, invoice no. 4, terms 2/10, n/30.

20   Purchased delivery truck on account from Sam Katz Garage, $2,500, invoice no. 111, dated March 21 (no discount).

22   Sold to Bill Burton merchandise on account, $2,000, invoice no. 5, terms 2/10, n/30.

23   Paid Minnie Katz balance owed, check no. 5.

24   Sold toy merchandise on account to Amy Rose, $2,000, invoice no. 6, terms 2/10, n/30.

25   Purchased toy merchandise, $800, check no. 6.

26   Purchased toy merchandise from Woody Smith on account, $5,900, invoice no. 211, dated March 27, terms 2/10, n/30.

28   Bill Burton paid invoice no. 5, dated March 22.

28   Amy Rose paid invoice no. 6, dated March 24.

28   Abby invested an additional $3,000 in the business.

28   Purchased merchandise from Earl Miller Co., $4,200, invoice no. 436, dated March 29, terms 2/10, n/30.

30   Paid Earl Miller Co. invoice no. 436, check no. 7.

30   Sold merchandise to Bonnie Flow Company on account, $3,200, invoice no. 7, terms 2/10, n/30.

Real-World Applications

10R-1. Angie Co. bought merchandise for $1,000 with credit terms of 2/10, n/30. Owing to the bookkeeper's incompetence, the 2% cash discount was missed. The bookkeeper told Pete Angie, the owner, not to get excited. After all, it was a $20 discount that was missed, not hundreds of dollars. Could you please act as Mr. Angie's assistant and show the bookkeeper that his $20 represents a sizable equivalent interest cost? In your calculation assume a 360-day year. Make some written recommendations so that this situation will not happen again.

10R-2. Jeff Ryan completed an Accounting I course and was recently hired as the bookkeeper of Spring Co. The special journals have not been posted, nor are Dr. and Cr. used on the column headings. Please assist Jeff by marking, in Figure 10-26, the Dr. and Cr. headings as well as setting up and posting to the general ledger and recording to the subsidiary ledger. (Only post or record the amounts, because no chart of accounts is provided.) Make some written recommendations on how a new computer system may lessen the need for posting.

Hint: $R = \dfrac{I}{PT}$

YOU make the call

Critical Thinking/Ethical Case

10R-3. Spring Co. bought merchandise from All Co. with terms 2/10, n/30. Joanne Ring, the bookkeeper, forgot to pay the bill within the first 10 days. She went to Mel Ryan, head accountant, who told her to backdate the check so that it looked like the bill was paid within the discount period. Joanne told Mel that she thought they could get away with it. Should Joanne and Mel backdate the check to take advantage of the discount? You make the call. Write down your specific recommendations to Joanne.

Figure 10-26
Special and General
Journals

SALES JOURNAL		
Account	PR	
Blue Co.		4 8 0 0 00
Jon Co.		5 6 0 0 00
Roff Co.		6 4 0 0 00
Totals		16 8 0 0 00

PURCHASES JOURNAL		
Account	PR	
Ralph Co.		4 0 0 0 00
Sos Co.		6 0 0 0 00
Jingle Co.		8 0 0 0 00
Totals		18 0 0 0 00

GENERAL JOURNAL			
Sales Returns and Allowances		1 6 0 0 00	
Accounts Receivable, Jon Co.			1 6 0 0 00
Customer returned merchandise			
Accounts Payable, Jingle Co.		8 0 0 00	
Purchases, Returns, and Allowances			8 0 0 00
Returned defective merchandise			

CASH RECEIPTS JOURNAL*						
Cash Dr.	Sales Discount Dr.	Accounts Receivable Cr.	Sales Cr.	Sundry-Dr.		
				Account Name	PR	Amount Cr.
4 7 0 4 00	9 6 00	4 8 0 0 00		Blue Co.		
1 9 6 0 00	4 0 00	2 0 0 0 00		Jon Co.		
5 0 0 0 00			5 0 0 0 00	Sales		
20 0 0 0 00				Notes Payable		20 0 0 0 00
3 1 3 6 00	6 4 00	3 2 0 0 00		Roff Co.		
4 6 0 0 00			4 6 0 0 00	Sales		
39 4 0 0 00	2 0 0 00	10 0 0 0 00	9 6 0 0 00	Totals		20 0 0 0 00

Note: This company's set of columns differs from that shown in the chapter.

CASH PAYMENTS JOURNAL					
Account	PR	Sundry	Accounts Payable	Purchases Discount	Cash
Sos Co.			3 0 0 0 00	6 0 00	2 9 4 0 00
Salaries Expense		2 6 0 0 00			2 6 0 0 00
Jingle Co.			4 0 0 0 00	8 0 00	3 9 2 0 00
Salaries Expense		2 6 0 0 00			2 6 0 0 00
Totals		5 2 0 0 00	7 0 0 0 00	1 4 0 00	12 0 6 0 00

Internet Exercises: L. L. Bean; Amazon.com

EX-1. [www.llbean.com] Each holiday season an extraordinary amount of merchandise is moved from online retailers like L. L. Bean from their warehouses to their customers. In the previous chapter you learned about the handling of sales and cash receipts transactions. In this chapter you learned about the other side of those transactions, Purchases and Cash Payments, using the related special journals.

Retailers wish to know their profits by product line or by department. From your examination of this Web site, suggest several columns that might appear in a purchases journal. For each suggestion state whether it would be a "debit" or "credit" column.

EX-2. [www.amazon.com] When merchandise for resale is paid for by the seller, the transaction is recorded in the cash payments journal. At the same time, an entry is made on the subsidiary ledger of the vendor. When all of the transactions are journalized and posted a schedule of accounts payable may be prepared. In a manual accounting system, individual ledger cards for vendors can become misplaced. If your coworker were to find a subsidiary ledger card but did not know whether to return it to Accounts Payable or the Accounts Receivable Department, how could you assist in getting it to the right place? Which columns of the ledger card could you examine to answer this dilemma?

Continuing Problem

Eldorado Computer Center

Tony was very happy to see the progress made by using the specialized journals. For the month of February he will add two more journals (purchases journal and cash payments journal). To assist you in recording the transactions, the following is an updated schedule of accounts payable as of January 31, 200X.

Schedule of Accounts Payable		
Office Depot	$	50
System Design Furniture		1,400
Pac Bell		150
Multi Systems, Inc.		450
Total Accounts Payable	$2,050	

Assignment

(See pages 356–361 in the *Study Guide and Working Papers*.)

1. Journalize the transactions in the appropriate journals (cash payments, purchases journal, or general journal).
2. Record in the accounts payable subsidiary ledger and post to the general ledger as appropriate. A partial general ledger is included in the *Study Guide and Working Papers*.
3. Prepare a schedule of accounts payable as of February 28, 200X.

The transactions for the month of February are as follows:

200X
Feb.

1 Prepaid the rent for the months of February, March, and April, $1,200, check no. 2585.

4 Bought merchandise on account from Multi Systems, Inc., purchase order no. 4010, $450; terms are 3/10, n/30.

8 Bought office supplies on account from Office Depot, purchase order no. 4011, $250; terms are n/30.

9 Purchased merchandise on account from Computer Connection, purchase order no. 4012, $500; terms are 1/30, n/60.

15 Paid purchase order no. 4010 in full to Multi Systems, Inc.; check no. 2586.

21 Issued debit memorandum no. 10 to Computer Connection for merchandise returned from purchase order no. 4012, $100.

27 Paid for office supplies, $50, check no. 2587.

APPENDIX

WHAT SPECIAL JOURNALS WOULD LOOK LIKE IN A PERPETUAL ACCOUNTING SYSTEM

Figure A-1

A Sales Journal under a Perpetual System

ART'S WHOLESALE CLOTHING COMPANY
SALES JOURNAL

Page 1

Date		Account Debited	Terms	Invoice No.	Post Ref.	Dr. Acc. Rec Cr. Sales	Cost of Goods Sold Dr. Merchandise Inventory Cr.
200X Apr.	3	Hal's Clothing	2/10, n/30	1	✔	800 00	560 00
	6	Bevans Company	2/10, n/30	2	✔	1600 00	1120 00
	18	Roe Company	2/10, n/30	3	✔	2000 00	1400 00
	24	Roe Company	2/10, n/30	4	✔	500 00	350 00
	28	Mel's Dept. Store	2/10, n/30	5	✔	900 00	630 00
	29	Mel's Dept. Store	2/10, n/30	6	✔	700 00	490 00
	30						
						6500 00	4550 00
						(113) (411)	(510) (114)

What's new:

In journal: New columns for Cost of Goods Sold (Dr.) and Inventory (Cr.). Each time a charge sale is earned, the Cost of Goods Sold increases and the amount of Inventory at cost is reduced.

In general ledger: New ledger accounts for Inventory and Cost of Goods Sold.

Example: On April 3, Art's Wholesale sold Hal's Clothing $800 of merchandise on account. This sale cost Art $560 to bring this merchandise into the store.

ART'S WHOLESALE CLOTHING COMPANY
CASH RECEIPTS JOURNAL

Page 1

Date		Cash Dr.	Sales Discount Dr.	Accounts Receivable Cr.	Sales Cr.	Sundry Account Name	Post Ref.	Amount Cr.	Costs of Goods Sold Dr. Merchandise Inventory Cr.
200X Apr.	1	8000 00				Art Newner, Capital	311	8000 00	
	4	784 00	16 00	800 00		Hal's Clothing	✔		
	15	900 00			900 00	Cash Sales	x		630 00
	16	980 00	20 00	1000 00		Bevans Company	✔		
	22	1960 00	40 00	2000 00		Roe Company	✔		
	27	500 00				Store Equipment	121	500 00	
	30	1200 00			1200 00	Cash Sales	x		840 00
		14324 00	76 00	3800 00	2100 00			8500 00	1470 00
		(111)	(413)	(113)	(411)			(X)	(510) (114)

Figure A-2 A Cash Receipts Journal under a Perpetual System

What's new:

In journal: New columns for Cost of Goods Sold (Dr.) and Inventory (Cr.). Each time a cash sale is earned, the Cost of Goods Sold increases and the amount of Inventory at cost is reduced.

In general ledger: New ledger accounts for Inventory and Cost of Goods Sold.

Example: On April 15, Art's Wholesale made cash sales for $900. These sales cost Art $630 to bring them into the store.

ART'S WHOLESALE CLOTHING COMPANY
PURCHASES JOURNAL

Date	Account Credited	Date of Invoice	Inv. No.	Terms	Post Ref.	Accounts Payable Credits	Merchandise Inventory Debit	Sundry–Dr. Account	Post Ref.	Amount
200X Apr. 3	Abby Blake Company	April 3	228	2/10, n/60	✔	5 0 5 0 00	5 0 0 0 00	Freight-In	514	5 0 00
4	Joe Francis Company	April 5	388		✔	4 0 0 0 00		Equip.	121	4 0 0 0 00
6	Thorpe Company	April 6	415	1/10, n/30	✔	8 0 0 00	8 0 0 00			
7	John Sullivan Company	April 6	516	n/10, EOM*	✔	9 8 0 00	9 8 0 00			
12	Abby Blake Company	April 13	242	1/10, n/30	✔	6 0 0 00	6 0 0 00			
25	John Sullivan Company	April 26	612		✔	5 0 0 00		Supplies	115	5 0 0 00
30										
						11 9 3 0 00	7 3 8 0 00			4 5 5 0 00
						(211)	(114)			(X)

Figure A-3 A Purchases Journal under a Perpetual System

What's new:

In journal: The column for Purchases is replaced with a column for Inventory. The cost of all merchandise bought on account for resale is debited to Inventory.

In ledger: New ledger account for Inventory.

Example: On April 7, Art's Wholesale bought $980 of merchandise for resale to customers from John Sullivan Company.

ART'S WHOLESALE CLOTHING COMPANY
CASH PAYMENTS JOURNAL

Page 1

Date	Ck. No.	Account Debited	Post Ref.	Sundry Accounts Dr.	Accounts Payable Dr.	Merchandise Inventory Cr.	Cash Cr.
200X Apr. 2	1	Prepaid Insurance	116	9 0 0 00			9 0 0 00
7	2	Joe Francis Company	✔		4 0 0 0 00		4 0 0 0 00
9	3	Merchandise Inventory	114	8 0 0 00			8 0 0 00
12	4	Thorpe Company	✔		6 0 0 00	6 00	5 9 4 00
28	5	Salaries Expense	611	7 0 0 00			7 0 0 00
30							
				2 4 0 0 00	4 6 0 0 00	6 00	6 9 9 4 00
				(X)	(211)	(114)	(111)

Figure A-4 A Cash Payments Journal under a Perpetual System

What's new:

In journal: New column for Merchandise Inventory replaces the Purchase Discount column. In the perpetual system, a purchase discount reduces the cost of merchandise inventory.

In general ledger: New ledger account for Merchandise Inventory.

Example: On April 12, Art's wholesale paid Thorpe Company the amount owed less a 1% discount.

COMPUTERIZED ACCOUNTING APPLICATION FOR CHAPTER 10

PART A: *Recording Transactions in the Sales, Receipts, Purchases, and Payments Journals*

PART B: *Computerized Accounting Instructions for Abby's Toy House (Problem 10A-4)*

Before starting on this assignment, read and complete the tasks discussed in Parts A, B, and F of the Computerized Accounting appendix at the back of this book and complete the Computerized Accounting Application assignments for Chapter 3, Chapter 4, the Valdez Realty Mini Practice Set (Chapter 5), and the Pete's Market Mini Practice Set (Chapter 8).

PART A: RECORDING TRANSACTIONS IN THE SALES, RECEIPTS, PURCHASES, AND PAYMENTS JOURNALS

Where to Record Sales and Cash Receipts

The Sales/Invoicing and Receipts features in Peachtree Complete Accounting were designed to work with the accounts receivables and general ledger modules in an integrated fashion. When transactions are recorded in the Sales/Invoicing and Receipts windows, the program automatically posts the customer's account in the accounts receivable subsidiary ledger, records the journal entry, and posts all accounts affected in the general ledger. However, the type of transactions recorded in the Sales/Invoicing and Receipts windows in Peachtree Complete Accounting differ from the types of transactions recorded in these journals in a manual accounting system. An explanation of the differences appears in the following chart:

Name of Computerized Entry Window	Types of Transactions Recorded in Computerized Journal
Sales/Invoicing	Sales of merchandise on account Sales returns and allowances
Receipts	Cash sales and payments from credit customers on account

Computerized Aged Receivables

An Aged Receivables report (the computerized version of a schedule of accounts receivable) for The Mars Company appears below (terms of 2/10, n/30 are offered to all credit customers of The Mars Company):

The Mars Company: Customer Aged Detail as at 3/1/04

	Total	Current	31 to 60	61 to 90	91+
John Dunbar					
910 2/25/04 Invoice	500.00	500.00	—	—	—
Kevin Tucker					
912 2/26/04 Invoice	550.00	550.00	—	—	—
	1,050.00	1,050.00			

Where to Record Purchases and Cash Payments

The Purchases and Payments windows in Peachtree Complete Accounting are designed to work with the accounts payable and general ledger modules in an integrated fashion.

When transactions are recorded in the Purchases and Payments windows, the program automatically posts the vendor's account in the accounts payable subsidiary ledger, records the journal entry, and posts all accounts affected in the general ledger. However, the type of transactions recorded in the Purchases and Payments windows in

Peachtree Complete Accounting differ from the types of transactions recorded in these journals in a manual accounting system. An explanation of the differences appears in the following chart:

Name of Computerized Journal	Types of Transactions Recorded in Computerized Journal
Purchases Window	Purchases of merchandise and other items on account Purchase returns and allowances
Payments Journal	Cash payments to credit and cash vendors

An Aged Payables report (the computerized version of a schedule of accounts payable) for The Mars Company appears below:

Aged Payables

The Mars Company: Vendor Aged Detail as at 3/1/04

	Total	Current	31 to 60	61 to 90	91+
Laurie Snyder					
569 2/27/04 Invoice	435.00	435.00	—	—	—
Young's Space Simulations					
790 2/25/04 Invoice	112.00	112.00	—	—	—
	547.00	547.00			

1. Click on the Start button. Point to Programs; point to the Peachtree folder and select Peachtree Complete Accounting. Your desktop may have the Peachtree icon allowing for a quicker entrance into the program.

Open the Company Data Files

2. Follow the "Open a File" instructions in Part A of the Computerized Accounting appendix at the back of this book to open **Mars Company.**

3. Click on the **Maintain** menu option. Then select **Company Information.** The program will respond by bringing up a dialogue box allowing the user to edit/add information about the company. In the **Company Name** entry field at the end of **Mars Company,** add a dash and your name "**-Student Name**" to the end of the company name. Click on the OK button to return to the Menu Window.

Add Your Name to the Company Name

4. On March 1, 2004 sold merchandise to Kevin Tucker on account, $800, invoice #913, terms 2/10, n/30 consisting of the following:

How to Record a Sale on Account

Stock #	Description	Quantity
001	Space Age Lamp	2
002	Solar Clock	5
005	Space Shuttle Model	1

5. Select **Sales/Invoicing** from the **Tasks** menu. Using the magnifying glass next to the **Customer ID** field, select Kevin Tucker by double clicking on his name. You are then moved to the **Invoice #** field. Type in "913". Press the TAB key that then moves you to the **Date** field. It should already reflect Mar 1, 2004 but if not, type in the date or use the calendar to the right of the field to select this date. TAB until you reach the **Quantity** field. Type in "2" and click TAB. This will move you to the **Item** field. Using the pull down menu, select the first item 001 Space Age Lamp by double clicking on it. This moves you to the **Description** field that will automatically fill in with information stored in the Inventory module. In fact, Peachtree will fill in all of the remaining fields as you tab through them until you are back to the **Quantity**

field. Enter the remaining items from the above table in the same manner as the Lamp. Your screen should look like this:

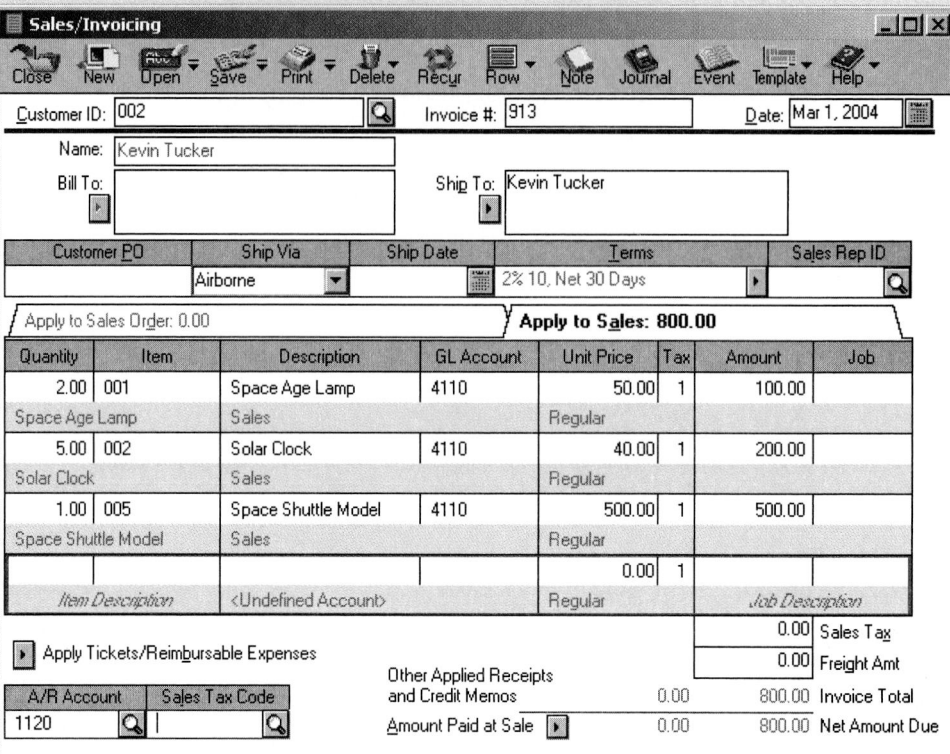

6. Before printing this transaction, you may wish to see how Peachtree will record the transaction. Click on the **Journal** icon on the tool bar. This activates a feature of Peachtree called "Accounting Behind the Screens" and allows the user a look at the workings of the program. It will bring up a Sales Journal showing exactly how it will post this invoice. That is to say, it will show you what accounts will be debited and which accounts credited. Note that Peachtree uses a perpetual inventory system and has created the entries to move the goods sold out of the Inventory account and into the Cost of Sales (COGS) account.

7. Close the Sales Journal window. If you have made an error anywhere on the invoice, simply click in the field containing the error and correct it.

8. After verifying that the journal entry is correct, click on the **Print** icon to print this invoice. You will be asked to select a form. As with the payroll checks, Peachtree supports a variety of blank invoice formats. It will also print its own format on plain paper. Select **Invoice Plain** (default) for your printing. Peachtree will both print and post the transaction in one step. A blank invoice is displayed, ready for additional transactions to be recorded. If you wish to batch print later, you can simply hit the **Save** icon which will store the invoice for printing using the **Select a Report** option under the **Accounts Receivable** reports. We will print all our invoices as we create them.

9. On March 5, 2004 issued credit memorandum #CM14 to Kevin Tucker for the return of one of the lamps he purchased. Peachtree uses the same entry window, **Sales/Invoicing,** to record credits issued to customers. There are two primary differences. One is that quantities will be entered as negative amounts and the second is that the printing will be accomplished with a Credit form rather than an Invoice form.

10. Select **Sales/Invoicing** from the **Tasks** menu. Using the magnifying glass next to the **Customer ID** field, select Kevin Tucker by double clicking on his name. You are then moved to the **Invoice #** field. Type in "CM14". Press the TAB key that then moves you to the **Date** field. Type in the date "Mar 5, 2004" or use the calendar to the right

How to Preview a Sales Journal

How to Edit a Sale or Purchase Entry Prior to Posting

How to Print/Post a Sales Entry

How to Record a Credit Memo

of the field to select this date. TAB until you reach the **Quantity** field. Type in "−1" (negative one) and click TAB. This will move you to the **Item** field. Using the pull down menu, select the first item 001 Space Age Lamp by double clicking on it. This moves you to the **Description** field that will automatically fill in with information stored in the Inventory module. In fact, Peachtree will fill in all of the remaining fields as you tab through them until you are back to the **Quantity** field. Your screen should look like this:

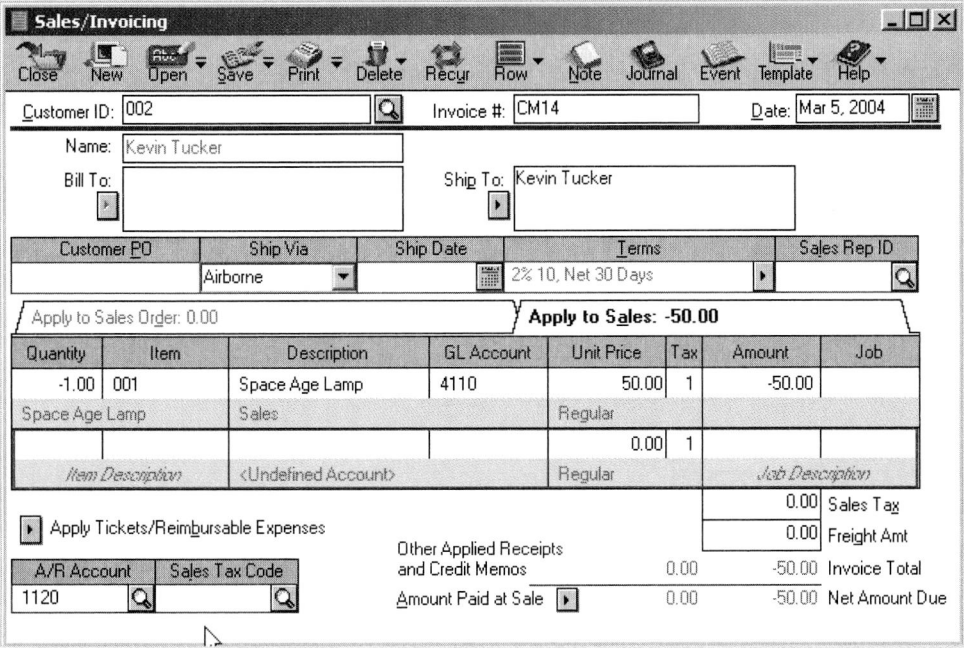

11. You may again use the **Journal** icon to see what this entry will look like in the Sales Journal.

> Preview the Entry

12. Close the Sales Journal window; then make any editing corrections that may be required.
13. After verifying that the journal entry is correct, click on the Print icon to print this transaction. Select **Credit Plain** as the form on which to print the credit memo. When you are finished, close the **Sales/Invoicing** box.

> Print the Credit Memo

14. On March 7, 2004 received check #1634 from Kevin Tucker in the amount of $735 in payment of invoice #913 ($800), dated March 1, less credit memorandum #CM14 ($50), less 2 percent discount ($16 − 1 = $15 net sales discount). Select **Receipts** from the **Tasks** menu. Peachtree will place the current date in the **Deposit ticket ID** field. You can accept this or change it to the date of the transaction. We will use the date of the transaction throughout the book. Using the magnifying glass, select customer Kevin Tucker. This will bring up a listing of the invoices and credits currently open in his account. The cursor will automatically move to the **Reference** field. We can enter Kevin's check number, 1634, in this field. The **Receipt Number** is similar to an invoice number and we will start with #105. We can now select the invoices and/or credits that are included in Kevin's payment. In the column marked **Pay** are small boxes that can be checked by clicking on them with the mouse. This marks the invoices selected for payment with the check received. We will check the boxes at the end of the lines containing invoice #913 and credit memo #CM14 which is associated with this invoice. Note that the field for **Receipt Amount** automatically reflects the amount of his payment. Please note that if we were receiving cash as the result of a cash sale or for any other reason rather than a payment on account, we would use the **Apply to Revenues** tab instead of the **Apply to Invoices** tab. In that screen, we can use any GL account we like to offset the

> How to Record a Cash Receipt from a Credit Customer

receipt of the cash. If you recorded this payment on account correctly, your screen should look like this:

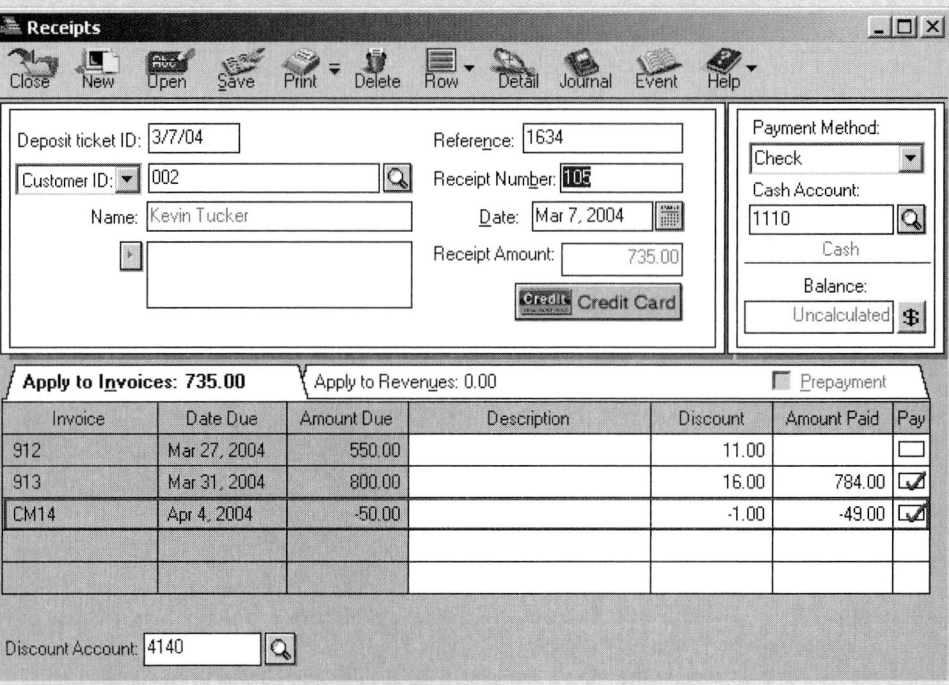

15. As before, we can preview how Peachtree will handle this transaction behind the screens by clicking on the **Journal** icon. This will bring up a Receipts Journal reflecting the accounts that will be affected by this entry.

16. Close the Sales Journal window. If you have made an error anywhere on the invoice, simply click in the field containing the error and correct it.

17. After verifying that the journal entry is correct, click on the **Print** icon to post this transaction. You could also click on **Save** to post but not print the receipt. A blank Receipts Journal dialog box is displayed, ready for additional Receipts transactions to be recorded. Close the Receipts dialog box when you are finished.

18. On March 15, 2004 purchased merchandise from Young's Space Simulations on account, $278, invoice #796, terms 2/10, n/30 consisting of the following:

Stock #	Description	Quantity
001	Space Age Lamp	5
003	Martian Landscape Lithograph	5
004	Simulated Moon Rock	9

19. Select **Purchases/Receive Inventory** from the **Tasks** menu. Using the magnifying glass next to the **Customer ID** field, select 002 Young's Space Simulations by double clicking on his name. You are then moved to the **Invoice #** field. Type in "796". Press the TAB key that then moves you to the **Date** field. Type in the date "Mar 15, 2004" or use the calendar to the right of the field to select this date. TAB until you reach the **Quantity** field. Type in "5" and click TAB. This will move you to the **Item** field. Using the pull down menu, select the first item 001 Space Age Lamp by double clicking on it. This moves you to the **Description** field that will automatically fill in with information stored in the Inventory module. In fact, Peachtree will fill in all of the remaining fields as you tab through them until you are back to the **Quantity** field. Should your Unit Price be different than that brought up by Peachtree, you can easily change the amount rather than tabbing through that field. If we were purchasing something besides merchandise inventory, we would skip over the Quantity and Item fields and fill in the Description, GL Account, and Amount fields based on

How to Preview the Receipts Journal

How to Post a Receipts Entry

How to Record a Purchase on Account

what we purchased and its cost. If you entered our inventory purchase correctly, your screen should look like this:

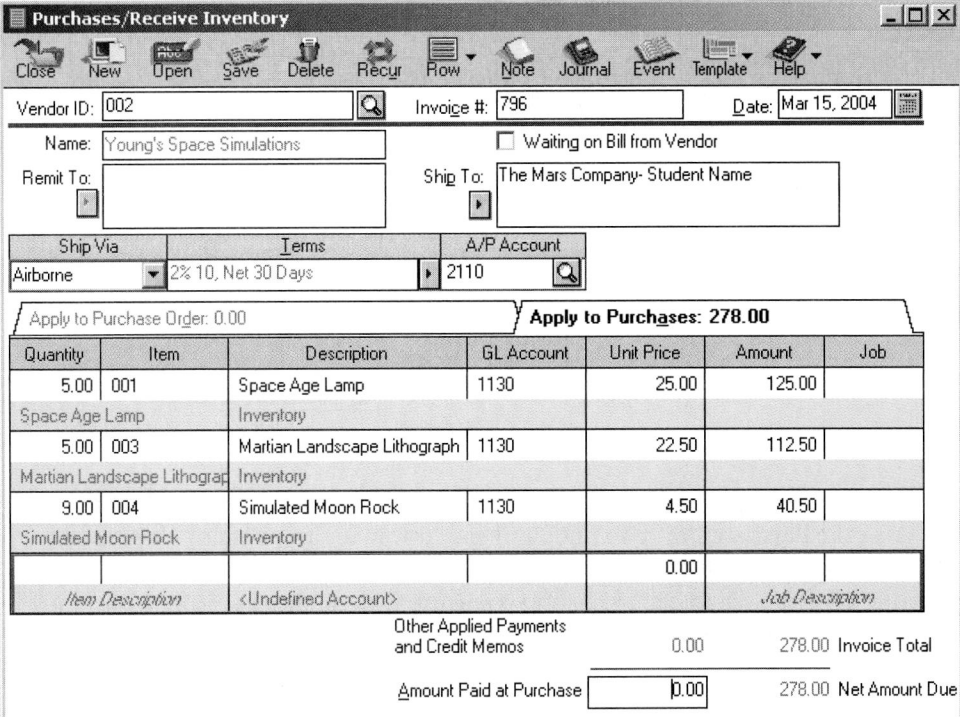

20. Before posting this transaction, you may wish to see how Peachtree will record the transaction. Click on the **Journal** icon on the tool bar. This activates a feature of Peachtree called "Accounting Behind the Screens" and allows the user a look at the workings of the program. It will bring up a Purchases Journal showing exactly how it will post this invoice. That is to say, it will show you what accounts will be debited and which accounts credited.

21. Close the Purchases Journal window. If you have made an error anywhere on the invoice, simply click in the field containing the error and correct it.

22. After verifying that the journal entry is correct, click on the **Save** icon to post this transaction. A blank Purchases screen is displayed, ready for additional Purchase transactions to be recorded.

23. On March 17, 2004 returned two of the Space Age Lamps to Young's Space Simulations with a value of $50. Issued debit memo #DM27. Select **Purchases/Receive Inventory** from the **Tasks** menu. Using the magnifying glass next to the **Customer ID** field, select 002 Young's Space Simulations by double clicking on his name. You are then moved to the **Invoice #** field. Type in "DM27". Press the TAB key that then moves you to the **Date** field. Type in the date "Mar 17, 2004" or use the calendar to the right of the field to select this date. TAB until you reach the **Quantity** field. Type in "−2" (negative two) and click TAB. This will move you to the **Item** field. Using the pull down menu, select the first item 001 Space Age Lamp by double clicking on it. This moves you to the **Description** field that will automatically fill in with information stored in the Inventory module. In fact, Peachtree will fill in all of the remaining fields as you tab through them until you are back to the **Quantity** field. Your screen should look like the screen on page 430.

24. Before posting this transaction, you may wish to see how Peachtree will record the transaction. Click on the **Journal** icon on the tool bar. This activates a feature of Peachtree called "Accounting Behind the Screens" and allows the user a look at the workings of the program. It will bring up a Purchases Journal showing exactly how it will post this invoice. That is to say, it will show you what accounts will be debited and which accounts credited.

How to Preview a Purchases Journal Entry

How to Post a Purchases Journal Entry

How to Record a Debit Memo

How to Preview a Purchases Journal Entry

25. Close the Purchases Journal window. If you have made an error anywhere on the invoice, simply click in the field containing the error and correct it.

Post the Entry

26. After verifying that the journal entry is correct, click on the **Save** icon to post this transaction; then close the Purchases window.

How to Record a Cash Payment to a Credit Vendor

27. On March 25, 2004 issued check #1007 to Young's Space Simulations in the amount of $223.44 in payment of invoice #796 ($278), dated March 15, less debit memorandum #DM27 ($50), less 2 percent discount ($5.56 − 1.00 = $4.56 net purchases discount). Select **Payments** from the **Tasks** menu. Using the magnifying glass, select vendor Young's Space Simulations. This will bring up a listing of the invoices and credits currently open in this account. TAB to the **Date** field and type in "March 25, 2004" or use the calendar to select this date. In the column marked **Pay** are small boxes that can be checked by clicking on them with the mouse. This marks the invoices selected for payment with the check you are creating. We will check the boxes at the end of the lines containing invoice #796 and debit memo #DM27 which is associated with this invoice. If we need to make a payment for something that is not already recorded in our accounts payable, we can use the **Apply to Expenses** tab instead of the **Apply to Invoices** tab that we are using. We can write a check for any purpose, including prepaid expenses, using this feature. With our payment, note that the field for the amount of the check automatically reflects the amount of this payment. Also note that the **Check Number** field is left blank. This field is used only to enter a check that has already been written or printed. We will enter the check number when we print the check. Your screen should look like the Payments screen on page 431.

How to Preview a Disbursements Journal Entry

28. Before printing this check, you may wish to see how Peachtree will record the transaction. Click on the **Journal** icon on the tool bar. It will bring up a Disbursements Journal showing exactly how it will post this payment. That is to say, it will show you what accounts will be debited and which accounts credited.

29. Close the Disbursements Journal window. If you have made an error anywhere on the check, simply click in the field containing the error and correct it. If you need to change which invoice to pay, click on the red check for the incorrect invoice to deselect it and reselect the correct invoice.

How to Print a Check

30. After verifying that the check is correct, click on the **Print** icon to print this check. You will be presented with a Print Forms: Disbursement Checks selection box. As before, Peachtree has the ability to print on a variety of different blank check forms. Since we will be printing on plain white paper, it does not matter which form we choose. Accept the default. Start with check #1007. Click on **Print** to continue. The check will now print. You may need to tell your printer to continue since it may want you to insert the blank check forms. A blank Payment window

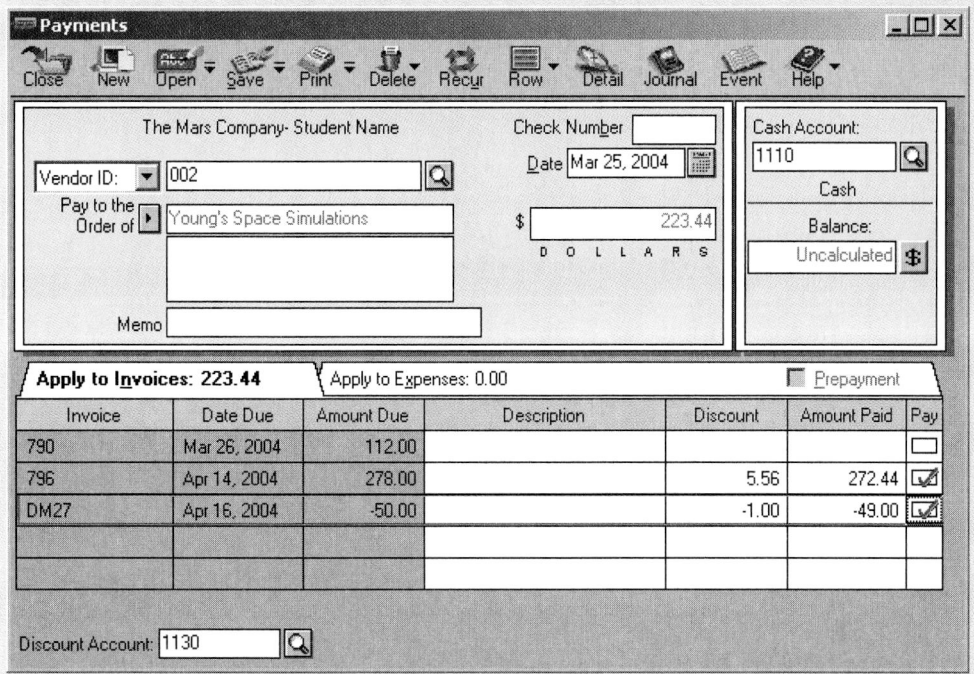

is displayed, ready for additional Payments transactions to be recorded. Close the Payments dialog box.

31. From the **Reports** menu, select **Accounts Receivable.** This will bring up a Select a Report dialogue box containing a list of several receivables related reports available to us. Select **Aged Receivables** to bring up the schedule of receivables still owed to Mars Company. Click on the **Print** icon to print the report.

How to Display and Print a Customer Aged Receivables Report

32. Close the Aged Receivables window. From the Select A Report dialogue box, select Accounts Payable from the **Report Area** portion of the window. This will bring up a selection of payables related reports. Select **Aged Payables** to bring up the schedule of payables still owed by the Mars Company. Click on the **Print** icon to print the report.

How to Display and Print a Vendor Aged Payables Report

33. Close the Aged Payables window. From the Select A Report dialogue box, select General Ledger from the **Report Area** portion of the window then print the following reports:

Print Reports

   a. General Ledger Trial Balance (Totals = 16,201.00)
   b. General Ledger Report (Cash = $10,511.56)

34. You may wish to experiment with some of the other reports that are available in the various areas of Peachtree's report area. Some examples you might want to see are a Sales Journal, Purchases Journal, Cash Receipts Journal, etc. Exit the program when you are finished.

PART B: COMPUTERIZED ACCOUNTING INSTRUCTIONS FOR ABBY'S TOY HOUSE (PROBLEM 10A-4)

1. Click on the Start button. Point to Programs; point to the Peachtree folder and select Peachtree Complete Accounting. Your desktop may have the Peachtree icon allowing for a quicker entrance into the program.

2. Follow the "Open a File" instructions in Part A of the Computerized Accounting appendix at the back of this book to open **Abby's Toy House.**

Open the Company Data Files

3. Click on the **Maintain** menu option. Then select **Company Information.** The program will respond by bringing up a dialogue box allowing the user to edit/add information about the company. In the **Company Name** entry field at the end of **Abby's Toy House,** add a dash and your name "**-Student Name**" to the end of the company name. Click on the OK button to return to the Menu Window.

Add Your Name to the Company Name

Record Transactions

4. Record the following transactions for March using the appropriate General(G), Sales/Invoicing(S), Receipts(R), Purchases(PU), and Payments(PA) windows. Use the same forms when printing invoices, credits, and checks as in Part A, changing the starting numbers as needed.

2004

Mar.

1   Abby Ellen invested $8,000 in the toy store. (G)

1   Paid three month's rent in advance, check #1, $3,000. (G)

1   Purchased merchandise from Earl Miller Company on account, $4,000, invoice #410, terms 2/10, n/30 consisting of the following: 6- Mountain Bikes, 12- Bike Carriers, 8- Deluxe Bike Seats. (PU)

3   Sold merchandise to Bill Burton on account, $1,000, invoice #1, terms 2/10, n/30 consisting of the following: 1- Mountain Bike, 1- Bike Carrier. (S)

6   Sold merchandise to Jim Rex on account, $700, invoice #2, terms 2/10, n/30 consisting of the following: 3- Bike Carriers, 1- Deluxe Bike Seat. (S)

8   Purchased merchandise from Earl Miller Co. on account $1,200, invoice #415, terms 2/10, n/30 consisting of the following: 2- Mountain Bikes, 4- Bike Carriers. (PU)

9   Sold merchandise to Bill Burton on account, $600, invoice #3, terms 2/10, n/30 consisting of the following: 3- Bike Carriers. (S)

9   Paid cleaning service $300, check #2. (G)

10 Jim Rex returned merchandise that cost $300 to Abby's Toy House consisting of the following: 1- Bike Carrier, 1- Deluxe Bike Seat. Abby issued credit memorandum #1 to Jim Rex for $300. Remember to use negative quantities. (S)

10 Purchased merchandise from Minnie Katz on account, $4,000, invoice #311, terms 1/15, n/60 consisting of the following: 2- Doll Houses w/ Furniture, 4- Porcelain Face Dolls, 10- Yo Yo's, Designer, 10- Magic Kits. (PU)

12 Issued check #3 to Earl Miller Co. in the amount of $3,920 in payment of invoice #410 ($4,000), dated March 2, less 2 percent discount ($80). (PA)

13 Sold $1,300 of toy merchandise for cash consisting of the following: 1- Doll House w/ Furniture, 1- Magic Kit. (Use the Receipts window with Customer Name and Reference fields reflecting "Cash". Receipt #101. Change Payment Method to Cash. Use the Apply to Revenues tab and list the items sold accepting all other defaults.) (R)

13 Paid salaries, $600, check #4. (G)

14 Returned merchandise to Minnie Katz in the amount of $1,000 consisting of the following: 1- Doll House w/ Furniture, 2 Porcelain Face Dolls. Debit memorandum #DM1. (PU)

15 Sold merchandise for $4,000 cash consisting of the following: 3- Mountain Bikes, 3- Bike Carriers, 2- Magic Kits, 4- Yo Yo's, Designer. See 13th for cash sale. Receipt #102. (R)

16 Received check #9823 from Jim Rex in the amount of $392 (receipt #103) in payment of invoice #2 ($700), dated March 6, less credit memorandum #CM1 ($300), less 2 percent discount ($14 − 6 = $8 net sales discount). Change payment method to Check. (R)

16 Received check # 4589 from Bill Burton in the amount of $1,000 (receipt #104) in payment of invoice #1, dated March 2. Notice how Peachtree does not factor in the discount since it is past the discount date. (R)

16 Sold merchandise to Amy Rose on account, $4,000, invoice #4, terms 2/10, n/30 consisting of the following: 1- Porcelain Face Doll, 3- Mountain Bikes, 4- Bike Carriers, 3- Deluxe Bike Seats. (S)

20 Purchased delivery truck on account from Sam Katz Garage, $3,000, invoice #111 (no discount). (PU) Since this is not an inventory item, you do not need to fill in the **Quantity** or **Item** fields. You must type in the

Description. Peachtree will default the GL code to a truck since this vendor was set up to do so. You will need to type in the purchase price in the **Amount** field. (PU)

22 Sold to Bill Burton merchandise on account, $900, invoice #5, terms 2/10, n/30 consisting of the following: 3- Magic Kits. (S)

23 Issued check #5 to Minnie Katz in the amount of $2,970 in payment of invoice #311 ($4,000), dated March 10, less debit memorandum #DM1 ($1,000), less 1 percent discount ($40 − 10 = $30 net purchases discount). (PA)

24 Sold toy merchandise on account to Amy Rose, $1,100, invoice #6, terms 2/10, n/30 consisting of the following: 1- Porcelain Face Doll, 1- Magic Kit, 3- Yo Yo's, Designer. We will allow the customer to exceed her credit limit. (S)

25 Purchased toy merchandise for cash from Woody Smith while waiting for an account to be approved, $600, check #6 consisting of the following: 2- Marionettes, Hand Carved. (Use the Payments window, Apply to Expenses tab and list the items purchased) (PA)

26 Purchased toy merchandise from Woody Smith on account, $4,800 (receipt #105), invoice #211, terms 2/10, n/30 consisting of the following: 16- Marionettes, Hand Carved. (PU)

28 Received check #4598 from Bill Burton in the amount of $882 (receipt #106) in payment of invoice #5 ($900), dated March 22, less 2 percent discount ($18). (R)

28 Received check #3217 from Amy Rose in the amount of $1,078 in payment of invoice #6, dated March 24, less 2 percent discounts ($22). (R)

28 Abby invested an additional $5,000 in the business. (G)

28 Purchased merchandise from Earl Miller Co. $1,400, invoice #436, terms 2/10, n/30 consisting of the following: 3- Mountain Bikes, 2- Bike Carriers. (PU)

30 Issued check #7 to Earl Miller Co. in the amount of $1,372 in payment of invoice #436 ($1,400), dated March 28, less 2 percent discount ($28). (PA)

30 Sold merchandise to Bonnie Flow Company on account, $3,000, invoice #7, terms 2/10, n/30 consisting of the following: 5- Marionettes, Hand Carved. (S)

5. Print the following reports accepting all defaults:

a. Aged Receivables
b. Aged Payables
c. General Journal
d. General Ledger Report

Print Reports

Preparing a Worksheet for a Merchandise Company

With Special Appendix on What Worksheets Look Like in a Perpetual Inventory System

Jessica is a classmate of yours who recently got a part-time job at Hansen's Pharmacy. She told you the other day that she and the other employees of Hansen's recently completed a physical inventory of the store. As Jessica said, "You wouldn't believe it, but everything in the store had to be counted last Saturday night after we closed. We kept track of the quantity of each item and its price. It was a lot of work and I'm glad it's over."

You begin to realize that good accounting not only depends on following accounting rules and practices but also relies on activities such as an accurate physical count of inventory. Whether Jessica knew it or not, she played an important role in the accounting cycle for her employer by helping to take inventory on that Saturday night.

Hansen's Pharmacy is no different than thousands of other businesses which maintain an inventory. A physical inventory must be periodically taken to adjust the accounting records for inventory amounts. Other accounting adjustments must also be made by most businesses for rent, supplies, insurance, depreciation, and wages.

In Chapter 11, we will learn how to make various adjustments to the accounts of a merchandising business such as Hansen's Pharmacy. We also will discover in this chapter that the ideal way to properly track the adjustments made to the accounts of a merchandising business is to use a device called a *worksheet.* After completing this chapter, you will have a much richer understanding of the role of the worksheet in accounting and the adjustment process for a business.

Learning Objectives

- Figuring adjustments for merchandise inventory, unearned rent, supplies used, insurance expired, depreciation expense, and salaries accrued. (p. 436)

- Preparing a worksheet for a merchandise company. (p. 439)

In Chapters 9 and 10 we discussed the special journals and subsidiary ledgers of a merchandise company. Appendix material provided an introduction to perpetual inventory. Now we shift our attention to recording adjustments and completing a worksheet for a merchandise company. Note that the appendix at the end of the chapter shows worksheets for a perpetual system.

Learning Unit 11-1   Adjustments for Merchandise Inventory and Unearned Rent

Gross sales
– Sales Ret. + Allow.
– Sales Discount
= Net sales

The Merchandise Inventory account shows the goods that a merchandise company has available to sell to customers. There are several ways of keeping track of the cost of goods sold (the total cost of the goods sold to customers) and the quantity of inventory that a company has on hand. In this chapter we discuss the periodic inventory system, in which the balance in inventory is updated only at the end of the accounting period.* This system is used by companies like Art's Wholesale Clothing Company, which sell a variety of merchandise with low unit prices.

Assume Art's Wholesale Clothing Company started the year with $19,000 worth of merchandise. This merchandise is called beginning merchandise inventory or simply beginning inventory. The balance of beginning inventory never changes. Instead, all purchases of merchandise are recorded in the Purchases account. During the accounting period $52,000 worth of such purchases were made and recorded in the Purchases account.

Net sales
– Cost of goods sold
= Gross profit
– Operating expenses
= Net income

At the end of the period, the company takes a physical count of the merchandise in stock; this amount is called ending merchandise inventory or simply ending inventory. It is calculated on an inventory sheet as shown in Figure 11-1. This $4,000, which is the ending inventory for this period, will be the beginning inventory for the next period.

When the income statement is prepared, the cost of goods sold section requires two distinct numbers for inventory. The beginning inventory adds to the cost of goods sold, and the ending inventory is subtracted from the cost of goods sold (see margin aids at right). Remember that the two figures for beginning and ending inventory were calculated months apart. Thus, combining these amounts to come up with one inventory figure would not be accurate.

Cost of goods sold
Beginning inventory
+ Net purchases
+ Freight-in
– Ending inventory
= Cost of goods sold

Note that in the calculation (in the margin) of cost of goods sold a new title called Freight-In is shown. Freight-in is a cost of goods sold account that records the shipping cost to the buyer. Note that net sales less cost of goods sold equals gross profit. Subtracting operating expenses from gross profits equals net income.

ADJUSTMENT FOR MERCHANDISE INVENTORY

First adjustment transfers the amount in beginning inventory from Merchandise inventory to Income Summary.

Adjusting the Merchandise Inventory account is a two-step process because we must record the beginning inventory and ending inventory amounts separately. The first step deals with beginning merchandise inventory.

Given: Beginning Inventory, $19,000

Note that Income Summary has no normal balance of debit or credit.

Our first adjustment removes beginning inventory from the asset account (Merchandise Inventory) and transfers it to Income Summary. We do so by crediting Merchandise Inventory for $19,000 and debiting Income Summary for the same amount. This adjustment is shown on page 437 in T account form and on a transaction analysis chart:

---

*For a discussion of the perpetual inventory system, see the appendix at the end of Chapter 9, page 380.

Figure 11-1
Ending Inventory Sheet

ART'S WHOLESALE CLOTHING COMPANY ENDING INVENTORY SHEET AS OF DECEMBER 31, 20X2			
Amount	Explanation	Unit Cost	Total
20	Ladies' Jackets code 14-0	$50	$1,000
10	Men's Hats code 327	10	100
90	Men's Shirts code 423	10	900
100	Ladies' Blouses code 481	20	2,000
			$4,000

Counted by _____   Checked and priced by _____

```
   Merchandise Inventory 114              Income Summary 313
  Bal.   19,000 | Adj.   19,000       Adj.   9,000 |
                                                   ↑
                        (A)
```

Accounts Affected	Category	↑ ↓	Rules
Income Summary	—	—	Dr.
Merchandise Inventory	Asset	↓	Cr.

(The adjusting entries would be recorded first on the worksheet and then in the general journal.)

The second step is entering the amount of ending inventory ($4,000) in the Merchandise Inventory account. This step is done to record the amount of goods on hand at the end of the period as an asset and to subtract this amount from the cost of goods sold (because we have not sold this inventory yet). To do so, we debit Merchandise Inventory for $4,000 and credit Income Summary for the same amount. This adjustment is shown below in T account form and on a transaction analysis chart:

```
   Merchandise Inventory 114              Income Summary 313
  Bal.   19,000 | Adj.   19,000       Adj.   19,000 | Adj.   4,000
  Adj.    4,000 |                                                ↑
        ↑
                        (B)
```

Let's look at how this process or method of recording merchandise inventory is reflected in the balance sheet and income statement (see Figure 11-2). Note that the $19,000 of beginning inventory is assumed sold and is shown on the income statement as part of the cost of goods sold. The ending inventory of $4,000 is assumed not to be sold and is subtracted from the cost of goods sold on the income statement. The ending inventory becomes next month's beginning inventory on the balance sheet. When the income statement is prepared, we will need a figure for beginning inventory as well as a figure for ending inventory.

ADJUSTMENT FOR UNEARNED RENT

A second new account we have not seen before is a liability called Unearned Rent or Rent Received in Advance. This account records the amount collected for rent before the service (renting the space) has been provided.

Suppose Art's Wholesale Clothing Company is subletting a portion of its space to Jesse Company for $200 per month. Jesse Company sends Art a check for $600 for three

> Second adjustment updates inventory account with a figure for ending inventory.

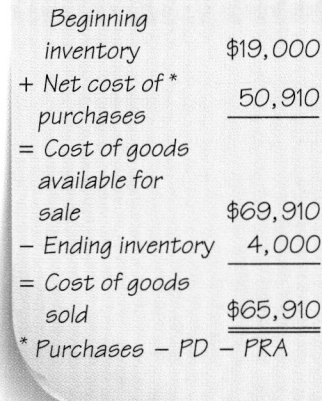

Beginning inventory	$19,000
+ Net cost of * purchases	50,910
= Cost of goods available for sale	$69,910
− Ending inventory	4,000
= Cost of goods sold	$65,910

* Purchases − PD − PRA

> Note:
> If Freight-In was involved, it would have been added to net cost of purchases.

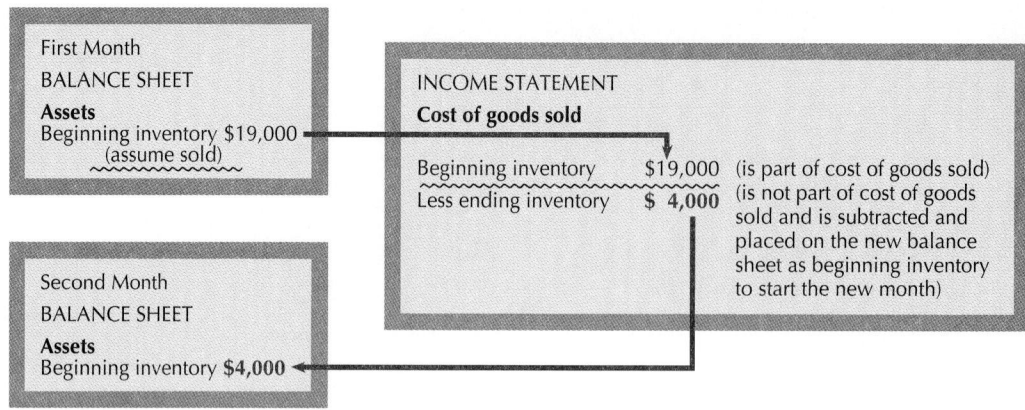

Figure 11-2
Recording Inventory on a Partial Balance Sheet and Income Statement

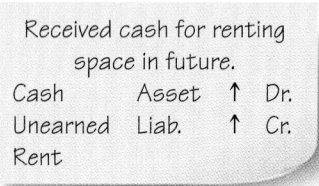

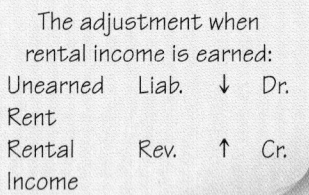

months' rent paid in advance. This unearned rent ($600) is a liability on the balance sheet because Art's Wholesale owes Jesse Company three months' worth of occupancy.

When Art's Wholesale fulfills a portion of the rental agreement—when Jesse Company has been in the space for a period of time—this liability account will be reduced and the Rental Income account will be increased. Rental Income is another type of revenue for Art's Wholesale.

Remember that under accrual accounting, revenue is recognized when it is earned, whether payment is received then or not. Here, Art's Wholesale collected cash in advance for a service that it has not performed as yet. A liability called Unearned Rent is the result. Art's Wholesale may have the cash, but the Rental Income is not recorded until it is earned. There are other types of unearned revenue besides unearned rent. Examples are subscriptions for magazines, legal fees collected before the work is performed, and insurance.

Learning Unit 11-1 Review

AT THIS POINT you should be able to

- Define the periodic method of inventory accounting. (p. 436)
- Explain why beginning and ending inventory are two separate figures in the cost of goods sold section on the income statement. (p. 436)
- Calculate net sales, cost of goods sold, gross profit, and net income. (p. 437)
- Show how to calculate a figure for ending inventory. (p. 437)
- Explain why Unearned Rent is a *liability* account. (p. 438)

SELF-REVIEW QUIZ 11-1

(The forms you need are on page 362 of the *Study Guide and Working Papers*.)
    Given the following, prepare the two *adjusting* entries for Merchandise Inventory on 12/31/0X.

Merchandise Inventory, 1/1/0X	$ 8,000
Purchases	9,000
Merchandise Inventory, 12/31/0X	4,000
Cost of Goods Sold	10,000
Unearned Magazine Subscriptions	8,000

SOLUTION TO SELF-REVIEW QUIZ 11-1

Dec.	31	Income Summary	8 0 0 0 00		
		Merchandise Inventory		8 0 0 0 00	
	31	Merchandise Inventory	4 0 0 0 00		
		Income Summary		4 0 0 0 00	

Figure 11-3 Merchandise Inventory Adjustments

Accounting in the Reel World

Even Accountants Wear Tevas . . .

Invented in the 1980s for hardcore water sports enthusiasts, Tevas sandals are now so ubiquitous that everyone from kayakers to couch potatoes (and yes, even accountants) wear them. Chances are, you probably have some Tevas (from Hebrew for "nature") in your closet. Where did you buy them? In the local shoe store or online? How many styles did you get to choose between?

As you'll see in the Tevas on-location video on your DVD, the company sells its sandals through retailers and online. Pay attention to the challenges presented by selling Tevas online,

particularly as they relate to managing inventory. And then, after you have watched this short video, answer the questions below:

1. How are the needs for forecasting Tevas inventory different for retailers and for the company's e-commerce Web site?
2. What inventory system—periodic or perpetual—do you think would work best for the online Tevas store and why?
3. What are the main challenges in keeping Tevas' e-commerce Web site humming and how do these challenges translate into expenses for the company?

Learning Unit 11-2   Completing the Worksheet

In this unit we prepare a worksheet for Art's Wholesale Clothing Company. For convenience, we reproduce the company's chart of accounts in Figure 11-4.

Figure 11-5 (p. 441) shows the trial balance that was prepared on December 1, 200X, from the special journals of Art's Wholesale. (Note that it is placed directly in the first two columns of the worksheet.)

In looking at the trial balance, we see many new titles that have appeared since we completed a trial balance for a service company in Chapter 5. Let's look specifically at these new titles in the summary in Table 11-1, p. 442.

Note the following:

- **Mortgage Payable** is a liability account that records the increases and decreases in the amount of debt owed on a mortgage. We discuss this account more in the next chapter, when financial reports are prepared.
- **Interest Expense** represents a nonoperating expense for Art's Wholesale and thus is categorized as Other Expense. The interest would be a regular expense if it were incurred for business purposes. We look at this expense in the next chapter.
- **Unearned Revenue** is a liability account that records receipt of payment for goods and services in advance of delivery. Unearned Rent is a particular example of this general type of account.

Figure 11-4
Art's Wholesale Clothing
Company Chart of
Accounts

CHART OF ACCOUNTS

Assets 100–199
111   Cash
112   Petty Cash
113   Accounts Receivable
114   Merchandise Inventory
115   Supplies
116   Prepaid Insurance
121   Store Equipment
122   Accum. Depreciation, Store
       Equipment

Liabilities 200–299
211   Accounts Payable
212   Salaries Payable
213   Federal Income Tax Payable
214   FICA—Social Security Payable
215   FICA—Medicare Payable
216   State Income Tax Payable
217   SUTA Tax Payable
218   FUTA Tax Payable
219   Unearned Rent*
220   Mortgage Payable

Owner's Equity 300–399
311   Art Newner, Capital
312   Art Newner, Withdrawals
313   Income Summary

Revenue 400–499
411   Sales
412   Sales Returns and Allowances
413   Sales Discount
414   Rental Income

Cost of Goods Sold 500–599
511   Purchases
512   Purchases Discount
513   Purchases Returns and
       Allowances
514   Freight-In

Expenses 600–699
611   Salaries Expense
612   Payroll Tax Expense
613   Depreciation Expense, Store
       Equipment
614   Supplies Expense
615   Insurance Expense
616   Postage Expense
617   Miscellaneous Expense
618   Interest Expense
619   Cleaning Expense
620   Delivery Expense

*Although Unearned Rent is the only term under Liabilities not using payable, it is a liability.

We have already discussed adjustments (p. 437), which make up the two-step process involved in adjusting Merchandise Inventory at the end of the accounting period. Now we show T accounts and transaction analysis charts for some more adjustments that need to be made at this point for a merchandise firm, just as they must for a service company.

Adjustment C: Rental Income Earned by Art's Wholesale, $200

A month ago, Cash was increased by $600, as was a liability, Unearned Rent. Art's Wholesale received payment in advance but had not earned the rental income. Now, because $200 has been earned, the liability is reduced and Rental Income can be recorded for the $200. This step is shown as follows:

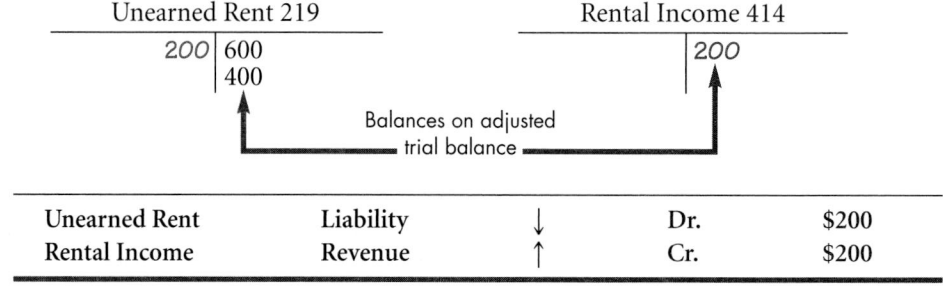

| Unearned Rent | Liability | ↓ | Dr. | $200 |
| Rental Income | Revenue | ↑ | Cr. | $200 |

Adjustment D: Supplies on Hand, $300

$500 worth of supplies has been used up; thus there is a need to increase Supplies Expense and decrease the asset Supplies.

Figure 11-5
Trial Balance Section of the Worksheet

	Trial Balance	
	Dr.	Cr.
Cash	12 9 2 0 00	
Petty Cash	1 0 0 00	
Accounts Receivable	14 5 0 0 00	
Merchandise Inventory	19 0 0 0 00	
Supplies	8 0 0 00	
Prepaid Insurance	9 0 0 00	
Store Equipment	4 0 0 0 00	
Acc. Dep., Store Equipment		4 0 0 00
Accounts Payable		17 9 0 0 00
Federal Income Tax Payable		8 0 0 00
FICA-Soc. Sec. Payable		4 5 4 00
FICA-Medicare Payable		1 0 6 00
State Income Tax Payable		2 0 0 00
SUTA Tax Payable		1 0 8 00
FUTA Tax Payable		3 2 00
Unearned Rent		6 0 0 00
Mortgage Payable		2 3 2 0 00
Art Newner, Capital		7 9 0 5 00
Art Newner, Withdrawals	8 6 0 0 00	
Income Summary		
Sales		95 0 0 0 00
Sales Returns and Allowances	9 5 0 00	
Sales Discount	6 7 0 00	
Purchases	52 0 0 0 00	
Purchases Discount		8 6 0 00
Purchases Returns and Allowances		6 8 0 00
Freight-In	4 5 0 00	
Salaries Expense	11 7 0 0 00	
Payroll Tax Expense	4 2 0 00	
Postage Expense	2 5 00	
Miscellaneous Expense	3 0 00	
Interest Expense	3 0 0 00	
	127 3 6 5 00	127 3 6 5 00

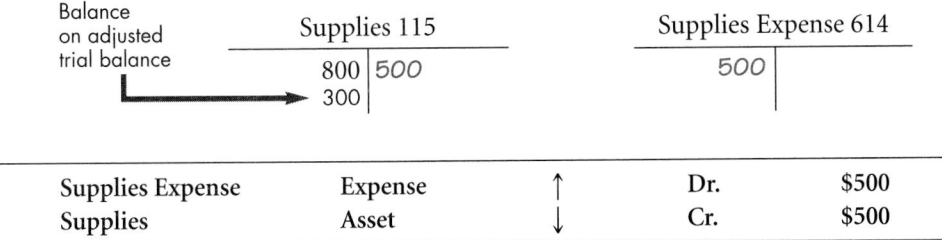

Supplies Expense	Expense	↑	Dr.	$500
Supplies	Asset	↓	Cr.	$500

Adjustment E: Insurance Expired, $300

Because insurance has expired by $300, Insurance Expense is increased by $300 and the asset Prepaid Insurance is decreased by $300.

Balance on adjusted trial balance

Prepaid Insurance 116
900 | 300
→ 600 |

Insurance Expense 615
300 |

TABLE 11-1 Summary of New Account Titles

Title	Category	Report(s) Found on	Normal Balance	Temporary or Permanent
Petty Cash	Asset	Balance Sheet	Dr.	Permanent
Merchandise Inventory* (Beginning)	Asset	Balance Sheet from prior period	Dr.	Permanent
	Cost of Goods Sold	Income Statement of current period		
Federal Income Tax Payable	Liability	Balance Sheet	Cr.	Permanent
FICA—Social Security Payable	Liability	Balance Sheet	Cr.	Permanent
FICA—Medicare Payable	Liability	Balance Sheet	Cr.	Permanent
State Income Tax Payable	Liability	Balance Sheet	Cr.	Permanent
SUTA Tax Payable	Liability	Balance Sheet	Cr.	Permanent
FUTA Tax Payable	Liability	Balance Sheet	Cr.	Permanent
Unearned Rent†	Liability	Balance Sheet	Cr.	Permanent
Mortgage Payable	Liability	Balance Sheet	Cr.	Permanent
Sales	Revenue	Income Statement	Cr.	Temporary
Sales Returns and Allowances	Contra Revenue	Income Statement	Dr.	Temporary
Sales Discount	Contra Revenue	Income Statement	Dr.	Temporary
Purchases§	Cost of Goods Sold	Income Statement	Dr.	Temporary
Purchases Discount	Contra-Cost of Goods Sold	Income Statement	Cr.	Temporary
Purchases Returns and Allowances	Contra-Cost of Goods Sold	Income Statement	Cr.	Temporary
Freight-In	Cost of Goods Sold	Income Statement	Dr.	Temporary
Payroll Tax Expense	Expense	Income Statement	Dr.	Temporary
Postage Expense	Expense	Income Statement	Dr.	Temporary
Interest Expense	Other Expense	Income Statement	Dr.	Temporary

*The ending inventory of current period is a contra-cost of goods sold on the income statement and will be an asset on the balance sheet for next period.

†Referred to as Unearned Revenue.

§Note that the category for Purchases and Freight-In are Cost of Goods Sold, whereas Purchases Discounts and Purchases Returns and Allowances are Contra-Cost of Goods Sold.

Insurance Expense	Expense	↑	Dr.	$300
Prepaid Insurance	Asset	↓	Cr.	$300

Adjustment F: Depreciation Expense, $50

When depreciation is taken, Depreciation Expense and Accumulated Depreciation are both increased by $50. Note that the cost of the store equipment remains the same.

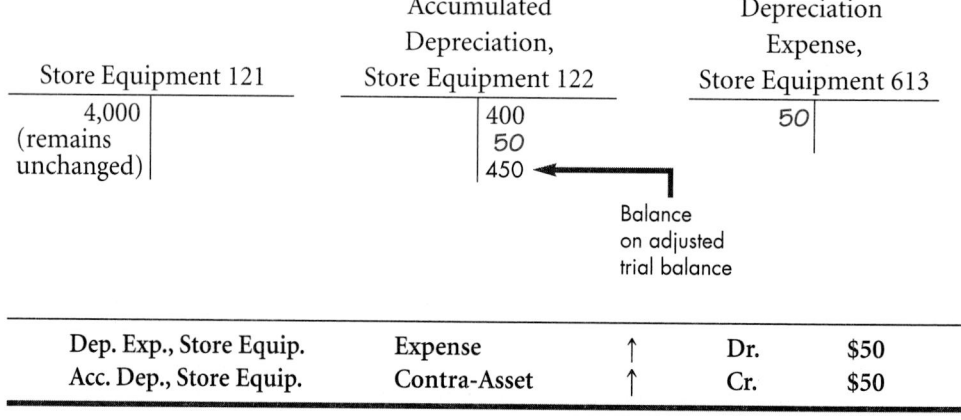

Dep. Exp., Store Equip.	Expense	↑	Dr.	$50
Acc. Dep., Store Equip.	Contra-Asset	↑	Cr.	$50

Adjustment G: Salaries Accrued, $600

The $600 in Salaries Accrued causes an increase in Salaries Expense and Salaries Payable.

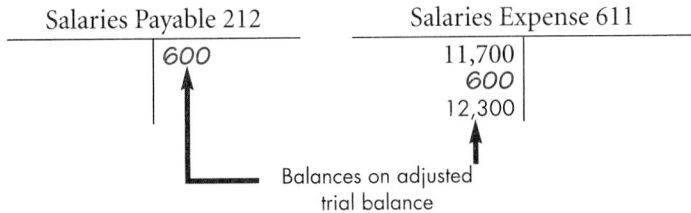

(Cont. on page 445)

	Trial Balance		Adjustments		Adjusted Trial Balance	
	Dr.	Cr.	Dr.	Cr.	Dr.	Cr.
Cash	1 2 9 2 0 00				1 2 9 2 0 00	
Petty Cash	1 0 0 00				1 0 0 00	
Accounts Receivable	1 4 5 0 0 00		(B)	(A)	1 4 5 0 0 00	
Merchandise Inventory	1 9 0 0 0 00		4 0 0 0 00	1 9 0 0 0 00	4 0 0 0 00	
Supplies	8 0 0 00			(D) 5 0 0 00	3 0 0 00	
Prepaid Insurance	9 0 0 00			(E) 3 0 0 00	6 0 0 00	
Store Equipment	4 0 0 0 00				4 0 0 0 00	
Acc. Dep., Store Equipment		4 0 0 00		(F) 5 0 00		4 5 0 00
Accounts Payable		1 7 9 0 0 00				1 7 9 0 0 00
Federal Income Tax Payable		8 0 0 00				8 0 0 00
FICA-Soc. Sec. Payable		4 5 4 00				4 5 4 00
FICA-Medicare Payable		1 0 6 00				1 0 6 00
State Income Tax Payable		2 0 0 00				2 0 0 00
SUTA Tax Payable		1 0 8 00				1 0 8 00
FUTA Tax Payable		3 2 00				3 2 00
Unearned Rent		6 0 0 00	(C) 2 0 0 00			4 0 0 00
Mortgage Payable		2 3 2 0 00				2 3 2 0 00
Art Newner, Capital		7 9 0 5 00				7 9 0 5 00
Art Newner, Withdrawals	8 6 0 0 00		(A)	(B)	8 6 0 0 00	
Income Summary			1 9 0 0 0 00	4 0 0 0 00	1 9 0 0 0 00	4 0 0 0 00
Sales		9 5 0 0 0 00				9 5 0 0 0 00
Sales Returns and Allowances	9 5 0 00				9 5 0 00	
Sales Discount	6 7 0 00				6 7 0 00	
Purchases	5 2 0 0 0 00				5 2 0 0 0 00	
Purchases Discount		8 6 0 00				8 6 0 00
Purchases Returns and Allowances		6 8 0 00				6 8 0 00
Freight-In	4 5 0 00				4 5 0 00	
Salaries Expense	1 1 7 0 0 00		(G) 6 0 0 00		1 2 3 0 0 00	
Payroll Tax Expense	4 2 0 00				4 2 0 00	
Postage Expense	2 5 00				2 5 00	
Miscellaneous Expense	3 0 00				3 0 00	
Interest Expense	3 0 0 00				3 0 0 00	
	1 2 7 3 6 5 00	1 2 7 3 6 5 00				
Rental Income				(C) 2 0 0 00		2 0 0 00
Supplies Expense			(D) 5 0 0 00		5 0 0 00	
Insurance Expense			(E) 3 0 0 00		3 0 0 00	
Depreciation Expense, Store Equip.			(F) 5 0 00		5 0 00	
Salaries Payable				(G) 6 0 0 00		6 0 0 00
			2 4 6 5 0 00	2 4 6 5 0 00	1 3 2 0 1 5 00	1 3 2 0 1 5 00

Figure 11-6 Worksheet with Three Columns Filled Out

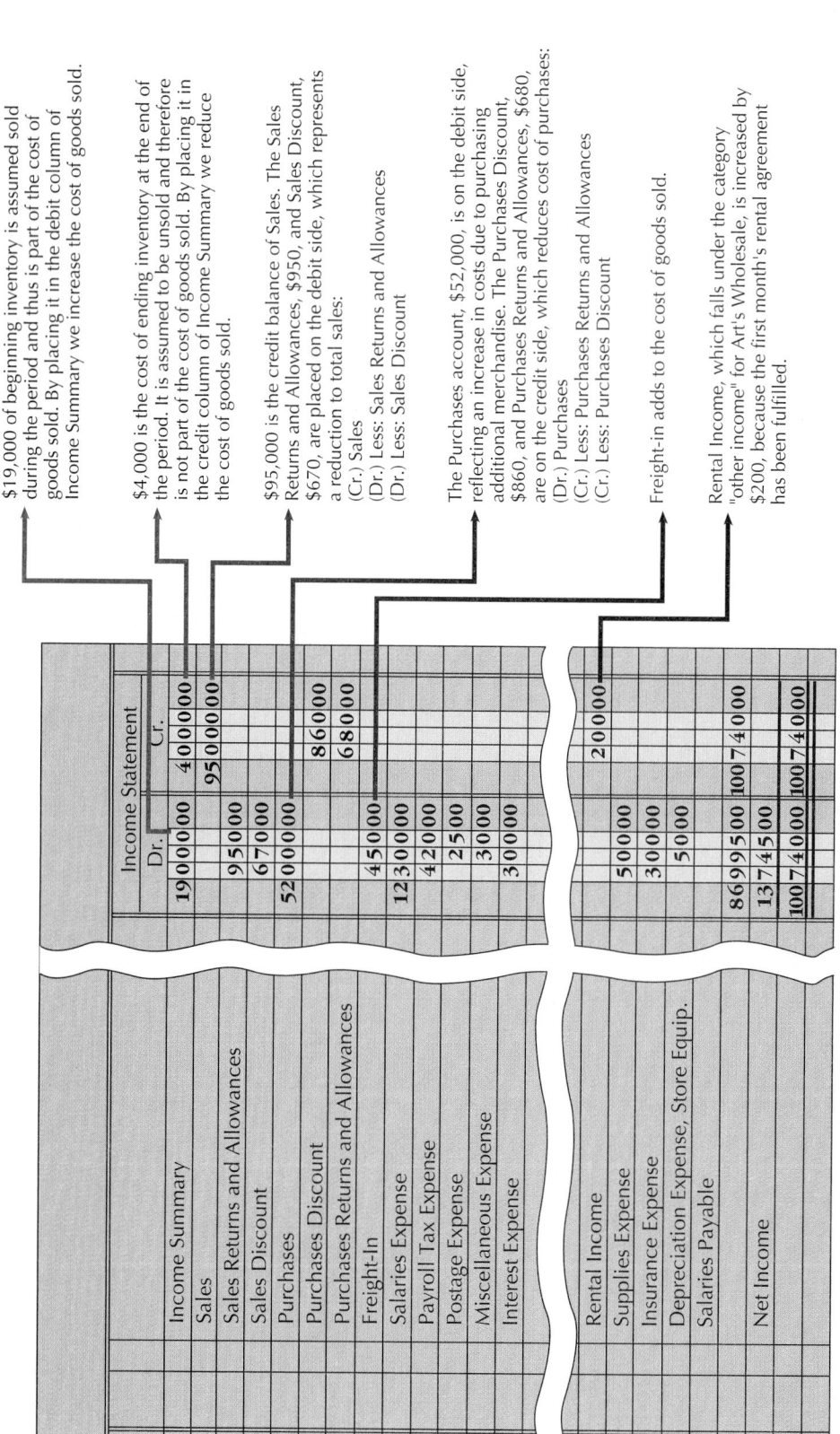

$19,000 of beginning inventory is assumed sold during the period and thus is part of the cost of goods sold. By placing it in the debit column of Income Summary we increase the cost of goods sold.

$4,000 is the cost of ending inventory at the end of the period. It is assumed to be unsold and therefore is not part of the cost of goods sold. By placing it in the credit column of Income Summary we reduce the cost of goods sold.

$95,000 is the credit balance of Sales. The Sales Returns and Allowances, $950, and Sales Discount, $670, are placed on the debit side, which represents a reduction to total sales:
(Cr.) Sales
(Dr.) Less: Sales Returns and Allowances
(Dr.) Less: Sales Discount

The Purchases account, $52,000, is on the debit side, reflecting an increase in costs due to purchasing additional merchandise. The Purchases Discount, $860, and Purchases Returns and Allowances, $680, are on the credit side, which reduces cost of purchases:
(Dr.) Purchases
(Cr.) Less: Purchases Returns and Allowances
(Cr.) Less: Purchases Discount

Freight-in adds to the cost of goods sold.

Rental Income, which falls under the category "other income" for Art's Wholesale, is increased by $200, because the first month's rental agreement has been fulfilled.

	Income Statement	
	Dr.	Cr.
Income Summary	19 000 00	4 000 00
Sales		95 000 00
Sales Returns and Allowances	950 00	
Sales Discount	670 00	
Purchases	52 000 00	
Purchases Discount		860 00
Purchases Returns and Allowances		680 00
Freight-In	450 00	
Salaries Expense	12 300 00	
Payroll Tax Expense	420 00	
Postage Expense	25 00	
Miscellaneous Expense	30 00	
Interest Expense	300 00	
Rental Income		200 00
Supplies Expense	500 00	
Insurance Expense	300 00	
Depreciation Expense, Store Equip.	50 00	
Salaries Payable		
	86 995 00	100 740 00
Net Income	13 745 00	
	100 740 00	100 740 00

Figure 11-7 Income Statement Section of the Worksheet

| Salaries Expense | Expense | ↑ | Dr. | $600 |
| Salaries Payable | Liability | ↑ | Cr. | $600 |

Figure 11-6, p. 443, shows the worksheet with the adjustments and adjusted trial balance column filled out. Note that the adjustment numbers in Income Summary from beginning and ending inventory are also carried over to the adjusted trial balance and are not combined.

The next step in completing the worksheet is to fill out the income statement columns from the adjusted trial balance, as shown in Figure 11-7, p. 444.

The next step in completing the worksheet is to fill out the balance sheet columns (Fig. 11-8). Note how ending inventory is carried over to the balance sheet from the adjusted trial balance column. Take time also to look at the placement of the payroll tax liabilities as well as Unearned Rent on the worksheet.

Figure 11-9, on pages 446–447, is the completed worksheet.

> *Remember:*
> We do not combine the $19,000 and $4,000 in Income Summary. When we prepare the cost of goods sold section for the formal financial statement, we will need both a beginning and an ending figure for inventory.

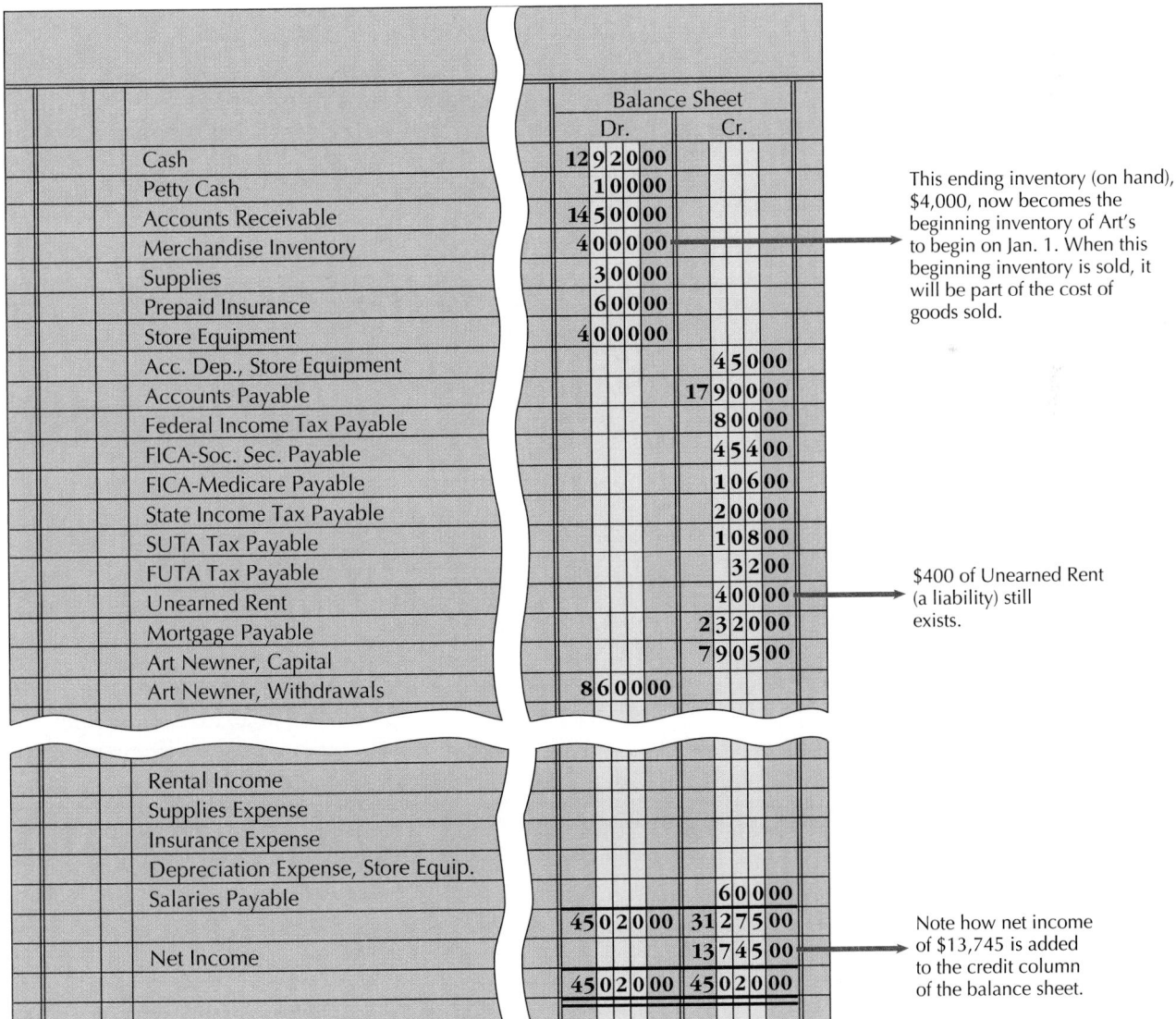

	Balance Sheet	
	Dr.	Cr.
Cash	12 9 2 0 00	
Petty Cash	1 0 0 00	
Accounts Receivable	14 5 0 0 00	
Merchandise Inventory	4 0 0 0 00	
Supplies	3 0 0 00	
Prepaid Insurance	6 0 0 00	
Store Equipment	4 0 0 0 00	
Acc. Dep., Store Equipment		4 5 0 00
Accounts Payable		17 9 0 0 00
Federal Income Tax Payable		8 0 0 00
FICA-Soc. Sec. Payable		4 5 4 00
FICA-Medicare Payable		1 0 6 00
State Income Tax Payable		2 0 0 00
SUTA Tax Payable		1 0 8 00
FUTA Tax Payable		3 2 00
Unearned Rent		4 0 0 00
Mortgage Payable		23 2 0 0 00
Art Newner, Capital		79 0 5 00
Art Newner, Withdrawals	8 6 0 0 00	
Rental Income		
Supplies Expense		
Insurance Expense		
Depreciation Expense, Store Equip.		
Salaries Payable		6 0 0 00
	45 0 2 0 00	31 2 7 5 00
Net Income		13 7 4 5 00
	45 0 2 0 00	45 0 2 0 00

This ending inventory (on hand), $4,000, now becomes the beginning inventory of Art's to begin on Jan. 1. When this beginning inventory is sold, it will be part of the cost of goods sold.

$400 of Unearned Rent (a liability) still exists.

Note how net income of $13,745 is added to the credit column of the balance sheet.

Figure 11-8 Balance Sheet Section of the Worksheet

WORKSHEET
FOR YEAR ENDED DECEMBER 31, 200X

	Trial Balance Dr.	Trial Balance Cr.	Adjustments Dr.	Adjustments Cr.
Cash	12 92 0 00			
Petty Cash	1 0 0 00			
Accounts Receivable	14 50 0 00			
Merchandise Inventory	19 00 0 00		(B)4 0 0 00	(A)19 0 0 00
Supplies	8 0 0 00			(D)5 0 0 00
Prepaid Insurance	9 0 0 00			(E)3 0 0 00
Store Equipment	4 00 0 00			
Acc. Dep., Store Equipment		4 0 0 00		(F) 5 0 00
Accounts Payable		17 90 0 00		
Federal Income Tax Payable		8 0 0 00		
FICA—Social Security Payable		4 5 4 00		
FICA—Medicare Payable		1 0 6 00		
State Income Tax Payable		2 0 0 00		
SUTA Tax Payable		1 0 8 00		
FUTA Tax Payable		3 2 00		
Unearned Rent		6 0 0 00	(C)2 0 0 00	
Mortgage Payable		23 2 0 00		
Art Newner, Capital		79 0 5 00		
Art Newner, Withdrawals	8 60 0 00			
Income Summary			(A)19 0 0 00	(B)4 0 0 00
Sales		95 00 0 00		
Sales Returns and Allowances	9 5 0 00			
Sales Discount	6 7 0 00			
Purchases	52 00 0 00			
Purchases Discount		8 6 0 00		
Purchases Returns and Allowances		6 8 0 00		
Freight-In	4 5 0 00			
Salaries Expense	11 70 0 00		(G)6 0 0 00	
Payroll Tax Expense	4 2 0 00			
Postage Expense	2 5 00			
Miscellaneous Expense	3 0 00			
Interest Expense	3 0 0 00			
	127 36 5 00	127 36 5 00		
Rental Income				(C)2 0 0 00
Supplies Expense			(D)5 0 0 00	
Insurance Expense			(E)3 0 0 00	
Depreciation Expense, Store Equip.			(F) 5 0 00	
Salaries Payable				(G)6 0 0 00
			24 65 0 00	24 65 0 00
Net Income				

Figure 11-9 Completed Worksheet

Adjusted Trial Bal. Dr.	Adjusted Trial Bal. Cr.	Income Statement Dr.	Income Statement Cr.	Balance Sheet Dr.	Balance Sheet Cr.
1292000				1292000	
10000				10000	
1450000				1450000	
40000				40000	
3000				3000	
6000				6000	
40000				40000	
	45000				45000
	1790000				1790000
	80000				80000
	45400				45400
	10600				10600
	20000				20000
	10800				10800
	3200				3200
	40000				40000
	232000				232000
	790500				790500
860000				860000	
1900000	400000	1900000	400000		
	9500000		9500000		
95000		95000			
67000		67000			
5200000		5200000			
	86000		86000		
	68000		68000		
45000		45000			
1230000		1230000			
42000		42000			
2500		2500			
3000		3000			
30000		30000			
	20000		20000		
50000		50000			
30000		30000			
5000		5000			
	60000				60000
13201500	13201500	8699500	10074000	4502000	3127500
		1374500			1374500
		10074000	10074000	4502000	4502000

Figure 11-9 (*continued*)

Learning Unit 11-2 Review

AT THIS POINT you should be able to

- Complete adjustments for a merchandise company. (p. 440)
- Complete a worksheet. (pp. 446–447)

SELF-REVIEW QUIZ 11-2

(Use the foldout worksheet at the end of the *Study Guide and Working Papers*.)

From the trial balance shown on Figure 11-10, complete a worksheet for Ray Company. Additional data include the following: (A and B) On December 31, 200X, ending inventory was calculated as $200; (C) Storage Fees Earned, $516; (D) Rent Expired, $100; (E) Depreciation Expense, Office Equipment, $60; (F) Salaries Accrued, $200.

Figure 11-10
Trial Balance of Ray Company

Account Title	Trial Balance Dr.	Trial Balance Cr.
Cash	2 4 8 6 00	
Merchandise Inventory	8 2 4 00	
Prepaid Rent	1 1 5 2 00	
Prepaid Insurance	6 0 00	
Office Equipment	2 1 6 0 00	
Accumulated Depreciation, Office Equipment		5 6 0 00
Unearned Storage Fees		2 5 1 6 00
Accounts Payable		1 0 0 00
B. Ray, Capital		1 9 3 2 00
Income Summary		
Sales		1 1 0 4 0 00
Sales Returns and Allowances	5 4 6 00	
Sales Discount	2 1 6 00	
Purchases	5 2 5 6 00	
Purchases Returns and Allowances		1 6 8 00
Purchases Discount		1 0 2 00
Salaries Expense	2 0 1 6 00	
Insurance Expense	1 3 9 2 00	
Utilities Expense	9 6 00	
Plumbing Expense	2 1 4 00	
	1 6 4 1 8 00	1 6 4 1 8 00

SOLUTION TO SELF-REVIEW QUIZ 11-2

The solution is shown on page 449 in Figure 11-11.

Quiz Tip:
The ending inventory of $200 becomes next month's beginning inventory.

RAY COMPANY
WORKSHEET
FOR YEAR ENDED DECEMBER 31, 200X

	Trial Balance Dr.	Trial Balance Cr.	Adjustments Dr.	Adjustments Cr.	Adjusted Trial Balance Dr.	Adjusted Trial Balance Cr.	Income Statement Dr.	Income Statement Cr.	Balance Sheet Dr.	Balance Sheet Cr.
Cash	248600				248600				248600	
Merchandise Inventory	82400		(B) 200000	(A) 82400	200000				200000	
Prepaid Rent	205200			(D) 100000	105200				105200	
Prepaid Insurance	6000				6000				6000	
Office Equipment	216000				216000				216000	
Acc. Dep., Store Equipment		56000		(E) 6000		62000				62000
Unearned Storage Fees		251600	(C) 51600			200000				200000
Accounts Payable		10000				10000				10000
B. Ray, Capital		193200				193200				193200
Income Summary			(A) 82400	(B) 200000	82400	200000	82400	200000		
Sales		1104000				1104000		1104000		
Sales Returns and Allowances	54600				54600		54600			
Sales Discount	21600				21600		21600			
Purchases	525600				525600		525600			
Purchases Returns and Allowances		16800				16800		16800		
Purchases Discount		10200				10200		10200		
Salaries Expense	201600		(F) 20000		221600		221600			
Insurance Expense	139200				139200		139200			
Utilities Expense	9600				9600		9600			
Plumbing Expense	21400				21400		21400			
	1641800	1641800								
Storage Fees Earned				(C) 51600		51600		51600		
Rent Expense			(D) 100000		100000		100000			
Depreciation Expense, Equipment			(E) 6000		6000		6000			
Salaries Payable				(F) 20000		20000				20000
			190000	190000	1687800	1687800	1092000	1202600	595800	485200
Net Income							110600			110600
							1202600	1202600	595800	595800

Figure 11-11 Worksheet for Ray Company

Chapter Review

Summary of Key Points

Learning Unit 11-1

1. The periodic inventory system updates the record of goods on hand only at the *end* of the accounting period. This system is used for companies with a variety of merchandise with low unit prices.
2. In the periodic inventory system, additional purchases of merchandise during the accounting period will be recorded in the Purchases account. The amount in beginning inventory will remain unchanged during the accounting period. At the end of the period, a new figure for ending inventory will be calculated.
3. Beginning inventory at the end of the accounting period is part of the cost of goods sold, whereas ending inventory is a reduction to cost of goods sold.
4. The perpetual inventory system keeps a continuous record of inventory. It is used by companies with high amounts of inventory.
5. Net sales less cost of goods sold equals gross profit. Gross profit less operating expenses equals net income.
6. Unearned Revenue is a liability account that accumulates revenue that has *not* been earned yet, although the cash has been received. It represents a liability to the seller until the service or product is performed or delivered.

Learning Unit 11-2

1. Two important adjustments in the accounting for a merchandise company deal with the Merchandise Inventory account and with the Unearned Revenue account (unearned rent).
2. When a company delivers goods or services for which it has been paid in advance, an adjustment is made to reduce the liability account Unearned Revenue and to increase an earned revenue account.

Key Terms

Beginning merchandise inventory (beginning inventory) The cost of goods on hand in a company to *begin* an accounting period.

Cost of goods sold Total cost of goods sold to customers.

Ending merchandise inventory (ending inventory) The cost of goods that remain unsold at the *end* of the accounting period. It is an asset on the new balance sheet.

Freight-in A cost of goods sold account that records shipping cost to buyer.

Gross profit Net sales less cost of goods sold.

Interest Expense The cost of borrowing money.

Mortgage Payable A liability account showing amount owed on a mortgage.

Periodic inventory system An inventory system that, at the *end* of each accounting period, calculates the cost of the unsold goods on hand by taking the cost of each unit times the number of units of each product on hand.

Perpetual inventory system An inventory system that keeps *continual track* of each type of inventory by recording units on hand at the beginning, units sold, and the current balance after each sale or purchase.

Unearned Revenue A liability account that records receipt of payment for goods or services in advance of delivery.

Blueprint: A Worksheet for a Merchandise Company

Account Titles	Adjustments Dr.	Adjustments Cr.	Adjusted Trial Balance Dr.	Adjusted Trial Balance Cr.	Income Statement Dr.	Income Statement Cr.	Balance Sheet Dr.	Balance Sheet Cr.
Cash			X				X	
Petty Cash			X				X	
Accounts Receivable			X				X	
Merchandise Inventory	X-E	X-B	X-E				X-E	
Supplies			X				X	
Equipment			X				X	
Acc. Dep., Store Equipment				X				X
Accounts Payable				X				X
Federal Income Tax Payable				X				X
FICA-Social Security Payable				X				X
FICA-Medicare Payable				X				X
State Income Tax Payable				X				X
SUTA Tax Payable				X				X
FUTA Tax Payable				X				X
Unearned Sales				X				X
Mortgage Payable				X				X
A. Flynn, Capital				X				X
A. Flynn, Withdrawals			X				X	
Income Summary*	X-B	X-E	X-B	X-E	X-B	X-E		
Sales				X		X		
Sales Returns and Allow.			X		X			
Sales Discount			X		X			
Purchases			X		X			
Purchases Ret. and Allow.				X		X		
Purchases Discount				X		X		
Freight-In			X		X			
Salaries Expense			X		X			
Payroll Tax Expense			X		X			
Insurance Expense			X		X			
Depreciation Expense			X		X			
Salaries Payable				X				X
Rental Income				X		X		

* Note that the figures for beginning (X-B) and ending inventory (X-E) are never combined on the Income Summary line of the worksheet. When the formal income statement is prepared, two distinct figures for inventory will be used to explain and calculate cost of goods sold. Beginning inventory adds to cost of goods sold; ending inventory reduces cost of goods sold.

Questions, Mini Exercises, Exercises, and Problems

Discussion Questions

1. What is the function of the Purchases account?
2. Explain why Unearned Revenue is a liability account.
3. In a periodic system of inventory, the balance of beginning inventory will remain unchanged during the period. True or false?

4. What is the purpose of an inventory sheet?

5. Why do many Unearned Revenue accounts have to be adjusted?

6. Explain why figures for beginning and ending inventory are not combined on the Income Summary line of the worksheet.

Mini Exercises

(The forms you need are on page 364 of the *Study Guide and Working Papers.*)

Adjustment for Merchandise Inventory

1. Given the following, journalize the adjusting entries for merchandise inventory. Note that ending inventory has a balance of $14,000.

Merchandise Inventory 114	Income Summary 313
30,000	

Adjustment for Unearned Fees

2.

    a. Given the following, journalize the adjusting entry. By December 31, $300 of the unearned dog walking fees were earned.

Unearned Dog Walking Fees 225	Earned Dog Walking Fees 441
650 12/1/XX	4,000 12/1/XX

    b. What is the category of unearned dog walking fees?

Worksheet

3. Match the following:
    1. Located on the Income Statement debit column of the worksheet.
    2. Located on the Income Statement credit column of the worksheet.
    3. Located on the Balance Sheet debit column of the worksheet.
    4. Located on the Balance Sheet credit column of the worksheet.
    _____ a. Ending Merchandise Inventory
    _____ b. Unearned Rent
    _____ c. Sales Discount
    _____ d. Purchases
    _____ e. Rental Income
    _____ f. Petty Cash

Merchandise Inventory Adjustment on Worksheet

4. Adjustment column of a worksheet:

    Merchandise Inventory
    Income Summary
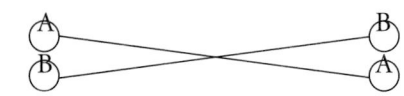

    Explain what the letters A and B represent. Why are they never combined?

Income Summary on the Worksheet

5.

	Adj.		ATB		Income Statement	
	Dr.	Cr.	Dr.	Cr.	Dr.	Cr.
Income Summary	A	B	C	D	E	F

Given a figure of beginning inventory of $500 and a $700 figure for ending inventory, place these numbers on the Income Summary line of this partial worksheet.

Exercises

(The forms you need are on page 365 of the *Study Guide and Working Papers*.)

11-1. Indicate the normal balance and category of each of the following accounts.

Categorizing account titles.

   a. Unearned Revenue
   b. Merchandise Inventory (beginning of period)
   c. Freight-in
   d. Payroll Tax Expense
   e. Purchases Discount
   f. Sales Discount
   g. FICA—Social Security Payable
   h. Purchases Returns and Allowances

11-2. From the following, calculate (a) net sales, (b) cost of goods sold, (c) gross profit, and (d) net income: Sales, $22,000; Sales Discount, $500; Sales Returns and Allowances, $250; Beginning Inventory, $650; Net Purchases, $13,200; Ending Inventory, $510; Operating Expenses, $3,600.

Calculating net sales, cost of goods sold, gross profit, and net income.

11-3. Allan Co. had the following balances on December 31, 200X:

Unearned revenue.

Cash		Unearned Janitorial Service
2,100		600

Janitorial Service
7,200

The accountant for Allan has asked you to make an adjustment, because $400 of janitorial services has just been performed for customers who had paid two months. Construct a transaction analysis chart.

11-4. Lesan Co. purchased merchandise costing $400,000. Calculate the cost of goods sold under the following different situations:

Calculating cost of goods sold.

   a. Beginning inventory $40,000 and no ending inventory.
   b. Beginning inventory $50,000 and a $60,000 ending inventory.
   c. No beginning inventory and a $30,000 ending inventory.

11-5. Prepare a worksheet from the following information using Figure 11-12, p. 454:

Preparing a worksheet.

a/b.	Merchandise Inventory, ending	13
c.	Store Supplies on hand	4
d.	Depreciation on Store Equipment	4
e.	Accrued Salaries	2

Group A Problems

(The forms you need are on page 366 of the *Study Guide and Working Papers*. You can also use the foldout worksheets at the end of the *Study Guide and Working Papers*.)

Calculating net sales, cost of goods sold, gross profit, and net income.

11A-1. Based on the following accounts, calculate:

   a. Net sales.
   b. Cost of goods sold.
   c. Gross profit.
   d. Net income.

Check Figure:
Net income. $1,958

Figure 11-12
Trial Balance for
Moore Co.

MOORE CO. TRIAL BALANCE DECEMBER 31, 200X	Dr.	Cr.
Cash	8 00	
Accounts Receivable	5 00	
Merchandise Inventory	1 1 00	
Store Supplies	1 0 00	
Store Equipment	2 0 00	
Accumulated Depreciation, Store Equipment		6 00
Accounts Payable		5 00
J. Moore, Capital		3 4 00
Income Summary	—	—
Sales		6 4 00
Sales Returns and Allowances	9 00	
Purchases	2 3 00	
Purchases Discount		3 00
Freight-In	3 00	
Salaries Expense	1 0 00	
Advertising Expense	1 3 00	
Totals	1 1 2 00	1 1 2 00

Accounts Payable	$ 4,800
Operating Expenses	1,500
Lang.com, Capital	18,200
Purchases	1,300
Freight-In	70
Ending Merchandise Inventory, Dec. 31, 200X	55
Sales	5,000
Accounts Receivable	400
Cash	700
Purchases Discount	40
Sales Returns and Allowances	210
Beg. Merchandise Inventory, Jan. 1, 200X	75
Purchases Returns and Allowances	66
Sales Discount	48

Comprehensive Problem: Completing a worksheet for a merchandise company.

11A-2. From the trial balance in Figure 11-13, p. 455, complete a worksheet for Jim's Hardware. Assume the following:

a/b. Ending inventory on December 31 is calculated at $310.
  c. Insurance expired, $150.
  d. Depreciation on store equipment, $60.
  e. Accrued wages, $90.

Comprehensive Problem: Completing a worksheet.

11A-3. The owner of Waltz Company has asked you to prepare a worksheet from the trial balance in Figure 11-14, p. 455.
Additional data:

a/b. Ending merchandise inventory on December 31, $1,805.
  c. Office supplies used up, $210.
  d. Rent expired, $195.
  e. Depreciation expense on office equipment, $550.
  f. Office salaries earned but not paid, $310.

JIM'S HARDWARE
TRIAL BALANCE
DECEMBER 31, 200X

	Dr.	Cr.
Cash	7 8 6 00	
Accounts Receivable	1 1 5 2 00	
Merchandise Inventory	6 0 0 00	
Prepaid Insurance	6 8 4 00	
Store Equipment	2 1 6 0 00	
Accumulated Depreciation, Store Equipment		6 6 0 00
Accounts Payable		5 1 6 00
Jim Spool, Capital		1 6 3 2 00
Income Summary		
Hardware Sales		1 1 0 4 0 00
Hardware Sales Returns and Allowances	5 4 6 00	
Hardware Sales Discount	2 1 6 00	
Purchases	5 2 5 6 00	
Purchases Discount		1 6 8 00
Purchases Returns and Allowances		1 0 2 00
Wages Expense	1 7 1 6 00	
Rent Expense	7 9 2 00	
Telephone Expense	1 1 4 00	
Miscellaneous Expense	9 6 00	
	1 4 1 1 8 00	1 4 1 1 8 00

Figure 11-13
Trial Balance for Jim's Hardware

Check Figure:
Net income $1,984

WALTZ COMPANY
TRIAL BALANCE
DECEMBER 31, 200X

	Dr.	Cr.
Cash	5 4 0 8 00	
Petty Cash	2 4 0 00	
Accounts Receivable	2 5 1 2 00	
Beginning Merchandise Inventory, Jan. 1	5 0 9 2 00	
Prepaid Rent	6 1 6 00	
Office Supplies	9 4 4 00	
Office Equipment	9 2 8 0 00	
Accumulated Depreciation, Office Equipment		7 6 0 0 00
Accounts Payable		5 9 6 4 00
K. Waltz, Capital		5 4 7 6 00
K. Waltz, Withdrawals	4 8 0 0 00	
Income Summary		
Sales		5 2 4 8 4 00
Sales Returns and Allowances	9 6 00	
Sales Discount	2 4 0 0 00	
Purchases	2 9 3 1 6 00	
Purchases Discount		1 6 00
Purchases Returns and Allowances		3 4 8 00
Office Salaries Expense	7 4 0 8 00	
Insurance Expense	2 4 0 0 00	
Advertising Expense	8 0 0 00	
Utilities Expense	5 7 6 00	
	7 1 8 8 8 00	7 1 8 8 8 00

Figure 11-14
Trial Balance for Waltz Company

Check Figure:
Net income $5,300

Figure 11-15
Trial Balance for Ron's
Wholesale Clothing
Company

RON'S WHOLESALE CLOTHING COMPANY TRIAL BALANCE DECEMBER 31, 200X	Dr.	Cr.
Cash	4 4 6 0 00	
Petty Cash	3 0 0 00	
Accounts Receivable	7 5 0 0 00	
Merchandise Inventory	9 0 0 0 00	
Supplies	1 0 0 0 00	
Prepaid Insurance	8 5 0 00	
Store Equipment	2 5 0 0 00	
Acc. Dep., Store Equipment		1 5 0 0 00
Accounts Payable		10 6 3 5 00
Federal Income Tax Payable		5 0 0 00
FICA—Social Security Payable		4 5 4 00
FICA—Medicare Payable		1 0 6 00
State Income Tax Payable		1 5 0 00
SUTA Tax Payable		1 0 8 00
FUTA Tax Payable		3 2 00
Unearned Storage Fees		3 2 5 00
Ron Win, Capital		12 5 0 0 00
Ron Win, Withdrawals	4 3 0 0 00	
Income Summary	—	—
Sales		45 0 0 0 00
Sales Returns and Allowances	1 4 7 5 00	
Sales Discount	1 3 3 5 00	
Purchases	26 0 0 0 00	
Purchases Discount		5 5 0 00
Purchases Returns and Allowances		4 0 0 00
Freight-In	2 2 5 00	
Salaries Expense	12 0 0 0 00	
Payroll Tax Expense	4 2 0 00	
Interest Expense	8 9 5 00	
	72 2 6 0 00	72 2 6 0 00

*Comprehensive Problem:
Completing a worksheet
with payroll and unearned
revenue.*

*Check Figure:
Net loss $824*

11A-4. From the trial balance in Figure 11-15 and additional data, complete the worksheet for Ron's Wholesale Clothing Company.
Additional data:

a/b. Ending merchandise inventory on December 31, $6,000.
  c. Supplies on hand, $400.
  d. Insurance expired, $600.
  e. Depreciation on store equipment, $400.
  f. Storage fees earned, $176.

Group B Problems

(The forms you need are on page 366 of the *Study Guide and Working Papers.*)

11B-1. From the following accounts, calculate (a) net sales, (b) cost of goods sold, (c) gross profit, and (d) net income.

*Calculating net sales, cost
of goods sold, gross profit,
and net income.*

Sales Discount	$ 452
Purchases Returns and Allowances	64
Beginning Merchandise Inventory, Jan 1, 200X	79
Sales Returns and Allowances	191

Purchases Discounts	42
Cash	3,895
Accounts Receivable	441
Sales	3,950
Ending Merchandise Inventory, Dec. 31, 200X	75
Freight-In	41
Purchases	1,152
R. Roland, Capital	1,950
Operating Expenses	895
Accounts Payable	129

Check Figure:
Net income $1,321

11B-2. As the accountant for Jim's Hardware, you have been asked to complete a worksheet from the trial balance in Figure 11-16 as well as additional data. Additional data:

a/b. Cost of ending inventory on December 31, $480.
  c. Insurance expired, $112.
  d. Depreciation on store equipment, $90.
  e. Accrued wages, $150.

Comprehensive Problem:
Completing a worksheet for a merchandise company.

11B-3. From Figure 11-17, p. 458, complete a worksheet for Waltz Company. Additional data:

a/b. Ending merchandise inventory on December 31, $1,600.
  c. Office supplies on hand, $90.
  d. Rent expired, $110.
  e. Depreciation expense on office equipment, $250.
  f. Salaries accrued, $180.

Comprehensive Problem:
Completing a worksheet.

11B-4. From the trial balance in Figure 11-18, p. 459, and additional data, complete the worksheet for Ron's Wholesale Clothing Company.

Comprehensive Problem:
Completing a worksheet with payroll and unearned revenue.

Figure 11-16
Trial Balance for Jim's Hardware

JIM'S HARDWARE TRIAL BALANCE DECEMBER 31, 200X		
	Dr.	Cr.
Cash	9 6 0 00	
Accounts Receivable	1 6 0 0 00	
Merchandise Inventory	7 3 6 00	
Prepaid Insurance	1 1 1 2 00	
Store Equipment	3 2 0 0 00	
Accumulated Depreciation, Store Equipment		1 6 8 0 00
Accounts Payable		1 4 0 8 00
J. Spool, Capital		2 5 7 6 00
Income Summary		
Hardware Sales		1 4 8 0 0 00
Hardware Sales Returns and Allowances	7 2 8 00	
Hardware Sales Discount	6 8 8 00	
Purchases	7 0 8 8 00	
Purchases Discounts		2 4 0 00
Purchases Returns and Allowances		2 4 8 00
Wages Expense	2 3 0 4 00	
Rent Expense	1 8 4 0 00	
Telephone Expense	5 5 2 00	
Miscellaneous Expense	1 4 4 00	
	2 0 9 5 2 00	2 0 9 5 2 00

Check Figure:
Net income $8,686

Figure 11-17
Trial Balance for Waltz
Company

WALTZ COMPANY TRIAL BALANCE DECEMBER 31, 200X		
	Dr.	Cr.
Cash	3 8 0 0 00	
Petty Cash	1 0 0 00	
Accounts Receivable	3 4 0 0 00	
Merchandise Inventory	5 2 0 4 00	
Prepaid Rent	1 2 0 0 00	
Office Supplies	1 3 6 0 00	
Office Equipment	9 6 8 0 00	
Accumulated Depreciation, Office Equipment		4 0 4 0 00
Accounts Payable		7 9 6 4 00
K. Waltz, Capital		5 4 7 6 00
K. Waltz, Withdrawals	5 0 0 0 00	
Income Summary	—	—
Sales		5 2 4 6 2 00
Sales Returns and Allowances	1 1 6 00	
Sales Discount	2 2 0 0 00	
Purchases	2 9 2 9 6 00	
Purchases Discounts		1 2 0 8 00
Purchases Returns and Allowances		1 3 5 0 00
Office Salaries Expense	7 4 0 8 00	
Insurance Expense	2 2 0 0 00	
Advertising Expense	8 0 0 00	
Utilities Expense	7 3 6 00	
	7 2 5 0 0 00	7 2 5 0 0 00

Check Figure:
Net income $6,850

Additional data:

a/b. Ending merchandise inventory on December 31, $9,000.
  c. Supplies on hand, $50.
  d. Insurance expired, $55.
  e. Depreciation on store equipment, $100.
  f. Storage fees earned, $115.

Real-World Applications

11R-1. Kim Andrews prepared the income statement in Figure 11-19 (p. 459) on a cash basis for Ed Sloan, M.D.

Dr. Sloan has requested written information from Kim as to what his professional fees earned would be under the accrual-basis system of accounting. Kim has asked you to provide Dr. Sloan with this information, based on the following facts that Kim ignored in the original preparation of the financial report:

	20X1	20X2
Accrued Professional Fees	$4,200	$5,300
Unearned Professional Fees	6,200	4,250

Make a written recommendation about the advantages of an accrual system to Dr. Sloan.

RON'S WHOLESALE CLOTHING COMPANY TRIAL BALANCE DECEMBER 31, 200X	Dr.	Cr.
Cash	2 6 0 0 00	
Petty Cash	3 0 00	
Accounts Receivable	3 0 0 0 00	
Merchandise Inventory	3 6 0 0 00	
Supplies	2 7 0 00	
Prepaid Insurance	1 8 0 00	
Store Equipment	1 0 0 0 00	
Accumulated Depreciation, Store Equipment		4 9 6 00
Accounts Payable		4 5 9 0 00
FIT Payable		3 5 0 00
FICA—Social Security Payable		1 9 4 00
FICA—Medicare Payable		4 6 00
SIT Payable		1 0 0 00
SUTA Tax Payable		6 0 00
FUTA Tax Payable		1 4 00
Unearned Storage Fees		3 5 0 00
Ron Win, Capital		2 7 3 4 00
Ron Win, Withdrawals	1 8 0 0 00	
Income Summary	—	—
Sales		1 9 4 0 0 00
Sales Returns and Allowances	5 6 0 00	
Sales Discount	4 8 0 00	
Purchases	8 6 0 0 00	
Purchases Discount		2 4 0 00
Purchases Returns and Allowances		1 6 0 00
Freight-In	1 0 0 00	
Salaries Expense	6 0 0 0 00	
Payroll Tax Expense	1 9 4 00	
Interest Expense	3 2 0 00	
	28 7 3 4 00	28 7 3 4 00

Figure 11-18 Trial Balance for Ran's Wholesale Clothing Company

Check Figure:
Net loss $8,686

ED SLOAN, M.D. INCOME STATEMENT FOR YEAR ENDED DECEMBER 31, 20X2		
Professional Fees Earned	5 0 0 0 0 00	
Expenses	1 8 0 0 0 00	
Net Income	32 0 0 0 00	

Figure 11-19 Income Statement for Ed Sloan, M. D.

11R-2. Abby Jay is having a difficult time understanding the relationship of sales, cost of goods sold, gross profit, and net income for a merchandise company. As the accounting lab tutor, you have been asked to sit down with Abby and explain how to calculate the missing amounts in each situation listed here. Keep in mind that each situation is a distinct and separate business problem.

	Sales	Beg. Inv.	Purchases	End Inv.	Cost of Goods Sold	Gross Profit	Expense	Net Income or Loss
Sit. 1	320,000	200,000	160,000	?	260,000	?	80,000	?
Sit. 2	380,000	140,000	?	180,000	200,000	?	100,000	80,000
Sit. 3	480,000	200,000	?	160,000	?	220,000	140,000	80,000
Sit. 4	?	160,000	280,000	140,000	?	160,000	140,000	?
Sit. 5	440,000	160,000	260,000	?	240,000	?	100,000	?
Sit. 6	280,000	120,000	?	140,000	160,000	?	?	40,000
Sit. 7	?	160,000	200,000	120,000	?	160,000	?	−20,000
Sit. 8	320,000	?	200,000	140,000	?	120,000	?	40,000

Explain in writing why gross profit does not always mean cash.

YOU make the call

Critical Thinking/Ethical Case

11R-3. Jim Heary is the custodian of petty cash. Jim, who is short of personal cash, decided to pay his home electrical and phone bill from petty cash. He plans to pay it back next month. Do you feel Jim should do so? You make the call. Write down your specific recommendations to Jim.

Internet Exercises: Saturn

EX-1. [www.saturn.com] An automobile dealer with a large inventory has a huge amount of cash invested in his product. The investment requires careful accounting to safeguard the asset both from a physically safe viewpoint and from a safe accounting standpoint. Because each of the individual units in an automobile inventory is identifiable, automobile inventories lend themselves as excellent candidates for perpetual inventory accounting.

At the end of an accounting period, what procedures would a car dealer like Saturn take to determine if all of the units in its perpetual inventory are accounted for? How would you adjust the inventory for an extra unit found on the sales lot, if the unit was not in the perpetual inventory records?

EX-2. [www.saturn.com] In the previous example you determined what entries to make for inventory that was not on the accounting records or for inventory that was in the accounting records but not on the location.

In this exercise, state how each of the following independent cases would affect gross profit. State whether gross profit is UNDERSTATED or OVERSTATED and give a reason for the answer you choose in each case.

    a. One unit of inventory in the accounting records is not on the location.
    b. One unit of inventory on the location is not in the accounting records.
    c. One unit shown as a sale in the accounting records is on the location.

Continuing Problem

Eldorado Computer Center

The first six months of the year have concluded for Eldorado Computer Center, and Tony wants to make the necessary adjustments to his accounts to prepare accurate financial statements.

Assignment

(The worksheet is in the envelope at the end of the *Study Guide and Working Papers*.)

To prepare these adjustments, use the trial balance in Figure 11-20, p. 462, and the following inventory that Tony took at the end of March:

10 dozen $\frac{1}{4}$" screws at a cost of $10 a dozen.

5 dozen $\frac{1}{2}$" screws at a cost of $7 a dozen.

2 feet of coaxial cable at a cost of $5 per foot.

There was $300 worth of merchandise left in stock.

Depreciation of computer equipment:

Computer depreciates at $33 a month; purchased July 5.

Computer workstations depreciate at $20 per month; purchased September 17.

Shop benches depreciate at $25 per month; purchased November 5.

Depreciation of office equipment:

Office equipment depreciates at $10 per month; purchased July 17.

Fax machine depreciates at $10 per month; purchased November 20.

Six months' worth of rent at a rental rate of $400 per month has expired.

Remember: If any long-term asset is purchased in the first 15 days of the month, Tony will charge depreciation for the full month. If an asset is purchased later than the 16th, he will not charge depreciation in the month it was purchased.

Complete the 10-column worksheet for the six months ended March 31, 200X.

Account Titles	Trial Balance	
	Dr.	Cr.
Cash	12 51 6 65	
Petty Cash	1 00 00	
Accounts Receivable	11 90 0 00	
Prepaid Rent	2 80 0 00	
Supplies	4 32 00	
Merchandise Inventory		
Computer Shop Equipment	3 80 0 00	
Accumulated Depr. CS Equip.		9 9 00
Office Equipment	1 05 0 00	
Accum. Depr. Office Equip.		20 00
Accounts Payable		2 84 0 00
T. Freedman, Capital		7 40 6 00
T. Freedman, Withdrawals	2 01 5 00	
Income Summary		
Service Revenue		19 80 0 00
Sales		9 70 0 00
Sales Return and Allowances	4 00 00	
Sales Discounts	2 20 00	
Advertising Exp.	8 00 00	
Rent Exp.		
Utilities Exp.	2 90 00	
Phone Exp.	1 50 00	
Supplies Exp.		
Insurance Exp.	1 00 00	
Postage Exp.	1 75 00	
Depreciation Exp. C.S. Equip.		
Depreciation Exp. Office Equip.		
Miscellaneous Exp.	10 00	
Wage Expense	2 03 0 00	
Payroll Tax Expense	2 26 35	
Purchases	9 50 00	
Purch. Ret. & Allow.		10 0 00
Totals	39 96 5 00	39 96 5 00

Figure 11-20
Trial Balance for Eldorado Computer March 31, 200X

APPENDIX

A WORKSHEET FOR ART'S WHOLESALE CLOTHING CO. USING A PERPETUAL INVENTORY SYSTEM

What's New: The Merchandise Inventory account does not need to be adjusted. The $4,000 figure for merchandise is the up-to-date balance in the account. The difference between beginning inventory and ending inventory will be part of a new account called *Cost of Goods Sold* on the worksheet.

How the $65,910 of Cost of Goods Sold was calculated from a periodic setup:

	Purchases	$52,000	←	**Assumed sold; part of cost**
+	Merchandise Inventory	$15,000	←	**Beg. Inv. – Ending Inv.**
				$19,000 – $4,000
−	Purchases Discount	860	→	**Reduces costs**
−	Purchases Returns and Allowances	680	↗	
+	Freight-in	450	→	**Adds to cost**
		$65,910		**Cost of Goods Sold**

What's Deleted from the Periodic Worksheet: Account titles for Purchases, Purchases Discounts, Purchases Returns and Allowances, and Freight-in.

Note: Net income is the same on the periodic and the perpetual worksheets.

PROBLEM FOR APPENDIX

Using the solution to Self-Review Quiz 11-2 (p. 448), convert this worksheet to a perpetual inventory system worksheet. (The worksheet is in the envelope at the end of the *Study Guide and Working Papers.*)

ART'S WHOLESALE CLOTHING CO.
WORKSHEET
FOR YEAR ENDED DECEMBER 31, 200X

Account Titles	Trial Balance Dr.	Trial Balance Cr.	Adjustments Dr.	Adjustments Cr.	Adjusted Trial Balance Dr.	Adjusted Trial Balance Cr.	Income Statement Dr.	Income Statement Cr.	Balance Sheet Dr.	Balance Sheet Cr.
Cash	4,820.00				4,820.00				4,820.00	
Petty Cash	100.00				100.00				100.00	
Accounts Receivable	14,500.00				14,500.00				14,500.00	
Merchandise Inventory	4,000.00				4,000.00				4,000.00	
Supplies	3,500.00			(B) 500.00	3,000.00				3,000.00	
Prepaid Insurance	6,300.00			(C) 300.00	6,000.00				6,000.00	
Store Equipment	4,000.00				4,000.00				4,000.00	
Acc. Dep., Store Equip.		4,000.00		(D) 50.00		4,050.00				4,050.00
Accounts Payable		8,900.00				8,900.00				8,900.00
Federal Income Tax		800.00				800.00				800.00
FICA—Social Security		454.00				454.00				454.00
FICA—Medicare		106.00				106.00				106.00
State Income Tax		200.00				200.00				200.00
SUTA Tax		108.00				108.00				108.00
FUTA Tax Payable		32.00				32.00				32.00
Unearned Rent		6,000.00	(A) 200.00			5,800.00				5,800.00
Mortgage Payable		2,320.00				2,320.00				2,320.00
Art Newner, Capital		7,905.00				7,905.00				7,905.00
Art Newner, Withdrawal	8,600.00				8,600.00				8,600.00	
Sales		95,000.00				95,000.00		95,000.00		
Sales Returns and Allow.	950.00				950.00		950.00			
Sales Discount	670.00				670.00		670.00			
Cost of Goods Sold	65,910.00				65,910.00		65,910.00			
Salaries Expense	11,700.00		(E) 600.00		12,300.00		12,300.00			
Payroll Tax Expense	420.00				420.00		420.00			
Postage Expense	25.00				25.00		25.00			
Miscellaneous Expense	30.00				30.00		30.00			
Interest Expense	300.00				300.00		300.00			
	125,825.00	**125,825.00**								
Rental Income				(A) 200.00		200.00		200.00		
Supplies Expense			(B) 500.00		500.00		500.00			
Insurance Expense			(C) 300.00		300.00		300.00			
Dep. Exp., Store Equip.			(D) 50.00		50.00		50.00			
Salaries Payable				(E) 600.00		600.00				600.00
			1,650.00	**1,650.00**	**126,475.00**	**126,475.00**	**81,455.00**	**95,200.00**	**45,020.00**	**31,275.00**
Net Income							**13,745.00**			**13,745.00**
							95,200.00	**95,200.00**	**45,020.00**	**45,020.00**

Figure A-1   Worksheet for Art's Wholesale Clothing Co.

RAY COMPANY
WORKSHEET
FOR YEAR ENDED DECEMBER 31, 200X

Account Titles	Trial Balance Dr.	Trial Balance Cr.	Adjustments Dr.	Adjustments Cr.	Adjusted Trial Balance Dr.	Adjusted Trial Balance Cr.	Income Statement Dr.	Income Statement Cr.	Balance Sheet Dr.	Balance Sheet Cr.
Cash	248600				248600				248600	
Merchandise Inventory	20000				20000				20000	
Prepaid Rent	115200			(B)10000	105200				105200	
Prepaid Insurance	6000				6000				6000	
Office Equipment	216000				216000				216000	
Accumulated Dep., Off. Equip.		56000		(C)6000		62000				62000
Unearned Storage Fees		251600	(A)51600			200000				200000
Accounts Payable		10000				10000				10000
B. Ray, Capital		193200				193200				193200
Sales		1104000				1104000		1104000		
Sales Returns and Allowances	54600				54600		54600			
Sales Discounts	21600				21600		21600			
Cogs*	561000				561000		561000			
Salaries Expense	201600		(D)20000		221600		221600			
Insurance Expense	139200				139200		139200			
Utilities Expense	9600				9600		9600			
Plumbing Expense	21400				21400		21400			
	1614800	1614800								
Storage Fees Earned				(A)51600		51600		51600		
Rent Expense			(B)10000		10000		10000			
Dep. Expense, Equip.			(C)6000		6000		6000			
Salaries Payable				(D)20000		20000				20000
			87600	87600	1640800	1640800	1045000	1155600	595800	485200
Net Income							110600			110600
							1155600	1155600	595800	595800

*$624 ($824 − $200) + $5,256 − $168 − $102.

Figure A-2 Worksheet for Ray Company

CHAPTER 12

Completion of the Accounting Cycle for a Merchandise Company

One thing about school that you like and at the same time dislike are tests. Tests are good because they provide you with feedback on your progress, which may make you feel that you've learned something. At the same time, you know that tests are not the most enjoyable thing about going to school, and studying for tests becomes a lot of hard work.

The same thing happens in accounting for a business. Generally, the "test" of whether a business is doing well or poorly depends on if it is earning a profit. Accounting provides feedback about this critical "test." And accounting can also help a business to evaluate how much cash it has in the bank, how much it has invested, its amount of property, plant, and equipment, and what it owes to others on a regular basis. Accounting does this through the use of financial statements.

Whether a business is small like James Hardware and Lumber Company or Hansen's Pharmacy, or gigantic like Microsoft or General Motors, a business will prepare financial statements on a regular basis. The income statement provides results about whether a business is earning or losing money, while the balance sheet is used to evaluate the financial position of a business at a particular point in time.

In Chapter 12 we will learn how to use the worksheet to prepare the financial statements for a business. We will also discuss preparing adjusting and closing entries, the post-closing trial balance, and reversing entries.

After you complete this chapter, you will better understand how accounting reports the results of the test of profit or loss from operating a business and be able to evaluate its financial position. And now you know that tests don't end when you graduate; they exist for all companies in business today.

Learning Objectives

- Preparing financial statements for a merchandise company. (p. 468)

- Recording adjusting and closing entries. (p. 477)

- Preparing post-closing trial balance. (p. 482)

- Completing reversing entries. (p. 483)

In this chapter we discuss the steps involved in completing the accounting cycle for a merchandise company. The steps involved include preparing financial reports, journalizing and posting adjusting and closing entries, preparing a post-closing trial balance, and reversing entries.

Learning Unit 12-1   Preparing Financial Statements

As we discussed in Chapter 5, when we were dealing with a service company rather than a merchandise company, the three financial statements can be prepared from the worksheet. Let's begin by looking at how Art's Wholesale Clothing Company prepares the income statement.

THE INCOME STATEMENT

Art is interested in knowing how well his shop performed for the year ended December 31, 200X. What were its net sales? Were there many returns of goods from dissatisfied customers? What was the cost of the goods brought into the store versus the selling price received? How many goods were returned to suppliers? What is the cost of the goods that have not been sold? What was the cost of the Freight-in account? The income statement in Figure 12-1 (p. 469) is prepared from the income statement columns of the worksheet. Note that there are no debit or credit columns on the formal income statement; the inside columns in financial reports are used for subtotaling, not for debit and credit.

The income statement is broken down into several sections. Remembering the sections can help you set it up correctly on your own. The income statement shows

$$
\begin{array}{l}
\ \text{Net Sales} \\
-\ \text{Cost of Goods Sold} \\
\hline
=\ \text{Gross Profit} \\
-\ \text{Operating Expenses} \\
\hline
=\ \text{Net Income from Operations} \\
+\ \text{Other Income} \\
-\ \text{Other Expenses} \\
\hline
=\ \text{Net Income}
\end{array}
$$

Let's take these sections one at a time and see where the figures come from on the worksheet.

Revenue Section

Net Sales   The first major category of the income statement shows net sales. The figure here—$93,380—is not on the worksheet. Instead, the accountant must combine the amounts for gross sales, sales returns and allowances, and sales discount found on the worksheet to arrive at a figure for net sales. Thus these individual amounts are not summarized in a single figure for net sales until the formal income statement is prepared.

$$
\begin{array}{l}
\ \textit{Sales} \\
-\ \textit{Sales Ret. \& Allow.} \\
-\ \textit{Sales Discount} \\
\hline
=\ \textit{Net Sales}
\end{array}
$$

ART'S WHOLESALE CLOTHING COMPANY
INCOME STATEMENT
FOR YEAR ENDED DECEMBER 31, 200X

Revenue:			
Gross Sales			$95 000 00
Less: Sales Ret. and Allow.		$ 95000	
Sales Discount		67000	162000
Net Sales			$93 380 00
Cost of Goods Sold:			
Merchandise Inventory, 1/1/0X		$19 000 00	
Purchases	$52 000 00		
Less: Purch. Discount	$ 86000		
Purch. Ret. and Allow.	68000	154000	
Net Purchases	$50 460 00		
Add: Freight-In	45000		
Net Cost of Purchases		50 910 00	
Cost of Goods Available for Sale		$69 910 00	
Less: Merch. Inv., 12/31/0X		400000	
Cost of Goods Sold			65 910 00
Gross Profit			$27 470 00
Operating Expenses:			
Salaries Expense		$12 300 00	
Payroll Tax Expense		42000	
Dep. Exp., Store Equip.		5000	
Supplies Expense		50000	
Insurance Expense		30000	
Postage Expense		2500	
Miscellaneous Expense		3000	
Total Operating Expenses			13 625 00
Net Income from Operations			$13 845 00
Other Income:			
Rental Income		$ 20000	
Other Expenses:			
Interest Expense		30000	10000
Net Income			$13 745 00

ART'S WHOLESALE CLOTHING COMPANY
PARTIAL WORKSHEET
FOR YEAR ENDED DECEMBER 31, 200X

	Income Statement	
	Dr.	Cr.
Income Summary	19 000 00	400000
Sales		95 000 00
Sales Returns and Allowances	95000	
Sales Discount	67000	
Purchases	52 000 00	
Purchases Discount		86000
Purchases Returns and Allowances		68000
Freight-In	45000	
Salaries Expense	12 300 00	
Payroll Tax Expense	42000	
Postage Expense	2500	
Miscellaneous Expense	3000	
Interest Expense	30000	
Rental Income		20000
Supplies Expense	50000	
Insurance Expense	30000	
Depreciation Expense, Store Equip.	5000	
Salaries Payable		
	86 995 00	100 74 000
Net Income	13 745 00	
	100 74 000	100 74 000

Figure 12-1 Partial Worksheet and Income Statement

Cost of Goods Sold Section

The figures for Merchandise Inventory are shown separately on the worksheet. The $19,000 represents the beginning inventory of the period, and the $4,000, calculated from an inventory sheet is the ending inventory. Note on the financial report that the cost of goods sold section uses two separate figures for inventory.

Note that the following numbers are not found on the worksheet but are shown on the formal income statement (they are combined by the accountant in preparing the income statement):

- Net Purchases: $50,460 (Purchases − Purchases Discount − Purchases Returns and Allowances)
- Net Cost of Purchases: $50,910 (Net Purchases + Freight-in)
- Cost of Goods Available for Sale: $69,910 (Beginning Inventory + Net Cost of Purchases)
- Cost of Goods Sold: $65,910 (Cost of Goods Available for Sale − Ending Inventory)

> Beg. Inventory
> \+ Net Cost of Puchases
> − Ending Inventory
> ————————————
> = Cost of Goods Sold

> Remember:
> In the periodic inventory system, goods brought in during the accounting period are added to the Purchases account, not to the Merchandise Inventory account.

Gross Profit

Gross profit ($27,470) is calculated by subtracting the cost of goods sold from net sales ($93,380 − $65,910). The amount is not found on the worksheet.

> Net Sales
> − Cost of Goods Sold
> ————————————
> = Gross Profit

Operating Expenses Section

Like the other figures we have discussed, the business's operating expenses do not appear on the worksheet. To get this figure ($13,625), the accountant adds up all the expenses on the worksheet.

Many operating companies break expenses down into those directly related to the selling activity of the company (selling expenses) and those related to administrative or office activity (administrative expenses or general expenses). Here's a sample list broken down into these two categories:

Operating Expenses

- Selling Expenses:
    Sales Salaries Expense
    Delivery Expense
    Advertising Expense
    Depreciation Expense, Store Equipment
    Insurance Expense
        Total Selling Expenses
- Administrative Expenses:
    Rent Expense
    Office Salaries Expense
    Utilities Expense
    Supplies Expense
    Depreciation Expense, Office Equipment
        Total Administrative Expenses
            Total Operating Expenses

Other Income (or Other Revenue) Section

The Other Income or Other Revenue section is used to record any revenue other than revenue from sales. For example, Art's Wholesale makes a profit from subletting a portion of a building. The $200 of rental income the company earns from this is recorded in the Other Income section.

Other Expenses Section

The Other Expenses section is used to record nonoperating expenses, that is, expenses that are not related to the main operating activities of the business. For example, Art's Wholesale owes $300 interest on money it has borrowed. That expense is shown in the Other Expenses section.

STATEMENT OF OWNER'S EQUITY

The information used to prepare the statement of owner's equity comes from the balance sheet columns of the worksheet. Keep in mind that the capital account in the ledger should be checked to see whether any additional investments have occurred during the period. Figure 12-2 below shows how the worksheet aids in this step. The

> The statement of owner's equity is the same for a merchandise business as for a service firm.

Figure 12-2
Preparing Statement of Owner's Equity from the Worksheet

> Any additional investment by the owner would be added to his or her beginning capital amount.

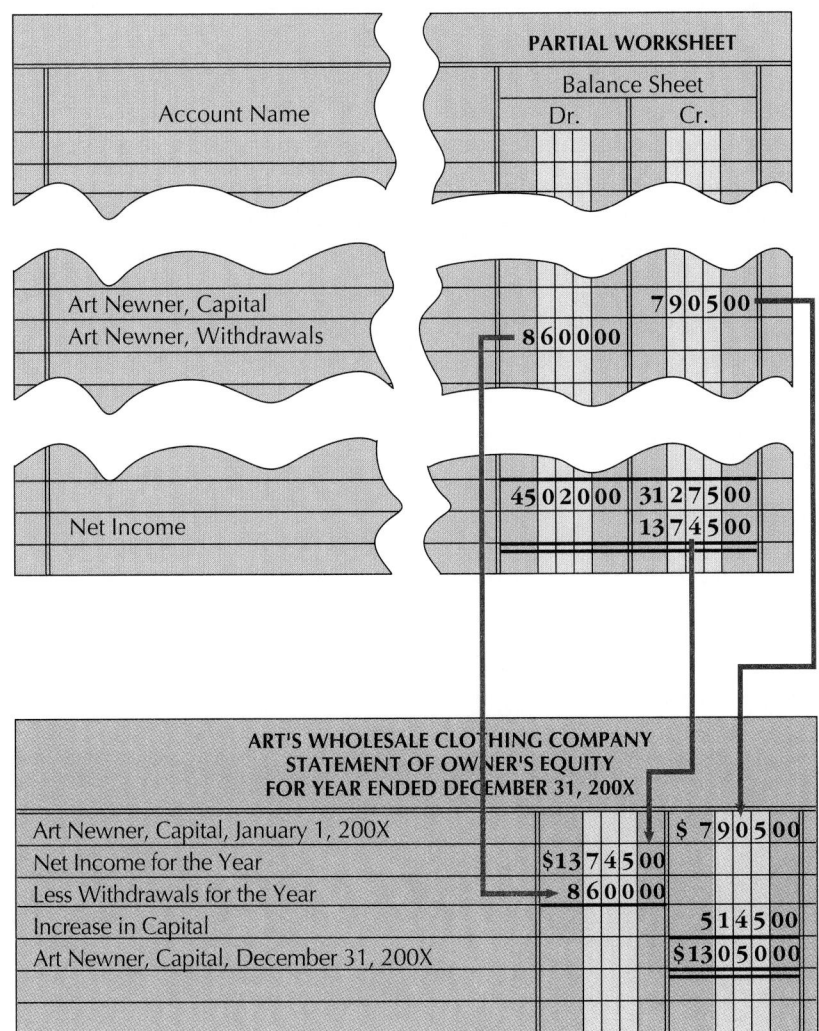

PARTIAL WORKSHEET		
Account Name	Balance Sheet Dr.	Balance Sheet Cr.
Art Newner, Capital		7 9 0 5 00
Art Newner, Withdrawals	8 6 0 0 00	
	45 0 2 0 00	31 2 7 5 00
Net Income		13 7 4 5 00

ART'S WHOLESALE CLOTHING COMPANY STATEMENT OF OWNER'S EQUITY FOR YEAR ENDED DECEMBER 31, 200X		
Art Newner, Capital, January 1, 200X		$ 7 9 0 5 00
Net Income for the Year	$13 7 4 5 00	
Less Withdrawals for the Year	8 6 0 0 00	
Increase in Capital		5 1 4 5 00
Art Newner, Capital, December 31, 200X		$13 0 5 0 00

ending figure of $13,050 for Art Newner, Capital, is carried over to the balance sheet, which is the final report we look at in this chapter.

THE BALANCE SHEET

Figure 12-3 on p. 473 shows how a worksheet is used to aid in the preparation of a classified balance sheet. A classified balance sheet breaks down the assets and liabilities into more detail. Classified balance sheets provide management, owners, creditors, and suppliers with more information about the company's ability to pay current and long-term debts. They also provide a more complete financial picture of the firm.

The categories on the classified balance sheet are as follows:

- **Current assets** are defined as cash and assets that will be converted into cash or used up during the normal operating cycle of the company or one year, whichever is longer. (Think of the operating cycle as the time period it takes a company to buy and sell merchandise and then collect accounts receivable.)

  Accountants list current assets in order of how easily they can be converted into cash (called *liquidity*). In some cases, Accounts Receivable can be turned into cash more quickly than Merchandise Inventory. For example, it can be quite difficult to sell an outdated computer in a computer store or to sell last year's model car this year.

- **Plant and Equipment** are long-lived assets that are used in the production or sale of goods or services. Art's Wholesale has only one plant asset, store equipment; other plant assets could include buildings and land. The assets are usually listed in order according to how long they will last; the shortest-lived assets are listed first. Land would always be the last asset listed (and land is never depreciated). Note that we still show the cost of the asset less its accumulated depreciation.

- **Current liabilities** are the debts or obligations of Art's Wholesale that must be paid within one year or one operating cycle. The order of listing accounts in this section is not always the same; many times companies will list their liabilities in the order they expect to pay them off. Note that the current portion of the mortgage, $320 (that portion due within one year), is listed before Accounts Payable.

- **Long-term liabilities** are debts or obligations that are not due and payable for a comparatively long period, usually for more than one year. For Art's Wholesale there is only one long-term liability, Mortgage Payable. The long-term portion of the mortgage is listed here; the current portion, due within one year, is listed under current liabilities.

Mortgage Payable:
$2,320
−   320 current portion
$2,000 long-term liability

ART'S WHOLESALE CLOTHING COMPANY
CLASSIFIED BALANCE SHEET
FOR YEAR ENDED DECEMBER 31, 200X

Assets

Current Assets:			
Cash	$12920 00		
Petty Cash	100 00		
Accounts Receivable	14500 00		
Merchandise Inventory	4000 00		
Supplies	300 00		
Prepaid Insurance	600 00		
Total Current Assets			$32420 00
Plant and Equipment:			
Store Equipment	$4000 00		
Less: Accum. Depreciation	450 00		3550 00
Total Assets			$35970 00

Liabilities

Current Liabilities:			
Mortgage Payable (current portion)	$ 320 00		
Accounts Payable	17900 00		
Federal Income Tax Payable	800 00		
FICA–Social Security Payable	4544 00		
FICA–Medicare Payable	1060 00		
State Income Tax Payable	200 00		
SUTA Tax Payable	1080 00		
FUTA Tax Payable	32 00		
Salaries Payable	600 00		
Unearned Rent	400 00		
Total Current Liabilities			$20920 00
Long-Term Liabilities:			
Mortgage Payable			2000 00
Total Liabilities			$22920 00

Owner's Equity

Art Newner, Capital, December 31, 200X		13050 00
Total Liabilities and Owner's Equity		$35970 00

ART'S WHOLESALE CLOTHING COMPANY
WORKSHEET
FOR YEAR ENDED DECEMBER 31, 200X

	Balance Sheet	
	Dr.	Cr.
Cash	12920 00	
Petty Cash	100 00	
Accounts Receivable	14500 00	
Merchandise Inventory	4000 00	
Supplies	300 00	
Prepaid Insurance	600 00	
Store Equipment	4000 00	
Acc. Dep., Store Equipment		450 00
Accounts Payable		17900 00
Federal Income Tax Payable		800 00
FICA-Social Security Payable		4544 00
FICA-Medicare Payable		1060 00
State Income Tax Payable		200 00
SUTA Tax Payable		1080 00
FUTA Tax Payable		32 00
Unearned Rent		400 00
Mortgage Payable		2320 00
Art Newner, Capital		7905 00
Salaries Payable		600 00
	45020 00	31275 00
Net Income		13745 00
	45020 00	45020 00

Figure 12-3 Partial Worksheet and Classified Balance Sheet

Learning Unit 12-1 Review

AT THIS POINT you should be able to

- Prepare a detailed income statement from the worksheet. (p. 469)
- Explain the difference between selling and administrative expenses. (p. 470)
- Explain which columns of the worksheet are used in preparing a statement of owner's equity. (p. 471)
- Explain as well as compare current assets with plant and equipment. (p. 472)
- Using Mortgage Payable as an example, explain the difference between current and long-term liabilities. (p. 472)
- Prepare a classified balance sheet from a worksheet. (p. 473)

SELF-REVIEW QUIZ 12-1

(The forms you need are on pages 372–374 of the *Study Guide and Working Papers.*)

Using the worksheet on page 449 from Self-Review Quiz 11-2, prepare in proper form (1) an income statement, (2) a statement of owner's equity, (3) a classified balance sheet for Ray Company.

SOLUTIONS TO SELF-REVIEW QUIZ 12-1

1.

RAY COMPANY INCOME STATEMENT FOR YEAR ENDED DECEMBER 31, 200X					
Revenue:					
Sales					$11 04 0 00
Less: Sales Ret. and Allow.				$ 5 46 00	
Sales Discount				2 16 00	76 2 00
Net Sales					$10 27 8 00
Cost of Goods Sold:					
Merchandise Inventory, 1/1/0X				$ 8 24 00	
Purchases			$5 25 6 00		
Less: Pur. Ret. and Allow.	$ 1 68 00				
Purchases Discount	1 02 00		27 0 00		
Net Purchases				4 98 6 00	
Cost of Goods Available for Sale				$ 5 81 0 00	
Less: Merchandise Inv., 12/31/0X				20 0 00	
Cost of Goods Sold					5 61 0 00
Gross Profit					$ 4 66 8 00
Operating Expenses:					
Salaries Expense			$ 2 21 6 00		
Insurance Expense			1 39 2 00		
Utilities Expense			9 6 00		
Plumbing Expense			2 1 4 00		
Rent Expense			1 0 0 00		
Depreciation Exp., Equip.			6 0 00		
Total Operating Expenses					4 07 8 00
Net Income from Operations					$ 59 0 00
Other Income:					
Storage Fees					5 16 00
Net Income					$ 1 10 6 00

Figure 12-4 Income Statement for Ray Company

Quiz Tip:
Note that Cost of Goods Sold has a separate figure for beginning inventory and ending inventory.

2.

Figure 12-5
Statement of Owner's
Equity for Ray Company

RAY COMPANY STATEMENT OF OWNER'S EQUITY FOR YEAR ENDED DECEMBER 31, 200X		
B. Ray, Capital, 1/1/0X	$1 9 3 2 00
Net Income for the Year	1 1 0 6 00
B. Ray, Capital, 12/31/0X	$3 0 3 8 00

3.

RAY COMPANY BALANCE SHEET DECEMBER 31, 200X			
Assets			
Current Assets:			
Cash	$2 4 8 6 00		
Merchandise Inventory	2 0 0 00		
Prepaid Rent	1 0 5 2 00		
Prepaid Insurance	6 0 00		
Total Current Assets		$3 7 9 8 00	
Plant and Equipment:			
Office Equipment	$2 1 6 0 00		
Less: Accumulated Depreciation	6 2 0 00	1 5 4 0 00	
Total Assets		$5 3 3 8 00	
Liabilities			
Current Liabilities			
Accounts Payable	$ 1 0 0 00		
Salaries Payable	2 0 0 00		
Unearned Storage Fees	2 0 0 0 00		
Total Liabilities		$2 3 0 0 00	
Owner's Equity			
B. Ray, Capital, December 31, 200X		3 0 3 8 00	
Total Liabilities and Owner's Equity		$5 3 3 8 00	

Figure 12-6 Balance Sheet for Ray Company

Learning Unit 12-2
Journalizing and Posting Adjusting and Closing Entries; Preparing the Post-Closing Trial Balance

JOURNALIZING AND POSTING ADJUSTING ENTRIES

From the worksheet of Art's Wholesale (repeated here in Fig. 12-7, p. 478, for your convenience), the adjusting entries can be journalized from the adjustments column and posted to the ledger. Keep in mind that the adjustments have been placed only on the worksheet, not in the journal or in the ledger. At this point, the journal does not reflect adjustments and the ledger still contains only unadjusted amounts.

Partial Ledger

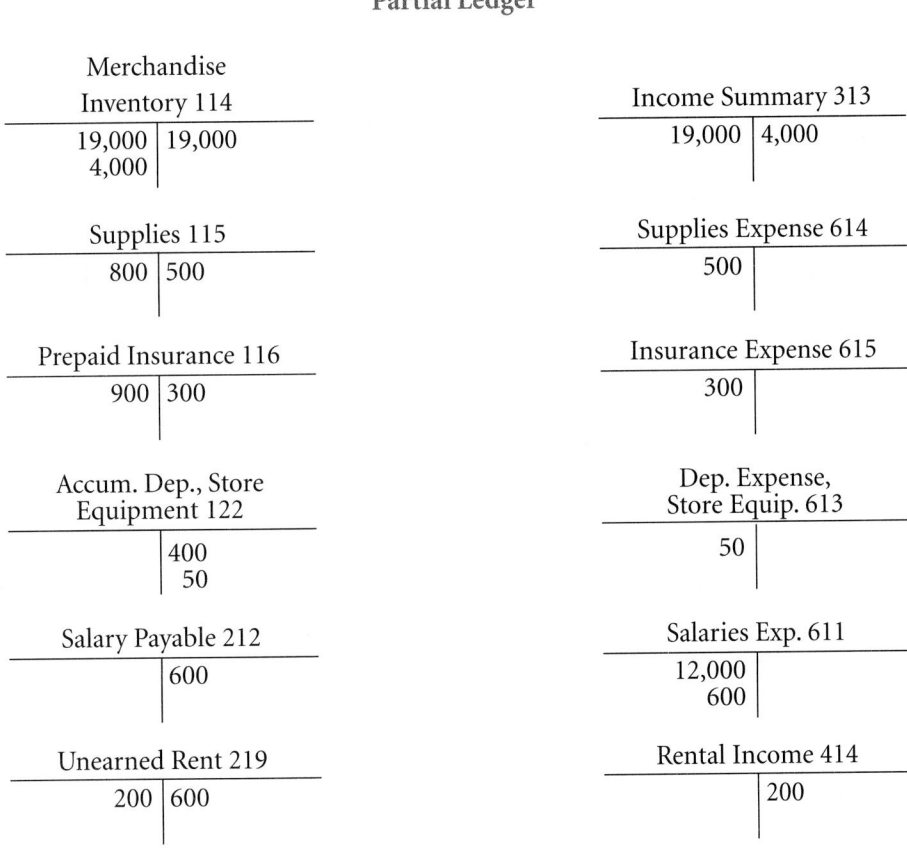

The journalized and posted adjusting entries are shown in Figure 12-8. Note that the liability Unearned Rent is reduced by $200 and Rental Income has increased by $200.

ART'S WHOLESALE CLOTHING CO.
WORKSHEET
FOR YEAR ENDED DECEMBER 31, 200X

	Trial Balance Dr.	Trial Balance Cr.	Adjustments Dr.	Adjustments Cr.
Cash	12920 00			
Petty Cash	100 00			
Accounts Receivable	1450 00			
Merchandise Inventory	19000 00		(B) 4000 00	(A) 19000 00
Supplies	800 00			(D) 500 00
Prepaid Insurance	900 00			(E) 300 00
Store Equipment	4000 00			
Acc. Dep., Store Equipment		400 00		(F) 50 00
Accounts Payable		17900 00		
Federal Income Tax Payable		800 00		
FICA—Social Security Payable		454 00		
FICA—Medicare Payable		106 00		
State Income Tax Payable		200 00		
SUTA Tax Payable		108 00		
FUTA Tax Payable		32 00		
Unearned Rent		600 00	(C) 200 00	
Mortgage Payable		2320 00		
Art Newner, Capital		7905 00		
Art Newner, Withdrawals	8600 00			
Income Summary			(A) 19000 00	(B) 4000 00
Sales		95000 00		
Sales Returns and Allowances	950 00			
Sales Discount	670 00			
Purchases	52000 00			
Purchases Discount		860 00		
Purchases Returns and Allowances		680 00		
Freight-In	450 00			
Salaries Expense	11700 00		(G) 600 00	
Payroll Tax Expense	420 00			
Postage Expense	25 00			
Miscellaneous Expense	30 00			
Interest Expense	300 00			
	127365 00	127365 00		
Rental Income				(C) 200 00
Supplies Expense			(D) 500 00	
Insurance Expense			(E) 300 00	
Depreciation Expense, Store Equip.			(F) 50 00	
Salaries Payable				(G) 600 00
			2465 00	2465 00
Net Income				

Figure 12-7 Completed Worksheet

Adjusted Trial Bal. Dr.	Adjusted Trial Bal. Cr.	Income Statement Dr.	Income Statement Cr.	Balance Sheet Dr.	Balance Sheet Cr.
12 920 00				12 920 00	
100 00				100 00	
14 500 00				14 500 00	
4 000 00				4 000 00	
300 00				300 00	
600 00				600 00	
400 00				400 00	
	450 00				450 00
	17 900 00				17 900 00
	800 00				800 00
	454 00				454 00
	106 00				106 00
	200 00				200 00
	108 00				108 00
	32 00				32 00
	400 00				400 00
	2 320 00				2 320 00
	7 905 00				7 905 00
8 600 00				8 600 00	
19 000 00	4 000 00	19 000 00	4 000 00		
	95 000 00		95 000 00		
950 00		950 00			
670 00		670 00			
52 000 00		52 000 00			
	860 00		860 00		
	680 00		680 00		
450 00		450 00			
12 300 00		12 300 00			
420 00		420 00			
25 00		25 00			
30 00		30 00			
300 00		300 00			
	200 00		200 00		
500 00		500 00			
300 00		300 00			
50 00		50 00			
	600 00				600 00
132 015 00	132 015 00	86 995 00	100 740 00	45 020 00	31 275 00
		13 745 00			13 745 00
		100 740 00	100 740 00	45 020 00	45 020 00

Figure 12-7 (continued)

Figure 12-8
Journalized and Posted
Adjusting Entries

		ART'S WHOLESALE CLOTHING CO. GENERAL JOURNAL			
					Page 2
	Date	Account Titles and Description	PR	Dr.	Cr.
		Adjusting Entries			
	31	Income Summary	313	1900000	
		Merchandise Inventory	114		1900000
		Transferred beginning inventory			
		to Income Summary			
	31	Merchandise Inventory	114	400000	
		Income Summary	313		400000
		Records cost of ending inventory			
	31	Unearned Rent	219	20000	
		Rental Income	414		20000
		Rental Income earned			
	31	Supplies Expense	614	50000	
		Supplies	115		50000
		Supplies consumed			
	31	Insurance Expense	615	30000	
		Prepaid Insurance	116		30000
		Insurance expired			
	31	Dep. Exp., Store Equipment	613	5000	
		Acc. Dep., Store Equipment	122		5000
		Depreciation on equipment			
	31	Salaries Expense	611	60000	
		Salaries Payable	212		60000
		Accrued salaries			

JOURNALIZING AND POSTING CLOSING ENTRIES

In Chapter 5, we discussed the closing process for a service company. The goals of closing are the same for a merchandise company. These goals are (1) to clear all temporary accounts in the ledger to zero and (2) to update capital in the ledger to its latest balance. The company must use the worksheet and the steps listed here to complete the closing process.

Step 1: Close all balances on the income statement credit column of the worksheet, except Income Summary, by debits.
Then credit the total to the Income Summary account.

Step 2: Close all balances on the income statement debit column of the worksheet, except Income Summary, by credits.
Then debit the total to the Income Summary account.

Step 3: Transfer the balance of the Income Summary account to the Capital account.

Step 4: Transfer the balance of the owner's Withdrawal account to the Capital account.

Figure 12-9
General Journal Closing
Entries

Date		Account Titles and Description	PR	Dr.	Cr.
		Closing Entries			
	31	Sales	411	95 0 0 0 00	
		Rental Income	414	2 0 0 00	
		Purchases Discount	512	8 6 0 00	
		Purchases Ret. and Allow.	513	6 8 0 00	
		Income Summary	313		96 7 4 0 00
		Transfers credit account balances			
		on income statement column of			
		worksheet to Income Summary			
	31	Income Summary	313	67 9 9 5 00	
		Sales Returns and Allowances	412		9 5 0 00
		Sales Discount	413		6 7 0 00
		Purchases	511		52 0 0 0 00
		Freight-In	514		4 5 0 00
		Salaries Expense	611		12 3 0 0 00
		Payroll Tax Expense	612		4 2 0 00
		Postage Expense	616		2 5 00
		Miscellaneous Expense	617		3 0 00
		Interest Expense	618		3 0 0 00
		Supplies Expense	614		5 0 0 00
		Insurance Expense	615		3 0 0 00
		Depreciation Expense, Store Equip.	613		5 0 00
		Transfers all expenses, and			
		deductions to Sales are			
		closed to Income Summary			
	31	Income Summary	313	13 7 4 5 00	
		A. Newner, Capital	311		13 7 4 5 00
		Transfer of net income to			
		Capital from Income Summary			
	31	A. Newner, Capital	311	8 6 0 0 00	
		A. Newner, Withdrawals	312		8 6 0 0 00
		Closes withdrawals to			
		Capital Account			

ART'S WHOLESALE CLOTHING CO.
GENERAL JOURNAL

Page 2

Let's look now at the journalized closing entries in Figure 12-9. When these entries are posted, all the temporary accounts will have zero balances in the ledger, and the Capital account will be updated with a new balance.

Let's take a moment to look at the Income Summary account in T account form:

```
                  Income Summary 313
         Adj.      19,000  |  4,000    Adj.
         Clos.     67,995  | 96,740    Clos.
                   86,995  |100,740

Net Income → Clos.  13,745
```

Note that Income Summary before the closing process contains the adjustments for Merchandise Inventory. The end result is that the net income of $13,745 is closed to the Capital account.

THE POST-CLOSING TRIAL BALANCE

The post-closing trial balance shown in Figure 12-10 is prepared from the general ledger. Note first that all temporary accounts have been closed and thus are not shown on this post-closing trial balance. Note also that the ending inventory figure of the last accounting period, $4,000, becomes the beginning inventory figure on January 1, 20X3.

Figure 12-10
Post-Closing Trial Balance for Art's Wholesale Clothing Company

ART'S WHOLESALE CLOTHING COMPANY POSTCLOSING TRIAL BALANCE DECEMBER 31, 200X	Dr.	Cr.
Cash	12 9 2 0 00	
Petty Cash	1 0 0 00	
Accounts Receivable	14 5 0 0 00	
Merchandise Inventory	4 0 0 0 00	
Supplies	3 0 0 00	
Prepaid Insurance	6 0 0 00	
Store Equipment	4 0 0 0 00	
Accum. Depreciation, Store Equipment		4 5 0 00
Accounts Payable		17 9 0 0 00
Federal Income Tax Payable		8 0 0 00
FICA—Social Security Payable		4 5 4 00
FICA—Medicare Payable		1 0 6 00
State Income Tax Payable		2 0 0 00
SUTA Tax Payable		1 0 8 00
FUTA Tax Payable		3 2 00
Salary Payable		6 0 0 00
Unearned Rent		4 0 0 00
Mortgage Payable		2 3 2 0 00
Art Newner, Capital		13 0 5 0 00
	36 4 2 0 00	36 4 2 0 00

Learning Unit 12-2 Review

AT THIS POINT you should be able to

- Journalize and post adjusting entries for a merchandise company. (p. 477)
- Explain the relationship of the worksheet to the adjusting and closing process. (p. 480)
- Complete the closing process for a merchandise company. (p. 481)
- Prepare a post-closing trial balance and explain why ending merchandise inventory is not a temporary account. (p. 482)

SELF-REVIEW QUIZ 12-2

(The forms you need are on page 375 of the *Study Guide and Working Papers.*)

Using the worksheet on page 449 from Self-Review Quiz 11-2, journalize the closing entries.

SOLUTION TO SELF-REVIEW QUIZ 12-2

Figure 12-11
Closing Entries Journalized

Date		Account Titles and Description	PR	Dr.	Cr.
					Page 2
		Closing			
Dec.	31	Sales		11 04 00 0	
		Storage Fees Earned		5 16 00	
		Purchases Returns and Allowances		1 68 00	
		Purchases Discount		1 02 00	
		Income Summary			11 82 6 00
	31	Income Summary		10 09 6 00	
		Sales Returns and Allowances			5 46 00
		Sales Discount			2 16 00
		Purchases			5 25 6 00
		Salaries Expense			2 21 6 00
		Insurance Expense			1 39 2 00
		Utilities Expense			9 6 00
		Plumbing Expense			2 14 00
		Rent Expense			1 00 00
		Depreciation Exp., Equipment			6 0 00
	31	Income Summary		1 10 6 00	
		B. Ray, Capital			1 10 6 00

Quiz Tip:
Note in the first closing entry that the four account titles (now listed as debits) were found on the worksheet as credits in the income statement column.

Learning Unit 12-3   Reversing Entries (Optional Section)

The accounting cycle for Art's Wholesale Clothing Company is completed. Now let's look at **reversing entries**, an optional way of handling some adjusting entries. Reversing entries are general journal entries that are the opposite of adjusting entries. Reversing entries help reduce potential errors and simplify the recordkeeping process. If Art's accountant does reversing entries, routine transactions can be done in the usual steps.

Reversing entries are an option; they are not mandatory.

To help explain the concept of reversing entries, let's look at these two adjustments that could be reversed:

1. When there is an increase in an asset account (no previous balance).
   Example: Interest Receivable
   　　　　　Interest Income
   (Interest earned but not collected is covered in later chapters.)

2. When there is an increase in a liability account (no previous balance).
   Example: Wages Expense
   　　　　　Wages Payable

With the exception of businesses in their first year of operation, accounts such as Accumulated Depreciation or Inventory cannot be reduced because they have previous balances.

Art's bookkeeper handles an entry without reversing for salaries at the end of the year (see Fig. 12-12). Note that the permanent account, Salaries Payable, carries over to the new accounting period a $600 balance. Remember that the $600 was an expense of the prior year.

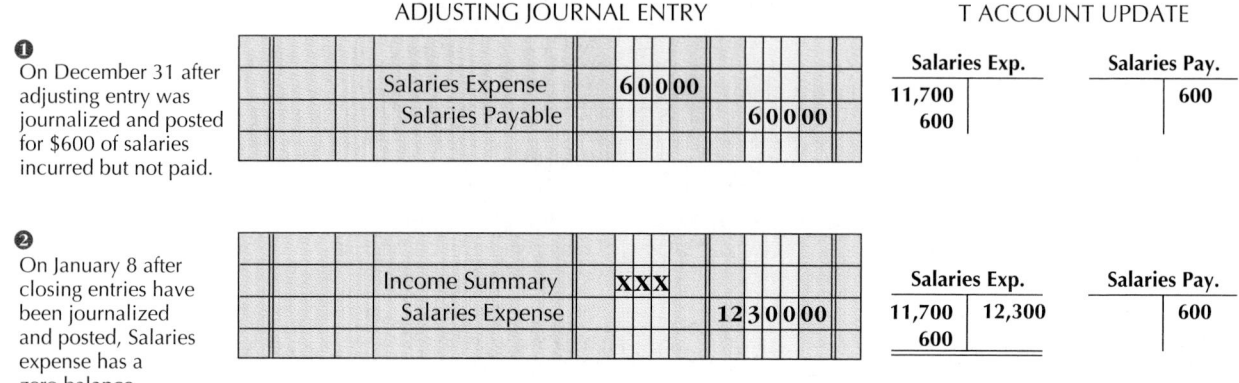

Figure 12-12 Reversing Entries Not Used

		Salaries Exp.	Salaries Pay.	Cash
Salaries Payable	600 00	1,400		600	600		2,000
Salaries Expense	1400 00						
Cash		2000 00					

Figure 12-13 Entry When Optional Reversing Entry Is Not Used

❶ On December 31 adjustment for salary was recorded.

Salaries Exp.		Salaries Pay.	
11,700			600
600			

❷ Closing entry on December 31.

Salaries Exp.		Salaries Pay.	
11,700	12,300		600
600			

❸ On January 1 (first day of the following fiscal period) reverse adjusting entry was made for salary on December 31 (a "flipping" adjustment).

					Salaries Exp.		Salaries Pay.	
Jan.	1	Salaries Payable	600 00			600	600	600
		Salaries Expense		600 00				

This way, the liability is reduced to 0. We know it will be paid in this new period, but the Salaries Expense has a credit balance of $600 until the payroll is paid. When the payroll of $2,000 is paid, the following results:

❹ Paid Payroll $2,000.

					Salaries Exp.		Cash	
Jan.	1	Salaries Expense	2000 00		2,000	600		2,000
		Cash		2000 00				

Figure 12-14 Reversing Entries Used

On January 8 of the new year, the payroll to be paid is $2,000. If the optional reversing entry is *not* used, the bookkeeper must make the journal entry in Figure 12-13.

To do so, the bookkeeper has to refer back to the adjustment on December 31 to determine how much of the salary of $2,000 is indeed a new salary expense and what portion was shown in the old year although not paid. It is easy to see how potential errors can result if the bookkeeper pays the payroll but forgets about the adjustment in the previous year. In this way, reversing entries can help avoid potential errors.

Figure 12-14 shows the four steps the bookkeeper would take if reversing entries were used. Note that Steps 1 and 2 are the same whether the accountant uses reversing entries or not.

Note that the balance of Salaries Expense is indeed only $1,400, the *true* expense in the new year. Reversing results in switching the adjustment the first day of the new period. Also note that each of the accounts ends up with the same balance no matter which method is chosen. Using a reversing entry for salaries, however, allows the accountant to make the normal entry when it is time to pay salaries.

Learning Unit 12-3 Review

AT THIS POINT you should be able to

- Explain the purpose of reversing entries. (p. 484)
- Complete a reversing entry. (p. 484)
- Explain when reversing entries can be used. (p. 484)

SELF-REVIEW QUIZ 12-3

Explain which of the following situations could be reversed:

1.

Supplies Exp.		Supplies	
200		800	200

2.

Wages Exp.		Wages Payable	
3,200			200
200			

3.

Sales		Unearned Sales	
	4,000	50	200
	50		

SOLUTIONS TO SELF-REVIEW QUIZ 12-3

(The forms you need are on page 376 of the *Study Guide and Working Papers.*)

1. Not reversed: asset Supplies is decreasing, not increasing.
2. Reversed: liability is increasing and no previous balance exists.
3. Not reversed: liability is decreasing and a previous balance exists.

Chapter Review

Summary of Key Points

Learning Unit 12-1

1. The formal income statement can be prepared from the income statement columns of the worksheet.
2. There are no debit or credit columns on the formal income statement.
3. The cost of goods sold section has a figure for beginning inventory and a separate figure for ending inventory.
4. Operating expenses could be broken down into selling and administrative expenses.
5. The ending figure for Capital is not found on the worksheet. It comes from the statement of owner's equity.
6. A classified balance sheet breaks assets into current and plant and equipment. Liabilities are broken down into current and long-term.

Learning Unit 12-2

1. The information for journalizing, adjusting, and closing entries can be obtained from the worksheet.
2. In the closing process all temporary accounts will be zero and the Capital account is brought up to its new balance.
3. Inventory is not a temporary account. The ending inventory, along with other permanent accounts, will be listed in the post-closing trial balance.

Learning Unit 12-3

1. Reversing entries are optional. They could aid in reducing potential errors and can simplify the recordkeeping process.
2. The reversing entry "flips" the adjustment on the first day of a new fiscal period. Thus, the bookkeeper need *not* look back at what happened in the old year when recording the current year's transactions.
3. Reversing entries are only used if (a) assets are increasing and have no previous balance or (b) liabilities are increasing and have no previous balance.

Key Terms

Administrative expenses (general expenses) Expenses such as general office expenses that are incurred indirectly in the selling of goods.

Classified balance sheet A balance sheet that categorizes assets as current or plant and equipment and groups liabilities as current or long-term.

Current assets Assets that can be converted into cash or used within one year or the normal operating cycle of the business, whichever is longer.

Current liabilities Obligations that will come due within one year or within the operating cycle, whichever is longer.

Long-term liabilities Obligations that are not due or payable for a long time, usually for more than a year.

Operating cycle Average time it takes to buy and sell merchandise and then collect accounts receivable.

Other expenses Nonoperating expenses that do not relate to the main operating activities of the business; they appear in a separate section on the income statement. One example given in the text is Interest Expense, interest owed on money borrowed by the company.

Other income Any revenue other than revenue from sales. It appears in a separate section on the income statement. Examples: Rental Income and Storage Fees.

Plant and equipment Long-lived assets such as buildings or land that are used in the production or sale of goods or services.

Reversing entries Optional bookkeeping technique in which certain adjusting entries are reversed or switched on the first day of the new accounting period so that transactions in the new period can be recorded without referring back to prior adjusting entries.

Selling expenses Expenses directly related to the sale of goods.

Questions, Mini Exercises, Exercises, and Problems

Discussion Questions

1. Which columns of the worksheet aid in the preparation of the income statement?
2. Explain the components of cost of goods sold.
3. Explain how operating expenses can be broken down into different categories.
4. What is the difference between current assets and plant and equipment?
5. What is an operating cycle?
6. Why journalize adjusting entries *after* the formal reports in a manual system have been prepared?
7. Explain the steps of closing for a merchandise company.
8. Temporary accounts could appear on a post-closing trial balance. Agree or disagree.
9. What is the purpose of using reversing entries? Are they mandatory? When should they be used?

Mini Exercises

(The forms you need are on page 378 of the *Study Guide and Working Papers.*)

Calculate Net Sales

1. From the following, calculate net sales:

Purchases	$ 80	Sales Discount	$ 5
Gross Sales	140	Operating Expenses	25
Sales Returns and Allowances	10		

Calculate Cost of Goods Sold

2. Calculate Cost of Goods Sold:

Freight-in	$ 5	Ending Inventory	$15
Beginning Inventory	20	Net Purchases	50

Calculate Gross Profit and Net Income

3. Using Mini Exercises 1 and 2, calculate

   a. Gross Profit.
   b. Net Income or Net Loss.

Blueprint: Financial Statements

(1) INCOME STATEMENT				
Revenue:				
Sales				$ XXX
Less: Sales Ret. and Allow.			$ XXX	
Sales Discount			XXX	XXX
Net Sales				$ XXXX
Cost of Goods Sold:				
Merchandise Inventory, 1/1/0X			$ XXX	
Purchases		$XXX		
Less: Purchases Discount	$XXX			
Purch. Ret. and Allow.	XXX	XXX		
Net Purchases		XXX		
Add: Freight-In		XXX		
Net Cost of Purchases			XXX	
Cost of Goods Avail. for Sale			$XXXX	
Less: Merch. Inv., 12/31/0X			XXX	
Cost of Goods Sold				XXXX
Gross Profit				$XXXX
Operating Expenses:				
~~			$XXX	
~~			XXX	
~~			XXX	
Total Operating Expenses				XXX
Net Income from Operations				$ XXX
Other Income:				
Rental Income			$ XXX	
Storage Fees Income			XXX	
Total Other Income			$ XXX	
Other Expenses:				
Interest Expenses			XXX	XXX
Net Income:				$ XXX

(2) STATEMENT OF OWNER'S EQUITY		
Beginning Capital		$XXX
Additional Investments		XXX
Total Investment		$XXX
Net Income	$XXX	
Less: Withdrawals	XXX	
Increase in Capital		XXX
Ending Capital		$XXX

(3) BALANCE SHEET				
Assets				
Current Assets:				
Cash		$ XXXX		
Acccounts Receivable		XXXX		
Merchandise Inventory		XXXX		
Prepaid Insurance		XXX		
Total Current Assets			$ XXXX	
Plant and Equipment:				
Store Equipment	$XXXX			
Less Accumulated Depreciation	XXXX	$XXXX		
Office Equipment	$XXXX			
Less Accumulated Depreciation	XXX	XXX		
Total Plant and Equipment			XXXX	
Total Assets			$XXXX	
Liabilities				
Current Liabilities:				
Unearned Revenue		$XXX		
Mortgage Payable (current portion)		XXX		
Accounts Payable		XXX		
Salaries Payable		XX		
FICA—Social Security Payable		XX		
FICA—Medicare Payable		XX		
Income Taxes Payable		XX		
Total Current Liabilities			$XXX	
Long-Term Liabilities				
Mortgage Payable			$XXX	
Total Liabilities			$XXXX	
Owner's Equity				
Capital*			XXXX	
Total Liabilities and Owner's Equity			$XXXX	

* From statement of owner's equity

Classification of Accounts

4. Match the following categories to each account listed below:
   1. Current Asset.
   2. Plant and Equipment.
   3. Current Liabilities.
   4. Long-Term Liabilities.

_____ **a.** Merchandise Inventory   _____ **f.** Mortgage Payable (Not Current)
_____ **b.** Unearned Rent   _____ **g.** FUTA Payable
_____ **c.** Prepaid Insurance   _____ **h.** Accumulated Depreciation
_____ **d.** SUTA Payable   _____ **i.** FICA-Social Security Payable
_____ **e.** Store Equipment   _____ **j.** Petty Cash

Reversing Entries

5. a. On January 1, prepare a reversing entry. On January 8, journalize the entry to record the paying of salary expense, $900.
    b. What will be the balance in Salaries Expense on January 8 (after posting)?

December 31:

Salaries Expense		Salaries Payable
900	1,200 closing	300 Adj.
Adj. 300		

Exercises

(The forms you need are on pages 378–380 of the *Study Guide and Working Papers.*)

Preparing cost of goods sold section.

12-1. From the following accounts, prepare a cost of goods sold section in proper form: Merchandise Inventory, 12/31/X1, $6,000; Purchases Discount, $900; Merchandise Inventory, 12/1/X1, $4,000; Purchases, $58,000; Purchases Returns and Allowances, $1,000; Freight-in, $300.

Categorizing and classifying account titles.

12-2. Give the category, the classification, and the report(s) on which each of the following appears (for example: Cash—asset, current asset, balance sheet):

    a. Salaries Payable.   **e.** SIT Payable.
    b. Accounts Payable.   **f.** Office Equipment.
    c. Mortgage Payable.   **g.** Land.
    d. Unearned Legal Fees.

Journalizing closing entries.

12-3. From the partial worksheet in Fig. 12-15, on p. 491, journalize the closing entries of December 31 for A. Slow Co.

Preparing partially completed balance sheet.

12-4. From the worksheet in Exercise 12-3, prepare the assets section of a classified balance sheet.

Reversing entry.

12-5. On December 31, 20X1, $300 of salaries has been accrued. (Salaries before the accrued amount totaled $26,000.) The next payroll to be paid will be on February 3, 20X2, for $6,000. Please do the following:

    a. Journalize and post the adjusting entry (use T accounts).
    b. Journalize and post the reversing entry on January 1.
    c. Journalize and post the payment of the payroll. Cash has a balance of $15,000 before the payment of payroll on February 3.

Account Titles	A. SLOW CO. WORKSHEET FOR YEAR ENDED DECEMBER 31, 200X			
	Income Statement		Balance Sheet	
	Dr.	Cr.	Dr.	Cr.
Cash			1 9 3 00	
Merch. Inventory			4 5 0 00	
Prepaid Advertising			5 6 1 00	
Prepaid Insurance			3 0 00	
Office Equipment			1 0 8 0 00	
Accum. Depr., Office Equip.				2 1 0 00
Accounts Payable				2 5 8 00
A. Slow, Capital				9 6 6 00
Income Summary	3 6 2 00	4 5 0 00		
Sales		5 5 2 0 00		
Sales Returns and Allowances	2 2 3 00			
Sales Discount	1 0 8 00			
Purchases	2 6 2 8 00			
Purchases Returns and Allow.		3 4 00		
Purchases Discount		5 1 00		
Salaries Expense	1 0 8 3 00			
Insurance Expense	6 9 6 00			
Utilities Expense	4 8 00			
Plumbing Expense	5 7 00			
Advertising Expense	1 5 00			
Depr. Expenses, Office Equip.	3 0 00			
Salaries Payable				7 5 00
	5 2 5 0 00	6 0 5 5 00	2 3 1 4 00	1 5 0 9 00
Net Income	8 0 5 00			8 0 5 00
	6 0 5 5 00	6 0 5 5 00	2 3 1 4 00	2 3 1 4 00

Figure 12-15 Worksheet for A. Slow Co.

Group A Problems

(The forms you need are on pages 381–391 of the *Study Guide and Working Papers.*)

12A-1. Prepare a formal income statement from the partial worksheet for Ring.com in Figure 12-16 on p. 492.

Check Figure:
Net Income from operations $761

12A-2. Prepare a statement of owner's equity and a classified balance sheet from the worksheet for James Company in Figure 12-17 on p. 492. *Note:* Of the Mortgage Payable, $200 is due within one year.

12A-3. a. Complete the worksheet for Jay's Supplies in Figure 12-18 on p. 493.
   b. Prepare an income statement, a statement of owner's equity, and a classified balance sheet. (*Note:* The amount of the mortgage due the first year is $800.)
   c. Journalize the adjusting and closing entries.

Check Figure:
Total Assets $33,340

12A-4. Using the ledger balances and additional data shown on page 493, do the following for Callahan Lumber for the year ended December 31, 200X:

   1. Prepare the worksheet.
   2. Prepare the income statement, statement of owner's equity, and balance sheet.
   3. Journalize and post adjusting and closing entries. (Be sure to put beginning balances in the ledger first.)

Check Figure:
Net Income $4,340

Figure 12-16
Partial Worksheet for
Ring.Com

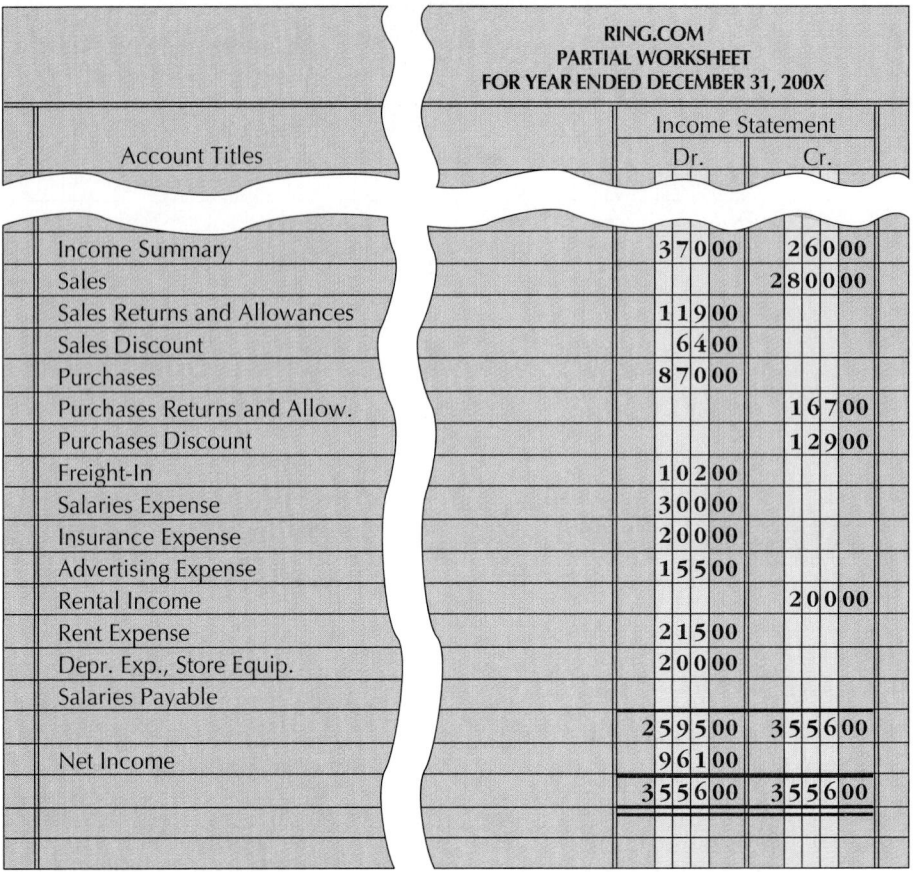

RING.COM
PARTIAL WORKSHEET
FOR YEAR ENDED DECEMBER 31, 200X

Account Titles	Income Statement Dr.	Income Statement Cr.
Income Summary	370 00	260 00
Sales		2800 00
Sales Returns and Allowances	119 00	
Sales Discount	64 00	
Purchases	870 00	
Purchases Returns and Allow.		167 00
Purchases Discount		129 00
Freight-In	102 00	
Salaries Expense	300 00	
Insurance Expense	200 00	
Advertising Expense	155 00	
Rental Income		200 00
Rent Expense	215 00	
Depr. Exp., Store Equip.	200 00	
Salaries Payable		
	2595 00	3556 00
Net Income	961 00	
	3556 00	3556 00

Figure 12-17
Partial Worksheet for
James Company

Preparing a statement of owner's equity and a classified balance sheet from a worksheet.

JAMES COMPANY
WORKSHEET
FOR YEAR ENDED DECEMBER 31, 200X

Account Titles	Balance Sheet Dr.	Balance Sheet Cr.
Cash	2350 00	
Petty Cash	90 00	
Accounts Receivable	135 00	
Merchandise Inv.	400 00	
Supplies	325 00	
Prepaid Insurance	500 00	
Store Equipment	2800 00	
Acc. Dep., Store Eq.		700 00
Automobile	1700 00	
Acc. Dep., Auto.		225 00
Accounts Payable		2800 00
Taxes Payable		2400 00
Unearned Rent		1850 00
Mortgage Payable		450 00
H. James, Capital		1240 00
H. James, With.	100 00	
Salaries Payable		60 00
	3436 500	3807 500
Net Loss	371 000	
	3807 500	3807 500

JAY'S SUPPLIES
WORKSHEET
FOR YEAR ENDED DECEMBER 31, 200X

Account Titles	Trial Balance Dr.	Trial Balance Cr.	Adjustments Dr.	Adjustments Cr.
Cash	2 000 00			
Accounts Receivable	3 000 00			
Merch. Inv., 1/1/XX	11 000 00	(B)	10 400 00	11 000 00 (A)
Prepaid Insurance	1 880 00			500 00 (E)
Equipment	3 400 00			
Accum. Dep., Equipment		1 080 00		400 00 (D)
Accounts Payable		5 080 00		
Unearned Training Fees		2 120 00	(C) 320 00	
Mortgage Payable		1 200 00		
P. Jay, Capital		10 560 00		
P. Jay, Withdrawals	4 280 00			
Income Summary		(A)	11 000 00	10 400 00 (B)
Sales		95 800 00		
Sales Returns and Allowances	3 200 00			
Sales Discount	2 600 00			
Purchases	63 600 00			
Purchases Returns and Allow.		13 600 00		
Purchases Discount		3 200 00		
Freight-In	2 680 00			
Advertising Expense	11 400 00			
Rent Expense	10 000 00			
Salaries Expense	13 600 00			
	132 640 00	132 640 00		
Training Fees Earned				320 00 (C)
Dep. Exp., Equipment			(D) 400 00	
Insurance Expense			(E) 500 00	
			22 620 00	22 620 00

Figure 12-18 Worksheet for Jay's Supplies

4. Prepare a post-closing trial balance.
5. Journalize the reversing entry for wages.

Acct. No.

110	Cash	$ 1,340
111	Accounts Receivable	1,300
112	Merchandise Inventory	4,550
113	Lumber Supplies	269
114	Prepaid Insurance	218
121	Lumber Equipment	3,000
122	Accum. Depr., Lumber Equipment	490
220	Accounts Payable	1,160
221	Wages Payable	—
330	J. Callahan, Capital	7,352
331	J. Callahan, Withdrawals	3,000
332	Income Summary	—
440	Sales	22,800
441	Sales Returns and Allowances	200
550	Purchases	14,800

*Comprehensive Problem.
Worksheet preparation:
preparing financial reports,
journalizing and posting
adjusting and closing
entries, preparing a post-
closing trial balance, and
journalizing reversing entry.*

*Check Figure:
Net Income $4,336*

551	Purchases Discount	285
552	Purchases Returns and Allowances	300
660	Wages Expense	2,480
661	Advertising Expense	400
662	Rent Expense	830
663	Dep. Expense, Lumber Equipment	—
664	Lumber Supplies Expense	—
665	Insurance Expense	—

Additional Data

a./b.	Merchandise inventory, December 31	$ 4,900
c.	Lumber supplies on hand, December 31	75
d.	Insurance expired	150
e.	Depreciation for the year	250
f.	Accrued wages on December 31	95

Group B Problems

(The forms you need are on pages 381–391 of the *Study Guide and Working Papers.*)

12B-1. From the partial worksheet shown in Figure 12-19, prepare a formal income statement.

12B-2. From the worksheet shown in Figure 12-20 on p. 494, complete

    a. Statement of owner's equity.
    b. Classified balance sheet.

Note: Of the Mortgage Payable, $3,000 is due within one year.

Preparing an income statement from a worksheet.

Preparing a statement of owner's equity and a classified balance sheet from a worksheet.

Figure 12-19
Partial Worksheet of Ring.Com

Check Figure:
Net income from operations
$845

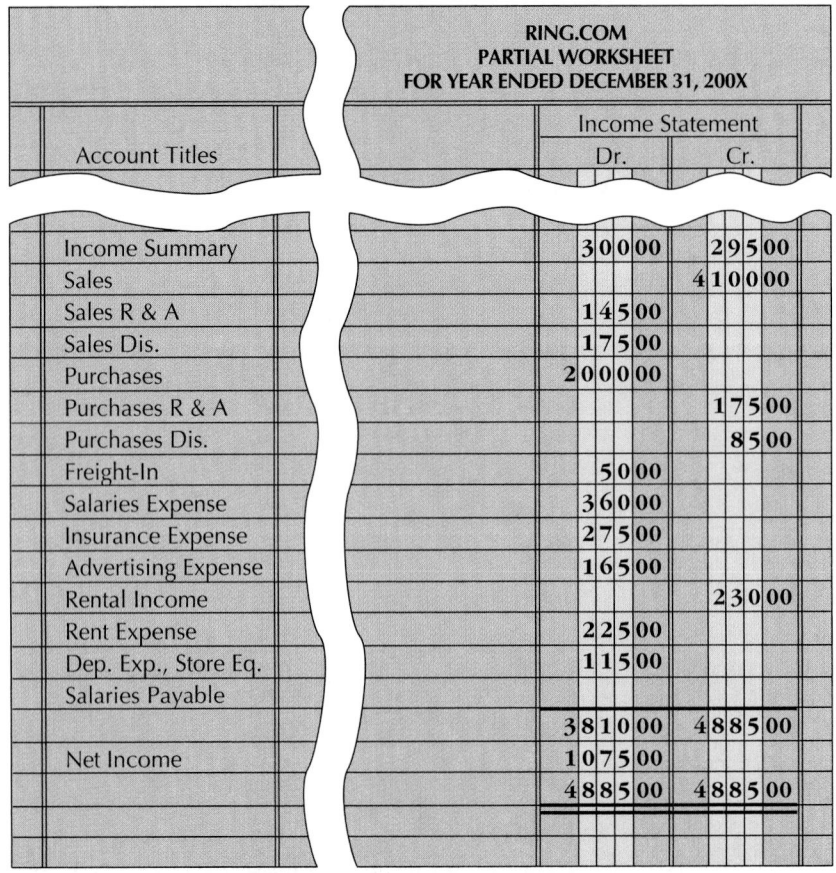

RING.COM
PARTIAL WORKSHEET
FOR YEAR ENDED DECEMBER 31, 200X

Account Titles	Income Statement Dr.	Income Statement Cr.
Income Summary	3 0 0 00	2 9 5 00
Sales		4 1 0 0 00
Sales R & A	1 4 5 00	
Sales Dis.	1 7 5 00	
Purchases	2 0 0 0 00	
Purchases R & A		1 7 5 00
Purchases Dis.		8 5 00
Freight-In	5 0 00	
Salaries Expense	3 6 0 00	
Insurance Expense	2 7 5 00	
Advertising Expense	1 6 5 00	
Rental Income		2 3 0 00
Rent Expense	2 2 5 00	
Dep. Exp., Store Eq.	1 1 5 00	
Salaries Payable		
	3 8 1 0 00	4 8 8 5 00
Net Income	1 0 7 5 00	
	4 8 8 5 00	4 8 8 5 00

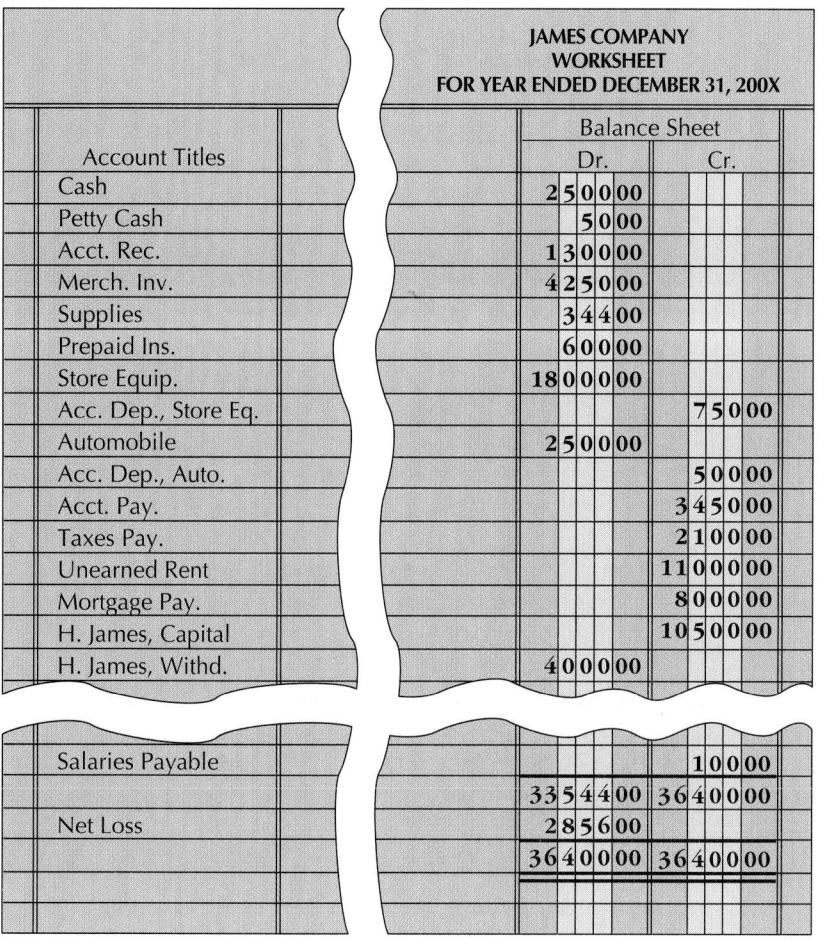

Figure 12-20
Worksheet for James Company

JAMES COMPANY
WORKSHEET
FOR YEAR ENDED DECEMBER 31, 200X

Account Titles	Balance Sheet Dr.	Balance Sheet Cr.
Cash	2 5 0 0 00	
Petty Cash	5 0 00	
Acct. Rec.	1 3 0 0 00	
Merch. Inv.	4 2 5 0 00	
Supplies	3 4 4 00	
Prepaid Ins.	6 0 0 00	
Store Equip.	1 8 0 0 0 00	
Acc. Dep., Store Eq.		7 5 0 00
Automobile	2 5 0 0 00	
Acc. Dep., Auto.		5 0 0 00
Acct. Pay.		3 4 5 0 00
Taxes Pay.		2 1 0 0 00
Unearned Rent		1 1 0 0 0 00
Mortgage Pay.		8 0 0 0 00
H. James, Capital		1 0 5 0 0 00
H. James, Withd.	4 0 0 0 00	
Salaries Payable		1 0 0 00
	3 3 5 4 4 00	3 6 4 0 0 00
Net Loss	2 8 5 6 00	
	3 6 4 0 0 00	3 6 4 0 0 00

Check Figure:
Total Assets $28,294

Completing the worksheet;
preparing financial reports;
and journalizing adjusting
and closing entries.

Check Figure:
Net Loss $12,050

Comprehensive Problem:
Worksheet preparation,
preparing financial reports,
journalizing and posting
adjusting and closing
entries, preparing a post-
closing trial balance, and
journalizing reversing entry.

Check Figure:
Net Income $2,730

12B-3. From the partial worksheet in Figure 12-21 on p. 495, your tasks are to

1. Complete the worksheet.
2. Prepare the income statement, statement of owner's equity, and classified balance sheet. The amount of the mortgage due the first year is $800.
3. Journalize the adjusting and closing entries.

12B-4. From the following ledger balances and additional data on pages 494–495, do the following:

1. Prepare the worksheet.
2. Prepare the income statement, statement of owner's equity, and balance sheet.
3. Journalize and post adjusting and closing entries. (Be sure to put beginning balances in the ledger first.)
4. Prepare a post-closing trial balance.
5. Journalize the reversing entry for wages.

Acct. No.

110	Cash	$ 940
111	Accounts Receivable	1,470
112	Merchandise Inventory	5,600
113	Lumber Supplies	260
114	Prepaid Insurance	117
121	Lumber Equipment	2,600
122	Acc. Dep., Lumber Equipment	340
220	Accounts Payable	1,330

JAY'S SUPPLIES
WORKSHEET
FOR YEAR ENDED DECEMBER 31, 200X

Account Titles	Trial Balance Dr.	Trial Balance Cr.	Adjustments Dr.	Adjustments Cr.
Cash	3 0 0 00			
Accounts Receivable	3 0 0 00			
Merch. Inventory, 1/1/XX	11 7 0 0 00		(B) 8 0 0 00	11 7 0 0 00 (A)
Prepaid Insurance	1 0 0 00			3 5 0 00 (E)
Equipment	5 0 0 00			
Accum. Dep., Equipment		1 9 0 00		5 0 0 00 (D)
Accounts Payable		2 1 0 00		
Unearned Training Fees		1 4 5 0 00	(C) 4 0 0 00	
Mortgage Payable		2 4 0 0 00		
P. Jay, Capital		27 7 5 0 00		
P. Jay, Withdrawals	4 0 0 00			
Income Summary			(A) 11 7 0 0 00	8 0 0 00 (B)
Sales		100 8 0 0 00		
Sales Returns and Allowances	4 1 0 0 00			
Sales Discount	2 8 0 0 00			
Purchases	70 0 0 0 00			
Purchases Returns and Allow.		2 0 0 0 00		
Purchases Discounts		1 4 0 0 00		
Freight-In	2 7 0 0 00			
Advertising Expense	8 0 0 00			
Rent Expense	8 5 0 0 00			
Salaries Expense	16 0 0 0 00			
	139 8 0 0 00	139 8 0 0 00		
Training Fees Earned				4 0 0 00 (C)
Dep. Exp., Equipment			(D) 5 0 0 00	
Insurance Expense			(E) 3 5 0 00	
			20 9 5 0 00	20 9 5 0 00

Figure 12-21 Worksheet for Jay's Supplies

221	Wages Payable	
330	J. Callahan, Capital	7,562
331	J. Callahan, Withdrawals	3,500
332	Income Summary	—
440	Sales	23,000
441	Sales Returns and Allowances	400
550	Purchases	14,700
551	Purchases Discount	440
552	Purchases Returns and Allowances	545
660	Wages Expense	2,390
661	Advertising Expense	400
662	Rent Expense	840
663	Dep. Exp., Lumber Equipment	—
664	Lumber Supplies Expense	—
665	Insurance Expense	—

Additional Data

a./b. Merchandise inventory, December 31	$ 3,900
c. Lumber supplies on hand, December 31	60

d. Insurance expired   50
e. Depreciation for the year   400
f. Accrued wages on December 31   175

Real-World Applications

12R-1. Chan Company recently had most of its records destroyed in a fire. The information for 20X1 (Fig. 12-22) was discovered by the bookkeeper. Please assist the bookkeeper in reconstructing an income statement for 20X1.

12R-2. Hope Lang, a junior accountant, has the December 31, 200X trial balance of Gregot Company sitting on her desk. Attached is a memo from her supervisor requesting that a classified balance sheet be prepared. Hope gathers the following data:

1. A physical inventory at December 31 showed $80,000 on hand.
2. Office supplies on hand was $600.
3. Insurance unexpired was $750.
4. Depreciation (straight-line) is based on a 25-year life.

Using the trial balance of Gregot Co. in Figure 12-23 on p. 497, please assist Hope with this project. *Hint:* Ending figure for capital is $115,850.

CHAN COMPANY
GENERAL JOURNAL

Page 2

Date		Description	PR	Dr.	Cr.
Dec.	31	Income Summary	312	3 6 3 0 00	
		Sales Returns and Allowances	420		1 4 0 00
		Sales Discount	430		3 0 00
		Purchases	500		2 4 0 0 00
		Delivery Expense	600		9 0 00
		Salaries Expense	610		8 4 0 00
		Rent Expense	620		3 0 00
		Office Supplies Expense	630		5 0 00
		Advertising Expense	640		1 0 00
		Dep. Exp., Store Equipment	650		4 0 00
	31	Sales	410	5 5 4 2 00	
		Purchases Discount	510	1 2 0 00	
		Purchases Returns and Allowances	520	1 0 0 00	
		Income Summary	312		5 7 6 2 00
	31	Income Summary	312	3 7 3 2 00	
		J. Chan, Capital	310		3 7 3 2 00

Beg. Inv. $1,400
End. Inv. 3,000

Figure 12-22 General Journal for Chan Company

GREGOT COMPANY TRIAL BALANCE DECEMBER 31, 200X		
	Dr.	Cr.
Cash	11 0 0 0 00	
Accounts Receivable	38 0 0 0 00	
Inventory, Jan. 1	80 0 0 0 00	
Prepaid Insurance	2 0 0 0 00	
Office Supplies	1 0 0 0 00	
Land	17 5 0 0 00	
Building	50 0 0 0 00	
Accumulated Depreciation, Building		10 0 0 0 00
Notes Payable		40 0 0 0 00
Accounts Payable		30 0 0 0 00
G. Gregot, Capital		98 4 0 0 00
G. Gregot, Withdrawals	13 0 0 0 00	
Income Summary	—	—
Retail Sales		329 0 0 0 00
Sales Returns and Allowances	21 0 0 0 00	
Sales Discount	8 0 0 0 00	
Purchases	215 5 0 0 00	
Purchases Returns and Allowances		11 6 0 0 00
Purchases Discount		4 0 0 0 00
Transportation-In	5 0 0 0 00	
Advertising Expense	2 5 0 0 00	
Wage Expense	55 0 0 0 00	
Utilities Expense	3 5 0 0 00	
	523 0 0 0 00	523 0 0 0 00

Figure 12-23 Trial Balance for Gregot Company

YOU make the call

Critical Thinking/Ethical Case

12R-3. Janet Flynn, owner of Reel Company, plans to apply for a bank loan at Petro National Bank. Because the company has a lot of debt on its balance sheet, Janet does not plan to show the loan officer the balance sheet. She plans only to bring the income statement. Do you feel that this move is a sound financial move by Janet? You make the call. Write down your specific recommendations to Janet.

Internet Exercises: Aware; ExxonMobil

EX-1. [www.aware.com] Aware is an electronics firm that claims to be positioning itself for rapid growth in the DSL technology market. The financial statements it presents are straightforward. Look over the 2001 balance sheet and comment on its classifications, using those presented in this chapter as a guide.

EX-2. [**www.exxonmobil.com.financials.html**]   This is another exercise in looking at the classifications in classified balance sheets. ExxonMobil is a vastly different company from Aware in Exercise 1. Observe, however, the classifications in the balance sheet of ExxonMobil. How does it compare to that of Aware? How is it different? Notice how they are basically the same as presented in this chapter.

Continuing Problem

Eldorado Computer Center

Using the worksheet in Chapter 11 for Eldorado Computer Center, journalize and post the adjusting entries and prepare the financial statements. (See page 402 in the *Study Guide and Working Papers.*)

THE CORNER DRESS SHOP

Reviewing the Accounting Cycle for a Merchandise Company

(The forms you need are on pages 415–437 of the *Study Guide and Working Papers*. This practice set will help you review all the key concepts of a merchandise company, along with the integration of payroll, including the preparation of Form 941.)

Because you are the bookkeeper of The Corner Dress Shop, we have gathered the following information for you. It will be your task to complete the accounting cycle for March.

THE CORNER DRESS SHOP POSTCLOSING TRIAL BALANCE FEBRUARY 28, 200X	1	2
Cash	2 3 3 4 90	
Accounts Receivable	2 2 0 0 00	
Petty Cash	3 5 00	
Merchandise Inventory	5 6 0 0 00	
Prepaid Rent	1 8 0 0 00	
Delivery Truck	6 0 0 0 00	
Accumulated Depreciation, Truck		1 5 0 0 00
Accounts Payable		1 9 0 0 00
FIT Payable		1 1 1 6 00
FICA—Social Security Payable		1 3 3 9 20
FICA—Medicare Payable		3 1 3 20
SIT Payable		7 5 6 00
SUTA Payable		9 7 9 20
FUTA Payable		1 6 3 20
Unearned Rent		8 0 0 00
B. Loeb, Capital		9 1 0 3 10
	17 9 6 9 90	17 9 6 9 90

Betty Loeb's dress shop is located at 1 Milgate Rd., Marblehead, MA 01945. Its identification number is 33-4158215.

Balances in subsidiary ledgers as of March 1 are as follows:

Accounts Receivable		Accounts Payable	
Bing Co.	$ 2,200	Blew Co.	$ 1,900
Blew Co.	—	Jones Co.	—
Ronald Co.	—	Moe's Garage	—
		Morris Co.	—

Payroll is paid monthly:

FICA rate	Social Security 6.2% on $87,000
	Medicare 1.45% on all earnings
SUTA rate	4.8% on $7,000
FUTA rate	.8% on $7,000
SIT rate	7%
FIT	Use table provided on page 503.

The payroll register for January and February is provided. In March, salaries are as follows:

Mel Case	$3,325
Jane Holl	4,120
Jackie Moore	4,760

Your tasks are to

1. Set up a general ledger, accounts receivable subsidiary ledger and accounts payable subsidiary ledger, auxiliary petty cash record, and payroll register. (Be sure to update ledger accounts based on information given in the post-closing trial balance for February 28 before beginning.)
2. Journalize the transactions and prepare the payroll register.
3. Update the accounts payable and accounts receivable subsidiary ledgers.
4. Post to the general ledger.
5. Prepare a trial balance on a worksheet and complete the worksheet.
6. Prepare an income statement, statement of owner's equity, and classified balance sheet.
7. Journalize the adjusting and closing entries.
8. Post the adjusting and closing entries to the ledger.
9. Prepare a post-closing trial balance.
10. Complete Form 941 and sign it as of the last day in April.

CHART OF ACCOUNTS
FOR THE CORNER DRESS SHOP

Assets

110	Cash
111	Accounts Receivable
112	Petty Cash
114	Merchandise Inventory
116	Prepaid Rent
120	Delivery Truck
121	Accumulated Depreciation, Truck

Liabilities

210	Accounts Payable
212	Salaries Payable
214	Federal Income Tax Payable
216	FICA — Soc. Sec. Payable
218	FICA — Medicare Payable
220	State Income Tax Payable
222	SUTA Tax Payable
224	FUTA Tax Payable
226	Unearned Rent

Owner's Equity

310	B. Loeb, Capital
320	B. Loeb, Withdrawals
330	Income Summary

Revenue

410	Sales
412	Sales Returns and Allowances
414	Sales Discount
416	Rental Income

Cost of Goods Sold

510	Purchases
512	Purchases Returns and Allowances
514	Purchase Discount

Expenses

610	Sales Salaries Expense
611	Office Salaries Expense
612	Payroll Tax Expense
614	Cleaning Expense
616	Depreciation Expense, Truck
618	Rent Expense
620	Postage Expense
622	Delivery Expense
624	Miscellaneous Expense

THE CORNER DRESS SHOP
PAYROLL REGISTER
JANUARY AND FEBRUARY 200X

Employees	Allow. and Marital Status	Cum. Earnings	Salary	Earnings			Cum. Earnings
				Reg.	O/T	Gross	
Mel Case	M – 2		3300 00	3300 00		3300 00	3300 00
Jane Holl	M – 1		3400 00	3400 00		3400 00	3400 00
Jackie Moore	M – 0		4100 00	4100 00		4100 00	4100 00
Totals for Jan.			10800 00	10800 00		10800 00	10800 00
Mel Case	M – 2	3300 00	3300 00	3300 00		3300 00	6600 00
Jane Holl	M – 1	3400 00	3400 00	3400 00		3400 00	6800 00
Jackie Moore	M – 0	4100 00	4100 00	4100 00		4100 00	8200 00
Totals for Feb.		10800 00	10800 00	10800 00		10800 00	21600 00

PAYROLL REGISTER

Taxable Earnings			Deductions					Ck. No.	Distribution	
	FICA		FICA						Office Salary Expense	Sales Salary Expense
Unemp.	Soc. Sec.	Medicare	Soc. Sec.	Medicare	FIT	SIT	Net Pay			
3300 00	3300 00	3300 00	204 60	47 85	288 00	231 00	2528 55		3300 00	
3400 00	3400 00	3400 00	210 80	49 30	344 00	238 00	2557 90			3400 00
4100 00	4100 00	4100 00	254 20	59 45	484 00	287 00	3015 35			4100 00
10800 00	10800 00	10800 00	669 60	156 60	1116 00	756 00	8101 80		3300 00	7500 00
3300 00	3300 00	3300 00	204 60	47 85	288 00	231 00	2528 55		3300 00	
3400 00	3400 00	3400 00	210 80	49 30	344 00	238 00	2557 90			3400 00
4100 00	4100 00	4100 00	254 20	59 45	484 00	287 00	3015 35			4100 00
10800 00	10800 00	10800 00	669 60	156 60	1116 00	756 00	8101 80		3300 00	7500 00

200X

Mar.

1   Bing paid balance owed, no discount.

2   Purchased merchandise from Morris Company on account, $10,000, terms 2/10, n/30.

2   Paid $6 from the petty cash fund for cleaning package, voucher no. 18 (consider it a cleaning expense).

3   Sold merchandise to Ronald Company on account, $7,000, invoice no. 51, terms 2/10, n/30.

5   Paid $3 from the petty cash fund for postage, voucher no. 19.

6   Sold merchandise to Ronald Company on account, $5,000, invoice no. 52, terms 2/10, n/30.

MARRIED Persons—MONTHLY Payroll Period
(For Wages Paid in 200X)

If the wages are—		And the number of withholding allowances claimed is—										
At least	But less than	0	1	2	3	4	5	6	7	8	9	10
		The amount of income tax to be withheld is—										
$3,240	$3,280	$358	$320	$282	$244	$206	$168	$130	$94	$69	$44	$18
3,280	3,320	364	326	288	250	212	174	136	98	73	48	22
3,320	3,360	370	332	294	256	218	180	142	104	77	52	26
3,360	3,400	376	338	300	262	224	186	148	110	81	56	30
3,400	3,440	382	344	306	268	230	192	154	116	85	60	34
3,440	3,480	388	350	312	274	236	198	160	122	89	64	38
3,480	3,520	394	356	318	280	242	204	166	128	93	68	42
3,520	3,560	400	362	324	286	248	210	172	134	97	72	46
3,560	3,600	406	368	330	292	254	216	178	140	101	76	50
3,600	3,640	412	374	336	298	260	222	184	146	107	80	54
3,640	3,680	418	380	342	304	266	228	190	152	113	84	58
3,680	3,720	424	386	348	310	272	234	196	158	119	88	62
3,720	3,760	430	392	354	316	278	240	202	164	125	92	66
3,760	3,800	436	398	360	322	284	246	208	170	131	96	70
3,800	3,840	442	404	366	328	290	252	214	176	137	100	74
3,840	3,880	448	410	372	334	296	258	220	182	143	105	78
3,880	3,920	454	416	378	340	302	264	226	188	149	111	82
3,920	3,960	460	422	384	346	308	270	232	194	155	117	86
3,960	4,000	466	428	390	352	314	276	238	200	161	123	90
4,000	4,040	472	434	396	358	320	282	244	206	167	129	94
4,040	4,080	478	440	402	364	326	288	250	212	173	135	98
4,080	4,120	484	446	408	370	332	294	256	218	179	141	103
4,120	4,160	490	452	414	376	338	300	262	224	185	147	109
4,160	4,200	496	458	420	382	344	306	268	230	191	153	115
4,200	4,240	502	464	426	388	350	312	274	236	197	159	121
4,240	4,280	508	470	432	394	356	318	280	242	203	165	127
4,280	4,320	514	476	438	400	362	324	286	248	209	171	133
4,320	4,360	520	482	444	406	368	330	292	254	215	177	139
4,360	4,400	528	488	450	412	374	336	298	260	221	183	145
4,400	4,440	539	494	456	418	380	342	304	266	227	189	151
4,440	4,480	550	500	462	424	386	348	310	272	233	195	157
4,480	4,520	561	506	468	430	392	354	316	278	239	201	163
4,520	4,560	572	512	474	436	398	360	322	284	245	207	169
4,560	4,600	582	518	480	442	404	366	328	290	251	213	175
4,600	4,640	593	525	486	448	410	372	334	296	257	219	181
4,640	4,680	604	535	492	454	416	378	340	302	263	225	187
4,680	4,720	615	546	498	460	422	384	346	308	269	231	193
4,720	4,760	626	557	504	466	428	390	352	314	275	237	199
4,760	4,800	636	568	510	472	434	396	358	320	281	243	205
4,800	4,840	647	579	516	478	440	402	364	326	287	249	211
4,840	4,880	658	589	522	484	446	408	370	332	293	255	217
4,880	4,920	669	600	532	490	452	414	376	338	299	261	223
4,920	4,960	680	611	542	496	458	420	382	344	305	267	229
4,960	5,000	690	622	553	502	464	426	388	350	311	273	235
5,000	5,040	701	633	564	508	470	432	394	356	317	279	241
5,040	5,080	712	643	575	514	476	438	400	362	323	285	247
5,080	5,120	723	654	586	520	482	444	406	368	329	291	253
5,120	5,160	734	665	596	528	488	450	412	374	335	297	259
5,160	5,200	744	676	607	539	494	456	418	380	341	303	265
5,200	5,240	755	687	618	549	500	462	424	386	347	309	271
5,240	5,280	766	697	629	560	506	468	430	392	353	315	277
5,280	5,320	777	708	640	571	512	474	436	398	359	321	283
5,320	5,360	788	719	650	582	518	480	442	404	365	327	289
5,360	5,400	798	730	661	593	524	486	448	410	371	333	295
5,400	5,440	809	741	672	603	535	492	454	416	377	339	301
5,440	5,480	820	751	683	614	546	498	460	422	383	345	307
5,480	5,520	831	762	694	625	556	504	466	428	389	351	313
5,520	5,560	842	773	704	636	567	510	472	434	395	357	319
5,560	5,600	852	784	715	647	578	516	478	440	401	363	325
5,600	5,640	863	795	726	657	589	522	484	446	407	369	331
5,640	5,680	874	805	737	668	600	531	490	452	413	375	337
5,680	5,720	885	816	748	679	610	542	496	458	419	381	343
5,720	5,760	896	827	758	690	621	553	502	464	425	387	349
5,760	5,800	906	838	769	701	632	563	508	470	431	393	355
5,800	5,840	917	849	780	711	643	574	514	476	437	399	361

$5,840 and over   Use Table 4(b) for a **MARRIED** person on page 34. Also see the instructions on page 32.

8   Paid $10 from the petty cash fund for first aid emergency, voucher no. 20.

9   Purchased merchandise from Morris Company on account, $5,000, terms 2/10, n/30.

9   Paid $5 for delivery expense from petty cash fund, voucher no. 21.

9   Sold more merchandise to Ronald Company on account, $3,000, invoice no. 53, terms 2/10, n/30.

9   Paid cleaning service, $300, check no. 110.

10   Ronald Company returned merchandise costing $1,000 from invoice no. 52; The Corner Dress shop issued credit memo no. 10 Ronald Company for $1,000.

11   Purchased merchandise from Jones Company on account, $10,000, terms 1/15, n/60.

12   Paid Morris Company invoice dated March 2, check no. 111.

13   Sold $7,000 of merchandise for cash.

14   Returned merchandise to Jones Company in amount of $2,000; The Corner Dress Shop issued debit memo no. 4 to Jones Company.

14   Paid $5 from the petty cash fund for delivery expense, voucher no. 22.

15   Paid taxes due for FICA (Social Security and Medicare) and FIT for February payroll, check no. 112.

15   Sold Merchandise for $29,000 cash.

15   Betty withdrew $100 for her own personal expenses, check no. 113.

15   Paid state income tax for February payroll, check no. 114.

16   Received payment from Ronald Company for invoice no. 52, less discount.

16   Ronald Company paid invoice no. 51, $7,000.

16   Sold merchandise to Bing Company on account, $3,200, invoice no. 54, terms 2/10, n/30.

21   Purchased delivery truck on account from Moe's Garage, $17,200.

22   Sold merchandise to Ronald Company, on Account, $4,000, Invoice no. 55, terms 2/10, n/30.

23   Paid Jones Company the balance owed, check no. 115.

24   Sold merchandise to Ronald Company on Account, $4,000, Invoice no. 55, terms 2/10, n/30.

25   Purchased merchandise for $1,000 check no. 116.

27   Purchased merchandise from Blew Company on account, $6,000, terms 2/10, n/30.

27   Paid $2 postage from the petty cash fund, voucher no. 23.

28   Ronald Company paid invoice no. 55 dated March 22, less discount.

28   Bing Company paid invoice no. 54 dated March 16.

29   Purchased merchandise from Morris Company on acount, $9,000, terms 2/10, n/30.

30   Sold merchandise to Blew Company on account, $10,000, invoice no. 57, terms 2/10, n/30.

30   Issued check no. 117 to replenish to the same level the petty cash fund.

30   Recorded payroll in payroll register.

30   Journalized payroll entry (to be paid on 31st).

30   Journalized employer's payroll tax expense.

31   Paid payroll checks no. 118, no. 119, and no. 120.

Additional Data

a./b. Ending merchandise inventory, $13,515.

 c. During March, rent expired, $600.

 d. Truck depreciated, $150.

 e. Rental income earned, $200 (one month's rent from subletting).

COMPUTERIZED ACCOUNTING APPLICATION FOR THE CORNER DRESS SHOP MINI PRACTICE SET (CHAPTER 12)

ACCOUNTING CYCLE FOR A MERCHANDISE COMPANY

Before starting on this assignment, read and complete the tasks discussed in Parts A, B, and F of the Computerized Accounting appendix at the back of this book and complete the Computerized Accounting Application assignments for Chapter 3, Chapter 4, Valdez Realty Mini Practice Set (Chapter 5), Pete's Market Mini Practice Set (Chapter 8), and Chapter 10.

    This practice set will help you review all the key concepts of a merchandise company along with the integration of payroll, including the preparation of Form 941.

    Since you are the bookkeeper for The Corner Dress Shop, we have gathered the following information for you. It will be your task to complete the accounting cycle for March.

The Corner Dress Shop: Trial Balance As at 3/1/04

		Debits	Credits
1110	Cash	$ 2,502.90	$ —
1115	Petty Cash	35.00	—
1120	Accounts Receivable	2,200.00	—
1130	Inventory	5,600.00	—
1140	Prepaid Rent	1,800.00	—
1250	Delivery Truck	6,000.00	—
1251	Accum. Dep — Delivery Truck	—	1,500.00
2110	Accounts Payable	—	1,900.00
2310	Federal Income Tax Payable	—	1,284.00
2320	State Income Tax Payable	—	756.00
2330	FICA — Soc. Sec. Payable	—	1,339.20
2335	FICA — Medicare Payable	—	313.20
2340	FUTA Payable	—	163.20
2350	SUTA Payable	—	979.20
2400	Unearned Rent	—	800.00
3110	Betty Loeb, Capital	$ —	$ 9,103.10
		$ 18,137.90	$18,137.90

The Corner Dress Shop: Customer Aged Detail As at 3/1/04

				Total	Current	31 to 60	61 to 90
Bing Co.							
12	1/1/04	Invoice		2,200.00	—	2,200.00	—

The Corner Dress Shop: Vendor Aged Detail As at 3/1/04

				Total	Current	31 to 60	61 to 90
Blew Co.							
422	2/16/04	Invoice		1,900.00	1,900.00	—	—

The Corner Dress Shop, owned by Betty Loeb, is located at 1 Milgate Road, Marblehead, Massachusetts, 01945. Her employer identification number is 33-4158215. Federal Income Tax (FIT), State Income Tax (SIT), Social Security, Medicare, FUTA, and SUTA are all calculated automatically by the program based on the following assumptions and built-in tax rates:

- FICA: Social Security, 6.2 percent on $84,900; Medicare, 1.45 percent on all earnings.
- SUTA: 4.8 percent on the first $7,000 in earnings.
- FUTA: .8 percent on the first $7,000 in earnings.
- Employees are paid monthly. The payroll is recorded and paid on the last day of each month.
- FIT is calculated automatically by the program based on the marital status and number of exemptions claimed by each employee.
- SIT for Massachusetts is calculated automatically by the program based on the marital status and number of exemptions claimed by each employee. Note that since Peachtree uses a different method for calculating FIT and SIT, your answers may not match the manual practice set causing slight differences in the payroll checks.

1. Click on the Start button. Point to Programs; point to the Peachtree folder and select Peachtree Complete Accounting. Your desktop may have the Peachtree icon allowing for a quicker entrance into the program.

   Open the Company Data Files

2. Follow the "Open a File" instructions in Part A of the Computerized Accounting appendix at the back of this book to open **The Corner Dress Shop**.

3. Click on the **Maintain** menu option. Then select **Company Information**. The program will respond by bringing up a dialogue box allowing the user to edit/add information about the company. In the **Company Name** entry field at the end of **The Corner Dress Shop**, add a dash and your name "-**Student Name**" to the end of the company name. Click on the OK button to return to the Menu Window.

   Add Your Name to the Company Name

4. To see what inventory items The Corner Dress Shop has available, let's print a listing. Select **Inventory** from the **Reports** menu. Select **Inventory Valuation Report** from the **Reports** List. Accept all defaults and print the resulting report. You will see that we have 6 items in our inventory. In addition, we can see our current cost on each item. Save this report to compare with a similar report you will print at the end of this practice set.

   Printing an Inventory Valuation Report

5. Peachtree's Inventory module allows the user to easily add new items or make changes to existing items such as recording price changes. Since you will be asked to change prices later in the practice set, let's take a look at how that works now. Do not actually change any of the fields for the item we will be looking at.

   Maintain Inventory Items

   - Select **Inventory Items** from the **Maintain** menu.
   - In the **Item ID** field, select "6000" using the Look Up feature.
   - In the **Description** field, you will see the current description of this inventory item. Should a change be needed, we would simply place the cursor where the change needs to be made and edit as needed.
   - Under the **General** Tab is a field where we can select and then enter a longer description of this item that will appear on sales and/or purchase invoices when we include this item on sales or purchase invoices.
   - The current selling price for this item is kept in the **Sales Price #1** field. Peachtree has the capability of storing multiple prices for an item. This feature can be activated by clicking on the arrow to the right of the **Sales Price #1** field. Go ahead and click on this arrow. A table is presented which allows us to enter up to 5 different selling prices. Different customers can be assigned to different price levels in this manner. Since we have only one price, we can **Cancel** the Multiple Pricing Level box to return to the Maintain Inventory Items window. When you are

prompted to change prices later in the practice set, you will simply change the price in the **Sales Price #1** field rather than add multiple prices.

- Unit/Measure, Item Type, and Location are sorting and information fields that can be used as needed and have no restrictions as to content except length.
- The **Cost Method** field is where we can select the cost assumption to use with this item. Using the pull down menu, you can see our selection consists of FIFO, LIFO, or Average. We will leave the setting at "Average". These cost assumptions will be discussed in greater detail in Chapter 16.
- Peachtree has used default information to select the GL accounts needed for an inventory transaction. If there is some need to change these, we can decline the defaults and select any account we may need. Since there is no need to change these accounts, we will leave them at their default settings.
- We could also establish a minimum stock level and have Peachtree warn us when we fall below this level. We can also establish a reorder point that Peachtree can use to generate an inventory reorder listing.
- We can also select the vendor from whom we would normally order this item. Peachtree uses this and all the information we can see in this window to work interactively with Peachtree's other modules and report features.
- Your screen should look like this:

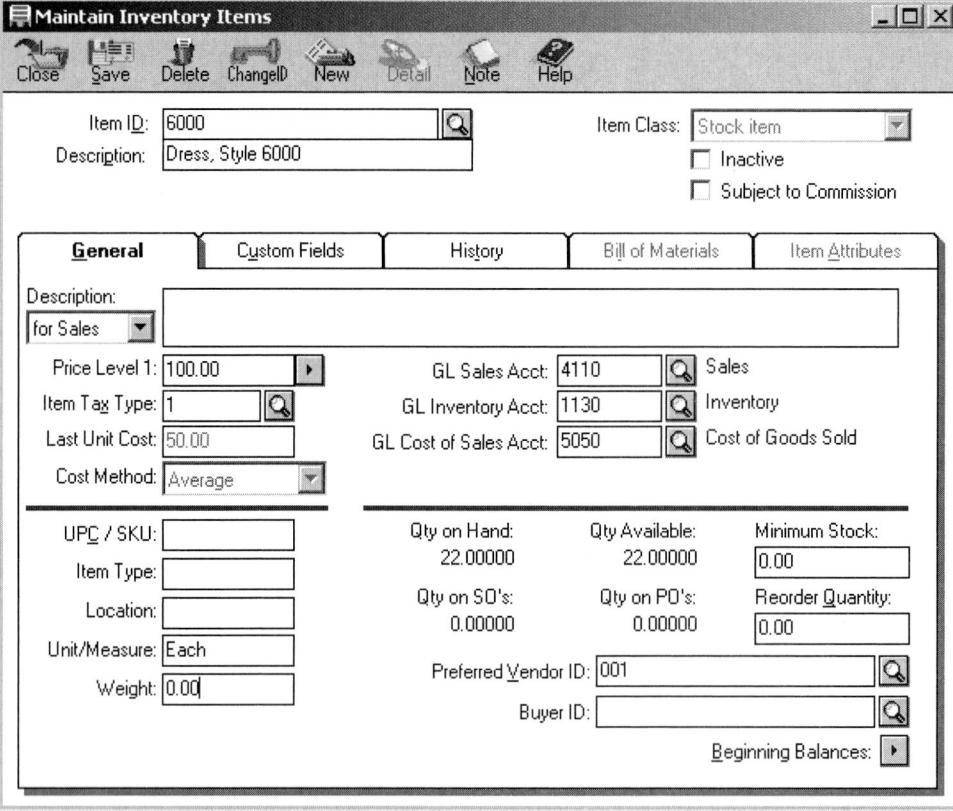

6. Record the following transactions for March using the appropriate General (G), Sales/Invoicing (S), Receipts (R), Purchases (PU), and Payments (PA) windows. Use the same forms when printing invoices, credits and checks as in Chapter 10 changing the starting numbers as needed. Accept defaults for any field for which you are not given data. Use the date of the transaction for the Deposit Ticket ID field.

Record March
Transactions

2004

Mar. 1 Received check #7634 from the Bing Co. in the amount of $2,200 in payment of invoice #12 ($2,200), dated January 1. If prompted, accept Cash as the cash account. Receipt #101. (R)

2 Purchased merchandise from the Morris Co. on account, $10,000, invoice #1210, terms 2/10, n/30 consisting of 184- Style 1000 and 180- Style 2000 dresses. (P)

3 Sold merchandise to the Ronold Co. on account, $7,000, invoice no. 51, terms 2/10, n/30 consisting of 48- Style 1000, 30- Style 2000, 8- Style 3000, 9- Style 4000, 8- Style 5000, and 8- Style 6000 dresses. (S)

6 Sold merchandise to the Ronold Co. on account, $5,000, invoice #52, terms 2/10, n/30 consisting of 48- Style 1000, 24- Style 2000, 5- Style 3000, 3- Style 4000, 3- Style 5000, and 3- Style 6000 dresses. (S)

9 Purchased merchandise from the Morris Co. on account, $5,000, invoice #1286, terms 2/10, n/30 consisting of 92- Style 1000 and 90- Style 2000 dresses. (P)

9 Sold merchandise to the Ronold Co. on account $3,000, invoice #53, terms 2/10, n/30 consisting of 20- Style 1000, 20- Style 2000, 4- Style 3000, 2- Style 4000, and 4- Style 5000 dresses. (S)

9 Paid cleaning service $300, check #110 to Ronda's Cleaning Service. In the Payments window selecting Cash as the cash account:

- Enter Ronda's name in the Pay To field
- Enter a description of the payment in the Description column
- Select the correct GL account for this line (Cleaning Expense)
- Enter the amount in the Amount column.
- Print the check as you did in Chapter 10. (PA)

10 Ronold Co. returned merchandise that cost $1,000 from invoice #52 consisting of 4- Style 1000, 5- Style 2000, 2- Style 3000, 1- Style 4000, 2- Style 5000, and 1- Style 6000 dresses. The Corner Dress Shop issued credit memorandum #CM 10 to the Ronald Co. for $1,000. Remember to use negative quantities for returns. (S)

11 Purchased merchandise from the Jones Co. on account $10,000, invoice #4639, terms 1/15, n/60 consisting of 144- Style 3000 and 124- Style 4000 dresses. (P)

12 Issued check #111 to the Morris Co. in the amount of $9,800 in payment of invoice #1210 ($10,000), dated March 2, less 2 percent discount ($200). (PA)

13 Sold $7,000 of merchandise for cash consisting of 24- Style 1000, 30- Style 2000, 24- Style 3000, and 29- Style 4000 dresses. Be sure to use CASH for the customer name and for the Reference fields. Use Receipt #102. (R)

14 Returned merchandise to the Jones Co. in the amount of $2,000 consisting of 32- Style 3000 and 22- Style 4000 dresses. Remember to use negative quantities for returns. Assign DM4 as the invoice number. (P)

15 Paid FIT, Social Security, and Medicare taxes due for February payroll, check #112 in the amount of $2,936.40. Make the check payable to the IRS. You may wish to print a General Trial Balance first to determine how much to pay for each account. Use the procedure established with your payment on the 9th adding as many lines as you need to pay all the liability accounts needed. (PA)

15 Due to increased operating costs, The Corner Dress Shop must raise its selling prices as follows:

Style 1000	$ 60.00
Style 2000	$ 70.00
Style 3000	$ 80.00
Style 4000	$ 90.00
Style 5000	$110.00
Style 6000	$120.00

Make these changes using the procedures discussed at the start of this practice set before continuing.

15   Sold merchandise for $29,000 cash consisting of 124- Style 1000, 144- Style 2000, 72- Style 3000, 61- Style 4000, 1- Style 5000, and 1- Style 6000 dresses. Use CASH for the Name and Reference fields. If you do not end up with $29,000 as your total, check to make sure you accomplished the price changes correctly. Receipt #103. (R)

15   B. Loeb withdrew $100 for her own personal expenses, check #113. (PA)

15   Paid SIT tax for February payroll, check #114. Make the check payable to the State of Massachusetts. (PA)

16   Received check #5432 from the Ronold Co. in the amount of $3,920 in payment of invoice no. 52 ($5,000), dated March 6, less credit memo CM 10 ($1,000), less 2 percent discount ($100 − 20 = $80, net sales discount). Receipt #104. (R)

16   Received check #5447 from the Ronold Co. in the amount of $7,000 in payment of invoice no. 51, dated March 3. Receipt #105. (R)

16   Sold merchandise to the Bing Co. on account, $3,200, invoice #54, terms 2/10, n/30 consisting of 12- Style 1000, 10- Style 2000, 11- Style 3000, and 10- Style 4000 dresses. Be sure to use the correct invoice number when printing. (S)

21   Purchased delivery truck on account from Moe's Garage, invoice #7113, $17,200.

- Select Moe's Garage in the Vendor ID field
- Enter the invoice number and date
- Ship via Customer Pickup
- Enter a description of the payment in the Description column
- Verify the correct GL account for this line (Delivery Truck)
- Enter the amount in the Amount column. (PU)

22   Sold merchandise to the Ronold Co. on account $4,000, invoice #55, terms 2/10, n/30 consisting of 24- Style 1000, 24- Style 2000, 3- Style 3000, 2- Style 4000, 2- Style 5000, and 2- Style 6000 dresses. (S)

23   Issued check #115 to the Jones Co. in the amount of $7,920 in payment of invoice #4639 ($10,000), dated March 11, less debit memo #DM4 ($2,000), less 1 percent discount ($100 − 20 = $80 net purchases discount). (PA)

24   Sold merchandise to the Bing Co. on account, $2,000, invoice #56, terms 2/10 n/30 consisting of 1- Style 2000, 10- Style 3000, 10- Style 4000, 1- Style 5000, and 1- Style 6000 dresses. (S).

25   Purchased merchandise for $1,000 cash from the Jones Company, check #116, consisting of 16- Style 3000 and 11- Style 4000 dresses. Use the Quantity and Item fields in the Payments window just as you would in the Purchases window. (PA)

27   Purchased merchandise from the Blew Co. on account, $6,000, invoice #437, terms 2/10, n/30 consisting of 60- Style 5000 and 66- Style 6000 dresses. (P)

28   Received check no. 5562 from the Ronold Co. in the amount of $3,920 in payment of invoice 55 ($4,000), dated March 22, less 2 percent discount ($80). Receipt #106. (R)

28   Received check #8127 from the Bing Co. in the amount of $3,200 in payment of invoice #54, dated March 16. (R)

29   Purchased merchandise from the Morris Co. on account, $9,000, invoice #1347, terms 2/10, n/30 consisting of 150- Style 1000 and 150- Style 2000

dresses. The vendor has changed his prices on these items so instead of accepting Peachtree's default for the unit prices, enter $28.00 and $32.00 for the Style 1000 and Style 2000, respectively. (P)

30   Sold merchandise to the Blew Co. on account, $10,000, invoice #57, terms 2/10, n/30 consisting of 6- Style 3000, 5- Style 4000, 41- Style 5000, and 38- Style 6000 dresses. (S).

30   The Auxiliary Petty Cash Record for March listed the following: Postage Expense, $5; Delivery Expense, $10; Cleaning Expense, $6; Miscellaneous Expense, $10. Issued check #117 to replenish the petty cash fund. The check should be made out to CASH. (PA)

31   Issued payroll checks for March wages as follows:

Employee	March Wages	Check no.
Case, Mel	$3,325	118
Holl, Jane	$4,120	119
Moore, Jackie	$4,760	120

Use **Select for Payroll Entry** under the **Tasks** menu. Use 31 March as the Pay End date as well as for the check date.

7. Print the following reports:

   a. General Ledger Trial Balance
   b. Aged Receivables
   c. Aged Payables
   d. Payroll Register
   e. 941 (FedForm 941 2002). Print this report on plain paper unless you have the blank forms available.

Print Reports

8. Open the General Journal; then record adjusting journal entries based on the following adjustment data:

   a. During March, rent expired, $600.
   b. Truck depreciated $150.
   c. Rental income earned, $200 (one month's rent from subletting). This is an unearned income adjustment.

Record March Adjusting Entries

9. After you have posted the adjusting journal entries, close the General Journal, then print the following reports:

   a. General Journal
   b. General Ledger Trial Balance
   c. General Ledger Report
   d. Income Statement
   e. Balance Sheet
   f. Inventory Valuation Report

Print Reports

10. Compare the Inventory Valuation Report with the one created at the start of this practice set. Note that the first two items, the ones whose cost price changed when we last purchased them, have neither the original prices of $25.00 and $30.00 nor the new prices of $28.00 and $32.00, respectively. Peachtree has created a weighted-average for these items. You will study the mechanics behind this calculation in Chapter 16.

11. Peachtree contains dozens of reports that you could examine at this time. Feel free to experiment with looking at the various report options available to you in the Reports menu.

Other Reports

12. In order to close the accounting period we must now advance the period.

   Using your mouse, click on **System** from the **Tasks** menu. Select **Change Accounting Periods**.

Advance Dates

- Using the pull down menu, select period 4 - Apr 1, 2004 to Apr 30, 2004 and click on **OK.**
- You will be asked whether you wish to print reports before continuing. Since we have already printed our reports, we can answer "No".
- Note that the status bar at the bottom of the screen now reflects that you are in period 4. You would be ready to start recording the April transactions.

How Companies Record Credit Card Sales in Their Special Journals

RECORDING BANK CREDIT CARDS

Example: Credit Card Sale of $100, MasterCard: It is interesting to note that for bank credit cards (MasterCard, Visa), the sales are recorded in the seller's Cash Receipts Journal, because the slips are converted into cash immediately. Bank credit cards are not treated as accounts receivable. The fee the bank charges, $2\frac{1}{2}$ to 6 percent, is usually deducted, and the bank credits the depositor's account immediately for the net. The end result for the seller is as follows:

Accounts Affected	Category	↑ ↓	Rules
Cash	Asset	↑	Dr. $94.
Credit Card Expense	Expense	↑	Dr. 6
Sales	Revenue	↑	Cr. 100

				CASH RECEIPTS JOURNAL			Sundry	
Date	Cash Dr.	Credit Card Expense Dr.	Accounts Receivable Cr.	Sales Credited	Sales Tax Payable Cr.		Account Name	Amount Cr.
	94 00	6 00		100 00				

It is the responsibility of the credit card company to sustain any losses (bad debts) from customers' nonpayment. If the bank waits to take the discount until the end of the month, the seller makes a nonpayment entry in the cash payment journal to record the credit card expense; the end result would be credit card expense up and cash balance down. Usually, the bank sends the charge on the monthly statement. *Remember: Bank credit cards are not treated as accounts receivable.*

RECORDING PRIVATE COMPANY CREDIT CARDS

Private companies such as American Express are considered by sellers as accounts receivable. The seller periodically summarizes the sales slips and submits them to the private credit card company for payment (which the company will pay quickly). Let's look at two situations to show how a company would handle its accounting procedures for these credit sales transactions.

Situation 1: On May 4, Morris Company sold merchandise on account of $53 to Bill Blank. Bill used American Express. Assume Morris Company has a low dollar volume and few transactions.

Note in Figure A-1 how the sale of $53 is recorded in the sales journal. Keep in mind that Morris is treating American Express, not Bill Blank, as the accounts receivable. In Figure A-2 we see on June 8 payment is received from American Express and results in the following:

1. Cash increasing by $50.35.
2. Credit card expense rising by $2.65.
3. Accounts receivable being reduced by the $53 originally owed by American Express.

Situation 2: On March 31, Blue Company summarized its credit card sales for American Express. Payment was received on April 13 from American Express. Assume Blue Company has a high dollar volume and many transactions.

Note in Figure A-3 how each credit company has its own column set up. In the ledger there is an account set up for each as well; the posting to the ledger would be done at the end of the month. With high volume and the need to record many transactions, the use of these additional columns (versus Figure A-1) will result in increased efficiency. Figure A-4 shows the receipt of money from American Express less the credit card expense charge.

Figure A-1
Morris Co. Sales Journal

			MORRIS COMPANY SALES JOURNAL				
Date	Invoice	Description of Accounts Receivable	PR	Accounts Receivable Dr.	Sales Tax* Payable Cr.	Sales Cr.	
May 4	692	American Express		53 00	3 00	50 00	
		(Bill Blank)					

* Assume a 6% sales tax.

			MORRIS COMPANY CASH RECEIPTS JOURNAL					
Date	Cash Dr.	Sales Discount Dr.	Credit Card Expense Dr.	Accounts Receivable Cr.	Sales Tax Payable Cr.	Sundry — Account Name	PR	Amount Cr.
June 8	50 35		2 65*	53 00		American Express		
						(Bill Blank)		

* Assume credit card expense of 5%. Note that the $2.56 is 5% × $53.

Figure A-2 Morris Co. Cash Receipts Journal

BLUE COMPANY SALES JOURNAL

Date	Invoice Number	Description of Accounts Receivable	PR	Accounts Receivable Dr.	Credit Cards — American Express Dr.	Credit Cards — Diners Club Dr.	Sales Tax Payable Cr.	Credit Card Sales Cr.	Sales Cr.
Mar. 31		Summary of American Express			11970 00		570 00	11400 00	
					(112)			(401)	

Figure A-3 Blue Co. Sales Journal

BLUE COMPANY CASH RECEIPTS JOURNAL

Date	Cash Dr.	Sales Discount Dr.	Credit Card Expense Dr.	Accounts Receivable Cr.	Credit Card Accounts Rec. — American Express Cr.	Credit Card Accounts Rec. — Diners Club Cr.	Sales Cr.	Sales Tax Payable Cr.	Sundry — Account Name	Sundry — PR	Sundry — Amount Cr.
Apr. 13	11251 80		718 20		11970 00				Summary of American Express payments		

Figure A-4 Blue Co. Cash Receipts Journal

Computerized Accounting

Part A   AN INTRODUCTION

Accounting procedures are essentially the same whether they are performed manually or on a computer. The following is a list of the account cycle steps in a manual accounting system as compared to the steps in a computerized accounting system.

STEPS OF THE ACCOUNTING CYCLE

Manual Accounting System

1. Business transactions occur and generate source documents.
2. Analyze and record business transactions in a manual journal.
3. Post or transfer information from journal to ledger.
4. Prepare a trial balance.
5. Prepare a worksheet.
6. Prepare financial statements.
7. Journalize and post adjusting entries.
8. Journalize and post closing entries.
9. Prepare a post-closing trial balance.

Computerized Accounting System

1. Business transactions occur and generate source documents.
2. Analyze and record business transactions in a computerized journal.
3. Computer automatically posts information from journal to ledger.
4. Trial balance is prepared automatically.
5. Enter necessary adjustments directly.
6. Financial statements are prepared automatically.
7. Completed prior to preparation of financial statements.
8. Closing procedures are completed automatically.
9. Trial balance is automatically prepared as needed.

The accounting cycle comparison shows that the accountant's task of initially analyzing business transactions in terms of debits and credits (both routine business transactions and adjusting entries) is required in both manual and computerized accounting systems. However, in a computerized accounting system, the "drudge" work of posting transactions, creating and completing worksheets and financial statements, and performing the closing procedures is all handled automatically by the computerized accounting system.

In addition, computerized accounting systems can perform accounting procedures at greater speeds and with greater accuracy than can be achieved in a manual accounting system. It is important to recognize, however, that the computer is only a tool that can accept and process information supplied by the accountant. Each business transaction and adjusting entry must first be analyzed and recorded in a computerized journal correctly; otherwise, the financial statements generated by the computerized accounting system will contain errors and will not be useful to the business.

Before a business can begin to use a computerized accounting system, and specifically the Peachtree Complete Accounting system, it must have the following items in place:

1. A computer system
2. Computer software
    a. Operating system software
    b. Peachtree Complete Accounting (any version)

COMPUTER SYSTEM

A computer system consists of several electronic components that together have the ability to accept user-supplied data; input, store, and execute programmed instructions; and output results according to user specifications. The physical computer and its related devices are the hardware, while the stored program that supplies the instructions is called the software.

To understand how a computer system works, we must first look at a conceptual computer that demonstrates the major components and functions of a computer system. The conceptual computer shown in Figure B-1 has four major elements—input devices, processing/internal memory unit, secondary storage devices, and output devices. The illustration also shows the flow of data into the computer and of processed information out of the computer.

Input devices are used to feed data and instructions into the computer. Once the data and instructions are entered, the computer must be able to store them internally and then process the data based on the instructions. Storage and processing occur in the processing/internal memory unit.

There are two types of internal computer memory: random-access memory (RAM) and read-only memory (ROM). RAM is the largest portion of the memory but still has limited capacity; consequently, secondary storage devices are needed. In addition, RAM is temporary—anything stored in RAM is erased when power to the computer is interrupted. Therefore, data stored in RAM must be saved to a secondary storage medium through the use of a secondary storage device before the power is turned off. ROM is permanent memory and consists of those instruction sets necessary to start the computer and receive initial messages from input devices. ROM takes up only a small portion of the total internal memory capacity of a computer system.

Figure B-1
Conceptual Computer

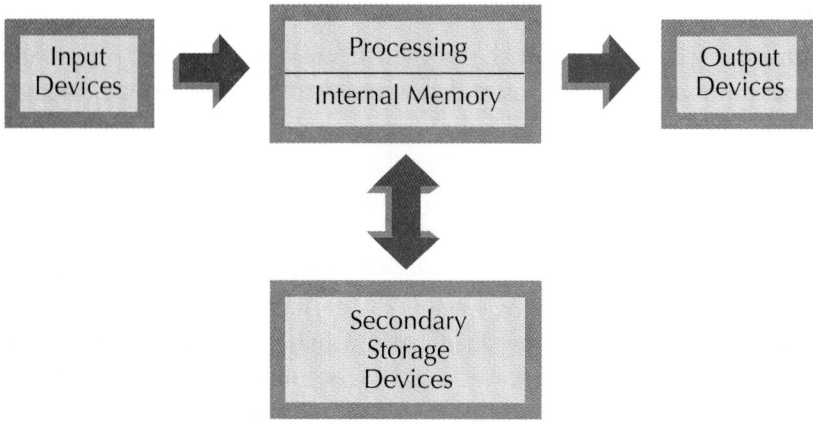

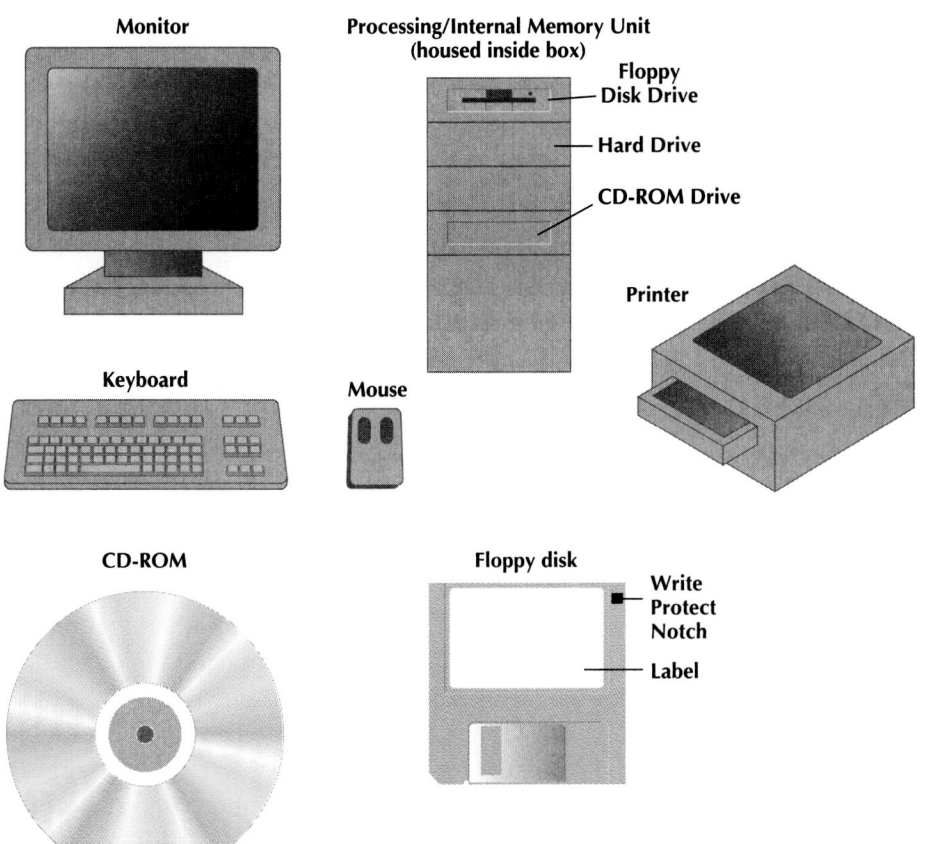

Figure B-2
Typical Configuration of a Microcomputer System

Figure B-3
Storage Media

Finally, the results of processing must be made available to computer users through output devices. These components form a collection of devices referred to as computer hardware because they have physical substance. In a typical microcomputer system (see Figure B-2) a keyboard and mouse are used for input and a printer and monitor are used for output. The processing/internal memory unit is housed inside a box along with secondary storage devices consisting of a hard drive unit, one or more floppy disk drives, and a CD-ROM drive.

Computer hardware can do nothing without a computer program. Computer programs are supplied on floppy disks or CD-ROMs, which are secondary storage media used in floppy disk or CD-ROM drives. Figure B-3 shows an example of a floppy disk and a CD-ROM.

To operate a particular computer program you must first load the program into the system's internal memory (RAM) through the use of a floppy disk or CD-ROM drive or by accessing the program that has been installed and stored on the system's hard drive. Once RAM accesses a program, the computer can execute the program instructions and process data as directed by the user through the keyboard or mouse. At the end of a processing session, the results may be viewed on the monitor, printed on the printer, and/or stored permanently on a floppy disk or hard drive.

COMPUTER SOFTWARE

The computer can do nothing without a computer program. Computer programs control the input, processing, storage, and output operations of a computer. Computer programmers write the instructions that tell the computer to execute certain procedures and process data. There are two broad categories of computer software; operating system software and applications software.

Operating System Software

Operating system software provides the link between the computer hardware, applications software, and the computer user. It consists of programs that start up the computer, retrieve applications programs, and allow the computer operator to store and retrieve data. Operating system software controls access to input and output devices and access to applications programs. There are several popular operating systems for microcomputers. They include Windows 95/98/2000/XP, DOS, DOS combined with Windows 3.XX, OS/2, the Macintosh operating system, and UNIX.

Applications Software

Applications software refers to programs designed for a specific use. The five most common types of business applications software are database management, spreadsheet, work processing, communications, and graphics. Spreadsheet software allows the manipulation of data and has the ability to project answers to "what if" questions. For example, a spreadsheet program could project a company's profit next year if sales increased by 10 percent and expenses increased by 6 percent. Word processing software enables the user to write and print letters, memos, and other documents. Graphic software displays data visually in the form of graphic images, and communications software allows your computer to "talk" to other computers. But to accomplish communications you need additional hardware: a modem to transmit and receive data over telephone lines. Database management software stores, retrieves, sorts, and updates an organized body of information. Most computerized accounting systems are designed as database management software. Accounting information is data that must be organized and stored in a common base of data. This allows the entry of data and the retrieval of information in an organized and systematic way.

Applications software is frequently linked with a particular operating system. Database management, spreadsheet, word processing, graphics, communication, accounting, and other software applications are available in versions that work with most of the popular operating systems. For example, if your computer system is using Windows XP you would purchase the Windows XP version of a word processing program. If you were using a Macintosh computer and operating system you would purchase the Macintosh version of a spreadsheet program.

Accounting Applications Software   Most computerized accounting software is organized into modules. Each module is designed to process a particular type of accounting data such as accounts receivable, accounts payable, or payroll. Each module is also designed to work in conjunction with the other modules. When modules are designed to work together in this manner, they are referred to as integrated software. In an integrated accounting system each module handles a different function but also communicates with the other modules. For example, to record a sale on account, you would make an entry into the accounts receivable module. The integration feature automatically records this entry in the sales journal, updates the customer's account in the accounts receivable subsidiary ledger, and posts all accounts affected in the general ledger. Thus in an integrated accounting system, transaction data are only entered once. All of the other accounting procedures required to bring the accounting records up-to-date are performed automatically through the integration function.

Peachtree Complete Accounting   The most current version of Peachtree Complete Accounting has been selected for use in this text to demonstrate and help you learn how to use a computerized accounting system. It is easy to use, fully integrated, and available in versions that work with several different operating systems. The program can be used to maintain the accounting data for a sole proprietorship, a partnership or a corporation. It will accommodate service, merchandising, and manufacturing businesses. The payroll functions in this version are based on the federal and state tax laws in effect in 2003 and contain educational version tax tables for working in those chapters that require them. They are not intended to be accurate but rather are intended to demonstrate the process used by Peachtree. The workshops contained in this text are designed to illustrate how manual accounting concepts will be handled by a computerized accounting system. They are not intended to provide a comprehensive course of study for a computerized accounting system.

WORKING WITH PEACHTREE COMPLETE ACCOUNTING

Before you begin to work with Peachtree Complete Accounting you need to be familiar with your computer hardware and the Windows operating system. When you are running Windows, your work takes place on the desktop. Think of this area as resembling the surface of a desk. There are physical objects on your real desk and there are windows and icons on the Windows desktop. There are minor differences between the various versions of Windows. The figures will reflect a typical Windows 2000 Desktop. Other Windows versions will have small differences but will be essentially the same.

A mouse is an essential input device for all Windows applications. A mouse is a pointing device that assumes different shapes on your monitor as you move the mouse on your desk. According to the nature of the current action, the mouse pointer may appear as a small arrowhead, an hourglass, or a hand. There are five basic mouse techniques:

◉	Click	To quickly press and release the left mouse button.
◉	Double-click	To click the left mouse button twice in rapid succession.
◉	Drag	To hold down the left mouse button while you move the mouse.
◉	Point	To position the mouse pointer over an object without clicking a button.
◉	Right-click	To quickly press and release the right mouse button.

The Windows 2000 Desktop

Figure B-4 shows a typical opening Windows 2000 screen. Your desktop may be different, just as your real desk is arranged differently from those of your colleagues.

- **Desktop icons:** Graphic representations of drives, files, and other resources. The desktop icons that display will vary depending on your computer setup.
- **Start button:** Clicking on the Start button displays the start menu and lets you start applications.
- **Taskbar:** Contains the Start button and other buttons representing open applications.

Applications Window

As you work with Peachtree Complete Accounting two kinds of windows will appear on your desktop. The Main Menu window is where all activities in Peachtree will begin. An application window contains a running application. The name of the application and the application's menu bar will appear at the top of the application

Figure B-4
Windows 2000 Desktop
(Partial)

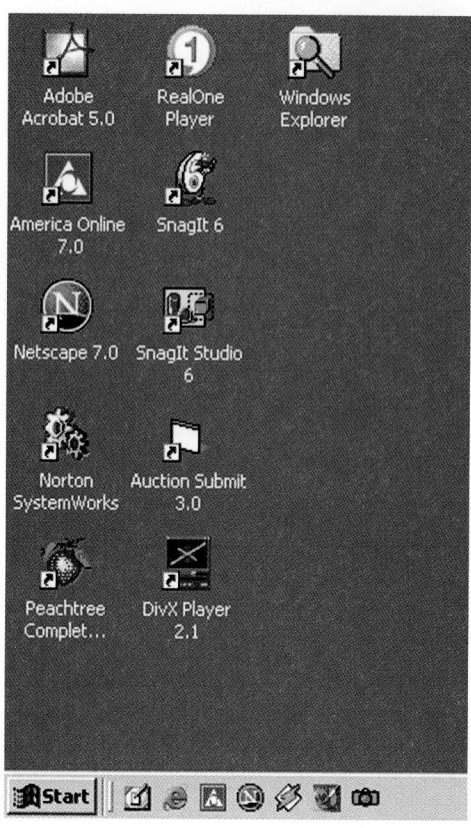

Figure B-5
Peachtree Main Menu
Application Window

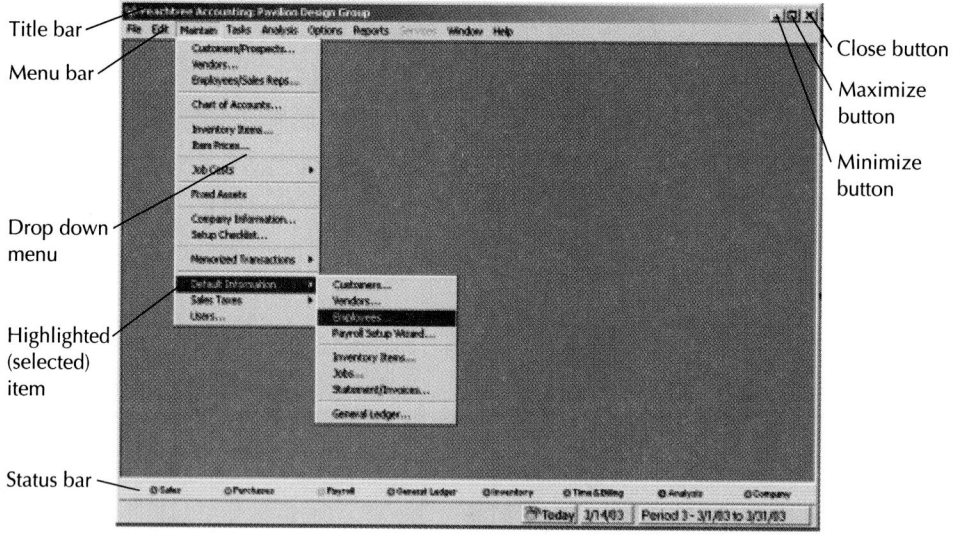

window. Regardless of the windows that are open on your desktop, most windows have certain elements in common. See Figure B-5 above.

- **Minimize button:** Clicking on this button minimizes a window and displays it as a task button on the taskbar.

- **Maximize button:** Clicking on this button enlarges the window so that it fills the entire desktop. After you enlarge a window, the Maximize button is replaced by a Restore button (a double box, not shown) that returns the window to the size it was before it was maximized.

- **Close button:** Clicking on this button will close the window.
- **Title bar:** Displays the name of the application.
- **Menu bar:** This window element lists the available menus for the window.
- **Drop down menu:** Shows the options available under each menu option.
- **Highlighted (selected) item:** The active selection in a Drop down menu.
- **Status bar:** A line of text at the bottom of many windows that gives more information about a field. If you are unsure of what to enter in a field, select it with your mouse and read the status bar.

Dialog Boxes

A dialog box appears when additional information is needed to execute a command. There are different ways to supply that information; consequently, there are different types of dialog boxes. Most dialog boxes (see Fig. B-6) are for specific functions and tasks and require you to supply the data for that task. After you supply the needed information, you can choose a command button to carry out a command such as to Post or Print.

- **Folder tabs:** Some dialog boxes have multiple pages of entry fields available to them. These tabs allow you to switch between available screens.
- **Arrow button:** A button with an arrow will generally bring up a pull down menu of options for that field.
- **Text box:** When you move to an empty text box, an insertion point appears in the far left-hand side of the box. The text you type starts at the insertion point. If the box you move to already contains text, this text is selected

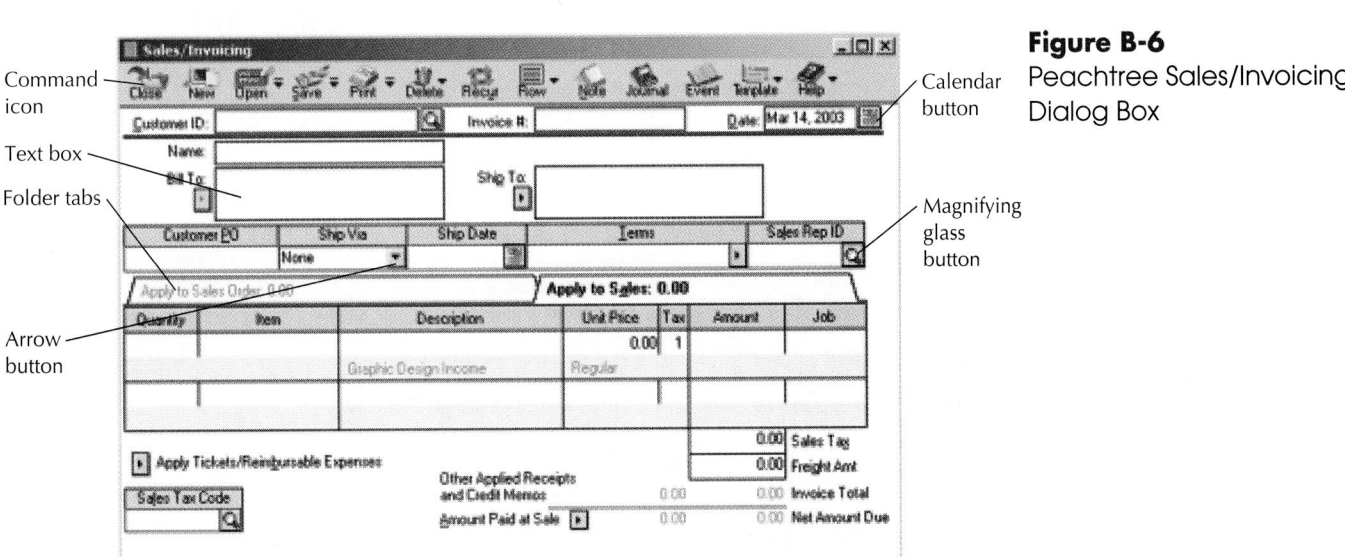

Figure B-6

Peachtree Sales/Invoicing Dialog Box

(highlighted), and any text you type replaces it. You can also delete the selected text by pressing the DELETE or BACKSPACE key.

● **Command icons:** Choose (click) on a command icon to initiate an immediate action such as carrying out or canceling a command. The Close, Print and Post buttons are common command buttons.

● **Magnifying glass button:** Click on this button to pull down a list of choices. Some fields will not show the magnifying glass until the field has been selected.

● **Calendar button:** Click on this button to bring up a calendar in order to select the date to be inserted in the field next to the button.

Other dialog boxes (see Fig. B-7) may require that choices be made, request additional information, provide warnings, or give messages indicating why a requested task cannot be accomplished.

● **Highlighted (selected) item:** To highlight and/or select an item in a displayed list, click on the item. Some may require a double-click to select. In Figure B-7, highlighting an item in the Report Area will bring up a list associated with that item in the Report List box. Highlighting an item in the Report List box will bring up a description in the Report Description box.

● **Scroll bar:** A bar that may appear at the bottom and/or right side of a window or dialog box if there is more text than can be displayed at one time within the window.

● **Scroll arrow:** A small arrow at the end of a scroll bar that you click on to move to the next item in the list. The top and left arrow scroll to the previous item; the bottom and right arrows scroll to the next item.

● **Scroll box:** A small box in a scroll bar. You can use the mouse to drag the scroll box left or right, or up or down. The scroll box indicates the relative position in the list.

Figure B-7
Peachtree Select a Report
Dialog Box

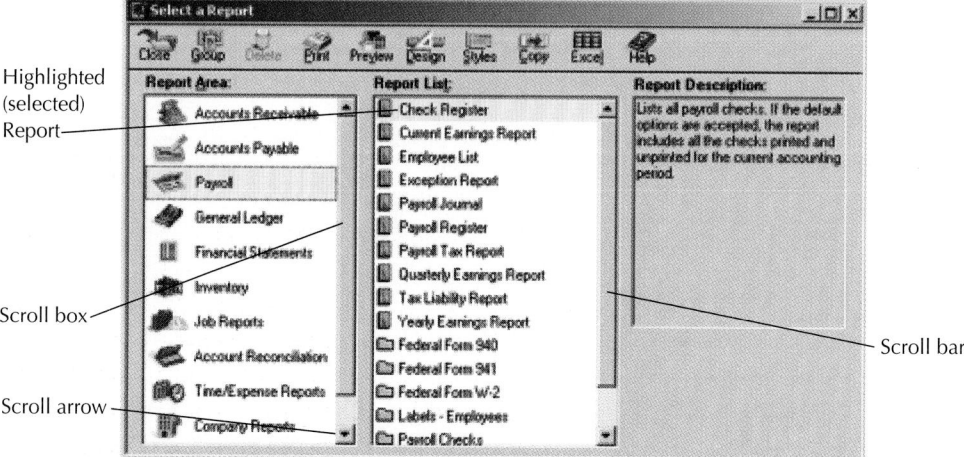

Open Company...	Ctrl+O
New Company...	Ctrl+N
Print...	Ctrl+P
Print Preview	Ctrl+W
Page Setup...	
Back Up...	Ctrl+B
Restore...	Ctrl+R
Online Backup...	
Select Import/Export...	
Data Verification...	
Payroll Tax Tables	▶
Exit	

Figure B-8
Peachtree **File** Menu

Using Menus

Commands are listed on menus, as shown in Figure B-8. Each item on the **Main Menu bar** has its own menus, which are listed by selecting the menu. When a menu is displayed, choose a command by clicking on it or by typing the **Underlined letter** to execute the command. You can also bypass the menu entirely if you know the **Keyboard equivalent** shown to the right of the command when the menu is displayed.

A **Dimmed command** indicates that a command is not currently executable; some additional action has to be taken for the command to become available. Some commands are followed by **Ellipses** (. . .) to indicate that more information is required to execute the command. The additional information can be entered into a dialog box, which will appear immediately after the command has been selected.

Although Peachtree has 10 menu options available on the **Main Menu bar,** most of your activities will involve the **Maintain, Tasks,** or **Reports** menus. The **Tasks** menu contains all of our routine, day to day activities such as invoicing customers, paying vendors, generating payroll, et al. The **Maintain** menu allows us to add, delete and edit customers, vendors, employees and default options, et al. The **Reports** menu allows us to generate the information contained in Peachtree in a variety of formats including custom designed ones.

Working in the Windows 2000 Environment

You can use a combination of mouse and keyboard techniques to navigate within the Windows 2000 environment. For example, you can click on an item to select it, and then press the ENTER key to choose it, or you can just double-click on the item. Peachtree Complete Accounting is designed for a mouse, but it also provides keyboard equivalents for almost every command. It may seem confusing at first that there are several different ways to do the same thing. You will find this flexibility useful. For example, if your hands are already on the keyboard, it may be faster to use the keyboard equivalent of a mouse command. Alternatively, if your hand is already on the mouse, it may be faster to use the mouse technique to carry out a command. When a procedure in an assignment says to select or choose an item, generally use whichever method you prefer. Alternative procedures are often provided as well. It is not necessary to memorize any particular technique, just be flexible and willing to experiment. As you gain experience with the program, you will develop personal preferences, and the various techniques will become second nature.

Opening a File in Peachtree Complete

As with any other Windows program, files in Peachtree are opened by using the **Open Company** option from the **File** menu. Peachtree will then open up an Open Company dialog box where you can tell Peachtree where to find the files you need. The files that have been supplied with this text for the sample companies should reside in the same directory as the Peachtree program files, generally "Peachw". Each company will have its own folder that can be read by the Open Company dialog box. If you do not see these files when you first open the box, you may need to change the directory or drive to one your instructor will specify.

Before starting any assignment, it is suggested that you create a backup of the files for that sample company in the event you need to restore back to the beginning of the assignment.

Backing Up a File in Peachtree Complete

Peachtree has the capability to quickly and easily back up your data to protect against accidental loss.

1. You must have already opened the files of the company you wish to back up. Let's say we wish to backup Bellwether Garden Supply. We would open that company using the **Open** feature from the **File** menu option.

2. While in the Menu Window, select **Back Up** from the **File** menu option. This will bring up the Back Up Company dialogue box as follows:

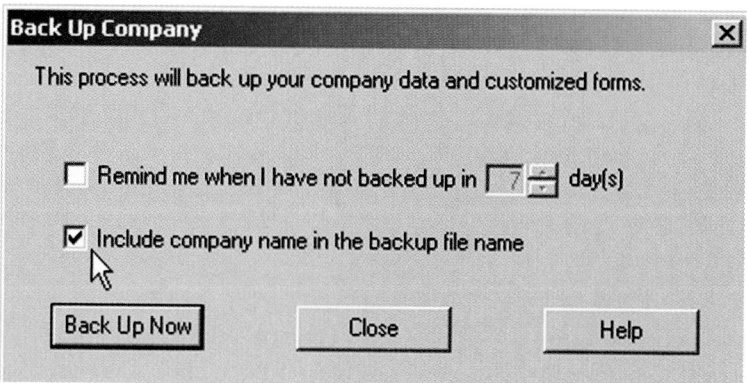

3. Click in the box next to **Include company name in the backup file name.** This will make Peachtree use the company name in the filename it selects for the backup. You could also use this dialogue box to have Peacthree provide a reminder at periodic intervals but we will leave this option alone for now. Press **Back Up Now** to continue.

4. You are now presented with a Save Back Up for Bellwether Garden Supply as: dialog box:

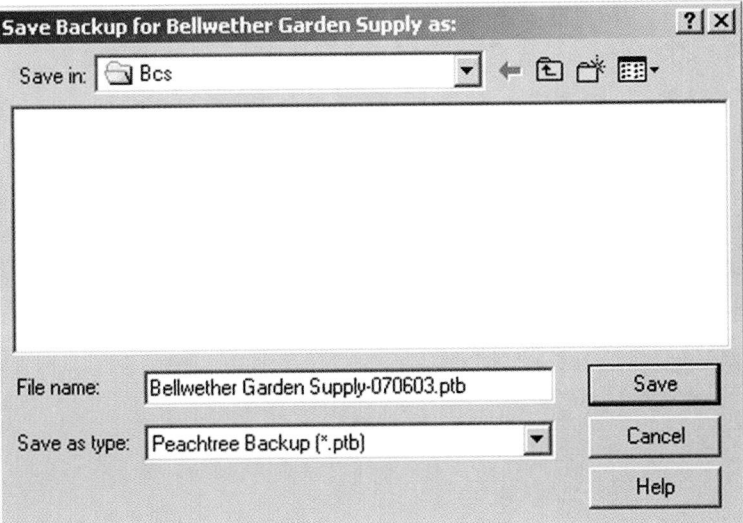

5. Click **Save.**

6. Peachtree will save your data files into one compressed .ptb file to any drive or path you specify including a floppy drive. It defaults to the location where the program files are stored and specifically to the folder where the company files are kept. It will also default to the company name followed by the date. You can change the name if desired. Use the **Save in** pull down menu to save the files to a location specified by your instructor. This could be a network drive, a student floppy disk, or even the local hard drive. Click **Save** and then **Ok** to complete the process. You now have a back up of your data. You should consider saving each and every day to protect yourself against possible loss. Peachtree will use the date as part of the backup's name so you could have a separate backup for each day. You do not have to accept the name Peachtree assigns and you can use a name with more meaning to you.

See Parts C and D of this appendix for information on using these backups.

Part B   INSTALLING PEACHTREE COMPLETE ACCOUNTING/STUDENT DATA FILES

This section of the appendix discusses several basic operations that you need to complete to install the Peachtree Complete Accounting program and the student data files disk for use in completing the computer Workshop assignments in this text.

SYSTEM REQUIREMENTS

The recommended minimum software and hardware requirements your computer system needs to run both Windows and Peachtree Complete Accounting successfully are:

- Microsoft Windows XP, 2000, 98, 95, or Windows NT 4.0 with Service Pack 5 or 6.
- A personal computer with a Pentium 233 MHz or higher processor is required but 350 MHz or better is recommended.
- A hard disk with 80–110 MB of free disk space.
- One 3.5 inch high-density floppy disk drive (if student floppy backups are desired).

- A CD-ROM drive (optional if installed on a network).
- 48 MB RAM required but 128 MB RAM is recommended.
- A 256 color SVGA or similar high-resolution monitor that is supported by Windows with a resolution of at least 800 × 600.
- Internet Explorer 5.x or higher installed.
- A printer that is supported by Windows.
- A mouse that is supported by Windows.

CD-ROM CONTENTS

The Peachtree Complete Accounting installation and program files (in condensed form) and the Student Data Files for use in completing the Computer Workshops are on the CD-ROM that accompanies this text.

Installation Procedures

To install Peachtree Complete Accounting on your hard disk, follow these instructions:

1. Start Windows.
2. Make sure that no other programs are running on your system.
3. Insert the CD-ROM in your CD-ROM drive.
4. Click on the Start button; then click on Run.
5. Type d:setup and press the ENTER key. For d, substitute the letter of your CD-ROM drive.
6. Select the items you wish to install and install them.
7. Put your CD-ROM away for safekeeping.

Installing Peachtree Complete Accounting on a Network

Peachtree Complete Accounting can be used in a network environment as long as each student uses a separate Student Data Files source to store his or her data files. Students should consult with their instructor and/or network administrator for specific procedures regarding program installation and any special printing procedures required for proper network operation.

Student Data File Integrity

Peachtree will run most efficiently if the student data files are installed on a hard drive. This can occur on the local hard drive or in a student folder on a network drive. Since it is possible that student files may be tampered with between class sessions, it is recommended that students back up and restore their files with a floppy disk each class day. Each student can also have a separate, password protected storage area on the network for the company files. Peachtree's back up and restore functions are quick and easy. The specific procedures will be discussed in Part A and E of this appendix.

Installation Default Settings

In the 2003 version of Peachtree Complete Accounting, you may encounter some differences in your screens to the screen captures contained in this book. This is due in part to the fact that Peachtree will install to one set of settings on a machine that has contained a previous version of Peachtree and to a second set of setting on a machine to which you are installing Peachtree for the first time. In order to ensure that your screens will be the same as those in this book, make or confirm the following selections from the Options menu item:

Open any company within Peachtree Complete Accounting 2003. Select Global from the Options menu.

1. Select the Accounting tab.

2. In the section entitled Hide General Ledger Accounts, remove any checkmarks from the three boxes in that section by left clicking on the checkmark.

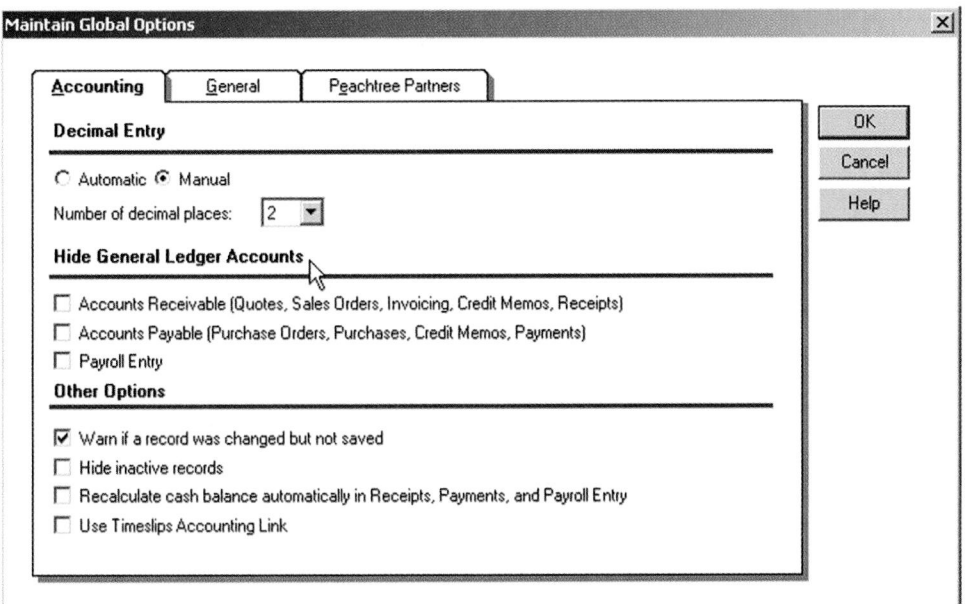

3. Click on the General tab of this same screen.

4. In the Color Scheme section, click on the radio button next to Classic.

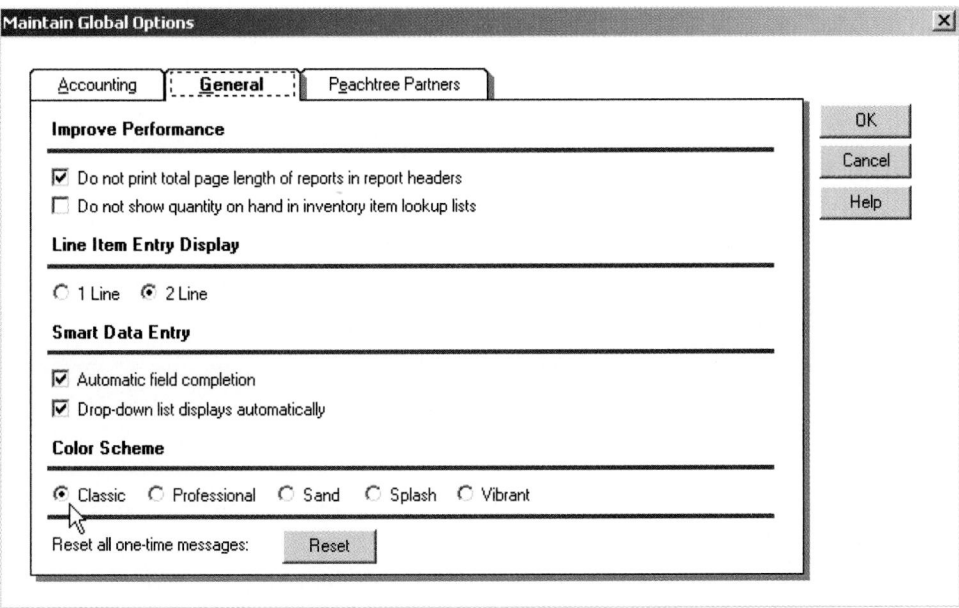

5. Click OK and exit Peachtree to make the changes permanent.

You can see the differences in the following illustrations that show both configurations.

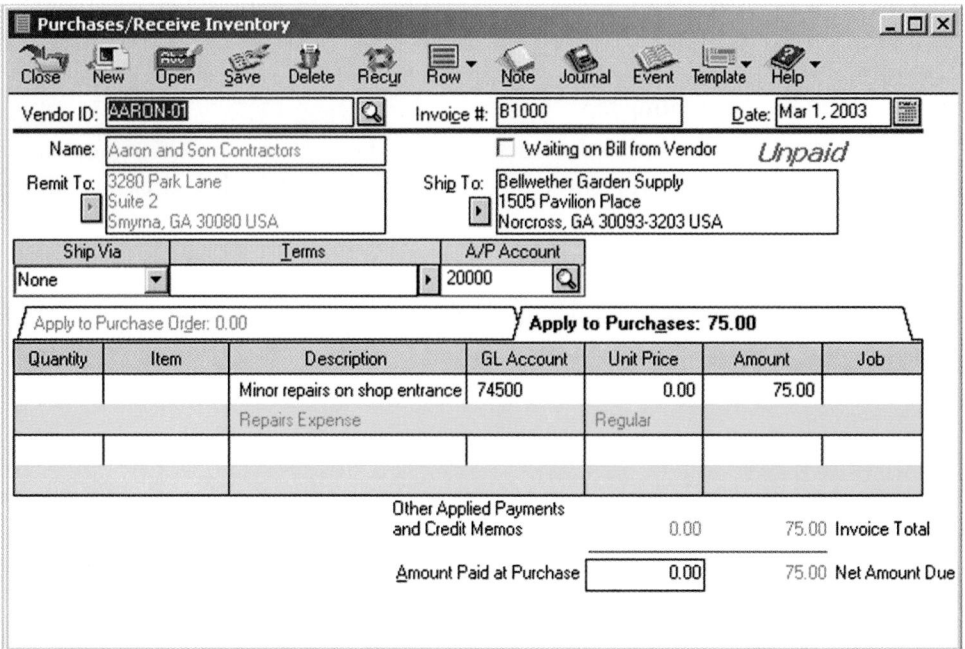

Sand with GL accounts hidden.

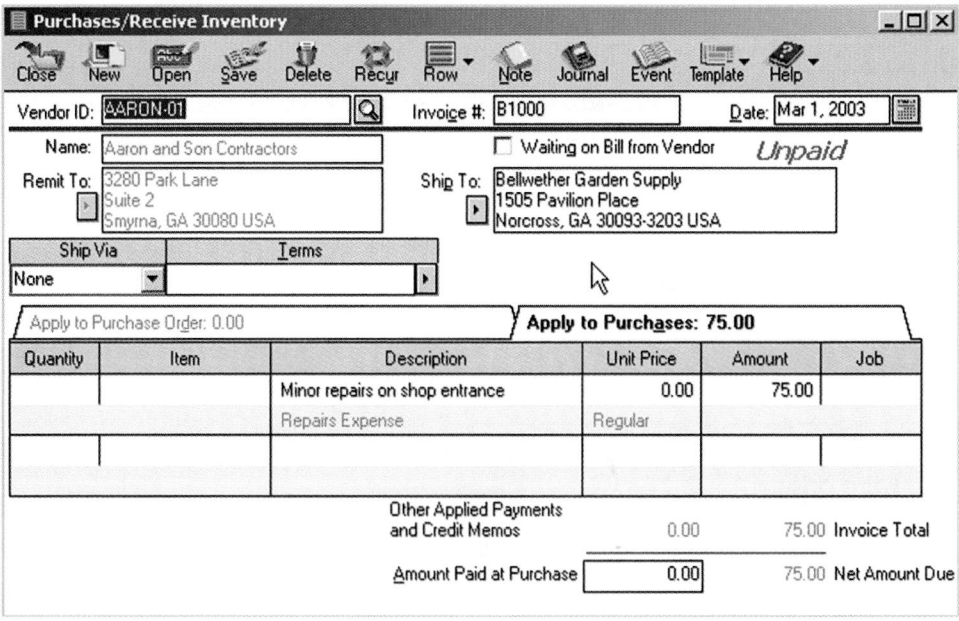

Classic with GL accounts displayed.

Part C   CORRECTING TRANSACTIONS

Once a transaction is posted in Peachtree Complete Accounting, the journal entry will be reflected in the accounting records. You will, however, be allowed to freely edit transactions due to the way the program has been configured for you. Peachtree does have an audit feature that would not allow you to make corrections without creating an audit trail of all such changes. This feature of Peachtree Complete Accounting is designed to ensure that a good audit trail of all transactions is constantly maintained within the program. This feature is turned on and off in the **Company Information** of the **Maintain** menu option. In a real world working situation, this feature would be turned on. Unless your instructor has you turn this feature on, you will be able to correct errors quickly and easily without creating a record of those corrections.

Correcting Unposted Errors.

If you should detect an error while in any of Peachtree's input screens prior to posting or printing, you can quickly and easily correct the error prior to continuing with the transaction.

1. Using your mouse, click in the field that contains the error. This will highlight the selected text box information so that you can change it.

2. Type the correct information; then press the TAB key to enter it. You may then either TAB to other fields needing corrections or again use the mouse to click in the proper field.

3. If you have selected an incorrect account or any other type of look-up information, use the pull down menu to select the correct account or information. This will replace the incorrect account with the correct account.

4. To discard an entry and start over, click on the Delete icon. You will not be given the opportunity to verify this step so be sure you want to delete the transaction before selecting this option. This option may not be available on every input screen.

5. Review the entry for accuracy after any editing corrections.

6. Complete the transaction by posting or printing.

Correcting Posted Errors.

Should you detect an error after you have posted the transaction, it can still be quickly and easily corrected. The only additional step needed to correct a posted transaction is to find it and bring it up on your screen.

Generate an on-screen report which will contain the document needing correction. As an example, a sales invoice can be found in an Aged Receivables Report, an Invoice Register, or a Sales Journal. A General Journal entry can be found in a General Journal or a General Ledger report. While other ways to locate a document exist, this is the easiest to use.

Select the line of the report containing the item needing correction by single clicking the mouse cursor. This will place a blue box around the line and the cursor will turn into a magnifying glass with a Z in the center. Peachtree Complete 2003 comes packaged with a sample company called Bellwether Garden Supply. Looking at a General Journal report under the Reports menu, your screen will look like Figure B-9.

By double clicking on any selected line, you can bring up that particular transaction. If, for example, we double click the selection from Figure B-9, we are presented with the screen on Figure B-10.

We could now edit any field of this entry and **Save** it again. The procedures that were presented for correcting an unposted transaction can now be applied. You can experiment with this feature in the sample company if your program has Bellwether installed.

Part D   HOW TO REPEAT OR RESTART AN ASSIGNMENT

You always have the option to repeat an assignment for additional practice or start over on an assignment. You simply restore the sample company files back to their

Figure B-9
General Journal

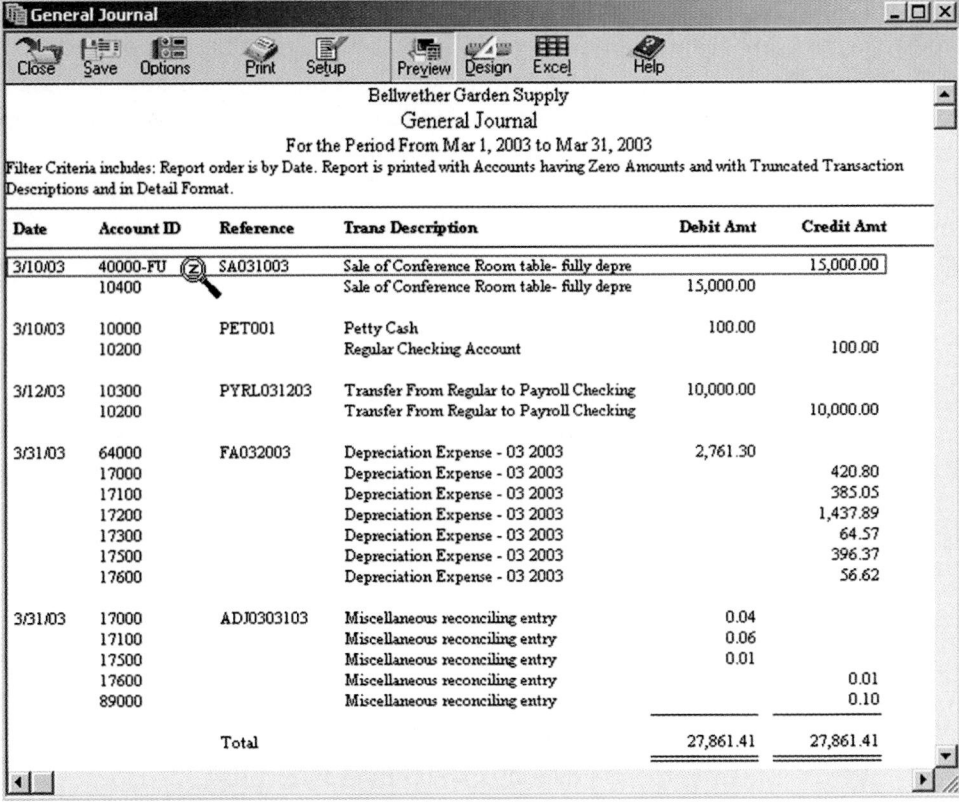

Figure B-10
General Journal Entry

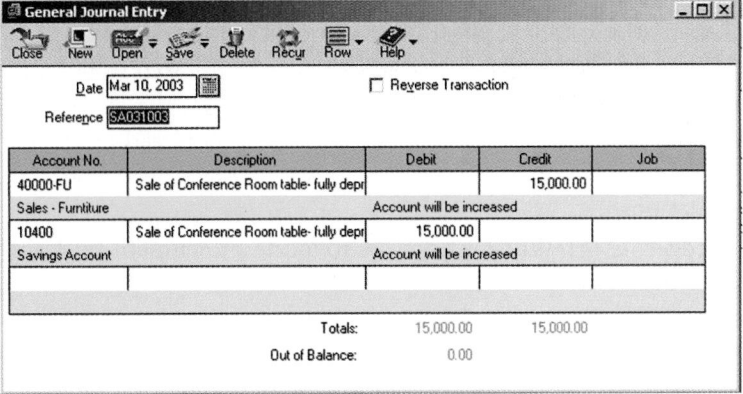

original state using the Backup created at the start of the assignment (see Part A). The procedure for restoring a file is very similar:

1. Open the company whose files you wish to restore. Let's say we wish to restore Bellwether Garden Supply. We would open that company using the **Open** feature from the **File** menu option.

2. While in the Menu Window, select **Restore** from the **File** menu option. This will bring up the Open Backup File dialogue box as shown at the top of page B-17.

3. Peachtree will default to the folder where the regular company files are kept. If you are keeping your backups on a floppy or on a drive/path other than the one Peachtree is defaulting to, you must use the **Look in** option to change the drive and select the correct path from the options given. You may have several backups made at different points in time so be sure to select the correct one. In the example above, there is only one backup so we would select Bellwether Garden Supply-070603.ptb (or the name you used in Part A). This was a backup made on July 6, 2003. After you have selected the correct filename, click on **Open**.

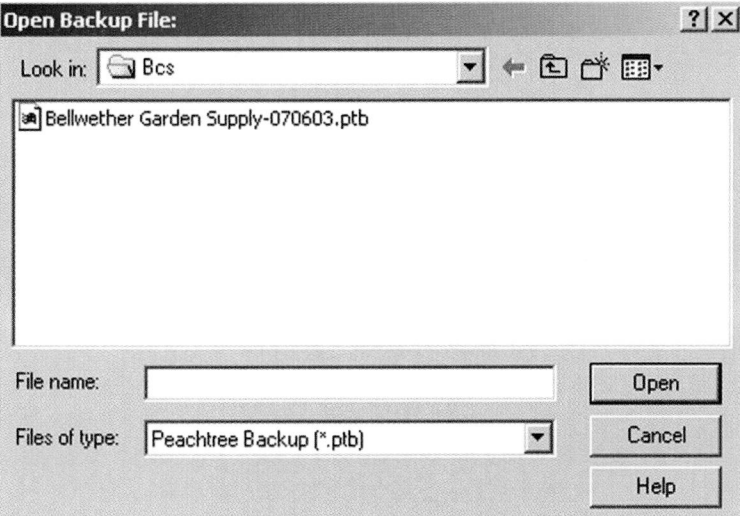

Part E   HOW AND WHEN TO USE THE BACKUP COPY OF A COMPANY'S DATA FILES

At certain times in the assignments you are asked to make a backup copy of a company's data files. There are several reasons why you might wish to access the backup copy of a company's data files. For example, you may not have printed a required report in an assignment before advancing the period to a new month or before adding additional transactions. You may have several errors and simply want to start an assignment over or to a point prior to the errors rather than correct the many mistakes.

If you backup your data using a different filename each day, you will have the option of restoring from any of these files. It would be wise to indicate in your text the point at which you created each backup so you will know what transactions have been completed at each of the backup's dates.

Part F   PRINT AND DISPLAY SETTING IN PEACHTREE COMPLETE

When you install Peachtree Accounting, the program automatically installs the printer established as the default Windows printer as the default printer for Peachtree Accounting. If you have not yet installed a default printer in Windows, you will need to do so prior to attempting to print any reports from the Peachtree Accounting program. Refer to your Windows manual for information on installing a printer.

The installation process for the Windows default printer does not ensure that the default printer and display settings within Peachtree Accounting will work to your satisfaction; consequently, you should test and if necessary adopt a different set of print settings. Changing the settings as detailed below does not result in a permanent change to the report and this process must be repeated each time you use a standard report. Custom reports can be created with permanent fonts.

If you need to change the font sizes or typefaces on your reports, you can do that from within Peachtree. Each report that you select will have an **Options** button as illustrated in Figure B-11.

Figure B-11
Options Button

Figure B-12
Fonts Tab

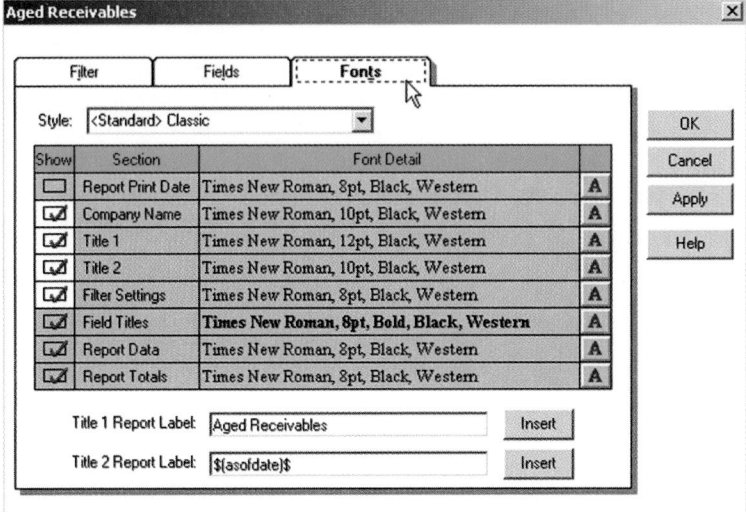

Selecting **Options** will bring up a dialog box with multiple tabs containing various parameters that can be changed for the report. One of these tabs is **Fonts** from which you can change the typeface and font for each item on the report. See Figure B-12.

Inventory and Depreciation

APPENDIX C

The method one uses to assign costs to ending inventory will have a direct effect on the company's cost of goods sold and profit. Look at the accompanying diagram and note that in each column that ending inventory has a different value assigned to it. Note also how this affects gross profit in each of the four columns.

	A		B		C		D	
Net sales		$50,000		$50,000		$50,000		$50,000
Beginning Inventory	$ 4,000		$ 4,000		$ 4,000		$ 4,000	
Net Purchases	20,000		20,000		20,000		20,000	
Cost of Goods Available for Sale	24,000		24,000		24,000		24,000	
Ending Inventory	5,000		6,000		7,000		8,000	
Cost of Goods Sold		19,000		18,000		17,000		16,000
Gross Profit		$31,000		$32,000		$33,000		$34,000

If all inventory brought into a store had the same cost, it would be simple to calculate ending inventory, and we would not have to include this appendix in the book. Unfortunately, things are not that easy; often the very same products are purchased and brought into the store at different costs during the same accounting period. Over the years there have developed four generally accepted methods to assign a cost to ending inventory. They are: (1) specific invoice, (2) weighted-average, (3) first-in, first-out, and (4) last-in, first-out. Each is based on the flow of costs, not the flow of goods (the actual physical movement of goods sold in a store).

SPECIFIC INVOICE METHOD

Jones Hardware sells rakes. At the end of the period 12 rakes remain unsold. Notice in the accompanying table on page C-2 that on January 1, at the start of the accounting period, 10 rakes were on hand, but during the period additional purchases of rakes were made. The price given is the purchase price paid by the store—it is not the same as the selling price, which is what the store charges its customers for the rakes. The selling price is not involved here. At the bottom of the chart you can see that 44 rakes cost Jones Hardware $543.

In the **specific invoice method,** one assigns the cost of ending inventory by identifying each item in that inventory by a specific purchase price and invoice number. Items can be identified by serial number, physical description, or location. Using this method, Jones Hardware knew that six of the rakes not sold were from the March 15 invoice and the other six were from the August 18 purchase. Thus $150 was assigned as the actual cost of ending inventory. If the total cost of goods available for sale is $543 and we subtract the actual cost of ending inventory ($150), this method provides a figure of $393 for cost of goods sold.

Specific Invoice Method

	Goods Available for Sale			Calculating Cost of Ending Inventory		
	Units	Cost	Total	Units	Cost	Total
January 1 Beg. Inventory	10	@ $10	= $100			
March 15 Purchased	9	@ 12	= 108	6	@ $12	$ 72
August 18 Purchased	20	@ 13	= 260	6	@ 13	78
November 15 Purchased	5	@ 15	= 75			
	44		$543	12		$150

Cost of Goods Available for Sale	$543
Less: Cost of Ending Inventory	150
= Cost of Goods Sold	$393

Let's look at pros and cons of this method:

Specific Invoice Method

Pros	Cons
1. Simple to use if company has small amount of high-cost goods — for example, autos, jewels, boats, antiques, etc.	1. Difficult to use for goods with large unit volume and small unit prices — for example, nails at a hardware store, packages of tooth paste at a drug store.
2. Flow of goods and flow of cost are the same.	
3. Costs are matched with the sales they helped to produce.	2. Difficult to use for decision-making purposes — ordinarily an impractical approach.

WEIGHTED-AVERAGE METHOD

The **weighted-average method** calculates an average unit cost by dividing the *total cost* of goods available for sale by the total *units* of goods available for sale. Since we don't know exactly *which* items are left in ending inventory, we will calculate the average of all the goods we have available in order to come up with a fair approximation of the cost of the ending inventory.

Weighted-Average Method

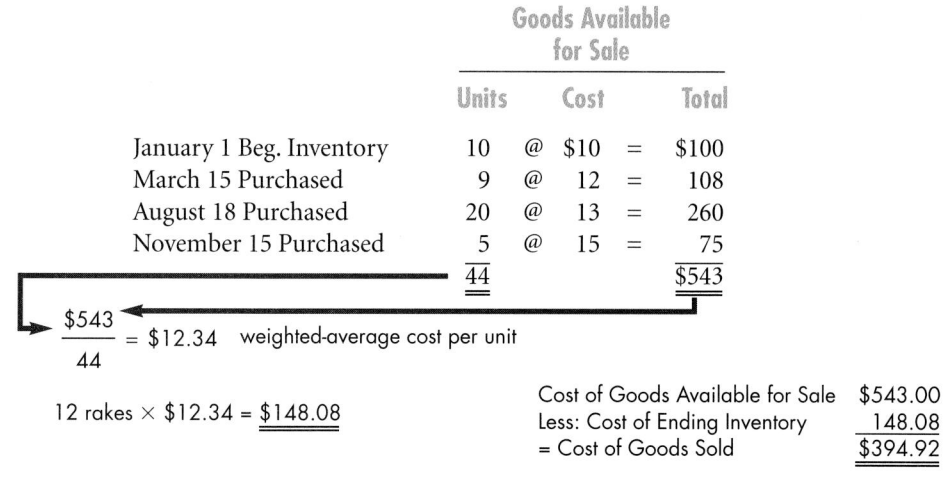

	Units	Cost			Total
January 1 Beg. Inventory	10	@	$10	=	$100
March 15 Purchased	9	@	12	=	108
August 18 Purchased	20	@	13	=	260
November 15 Purchased	5	@	15	=	75
	44				$543

$$\frac{\$543}{44} = \$12.34 \quad \text{weighted-average cost per unit}$$

12 rakes $\times$ $12.34 = $148.08

Cost of Goods Available for Sale	$543.00
Less: Cost of Ending Inventory	148.08
= Cost of Goods Sold	$394.92

The pros and cons of this method:

Weighted-Average Method

Pros	Cons
1. Weighted-average takes into account the number of units purchased at each amount, not a simple average cost. Good for products sold in large volume, such as grains and fuels.	1. Current prices have no more significance than prices of goods bought months earlier.
	2. Compared to other methods, the most recent costs are not matched with current sales.
2. Accountant assigns an equal unit cost to each unit of inventory; thus, when the income statement is prepared, net income will not fluctuate as much as with other methods.	3. Cost of ending inventory is not as up-to-date as it could be using another method.

FIRST-IN, FIRST-OUT METHOD (FIFO)

In the **FIFO method,** one assumes that the oldest goods (rakes, in this case) are sold first. In other words, the first merchandise brought into the store tends to be sold first. Indeed, it is often the sale of these items that prompts the store to buy more of them—as they start to run out, the store purchases more. When costs are assigned in the FIFO method, the cost of the last items brought into the store is assigned to ending inventory and the inventory sold is assigned to cost of goods sold. For example, using our Jones Hardware situation, the ending inventory of 12 rakes on hand are assigned a cost from the last two purchases of rakes (purchases made on November 15 and some purchases made on August 8), $166. Using the FIFO method, it is always assumed that it is the most recently purchased merchandise that has not been sold. Look at how this works out in the accompanying table on page C-4.

First-In, First-Out (FIFO) Method

	Goods Available for Sale			Calculating Cost of Ending Inventory		
	Units	Cost	Total	Units	Cost	Total
January 1 Beg. Inventory	10	@ $10	= $100			
March 15 Purchased	9	@ 12	= 108			
August 18 Purchased	20	@ 13	= 260	7	@ $13	= 91
November 15 Purchased	5	@ 15	= 75	5	@ 15	= 75
	44		$543	12		$166

Cost of Goods Available for Sale $543
Less: Cost of Ending Inventory   166
= Cost of Goods Sold $377

If you are having difficulty with this, think of the inventory as being taken from the bottom layer first, then the next one up, and the next one up, etc.

The pros and cons of this method:

First-In, First-Out (FIFO) Method

Pros	Cons
1. The cost flow tends to follow the physical flow (most businesses try to sell the old goods first — for example, perishables such as fruit or vegetables).	1. During inflation this method will produce higher income on the income statement — thus more taxes to be paid. (We will discuss this later in this appendix.)
2. The figure for ending inventory is made up of current costs on the balance sheet (since inventory left over is assumed to be from goods last brought into the store).	2. Recent costs are not matched with recent sales, since we assume old goods are sold first.

LAST-IN, FIRST-OUT METHOD (LIFO)

Under the **LIFO method,** it is assumed that the rakes *most recently acquired* by Jones are sold first. In other words, the last merchandise brought into the store is the first to be sold. As an example of this method, think of a barrel of nails. It is the most recently purchased nails, which are at the top of the barrel, that are sold first — the nails at the bottom of the barrel are sold last. Note in the accompanying table on page C-4 that the 12 rakes not sold were assigned costs based on the old inventory of January and March that totaled $124, giving Jones a cost of goods sold of $419.

Last-In, First-Out (LIFO) Method

	Goods Available for Sale			Calculating Cost of Ending Inventory		
	Units	Cost	Total	Units	Cost	Total
January 1 Beg. Inventory	10	@ $10	= $100	10	@ $10	= $100
March 15 Purchased	9	@ 12	= 108	2	@ 12	= $ 24
August 18 Purchased	20	@ 13	= 260			
November 15 Purchased	5	@ 15	= 75			
	44		$543	12		$124

Cost of Goods Available for Sale $543
Less: Cost of Ending Inventory   124
= Cost of Goods Sold $419

These are the pros and cons of this method:

Last-In, First-Out (LIFO) Method

Pros	Cons
1. Cost of goods sold is stated at or near current costs, since costs of *latest* goods acquired are used. 2. Matches current costs with current selling prices. 3. During periods of inflation this method produces the lowest net income, which is a tax advantage. (The lower cost of ending inventory means a higher cost of goods sold; with a higher cost of goods sold, gross profit and ultimately net income are smaller, and thus taxes are lower.)	1. Ending inventory is valued at very old prices. 2. Doesn't match physical flow of goods (but can still be used to calculate flow of costs).

Now we will compare the methods that could be used by Jones Hardware to see the cost of ending inventory and the assigned cost of goods sold.

Comparison of Methods for Jones Hardware

	Cost of Ending Inventory	Cost of Goods Sold
Specific Invoice	$150.00	$393.00
Weighted-Average	148.08	394.92
FIFO	166.00	377.00
LIFO	124.00	419.00

All four methods are acceptable accounting procedures, and each has its own virtues:

1. The specific invoice method matches exactly costs with revenue—as we have noted before, this is very important in the accrual basis of accounting.

2. The weighted-average method tends to smooth out the fluctuations between FIFO and LIFO.

3. FIFO provides an up-to-date picture of inventory on the balance sheet, since it uses the latest purchases to calculate ending inventory.

4. When prices are rising, LIFO shows the highest costs of goods sold and thus provides some tax advantages.

Learning Unit C-1 Review

PROBLEM (SOLUTION AT END OF APPENDIX)

Regis Company began the year with 300 units of product B in inventory with a unit cost of $40. The following additional purchases of the product were made:

FIFO, LIFO, weighted-average:

- April 1, 200 units @ $50 each
- July 5, 500 units @ $60 each
- Aug. 15, 400 units @ $70 each
- Nov. 20, 200 units @ $80 each

At end of year Regis Company had 400 units of its product unsold. Your task is to calculate cost of ending inventory as well as cost of goods sold by (a) FIFO, (b) LIFO, (c) weighted-average.

Learning Unit C-2   DEPRECIATION METHODS

In this unit we will look at different methods for computing depreciation. If you want to check any of the concepts of depreciation, you can refer back to Chapter 4.

When a company calculates its periodic depreciation expense, different methods will produce significantly different results. Thus the method of depreciation chosen will affect the net income for current as well as future periods, as well as the **book value** (cost of asset less accumulated depreciation) of the asset on the balance sheet.

Let's assume that Melvin Company purchased a truck on January 1, 19XX, for $20,000, with a **residual value** of $2,000 and an estimated life of 5 years. The following are the four depreciation methods that Melvin Company could use:

Think of residual value as trade-in value at end of estimated life.

1. Straight-line method.
2. Units-of-production method.
3. Sum-of-the-years'-digits method.
4. Declining-balance method.

STRAIGHT-LINE METHOD

The **straight-line method** is simple to use, because it allocates the cost of the asset (less residual value) evenly over its estimated useful life. (At the time an asset is acquired, an estimate is made of its usefulness or **useful life** in terms of number of years it would last, amount of output expected, etc.) Let's look at how Melvin Company calculates its depreciation expense for each of the estimated 5 years of usefulness using the straight-line method. Take a moment to read the key points in the parentheses below the accompanying table.

The formula:

$$\frac{\text{cost} - \text{residual value}}{\text{service useful life in years}} = \frac{\$20,000 - \$2,000}{5} = \$3,600$$

End of Year	Cost of Delivery Truck	Yearly* Depreciation Expense	Accumulated Depreciation, End of Year	Book Value, End of Year (Cost − Accum. Dep.)
1	$20,000	$3,600	$ 3,600	$16,400
2	20,000	3,600	7,200	12,800
3	20,000	3,600	10,800	9,200
4	20,000	3,600	14,400	5,600
5	20,000	3,600	18,000	2,000
	↑	↑	↑	↑
	(Cost of machine doesn't change)	(Note that depreciation expense is the same each year)	(Accumulated depreciation increases by $3,600 each year)	(Book value each year is lowered by $3,600 until residual value of $2,000 is reached)

*The depreciation rate is 100 percent ÷ 5 years = 20 percent. The 20 percent is then multiplied times the cost minus the residual value.

UNITS-OF-PRODUCTION METHOD

With the **units-of-production method** it is assumed that *passage of time* does not determine the amount of depreciation taken. Depreciation expense is based on *use*, be it total estimated miles, tons hauled, or estimated units of production—for example, the number of shoes a machine could produce in its expected useful life. The accompanying table shows the calculations that Melvin Company makes for its truck using the units-of-production method (note that the truck is assumed to have an estimated life of 90,000 miles).

> Depreciation expense is directly related to use, not to passage of time.

The formula:

$$\frac{\text{cost} - \text{residual value}}{\text{estimated units of production}} = \frac{\$20,000 - \$2,000}{90,000 \text{ miles}} = \$.20 \text{ per mile}$$

$$(\$.20) \times (\text{no. of miles driven}) = \text{Depreciation expense for period}$$

End of Year	Cost of Delivery Truck	Miles Driven in Year	Yearly Depreciation Expense	Accumulated Depreciation, End of Year	Book Value, End of Year (Cost − Accum. Dep.)
1	$20,000	30,000	$6,000	$ 6,000	$14,000
2	20,000	21,000	4,200	10,200	9,800
3	20,000	15,000	3,000	13,200	6,800
4	20,000	5,000	1,000	14,200	5,800
5	20,000	19,000	3,800	18,000	2,000
		↑	↑		
		(After 5 years, truck has been driven 90,000 miles)	(Depreciation expense is directly related to number of miles driven)		

SUM-OF-THE-YEARS'-DIGITS METHOD

The **sum-of-the-years'-digits method** places more depreciation expense in the early years rather than the later years in order to better match revenue and expenses, since an asset's productivity may be reduced in later years. For this reason it is called an

accelerated depreciation method. To use it, you multiply cost minus residual times a certain fraction. This fraction is made up of the following:

1. *The denominator:* The denominator is based on how many years the asset is likely to last (say 5). You then add the sum of the digits of 5 years $(1 + 2 + 3 + 4 + 5)$, which equals 15; 15 is the denominator. [There is also a formula to use for the denominator: $N(N + 1)/2$, where N stands for number of years of useful life (in our case, 5 years). In our case the formula would look like this: $5(5 + 1)/2 = 15$.]

2. *The numerator:* The years in reverse order are the numerator (in our case, 5, 4, 3, 2, 1).

Thus, in year 1 the fraction would be 5/15; in year 2, 4/15; in year 3, 3/15; in year 4, 2/15; in year 5, 1/15. And in each year you would multiply this fraction times cost minus residual to find the depreciation expense. This is shown in the accompanying table.

End of Year	$\begin{pmatrix} \text{Cost} \\ \text{Minus} \\ \text{residual} \end{pmatrix}$	$\times$	$\begin{pmatrix} \text{Fraction} \\ \text{for Year} \end{pmatrix}$	=	Yearly Depreciation Expense	Accumulated Depreciation, End of Year	Book Value, End of Year (Cost — Accum. Dep.)
1	$18,000	$\times$	$\dfrac{5}{15}$	=	$6,000	$ 6,000	$14,000 ($20,000 − $6,000)
	(20,000 − 2,000)						
2	18,000	$\times$	$\dfrac{4}{15}$	=	4,800	10,800	9,200
3	18,000	$\times$	$\dfrac{3}{15}$	=	3,600	14,400	5,600
4	18,000	$\times$	$\dfrac{2}{15}$	=	2,400	16,800	3,200
5	18,000	$\times$	$\dfrac{1}{15}$	=	1,200	18,000	2,000
		↑			↑	↑	↑
		(Fraction for year is multiplied times cost minus residual)			(Depreciation expense in first year is highest)	(Each year depreciation accumulates by a smaller amount)	(Book value goes down each year until residual is reached)

Take a moment to make sure you see how the figures for these calculations are arrived at before moving on to the next method.

DOUBLE DECLINING-BALANCE METHOD

The **double declining-balance method** is also an accelerated method, in which a larger depreciation expense is taken in earlier years and smaller amounts in later years. This method uses twice the straight-line rate, which is why it is called the *double declining-balance method*.

A key point in this method is that *residual value* is *not* deducted from cost in the calculations, although the asset cannot be depreciated below its residual value. To calculate depreciation, take the following steps:

1. Calculate the straight-line rate and double it:

$$\frac{100\%}{\text{useful life}} \times 2$$

2. At the *end of each year* multiply rate times book value of asset at beginning of year.

Let's look at how Melvin Company calculates the depreciation on its truck using this method.

Note rate of .40 is not changed (20% × 2)
↓

End of Year	Cost	Accumulated Depreciation, Beg. of Year	Book Value Beg. of Year (Cost − Acc. Dep.)	Dep. Exp. (B.V. Beg. of Year × Rate)	Accumulated Depreciation, End of Year	Book Value, End of Year (Cost − Acc. Dep.)
1	$20,000		$20,000	$8,000 ($20,000 × .40)	$ 8,000	$12,000 (20,000 − 8,000)
2	20,000	$ 8,000	12,000	4,800 (12,000 × .40)	12,800 (8,000 + 4,800)	7,200
3	20,000	12,800	7,200	2,880 (7,200 × .40)	15,680	4,320
4	20,000	15,680	4,320	1,728 (4,320 × .40)	17,408	2,592
5	20,000	17,408	2,592	592	18,000	2,000

↑ (Original cost remains the same)

↑ Depreciation is limited to $592, since the asset cannot depreciate below the residual value)

↑ (The book value now equals the residual value)

Be sure to note the $592 in year 5 of depreciation expense. We could not take more than the $592, or we would have depreciated the asset below the residual value.

DEPRECIATION FOR TAX PURPOSES BEFORE THE TAX REFORM ACT OF 1986

Over the years, the methods we have discussed have been used for *financial* reporting; they have not been used for *tax* purposes. For tangible assets bought prior to 1981, tax law allowed companies to use the declining-balance or sum-of-the-years'-digits methods for tax reporting. Beginning in 1981, the Accelerated Cost Recovery System (MACRS) began to be used. The MACRS is a simpler system, meant to stimulate economic growth by faster cost recovery.

MACRS eliminates the concept of useful life and salvage value and establishes classes of depreciable property, dividing it into 3-, 5-, 10-, 18-, or 19-year property. The deductions for depreciation MACRS allows are shown in Table C-1 on page C-10. Using this table, you can see that if Melvin Company used ACRS for its $20,000 truck (a light truck in the 3-year class) bought on January 1, the following depreciation would be recorded:

Note that Table C-1 is before the Tax Reform Act of 1986.

$$
\begin{array}{lll}
19X1 & .25 \times \$20,000 = & \$ 5,000 \\
19X2 & .38 \times \ \ 20,000 = & \ \ 7,600 \\
19X3 & .37 \times \ \ 20,000 = & \ \ 7,400 \\
\hline
& & \$20,000 \\
\end{array}
$$

The important points to remember are:

1. ACRS is generally not acceptable in preparing financial reports, because it allocates depreciation over a much shorter period than estimated useful life.

2. ACRS for tax reporting defers payment of income tax, since large amounts of depreciation are charged to earlier years.

TABLE C-1 Accelerated Cost Recovery System: Annual Depreciation as a Percentage of Original Cost

	For Property in the		
	Three-Year Class[1]	Five-Year Class[2]	Ten-Year Class[3]
1st year	25	15	8
2nd year	38	22	14
3rd year	37	21	12
4th year		21	10
5th year		21	10
6th year			10
7th year			9
8th year			9
9th year			9
10th year			9

[1]Three-year class includes autos, some tools, and light trucks.

[2]Five-year class includes most machinery and equipment.

[3]Ten-year class includes amusement parks, pipelines, and nuclear plants.

MACRS AFTER THE TAX REFORM ACT OF 1986 (GENERAL DEPRECIATION SYSTEM)

This tax act generally overhauls the depreciation setup of property placed in service after December 31, 1986. Look for a moment at Figure C-1. This is a chart that summarizes the Tax Reform Act update. As you can see, some new classes are introduced (7- and 20-year property); cars and light trucks are moved from the 3-year class to the 5-year class; and office equipment moves from the 5-year class to the 7-year class.

According to this act, classes 3, 5, 7, and 10 use 200 percent declining-balance, switching to straight-line, while classes 15 and 20 use 150 percent declining-balance, switching to straight-line. Both residential and nonresidential real property must use straight-line. Note that the recovery period is extended to $27\frac{1}{2}$ years for residential property and to $31\frac{1}{2}$ years for nonresidential property.

Let's use Table C-2 (which was developed for this tax law) to calculate depreciation on the purchase of a nonluxury car for $5,000 on March 19, 1987.

Using Table C-2 to figure our example, we get the following:

Year	Depreciation
1	$.20 \times \$5,000 = \$1,000$
2	$.32 \times \$5,000 = 1,600$
3	$.1920 \times \$5,000 = 960$
4	$.1152 \times \$5,000 = 576$
5	$.1152 \times \$5,000 = 576$
6	$.0576 \times \$5,000 = 288$

The following classes use a 200 percent declining-balance, switching to straight-line:

- 3-year: Race horses more than two years old or any horse other than a race horse that is more than 12 years old at time placed into service; special tools of certain industries.

- 5-year: Automobiles (not luxury); taxis; light general-purpose trucks, semiconductor manufacturing equipment; computer-based telephone central office switching equipment; qualified technological equipment; property used in connection with research and experimentation.

- 7-year: Railroad track; single-purpose agricultural (pigpens) or horticultural structure; fixtures, equipment, and furniture.

- 10-year: The 1986 law doesn't add any specific property under this class.

The following classes use a 150 percent declining-balance, switching to straight-line:

- 15-year: Municipal wastewater treatment plants; telephone distribution plants and comparable equipment used for two-way exchange of voice and data communications.

- 20-year: Municipal sewers.

The following classes use straight-line:

- 27.5-year: Only residential rental property.
- 31.5-year: Only nonresidential real property.

Figure C-1 Summary of Classes for the Tax Reform Act Update

TABLE C-2 Annual Recovery (Percent of Original Depreciable Basis)

Recovery Year	3-Year Class (200% D.B.)	5-Year Class (200% D.B.)	7-Year Class (200% D.B.)	10-Year Class (200% D.B.)	15-Year Class (150% D.B.)	20-Year Class (150% D.B.)
1	33.00	20.00	14.28	10.00	5.00	3.75
2	45.00	32.00	24.49	18.00	9.50	7.22
3	15.00*	19.20	17.49	14.40	8.55	6.68
4	7.00	11.52*	12.49	11.52	7.69	6.18
5		11.52	8.93*	9.22	6.93	5.71
6		5.76	8.93	7.37	6.23	5.28
7			8.93	6.55*	5.90*	4.89
8			4.46	6.55	5.90	4.52
9				6.55	5.90	4.46*
10				6.55	5.90	4.46
11				3.29	5.90	4.46
12					5.90	4.46
13					5.90	4.46
14					5.90	4.46
15					5.90	4.46
16					5.90	4.46
17					3.00	4.46

*Identifies when switch is made to straight-line.

When we use this table, we do not have to decide which year we should switch from declining-balance to straight-line.

Learning Unit C-2 Review

PROBLEMS (SOLUTION AT END OF APPENDIX)

Depreciation schedule.

1. Agor Co., whose accounting period ends on December 31, purchased a machine for $34,000 on January 1 with an estimated residual value of $4,000 and estimated useful life of 10 years. Prepare depreciation schedules for the current as well as following year using (a) straight-line, (b) sum-of-the-years'-digits, and (c) declining-balance at twice the straight-line rate.

ACRS.

2. Jangles bought an amusement park for $200,000 on January 1, 19XX. Calculate his depreciation expense for tax purposes for the first three years using the Accelerated Cost Recovery System. (This is before the Tax Reform Act of 1986 came into effect.)

ACRS and Tax Reform Act of 1986.

3. Bill Moore Company bought a light general-purpose truck for $10,000 on March 8, 1987. Calculate the yearly depreciation using the ACRS method. (Remember that the Tax Reform Act of 1986 applies.)

4. On January 1, 19XX, a machine was installed at Zebrot Factory at a cost of $29,000. Its estimated residual value at the end of its estimated life of 4 years is $9,000. The machine is expected to produce 50,000 units with the following production schedule:

- 19X1: 8,000 units
- 19X2: 17,000 units
- 19X3: 15,000 units
- 19X4: 10,000 units

Complete depreciation schedules for (a) straight-line, (b) units of production, (c) sum-of-the-years'-digits, (d) declining balance at twice the straight-line rate.

SOLUTION TO PROBLEM ON INVENTORY

(See Learning Unit C-1 Review.)

		Units	Cost Per Unit	
Jan. 1	Beg. Inv.	300	$40	= $12,000
Apr. 1	Purchased	200	50	= 10,000
Jul. 5	Purchased	500	60	= 30,000
Aug. 15	Purchased	400	70	= 28,000
Nov. 20	Purchased	200	80	= 16,000
		1,600		$96,000

a. FIFO

200 × $80	= $16,000	COGAFS	$96,000
200 × $70	= 14,000	− Cost of End. Inv.	30,000
Cost of End. Inv.	$30,000	COGS	$66,000

b. LIFO

300 × $40	= $12,000	COGAFS		$96,000
100 × $50	= 5,000	− Cost of End. Inv.		17,000
Cost of End. Inv.	$17,000	COGS		$79,000

c. WEIGHTED-AVERAGE

$$\frac{\$96,000}{1,600 \text{ units}} = \$\ 60$$

400 × $60 = $24,000	Cost of Ending Inventory
COGAFS	$96,000
− Cost of End. Inv.	24,000
COGS	$72,000

SOLUTION TO DEPRECIATION PROBLEMS

(See Learning Unit C-2 Review.)

1. a. Straight-line

$$\frac{\$34,000 - \$4,000}{10} = \frac{\$30,000}{10} = \$3,000$$

Year	Cost	Dep. Exp.	Acc. Dep. E.O.Y.	Book Value E.O.Y.
1	$34,000	$3,000	$3,000	$31,000
2	34,000	3,000	6,000	28,000

b.

Year	Cost Less Residual	×	Fraction for Year	=	Yearly Deprec. Expense	Acc. Dep. E.O.Y.	Book Value E.O.Y.
1	$30,000		10/55	=	$5,454.55	$ 5,454.55	$28,545.45
2	30,000		9/55	=	4,909.09	10,363.64	23,636.36

c.

Year	Cost	Acc. Dep. B.O.Y.	Book Value B.O.Y.	Dep. Exp.	Acc. Dep. E.O.Y.	Book Value E.O.Y.
1	$34,000	—	$34,000	$6,800 (34,000 × .20)	$ 6,800	$27,200
2	34,000	$6,800	27,200	5,440	12,240	21,760

2. Amusement Parks—Ten-Year Class

Year

1	.08 × $200,000 = $16,000
2	.14 × 200,000 = 28,000
3	.12 × 200,000 = 24,000
Total Depreciation for Three Years	$68,000

3.
$$
\begin{array}{lcl}
.20 & \times\ \$10,000 = & \$\ 2,000 \\
.32 & \times\ \ 10,000 = & 3,200 \\
.1920 & \times\ \ 10,000 = & 1,920 \\
.1152 & \times\ \ 10,000 = & 1,152 \\
.1152 & \times\ \ 10,000 = & 1,152 \\
.0576 & \times\ \ 10,000 = & \underline{\ \ \ 576} \\
& & \overline{\underline{\$10,000}}
\end{array}
$$

4. a. $\dfrac{\$29,000 - \$9,000}{4\ \text{Years}} = \dfrac{\$20,000}{4} = \$5,000$

End of Year	Cost of Equipment	Yearly Depreciation Expense	Acc. Dep. E.O.Y.	Book Value E.O.Y.
19X1	$29,000	$5,000	$ 5,000	$24,000
19X2	29,000	5,000	10,000	19,000
19X3	29,000	5,000	15,000	14,000
19X4	29,000	5,000	20,000	9,000

b. $\dfrac{\$29,000 - \$9,000}{50,000\ \text{units}} = \dfrac{\$20,000}{50,000} = \$.40\ \text{per unit}$

End of Year	Cost of Equipment	Units Produced	Yearly Depreciation Expense	Acc. Dep. E.O.Y.	Book Value E.O.Y.
19X1	$29,000	$ 8,000	$3,200	$ 3,200	$25,800
19X2	29,000	17,000	6,800	10,000	19,000
19X3	29,000	15,000	6,000	16,000	13,000
19X4	29,000	10,000	4,000	20,000	9,000

c.

End of Year	Cost Less Residual	$\times$ Rate	=	Yearly Depreciation Expense	Acc. Dep. E.O.Y.	Book Value E.O.Y.
19X1	$20,000	× 4/10	=	$8,000	$ 8,000	$21,000
19X2	20,000	× 3/10	=	6,000	14,000	15,000
19X3	20,000	× 2/10	=	4,000	18,000	11,000
19X4	20,000	× 1/10	=	2,000	20,000	9,000

d.

End of Year	Cost	Acc. Dep. B.O.Y.	Book Value B.O.Y.	Dep. Exp.	Acc. Dep. E.O.Y.	Book Value E.O.Y.
1	$ 29,000	—	$29,000	$14,500 (29,000 × .50)	$14,500	$14,500
2	29,000	14,500	14,500	5,500	20,000	9,000

In year 2 we could only depreciate up to $5,500 so that Book Value does not go below Residual value of $9,000.

Index

Photo Credits

STUDY GUIDE AND WORKING PAPERS CHAPTERS 1-12

COLLEGE ACCOUNTING

Ninth Edition

Jeffrey Slater

North Shore Community College

PEARSON

Prentice Hall

Upper Saddle River, New Jersey 07458

Editor-in-Chief: PJ Boardman
Assistant Editor: Sam Goffinet
Manager, Print Production: Christy Mahon
Production Editor & Buyer: Carol O'Rourke
Printer/Binder: Courier Kendallville

10 9 8 7 6 5 4
ISBN 0-13-143963-4

Contents

INTRODUCTION TO ACCOUNTING CONCEPTS AND PROCEDURES

SELF-REVIEW QUIZ 1-1

GRACIE RYAN REAL ESTATE

	ASSETS		=	LIABILITIES	+	OWNER'S EQUITY
	Cash	+	Computer Equipment	=	Accounts Payable	+	Gracie Ryan, Capital
TRANSACTION 1						
NEW BALANCE				=		
TRANSACTION 2						
NEW BALANCE				=		
TRANSACTION 3						
ENDING BALANCE		+		=		+
				=		

SELF-REVIEW QUIZ 1-2

_____
_____
_____

ASSETS							LIABILITIES AND OWNER'S EQUITY						

SELF-REVIEW QUIZ 1-3

B. BING CO.

	ASSETS				=	LIABILITIES	+	OWNER'S EQUITY					
	Cash	+	Accounts Receivable	+	Cleaning Equipment	=	Accounts Payable	+	B. Bing, Capital	−	B. Bing Withd.	+	Revenue	−	Expenses
Beg. Balance	$10,000	+	$2,500	+	$6,500	=	$1,000	+	$11,800	−	$800	+	$9,000	−	$2,000
1.														
Balance						=								
2.														
Balance						=								
3.														
Balance						=								
4.														
Balance						=								
5.														
Ending Balance		+		+		=		+		−		+		−	

SG-3

SELF-REVIEW QUIZ 1-4

(1)

_____

_____

_____

(2)

_____

_____

_____

(3)

_____

_____

_____

_____

ASSETS					LIABILITIES AND OWNER'S EQUITY				

FORMS FOR COMPREHENSIVE DEMONSTRATION PROBLEM

(A)

MICHAEL BROWN, ATTORNEY AT LAW

	Cash	+	Accounts Receivable	+	Office Equipment	=	Accounts Payable	+	M. Brown, Capital	–	M. Brown Withd.	+	Legal fees	–	Expenses
	ASSETS					=	**LIABILITIES**	+	**OWNER'S EQUITY**						
1.																
Balance																
2.																
Balance																
3.																
Balance																
4.																
Balance																
5.																
Balance																
6.																
Balance																
7.																
Balance																
8.																
Balance																
9.																
Ending Balance																

COMPREHENSIVE PROBLEM (CONTINUED)

B-1

MICHAEL BROWN, ATTORNEY AT LAW
INCOME STATEMENT
FOR MONTH ENDED JUNE 30, 200X

B-2

MICHAEL BROWN, ATTORNEY AT LAW
STATEMENT OF OWNER'S EQUITY
FOR MONTH ENDED JUNE 30, 200X

B-3

MICHAEL BROWN, ATTORNEY AT LAW
BALANCE SHEET
JUNE 30, 200X

ASSETS   LIABILITIES AND OWNER'S EQUITY

YOU MAKE THE CALL: CRITICAL THINKING/ETHICAL CASE

_____
_____
_____
_____
_____
_____
_____
_____
_____
_____
_____
_____

INTERNET EXERCISES

_____
_____
_____
_____
_____
_____
_____
_____
_____
_____
_____
_____
_____
_____
_____
_____
_____

CHAPTER 1
FORMS FOR MINI EXERCISES

1. A. _____
   B. _____
   C. _____
   D. _____
   E. _____
   F. _____

2. A. _____ _____ _____
   B. _____
   C. _____

3. A. _____
   B. _____

4. _____
   _____
   _____

5. _____
   _____
   _____
   _____
   _____

6. _____
   _____
   _____
   _____

7. A. _____
   B. _____
   C. _____
   D. _____

8. A. _____
   B. _____
   C. _____
   D. _____
   E. _____
   F. _____
   G. _____
   H. _____

9. A. _____
   B. _____
   C. _____
   D. _____

FORMS FOR EXERCISES

1-1.

A. _____
B. _____
C. _____

1-2.

ASSETS	=	LIABILITIES	+	OWNER'S EQUITY
A.				
B.				
C.				

1-3.

AVON'S CLEANERS
BALANCE SHEET
NOVEMBER 30, 200X

ASSETS				LIABILITIES AND OWNER'S EQUITY		

EXERCISES (CONTINUED)

1-4.

	ASSETS			=	LIABILITIES	+			OWNER'S EQUITY			
			B. WONG									
	Cash	+	Accounts Receivable	+	Computer Equipment	=	Accounts Payable	+	B. Wong Capital	− B. Wong Withd.	+ Revenue	− Expenses
A.												
B.												
C.												
D.												
E.												
F.												
G.												
Ending Balance												

EXERCISES (CONTINUED)

1-5.

(A)

FRENCH REALTY
INCOME STATEMENT
FOR MONTH ENDED JUNE 30, 200X

(B)

FRENCH REALTY
STATEMENT OF OWNER'S EQUITY
FOR MONTH ENDED JUNE 30, 200X

(C)

FRENCH REALTY
BALANCE SHEET
JUNE 30, 200X

ASSETS   LIABILITIES AND OWNER'S EQUITY

END OF CHAPTER PROBLEMS

PROBLEM 1A-1 OR PROBLEM 1B-1

LEE'S NAIL CARE CENTER

	ASSETS			=	LIABILITIES	+	OWNER'S EQUITY
	Cash	+	Equipment	=	Accounts Payable	+	Lee Stone, Capital
TRANSACTION A							
NEW BALANCE							
TRANSACTION B							
NEW BALANCE							
TRANSACTION C							
NEW BALANCE							
TRANSACTION D							
ENDING BALANCE							

PROBLEM 1A-2 OR PROBLEM 1B-2

GREEN'S ADVERTISING SERVICE
BALANCE SHEET
SEPTEMBER 30, 200X

ASSETS	LIABILITIES AND OWNER'S EQUITY

PROBLEM 1A-3 OR PROBLEM 1B-3

RICK FOX
TYPING SERVICE

	ASSETS			= LIABILITIES +		OWNER'S EQUITY				
	Cash +	Accounts Receivable +	Office Equipment =		Accounts Payable +	R. Fox, Capital –	R. Fox, Withd. +	Typing Revenue –	Expenses
A.									
BALANCE									
B.									
BALANCE									
C.									
BALANCE									
D.									
BALANCE									
E.									
BALANCE									
F.									
BALANCE									
G.									
BALANCE									
H.									
ENDING BALANCE									

PROBLEM 1A-4 OR PROBLEM 1B-4

(A)

WEST STENCILING SERVICE
INCOME STATEMENT
FOR MONTH ENDED JUNE 30, 200X

(B)

WEST STENCILING SERVICE
STATEMENT OF OWNER'S EQUITY
FOR MONTH ENDED JUNE 30, 200X

PROBLEM 1A-4 OR PROBLEM 1B-4 (CONCLUDED)

WEST STENCILING SERVICE
BALANCE SHEET
JUNE 30, 200X

ASSETS		LIABILITIES AND OWNER'S EQUITY	

PROBLEM 1A-5 OR PROBLEM 1B-5

TOBEY'S CATERING SERVICE

	ASSETS				= LIABILITIES +		OWNER'S EQUITY				
	Cash	+	Accounts Receivable	+	Equipment	=	Accounts Payable	+	J. Tobey, Capital	−	J. Tobey, Withd.	+	Catering Revenue	−	Expenses
10/25											
BALANCE											
10/27											
BALANCE											
10/28											
BALANCE											
10/29											
BALANCE											
11/1											
BALANCE											
11/5											
BALANCE											
11/8											
BALANCE											
11/10											
BALANCE											
11/15											
BALANCE											
11/17											
BALANCE											
11/20											
BALANCE											
11/25											
BALANCE											
11/28											
BALANCE											
11/30											
END. BAL.											

PROBLEM 1A-5 OR PROBLEM 1B-5 (CONTINUED)

(B)

TOBEY'S CATERING SERVICE
BALANCE SHEET
OCTOBER 31, 200X

ASSETS				LIABILITIES AND OWNER'S EQUITY			

(C)

TOBEY'S CATERING SERVICE
INCOME STATEMENT
FOR MONTH ENDED NOVEMBER 30, 200X

PROBLEM 1A-5 OR PROBLEM 1B-5 (CONTINUED)

(D)

TOBEY'S CATERING SERVICE
STATEMENT OF OWNER'S EQUITY
FOR MONTH ENDED NOVEMBER 30, 200X

(E)

TOBEY'S CATERING SERVICE
BALANCE SHEET
NOVEMBER 30, 200X

ASSETS				LIABILITIES AND OWNER'S EQUITY			

CHAPTER 1
SUMMARY PRACTICE TEST:
INTRODUCTION TO ACCOUNTING CONCEPTS AND PROCEDURES

Part 1 Instructions

Fill in the blank(s) to complete the statement.

1. _____ is the recording function of the accounting process.

2. Assets = _____ + Owner's Equity

3. The owner's current investment or equity in the assets of a business is called _____.

4. A list of assets, liabilities, and owner's equity as of a particular date is reported on a _____ _____.

5. _____ create an outward or potential outward flow of assets.

6. Revenue earned on account creates an asset entitled _____ _____.

7. _____ record personal expenses that are not related to the business. They are a subdivision of owner's equity.

8. The _____ _____ reports how well a business performs for a period of time.

9. The _____ _____ _____ _____ is a report that shows changes in capital.

10. The ending figure for capital from the statement of owner's equity is placed on the _____ _____.

Part II Instructions

Answer true or false to the following statements.

1. Business transactions are recorded in monetary terms.
2. Assets less Liabilities equals Owner's Equity.
3. Revenue is an asset.
4. Capital means cash.
5. Bookkeeping is 50 percent of accounting.
6. The balance sheet lists assets, revenue, and owner's equity.
7. The balance sheet shows where we are now for a specific period of time.
8. Revenue creates an outward flow of assets.
9. Expenses are a subdivision of owner's equity.
10. Withdrawals are the only subdivision of owner's equity.
11. Withdrawals are listed on the income statement.
12. Revenue is a subdivision of owner's equity.

13. Revenues and withdrawals are listed on the income statement.
14. The income statement helps update the statement of owner's equity, and the statement of owner's equity helps update the balance sheet.
15. Withdrawals are listed on the statement of owner's equity.

Part III Instructions

In column B, record the appropriate code(s) that result from recording the transaction in column A.

1. Increase in assets
2. Decrease in assets
3. Increase in liabilities
4. Decrease in liabilities

5. Increase in capital
6. Increase in revenues
7. Increase in expenses
8. Increase in withdrawals

COLUMN A	COLUMN B
1. EXAMPLE: Jim Murray invested $1,000 in his business.	1,5
2. Bought equipment on account for $100.	
3. Paid salaries of $50	
4. Bought additional equipment for $500 cash.	
5. Paid rent expense of $50.	
6. Received $5,000 in cash from revenue earned.	
7. Paid heat expense of $15.	
8. Earned revenue of $500 that will not be received until next month.	
9. Paid amount owed on equipment previously purchased on account.	
10. Paid for cleaning supplies expense, $15.	
11. Customers paid $10 of amount previously owed.	
12. Bought additional equipment of $1,000, half paid in cash and half charged.	
13. Charged customer $100 for services performed.	
14. Jim paid home phone bill from the company's cash.	
15. Advertising expense incurred but not to be paid until next month.	

CHAPTER 1 SOLUTIONS TO SUMMARY PRACTICE TEST

Part I

1. bookkeeping
2. liabilities
3. capital
4. balance sheet

5. expenses
6. Accounts Receivable
7. withdrawals
8. income statement

9. statement of owner's equity
10. balance sheet

Part II

1.	true	**6.**	false	**11.**	false
2.	true	**7.**	false	**12.**	true
3.	false	**8.**	false	**13.**	false
4.	false	**9.**	true	**14.**	true
5.	false	**10.**	false	**15.**	true

Part III

1.	1,5	**6.**	1,6	**11.**	1,2
2.	1,3	**7.**	7,2	**12.**	1,2,3
3.	7,2	**8.**	1,6	**13.**	1,6
4.	1,2	**9.**	4,2	**14.**	8,2
5.	7,2	**10.**	7,2	**15.**	7,3

DEBITS AND CREDITS: ANALYZING AND RECORDING BUSINESS TRANSACTIONS

2

SELF-REVIEW QUIZ 2-1

1. _____	4. _____
2. _____	5. _____
3. _____	

SELF-REVIEW QUIZ 2-2

A.

1. Accounts Affected	2. Category	3. ⇅	4. Rules	5. T Account Update

B.

1. Accounts Affected	2. Category	3. ⇅	4. Rules	5. T Account Update

SG-25

C.	1. Accounts Affected	2. Category	3. ⇕	4. Rules	5. T Account Update

D.	1. Accounts Affected	2. Category	3. ⇕	4. Rules	5. T Account Update

E.	1. Accounts Affected	2. Category	3. ⇕	4. Rules	5. T Account Update

SELF-REVIEW QUIZ 2-3

Cash		111
4,500	300	
2,000	100	
1,000	1,200	
300	1,300	
	2,600	

Accounts Payable		211
300	700	

Salon Fees		411
	3,500	
	1,000	

Accounts Receivable		121
1,000	300	

Pam Jay, Capital		311
	4,000	

Rent Expense		511
1,200		

Salon Equipment		131
700		

Pam Jay, Withdrawals		321
100		

Salon Supplies Exp.		521
1,300		

Salaries Expense		531
2,600		

(1)

(2)

(3)

(4)

FORMS FOR COMPREHENSIVE DEMONSTRATION PROBLEM

(1,2,3)

Advertising Expense 511	Gas Expense 512	Salaries Expense 513	Telephone Expense 514

Accounts Payable 211	Mel Free, Capital 311	Mel Free, Withdrawals 312	Delivery Fees Earned 411

Cash 111	Accounts Receivable 112	Office Equipment 121	Delivery Trucks 122

FORMS FOR COMPREHENSIVE DEMONSTRATION PROBLEM (CONTINUED)

(4)

MEL'S DELIVERY SERVICE
TRIAL BALANCE
JULY 31, 200X

	Dr.	Cr.

(5A)

MEL'S DELIVERY SERVICE
INCOME STATEMENT
FOR MONTH ENDED JULY 31, 200X

FORMS FOR COMPREHENSIVE DEMONSTRATION PROBLEM (CONTINUED)

(5B)

MEL'S DELIVERY SERVICE
STATEMENT OF OWNER'S EQUITY
FOR MONTH ENDED JULY 31, 200X

(5C)

MEL'S DELIVERY SERVICE
BALANCE SHEET
JULY 31, 200X

ASSETS					LIABILITIES AND OWNER'S EQUITY				

FORMS FOR EXERCISES

2-1

_____
_____
_____
_____
_____
_____
_____
_____
_____
_____
_____
_____
_____
_____
_____
_____
_____
_____
_____
_____

2-2

1 Accounts Affected	2. Category	3 ↑ ↓	4 Rules	5 T-Account Update	

2-3

Account	Category	↑↓	Financial Statement

EXERCISES (CONTINUED)

2-4.

	Dr.	Cr.
A.	8	1
B.		
C.		
D.		
E.		
F.		
G.		
H.		
I.		

2-5.

(1)

HALL'S CLEANERS
INCOME STATEMENT
FOR MONTH ENDED JULY 31, 200X

(2)

HALL'S CLEANERS
STATEMENT OF OWNER'S EQUITY
FOR MONTH ENDED JULY 31, 200X

EXERCISES (CONTINUED)

(3)

HALL'S CLEANERS
BALANCE SHEET
JULY 31, 200X

ASSETS						LIABILITIES AND OWNER'S EQUITY				

END OF CHAPTER PROBLEMS

PROBLEM 2A-1 OR PROBLEM 2B-1

Accounts Affected	Category	Inc. Dec. ← →	Rules	T-Account Update	
A.					
B.					
C.					
D.					
E.					
F.					

PROBLEM 2A-2 OR PROBLEM 2B-2

Cash	111

M. Slater, Withdrawals	312

Office Equipment	121

Travel Fees Earned	411

Accounts Payable	211

Advertising Expense	511

M. Slater, Capital	311

Rent Expense	512

PROBLEM 2A-3 OR PROBLEM 2B-3

(A)

Cash 111	Accounts Payable 211	Fees Earned 411

Accounts Receivable 112	Mike Frank, Capital 311	Rent Expense 511

Office Equipment 121	Mike Frank, Withdrawals 312	Utilities Expense 512

(B)

MIKE'S WINDOW WASHING SERVICE
TRIAL BALANCE
MAY 31, 200X

	Dr.	Cr.

PROBLEM 2A-4 OR PROBLEM 2B-4

(A)

GRACIE LANTZ, ATTORNEY AT LAW
INCOME STATEMENT
FOR MONTH ENDED MAY 31, 200X

(B)

GRACIE LANTZ, ATTORNEY AT LAW
STATEMENT OF OWNER'S EQUITY
FOR MONTH ENDED MAY 31, 200X

Name _____ Class _____ Date _____

PROBLEM 2A-4 OR 2B-4 (CONCLUDED)

(C)

GRACIE LANTZ, ATTORNEY AT LAW
BALANCE SHEET
MAY 31, 200X

ASSETS

LIABILITIES AND OWNER'S EQUITY

PROBLEM 2A-5 OR PROBLEM 2B-5

(1,2,3)

Advertising Expense 511	Gas Expense 512	Salaries Expense 513	Telephone Expense 514

Accounts Payable 211	A. Angel, Capital 311	A. Angel, Withdrawals 312	Delivery Fees Earned 411

Cash 111	Accounts Receivable 112	Office Equipment 121	Delivery Trucks 122

(4)

ANGEL'S DELIVERY SERVICE
TRIAL BALANCE
MARCH 31, 200X

	Dr.	Cr.

(5A)

ANGEL'S DELIVERY SERVICE
INCOME STATEMENT
FOR MONTH ENDED MARCH 31, 200X

PROBLEM 2A-5 OR 2B-5 (CONCLUDED)

(5B)

ANGEL'S DELIVERY SERVICE
STATEMENT OF OWNER'S EQUITY
FOR MONTH ENDED MARCH 31, 200X

(5C)

ANGEL'S DELIVERY SERVICE
BALANCE SHEET
MARCH 31, 200X

ASSETS					LIABILITIES AND OWNER'S EQUITY				

CHAPTER 2
SUMMARY PRACTICE TEST:
DEBITS AND CREDITS: ANALYZING AND RECORDING
BUSINESS TRANSACTIONS

Part I Instructions

Fill in the blank(s) to complete the statement.

1. _____ accumulate information in a book called the ledger.
2. The left side of any T account is called the _____ _____.
3. Assets are increased by _____.
4. The process of balancing an account involves _____.
5. Transaction analysis charts are an aid in recording _____ _____.
6. The _____ _____ _____ indicates the names and numbering system of accounts.
7. A _____ is a group of accounts.
8. A _____ _____ is an informal report that lists accounts and their balances.
9. Withdrawals are increased by _____.
10. The income statement, statement of owner's equity, and balance sheet may be prepared from a _____ _____.
11. Cash, Accounts Receivable, and Equipment are examples of _____.
12. Increasing expenses ultimately cause owner's equity to _____.
13. An increase in rent expense is a _____ by the rules of debits and credits.
14. A debit to one asset and a credit to another asset for the same transaction reflect a _____ in assets.
15. The category of accounts payable is a/an _____.

Part II Instructions

Abby Lane opened a taxi company. From the following chart of accounts, indicate in column B (by account number) which account (s) will be debited or credited as related to the transaction in column A.

Chart of Accounts

ASSETS	LIABILITIES	EXPENSES
10 Cash	50 Accounts Payable	80 Advertising
20 Accounts Receivable		90 Gas
30 Equipment	OWNER'S EQUITY	100 Salaries
40 Taxi	60 A. Lane, Capital	110 Telephone
	62 A. Lane, Withdrawals	
	REVENUE	
	70 Taxi Fees Earned	

	COLUMN A	COLUMN B	
		DEBIT(S)	CREDIT(S)
1.	EXAMPLE: Abby Lane invested $25,000 in the taxi company.	10	60
2.	Purchased a taxi on account for $40,000.	_____	_____
3.	Bought equipment on account for $6,000.	_____	_____
4.	Advertising bill received, but not paid til next month.	_____	_____
5.	Abby paid home telephone bill from company checkbook, $20.	_____	_____
6.	Collected $100 in cash from daily taxi fees earned.	_____	_____
7.	Customer charged a taxi ride of $10.	_____	_____
8.	Received partial payment for Transaction #7 of $5.	_____	_____
9.	Paid business telephone bill, $32.	_____	_____
10.	Purchased additional equipment for cash, $550.	_____	_____
11.	Paid taxi driver salaries of $150.	_____	_____
12.	Drove customer on account to local train station for $6.	_____	_____
13.	Received $5 from customer who hired taxi for ride across town.	_____	_____
14.	Collected from past charged revenue, $15.	_____	_____
15.	Bought office equipment on account for $110.	_____	_____

Part III Instructions

Answer true or false to the following statements.

1. There are debit and credit columns found on the three financial statements.
2. A trial balance could balance but be wrong.
3. Withdrawals are listed on the credit column of the trial balance.
4. Double entry bookkeeping results in a system where the sum of all the debits is equal to the sum of all the credits.
5. The ledger is numbered like a textbook.

6. Withdrawals are always increased by credits.

7. An expense could create a liability.

8. A shift in assets means the total of assets must change.

9. The rules of debit and credit are constantly changing.

10. The transaction analysis chart is a teaching device.

11. The chart of accounts makes locating and identifying accounts easier.

12. The left side of any account is a credit.

13. A debit means all accounts are decreasing.

14. Financial statements are prepared from a trial balance.

15. The statement of owner's equity is prepared before the income statement.

16. Liabilities increase by credits.

17. Footings aid in balancing accounts.

18. Withdrawals are listed on the income statement.

19. The balance sheet contains the old figure for capital.

20. Think of a credit as always meaning something good.

CHAPTER 2
SOLUTIONS TO SUMMARY PRACTICE TEST

Part I

1. accounts

2. debit side

3. debits

4. footings

5. business transactions

6. chart of accounts

7. ledger (general)

8. trial balance

9. debits

10. trial balance

11. assets

12. decrease

13. debit

14. shift

15. liability

Part II

	Debit	Credit			Debit	Credit			Debit	Credit
1.	10	60	**6.**		10	70	**11.**		100	10
2.	40	50	**7.**		20	70	**12.**		20	70
3.	30	50	**8.**		10	20	**13.**		10	70
4.	80	50	**9.**		110	10	**14.**		10	20
5.	62	10	**10.**		30	10	**15.**		30	50

Part III

1. false

2. true

3. false

4. true

5. false

6. false

7. true

8. false

9. false

10. true

11. true

12. false

13. false

14. true

15. false

16. true

17. true

18. false

19. false

20. false

LOWE'S REPAIR SERVICE
GENERAL JOURNAL

PAGE 1 (cont'd)

Date	Account Titles and Description	PR	Dr.	Cr.

SELF-REVIEW QUIZ 3-2

CLARK'S WORD PROCESSING SERVICES
GENERAL JOURNAL

PAGE 1

Date 200x		Account Titles and Description	PR		Dr.					Cr.			
May	1	Cash	111	10	0	0	0	00					
		Brenda Clark, Capital	311						10	0	0	0	00
		Initial investment of cash by owner											
	1	Word Processing Equipment	121	6	0	0	0	00					
		Cash	111						1	0	0	0	00
		Accounts Payable	211						5	0	0	0	00
		Purchase of equip. from Ben Co.											
	1	Prepaid Rent	115	1	2	0	0	00					
		Cash	111						1	2	0	0	00
		Rent paid in advance (3 months)											
	3	Office Supplies	114		6	0	0	00					
		Accounts Payable	211							6	0	0	00
		Purchase of supplies on acct. from Norris											
	7	Cash	111	3	0	0	0	00					
		Word Processing Fees	411						3	0	0	0	00
		Cash received for services rendered											
	13	Office Salaries Expense	511		6	5	0	00					
		Cash	111							6	5	0	00
		Payment of office salaries											
	18	Advertising Expense	512		2	5	0	00					
		Accounts Payable	211							2	5	0	00
		Bill received but not paid from Al's News											
	20	Brenda Clark, Withdrawals	312		6	2	5	00					
		Cash	111							6	2	5	00
		Personal withdrawal of cash											
	22	Accounts Receivable	112	5	0	0	0	00					
		Word Processing Fees	411						5	0	0	0	00
		Billed Morris Co. for fees earned											

OFFICE SUPPLIES   ACCOUNT NO. <u>114</u>

Date		Explanation	Post Ref.	Debit	Credit	Balance	
						Debit	Credit

PREPAID RENT   ACCOUNT NO. <u>115</u>

Date		Explanation	Post Ref.	Debit	Credit	Balance	
						Debit	Credit

WORD PROCESSING EQUIPMENT   ACCOUNT NO. <u>121</u>

Date		Explanation	Post Ref.	Debit	Credit	Balance	
						Debit	Credit

ACCOUNTS PAYABLE   ACCOUNT NO. <u>211</u>

Date		Explanation	Post Ref.	Debit	Credit	Balance	
						Debit	Credit

BRENDA CLARK, CAPITAL   ACCOUNT NO. <u>311</u>

Date		Explanation	Post Ref.	Debit	Credit	Balance	
						Debit	Credit

BRENDA CLARK, WITHDRAWALS   ACCOUNT NO. <u>312</u>

Date		Explanation	Post Ref.	Debit	Credit	Balance	
						Debit	Credit

WORD PROCESSING FEES   ACCOUNT NO. <u>411</u>

Date		Explanation	Post Ref.	Debit	Credit	Balance	
						Debit	Credit

OFFICE SALARIES EXPENSE   ACCOUNT NO. <u>511</u>

Date		Explanation	Post Ref.	Debit	Credit	Balance	
						Debit	Credit

ADVERTISING EXPENSE   ACCOUNT NO. 512

Date	Explanation	Post Ref.	Debit	Credit	Balance Debit	Credit

TELEPHONE EXPENSE   ACCOUNT NO. 513

Date	Explanation	Post Ref.	Debit	Credit	Balance Debit	Credit

SELF-REVIEW QUIZ 3-3

1. _____

_____

_____

2.   P. 4

Date		Account Titles and Description	PR	Dr.		Cr.	

FORMS FOR COMPREHENSIVE DEMONSTRATION PROBLEM
(A, B)

ABBY'S EMPLOYMENT AGENCY
GENERAL JOURNAL

PAGE 1

Date	Account Titles and Description	PR	Dr.	Cr.

FORMS FOR COMPREHENSIVE DEMONSTRATION PROBLEM (CONTINUED)

GENERAL LEDGER OF ABBY'S PLACEMENT AGENCY

CASH   ACCOUNT NO. 111

Date	Explanation	Post Ref.	Debit	Credit	Balance Debit	Balance Credit

ACCOUNTS RECEIVABLE   ACCOUNT NO. 112

Date	Explanation	Post Ref.	Debit	Credit	Balance Debit	Balance Credit

SUPPLIES   ACCOUNT NO. 131

Date	Explanation	Post Ref.	Debit	Credit	Balance Debit	Balance Credit

EQUIPMENT   ACCOUNT NO. 141

Date	Explanation	Post Ref.	Debit	Credit	Balance Debit	Balance Credit

FORMS FOR COMPREHENSIVE DEMONSTRATION PROBLEM (CONTINUED)

ACCOUNTS PAYABLE · ACCOUNT NO. 211

Date	Explanation	Post Ref.	Debit	Credit	Balance Debit	Balance Credit

A. TODD, CAPITAL · ACCOUNT NO. 311

Date	Explanation	Post Ref.	Debit	Credit	Balance Debit	Balance Credit

A. TODD, WITHDRAWALS · ACCOUNT NO. 321

Date	Explanation	Post Ref.	Debit	Credit	Balance Debit	Balance Credit

EMPLOYMENT FEES EARNED · ACCOUNT NO. 411

Date	Explanation	Post Ref.	Debit	Credit	Balance Debit	Balance Credit

FORMS FOR COMPREHENSIVE DEMONSTRATION PROBLEM (CONTINUED)

WAGE EXPENSE   ACCOUNT NO. 511

Date	Explanation	Post Ref.	Debit	Credit	Balance Debit	Balance Credit

TELEPHONE EXPENSE   ACCOUNT NO. 521

Date	Explanation	Post Ref.	Debit	Credit	Balance Debit	Balance Credit

ADVERTISING EXPENSE   ACCOUNT NO. 531

Date	Explanation	Post Ref.	Debit	Credit	Balance Debit	Balance Credit

FORMS FOR COMPREHENSIVE DEMONSTRATION PROBLEM (CONTINUED)

ABBY'S EMPLOYMENT AGENCY
TRIAL BALANCE
MARCH 31, 200X

	Dr.	Cr.

YOU MAKE THE CALL: CRITICAL THINKING/ETHICAL CASE

_____

_____

_____

_____

_____

_____

_____

_____

_____

_____

_____

_____

_____

_____

_____

_____

_____

_____

INTERNET EXERCISES

_____

_____

_____

_____

_____

_____

_____

_____

_____

_____

_____

_____

_____

_____

_____

_____

3-2.

Date		Account Titles and Description	PR	Dr.	Cr.

EXERCISES (CONTINUED)

3-3.

Date		Account Titles and Description	PR	Dr.				Cr.			
200X											
April	6	Cash		15	0	0	0	—			
		A. King, Capital						15	0	0	0	—
		Cash investment									
	14	Equipment		9	0	0	0	—			
		Cash						4	0	0	0	—
		Accounts Payable						5	0	0	0	—
		Purchase of Equipment									

CASH ACCOUNT NO. 111

Date	Explanation	Post Ref.	Debit	Credit	Balance Debit	Credit

EQUIPMENT ACCOUNT NO. 121

Date	Explanation	Post Ref.	Debit	Credit	Balance Debit	Credit

ACCOUNTS PAYABLE ACCOUNT NO. 211

Date	Explanation	Post Ref.	Debit	Credit	Balance Debit	Credit

A. KING, CAPITAL ACCOUNT NO. 311

Date	Explanation	Post Ref.	Debit	Credit	Balance Debit	Credit

EXERCISES (CONTINUED)

3-4.

(A)

PAGE 1

Date		Account Titles and Description	PR	Dr.			Cr.		

(B)

CASH   **ACCOUNT NO. 111**

Date		Explanation	Post Ref.	Debit			Credit			Balance Debit		Credit	

ACCOUNTS RECEIVABLE   **ACCOUNT NO. 112**

Date		Explanation	Post Ref.	Debit			Credit			Balance Debit		Credit	

EXERCISES (CONTINUED)

EQUIPMENT   ACCOUNT NO. 121

Date		Explanation	Post Ref.	Debit	Credit	Balance	
						Debit	Credit

ACCOUNTS PAYABLE   ACCOUNT NO. 211

Date		Explanation	Post Ref.	Debit	Credit	Balance	
						Debit	Credit

J. LOWE, CAPITAL   ACCOUNT NO. 311

Date		Explanation	Post Ref.	Debit	Credit	Balance	
						Debit	Credit

J. LOWE, WITHDRAWALS   ACCOUNT NO. 312

Date		Explanation	Post Ref.	Debit	Credit	Balance	
						Debit	Credit

FEES EARNED   ACCOUNT NO. 411

Date		Explanation	Post Ref.	Debit	Credit	Balance	
						Debit	Credit

SALARIES EXPENSE   ACCOUNT NO. 511

Date		Explanation	Post Ref.	Debit	Credit	Balance	
						Debit	Credit

EXERCISES (CONTINUED)

(C)

LOWE COMPANY
TRIAL BALANCE
JULY 31, 200X

		Dr.	Cr.

3-5.

SUNG CO.
TRIAL BALANCE
MARCH 31, 200X

		Dr.	Cr.

3-6.

		Dr.	Cr.

END OF CHAPTER PROBLEMS

PROBLEM 3A-1 OR PROBLEM 3B-1

AL'S FITNESS CENTER
GENERAL JOURNAL

PAGE 1

Date	Account Titles and Description	PR	Dr.	Cr.

PROBLEM 3A-1 OR PROBLEM 3B-1 (CONCLUDED)

AL'S FITNESS CENTER
GENERAL JOURNAL

PAGE 2

Date	Account Titles and Description	PR	Dr.	Cr.

PROBLEM 3A-2 OR PROBLEM 3B-2
(A, B)

TAYLOR'S DANCE STUDIO
GENERAL JOURNAL

PAGE 1

Date		Account Titles and Description	PR	Dr.			Cr.		

PROBLEM 3A-2 OR PROBLEM 3B-2 (CONTINUED)

GENERAL LEDGER OF TAYLOR'S DANCE STUDIO

CASH   ACCOUNT NO. 111

Date	Explanation	Post Ref.	Debit	Credit	Balance Debit	Balance Credit

ACCOUNTS RECEIVABLE   ACCOUNT NO. 112

Date	Explanation	Post Ref.	Debit	Credit	Balance Debit	Balance Credit

PREPAID RENT   ACCOUNT NO. 114

Date	Explanation	Post Ref.	Debit	Credit	Balance Debit	Balance Credit

SUPPLIES   ACCOUNT NO. 121

Date	Explanation	Post Ref.	Debit	Credit	Balance Debit	Balance Credit

PROBLEM 3A-2 OR PROBLEM 3B-2 (CONTINUED)

EQUIPMENT   ACCOUNT NO. 131

Date		Explanation	Post Ref.	Debit	Credit	Balance	
						Debit	Credit

ACCOUNTS PAYABLE   ACCOUNT NO. 211

Date		Explanation	Post Ref.	Debit	Credit	Balance	
						Debit	Credit

MOLLY TAYLOR, CAPITAL   ACCOUNT NO. 311

Date		Explanation	Post Ref.	Debit	Credit	Balance	
						Debit	Credit

MOLLY TAYLOR, WITHDRAWALS   ACCOUNT NO. 312

Date		Explanation	Post Ref.	Debit	Credit	Balance	
						Debit	Credit

PROBLEM 3A-2 OR PROBLEM 3B-2 (CONTINUED)

FEES EARNED ACCOUNT NO. 411

Date	Explanation	Post Ref.	Debit	Credit	Balance Debit	Balance Credit

ELECTRICAL EXPENSE ACCOUNT NO. 511

Date	Explanation	Post Ref.	Debit	Credit	Balance Debit	Balance Credit

SALARIES EXPENSE ACCOUNT NO. 521

Date	Explanation	Post Ref.	Debit	Credit	Balance Debit	Balance Credit

TELEPHONE EXPENSE ACCOUNT NO. 531

Date	Explanation	Post Ref.	Debit	Credit	Balance Debit	Balance Credit

PROBLEM 3A-2 OR PROBLEM 3B-2 (CONCLUDED)

(C)

TAYLOR'S DANCE STUDIO
TRIAL BALANCE
JUNE 30, 200X

	Dr.	Cr.

PROBLEM 3A-3 OR PROBLEM 3B-3
(A, B)

A. FRENCH'S PLACEMENT AGENCY
GENERAL JOURNAL

P. 1

Date	Account Titles and Description	PR	Dr.	Cr.

PROBLEM 3A-3 OR PROBLEM 3B-3 (CONTINUED)

GENERAL LEDGER OF A. FRENCH'S PLACEMENT AGENCY

CASH   ACCOUNT NO. 111

Date	Explanation	Post Ref.	Debit	Credit	Balance Debit	Balance Credit

ACCOUNTS RECEIVABLE   ACCOUNT NO. 112

Date	Explanation	Post Ref.	Debit	Credit	Balance Debit	Balance Credit

SUPPLIES   ACCOUNT NO. 131

Date	Explanation	Post Ref.	Debit	Credit	Balance Debit	Balance Credit

EQUIPMENT   ACCOUNT NO. 141

Date	Explanation	Post Ref.	Debit	Credit	Balance Debit	Balance Credit

PROBLEM 3A-3 OR PROBLEM 3B-3 (CONTINUED)

ACCOUNTS PAYABLE — ACCOUNT NO. 211

Date	Explanation	Post Ref.	Debit	Credit	Balance Debit	Balance Credit

A. FRENCH, CAPITAL — ACCOUNT NO. 311

Date	Explanation	Post Ref.	Debit	Credit	Balance Debit	Balance Credit

A. FRENCH, WITHDRAWALS — ACCOUNT NO. 312

Date	Explanation	Post Ref.	Debit	Credit	Balance Debit	Balance Credit

PLACEMENT FEES EARNED — ACCOUNT NO. 411

Date	Explanation	Post Ref.	Debit	Credit	Balance Debit	Balance Credit

PROBLEM 3A-3 OR PROBLEM 3B-3 (CONTINUED)

WAGE EXPENSE ACCOUNT NO. 511

Date		Explanation	Post Ref.	Debit	Credit	Balance	
						Debit	Credit

TELEPHONE EXPENSE ACCOUNT NO. 521

Date		Explanation	Post Ref.	Debit	Credit	Balance	
						Debit	Credit

ADVERTISING EXPENSE ACCOUNT NO. 531

Date		Explanation	Post Ref.	Debit	Credit	Balance	
						Debit	Credit

PROBLEM 3A-3 OR PROBLEM 3B-3 (CONCLUDED)

(C)

A. FRENCH'S PLACEMENT AGENCY
TRIAL BALANCE
JUNE 30, 200X

	Dr.	Cr.

CHAPTER 3
SUMMARY PRACTICE TEST:
BEGINNING THE ACCOUNTING CYCLE: JOURNALIZING, POSTING, AND THE TRIAL BALANCE

1. A _____ _____ is an accounting period that runs for any 12 consecutive months.

2. _____ _____ are prepared for parts of a fiscal year (monthly, quarterly, etc.).

3. The _____ _____ _____ eliminates the need for footings.

4. The positive balance of each account is referred to as its _____ _____.

5. The process of recording transactions in a journal is called _____.

6. Entries are journalized in _____ _____.

7. A ledger is often called a _____ _____ _____ _____ .

8. The _____ portion of a journal entry is indented and placed below the _____ portion.

9. A journal entry requiring three or more accounts is called a _____ _____ _____.

10. Prepaid rent is a(n) _____ on the balance sheet.

11. When supplies are used up or consumed they become a(n) _____.

12. The book of original entry usually refers to a(n) _____.

13. The process of transferring information from a journal to a ledger is called _____.

14. _____ deals with the process of updating the PR of the journal from the account number of the ledger to indicate to which account in the ledger information has been posted.

15. Recording $885.000 as $88.50 is an example of a _____.

Part II Instructions

Match the term in column A to the definition, example, or phrase in column B. Be sure to use a letter only once.

COLUMN A

- __g__ **1.** EXAMPLE: Book of original entry
- _____ **2.** Withdrawals
- _____ **3.** Slide
- _____ **4.** Transposition
- _____ **5.** Posting
- _____ **6.** General Journal
- _____ **7.** Cross-reference
- _____ **8.** Journalizing
- _____ **9.** Balance Sheet prepared monthly
- _____ **10.** A fiscal year

COLUMN B

a. 118 — 1180

b. Transferring information from a general journal to a ledger

c. Chronological order

d. Increased by a credit

e. Non-business expense

f. Compound journal entry

g. General journal

h. Rearrangement of digits of a number by accident

i. Updating PR column of journal from ledger account

j. Trial balance

k. Place to record transactions

l. Accounting cycle

m. Accounting period

n. Interim statements

Part III Instructions

Answer true or false to the following statements.

1. 5,187 written by mistake as 5,178 is an example of a slide.

2. The totals of a trial balance may possibly not balance due to transpositions.

3. Withdrawals has a normal balance of a credit.

4. The running balance of an account can be kept in a four-column account.

5. The journal links debits and credits in alphabetical order.

6. The ledger accumulates information from the journal.

7. The post reference column of a ledger records the account number of that account.

8. An accounting cycle must be from January 1 to December 31.

9. The ledger is the book of original entry.

10. The income statement is prepared for a specific accounting period.

11. Interim statements are prepared for an entire fiscal year.

12. A calendar year could be a fiscal year.

13. 150 written by mistake as 1,500 is an example of a slide.

14. If the totals of a trial balance balance, the individual balance of items must be correct.

15. The equality of debits and credits on a trial balance does not guarantee that transactions have been properly recorded.

16. The trial balance is prepared from the journal.

17. Cross-referencing means never updating the post reference column of the journal.

18. Journals and ledgers are always in the same book.

19. The normal balance of each account is located on the same side that increases the acccount.

20. Ruling of four-column accounts is eliminated.

CHAPTER 3
SOLUTIONS TO SUMMARY PRACTICE TEST

Part I

1. fiscal year
2. interim statements
3. four-column ledger
4. normal balance
5. journalizing
6. chronological order
7. book of final entry
8. credit, debit
9. compound journal entry
10. asset
11. expense
12. journal
13. posting
14. cross-reference
15. slide

Part II

1. g
2. e
3. a
4. h
5. b
6. k
7. i
8. c
9. n
10. m

Part III

1. false
2. true
3. false
4. true
5. false
6. true
7. false
8. false
9. false
10. true
11. false
12. true
13. true
14. false
15. true
16. false
17. false
18. false
19. true
20. true

Name _____ Class _____ Date _____

SELF-REVIEW QUIZ 4-1

Use a blank fold-out worksheet located in envelope at the end of this study guide.

SELF-REVIEW QUIZ 4-2

(1) _____
_____
_____

(2) _____
_____

(3)

LIABILITIES AND OWNER'S EQUITY

ASSETS

FORMS FOR COMPREHENSIVE DEMONSTRATION PROBLEM

(1)
Use a blank fold-out worksheet located at the end of this study guide.

(2)

FROST COMPANY
INCOME STATEMENT
FOR MONTH ENDED DECEMBER 31, 200X

(2)

FROST COMPANY
STATEMENT OF OWNER'S EQUITY
FOR MONTH ENDED DECEMBER 31, 200X

COMPREHENSIVE DEMONSTRATION PROBLEM (CONCLUDED)

(2)

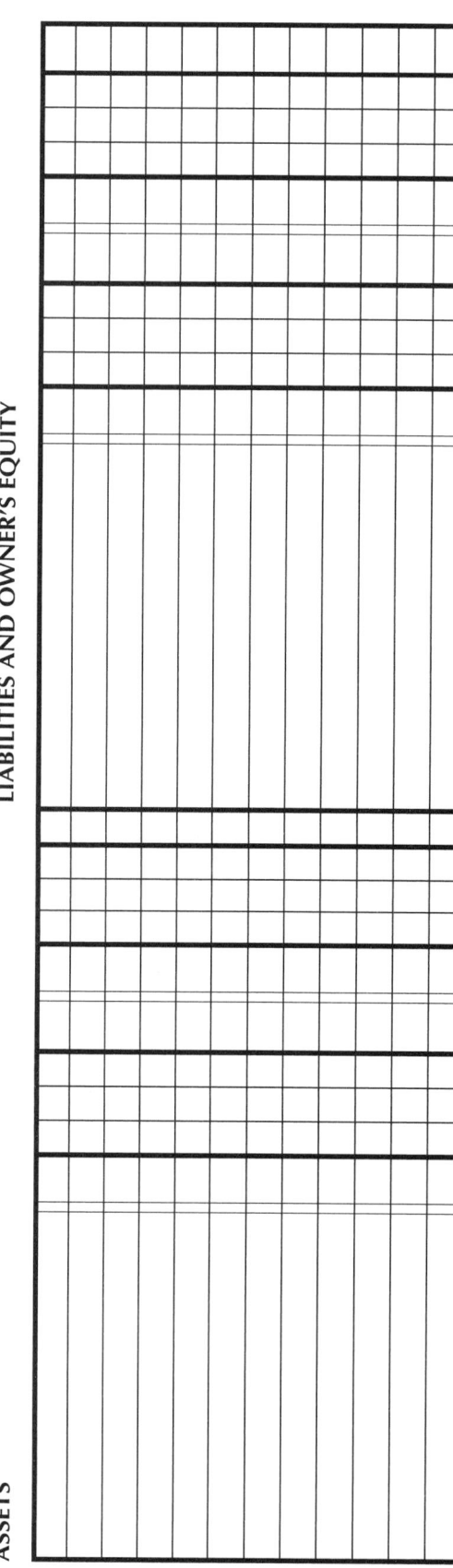

FROST COMPANY
BALANCE SHEET
DECEMBER 31, 200X

ASSETS

LIABILITIES AND OWNER'S EQUITY

EXERCISES (CONTINUED)

4-5.

(A)

J. TRENT
INCOME STATEMENT
FOR MONTH ENDED DECEMBER 31, 200X

(B)

J. TRENT
STATEMENT OF OWNER'S EQUITY
FOR MONTH ENDED DECEMBER 31, 200X

EXERCISES (CONTINUED)
(C)

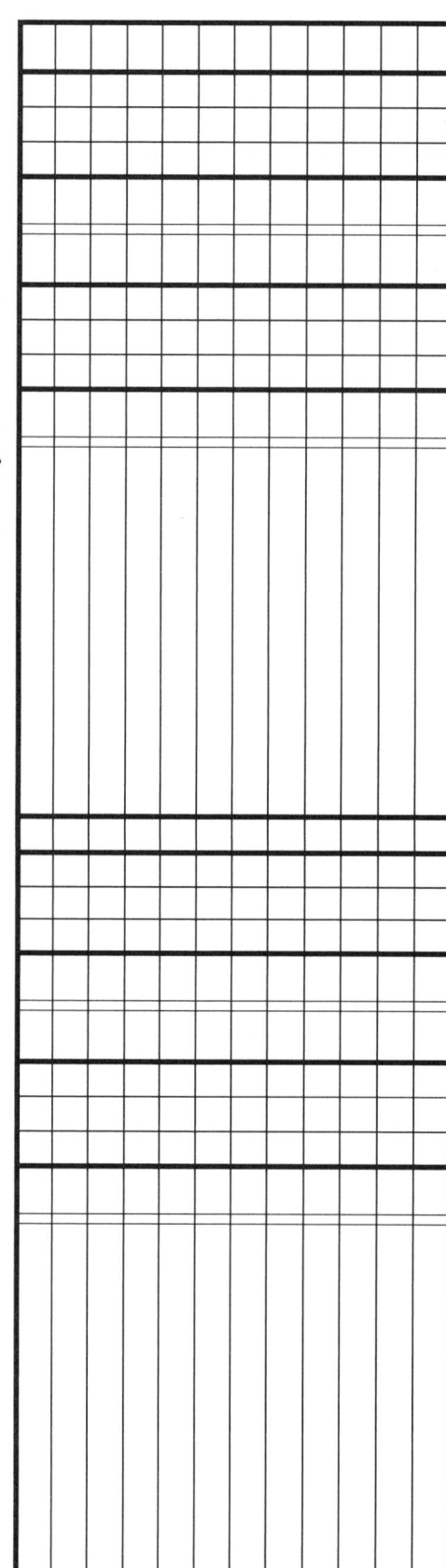

J. TRENT
BALANCE SHEET
DECEMBER 31, 200X

ASSETS

LIABILITIES AND OWNER'S EQUITY

END OF CHAPTER PROBLEMS

PROBLEM 4A-1 OR PROBLEM 4B-1

Use a blank fold-out worksheet located at the end of this study guide.

PROBLEM 4A-2 OR PROBLEM 4B-2

Use a blank fold-out worksheet located at the end of this study guide.

PROBLEM 4A-3 OR PROBLEM 4B-3

Use a blank fold-out worksheet located at the end of this study guide.

(2)

KEVIN'S MOVING CO.
INCOME STATEMENT
FOR MONTH ENDED OCTOBER 31, 200X

KEVIN'S MOVING CO.
STATEMENT OF OWNER'S EQUITY
FOR MONTH ENDED OCTOBER 31, 200X

(2)

Name _____ Class _____ Date _____

PROBLEM 4A-3 OR PROBLEM 4B-3

(2)

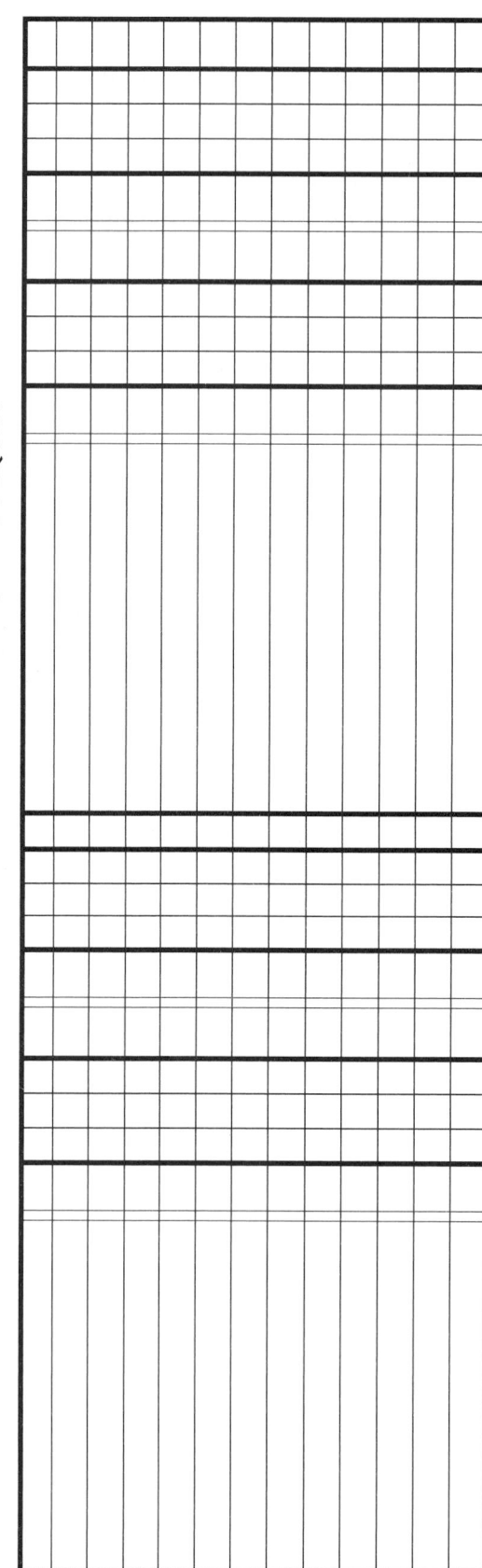

KEVIN'S MOVING CO.
BALANCE SHEET
OCTOBER 31, 200X

ASSETS

LIABILITIES AND OWNER'S EQUITY

PROBLEM 4A-4 OR PROBLEM 4B-4

Use a blank fold-out worksheet located at the end of this study guide.

(2)

DICK'S REPAIR SERVICE
INCOME STATEMENT
FOR MONTH ENDED NOVEMBER 30, 200X

(2)

DICK'S REPAIR SERVICE
STATEMENT OF OWNER'S EQUITY
FOR MONTH ENDED NOVEMBER 30, 200X

PROBLEM 4A-4 OR PROBLEM 4B-4 (CONCLUDED)

(2)

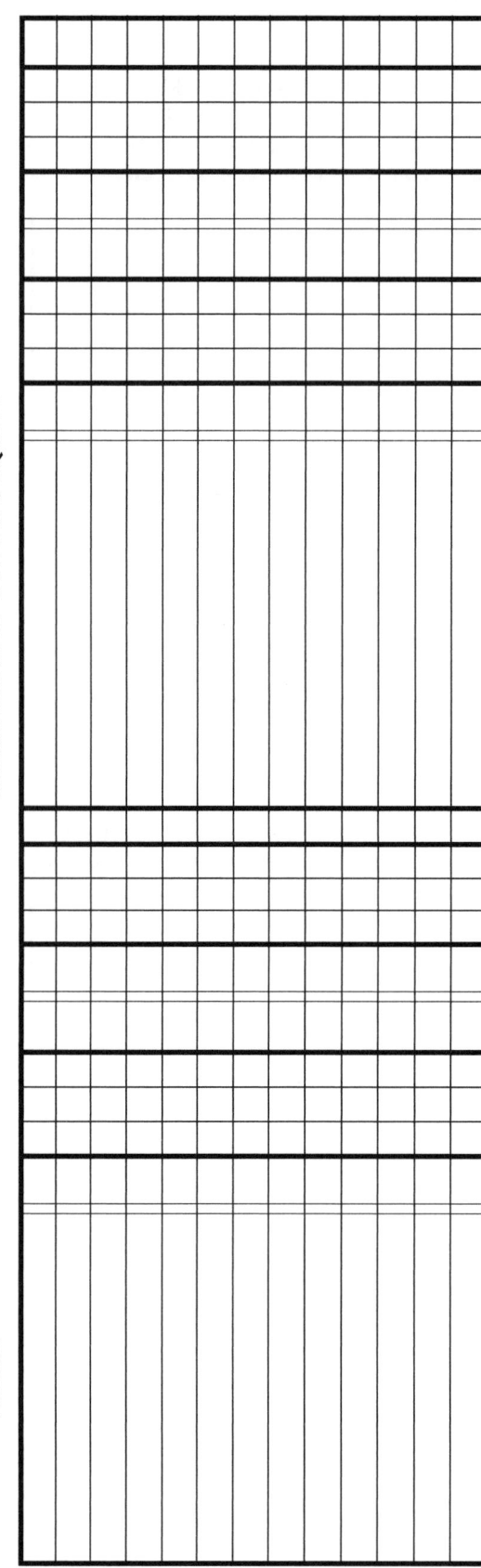

DICK'S REPAIR SERVICE
BALANCE SHEET
NOVEMBER 30, 200X

ASSETS

LIABILITIES AND OWNER'S EQUITY

CHAPTER 4
SUMMARY PRACTICE TEST:
THE ACCOUNTING CYCLE CONTINUED:
PREPARING WORKSHEETS AND FINANCIAL STATEMENTS

Part I Instructions

Fill in the blank(s) to complete the statement.

1. Adjustments are the result of _____ transactions.
2. A _____ will increase accumulated depreciation.
3. _____ affect both the income statement and balance sheet.
4. The adjustment for supplies reflects the amount of supplies _____.
5. Supplies Expense is found on the income statement. Supplies are found on
    _____ _____.
6. _____ _____ reflects the cost of equipment at time of purchase.
7. Depreciation Expense is found on the _____ _____.
8. _____ _____ is a contra asset that has a credit balance.
9. Accumulated Depreciation, a contra asset, is found on the _____ _____.
10. Historical or original cost of an auto less _____
    _____ reflects the unused amount of the auto on the accounting books.
11. Withdrawals are found in the _____ column of the balance sheet
    section of the worksheet.
12. Salaries Payable is a liability that will appear in the _____
    _____ _____ _____ of the worksheet.
13. The figure for net income on the worksheet is carried over to the _____
    column of the balance sheet.
14. A worksheet is a(n) _____ report.
15. _____ _____ are prepared after the
    completion of the worksheet.

Part II Instructions

Complete the following statements by circling the letter of the appropriate answer.

1. Adjustments will affect
   a. the balance sheet
   b. the income statement
   c. both a and b

2. The historical or original cost of an asset on the worksheet
   a. never changes
   b. sometimes changes
   c. continually changes

3. Net income on the worksheet is
   a. carried over to the trial balance
   b. carried over to the adjusted trial balance
   c. carried over to the balance sheet column

4. Accumulated Depreciation is found on
   a. a worksheet
   b. an income statement
   c. both a worksheet and an income statement

5. Accumulated Depreciation, a contra asset, is increased by a
   a. debit
   b. credit
   c. both a and b

6. A worksheet is usually competed
   a. one column at a time
   b. two columns at a time
   c. three columns at a time

7. Withdrawals on the worksheet are found in the
   a. debit column of the income statement
   b. debit column of the balance sheet
   c. both a and b

8. The worksheet specifically shows the
   a. beginning figure for owner capital
   b. ending figure for owner capital
   c. average figure for owner capital

9. The total of the assets on a formal balance sheet will _____ equal the total of the debit column of the balance sheet on the worksheet.
   a. always
   b. sometimes
   c. never

10. The adjustment for depreciation affects
    a. the income statement
    b. the balance sheet
    c. both a and b

11. The adjustment for supplies requires one to know
    a. beginning supplies plus supplies purchased
    b. supplies on hand
    c. both a and b

12. The purpose of adjustments is to

    a. bring general journals up to date

    b. bring ledger accounts up to proper balances in the journal

    c. bring ledger accounts to proper balance

13. Book values equals cost less

    a. expenses

    b. accumulated depreciation

    c. neither a nor b

14. The _____ is an informal report.

    a. income statement

    b. balance sheet

    c. worksheet

Part III Instructions

Answer true or false to the following statements.

1. The normal balance of accumulated depreciation is a debit.

2. Assets are only income statement accounts.

3. The total of the adjustments column may balance but be incorrect.

4. Prepaid rent is found on the income statement.

5. Rent expense is found on the income statement.

6. Debits and credits are found on financial statements.

7. Historical cost relates only to automobiles.

8. Accumulated Depreciation is found on the income statement.

9. As Accumulated Depreciation increases, the historical cost changes.

10. The adjustment for depreciation directly affects cash.

11. An expense is only recorded when it is paid.

12. The ending figure for owner capital does not have to be calculated from the worksheet.

13. Withdrawals have the same balance as Accumulated Depreciation.

14. Salaries Payable is an asset on the income statement.

15. Net loss would never be shown on a worksheet.

16. The net income on the worksheet is the same amount on the income statement.

17. Worksheets must use dollar signs.

18. The worksheet eliminates the need to prepare financial statements.

19. Cost less accumulated depreciation equals book value.

20. Accrued Salaries are expenses that have already been paid for.

CHAPTER 4
SOLUTIONS TO SUMMARY PRACTICE TEST

Part I

1. internal
2. credit
3. adjustments
4. used up
5. balance sheet
6. historical (original) cost
7. income statement
8. Accumulated Depreciation
9. balance sheet
10. accumulated depreciation
11. debit
12. balance sheet credit column
13. credit
14. informal
15. financial statements

Part II

1. c
2. a
3. c
4. a
5. b
6. b
7. b
8. a
9. c
10. c
11. c
12. c
13. b
14. c

Part III

1. false
2. false
3. true
4. false
5. true
6. false
7. false
8. false
9. false
10. false
11. false
12. true
13. false
14. false
15. false
16. true
17. false
18. false
19. true
20. false

THE ACCOUNTING CYCLE COMPLETED: ADJUSTING, CLOSING, AND THE POST-CLOSING TRIAL BALANCE

5

SELF-REVIEW QUIZ 5-1

(1)

PAGE 2

Date	Account Titles and Description	PR	Dr.	Cr.

(2) Partial Ledger

Depreciation Expense, Store Equipment 511	Accumulated Depreciation, Store Equipment 122
	4

Prepaid Insurance 116	Insurance Expense 516
3	

Store Supplies 114	Supplies Expense 514
5	

Salaries Expense 512	Salaries Payable 212
8	

SELF-REVIEW QUIZ 5-2

<table>
<tr><td></td><td></td><td></td><td></td><td></td><td></td><td></td><td></td><td></td></tr>
<tr><td></td><td></td><td></td><td></td><td></td><td></td><td></td><td></td><td></td></tr>
<tr><td></td><td></td><td></td><td></td><td></td><td></td><td></td><td></td><td></td></tr>
<tr><td></td><td></td><td></td><td></td><td></td><td></td><td></td><td></td><td></td></tr>
<tr><td></td><td></td><td></td><td></td><td></td><td></td><td></td><td></td><td></td></tr>
<tr><td></td><td></td><td></td><td></td><td></td><td></td><td></td><td></td><td></td></tr>
<tr><td></td><td></td><td></td><td></td><td></td><td></td><td></td><td></td><td></td></tr>
</table>

	P. Logan, Capital	310
	14	

	Revenue from Clients	410
	25	

	Supplies Expense	514
	4	

	P. Logan, Withdrawals	311
3		

	Depreciation Expense, Store Equipment	510
1		

	Insurance Expense	516
2		

	Income Summary	312

	Salaries Expense	512
11		

	Rent Expense	518
2		

(2) _____

_____

_____

SELF-REVIEW QUIZ 5-3

_____

_____

_____

FORMS FOR COMPREHENSIVE DEMONSTRATION PROBLEM

(Worksheet is a fold-out at end of study guide/working paper)

ROLO COMPANY
GENERAL JOURNAL

PAGE 1

Date	Account Titles and Description	PR	Dr.	Cr.

FORMS FOR COMPREHENSIVE DEMONSTRATION PROBLEM (CONTINUED)

ROLO COMPANY
GENERAL JOURNAL

PAGE 2

Date	Account Titles and Description	PR	Dr.	Cr.

FORMS FOR COMPREHENSIVE DEMONSTRATION PROBLEM (CONTINUED)

CASH   ACCOUNT NO. 111

Date	Explanation	Post Ref.	Debit	Credit	Balance Debit	Balance Credit

ACCOUNTS RECEIVABLE   ACCOUNT NO. 112

Date	Explanation	Post Ref.	Debit	Credit	Balance Debit	Balance Credit

PREPAID RENT   ACCOUNT NO. 114

Date	Explanation	Post Ref.	Debit	Credit	Balance Debit	Balance Credit

OFFICE SUPPLIES   ACCOUNT NO. 115

Date	Explanation	Post Ref.	Debit	Credit	Balance Debit	Balance Credit

FORMS FOR COMPREHENSIVE DEMONSTRATION PROBLEM (CONTINUED)

OFFICE EQUIPMENT **ACCOUNT NO. 121**

Date	Explanation	Post Ref.	Debit	Credit	Balance Debit	Balance Credit

ACCUMULATED DEPRECIATION, OFFICE EQUIPMENT **ACCOUNT NO. 122**

Date	Explanation	Post Ref.	Debit	Credit	Balance Debit	Balance Credit

ACCOUNTS PAYABLE **ACCOUNT NO. 211**

Date	Explanation	Post Ref.	Debit	Credit	Balance Debit	Balance Credit

Name _____ Class _____ Date _____

FORMS FOR COMPREHENSIVE DEMONSTRATION PROBLEM (CONTINUED)

SALARIES PAYABLE   ACCOUNT NO. 212

Date	Explanation	Post Ref.	Debit	Credit	Balance Debit	Balance Credit

ROLO KERN, CAPITAL   ACCOUNT NO. 311

Date	Explanation	Post Ref.	Debit	Credit	Balance Debit	Balance Credit

ROLO KERN, WITHDRAWALS   ACCOUNT NO. 312

Date	Explanation	Post Ref.	Debit	Credit	Balance Debit	Balance Credit

INCOME SUMMARY   ACCOUNT NO. 313

Date	Explanation	Post Ref.	Debit	Credit	Balance Debit	Balance Credit

FEES EARNED   ACCOUNT NO. 411

Date	Explanation	Post Ref.	Debit	Credit	Balance Debit	Balance Credit

FORMS FOR COMPREHENSIVE DEMONSTRATION PROBLEM (CONTINUED)

SALARIES EXPENSE   ACCOUNT NO. 511

Date	Explanation	Post Ref.	Debit	Credit	Balance Debit	Balance Credit

ADVERTISING EXPENSE   ACCOUNT NO. 512

Date	Explanation	Post Ref.	Debit	Credit	Balance Debit	Balance Credit

RENT EXPENSE   ACCOUNT NO. 513

Date	Explanation	Post Ref.	Debit	Credit	Balance Debit	Balance Credit

OFFICE SUPPLIES EXPENSE   ACCOUNT NO. 514

Date	Explanation	Post Ref.	Debit	Credit	Balance Debit	Balance Credit

DEPRECIATION EXPENSE, OFFICE EQUIPMENT   ACCOUNT NO. 515

Date	Explanation	Post Ref.	Debit	Credit	Balance Debit	Balance Credit

FORMS FOR COMPREHENSIVE DEMONSTRATION PROBLEM (CONTINUED)

ROLO COMPANY
INCOME STATEMENT
FOR MONTH ENDED JANUARY 31, 200X

ROLO COMPANY
STATEMENT OF OWNER'S EQUITY
FOR MONTH ENDED JANUARY 31, 200X

FORMS FOR COMPREHENSIVE DEMONSTRATION PROBLEM (CONCLUDED)

ROLO COMPANY
BALANCE SHEET
JANUARY 31, 200X

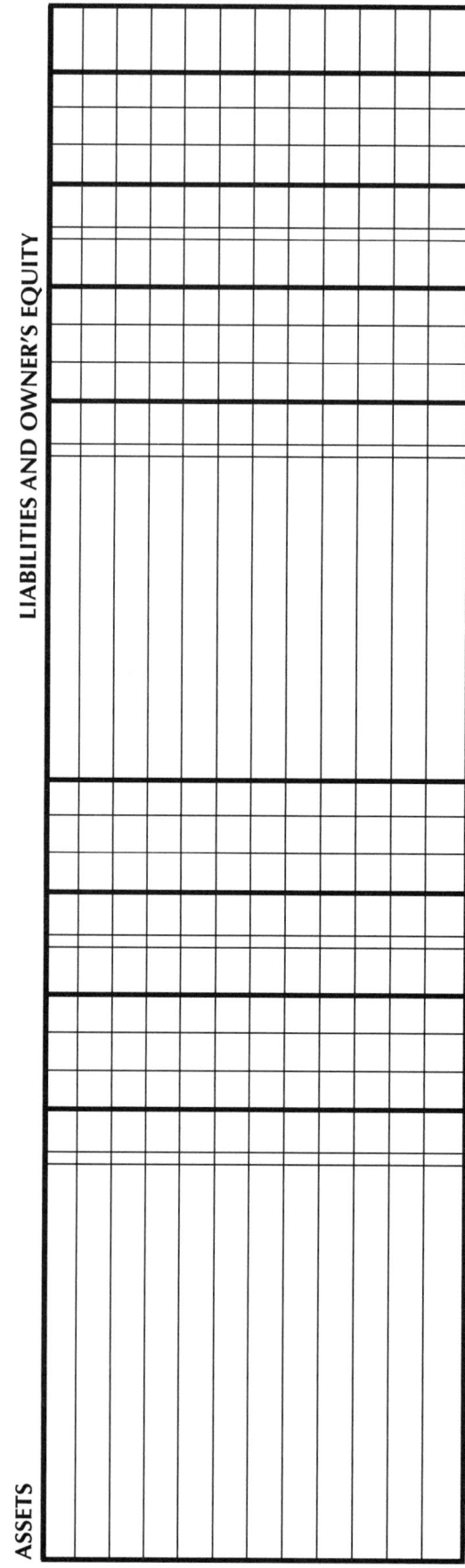

ASSETS

LIABILITIES AND OWNER'S EQUITY

FORMS FOR COMPREHENSIVE DEMONSTRATION PROBLEM (CONCLUDED)

ROLO COMPANY
POST-CLOSING TRIAL BALANCE
JANUARY 31, 200X

	Dr.	Cr.

YOU MAKE THE CALL: CRITICAL THINKING/ETHICAL CASE

INTERNET EXERCISES

FORMS FOR EXERCISES

5-1.

Date	Account Titles and Description	PR	Dr.	Cr.

5-2.

TEMPORARY	PERMANENT	WILL BE CLOSED

1. Income Summary
2. M. Bryant, Capital
3. Salary Expense
4. M. Bryant, Withdrawals
5. Fees Earned
6. Accounts Payable
7. Cash

5-3.

Date		Account Titles and Description	PR		Dr.		Cr.	

EXERCISES (CONTINUED)

5-4.

Date	Account Titles and Description	PR	Dr.	Cr.

5-5.

WEY CO.
POST-CLOSING TRIAL BALANCE
DECEMBER 31, 200X

		Dr.	Cr.

PROBLEM 5A-1 OR PROBLEM 5B-1

Use a blank fold-out worksheet located at the end of this study guide.

(2)

LOU'S CONSULTING SERVICE
GENERAL JOURNAL

PAGE 3

Date		Account Titles and Description	PR	Dr.	Cr.

PROBLEM 5A-2 OR PROBLEM 5B-2

(1)

POTTER CLEANING SERVICE
GENERAL JOURNAL

PAGE 2

Date	Account Titles and Description	PR	Dr.	Cr.

PROBLEM 5A-2 OR PROBLEM 5B-2 (CONTINUED)

CASH   ACCOUNT NO. <u>112</u>

Date	Explanation	Post Ref.	Debit	Credit	Balance Debit	Balance Credit

PREPAID INSURANCE   ACCOUNT NO. <u>114</u>

Date	Explanation	Post Ref.	Debit	Credit	Balance Debit	Balance Credit

CLEANING SUPPLIES   ACCOUNT NO. <u>115</u>

Date	Explanation	Post Ref.	Debit	Credit	Balance Debit	Balance Credit

AUTO   ACCOUNT NO. <u>121</u>

Date	Explanation	Post Ref.	Debit	Credit	Balance Debit	Balance Credit

ACCUMULATED DEPRECIATION, AUTO   ACCOUNT NO. <u>122</u>

Date	Explanation	Post Ref.	Debit	Credit	Balance Debit	Balance Credit

PROBLEM 5A-2 OR PROBLEM 5B-2 (CONTINUED)

ACCOUNTS PAYABLE   ACCOUNT NO. <u>212</u>

Date	Explanation	Post Ref.	Debit	Credit	Balance Debit	Balance Credit

SALARIES PAYABLE   ACCOUNT NO. <u>213</u>

Date	Explanation	Post Ref.	Debit	Credit	Balance Debit	Balance Credit

B. POTTER, CAPITAL   ACCOUNT NO. <u>312</u>

Date	Explanation	Post Ref.	Debit	Credit	Balance Debit	Balance Credit

B. POTTER, WITHDRAWALS   ACCOUNT NO. <u>313</u>

Date	Explanation	Post Ref.	Debit	Credit	Balance Debit	Balance Credit

INCOME SUMMARY   ACCOUNT NO. <u>314</u>

Date	Explanation	Post Ref.	Debit	Credit	Balance Debit	Balance Credit

PROBLEM 5A-2 OR PROBLEM 5B-2 (CONTINUED)

CLEANING FEES   ACCOUNT NO. 412

Date		Explanation	Post Ref.	Debit	Credit	Balance	
						Debit	Credit

SALARIES EXPENSE   ACCOUNT NO. 513

Date		Explanation	Post Ref.	Debit	Credit	Balance	
						Debit	Credit

TELEPHONE EXPENSE   ACCOUNT NO. 514

Date		Explanation	Post Ref.	Debit	Credit	Balance	
						Debit	Credit

ADVERTISING EXPENSE   ACCOUNT NO. 515

Date		Explanation	Post Ref.	Debit	Credit	Balance	
						Debit	Credit

GAS EXPENSE   ACCOUNT NO. 516

Date		Explanation	Post Ref.	Debit	Credit	Balance	
						Debit	Credit

PROBLEM 5A-2 OR PROBLEM 5B-2 (CONTINUED)

INSURANCE EXPENSE   ACCOUNT NO. <u>517</u>

Date	Explanation	Post Ref.	Debit	Credit	Balance Debit	Balance Credit

CLEANING SUPPLIES EXPENSE   ACCOUNT NO. <u>518</u>

Date	Explanation	Post Ref.	Debit	Credit	Balance Debit	Balance Credit

DEPRECIATION EXPENSE, AUTO   ACCOUNT NO. <u>519</u>

Date	Explanation	Post Ref.	Debit	Credit	Balance Debit	Balance Credit

PROBLEM 5A-2 OR PROBLEM 5B-2 (CONCLUDED)

POTTER CLEANING SERVICE
POST-CLOSING TRIAL BALANCE
MARCH 31, 200X

	Dr.	Cr.

PROBLEM 5A-3 OR PROBLEM 5B-3

Use a blank fold-out worksheet located at the end of this study guide.

PROBLEM 5A-3 OR PROBLEM 5B-3 (CONTINUED)

PETE'S PLOWING
GENERAL JOURNAL

PAGE 1

Date	Account Titles and Description	PR	Dr.	Cr.

PROBLEM 5A-3 OR PROBLEM 5B-3 (CONTINUED)

PETE'S PLOWING
GENERAL JOURNAL

PAGE 2

Date	Account Titles and Description	PR	Dr.	Cr.

PROBLEM 5A-3 OR PROBLEM 5B-3 (CONTINUED)

PETE'S PLOWING
GENERAL JOURNAL

PAGE 3

Date	Account Titles and Description	PR	Dr.	Cr.

PROBLEM 5A-3 OR PROBLEM 5B-3 (CONTINUED)

CASH   **ACCOUNT NO. 111**

Date	Explanation	Post Ref.	Debit	Credit	Balance Debit	Balance Credit

ACCOUNTS RECEIVABLE   **ACCOUNT NO. 112**

Date	Explanation	Post Ref.	Debit	Credit	Balance Debit	Balance Credit

PREPAID RENT   **ACCOUNT NO. 114**

Date	Explanation	Post Ref.	Debit	Credit	Balance Debit	Balance Credit

SNOW SUPPLIES   **ACCOUNT NO. 115**

Date	Explanation	Post Ref.	Debit	Credit	Balance Debit	Balance Credit

PROBLEM 5A-3 OR PROBLEM 5B-3 (CONTINUED)

OFFICE EQUIPMENT   ACCOUNT NO. 121

Date	Explanation	Post Ref.	Debit	Credit	Balance Debit	Credit

ACCUMULATED DEPRECIATION, OFFICE EQUIPMENT   ACCOUNT NO. 122

Date	Explanation	Post Ref.	Debit	Credit	Balance Debit	Credit

SNOW EQUIPMENT   ACCOUNT NO. 123

Date	Explanation	Post Ref.	Debit	Credit	Balance Debit	Credit

ACCUMULATED DEPRECIATION, SNOW EQUIPMENT   ACCOUNT NO. 124

Date	Explanation	Post Ref.	Debit	Credit	Balance Debit	Credit

ACCOUNTS PAYABLE   ACCOUNT NO. 211

Date	Explanation	Post Ref.	Debit	Credit	Balance Debit	Credit

PROBLEM 5A-3 OR PROBLEM 5B-3 (CONTINUED)

SALARIES PAYABLE   ACCOUNT NO. 212

Date	Explanation	Post Ref.	Debit	Credit	Balance Debit	Balance Credit

PETE MACK, CAPITAL   ACCOUNT NO. 311

Date	Explanation	Post Ref.	Debit	Credit	Balance Debit	Balance Credit

PETE MACK, WITHDRAWALS   ACCOUNT NO. 312

Date	Explanation	Post Ref.	Debit	Credit	Balance Debit	Balance Credit

INCOME SUMMARY   ACCOUNT NO. 313

Date	Explanation	Post Ref.	Debit	Credit	Balance Debit	Balance Credit

PLOWING FEES   ACCOUNT NO. 411

Date	Explanation	Post Ref.	Debit	Credit	Balance Debit	Balance Credit

PROBLEM 5A-3 OR PROBLEM 5B-3 (CONTINUED)

SALARIES EXPENSE　　　　　　　　　**ACCOUNT NO. 511**

Date		Explanation	Post Ref.	Debit	Credit	Balance	
						Debit	Credit

ADVERTISING EXPENSE　　　　　　　　**ACCOUNT NO. 512**

Date		Explanation	Post Ref.	Debit	Credit	Balance	
						Debit	Credit

TELEPHONE EXPENSE　　　　　　　　**ACCOUNT NO. 513**

Date		Explanation	Post Ref.	Debit	Credit	Balance	
						Debit	Credit

RENT EXPENSE　　　　　　　　　　**ACCOUNT NO. 514**

Date		Explanation	Post Ref.	Debit	Credit	Balance	
						Debit	Credit

SNOW SUPPLIES EXPENSE　　　　　　**ACCOUNT NO. 515**

Date		Explanation	Post Ref.	Debit	Credit	Balance	
						Debit	Credit

PROBLEM 5A-3 OR PROBLEM 5B-3 (CONTINUED)

DEPRECIATION EXPENSE, OFFICE EQUIPMENT   ACCOUNT NO. 516

Date	Explanation	Post Ref.	Debit	Credit	Balance Debit	Balance Credit

DEPRECIATION EXPENSE, SNOW EQUIPMENT   ACCOUNT NO. 517

Date	Explanation	Post Ref.	Debit	Credit	Balance Debit	Balance Credit

PROBLEM 5A-3 OR PROBLEM 5B-3 (CONTINUED)

PETE'S PLOWING
INCOME STATEMENT
FOR MONTH ENDED JANUARY 31, 200X

PETE'S PLOWING
STATEMENT OF OWNER'S EQUITY
FOR MONTH ENDED JANUARY 31, 200X

PROBLEM 5A-3 OR PROBLEM 5B-3 (CONCLUDED)

PETE'S PLOWING
BALANCE SHEET
JANUARY 31, 200X

ASSETS

LIABILITIES AND OWNER'S EQUITY

PROBLEM 5A-3 OR PROBLEM 5B-3 (CONCLUDED)

PETE'S PLOWING
POST-CLOSING TRIAL BALANCE
JANUARY 31, 200X

		Dr.					Cr.			

CHAPTER 5
SUMMARY PRACTICE TEST:
THE ACCOUNTING CYCLE COMPLETED:
ADJUSTING, CLOSING, AND
THE POST-CLOSING TRIAL BALANCE

Part I Instructions

Fill in the blank(s) to complete the statement.

1. Income summary is _____ by the end of the period.
2. Revenue, Expenses, and Withdrawals are examples of _____ _____.
3. _____ in temporary accounts will not be carried over to the next accounting period.
4. After closing entries are posted, owner's Capital in the ledger will contain the _____ _____.
5. Revenue is closed to Income Summary by a _____ to each revenue account and a _____ to Income Summary.
6. Expenses are closed to Income Summary by _____ the individual expenses and _____ Income Summary.
7. If the balance of Income Summary is a credit, it will be closed by _____ Income Summary and _____ owner's Capital.
8. The balance of Withdrawals is closed by a _____ and the amount transferred to owner's Capital by a _____.
9. At the end of the closing process, all temporary accounts in the ledger will have a _____ balance.
10. The _____ _____ _____ contains a list of permanent accounts after the adjusting and closing entries have been posted to the ledger from a journal.
11. Closing entries can be prepared from a _____.
12. After closing entries are posted, Income Summary will have a _____ balance.
13. Journalizing adjustments can be done from the _____.
14. Cash, Equipment, and Supplies are not part of the _____ process.
15. Income Summary is a _____ account.

Part II Instructions

The following is a chart of accounts for Jim's Fix-it Shop. From the chart, indicate in Column B (by account number) which accounts will be debited or credited as related to the transactions in Column A.

CHART OF ACCOUNTS

ASSETS	OWNER'S EQUITY
112 Cash	340 J. Fix, Capital
114 Accounts Receivable	341 J. Fix, Withdrawals
116 Prepaid Rent	342 Income Summary
118 Fix-It Supplies	
120 Truck	REVENUE
121 Accumulated Depreciation, Truck	450 Fix-It Fees Earned
LIABILITIES	EXPENSES
230 Accounts Payable	560 Salaries
232 Salaries Payable	562 Advertising
	564 Rent
	566 Fix-It Supplies
	568 Depreciation Expense, Truck

COLUMN A	COLUMN B	
	Debit(s)	Credit(s)
1. Closed balance in revenue account to Income Summary.	_____	_____
2. Closed balance in individual expenses to Income Summary	_____	_____
3. Closed balance in Income Summary to owner's Capital. (Assume that it is a net income.)	_____	_____
4. Closed Withdrawals to owner's Capital.	_____	_____
5. Recorded Fix-It supplies used up.	_____	_____
6. Recorded depreciation on truck.	_____	_____
7. Brought Salaries Expense up to date (an adjustment).	_____	_____

Part III Instructions

Answer true or false to the following statements.

1. All companies journalize and post closing entries before the end of their calendar year.
2. Adjustments are journalized before preparing the worksheet.
3. Closing entries can only clear permanent accounts.
4. Income summary is a temporary account.
5. Interim statements can be prepared from worksheets.
6. To clear expenses in the closing process, a compound entry is appropriate.
7. Withdrawals is a permanent account.
8. Income Summary helps update withdrawals.

9. Accumulated Depreciation is a temporary account.

10. Cash, Rent Expense, and Accounts Receivable need to be closed at the end of the period.

11. Closing entries do not relate to the worksheet.

12. Revenue is closed by a credit.

13. Expenses are placed on the debit side of the Income Summary account.

14. A post-closing trial balance closely resembles the ending balance sheet.

15. Accumulated Depreciation never has to be adjusted.

16. Interim statements are always prepared monthly.

17. A post-closing trial balance is prepared before adjustments are journalized.

18. Income Summary is shown on the balance sheet.

19. The process of closing entries will help update owner's Capital.

20. An increase in Income Summary is a debit.

21. An increase in Income Summary is a credit.

22. The income statement is listed in terms of debits and credits.

23. Closing updates only permanent accounts.

24. The completion of financial statements means that the Capital account in the ledger has been updated.

25. Withdrawals is closed to Income Summary.

SOLUTIONS TO SUMMARY PRACTICE TEST

Part I

1. closed
2. temporary accounts
3. balances
4. ending figure (balance)
5. debit, credit
6. crediting, debiting
7. debiting, crediting
8. credit, debit
9. zero
10. post-closing trial balance
11. worksheet
12. zero
13. worksheet
14. closing
15. temporary

Part II

	Debit	Credit
1.	450	342
2.	342	560, 562, 564, 566, 568
3.	342	340
4.	340	341
5.	566	118
6.	568	121
7.	560	232

BANKING PROCEDURES AND CONTROL OF CASH

SELF-REVIEW QUIZ 6-1

Situation	Add to Bank Balance	Deduct from Bank Balance	Add to Checkbook Balance	Deduct from Checkbook Balance
1				
2				
3				
4				
5				
6				
7				
8				

SELF-REVIEW QUIZ 6-2

PAGE 6

Date	Account Titles and Description	PR	Dr.	Cr.

AUXILIARY PETTY CASH RECORD

Date	Voucher No.	Description	Receipts	Payment	Category of Payment				
					Delivery Expense	General Expense	Account	Sundry Amount	

YOU MAKE THE CALL: CRITICAL THINKING/ETHICAL CASE

_____
_____
_____
_____
_____
_____
_____
_____
_____
_____
_____
_____
_____
_____
_____
_____
_____

INTERNET EXERCISES

_____
_____
_____
_____
_____
_____
_____
_____
_____
_____
_____
_____
_____
_____
_____
_____
_____
_____
_____
_____
_____

CHAPTER 6
FORMS FOR MINI EXERCISES

1.

   A. _____   E. _____

   B. _____   F. _____

   C. _____

   D. _____

2.

3.   _____ _____ _____ _____

JUNE CO.
BANK RECONCILIATION
MAY 31, 200X

Checkbook	Bank

4.

   A. _____ _____ _____   E. _____ _____ _____

   B. _____ _____ _____   F. _____ _____ _____

   C. _____ _____ _____

   D. _____ _____ _____

5.

6.

FORMS FOR EXERCISES

6-1.

LANG CO.
BANK RECONCILIATION AS OF JULY 31, 200X

CHECKBOOK BALANCE

Ending Checkbook Balance _____
  Deduct: _____
  Bank Service Charge _____
                    _____
                    _____
Reconciled Balance _____

BALANCE PER BANK

Ending Bank Statement Balance _____
  Add: _____
  Deposit in Transit _____
                    _____
  Deduct: _____
  Outstanding Checks _____
                    _____
Reconciled Balance _____

6-2.

6-3.

EXERCISES (CONTINUED)

6-4.

6-5.

    Beg. Change Fund
+Cash Register Total
=Cash should have on hand
− Counted Cash
= Cash Shortage

END OF CHAPTER PROBLEMS

PROBLEM 6A-1 OR PROBLEM 6B-1

ABLE.COM
BANK RECONCILIATION AS OF JULY 31, 200X

BALANCE PER BANK

Bank Statement Balance

  Add: _____

  Deduct: _____

      _____

Reconciled Balance _____

CHECKBOOK BALANCE

Checkbook Balance

  Add:

      _____

  Deduct:

      _____

Reconciled Balance _____

PROBLEM 6A-1 OR PROBLEM 6B-1 (CONCLUDED)

Date		Account Titles and Description	PR	Dr.	Cr.

PROBLEM 6A-2 OR PROBLEM 6B-2

LOWELL NATIONAL BANK
RIO MEAN BRAND
BUGNA, TEXAS   TELEPHONE 555-8311

This form is provided to help you balance your bank statement. If no errors are reported to auditors in ten days, the account will be considered correct.

Please notify us of any change in address.

Checks outstanding
(not charged to account)

Check No.	Amount
Total	

Sort the checks numerically or by date issued.
Check off on the stubs of your checkbook each check paid by bank.
List the numbers and amounts of checks still outstanding in the space provided at the left.
Verify the deposits in your checkbook with deposits credited on this statement. Bank balance show on this statement $_____

Plus: Deposits not
   credited on this statement $_____
      Subtotal $_____
Less: Checks outstanding $_____
Balance $_____

If your checkbook does not agree, enter any necessary adjustments:
_____
_____
_____
Correct checkbook balance $_____

PROBLEM 6A-2 OR PROBLEM 6B-2 (CONCLUDED)

GENERAL JOURNAL

Date	Account Titles and Description	PR	Dr.	Cr.

PROBLEM 6A-3 OR PROBLEM 6B-3

MERRY CO.
GENERAL JOURNAL

Date		Account Titles and Description	PR	Dr.	Cr.

PROBLEM 6A-3 OR PROBLEM 6B-3 (CONCLUDED)

MERRY CO.
AUXILIARY PETTY CASH RECORD

Date	Voucher No.	Description	Receipts	Payment	Category of Payment				
					Postage Expense	Office Supplies Expense	Sundry		
							Account	Amount

PROBLEM 6A-4 OR PROBLEM 6B-4

LOGAN CO.
GENERAL JOURNAL

Date		Account Titles and Description	PR	Dr.	Cr.

PROBLEM 6A-4 OR PROBLEM 6B-4

LOGAN CO.
AUXILIARY PETTY CASH RECORD

Date	Voucher No.	Description	Receipts	Payment	Category of Payment				
					Postage Expense	Delivery Expense	Account	Sundry Amount	

CHAPTER 6
SUMMARY PRACTICE TEST
BANKING PROCEDURES AND CONTROL OF CASH

Part I Instructions

Fill in the blank(s) to complete the statement.

1. _____ _____ limit any further negotiations of a check.
2. Deposits in transit are _____ to the bank balance.
3. All adjustments to the checkbook balance in the reconciliation process will require _____ _____.
4. Petty cash is an _____ found on the balance sheet.
5. The auxiliary petty cash record is not a _____.
6. A _____ _____ is an asset used to make change for customer.
7. A cash overage will be _____ _____ on the income statement.
8. _____ _____ represents checks not processed by the bank at the time the bank statement was prepared.
9. When a bank debits your account, your balance will _____.
10. _____ is a procedure whereby the bank does not return the processed checks.

Part II Instructions

Indicate which of the following procedures are involved in each of the transactions below

a. Recorded in General Journal
b. Recorded in both general journal and auxiliary petty cash record
c. Recorded only in auxiliary petty cash record
d. New check is written
e. Account petty cash is increased

1.	EXAMPLE: Check issued to establish petty cash	b,d,e
2.	Paid donation from petty cash	_____
3.	Paid postage from petty cash	_____
4.	Paid past purchases previously charged	_____
5.	Paid for business luncheon with petty cash	_____
6.	Issued check to pay for office supplies	_____
7.	Replenished petty cash	_____
8.	Paid local donation from petty cash	_____
9.	Paid for past purchases bought on account	_____
10.	Replenished petty cash	_____

Part III Instructions

Answer true or false to the following statements.

1. Checks outstanding have reached the bank but have not been recorded in the checkbook.
2. Petty cash is a liability found on the balance sheet.
3. Checks returned from the bank are placed in alphabetical order.
4. The General Journal has a record of all checks written.
5. Bank service charges represent an expense to the business.
6. The bank statement is the same as the bank reconciliation.
7. The balance in the company cash account will always equal the bank balance before the bank statement is received.
8. Deposit slips are needed in writing checks.
9. The signature must be presented when cashing a check.
10. The auxiliary petty cash record is posted monthly.
11. The petty cash account has a debit balance.
12. Replenishment of petty cash requires a new check.
13. The expenses paid from petty cash are journalized at time of replenishment.
14. Internal control only affects large companies.
15. A petty cash voucher records the expense into the ledger.
16. The petty cash fund must be replenished monthly.
17. The petty cash voucher identifies the account that will be charged.
18. The establishment of petty cash may require some judgment as to the amount of petty cash needed.
19. EFT is the same as safekeeping.
20. The drawer is the person who receives the check.
21. A debit memo will increase the depositor's balance.
22. A change fund uses only one denomination.
23. The payer is the person or company the check is payable to.

Part IV Instructions

Based on the following situation, prepare a bank reconciliation.

The checkbook balance of Moore Company is $3,763.08. The bank statement shows a bank balance of $6,480. The bank statement shows interest earned of $42 and a service charge of $29.76. There is a deposit in transit of $2,558.22. Outstanding checks total $3,762.90. The bank collected a note for Moore for $4,200. Moore Company forgot to deduct a check for $2,700 during the month.

SOLUTIONS TO SUMMARY PRACTICE TEST

PART I

1.	restrictive endorsements	**6.**	change fund
2.	added	**7.**	miscellaneous income
3.	journal entries	**8.**	checks outstanding
4.	asset	**9.**	decrease
5.	journal	**10.**	safekeeping

Part II

1.	b, d, e	**6.**	a, d
2.	c	**7.**	b, d
3.	c	**8.**	c
4.	a, d	**9.**	a, d
5.	c	**10.**	b, d

Part III

1.	false	**6.**	false	**11.**	true	**16.**	false	**21.**	false
2.	false	**7.**	false	**12.**	true	**17.**	true	**22.**	false
3.	false	**8.**	false	**13.**	true	**18.**	true	**23.**	false
4.	false	**9.**	true	**14.**	false	**19.**	false		
5.	true	**10.**	false	**15.**	false	**20.**	false		

Part IV

MOORE CO.			BANK BALANCE	
Checkbook Balance		$3,763.08	Bank Balance	$6,480.00
ADD:			ADD:	
			Deposit	
Interest	$ 42		in Transit	2,558.22
Collection of note	4,200	4,242.00		$9,038.22
		8,005.08		
DEDUCT:			DEDUCT:	
Service Chg.	$ 29.76		Check outstanding	$3,762.90
Error	2,700.00	2,729.76		
Reconciled Balance		$5,275.32	Reconciled Balance	$5,275.32

CONTINUING PROBLEM FOR CHAPTER 6

ELDORADO COMPUTER CENTER
GENERAL JOURNAL

PAGE 3

Date	Account Titles and Description	PR	Dr.	Cr.

CASH 　　　　　　　　**ACCOUNT NO. 1000**

Date		Explanation	Post Ref.	Debit	Credit	Balance Debit	Balance Credit
9/30	0X	Balance forward	✓			1 6 4 5 00	

PETTY CASH 　　　　　　　　**ACCOUNT NO. 1010**

Date		Explanation	Post Ref.	Debit	Credit	Balance Debit	Balance Credit

ACCOUNTS RECEIVABLE   ACCOUNT NO. <u>1020</u>

Date		Explanation	Post Ref.	Debit	Credit	Balance	
						Debit	Credit
9/30	0X	Balance forward	✓			2 6 0 0 00	

PREPAID RENT   ACCOUNT NO. <u>1025</u>

Date		Explanation	Post Ref.	Debit	Credit	Balance	
						Debit	Credit
9/30	0X	Balance forward	✓			4 0 0 00	

SUPPLIES   ACCOUNT NO. <u>1030</u>

Date		Explanation	Post Ref.	Debit	Credit	Balance	
						Debit	Credit
9/30	0X	Balance forward	✓			9 0 00	

COMPUTER SHOP EQUIPMENT   ACCOUNT NO. <u>1080</u>

Date		Explanation	Post Ref.	Debit	Credit	Balance	
						Debit	Credit
9/30	0X	Balance forward	✓			2 4 0 0 00	

ACCUMULATED DEPRECIATION, COMPUTER SHOP EQUIPMENT   ACCOUNT NO. 1081

Date		Explanation	Post Ref.	Debit	Credit	Balance Debit	Balance Credit
9/30	0X	Balance forward	✓				9 9

OFFICE EQUIPMENT   ACCOUNT NO. 1090

Date		Explanation	Post Ref.	Debit	Credit	Balance Debit	Balance Credit
9/30	0X	Balance forward	✓			6 0 0 00	

ACCUMULATED DEPRECIATION, OFFICE EQUIPMENT   ACCOUNT NO. 1091

Date		Explanation	Post Ref.	Debit	Credit	Balance Debit	Balance Credit
9/30	0X	Balance forward	✓				2 0 00

ACCOUNTS PAYABLE   ACCOUNT NO. 2000

Date		Explanation	Post Ref.	Debit	Credit	Balance Debit	Balance Credit
9/30	0X	Balance forward	✓				2 1 0 00

T. FREEDMAN, CAPITAL   ACCOUNT NO. <u>3000</u>

Date		Explanation	Post Ref.	Debit	Credit	Balance	
						Debit	Credit
9/30	0X	Balance forward	✓				7 4 0 6 00

T. FREEDMAN, WITHDRAWALS   ACCOUNT NO. <u>3010</u>

Date		Explanation	Post Ref.	Debit	Credit	Balance	
						Debit	Credit

INCOME SUMMARY   ACCOUNT NO. <u>3020</u>

Date		Explanation	Post Ref.	Debit	Credit	Balance	
						Debit	Credit

SERVICE REVENUE   ACCOUNT NO. <u>4000</u>

Date		Explanation	Post Ref.	Debit	Credit	Balance	
						Debit	Credit

ADVERTISING EXPENSE   ACCOUNT NO. <u>5010</u>

Date		Explanation	Post Ref.	Debit	Credit	Balance	
						Debit	Credit

RENT EXPENSE   ACCOUNT NO. <u>5020</u>

Date		Explanation	Post Ref.	Debit	Credit	Balance	
						Debit	Credit

UTILITIES EXPENSE   ACCOUNT NO. 5030

Date	Explanation	Post Ref.	Debit	Credit	Balance Debit	Balance Credit

PHONE EXPENSE   ACCOUNT NO. 5040

Date	Explanation	Post Ref.	Debit	Credit	Balance Debit	Balance Credit

SUPPLIES EXPENSE   ACCOUNT NO. 5050

Date	Explanation	Post Ref.	Debit	Credit	Balance Debit	Balance Credit

INSURANCE EXPENSE   ACCOUNT NO. 5060

Date	Explanation	Post Ref.	Debit	Credit	Balance Debit	Balance Credit

POSTAGE EXPENSE   ACCOUNT NO. <u>5070</u>

Date		Explanation	Post Ref.	Debit	Credit	Balance	
						Debit	Credit

DEPRECIATION EXPENSE, COMPUTER SHOP EQUIPMENT   ACCOUNT NO. <u>5080</u>

Date		Explanation	Post Ref.	Debit	Credit	Balance	
						Debit	Credit

DEPRECIATION EXPENSE, OFFICE EQUIPMENT   ACCOUNT NO. <u>5090</u>

Date		Explanation	Post Ref.	Debit	Credit	Balance	
						Debit	Credit

MISCELLANEOUS EXPENSE   ACCOUNT NO. <u>5100</u>

Date		Explanation	Post Ref.	Debit	Credit	Balance	
						Debit	Credit

ELDORADO COMPUTER CENTER
TRIAL BALANCE
OCTOBER 31, 200X

AUXILIARY PETTY CASH RECORD

Date	Voucher No.	Description	Receipts	Payment	Category of Payment					
					Postage Expense	Supplies Expense	Account	Sundry Amount		

Name _____ Class _____ Date _____

ELDORADO COMPUTER CENTER
BANK RECONCILIATION AS OF SEPTEMBER 30, 200X

BALANCE PER BANK

Bank Statement Balance

Add: _____

Deduct: _____

                              _____

Reconciled Balance   _____

CHECKBOOK BALANCE

Checkbook Balance

Add:

                                                    _____

Deduct:

                                                    _____

Reconciled Balance   _____

Name _____ Class _____ Date _____

YOU MAKE THE CALL: CRITICAL THINKING/ETHICAL CASE

_____
_____
_____
_____
_____
_____
_____
_____
_____
_____
_____
_____
_____
_____
_____
_____
_____
_____
_____
_____

INTERNET EXERCISES

_____
_____
_____
_____
_____
_____
_____
_____
_____
_____
_____
_____
_____
_____
_____
_____
_____
_____
_____
_____
_____
_____

FORMS FOR CHAPTER 7
MINI EXERCISES

1. A. _____
       _____
       _____
       _____

    B. _____
       _____
       _____
       _____

2. _____
    _____
    _____
    _____
    _____
    _____

3. _____
    _____
    _____
    _____
    _____

4. A. _____ D. _____
    B. _____ E. _____
    C. _____ F. _____

5.
    A. _____
    B. _____
    C. _____
    D. _____
    E. _____

FORMS FOR EXERCISES

7-1.

Jose _____

Jill _____
_____

Dale _____
_____

7-2. _____
_____
_____
_____
_____
_____
_____
_____
_____
_____
_____

7-3.

ACCOUNT	CATEGORY	↑ NORMAL BALANCE	STATEMENTS FOUND ON

7-4. _____
_____
_____
_____
_____
_____
_____

7-5.

END OF CHAPTER PROBLEMS

PROBLEM 7A-1 OR PROBLEM 7B-1

Employee	Hourly Rate	# of Hours Worked	Gross Earnings
A.			
B.			
C.			
D.			

A.   B.

C.   D.

PROBLEM 7A-2 OR PROBLEM 7B-2

Use the fold-out payroll register located at the end of this study guide.

PROBLEM 7A-3 OR PROBLEM 7B-3

Use the fold-out payroll register located at the end of this study guide.

PROBLEM 7A-3 OR PROBLEM 7B-3 (CONCLUDED)

GENERAL JOURNAL

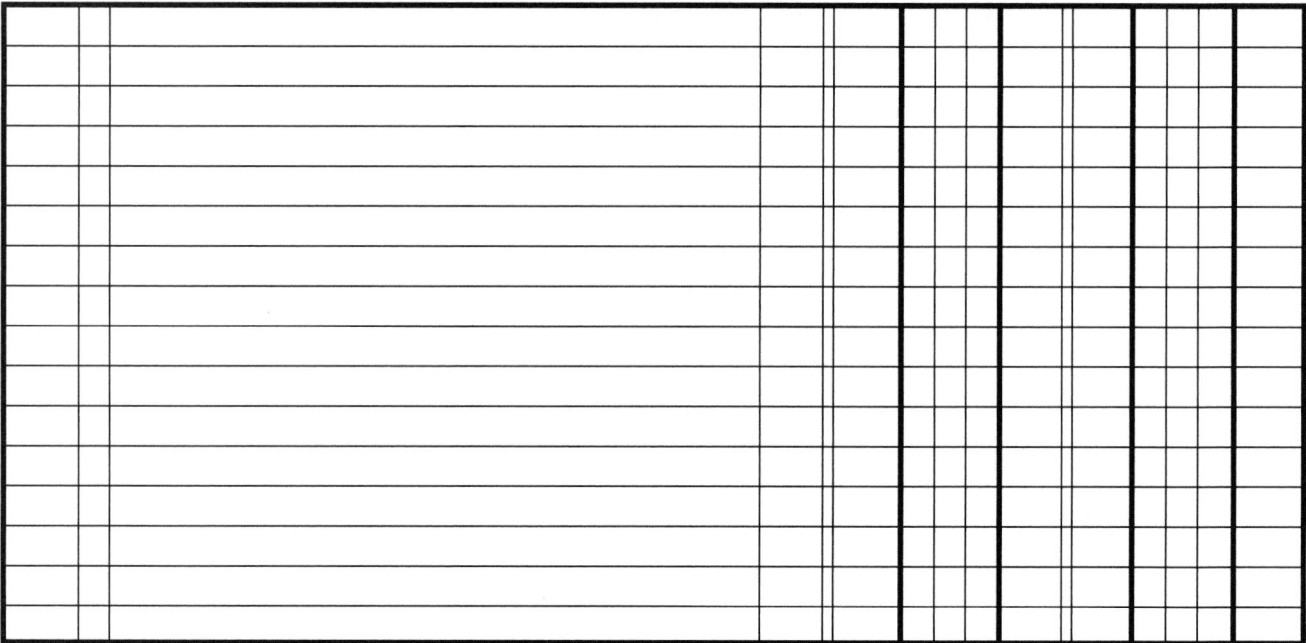

PROBLEM 7A-4 OR PROBLEM 7B-4

Use the fold-out payroll register located at the end of this study guide.

PROBLEM 7A-4 OR PROBLEM 7B-4 (CONTINUED)

GENERAL JOURNAL

Date	Account Titles and Description	PR	Dr.	Cr.

PROBLEM 7A-4 OR PROBLEM 7B-4 (CONTINUED)

PARTIAL GENERAL LEDGER

FICA—SOCIAL SECURITY PAYABLE   ACCOUNT NO. 210

Date	Explanation	Post Ref.	Debit	Credit	Balance Debit	Balance Credit

FICA—MEDICARE PAYABLE   ACCOUNT NO. 212

Date	Explanation	Post Ref.	Debit	Credit	Balance Debit	Balance Credit

FIT PAYABLE   ACCOUNT NO. 214

Date	Explanation	Post Ref.	Debit	Credit	Balance Debit	Balance Credit

SIT PAYABLE   ACCOUNT NO. 216

Date	Explanation	Post Ref.	Debit	Credit	Balance Debit	Balance Credit

PROBLEM 7A-4 OR PROBLEM 7B-4 (CONCLUDED)

UNION DUES PAYABLE   ACCOUNT NO. 218

Date	Explanation	Post Ref.	Debit	Credit	Balance Debit	Balance Credit

WAGES AND SALARIES PAYABLE   ACCOUNT NO. 220

Date	Explanation	Post Ref.	Debit	Credit	Balance Debit	Balance Credit

FACTORY SALARIES EXPENSE   ACCOUNT NO. 610

Date	Explanation	Post Ref.	Debit	Credit	Balance Debit	Balance Credit

OFFICE SALARIES EXPENSE   ACCOUNT NO. 612

Date	Explanation	Post Ref.	Debit	Credit	Balance Debit	Balance Credit

CHAPTER 7
SUMMARY PRACTICE TEST:
PAYROLL CONCEPTS AND PROCEDURES—EMPLOYEE TAXES

PART I INSTRUCTIONS

Fill in the blank (s) to complete the statement.

1. The _____ _____ _____
   _____ states the maximum hours a worker will work at regular rate of pay.

2. Form _____ aids the employer in knowing how much to deduct for federal income tax.

3. The base for FICA-Medicare will _____ _____ from year to year.

4. _____ _____ of the employer's tax guide has tables available for deductions for FIT and FICA (Social Security and Medicare).

5. _____ _____ _____ protects employees against losses due to injury or death incurred while on the job.

6. Data from the _____ _____ will provide the needed information to record the payroll entry in the general journal.

7. The _____ _____ _____
   _____ in the payroll register identifies how the total gross earnings are to be charged to specific accounts.

8. The credit to Wages and Salaries Payable in recording the payroll entry in the general journal represents _____ _____ .

9. FICA-Social Security Payable is a _____ found on the balance sheet.

10. Each quarter has _____ weeks.

Part II Instructions

Answer true or false to the following.

1. The individual earnings record is updated from the general journal.

2. The account distribution columns of the payroll register provide data to record which accounts will be debited to record the total payroll when a journal entry is prepared.

3. FICA-Medicare Payable is an asset for the employer.

4. Gross pay plus deductions equals net pay.

5. Form W-4 aids in calculating FICA-Social Security.

6. The employer will match the employee's contribution for FICA (Social Security and Medicare).

7. Each quarter has 13 weeks.

8. The normal balance of FIT Payable is a credit.

9. The Wage-Bracket Table makes it more difficult to calculate the amount of deductions for FIT.

10. A calendar year has no effect on taxes for FICA-Social Security.

Part III Instructions

Complete the chart below (use table in text as needed). Use the following information: Before this payroll John Roll had earned $86,900. This week John earned $900 for the past two weeks. Assume a FICA rate of Social Security of 6.2% up to $87,000. Medicare, 1.45%. John is single, claiming one deduction. The state income tax is 7 percent.

| GROSS PAY | TAXABLE FICA | DEDUCTIONS FICA | | FIT | SIT | NET PAY |
		Soc. Sec.	Med.			

CHAPTER 7
SOLUTIONS TO SUMMARY PRACTICE TEST

Part I

1. Fair Labors Standards Act
2. W-4
3. Not change
4. Circular E
5. Workers' Compensation Insurance

6. Payroll register
7. Labor distribution account numbers
8. Net earnings
9. Liability
10. 13

Part II

1. false
2. true
3. false
4. false
5. false

6. true
7. true
8. true
9. false
10. false

Part III

```
FICA
Social Security    $100 x.062 =     $ 6.20
Medicare           900 x.0145 =      13.05
FIT                by table          92.000      $900.00
SIT                900 x.07           63.00      - 174.25
Total deductions                    $174.25      $725.75
```

CONTINUING PROBLEM FOR CHAPTER 7*

ELDORADO COMPUTER CENTER
GENERAL JOURNAL

PAGE 4

Date		Account Titles and Description	PR		Dr.		Cr.	

* Payroll register is located in envelope at end of study guide/working papers.

ELDORADO COMPUTER CENTER
GENERAL JOURNAL

Date	Account Titles and Description	PR	Dr.	Cr.

CASH   ACCOUNT NO. **1000**

Date		Explanation	Post Ref.	Debit	Credit	Balance								
								Debit				Credit		
10/31	0X	Balance forward	√			4	2	9	3	00				

PETTY CASH   ACCOUNT NO. **1010**

Date		Explanation	Post Ref.	Debit	Credit	Balance								
								Debit				Credit		
10/31	0X	Balance forward	√				1	0	0	00				

ACCOUNTS RECEIVABLE   ACCOUNT NO. **1020**

Date		Explanation	Post Ref.	Debit	Credit	Balance								
								Debit				Credit		
10/31	0X	Balance forward	√			4	2	0	0	00				

PREPAID RENT   ACCOUNT NO. <u>1025</u>

Date		Explanation	Post Ref.	Debit	Credit	Balance	
						Debit	Credit
10/31	0X	Balance forward	√			1 6 0 0 00	

SUPPLIES   ACCOUNT NO. <u>1030</u>

Date		Explanation	Post Ref.	Debit	Credit	Balance	
						Debit	Credit
10/31	0X	Balance forward	√			1 3 2 00	

COMPUTER SHOP EQUIPMENT   ACCOUNT NO. <u>1080</u>

Date		Explanation	Post Ref.	Debit	Credit	Balance	
						Debit	Credit
10/31	0X	Balance forward	√			2 4 0 0 00	

ACCUMULATED DEPRECIATION, COMPUTER SHOP EQUIPMENT   ACCOUNT NO. <u>1081</u>

Date		Explanation	Post Ref.	Debit	Credit	Balance	
						Debit	Credit
10/31	0X	Balance forward	√				9 9 00

OFFICE EQUIPMENT

ACCOUNT NO. 1090

Date		Explanation	Post Ref.	Debit	Credit	Balance	
						Debit	Credit
10/31	0X	Balance forward	√			6 0 0 00	

ACCUMULATED DEPRECIATION, OFFICE EQUIPMENT

ACCOUNT NO. 1091

Date		Explanation	Post Ref.	Debit	Credit	Balance	
						Debit	Credit
10/31	0X	Balance forward	√				2 0 00

ACCOUNTS PAYABLE

ACCOUNT NO. 2000

Date		Explanation	Post Ref.	Debit	Credit	Balance	
						Debit	Credit
10/31	0X	Balance forward	√				5 0 00

WAGES PAYABLE

ACCOUNT NO. 2010

Date		Explanation	Post Ref.	Debit	Credit	Balance	
						Debit	Credit

PARTIAL GENERAL LEDGER

FICA—SOCIAL SECURITY PAYABLE　　　　**ACCOUNT NO. 2020**

Date	Explanation	Post Ref.	Debit	Credit	Balance Debit	Balance Credit

FICA—MEDICARE PAYABLE　　　　**ACCOUNT NO. 2030**

Date	Explanation	Post Ref.	Debit	Credit	Balance Debit	Balance Credit

FIT PAYABLE　　　　**ACCOUNT NO. 2040**

Date	Explanation	Post Ref.	Debit	Credit	Balance Debit	Balance Credit

SIT PAYABLE　　　　**ACCOUNT NO. 2050**

Date	Explanation	Post Ref.	Debit	Credit	Balance Debit	Balance Credit

T. FREEDMAN CAPITAL   ACCOUNT NO. 3000

Date		Explanation	Post Ref.	Debit	Credit	Balance Debit	Balance Credit
10/31	0X	Balance forward	√				7 4 0 6 00

T. FREEDMAN WITHDRAWALS   ACCOUNT NO.

Date		Explanation	Post Ref.	Debit	Credit	Balance Debit	Balance Credit
10/31	0X	Balance forward	√			2 0 1 5 00	

SERVICE REVENUE   ACCOUNT NO. 4000

Date		Explanation	Post Ref.	Debit	Credit	Balance Debit	Balance Credit
10/31	0X	Balance forward	√				7 8 0 0 00

ADVERTISING EXPENSE   ACCOUNT NO. 5010

Date		Explanation	Post Ref.	Debit	Credit	Balance Debit	Balance Credit

RENT EXPENSE   ACCOUNT NO. 5020

Date		Explanation	Post Ref.	Debit	Credit	Balance Debit	Balance Credit

UTILITIES EXPENSE   ACCOUNT NO. 5030

Date		Explanation	Post Ref.	Debit	Credit	Balance	
						Debit	Credit

PHONE EXPENSE   ACCOUNT NO. 5040

Date		Explanation	Post Ref.	Debit	Credit	Balance	
						Debit	Credit

SUPPLIES EXPENSE   ACCOUNT NO. 5050

Date		Explanation	Post Ref.	Debit	Credit	Balance	
						Debit	Credit

INSURANCE EXPENSE   ACCOUNT NO. 5060

Date		Explanation	Post Ref.	Debit	Credit	Balance	
						Debit	Credit

POSTAGE EXPENSE   ACCOUNT NO. 5070

Date		Explanation	Post Ref.	Debit	Credit	Balance	
						Debit	Credit
10/31	0X	Balance forward	√			2 5 00	

DEPRECIATION EXPENSE C. S. EQUIPMENT **ACCOUNT NO. 5080**

Date		Explanation	Post Ref.	Debit	Credit	Balance	
						Debit	Credit

DEPRECIATION EXPENSE OFFICE EQUIPMENT **ACCOUNT NO. 5090**

Date		Explanation	Post Ref.	Debit	Credit	Balance	
						Debit	Credit

MISCELLANEOUS EXPENSE **ACCOUNT NO. 5100**

Date		Explanation	Post Ref.	Debit	Credit	Balance	
						Debit	Credit
10/31	0X	Balance forward	√			1 0 00	

WAGES EXPENSE **ACCOUNT NO. 5110**

Date		Explanation	Post Ref.	Debit	Credit	Balance	
						Debit	Credit

ELDORADO COMPUTER CENTER
TRIAL BALANCE
NOVEMBER 30, 200X

	Dr.	Cr.

The Employer's Tax Responsibilities: Principles and Procedures

8

SELF-REVIEW QUIZ 8-1

GENERAL JOURNAL

Date	Account Titles and Description	PR	Dr.	Cr.

SELF-REVIEW QUIZ 8-2

1.

2.

SELF-REVIEW QUIZ 8-3

1. _____ 2. _____ 3. _____ 4. _____ 5. _____ 6. _____

YOU MAKE THE CALL: CRITICAL THINKING/ETHICAL CASE

_____
_____
_____
_____
_____
_____
_____
_____
_____
_____
_____
_____
_____
_____
_____
_____
_____
_____
_____

INTERNET EXERCISES

_____
_____
_____
_____
_____
_____
_____
_____
_____
_____
_____
_____
_____
_____
_____
_____
_____
_____
_____
_____
_____
_____

Name _____ Class _____ Date _____

FORMS FOR MINI EXERCISES

1.

A. B. C. D. E.			

2.

_____

_____

_____

_____

3.

A. _____

B. _____

C. _____

D. _____

4.

_____

_____

_____

_____

5.

A. _____

B. _____

C. _____

D. _____

E. _____

F. _____

G. _____

FORMS FOR EXERCISES

8-1.

8-2.

8-3.

EXERCISES (CONTINUED)

8-4. _____

_____

_____

_____

_____

_____

_____

_____

8-5. _____

_____

_____

_____

8-6. _____

_____

8-7. _____

_____

_____

8-8.

EXERCISES (CONTINUED)

8-9.

_____

_____

_____

_____

_____

8-10.

_____

_____

_____

_____

END OF CHAPTER PROBLEMS

PROBLEM 8A-1 OR PROBLEM 8B-1

Employee	Allowance & Marital Status	Gross	FICA		Federal Income Tax
			Soc. Sec.	Medicare	

(2)

PROBLEM 8A-2 OR PROBLEM 8B-2

Date	Account Titles and Description	PR	Dr.	Cr.

PROBLEM 8A-2 OR PROBLEM 8B-2 (CONCLUDED)

Date	Account Titles and Description	PR	Dr.	Cr.

PROBLEM 8A-3 OR PROBLEM 8B-3

Form **941**

Department of the Treasury
Internal Revenue Service

Employer's Quarterly Federal Tax Return

See separate instructions for information on completing this return.

Please type or print.

Enter state code for state in which deposits were made ONLY if different from state in address to the right (see page 2 of instructions).

Name (as distinguished from trade name)

Date quarter ended

Trade name, if any

Employer identification number

Address (number and street)

City, state, and ZIP code

OMB No. 1545-0029

| T |
| FF |
| FD |
| FP |
| I |
| T |

If address is different from prior return, check here

IRS Use

| 1 1 1 1 1 1 1 1 1 1 | 2 | 3 3 3 3 3 3 3 3 | 4 4 4 | 5 5 5 |
| 6 | 7 | 8 8 8 8 8 8 8 8 | 9 9 9 | 10 10 10 10 10 10 10 10 10 |

If you do not have to file returns in the future, check here ☐ and enter date final wages paid

If you are a seasonal employer, see **Seasonal employers** on page 1 of the instructions and check here ☐

1	Number of employees in the pay period that includes March 12th .	1		
2	Total wages and tips, plus other compensation		**2**	
3	Total income tax withheld from wages, tips, and sick pay		**3**	
4	Adjustment of withheld income tax for preceding quarters of calendar year		**4**	
5	Adjusted total of income tax withheld (line 3 as adjusted by line 4—see instructions) . . .		**5**	

6	Taxable social security wages	6a		12.4% (.124) =	6b	
	Taxable social security tips	6c		12.4% (.124) =	6d	
7	Taxable Medicare wages and tips . . .	7a		2.9% (.029) =	7b	

8	Total social security and Medicare taxes (add lines 6b, 6d, and 7b). Check here if wages are not subject to social security and/or Medicare tax . . . . ☐	**8**	
9	Adjustment of social security and Medicare taxes (see instructions for required explanation) Sick Pay $ _____ Fractions of Cents $ _____ Other $ _____ =	**9**	
10	Adjusted total of social security and Medicare taxes (line 8 as adjusted by line 9—see instructions)	**10**	
11	**Total taxes** (add lines 5 and 10)	**11**	
12	Advance earned income credit (EIC) payments made to employees	**12**	
13	Net taxes (subtract line 12 from line 11). **If $2,500 or more, this must equal line 17, column (d) below (or line D of Schedule B (Form 941))**	**13**	
14	Total deposits for quarter, including overpayment applied from a prior quarter	**14**	
15	**Balance due** (subtract line 14 from line 13). See instructions	**15**	

16 **Overpayment.** If line 14 is more than line 13, enter excess here $ _____

and check if to be: ☐ Applied to next return **OR** ☐ Refunded.

All filers: If line 13 is less than $1,000, you need not complete line 17 or Schedule B (Form 941).

Semiweekly schedule depositors: Complete Schedule B (Form 941) and check here . . . . ☐

Monthly schedule depositors: Complete line 17, columns (a) through (d), and check here. . . . . ☐

17	**Monthly Summary of Federal Tax Liability.** Do not complete if you were a semiweekly schedule depositor.			
	(a) First month liability	**(b)** Second month liability	**(c)** Third month liability	**(d)** Total liability for quarter

Sign Here

Under penalties of perjury, I declare that I have examined this return, including accompanying schedules and statements, and to the best of my knowledge and belief, it is true, correct, and complete.

Signature _____ Print Your Name and Title _____ Date _____

For Privacy Act and Paperwork Reduction Act Notice, see back of Payment Voucher. Cat. No. 17001Z Form **941**

PROBLEM 8A-4 OR PROBLEM 8B-4

Form **941**

Department of the Treasury
Internal Revenue Service

Employer's Quarterly Federal Tax Return

See separate instructions for information on completing this return.

Please type or print.

Enter state code for state in which deposits were made ONLY if different from state in address to the right (see page 2 of instructions).

Name (as distinguished from trade name)

Trade name, if any

Address (number and street)

Date quarter ended

Employer identification number

City, state, and ZIP code

OMB No. 1545-0029

T
FF
FD
FP
I
T

If address is different from prior return, check here

IRS Use

1	1	1	1	1	1	1	1	1	1	2	3	3	3	3	3	3	3	4	4	4	5	5	5
6	7	8	8	8	8	8	8	8	8		9	9	9	10	10	10	10	10	10	10	10	10	10

If you do not have to file returns in the future, check here ☐ and enter date final wages paid _____

If you are a seasonal employer, see **Seasonal employers** on page 1 of the instructions and check here ☐

1	Number of employees in the pay period that includes March 12th .	1	
2	Total wages and tips, plus other compensation	2	
3	Total income tax withheld from wages, tips, and sick pay	3	
4	Adjustment of withheld income tax for preceding quarters of calendar year	4	
5	Adjusted total of income tax withheld (line 3 as adjusted by line 4—see instructions) . . .	5	

6	Taxable social security wages	6a		12.4% (.124) =	6b	
	Taxable social security tips	6c		12.4% (.124) =	6d	
7	Taxable Medicare wages and tips . . .	7a		2.9% (.029) =	7b	

8	Total social security and Medicare taxes (add lines 6b, 6d, and 7b). Check here if wages are not subject to social security and/or Medicare tax . . . . ☐	8	
9	Adjustment of social security and Medicare taxes (see instructions for required explanation) Sick Pay $ _____ Fractions of Cents $ _____ Other $ _____ =	9	
10	Adjusted total of social security and Medicare taxes (line 8 as adjusted by line 9—see instructions)	10	
11	**Total taxes** (add lines 5 and 10)	11	
12	Advance earned income credit (EIC) payments made to employees	12	
13	Net taxes (subtract line 12 from line 11). **If $2,500 or more, this must equal line 17, column (d) below (or line D of Schedule B (Form 941))**	13	
14	Total deposits for quarter, including overpayment applied from a prior quarter	14	
15	**Balance due** (subtract line 14 from line 13). See instructions	15	
16	**Overpayment.** If line 14 is more than line 13, enter excess here ▶ $ _____		

and check if to be: ☐ Applied to next return **OR** ☐ Refunded.

All filers: If line 13 is less than $1,000, you need not complete line 17 or Schedule B (Form 941).

Semiweekly schedule depositors: Complete Schedule B (Form 941) and check here . . . . ☐

Monthly schedule depositors: Complete line 17, columns (a) through (d), and check here. . . . . ☐

17	**Monthly Summary of Federal Tax Liability.** Do not complete if you were a semiweekly schedule depositor.		
(a) First month liability	**(b)** Second month liability	**(c)** Third month liability	**(d)** Total liability for quarter

Sign Here

Under penalties of perjury, I declare that I have examined this return, including accompanying schedules and statements, and to the best of my knowledge and belief, it is true, correct, and complete.

Signature _____ Print Your Name and Title _____ Date _____

For Privacy Act and Paperwork Reduction Act Notice, see back of Payment Voucher.

Cat. No. 17001Z

Form **941**

Form **940-EZ**

Department of the Treasury
Internal Revenue Service   (99)

Employer's Annual Federal Unemployment (FUTA) Tax Return

See separate **Instructions for Form 940-EZ** for information on completing this form.

OMB No. 1545-1110

200X

T	
FF	
FD	
FP	
I	
T	

Name (as distinguished from trade name)   Calendar year

Trade name, if any

Address and ZIP code   Employer identification number

Answer the questions under **Who May Use Form 940-EZ** *on page 2. If you cannot use Form 940-EZ, you must use Form 940.*

A Enter the amount of contributions paid to your state unemployment fund. (See separate instructions.) . . . $ ------------------------------

B (1) Enter the name of the state where you have to pay contributions . . . . ------------------------------
    (2) Enter your state reporting number as shown on your state unemployment tax return

If you will not have to file returns in the future, check here (see **Who Must File** in separate instructions), **and complete and sign the return.** ☐

If this is an Amended Return, check here . . . . ☐

Part I — Taxable Wages and FUTA Tax

1	Total payments (including payments shown on lines 2 and 3) during the calendar year for services of employees	**1**	
2	Exempt payments. (Explain all exempt payments, attaching additional sheets if necessary.) ---------------------------------- ----------------------------------	**2**	
3	Payments of more than $7,000 for services. Enter only amounts over the first $7,000 paid to each employee. Do not include any exempt payments from line 2. (See separate instructions.) The $7,000 amount is the Federal wage base. Your state wage base may be different. **Do not use your state wage limitation**	**3**	
4	Total exempt payments (add lines 2 and 3)	**4**	
5	**Total taxable wages** (subtract line 4 from line 1)	**5**	
6	**FUTA tax.** Multiply the wages on line 5 by .008 and enter here. (**If the result is over $100, also complete Part II.**)	**6**	
7	Total FUTA tax deposited for the year, including any overpayment applied from a prior year	**7**	
8	**Balance due** (subtract line 7 from line 6). Pay to the **"United States Treasury"**	**8**	
	If you owe more than $100, see **Depositing FUTA tax** in separate instructions.		
9	**Overpayment** (subtract line 6 from line 7). Check if it is to be: ☐ **Applied to next return or** ☐ **Refunded**	**9**	

Part II — Record of Quarterly Federal Unemployment Tax Liability (Do not include state liability.) **Complete only if line 6 is over $100.**

Quarter	First (Jan. 1 – Mar. 31)	Second (Apr. 1 – June 30)	Third (July 1 – Sept. 30)	Fourth (Oct. 1 – Dec. 31)	Total for year
Liability for quarter					

Under penalties of perjury, I declare that I have examined this return, including accompanying schedules and statements, and, to the best of my knowledge and belief, it is true, correct, and complete, and that no part of any payment made to a state unemployment fund claimed as a credit was, or is to be, deducted from the payments to employees.

CHAPTER 8
SUMMARY PRACTICE TEST:
THE EMPLOYER'S TAX RESPONSIBILITIES—
PRINCIPLES AND PROCEDURES

Part I Instructions

Fill in the blank(s) to complete the statement.

1. Only the _____ completes the SS-4 Form.
2. The payroll tax expense for the employer is made up of _____, _____, and FUTA.
3. The employer is responsible for paying for _____.
4. SUTA is usually paid _____.
5. FUTA Payable is a _____ found on the _____ _____.
6. Form 941 summarizes the taxes owed for _____ and _____.
7. _____ _____ _____ will tell if a deposit is to be made monthly, or semi-weekly for FIT and Social Security.
8. Form _____ is prepared quarterly to summarize tax liabilities for FICA (Social Security and Medicare) and FIT
9. The _____ _____ _____ _____ is required to be given to employees by January 31 following the year employed.
10. Form 940EZ records the amount of tax liability for _____.

Part II Instructions

Answer true or false to the following.

1. Prepaid Workers' Compensation Insurance is an asset.
2. Workers' compensation need not be estimated at the beginning of the year.
3. Payroll Tax Expense is made up of FICA, SUTA, and FIT
4. Frequency of deposits relating to Form 941 is based on amount of tax liability in lookback periods.
5. The maximum tax credit for state unemployment tax is .8% against the FUTA tax.
6. The individual earnings record provides the data to prepare W-2's.
7. A tax calendar provides little help to the employer involving the payment of tax liabilities.
8. Form 941 is completed twice a year.
9. A year-end adjusting entry is needed for workers' compensation.
10. Form 8109 relates only to Form 940EZ.

Part III Instructions

Complete the following table:

ACCOUNT	CATEGORY	FOUND ON WHICH REPORT
1. Payroll Tax Expense		
2. FUTA Payable		
3. SUTA Payable		
4. FICA Tax Payable—Medicare		
5. FIT Payable		
6. Office Salaries Expense		

Part IV Instructions

Complete the following table:

	4 QUARTERS LOOK-BACK PERIOD LIABILITY	PAYROLL PAID WEEKLY	TAX PAID BY:
Sit. A	$40,000	October	?
Sit. B	75,000		
		on Wed.	?
		on Thurs.	?
		on Fri	?
		on Sat.	?
		on Sun.	?
		on Mon.	?
		on. Tues.	?

Why is Depositor in Situation A classified as a Monthly Depositor while in Situation B Depositor is classified as Semi-Weekly?

SOLUTIONS TO SUMMARY PRACTICE TEST

Part I

1. Employer
2. FICA (Social Security and Medicare), SUTA
3. FUTA (SUTA)
4. quarterly
5. liability, balance sheet
6. FICA (Social Security and Medicare), FIT
7. Look-Back Periods
8. 941
9. wage and tax statement
10. FUTA

Part II

1.	true	**6.**	true
2.	false	**7.**	false
3.	false	**8.**	false
4.	true	**9.**	true
5.	false	**10.**	false

Part III

1. Expense; Income Statement
2. Liability; Balance Sheet
3. Liability; Balance Sheet
4. Liability; Balance Sheet
5. Liability; Balance Sheet
6. Expense; Income Statement

Part IV

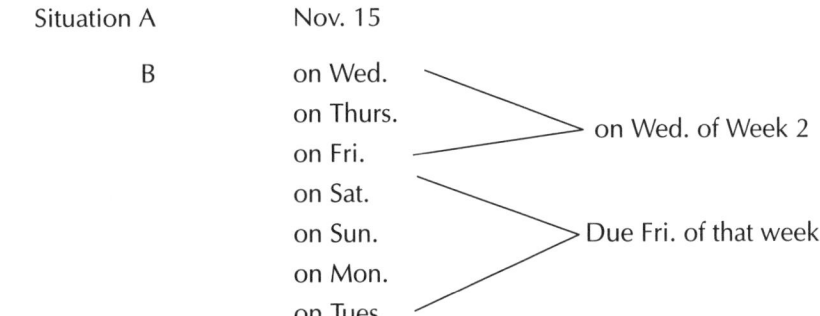

Situation A   Nov. 15

B

on Wed.
on Thurs.
on Fri. → on Wed. of Week 2
on Sat.
on Sun.
on Mon. → Due Fri. of that week
on Tues.

CONTINUING PROBLEM FOR CHAPTER 8
ELDORADO COMPUTER CENTER

ELDORADO COMPUTER CENTER
GENERAL JOURNAL

PAGE 9

Date	Account Titles and Description	PR	Dr.	Cr.

Form **941**

Department of the Treasury
Internal Revenue Service

Employer's Quarterly Federal Tax Return

See separate instructions for information on completing this return.

Please type or print.

Enter state code for state in which deposits were made ONLY if different from state in address to the right (see page 2 of instructions).

Name (as distinguished from trade name)	Date quarter ended
Trade name, if any	Employer identification number
Address (number and street)	City, state, and ZIP code

OMB No. 1545-0029

| T |
| FF |
| FD |
| FP |
| I |
| T |

If address is different from prior return, check here

IRS Use

| 1 | 1 | 1 | 1 | 1 | 1 | 1 | 1 | 1 | 1 | 2 | | 3 | 3 | 3 | 3 | 3 | 3 | 3 | 3 | | 4 | 4 | 4 | | 5 | 5 | 5 |
| 6 | | 7 | | 8 | 8 | 8 | 8 | 8 | 8 | 8 | | | 9 | 9 | 9 | | 10 | 10 | 10 | 10 | 10 | 10 | 10 | 10 | 10 | 10 |

If you do not have to file returns in the future, check here ☐ and enter date final wages paid _____

If you are a seasonal employer, see **Seasonal employers** on page 1 of the instructions and check here ☐

1	Number of employees in the pay period that includes March 12th .	**1**		
2	Total wages and tips, plus other compensation	**2**	
3	Total income tax withheld from wages, tips, and sick pay	**3**	
4	Adjustment of withheld income tax for preceding quarters of calendar year	**4**	
5	Adjusted total of income tax withheld (line 3 as adjusted by line 4—see instructions) . . .	**5**	
6	Taxable social security wages	**6a**		12.4% (.124) =	**6b**	
	Taxable social security tips	**6c**		12.4% (.124) =	**6d**	
7	Taxable Medicare wages and tips . . .	**7a**		2.9% (.029) =	**7b**	
8	Total social security and Medicare taxes (add lines 6b, 6d, and 7b). Check here if wages are not subject to social security and/or Medicare tax . . . . ☐	**8**	
9	Adjustment of social security and Medicare taxes (see instructions for required explanation) Sick Pay $ _____ Fractions of Cents $ _____ Other $ _____ =	**9**	
10	Adjusted total of social security and Medicare taxes (line 8 as adjusted by line 9—see instructions)	**10**	
11	**Total taxes** (add lines 5 and 10)	**11**	
12	Advance earned income credit (EIC) payments made to employees	**12**	
13	Net taxes (subtract line 12 from line 11). **If $2,500 or more, this must equal line 17, column (d) below (or line D of Schedule B (Form 941))**	**13**	
14	Total deposits for quarter, including overpayment applied from a prior quarter	**14**	
15	**Balance due** (subtract line 14 from line 13). See instructions	**15**	
16	**Overpayment.** If line 14 is more than line 13, enter excess here $ _____		

and check if to be: ☐ Applied to next return **OR** ☐ Refunded.

All filers: If line 13 is less than $1,000, you need not complete line 17 or Schedule B (Form 941).

Semiweekly schedule depositors: Complete Schedule B (Form 941) and check here . . . . ☐

Monthly schedule depositors: Complete line 17, columns (a) through (d), and check here. . . . . ☐

17	**Monthly Summary of Federal Tax Liability.** Do not complete if you were a semiweekly schedule depositor.			
(a) First month liability	**(b)** Second month liability	**(c)** Third month liability	**(d)** Total liability for quarter

Sign Here

Under penalties of perjury, I declare that I have examined this return, including accompanying schedules and statements, and to the best of my knowledge and belief, it is true, correct, and complete.

Signature _____ Print Your Name and Title _____ Date _____

For Privacy Act and Paperwork Reduction Act Notice, see back of Payment Voucher.   Cat. No. 17001Z   Form **941**

Name _____ Class _____ Date _____

Form **940-EZ**

Department of the Treasury
Internal Revenue Service (99)

Employer's Annual Federal Unemployment (FUTA) Tax Return

See separate Instructions for Form 940-EZ for information on completing this form.

200X

T	
FF	
FD	
FP	
I	
T	

Name (as distinguished from trade name)

Calendar year

Trade name, if any

Address and ZIP code

Employer identification number

*Answer the questions under **Who May Use Form 940-EZ** on page 2. If you cannot use Form 940-EZ, you must use Form 940.*

A   Enter the amount of contributions paid to your state unemployment fund. (See separate instructions.) . . . $ _____

B   (1) Enter the name of the state where you have to pay contributions . . . . _____
         (2) Enter your state reporting number as shown on your state unemployment tax return

If you will not have to file returns in the future, check here (see **Who Must File** in separate instructions), **and complete and sign the return.** ☐

If this is an Amended Return, check here . . . . ☐

Part I	**Taxable Wages and FUTA Tax**

1   Total payments (including payments shown on lines 2 and 3) during the calendar year for services of employees | **1**

2   Exempt payments. (Explain all exempt payments, attaching additional sheets if necessary.) _____ _____ | **2**

3   Payments of more than $7,000 for services. Enter only amounts over the first $7,000 paid to each employee. Do not include any exempt payments from line 2. (See separate instructions.) The $7,000 amount is the Federal wage base. Your state wage base may be different. **Do not use your state wage limitation** . . . . . . | **3**

4   Total exempt payments (add lines 2 and 3) . . . . | **4**

5   **Total taxable wages** (subtract line 4 from line 1) . . . . | **5**

6   **FUTA tax.** Multiply the wages on line 5 by .008 and enter here. **(If the result is over $100, also complete Part II.)** | **6**

7   Total FUTA tax deposited for the year, including any overpayment applied from a prior year . . . . . | **7**

8   **Balance due** (subtract line 7 from line 6). Pay to the **"United States Treasury"** . . . . | **8**
        If you owe more than $100, see **Depositing FUTA tax** in separate instructions.

9   **Overpayment** (subtract line 6 from line 7). Check if it is to be: ☐ **Applied to next return or** ☐ **Refunded** | **9**

Part II	**Record of Quarterly Federal Unemployment Tax Liability** (Do not include state liability.) **Complete only if line 6 is over $100.**

Quarter	First (Jan. 1 – Mar. 31)	Second (Apr. 1 – June 30)	Third (July 1 – Sept. 30)	Fourth (Oct. 1 – Dec. 31)	Total for year
Liability for quarter					

Under penalties of perjury, I declare that I have examined this return, including accompanying schedules and statements, and, to the best of my knowledge and belief, it is true, correct, and complete, and that no part of any payment made to a state unemployment fund claimed as a credit was, or is to be, deducted from the payments to employees.

MINI PRACTICE SET:
PETE'S MARKET

PETE'S MARKET
GENERAL JOURNAL

PAGE 6

Date	Account Titles and Description	PR	Dr.	Cr.

MINI PRACTICE SET:
PETE'S MARKET

PETE'S MARKET
GENERAL JOURNAL

PAGE 7

Date	Account Titles and Description	PR	Dr.	Cr.

Form **941**

Department of the Treasury
Internal Revenue Service

Employer's Quarterly Federal Tax Return

See separate instructions for information on completing this return.

Please type or print.

Enter state code for state in which deposits were made ONLY if different from state in address to the right (see page 2 of instructions).

Name (as distinguished from trade name)	Date quarter ended
Trade name, if any	Employer identification number
Address (number and street)	City, state, and ZIP code

OMB No. 1545-0029

| T |
| FF |
| FD |
| FP |
| I |
| T |

If address is different from prior return, check here ☐

IRS Use

| 1 | 1 | 1 | 1 | 1 | 1 | 1 | 1 | 1 | 1 | 2 | | 3 | 3 | 3 | 3 | 3 | 3 | 3 | 3 | | 4 | 4 | 4 | | 5 | 5 | 5 |

| 6 | 7 | 8 | 8 | 8 | 8 | 8 | 8 | 8 | 8 | | | 9 | 9 | 9 | | 10 | 10 | 10 | 10 | 10 | 10 | 10 | 10 | 10 | 10 |

If you do not have to file returns in the future, check here ☐ and enter date final wages paid

If you are a seasonal employer, see **Seasonal employers** on page 1 of the instructions and check here

1	Number of employees in the pay period that includes March 12th .	1		
2	Total wages and tips, plus other compensation		**2**	
3	Total income tax withheld from wages, tips, and sick pay		**3**	
4	Adjustment of withheld income tax for preceding quarters of calendar year		**4**	
5	Adjusted total of income tax withheld (line 3 as adjusted by line 4—see instructions) . . .		**5**	

6	Taxable social security wages	**6a**		12.4% (.124) =	**6b**	
	Taxable social security tips	**6c**		12.4% (.124) =	**6d**	
7	Taxable Medicare wages and tips . . .	**7a**		2.9% (.029) =	**7b**	

8	Total social security and Medicare taxes (add lines 6b, 6d, and 7b). Check here if wages are not subject to social security and/or Medicare tax . . . . ☐	**8**	
9	Adjustment of social security and Medicare taxes (see instructions for required explanation) Sick Pay $ _____ Fractions of Cents $ _____ Other $ _____ =	**9**	
10	Adjusted total of social security and Medicare taxes (line 8 as adjusted by line 9—see instructions)	**10**	
11	**Total taxes** (add lines 5 and 10)	**11**	
12	Advance earned income credit (EIC) payments made to employees	**12**	
13	Net taxes (subtract line 12 from line 11). **If $2,500 or more, this must equal line 17, column (d) below (or line D of Schedule B (Form 941))**	**13**	
14	Total deposits for quarter, including overpayment applied from a prior quarter	**14**	
15	**Balance due** (subtract line 14 from line 13). See instructions	**15**	
16	**Overpayment.** If line 14 is more than line 13, enter excess here $ _____ and check if to be: ☐ Applied to next return **OR** ☐ Refunded.		

All filers: If line 13 is less than $1,000, you need not complete line 17 or Schedule B (Form 941).

Semiweekly schedule depositors: Complete Schedule B (Form 941) and check here . . . . ☐

Monthly schedule depositors: Complete line 17, columns (a) through (d), and check here . . . . ☐

17	**Monthly Summary of Federal Tax Liability.** Do not complete if you were a semiweekly schedule depositor.			
	(a) First month liability	**(b)** Second month liability	**(c)** Third month liability	**(d)** Total liability for quarter

Sign Here

Under penalties of perjury, I declare that I have examined this return, including accompanying schedules and statements, and to the best of my knowledge and belief, it is true, correct, and complete.

Signature _____ Print Your Name and Title _____ Date _____

For Privacy Act and Paperwork Reduction Act Notice, see back of Payment Voucher. Cat. No. 17001Z Form **941**

COMPREHENSIVE REVIEW PROBLEM:
PETE'S MARKET

Use the fold-out payroll register located at the end of this study guide.

FICA Social Security Payable 210	
	410.90 (ee)
	410.90 (er)

FICA-Medicare Payable 212	
	100 (ee)
	100 (er)

FIT Payable 220	
	600

SIT Payable 225	
	150

FUTA Tax Payable 230	
	88

SUTA Payable 240	
	155

Special Journals: Sales and Cash Receipts

SELF-REVIEW QUIZ 9-1

1. _____ 2. _____ 3. _____ 4. _____ 5. _____

SELF-REVIEW QUIZ 9-2

1. _____ 2. _____ 3. _____ 4. _____ 5. _____ 6. _____ 7 _____ 8. _____

SELF-REVIEW QUIZ 9-3

SHOES.COM
SALES JOURNAL

PAGE 1

Date		Account Debited	Terms	Invoice No.	Post Ref.	Dr. Acc. Receivable Cr. Sales			

SHOES.COM
GENERAL JOURNAL

PAGE 1

Date		Account Titles and Description	PR	Dr.	Cr.

ACCOUNTS RECEIVABLE SUBSIDIARY LEDGER

NAME JANE COMPANY

ADDRESS 118 MORRIS RD., BOSTON, MA 01935

Date		Explanation	Post Ref.	Debit	Credit	Dr. Balance

NAME RALPH COMPANY

ADDRESS 31 NORRIS ROAD, BOSTON MA 01935

Date		Explanation	Post Ref.	Debit	Credit	Dr. Balance

PARTIAL GENERAL LEDGER

ACCOUNT RECEIVABLE   ACCOUNT NO. 112

Date	Explanation	Post Ref.	Debit	Credit	Balance Debit	Balance Credit

SALES   ACCOUNT NO. 411

Date	Explanation	Post Ref.	Debit	Credit	Balance Debit	Balance Credit

SALES RETURNS AND ALLOWANCES   ACCOUNT NO. 412

Date	Explanation	Post Ref.	Debit	Credit	Balance Debit	Balance Credit

SELF-REVIEW QUIZ 9-4

MOORE COMPANY

CASH RECEIPTS JOURNAL   PAGE 2

Date	Cash Dr.	Sales Discounts Dr.	Accounts Receivable Cr.	Sales Cr.	Account Name	Sundry Pr.	Amount Cr.

PARTIAL GENERAL LEDGER

CASH — ACCOUNT NO. 110

Date 200X		Explanation	Post Ref.	Debit	Credit	Balance Debit	Balance Credit
May	1	Balance	√			600 00	

ACCOUNTS RECEIVABLE — ACCOUNT NO. 120

Date 200X		Explanation	Post Ref.	Debit	Credit	Balance Debit	Balance Credit
May	1	Balance	√			700 00	

STORE EQUIPMENT — ACCOUNT NO. 130

Date 200X		Explanation	Post Ref.	Debit	Credit	Balance Debit	Balance Credit
May	1	Balance	√			600 00	

SALES — ACCOUNT NO. 410

Date 200X		Explanation	Post Ref.	Debit	Credit	Balance Debit	Balance Credit
May	1	Balance	√				700 00

SALES DISCOUNT   **ACCOUNT NO. 420**

Date 200X		Explanation	Post Ref.	Debit	Credit	Balance Debit	Balance Credit

ACCOUNTS RECEIVABLE SUBSIDIARY LEDGER

NAME   **IRENE WELCH**

ADDRESS   **10 RONG RD., BEVERLY, MA 01215**

Date 200X		Explanation	Post Ref.	Debit	Credit	Dr. Balance
May	1	Balance	√			5 0 0 00

NAME   **JANIS FROSS**

ADDRESS   **81 FOSTER RD., BEVERLY, MA 09125**

Date 200X		Explanation	Post Ref.	Debit	Credit	Dr. Balance
May	1	Balance	√			2 0 0 00

FORMS FOR COMPREHENSIVE DEMONSTRATION PROBLEM

WALTER LANTZE CO.
GENERAL JOURNAL

PAGE 1

Date	Account Titles and Description	PR	Dr.	Cr.

WALTER LANTZE CO.
SALES JOURNAL

PAGE 1

Date	Account Debited	Terms	Invoice No.	Post Ref.	Dr. Acc. Receivable Cr. Sales

WALTER LANTZE CO.

CASH RECEIPTS JOURNAL   PAGE 1

Date	Cash Dr.	Sales Discounts Dr.	Accounts Receivable Cr.	Sales Cr.	Sundry Account Name	Pr.	Amount Cr.

Name _____ Class _____ Date _____

PARTIAL GENERAL LEDGER

CASH **ACCOUNT NO. 111**

Date	Explanation	Post Ref.	Debit	Credit	Balance Debit	Balance Credit

ACCOUNTS RECEIVABLE **ACCOUNT NO. 112**

Date	Explanation	Post Ref.	Debit	Credit	Balance Debit	Balance Credit

WALTER LANTZ, CAPITAL **ACCOUNT NO. 311**

Date	Explanation	Post Ref.	Debit	Credit	Balance Debit	Balance Credit

SALES   **ACCOUNT NO. 411**

Date		Explanation	Post Ref.	Debit	Credit	Balance	
						Debit	Credit

SALES RETURNS AND ALLOWANCES   **ACCOUNT NO. 412**

Date		Explanation	Post Ref.	Debit	Credit	Balance	
						Debit	Credit

SALES DISCOUNT   **ACCOUNT NO. 413**

Date		Explanation	Post Ref.	Debit	Credit	Balance	
						Debit	Credit

ACCOUNTS RECEIVABLE SUBSIDIARY LEDGER

NAME BUZZARD CO.

ADDRESS 1000 BURBANK AVE., CALIF 53210

Date 200X		Explanation	Post Ref.	Debit	Credit	Debit Balance

NAME PANDA CO.

ADDRESS 400 GRACIE AVE., LYNN, MA 019417

Date 200X		Explanation	Post Ref.	Debit	Credit	Debit Balance

LANTZE CO.
SCHEDULE OF ACCOUNTS RECEIVABLE
JULY 31, 200X

YOU MAKE THE CALL: CRITICAL THINKING/ETHICAL CASE

_____
_____
_____
_____
_____
_____
_____
_____
_____
_____
_____
_____
_____
_____
_____
_____
_____

INTERNET EXERCISES

_____
_____
_____
_____
_____
_____
_____
_____
_____
_____
_____
_____
_____
_____
_____
_____
_____
_____
_____
_____

CHAPTER 9
FORMS FOR MINI EXERCISES

1.

2.

3.

A. _____   _____
B. _____   _____
C. _____   _____

4.

5.

A. _____
B. _____
C. _____
D. _____

BLUE CO.
SCHEDULE OF ACCOUNTS RECEIVABLE
MAY 31, 200X

FORMS FOR EXERCISES

9-1.

Amazon.com	Accounts Receivable 112

Bill Valley Co.	Sales 412

9-2.

SALES JOURNAL

PAGE 1

Date	Account Debited	Terms	Invoice No.	Post Ref.	Dr. Accounts Receivable Cr. Sales

Bass Co.	Sales 411

Ronald Co.	Accounts Receivable 112	Sales Returns & Allowances 412

GENERAL JOURNAL

PAGE 1

EXERCISES (CONTINUED)

9-3.

CASH RECEIPTS JOURNAL   PAGE 1

Date	Cash Dr.	Sales Discounts Dr.	Accounts Receivable Cr.	Sales Cr.	Sundry Account Names	Post Ref.	Amount Cr.

9-4.

SALES JOURNAL   PAGE 1

Date	Account Debited	Terms	Invoice No.	Post Ref.	Dr. Accounts Receivable Cr. Sales

CASH RECEIPTS JOURNAL   PAGE1

Date	Cash Dr.	Sales Discounts Dr.	Accounts Receivable Cr.	Sales Cr.	Sundry Account Names	Post Ref.	Amount Cr.

EXERCISES (CONTINUED)

GENERAL JOURNAL
PAGE 1

Date	Account Titles and Description	PR	Dr.	Cr.

ACCOUNTS RECEIVABLE SUBSIDIARY LEDGER

Boston Co.

Gary Co.

PARTIAL GENERAL LEDGER

Cash   111

Accounts Receivable   113

Edna Cares, Capital   311

Sales   411

Sales Returns &
Allowances   412

Sales Discount   413

EDNA CO.
SCHEDULE OF ACCOUNTS RECEIVABLE
JUNE 30, 200X

9-5.

END OF CHAPTER PROBLEMS

PROBLEM 9A-1 OR PROBLEM 9B-1

(1,2)

FOOD.COM
SALES JOURNAL

PAGE 1

Date		Account Debited	Invoice No.	PR.	Accounts Receivable Dr.	Pizza Sales Cr.	Grocery Sales Cr.

(1,2)

FOOD.COM
GENERAL JOURNAL

PAGE 1

Date		Account Titles and Description	PR	Dr.	Cr.

PROBLEM 9A-1 OR PROBLEM 9B-1 (CONTINUED)

ACCOUNTS RECEIVABLE SUBSIDIARY LEDGER

NAME   DUNCAN CO.

ADDRESS   942 MOSE ST., REVERE. MA 01938

Date	Explanation	Post Ref.	Debit	Credit	Dr. Balance

NAME   LONG CO.

ADDRESS   8 JOSS AVE., LYNN, MA 01947

Date	Explanation	Post Ref.	Debit	Credit	Dr. Balance

NAME   SUE MOORE CO.

ADDRESS   10 LOST RD., TOPSFIELD, MA 01998

Date	Explanation	Post Ref.	Debit	Credit	Dr. Balance

PROBLEM 9A-1 OR PROBLEM 9B-1 (CONTINUED)

FOOD.COM
GENERAL LEDGER

ACCOUNTS RECEIVABLE   **ACCOUNT NO. 112**

Date		Explanation	Post Ref.	Debit	Credit	Balance	
						Debit	Credit

PIZZA SALES   **ACCOUNT NO. 410**

Date		Explanation	Post Ref.	Debit	Credit	Balance	
						Debit	Credit

GROCERY SALES   **ACCOUNT NO. 411**

Date		Explanation	Post Ref.	Debit	Credit	Balance	
						Debit	Credit

SALES RETURNS AND ALLOWANCES   **ACCOUNT NO. 412**

Date		Explanation	Post Ref.	Debit	Credit	Balance	
						Debit	Credit

PROBLEM 9A-1 OR PROBLEM 9B-1 (CONCLUDED)

FOOD.COM
SCHEDULE OF ACCOUNTS RECEIVABLE
JUNE 30, 200X

PROBLEM 9A-2 OR PROBLEM 9B-2

(1,2)

TED'S AUTO SUPPLY
SALES JOURNAL

PAGE 4

Date	Customer's Name Account Receivable	Invoice No.	PR.	Accounts Receivable Dr.	Sales Tax Payable Cr.	Auto Parts Sales Cr.

PROBLEM 9A-2 OR PROBLEM 9B-2 (CONTINUED)

(1,2)

TED'S AUTO SUPPLY
GENERAL JOURNAL

PAGE 2

Date	Account Titles and Description	PR	Dr.	Cr.

PROBLEM 9A-2 OR PROBLEM 9B-2 (CONTINUED)

ACCOUNTS RECEIVABLE SUBSIDIARY LEDGER

NAME   LANCE CORNER

ADDRESS   9 ROE ST., BARTLETT, NH 01382

Date 200X		Explanation	Post Ref.	Debit	Credit	Dr. Balance
NOV	1	Balance	√			4 0 0 00

NAME   J. SETH

ADDRESS   22 REESE ST., LACONIA, NH 04321

Date 200X		Explanation	Post Ref.	Debit	Credit	Dr. Balance
NOV	1	Balance	√			2 0 0 00

NAME   R. VOLAN

ADDRESS   12 ASTER RD., MERIMACK, NH 02134

Date 200X		Explanation	Post Ref.	Debit	Credit	Dr. Balance
NOV	1	Balance	√			1 0 0 0 00

PROBLEM 9A-2 OR PROBLEM 9B-2 (CONTINUED)

TED'S AUTO SUPPLY
PARTIAL GENERAL LEDGER

ACCOUNTS RECEIVABLE   **ACCOUNT NO. 110**

Date 200X		Explanation	Post Ref.	Debit	Credit	Balance Debit	Balance Credit
NOV	1	Balance	√			1 6 0 0 00	

SALES TAX PAYABLE   **ACCOUNT NO. 210**

Date 200X		Explanation	Post Ref.	Debit	Credit	Balance Debit	Balance Credit
NOV	1	Balance	√				1 6 0 0 00

AUTO PARTS SALES   **ACCOUNT NO. 410**

Date		Explanation	Post Ref.	Debit	Credit	Balance Debit	Balance Credit

SALES RETURNS AND ALLOWANCES   **ACCOUNT NO. 420**

Date		Explanation	Post Ref.	Debit	Credit	Balance Debit	Balance Credit

PROBLEM 9A-2 OR PROBLEM 9B-2 (CONCLUDED)

(3)

TED'S AUTO SUPPLY
SCHEDULE OF ACCOUNTS RECEIVABLE
NOVEMBER 30, 200X

PROBLEM 9A-3 OR PROBLEM 9B-3

(1,2)

PEAKER'S SNEAKER SHOP
SALES JOURNAL

PAGE 5

Date		Customer's Name	Sales Ticket No.	Terms	PR.	Accounts Rec. - Dr. Sales - Cr.			

PROBLEM 9A-3 OR PROBLEM 9B-3 (CONTINUED)

PEAKER'S SNEAKER SHOP
CASH RECEIPTS JOURNAL

PAGE 2

Date	Cash Dr.	Sales Discounts Dr.	Accounts Receivable Cr.	Sales Cr.	Sundry			Amount Cr.
					Account Names	Pr.		

PROBLEM 9A-3 OR PROBLEM 9B-3 (CONTINUED)
(1,2)

PEAKER'S SNEAKER SHOP
GENERAL JOURNAL

PAGE 1

Date	Account Titles and Description	PR	Dr.	Cr.

ACCOUNTS RECEIVABLE SUBSIDIARY LEDGER

NAME   B. DALE

ADDRESS   1822 RIVER RD., MEMPHIS, TN 09111

Date 200X		Explanation	Post Ref.	Debit	Credit	Dr. Balance
MAY	1	Balance	√			4 0 0 00

NAME   RON LESTER

ADDRESS   18 MASS. AVE., SAN DIEGO, CA 01999

Date		Explanation	Post Ref.	Debit	Credit	Dr. Balance
MAY	1	Balance	√			8 0 0 00

PROBLEM 9A-3 OR PROBLEM 9B-3 (CONTINUED)

ACCOUNTS RECEIVABLE SUBSIDIARY LEDGER

NAME   PAM PRY

ADDRESS   918 MOORE DR., HOMEWOOD, IL 60430

Date 200X		Explanation	Post Ref.	Debit	Credit	Dr. Balance
MAY	1	Balance	√			6 0 0 00

NAME   JIM ZON

ADDRESS   2 CHESTNUT ST., SWAMPSCOTT, MA 01970

Date 200X		Explanation	Post Ref.	Debit	Credit	Dr. Balance
MAY	1	Balance	√			4 0 0 00

PEAKER'S SNEAKER SHOP
PARTIAL GENERAL LEDGER

CASH **ACCOUNT NO. 10**

Date 200X		Explanation	Post Ref.	Debit	Credit	Balance Debit	Balance Credit
MAY	1	Balance	√			15 5 0 0 00	

PROBLEM 9A-3 OR PROBLEM 9B-3 (CONTINUED)

ACCOUNTS RECEIVABLE   ACCOUNT NO. 12

Date 200X	Explanation	Post Ref.	Debit	Credit	Balance Debit	Balance Credit
MAY 1	Balance	√			2 2 0 0 00	

SNEAKER RACK EQUIPMENT   ACCOUNT NO. 14

Date 200X	Explanation	Post Ref.	Debit	Credit	Balance Debit	Balance Credit
MAY 1	Balance	√			1 0 0 0 00	

MARK PEAKER, CAPITAL   ACCOUNT NO. 30

Date 200X	Explanation	Post Ref.	Debit	Credit	Balance Debit	Balance Credit
MAY 1	Balance	√				40 0 0 0 00

SALES   ACCOUNT NO. 40

Date 200X	Explanation	Post Ref.	Debit	Credit	Balance Debit	Balance Credit
MAY 1	Balance	√				2 2 0 0 00

PROBLEM 9A-3 OR PROBLEM 9B-3 (CONCLUDED)

SALES DISCOUNT   ACCOUNT NO. 42

Date 200X	Explanation	Post Ref.	Debit	Credit	Balance Debit	Balance Credit

SALES RETURNS & ALLOWANCES   ACCOUNT NO. 44

Date 200X	Explanation	Post Ref.	Debit	Credit	Balance Debit	Balance Credit

(3)

PEAKER'S SNEAKER SHOP
SCHEDULE OF ACCOUNTS RECEIVABLE
MAY 31, 200X

PROBLEM 9A-4 OR PROBLEM 9B-4

BILL'S COSMETIC MARKET
SALES JOURNAL

PAGE 1

Date	Customer	Sales Ticket	PR.	Accounts Receivable Dr.	Sales Tax Payable Cr.	Lipstick Sales Cr.	Eyeshadow Sales Cr.

PROBLEM 9A-4 OR PROBLEM 9B-4 (CONTINUED)

BILL'S COSMETIC MARKET
CASH RECEIPTS JOURNAL

PAGE 1

Date	Cash Dr.	Accounts Receivable Dr.	Sales Tax Payable Cr.	Lipstick Sales Cr.	Eyeshadow Sales Cr.	Sundry		
						Account Names	PR.	Ammount Cr.

PROBLEM 9A-4 OR PROBLEM 9B-4 (CONTINUED)

(1,2)

**BILL'S COSMETIC MARKET
PARTIAL GENERAL LEDGER**

PAGE 1

Date	Account Titles and Description	PR	Dr.	Cr.

ACCOUNTS RECEIVABLE SUBSIDIARY LEDGER

NAME   ALICE KOY CO.

ADDRESS   2 RYAN RD., BUFFALO, NY 09113

Date	Explanation	Post Ref.	Debit	Credit	Debit Balance

PROBLEM 9A-4 OR PROBLEM 9B-4 (CONTINUED)

ACCOUNTS RECEIVABLE SUBSIDIARY LEDGER

NAME   RUSTY NEAL CO.

ADDRESS   4 REEL RD., LANCASTER, PA 04332

Date	Explanation	Post Ref.	Debit	Credit	Debit Balance

NAME   MARIKA SANCHEZ CO.

ADDRESS   14 BONE DR., ENGLEWOOD CLIFFS, NJ 07632

Date	Explanation	Post Ref.	Debit	Credit	Debit Balance

NAME   JEFF TONG CO.

ADDRESS   2 MARION RD., BOSTON, MA 01981

Date	Explanation	Post Ref.	Debit	Credit	Debit Balance

PROBLEM 9A-4 OR PROBLEM 9B-4 (CONTINUED)

BILL'S COSMETIC MARKET
GENERAL JOURNAL

CASH   **ACCOUNT NO. 10**

Date		Explanation	Post Ref.	Debit	Credit	Balance	
						Debit	Credit

ACCOUNTS RECEIVABLE   **ACCOUNT NO. 12**

Date		Explanation	Post Ref.	Debit	Credit	Balance	
						Debit	Credit

SALES TAX PAYABLE   **ACCOUNT NO. 20**

Date		Explanation	Post Ref.	Debit	Credit	Balance	
						Debit	Credit

BILL MURRAY, CAPITAL   **ACCOUNT NO. 30**

Date		Explanation	Post Ref.	Debit	Credit	Balance	
						Debit	Credit

PROBLEM 9A-4 OR PROBLEM 9B-4 (CONTINUED)

LIPSTICK SALES   ACCOUNT NO. 40

Date	Explanation	Post Ref.	Debit	Credit	Balance Debit	Balance Credit

SALES RETURNS & ALLOWANCES, LIPSTICK   ACCOUNT NO. 42

Date	Explanation	Post Ref.	Debit	Credit	Balance Debit	Balance Credit

EYESHADOW SALES   ACCOUNT NO. 44

Date	Explanation	Post Ref.	Debit	Credit	Balance Debit	Balance Credit

PROBLEM 9A-4 (CONCLUDED)

(3)

BILL'S COSMETIC MARKET
SCHEDULE OF ACCOUNTS RECEIVABLE
APRIL 30, 200X

CHAPTER 9
SUMMARY PRACTICE TEST
SPECIAL JOURNALS: SALES AND
CASH RECEIPTS

Part I Instructions

Fill in the blank(s) to complete the statement.

1. The normal balance of Sales Discounts is _____.
2. _____ _____ and _____ is a contra-revenue account.
3. Sales discount is a _____ account.
4. A discount period is less time than the _____ _____.
5. A _____ _____ records the sale of merchandise on account.
6. The _____ _____ _____ _____ lists in alphabetical order an account for each customer.
7. _____ _____ in the general ledger is called the controlling account.
8. The (√) in the sales journal indicates that the accounts receivable ledger has been updated _____ _____ _____.
9. The totals of the sales journal are posted at _____ _____ _____ _____ to the general ledger account.
10. In a wholesale company there is no _____ tax.
11. Sales Tax Payable is a _____ in the general ledger.
12. Issuing a _____ _____ results in the seller reducing its accounts receivable.
13. Sales Returns and Allowances is a _____ account.
14. The _____ _____ _____ records the receipt of cash from any source.
15. The total of the _____ column in the cash receipts journal is never posted.
16. _____ is a process that helps prove the accuracy of recording transactions in the cash receipts journal.
17. No _____ _____ are taken on sales tax.
18. A _____ _____ _____ lists the ending balances from the accounts receivable ledger.

Part II Instructions

From the following chart, complete the statements below.

CASH RECEIPTS JOURNAL

Cash Dr.				Sales Discounts Dr.				Accounts Receivable Cr.				Sales Cr.				Sundry Account Cr.			
			F												I				
		X	XX											X	XX				
							G				H								J
					X	XX			X	XX			X	XX			X	XX	
					X	XX			X	XX			X	XX					
	X	XX			X	XX			X	XX			X	XX			X	XX	
			E				D				C				B				A

1. **EXAMPLE:** *A is never posted*

2. B is posted at _____ _____
   _____ to the Sales account in the general ledger.

3. C is posted to _____ _____, the controlling account
   in the general ledger at the end of the month.

4. D has a _____ balance that is posted to Sales Discount in the
   general ledger at the end of the month.

5 E is posted a _____ _____ _____ to the Cash account in the
   general ledger.

6. F should _____ _____ _____, because the total will be posted
   to the Cash account in the general ledger at the end of the month.

7. G is _____ _____ during the month.

8. H is _____ recorded to the accounts receivable subsidiary ledger during the month.

9. I is _____ _____ during the month, because the total
   of the Sales column is posted at the end of the month to Sales in the general ledger.

10. J is posted to the _____ _____ during the month, as the total of sundry is
   never posted.

Part III Instructions

Answer true or false to the following statements.

1. A schedule of accounts receivable is prepared from the general ledger.

2. Cross-footing verifies the accuracy of recording transactions into special journals.
3. (X) means the accounts receivable ledger has been updated.
4. The total of the sundry column is posted at the end of the month.
5. The cash receipts journal records sales on account.
6. Issuing a credit memorandum results in Sales, Returns and Allowances decreasing with Accounts Receivable increasing.
7. A Periodic System continually monitors Inventory.
8. The sum of the accounts receivable subsidiary ledger is equal to the balance in the controlling account at the end of the month.
9. The sales journal records cash sales.
10. The accounts receivable subsidiary ledger is listed in numerical order.
11. Sales Returns and Allowances is a contra-revenue account.
12. Net sales = gross sales − SRA-SD.
13. All businesses must have a sales journal to record cash sales.
14. Discounts are taken on sales tax.
15. The total of the Sales Tax Payable is posted at the end of the month to the accounts receivable subsidiary ledger.
16. The accounts receivable subsidiary ledger is always located in the general ledger.
17. Gross profit plus operating expenses equals net income.
18. A credit period is longer than the discount period.
19. In the accounts receivable subsidiary ledger each account is debited to record amounts customers owe.
20. Special journals reduce posting labor.

CHAPTER 9
SOLUTIONS TO SUMMARY PRACTICE TEST

Part I

1. Debit
2. Sales Returns and Allowances
3. contra-revenue
4. credit period
5. sales journal
6. accounts receivable subsidiary ledger
7. Accounts Receivable
8. during the month
9. end of the month
10. sales
11. liability
12. credit memorandum
13. contra-revenue
14. cash receipts journal
15. sundry
16. cross-footing
17. cash discounts
18. schedule of accounts receivable

Part II

1. never posted
2. end of month
3. Accounts Receivable
4. debit
5. end of month
6. not be posted
7. not posted
8. immediately
9. not posted
10. general ledger

Part III

1.	false	11.	true
2.	true	12.	true
3.	false	13.	false
4.	false	14.	false
5.	false	15.	false
6.	false	16.	false
7.	false	17.	false
8.	true	18.	true
9.	false	19.	true
10.	false	20.	true

CONTINUING PROBLEM FOR CHAPTER 9

SALES JOURNAL   PAGE 1

Date	Account Debited	Terms	Invoice No.	Post Ref.	Dr. Accounts Receivable Cr. Sales

CASH RECEIPTS JOURNAL   PAGE 1

Date	Cash Dr.	Sales Discounts Dr.	Accounts Receivable Cr.	Sales Cr.	Sundry Account Names	Post Ref.	Amount Cr.

GENERAL JOURNAL   PAGE 10

Date	Account Titles and Description	PR	Dr.	Cr.

ELDORADO COMPUTER CENTER
SCHEDULE OF ACCOUNTS RECEIVABLE
1/31/0X

_____
_____
_____
_____

CASH   **ACCOUNT NO. 1000**

Date		Explanation	Post Ref.	Debit	Credit	Balance Debit	Balance Credit
1/1	0X	Balance Forward	√			3 3 3 6 65	

ELDORADO COMPUTER CENTER
PARTIAL GENERAL LEDGER

ACCOUNTS RECEIVABLE   ACCOUNT NO. 1020

Date		Explanation	Post Ref.	Debit	Credit	Balance Debit	Balance Credit
1/1	0X	Balance Forward				13 600 00	

SALES   ACCOUNT NO.

Date		Explanation	Post Ref.	Debit	Credit	Balance Debit	Balance Credit

SALES RETURN AND ALLOWANCES   ACCOUNT NO. 4020

Date		Explanation	Post Ref.	Debit	Credit	Balance Debit	Balance Credit

SALES DISCOUNTS   ACCOUNT NO. 4030

Date		Explanation	Post Ref.	Debit	Credit	Balance Debit	Balance Credit
			√				

NAME   TAYLOR GOLF   **ACCOUNT NO. 100**

ADDRESS   1010 MOCKINGBIRD LANE, CARLSBAD, CA 92008

Date		Explanation	Post Ref.	Debit	Credit	Dr. Balance
1/1	0X	Balance forward	√			2 9 0 0 00

NAME   VITA NEEDLE   **ACCOUNT NO. 101**

ADDRESS   144 CANTATA, IRVINE, CA 92606

Date		Explanation	Post Ref.	Debit	Credit	Dr. Balance
1/1	0X	Balance	√			6 8 0 0 00

NAME   ACCUPAC   **ACCOUNT NO. 103**

ADDRESS   1717 JORDAN ST., SAN CLEMENTE, CA 91607

Date		Explanation	Post Ref.	Debit	Credit	Dr. Balance
1/1	0X	Balance	√			3 9 0 0 00

ACCOUNTS RECEIVABLE SUBSIDIARY LEDGER

NAME   ANTHONY J. PITALE   **ACCOUNT NO. 104**

ADDRESS   600 NEWPORT BEACH, NEWPORT, CA 91600

Date	Explanation	Post Ref.	Debit	Credit	Dr. Balance

APPENDIX—PERPETUAL INVENTORY SYSTEM

GENREAL JOURNAL

PAGE 1

Date	Account Titles and Description	PR	Dr.	Cr.

GENREAL JOURNAL

PAGE 1

Date	Account Titles and Description	PR	Dr.	Cr.

Special Journals: Purchases and Cash Payments

SELF-REVIEW QUIZ 10-1

1. _____ 2. _____ 3. _____ 4. _____ 5. _____

SELF-REVIEW QUIZ 10-2

PAGE 2

MUNROE CO.
PURCHASES JOURNAL

Date	Account Credited	Date of Invoice	Inv. No.	Terms	PR	Accounts Payable Cr.	Purchases Dr.	Sundry Dr.		
								Account	PR	Amount

MUNROE CO.
GENERAL JOURNAL

PAGE 1

Date		Account Titles and Description	PR	Dr.	Cr.

ACCOUNTS PAYABLE SUBSIDIARY LEDGER

NAME   JOHN BUTLER COMPANY

ADDRESS   18 REED RD., HOMEWOOD, IL 60430

Date		Explanation	Post Ref.	Debit	Credit	Cr. Balance
.						

NAME   FLYNN COMPANY

ADDRESS   15 FOSS AVE., ENGLEWOOD CLIFFS, NJ 07632

Date		Explanation	Post Ref.	Debit	Credit	Cr. Balance

PARTIAL GENERAL LEDGER

EQUIPMENT   ACCOUNT NO. 121

Date		Explanation	Post Ref.	Debit	Credit	Balance Debit	Balance Credit

ACCOUNTS PAYABLE   ACCOUNT NO. 212

Date	Explanation	Post Ref.	Debit	Credit	Balance Debit	Balance Credit

PURCHASES   ACCOUNT NO. 512

Date	Explanation	Post Ref.	Debit	Credit	Balance Debit	Balance Credit

PURCHASES RETURNS AND ALLOWANCES   ACCOUNT NO. 513

Date	Explanation	Post Ref.	Debit	Credit	Balance Debit	Balance Credit

SELF-REVIEW QUIZ 10-3

MELISSA COMPANY
CASH PAYMENTS JOURNAL   PAGE 2

Date	Check No.	Accounts Debited	PR.	Sundry Account Dr.	Accounts Payable Dr.	Purchases Discounts Cr.	Cash Cr.

ACCOUNTS PAYABLE SUBSIDARY LEDGER

NAME   BOB FINKELSTEIN

ADDRESS   112 FLYING HIGHWAY, TRENTON, NJ 00861

Date 200X		Explanation	Post Ref.	Debit	Credit	Cr. Balance
June	1	Balance	√			3 0 0 00

NAME   AL JEEP

ADDRESS   118 WANG RD., SAUGUS, MA 01432

Date 200X		Explanation	Post Ref.	Debit	Credit	Cr. Balance
June	1	Balance	√			2 0 0 00

PARTIAL GENERAL LEDGER

CASH   **ACCOUNT NO. 110**

Date 200X		Explanation	Post Ref.	Debit	Credit	Balance Debit	Balance Credit
June	1	Balance	√			7 0 0 00	

ACCOUNTS PAYABLE   **ACCOUNT NO. 210**

Date 200X		Explanation	Post Ref.	Debit	Credit	Balance Debit	Balance Credit
June	1	Balance	√				5 0 0 00

PURCHASES DISCOUNT   **ACCOUNT NO. 511**

Date	Explanation	Post Ref.	Debit	Credit	Balance Debit	Balance Credit

ADVERTISING EXPENSE   **ACCOUNT NO. 610**

Date	Explanation	Post Ref.	Debit	Credit	Balance Debit	Balance Credit

FORMS FOR COMPREHENSIVE DEMONSTRATION PROBLEM

J. LING CO.
SALES JOURNAL

PAGE 1

Date	Account Debited	Terms	Invoice No.	Post Ref.	Dr. Acc. Receivable Cr. Sales

CASH RECEIPTS JOURNAL

PAGE 1

Date	Cash Dr.	Sales Discounts Dr.	Accounts Receivable Cr.	Sales Cr.	Sundry Account Name	Pr.	Amount Cr.

PURCHASES JOURNAL

PAGE 1

Date	Account Credited	Terms	PR	Accounts Payable Cr.	Purchases Dr.	Sundry Dr. Account	PR	Amount

CASH PAYMENTS JOURNAL

PAGE 1

Date	Check No.	Accounts Debited	PR.	Sundry Account Dr.	Accounts Payable Dr.	Purchases Discounts Cr.	Cash Cr.

GENERAL JOURNAL

Date	Account Titles and Description	PR	Dr.	Cr.

ACCOUNTS RECEIVABLE SUBSIDIARY LEDGER

NAME   BALDER CO.

ADDRESS   1 ROCK RD., DENVER, CO 66083

Date	Explanation	Post Ref.	Debit	Credit	Dr. Balance

NAME   LEWIS CO.

ADDRESS   15 SMITH AVE., REVERE, MA 01545

Date	Explanation	Post Ref.	Debit	Credit	Dr. Balance

ACCOUNTS PAYABLE SUBSIDIARY LEDGER

NAME CASE CO.

ADDRESS 1 LONG RD., MARLEBORO, MA 01545

Date		Explanation	Post Ref.	Debit	Credit	Cr. Balance

NAME NOONE CO.

ADDRESS 11 MILL RD., MALDEN, OK 01143

Date		Explanation	Post Ref.	Debit	Credit	Cr. Balance

PARTIAL GENERAL LEDGER

Cash	111	Sales	410	Purchases Discounts	530

Accounts Receivable	112	Sales Returns & Allowances	420	Salaries Expense	610

Equipment	116	Sales Discount	430		

Accounts Payable	210	Purchases	510		

J. Ling, Capital	310	Purchases Returns & Allowances	520		

YOU MAKE THE CALL: CRITICAL THINKING/ETHICAL CASE

_____
_____
_____
_____
_____
_____
_____
_____
_____
_____
_____
_____
_____
_____
_____
_____
_____
_____
_____

INTERNET EXERCISE

_____
_____
_____
_____
_____
_____
_____
_____
_____
_____
_____
_____
_____
_____
_____
_____
_____
_____
_____

CHAPTER 10
FORMS FOR MINI EXERCISES

1. A. _____
   B. _____
   C. _____
   D. _____
   E. _____
   F. _____
   G. _____
   H. _____

2.

3. _____

   _____

   _____

   _____

   _____

   _____

   _____

   _____

   _____

   _____

4. A. _____   _____   5. A. _____   E. _____
   B. _____   _____   B. _____   F. _____
   C. _____   _____   C. _____
                                  D. _____

6.

WEB.COM
SCHEDULE OF ACCOUNTS PAYABLE
MAY 31, 200X

FORMS FOR EXERCISES

10-1.

Rey.com	Equipment 120

Lane.com	Accounts Payable 210

Sail.com	Purchases 510

10-2.   PAGE 1

Reel Co.	Accounts Payable 211	Purchases Returns and Allowances 513

FORMS FOR EXERCISES (CONTINUED)

10-3.   PAGE 2

Date	Check No.	Accounts Debited	PR.	Sundry Account Dr.	Accounts Payable Dr.	Purchases Discounts Cr.	Cash Cr.

ACCOUNTS PAYABLE SUBSIDIARY LEDGER

A. James

	1,000

B. Foss

	400

J. Ranch

	900

B. Swanson

	100

PARTIAL GENERAL LEDGER

Cash   110

3,000	

Accounts Payable   210

	2,400

Purchases Discount   511

Advertising Expense   610

EXERCISES (CONTINUED)

10-4.

MORGAN'S CLOTHING
SCHEDULE OF ACCOUNTS PAYABLE
APRIL 30, 200X

_____

_____

_____

_____

_____   Accounts Payable   210

10-5.

Accounts Affected	Category	↑ ↓	Rules

10-6.

_____

_____

_____

_____

_____

_____

PROBLEM 10A-1 OR PROBLEM 10B-1

SKATES.COM
PURCHASES JOURNAL

PAGE 3

Date	Account Credited	Date of Invoice	Inv. No.	Terms	PR	Accounts Payable Cr.	Purchases Dr.	Sundry Dr.		
								Account	PR	Amount

PROBLEM 10A-1 OR PROBLEM 10B-1 (CONTINUED)

ACCOUNTS PAYABLE SUBSIDIARY LEDGER

NAME   MAIL.COM

ADDRESS   12 SMITH ST., DEARBORN, MI 09113

Date	Explanation	Post Ref.	Debit	Credit	Cr. Balance

NAME   NORTON CO.

ADDRESS   1 RANTOUL RD., CHARLOTTE, NC 01114

Date	Explanation	Post Ref.	Debit	Credit	Cr. Balance

NAME   ROLO CO.

ADDRESS   2 WEST RD., LYNN, MA 01471

Date	Explanation	Post Ref.	Debit	Credit	Cr. Balance

PARTIAL GENERAL LEDGER

STORE SUPPLIES   **ACCOUNT NO. 115**

Date	Explanation	Post Ref.	Debit	Credit	Balance Debit	Balance Credit

PROBLEM 10A-1 OR PROBLEM 10B-1 (CONCLUDED)

STORE EQUIPMENT   **ACCOUNT NO. 121**

Date	Explanation	Post Ref.	Debit	Credit	Balance Debit	Balance Credit

ACCOUNTS PAYABLE   **ACCOUNT NO. 210**

Date	Explanation	Post Ref.	Debit	Credit	Balance Debit	Balance Credit

PURCHASES   **ACCOUNT NO. 510**

Date	Explanation	Post Ref.	Debit	Credit	Balance Debit	Balance Credit

PROBLEM 10A-2 OR PROBLEM 10B-2

MABEL'S NATURAL FOOD STORE
PURCHASES JOURNAL

PAGE 10

Date	Account Credited	Date of Invoice	Inv. No.	Terms	PR	Accounts Payable Cr.	Purchases Dr.	Store Supplies Dr.	Sundry Dr.		
									Account	PR	Amount

PROBLEM 10A-2 OR PROBLEM 10B-2 (CONTINUED)

ACCOUNTS PAYABLE SUBSIDIARY LEDGER

NAME   ATON CO.

ADDRESS   11 LYNNWAY AVE., NEWPORT, RI 03112

Date 200X		Explanation	Post Ref.	Debit	Credit	Cr. Balance
MAY	1	Balance	√			4 0 0 00

NAME   BROWARD CO.

ADDRESS   21 RIVER ST., ANAHEIM, CA 43110

Date 200X		Explanation	Post Ref.	Debit	Credit	Cr. Balance
MAY	1	Balance	√			6 0 0 00

NAME   MIDDEN CO.

ADDRESS   10 ASTER RD., DUBUQUE, IA 80021

Date 200X		Explanation	Post Ref.	Debit	Credit	Cr. Balance
MAY	1	Balance	√			1 2 0 0 00

NAME   RELAR CO.

ADDRESS   22 GERALD RD., SMITH, CO 43138

Date 200X		Explanation	Post Ref.	Debit	Credit	Cr. Balance
MAY	1	Balance	√			5 0 0 00

PROBLEM 10A-2 OR PROBLEM 10B-2 (CONTINUED)

PARTIAL GENERAL LEDGER

STORE SUPPLIES   ACCOUNT NO. 110

Date	Explanation	Post Ref.	Debit	Credit	Balance Debit	Balance Credit

OFFICE EQUIPMENT   ACCOUNT NO. 120

Date	Explanation	Post Ref.	Debit	Credit	Balance Debit	Balance Credit

ACCOUNTS PAYABLE   ACCOUNT NO. 210

Date 200X	Explanation	Post Ref.	Debit	Credit	Balance Debit	Balance Credit
MAY 1	Balance	√				2 7 0 0 00

PURCHASES   ACCOUNT NO. 510

Date 200X	Explanation	Post Ref.	Debit	Credit	Balance Debit	Balance Credit
MAY 1	Balance	√			16 7 0 0 00	

PROBLEM 10A-2 OR PROBLEM 10B-2 (CONCLUDED)

PURCHASES RETURNS AND ALLOWANCES   ACCOUNT NO. 512

Date	Explanation	Post Ref.	Debit	Credit	Balance Debit	Balance Credit

GENERAL JOURNAL   PAGE 2

Date	Account Titles and Description	PR	Dr.	Cr.

MABEL'S NATURAL FOOD STORE
SCHEDULE OF ACCOUNTS PAYABLE
MAY 31, 200X

PROBLEM 10A-3 OR PROBLEM 10B-3

(1,2)

JONES' COMPUTER CENTER
CASH PAYMENTS JOURNAL

PAGE 5

Date	Check No.	Account Debited	PR.	Sundry Dr.	Accounts Payable Dr.	Computer Purchases Dr.	Computer Purchases Discount Cr.	Cash Cr.

PROBLEM 10A-3 OR PROBLEM 10B-3 (CONTINUED)

ACCOUNTS PAYABLE SUBSIDIARY LEDGER

NAME   ALVIN CO.

ADDRESS   1 REACH RD., IPSWICH, MA 01932

Date 200X		Explanation	Post Ref.	Debit	Credit	Cr. Balance
MAY	1	Balance	√			1 2 0 0 00

NAME   HENRY CO.

ADDRESS   1 RALPH RD., REVERE, MA 01321

Date 200X		Explanation	Post Ref.	Debit	Credit	Cr. Balance
MAY	1	Balance	√			6 0 0 00

NAME   SOY CO.

ADDRESS   7 PLYMOUTH AVE., GLENN, NH 01218

Date 200X		Explanation	Post Ref.	Debit	Credit	Cr. Balance
MAY	1	Balance	√			8 0 0 00

NAME   XON CO.

ADDRESS   22 REY RD., BOCA RATON, FL 99132

Date 200X		Explanation	Post Ref.	Debit	Credit	Cr. Balance
MAY	1	Balance	√			1 4 0 0 00

PROBLEM 10A-3 OR PROBLEM 10B-3 (CONTINUED)

PARTIAL GENERAL LEDGER

CASH ACCOUNT NO. 110

Date 200X		Explanation	Post Ref.	Debit	Credit	Balance Debit	Balance Credit
MAY	1	Balance	√			17 0 0 0 00	

DELIVERY TRUCK ACCOUNT NO. 150

Date 200X		Explanation	Post Ref.	Debit	Credit	Balance Debit	Balance Credit

ACCOUNTS PAYABLE ACCOUNT NO. 210

Date 200X		Explanation	Post Ref.	Debit	Credit	Balance Debit	Balance Credit
MAY	1	Balance	√				4 0 0 0 00

COMPUTER PURCHASES ACCOUNT NO. 510

Date 200X		Explanation	Post Ref.	Debit	Credit	Balance Debit	Balance Credit

PROBLEM 10A-3 OR PROBLEM 10B-3 (CONCLUDED)

COMPUTER PURCHASES DISCOUNT   ACCOUNT NO. 511

Date	Explanation	Post Ref.	Debit	Credit	Balance Debit	Balance Credit

RENT EXPENSE   ACCOUNT NO. 610

Date	Explanation	Post Ref.	Debit	Credit	Balance Debit	Balance Credit

UTILITIES EXPENSE   ACCOUNT NO. 620

Date	Explanation	Post Ref.	Debit	Credit	Balance Debit	Balance Credit

JONES, COMPUTER CENTER
SCHEDULE OF ACCOUNTS PAYABLE
MAY 31, 200X

PROBLEM 10A-4 OR PROBLEM 10B-4
(1,2,3)

PAGE 1

ABBY'S TOY HOUSE
PURCHASES JOURNAL

Date	Account Credited	Date of Inv.	Inv. No.	Terms	Pr.	Accounts Payable Cr.	Toy Purchases Dr.	Sundry Dr.		
								Accounts	PR	Amount

PROBLEM 10A-4 OR PROBLEM 10B-4 (CONTINUED)

ABBY'S TOY HOUSE
CASH RECEIPTS JOURNAL

PAGE 1

Date	Cash Dr.	Sales Discounts Dr.	Accounts Receivable Cr.	Toy Sales Cr.	Sundry Account	Pr.	Amount Cr.

PROBLEM 10A-4 OR PROBLEM 10B-4 (CONTINUED)

ABBY'S TOY HOUSE
CASH PAYMENTS JOURNAL

PAGE 1

Date	Check No.	Account Debited	PR.	Sundry Dr.	Accounts Payable Dr.	Purchases Discount Cr.	Cash Cr.

PROBLEM 10A-4 OR PROBLEM 10B-4 (CONTINUED)

ABBY'S TOY HOUSE
SALES JOURNAL
MARCH 31, 200X

PAGE 1

Date		Account Debited	Invoice No	Terms	PR.	Accounts Rec. - Dr. Toy Sales - Cr.		

ABBY'S TOY HOUSE
GENERAL JOURNAL
MARCH 31, 200X

PAGE 1

Date		Account Titles and Description	PR	Dr.			Cr.		

PROBLEM 10A-4 OR PROBLEM 10B-4 (CONTINUED)

(4)

ABBY'S TOY HOUSE
SCHEDULE OF ACCOUNTS RECEIVABLE
MARCH 31, 200X

(4)

ABBY'S TOY HOUSE
SCHEDULE OF ACCOUNTS PAYABLE
MARCH 31, 200X

PROBLEM 10A-4 OR PROBLEM 10B-4 (CONTINUED)

ACCOUNTS PAYABLE SUBSIDIARY LEDGER

NAME   MINNIE KATZ

ADDRESS   87 GARFIELD AVE., REVERE, MA 01245

Date	Explanation	Post Ref.	Debit	Credit	Cr. Balance

NAME   SAM KATZ GARAGE

ADDRESS   22 REGIS RD., BOSTON, MA 01950

Date	Explanation	Post Ref.	Debit	Credit	Cr. Balance

NAME   EARL MILLER CO.

ADDRESS   22 RETTER ST., SAN DIEGO, CA 01211

Date	Explanation	Post Ref.	Debit	Credit	Cr. Balance

NAME   WOODY SMITH

ADDRESS   2 SPRING ST., WEERS, ND 02118

Date	Explanation	Post Ref.	Debit	Credit	Cr. Balance

PROBLEM 10A-4 OR PROBLEM 10B-4 (CONTINUED)

ACCOUNTS RECEIVABLE SUBSIDIARY LEDGER

NAME   **BILL BURTON**

ADDRESS   **24 RYAN RD., BUIKE, OH 02183**

Date	Explanation	Post Ref.	Debit	Credit	Dr. Balance

NAME   **BONNIE FLOW CO.**

ADDRESS   **2 SMITH RD., DALLAS, TX 22210**

Date	Explanation	Post Ref.	Debit	Credit	Dr. Balance

NAME   **JIM REX**

ADDRESS   **1 SCHOOL ST., CLEVELAND, OH 22441**

Date	Explanation	Post Ref.	Debit	Credit	Dr. Balance

PROBLEM 10A-4 OR PROBLEM 10B-4 (CONTINUED)

NAME   AMY ROSE

ADDRESS   18 VEEK RD., CHESTER, CT 80111

Date		Explanation	Post Ref.	Debit	Credit	Dr. Balance

GENERAL LEDGER

CASH   ACCOUNT NO. 110

Date		Explanation	Post Ref.	Debit	Credit	Balance Debit	Balance Credit

ACCOUNTS RECEIVABLE   ACCOUNT NO. 112

Date		Explanation	Post Ref.	Debit	Credit	Balance Debit	Balance Credit

PREPAID RENT   ACCOUNT NO. 114

Date		Explanation	Post Ref.	Debit	Credit	Balance Debit	Balance Credit

PROBLEM 10A-4 OR PROBLEM 10B-4 (CONTINUED)

DELIVERY TRUCK   ACCOUNT NO. 121

Date	Explanation	Post Ref.	Debit	Credit	Balance Debit	Balance Credit

ACCOUNTS PAYABLE   ACCOUNT NO. 210

Date	Explanation	Post Ref.	Debit	Credit	Balance Debit	Balance Credit

A. ELLEN, CAPITAL   ACCOUNT NO. 310

Date	Explanation	Post Ref.	Debit	Credit	Balance Debit	Balance Credit

TOY SALES   ACCOUNT NO. 410

Date	Explanation	Post Ref.	Debit	Credit	Balance Debit	Balance Credit

PROBLEM 10A-4 OR PROBLEM 1013-4 (CONTINUED)

SALES RETURNS AND ALLOWANCES   ACCOUNT NO. 412

Date		Explanation	Post Ref.	Debit	Credit	Balance	
						Debit	Credit

SALES DISCOUNTS   ACCOUNT NO. 414

Date		Explanation	Post Ref.	Debit	Credit	Balance	
						Debit	Credit

TOY PURCHASES   ACCOUNT NO. 510

Date		Explanation	Post Ref.	Debit	Credit	Balance	
						Debit	Credit

PURCHASES RETURNS AND ALLOWANCES   ACCOUNT NO. 512

Date		Explanation	Post Ref.	Debit	Credit	Balance	
						Debit	Credit

PROBLEM 10A-4 OR PROBLEM 10B-4 (CONCLUDED)

PURCHASES DISCOUNT   ACCOUNT NO. 514

Date	Explanation	Post Ref.	Debit	Credit	Balance Debit	Balance Credit

SALARIES EXPENSE   ACCOUNT NO. 610

Date	Explanation	Post Ref.	Debit	Credit	Balance Debit	Balance Credit

CLEANING EXPENSE   ACCOUNT NO. 612

Date	Explanation	Post Ref.	Debit	Credit	Balance Debit	Balance Credit

CHAPTER 10
SUMMARY PRACTICE TEST
SPECIAL JOURNALS:
PURCHASES AND CASH PAYMENTS

Part I Instructions

Fill in the blank(s) to complete the statement.

1. F.O.B. shipping point means the _____ covers the shipping cost.

2. Purchases are categorized as _____.

3. The Purchases account has a _____ balance.

4. Purchases are defined as merchandise for _____ to customers.

5. The accounts payable subsidiary ledger represents a potential _____ of cash.

6. The controlling account in the general ledger for the accounts payable subsidiary ledger is called _____ _____.

7. The accounts payable subsidiary ledger would be recorded _____.

8. The balance in the Accounts Payable controlling account should be equal to the sum of the accounts payable ledger accounts _____ _____ _____ _____.

9. The total of the sundry column is _____ _____.

10. The √ in the reference column indicates that the _____ _____ _____ _____ has been updated.

11. A _____ _____ that is issued means the buyer owes less money, as merchandise is being returned or an allowance received.

12. A debit memorandum issued or a credit memorandum received results in a _____ to Accounts Payable and a credit to Purchases, Returns and Allowances.

13. List price - net price = _____ _____ amount.

14. The accounts payable ledger is listed in _____ _____.

15. Purchases Returns and Allowances is increased by a _____.

16. The cash payments journal records transactions that involve outward flows of _____.

17. The cash payments journal alleviates certain repetitive _____.

18. Purchases Discounts is increased by _____.

19. A _____ _____ provides the purchasing department the information to then prepare a purchase order.

20. A _____ _____ is made out after a company inspects received shipments.

21. The total of the cash column is posted at the _____ _____ _____ _____ to the general ledger.

Part II Instructions

From the following chart, complete the statements below.

CASH PAYMENTS JOURNAL

Sundry Dr.					Accounts Payable Dr.					Purchases Discounts Cr.					Cash Cr.			
					X	X	X			X	X	X			X	X	X	(E)
					X	X	X	(G)		X	X	X	(F)		X	X	X	
					X	X	X	(J)							X	X	X	
X	X	X	(H)												X	X	X	
X	X	X	(I)												X	X	X	
X	X	X			X	X	X			X	X	X			X	X	X	
	(A)					(B)					(C)					(D)		

1. EXAMPLE: A is *never posted*.

2. B is posted at _____ _____ _____ in the general ledger to Accounts Payable.

3. C is posted monthly to _____ _____ in the _____ _____ at the end of the month.

4. D is posted as a _____ balance at the end of the month to Cash in the general ledger.

5. E is _____ _____, because the total of cash is posted at the end of the month.

6. F need not be _____, as the column total is posted at the end of the month to the general ledger.

7. G is _____ _____ to the accounts payable ledger.

8. H is posted during the month to the _____ _____.

9. I is _____ the month to the general ledger.

10. J is recorded _____ to the accounts payable subsidiary ledger.

Part III Instructions

Answer true or false to the following statements.

1. F.O.B. shipping point means buyer is responsible to cover shipping costs.
2. The purchases account is a contra-cost of goods sold account.
3. Purchases Discounts are the result of paying for equipment within the discount period.
4. F.O.B. Destination means the seller is responsible to cover shipping costs.
5. Purchases Discounts are taken on freight.
6. The purchases journal records only the buying of merchandise.
7. The cash payments journal records the receipt of cash.
8. The balance in Accounts Payable, the controlling account, will be equal to the sum of the accounts receivable subsidiary ledger at the end of the month.
9. A purchase order is completed after the purchase requisition.
10. On receiving a purchase order, the seller may issue a sales invoice.
11. The normal balance of Purchases Discount is a debit balance.
12. The seller will often issue a debit memorandum to the buyer.
13. All credit memorandums must be recorded in general journals.
14. Returned equipment by a buyer results in a change in Purchases Returns and Allowances.
15. Trade discounts do not occur because of early payments of one's bills.
16. A seller's sales discount on purchases is the buyers purchases discount.
17. Buying of equipment on account is only recorded in the general ledger.
18. On receiving a debit memorandum, the seller will issue a credit memorandum.
19. Cash sales are recorded in the cash payments journal.
20. Purchases are contra costs.

CHAPTER 10
SOLUTIONS TO SUMMARY PRACTICE TEST

Part I

1. buyer (purchaser)
2. cost
3. debit
4. resale
5. outflow
6. accounts payable
7. daily
8. at end of month
9. never posted
10. accounts payable subsidiary ledger
11. debit memorandum
12. debit
13. trade discount
14. alphabetical order
15. credit
16. cash
17. postings
18. credits
19. purchase requisition
20. receiving report
21. end of the month

Part II

1. never posted
2. end of month
3. Purchases Discounts, general ledger
4. credit
5. not posted

6. posted
7. recorded immediatly (or daily)
8. general ledger
9. posted during
10. daily

Part III

1. true
2. false
3. false
4. true
5. false
6. false
7. false
8. false
9. true
10. true

11. false
12. false
13. false
14. false
15. true
16. true
17. false
18. true
19. false
20. false

CONTINUING PROBLEM FOR CHAPTER 10

PURCHASES JOURNAL

PAGE 1

Date	Account Credited	PR	Accounts Payable Cr.	Purchases Dr.	Sundry Dr.		
					Account	PR	Amount

CASH PAYMENTS JOURNAL

PAGE 1

Date	Account Titles and Description	PR	Dr.	Cr.

ELDORADO COMPUTER CENTER
GENERAL JOURNAL

PAGE 11

Date	Account Titles and Description	PR	Dr.	Cr.

PARTIAL GENERAL LEDGER

CASH   ACCOUNT NO. 1000

Date		Explanation	Post Ref.	Debit	Credit	Balance Debit	Balance Credit
2/1	0X	Balance forward	√			12 1 1 6 65	

SUPPLIES   ACCOUNT NO. 1030

Date		Explanation	Post Ref.	Debit	Credit	Balance Debit	Balance Credit
2/1	0X	Balance forward	√			1 3 2 00	

MERCHANDISE INVENTORY   ACCOUNT NO. 1040

Date		Explanation	Post Ref.	Debit	Credit	Balance Debit	Balance Credit

PREPAID RENT   ACCOUNT NO. 1025

Date		Explanation	Post Ref.	Debit	Credit	Balance Debit	Balance Credit
2/1	0X	Balance forward	√			1 6 0 0 00	

ACCOUNTS PAYABLE   ACCOUNT NO. 2000

Date		Explanation	Post Ref.	Debit	Credit	Balance Debit	Balance Credit
2/1	0X	Balance forward	√				2 0 5 0 00

PURCHASES   ACCOUNT NO. 6000

Date		Explanation	Post Ref.	Debit	Credit	Balance Debit	Balance Credit

PURCHASE RETURNS AND ALLOWANCES   ACCOUNT NO. 6010

Date		Explanation	Post Ref.	Debit	Credit	Balance Debit	Balance Credit

PURCHASE DISCOUNTS   ACCOUNT NO. 6020

Date		Explanation	Post Ref.	Debit	Credit	Balance Debit	Balance Credit

ELDORADO COMPUTER CENTER
SCHEDULE OF ACCOUNTS PAYABLE
2/28/0X

ACCOUNTS PAYABLE SUBSIDIARY LEDGER

NAME MULTI SYSTEMS   # 6A3

ADDRESS 1919 MORAN ST., ANAHEIM, CA 92606

Date		Explanation	Post Ref.	Debit	Credit	Cr. Balance
2/1	0X	Balance forward	√			4 5 0 00

NAME OFFICE DEPOT   # 6A4

ADDRESS 460 ESCONDIDO BLVD., ESCONDIDO, CA 92025

Date		Explanation	Post Ref.	Debit	Credit	Cr. Balance
2/1	0X	Balance forward	√			5 0 00

NAME   SAN DIEGO ELECTRIC   **# 6A5**

ADDRESS   606 INDUSTRIAL ST., SAN DIEGO, CA 92121

Date		Explanation	Post Ref.	Debit	Credit	Cr. Balance

NAME   PACIFIC BELL   **# 6A6**

ADDRESS   101 BELL AVE., SAN DIEGO, CA 92101

Date		Explanation	Post Ref.	Debit	Credit	Cr. Balance
2/1	0X	Balance forward	√			1 5 0 00

NAME   COMPUTER CONNECTION   **# 6A7**

ADDRESS   1020 WIL LANE, LOS ANGELES, CA 92405

Date		Explanation	Post Ref.	Debit	Credit	Cr. Balance

NAME   **SYSTEMS DESIGN FURNITURE**   # 6A8

ADDRESS   **2070 FIRST ST., SAN DIEGO, CA 92101**

Date		Explanation	Post Ref.	Debit					Credit					Cr. Balance				
2/1	0X	Balance forward	√											1	4	0	0	00

PREPARING A WORKSHEET FOR A MERCHANDISE COMPANY

SELF-REVIEW QUIZ 11-1

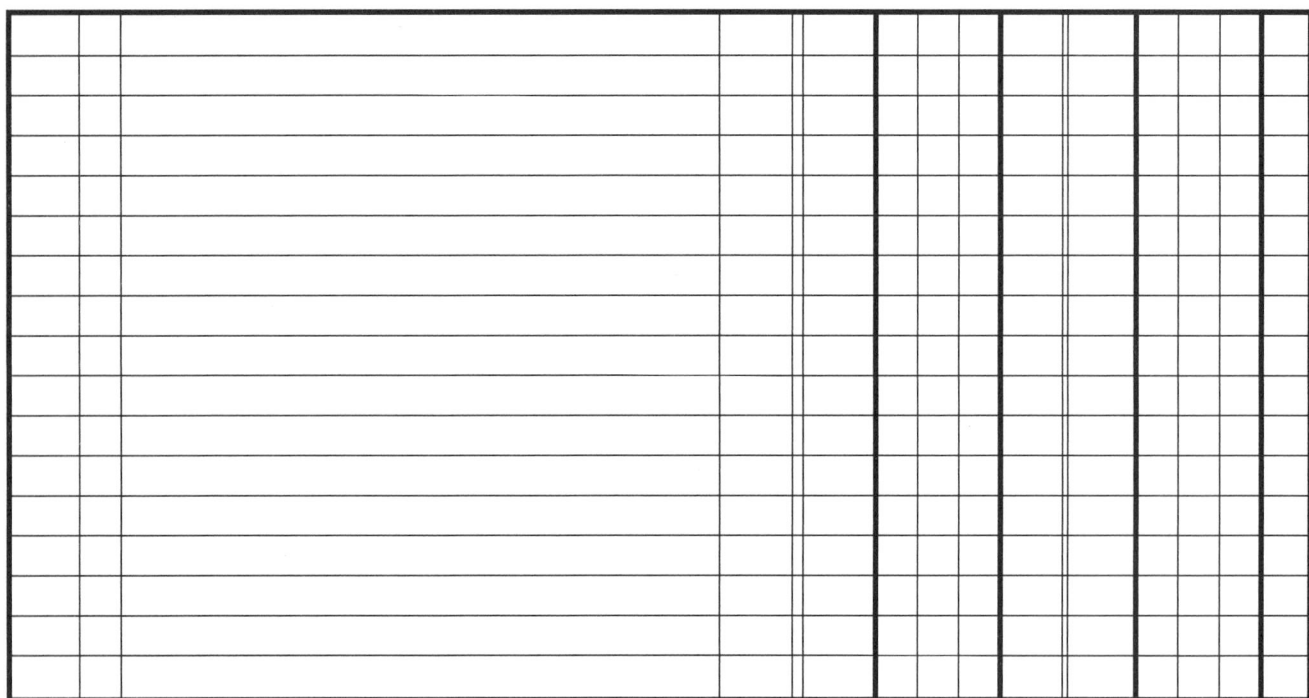

SELF-REVIEW QUIZ 11-2

Use a blank fold-out worksheet located at the end of this study guide.

YOU MAKE THE CALL: CRITICAL THINKING/ETHICAL CASE

_____

_____

_____

_____

_____

_____

_____

_____

_____

_____

_____

_____

_____

_____

_____

_____

_____

_____

_____

_____

INTERNET EXERCISES

_____

_____

_____

_____

_____

_____

_____

_____

_____

_____

_____

_____

_____

_____

_____

_____

_____

_____

_____

_____

FORMS FOR MINI EXERCISES

1.																		
2.																		

3. A. _____   E. _____
    B. _____   F. _____
    C. _____
    D. _____

4. _____
    _____
    _____
    _____
    _____
    _____
    _____

5.

    A. _____ B. _____ C. _____ D. _____ E. _____ F. _____

FORMS FOR EXERCISES

11-1.

A. _____

B. _____

_____

C. _____

D. _____

E. _____

F. _____

G. _____

H. _____

11-2.

A. _____

_____

_____

B. _____

_____

_____

C. _____

_____

_____

D. _____

_____

_____

11-3.

Accounts Affected	Category	↑ ↓	Rules

11-4.

A. _____

B. _____

C. _____

11-5.

Use a blank fold-out worksheet located at the end of this study guide.

END OF CHAPTER PROBLEMS

PROBLEM 11A-1 OR PROBLEM 11B-1

A.	
B.	
C.	
D.	

PROBLEM 11A-2 OR PROBLEM 11B-2;
PROBLEM 11A-3 OR PROBLEM 11B-3;
PROBLEM 11A-4 OR PROBLEM 11B-4

Use blank fold-out worksheets located at the end of this study guide.

CHAPTER 11
SUMMARY PRACTICE TEST:
PREPARING THE WORKSHEET
FOR A MERCHANDISE COMPANY

Part I Instructions

Fill in the blank(s) to complete the statement.

1. The _____ _____ system doesn't keep a continual track of the quantity and cost of the inventory on hand.

2. In the periodic inventory sytsem, all purchases of merchandise during the period is recorded in the _____ account.

3. A continuous record of inventory is kept in a _____ _____ system.

4. When using the periodic system, _____ _____ will remain unchanged.

5. _____ _____ represents a liability on the balance sheet and records money received for a sale or service not yet performed.

6. Freight-in is _____ to the cost of goods sold.

7. Net Sales less Cost of Goods Sold equals _____ _____.

8. _____ _____ equals Gross Sales less Sales Discounts and Sales Returns and Allowances.

9. Net Purchases equals Purchases less _____ _____ and _____ _____ _____ _____.

10. An _____ _____ helps calculate ending inventory.

11. Ending inventory is _____ from the cost of goods available for sale.

12. Net purchases are _____ to Beginning Inventory to get the cost of goods available for sale.

13. Gross Profit less _____ equals Net Income.

14. Purchase discounts _____ the total cost of merchandise sold.

15. Beginning inventory at the end of the period is assumed to be _____, and thus a _____.

16. The ending inventory of one period becomes the _____ _____ next period.

17. Ending inventory represents goods not _____.

18. The inventory account is _____ at the end of the period.

19. Purchases are increased by a _____.

20. Sales returns and allowances are used in calculating _____ _____.

21. Beginning Inventory plus Net Purchases equals _____ _____ _____ _____ _____ _____.

22. Beginning Inventory and Ending Inventory are never _____ on the worksheet.

Part II Instructions

Answer true or false to the following statements.

1. Unearned Revenue is an asset.
2. Perpetual inventory doesn't keep a continuous record of inventory.
3. Purchases reduce cost of goods sold.
4. Freight-in is subtracted from cost of good sold.
5. Figures for Beginning and Ending Inventory are combined on the work sheet.
6. A periodic system is used by companies with low volume and high unit prices.
7. Merchandise Inventory is a liability.
8. Unearned Revenue is a liability on the income statement.
9. Inventory is always taken 10 times per year.
10. Purchases replace ending inventory in a periodic system.
11. A trial balance may be placed directly on a worksheet.
12. The adjustment process updates the inventory account.
13. A post-closing trial balance has no temporary accounts.
14. Sales Discounts is a permanent account.
15. Gross sales are located on the balance sheet.
16. The Sales Returns and Allowances account has a normal balance of a credit.
17. Ending inventory of one period is the beginning inventory of the following period.
18. Net income always means cash.
19. Ending inventory increases cost of goods sold.
20. Net purchases is always the same as total purchases.
21. Gross profit plus expenses equals net income.
22. Unearned Storage Fees is a liability.
23. Merchandise inventory that is sold is assumed to be a cost.
24. Accumulated Depreciation is increased by a debit.
25. Merchandise Inventory can never be listed on a trial balance.
26. Ending Merchandise Inventory can only be found on a balance sheet.
27. The amount of rent expired is used in the adjustment process.
28. Adjustments help update individual ledger accounts.
29. Purchases Returns and Allowances is found on a balance sheet.
30. Beginning Merchandise Inventory found on the balance sheet from the prior period will also be placed in the cost of goods sold section of the balance sheet.
31. Sales always means cash received.
32. Ending Merchandise Inventory of the current period is found only on the balance sheet.
33. Purchases adds to the cost of goods sold.
34. Purchases discounts reduce the cost of purchases on the balance sheet.
35. Beginning inventory can never be assumed sold by the end of a period.

36. Ending inventory in one period becomes beginning inventory for the next two periods.

37. The ending inventory may be calculated from an inventory sheet.

38. Income Summary is used in the adjustment of merchandise inventory.

39. Ending inventory not sold is only placed in the credit column of the balance sheet section on the worksheet.

40. Purchases Discount is recorded in the credit column of the income statement section on the worksheet.

41. Gross profit and net income mean the same.

42. All companies must give sales discounts.

43. A merchandise company does not need a cost of goods sold section on the income statement.

44. Cost of goods available to sell less ending inventory equals cost of goods not sold.

SOLUTIONS TO SUMMARY PRACTICE TEST

Part I

1. periodic inventory
2. Purchases
3. perpetual inventory
4. beginning inventory
5. Unearned Revenue
6. added
7. Gross Profit
8. Net sales
9. Purchases Discounts, Purchases Returns and Allowances
10. Inventory sheet (record)
11. Subtracted
12. added
13. Expenses
14. reduce
15. sold, cost
16. begining inventory
17. sold
18. adjusted
19. debit
20. net sales
21. Cost of Goods Available for Sale
22. combined

Part II

1.	false	**12.**	true	**23.**	true	**34.**	false
2.	false	**13.**	true	**24.**	false	**35.**	false
3.	false	**14.**	false	**25.**	false	**36.**	false
4.	false	**15.**	false	**26.**	false	**37.**	true
5.	false	**16.**	false	**27.**	true	**38.**	true
6.	false	**17.**	true	**28.**	true	**39.**	false
7.	false	**18.**	false	**29.**	false	**40.**	true
8.	false	**19.**	false	**30.**	false	**41.**	false
9.	false	**20.**	false	**31.**	false	**42.**	false
10.	false	**21.**	false	**32.**	false	**43.**	false
11.	true	**22.**	true	**33.**	true	**44.**	false

CONTINUING PROBLEM FOR CHAPTER 11

Use blank fold-out worksheet located at the end of this study guide.

COMPLETION OF THE ACCOUNTING CYCLE FOR A MERCHANDISE COMPANY

12

Name _____ Class _____ Date _____

SELF-REVIEW QUIZ 12-1

(1)

(2)

(3)

SELF-REVIEW QUIZ 12-2

GENERAL JOURNAL PAGE 2

Date	Account Titles and Description	PR	Dr.	Cr.

SELF-REVIEW QUIZ 12-3

Situation 1

Situation 2

Situation 3

YOU MAKE THE CALL: CRITICAL THINKING/ETHICAL CASE

_____

_____

_____

_____

_____

_____

_____

_____

_____

_____

_____

_____

_____

_____

_____

_____

_____

INTERNET EXERCISES

_____

_____

_____

_____

_____

_____

_____

_____

_____

_____

_____

_____

_____

_____

_____

_____

_____

_____

_____

_____

_____

Name _____ Class _____ Date _____

FORMS FOR MINI EXERCISES

1.

_____
_____
_____
_____

2.

_____
_____
_____
_____

3.

_____
_____
_____
_____

4. A. _____   F. _____
    B. _____   G. _____
    C. _____   H. _____
    D. _____   I. _____
    E. _____   J. _____

5.

FORMS FOR EXERCISES

12-1.

COST OF GOODS SOLD

Merchandise Inv. 12/01/X1 _____

Purchases _____

Less: Purchases Disc. _____

   Purch. R. & A. _____

   _____

Net Purchases _____

   Add: Freight-in _____

Net Cost of Purchases _____

Cost of Goods Available for Sale _____

Less: Merchandise Inv. 12/31/X1 _____

   Cost of Goods Sold _____

12-2.

A. _____

B. _____

C. _____

D. _____

E. _____

F. _____

G. _____

12-3.

EXERCISES (CONTINUED)

12-4.

A. SLOW COMPANY
BALANCE SHEET
DECEMBER 31, 200X

12-5.

(A)

Salaries Expense   Salaries Payable

(B)

Salaries Expense   Salaries Expense

(C)

Salaries Expense   Cash

PROBLEM 12A-1 OR PROBLEM 12B-1

RING.COM
INCOME STATEMENT
FOR YEAR ENDED DECEMBER 31, 200X

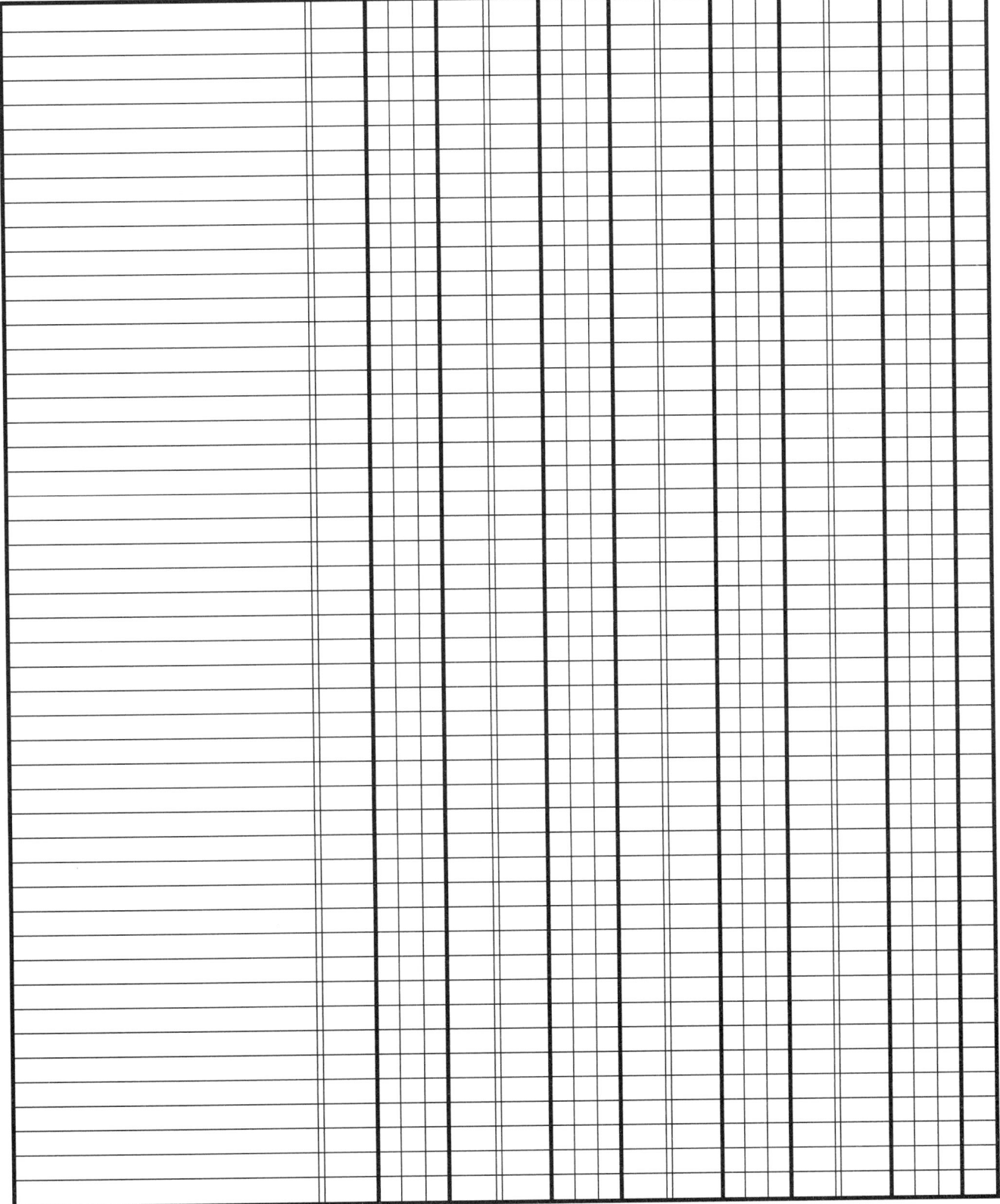

PROBLEM 12A-2 OR PROBLEM 12B-2

JAMES CO.
STATEMENT OF OWNER'S EQUITY
FOR MONTH ENDED DECEMBER 31, 200X

PROBLEM 12A-2 OR PROBLEM 12B-2 (CONCLUDED)

JAMES CO.
BALANCE SHEET
DECEMBER 31, 200X

PROBLEM 12A-3 OR PROBLEM 12B-3

Use a blank fold-out worksheet located at the end of this study guide.

JAY'S SUPPLIES
INCOME STATEMENT
FOR YEAR ENDED DECEMBER 31, 200X

PROBLEM 12A-3 OR PROBLEM 12B-3 (CONTINUED)

JAY'S SUPPLIES
STATEMENT OF OWNER'S EQUITY
FOR MONTH ENDED DECEMBER 31, 200X

PROBLEM 12A-3 OR PROBLEM 12B-3 (CONTINUED)

JAY'S SUPPLIES
BALANCE SHEET
DECEMBER 31, 200X

PROBLEM 12A-3 OR PROBLEM 12B-3 (CONTINUED)

GENERAL JOURNAL

PAGE 2

Date	Account Titles and Description	PR	Dr.	Cr.

Name _____ Class _____ Date _____

PROBLEM 12A-3 OR PROBLEM 12B-3 (CONCLUDED)

GENERAL JOURNAL

Date	Account Titles and Description	PR	Dr.	Cr.

PROBLEM 12A-4 OR PROBLEM 12B-4

Use a blank fold-out worksheet located at the end of this study guide.

CALLAHAN LUMBER
INCOME STATEMENT
FOR YEAR ENDED DECEMBER 31, 200X

PROBLEM 12A-4 OR PROBLEM 12B-4 (CONTINUED)

Use a blank fold-out worksheet located at the end of this study guide.

CALLAHAN LUMBER
STATEMENT OF OWNER'S EQUITY
FOR YEAR ENDED DECEMBER 31, 200X

PROBLEM 12A-4 OR PROBLEM 12B-4 (CONTINUED)

CALLAHAN LUMBER
BALANCE SHEET
DECEMBER 31, 200X

PROBLEM 12A-4 OR PROBLEM 12B-4 (CONTINUED)

GENERAL JOURNAL

Date	Account Titles and Description	PR	Dr.	Cr.

PROBLEM 12A-4 OR PROBLEM 12B-4 (CONTINUED)

CALLAHAN LUMBER
GENERAL LEDGER

CASH   ACCOUNT NO. 110

Date	Explanation	Post Ref.	Debit	Credit	Balance Debit	Balance Credit

ACCOUNTS RECEIVABLE   ACCOUNT NO. 111

Date	Explanation	Post Ref.	Debit	Credit	Balance Debit	Balance Credit

MERCHANDISE INVENTORY   ACCOUNT NO. 112

Date	Explanation	Post Ref.	Debit	Credit	Balance Debit	Balance Credit

LUMBER SUPPLIES   ACCOUNT NO. 112

Date	Explanation	Post Ref.	Debit	Credit	Balance Debit	Balance Credit

PROBLEM 12A-4 OR PROBLEM 12B-4 (CONTINUED)

PREPAID INSURANCE ACCOUNT NO. 114

Date		Explanation	Post Ref.	Debit	Credit	Balance	
						Debit	Credit

LUMBER EQUIPMENT ACCOUNT NO. 121

Date		Explanation	Post Ref.	Debit	Credit	Balance	
						Debit	Credit

ACCUMULATED DEPRECIATION, LUMBER EQUIPMENT ACCOUNT NO. 122

Date		Explanation	Post Ref.	Debit	Credit	Balance	
						Debit	Credit

ACCOUNTS PAYABLE ACCOUNT NO. 220

Date		Explanation	Post Ref.	Debit	Credit	Balance	
						Debit	Credit

WAGES PAYABLE ACCOUNT NO. 221

Date		Explanation	Post Ref.	Debit	Credit	Balance	
						Debit	Credit

PROBLEM 12A-4 OR PROBLEM 12B-4 (CONTINUED)

J. CALLAHAN, CAPITAL   ACCOUNT NO. 330

Date	Explanation	Post Ref.	Debit	Credit	Balance Debit	Balance Credit

J. CALLAHAN, WITHDRAWALS   ACCOUNT NO. 331

Date	Explanation	Post Ref.	Debit	Credit	Balance Debit	Balance Credit

INCOME SUMMARY   ACCOUNT NO. 332

Date	Explanation	Post Ref.	Debit	Credit	Balance Debit	Balance Credit

SALES   ACCOUNT NO. 440

Date	Explanation	Post Ref.	Debit	Credit	Balance Debit	Balance Credit

SALES RETURNS AND ALLOWANCES   ACCOUNT NO. 441

Date	Explanation	Post Ref.	Debit	Credit	Balance Debit	Balance Credit

PROBLEM 12A-4 OR PROBLEM 12B-4 (CONTINUED)

PURCHASES   ACCOUNT NO. 550

Date	Explanation	Post Ref.	Debit	Credit	Balance Debit	Balance Credit

PURCHASES DISCOUNT   ACCOUNT NO. 551

Date	Explanation	Post Ref.	Debit	Credit	Balance Debit	Balance Credit

PURCHASES RETURNS AND ALLOWANCES   ACCOUNT NO. 552

Date	Explanation	Post Ref.	Debit	Credit	Balance Debit	Balance Credit

WAGES EXPENSE   ACCOUNT NO. 660

Date	Explanation	Post Ref.	Debit	Credit	Balance Debit	Balance Credit

ADVERTISING EXPENSE   ACCOUNT NO. 661

Date	Explanation	Post Ref.	Debit	Credit	Balance Debit	Balance Credit

PROBLEM 12A-4 OR PROBLEM 12B-4 (CONTINUED)

RENT EXPENSE   ACCOUNT NO. 662

Date	Explanation	Post Ref.	Debit	Credit	Balance	
					Debit	Credit

DEPRECIATION EXPENSE, LUMBER EQUIPMENT   ACCOUNT NO. 663

Date	Explanation	Post Ref.	Debit	Credit	Balance	
					Debit	Credit

LUMBER SUPPLIES EXPENSE   ACCOUNT NO. 664

Date	Explanation	Post Ref.	Debit	Credit	Balance	
					Debit	Credit

INSURANCE EXPENSE   ACCOUNT NO. 665

Date	Explanation	Post Ref.	Debit	Credit	Balance	
					Debit	Credit

PROBLEM 12A-4 OR PROBLEM 12B-4 (CONCLUDED)

CALLAHAN LUMBER
POST-CLOSING TRIAL BALANCE
DECEMBER 31, 200X

	Dr.	Cr.

CHAPTER 12
SUMMARY PRACTICE TEST:
COMPLETION OF THE ACCOUNTING
CYCLE FOR A MERCHANDISE COMPANY

Part I

Fill in the blank(s) to complete the statement.

1. The inside columns for financial reports are used for _____.

2. The fomal income statement uses _____ _____ figures for inventory.

3. The gross profit figure _____ (is/is not) found on the worksheet.

4. _____ expenses are related to the selling activity.

5. _____ _____ are related to the administrative function.

6. _____ _____ could be broken down into selling and administrative expenses.

7. The _____ figure for capital is not found on the worksheet.

8. _____ _____ are cash or other assets that will be converted into cash during the normal operating cycle of the company or one year, whichever is longer.

9. _____ and _____ are long-lived assets used for the production or sale of other assets or services.

10. Debts or obligations that are to be paid with current assets within one year or one operating cycle are called _____ _____ _____.

11. Mortgage Payable is an example of a _____.

12. Ending merchandise inventory is a _____ _____.

13. By the adjusting process, the beginning inventory of the period is transferred to _____ _____.

14. The post-closing trial balance contains no _____ accounts.

15. A reversing entry involves certain _____ entries.

16. Reversing entries are used only if assets are _____ and have no previous balance and liabilities are _____ and have no balance.

Name _____ Class _____ Date _____

Part II Instructions

Match the term in the last column to the definition, example, or phrase in the right column. Be sure to use a letter only once.

____d____ **1.** EXAMPLE: Equipment
_____ **2.** Net Sales-Cost of Goods Sold
_____ **3.** Operating Cycle
_____ **4.** Subtotalling
_____ **5.** Gross Profit-Operating Expenses
_____ **6.** Operating Expenses
_____ **7.** Temporary Account
_____ **8.** FICA Tax Payable-Soc. Sec.
_____ **9.** Result of an adjusting entry
_____ **10.** Petty Cash
_____ **11.** An asset that is adjsuted
_____ **12.** Ending Capital
_____ **13.** A Liability showing revenue no earned
_____ **14.** Unearned training fees

a. Inside columns of financial reports
b. Unearned Revenue
c. Current asset
d. Plant and Equipment
e. Reversing Entry
f. Time Period
g. Net Income
h. Current Liability
i. When earned reduced by a debit
j. Gross Profit
k. Merchandise Inventory
l. Debit Balance
m. Not found on worksheet
n. Income Summary
o. Selling and Administrative

Part III Instructions

Answer true or false to the following statements.

1. Formal statements contain debit and credit columns.
2. Cost of goods sold contains only ending inventory.
3. Net sales less cost of goods sold equals gross profit.
4. Operating expenses can only be administrative.
5. Supplies is part of Plant and Equipment.
6. Unearned Rent is a liability.
7. An operating cycle of a business must be one year.
8. Accumulated Depreciation is a current asset.
9. Long-term liabilities are due within one year.
10. Merchandise Inventory is a temporary account.
11. The normal balance of merchandise inventory is a debit.
12. The post-closing trial balance will not contain any unearned revenue accounts.
13. Ending inventory is closed directly to Capital.
14. Reversing entries cannot be applied to all adjustments.
15. Reversing entries are optional at the end of each month before close of year.
16. Reversing entries switch closing entries on the first day of new period.
17. An adjusting entry with an asset decreasing with no prevoius balance cannot be reversed.
18. Closing entries will update the merchandise inventory account.
19. Beginning merchandise inventory of a period is assumed sold by end of the period.
20. An adjusting entry for Accrued Wages can be reversed.

CHAPTER 12
SOLUTIONS TO SUMMARY PRACTICE TEST

Part I

1. subtotalling
2. two separate
3. not
4. Selling
5. Administrative expenses
6. Operating expenses
7. ending
8. Current assets
9. Plant, Equipment
10. current liabilities
11. long-term liability
12. permanent account
13. Income Summary
14. temporary
15. adjusting
16. increasing, increasing

Part II

1. d
2. j
3. f
4. a
5. g
6. o
7. n
8. h
9. e
10. l
11. k
12. m
13. b
14. i

Part III

1. false
2. false
3. true
4. false
5. false
6. true
7. false
8. false
9. false
10. false
11. true
12. false
13. false
14. true
15. false
16. false
17. true
18. false
19. true
20. true

CONTINUING PROBLEM FOR CHAPTER 12

GENERAL JOURNAL   PAGE 1

Date	Account Titles and Description	PR	Dr.	Cr.

ELDORADO COMPUTER CENTER
GENERAL LEDGER

CASH   ACCOUNT NO. 1000

Date		Explanation	Post Ref.	Debit	Credit	Balance Debit	Balance Credit
3/1	0X	Balance forward	√			12 5 1 6 65	

PETTY CASH   ACCOUNT NO. 1010

Date		Explanation	Post Ref.	Debit	Credit	Balance Debit	Balance Credit
3/1	0X	Balance forward	√			1 0 0 00	

ACCOUNTS RECEIVABLE   ACCOUNT NO. 1020

Date		Explanation	Post Ref.	Debit	Credit	Balance Debit	Balance Credit
3/1	0X	Balance forward	√			11 9 0 0 00	

PREPAID RENT   ACCOUNT NO. 1025

Date		Explanation	Post Ref.	Debit	Credit	Balance Debit	Balance Credit
3/1	0X	Balance forward	√			2 8 0 0 00	

SUPPLIES   ACCOUNT NO. 1030

Date		Explanation	Post Ref.	Debit	Credit	Balance	
						Debit	Credit
3/1	0X	Balance forward	√			4 3 2 00	

MERCHANDISE INVENTORY   ACCOUNT NO. 1040

Date		Explanation	Post Ref.	Debit	Credit	Balance	
						Debit	Credit

COMPUTER SHOP EQUIPMENT   ACCOUNT NO. 1080

Date		Explanation	Post Ref.	Debit	Credit	Balance	
						Debit	Credit
3/1	0X	Balance forward	√			3 8 0 0	

ACCUMULATED DEPRECIATION, C.S. EQUIPMENT   ACCOUNT NO. 1081

Date		Explanation	Post Ref.	Debit	Credit	Balance	
						Debit	Credit
3/1	0X	Balance forward	√				9 9 00

OFFICE EQUIPMENT   ACCOUNT NO. 1090

Date		Explanation	Post Ref.	Debit	Credit	Balance	
						Debit	Credit
3/1	0X	Balance forward	√			1 0 5 0 00	

ACCUMULATED DEPRECIATION, OFFICE EQUIPMENT

ACCOUNT NO. 1091

Date		Explanation	Post Ref.	Debit	Credit	Balance Debit	Balance Credit
3/1	0X	Balance forward	√				2 0 00

ACCOUNTS PAYABLE

ACCOUNT NO. 2000

Date		Explanation	Post Ref.	Debit	Credit	Balance Debit	Balance Credit
3/1	0X	Balance forward	√				2 8 4 0 00

WAGES PAYABLE

ACCOUNT NO. 2010

Date		Explanation	Post Ref.	Debit	Credit	Balance Debit	Balance Credit

FICA S.S. PAYABLE

ACCOUNT NO. 2020

Date		Explanation	Post Ref.	Debit	Credit	Balance Debit	Balance Credit

FICA MEDICARE PAYABLE

ACCOUNT NO. 2030

Date		Explanation	Post Ref.	Debit	Credit	Balance Debit	Balance Credit

FIT PAYABLE   ACCOUNT NO. 2040

Date		Explanation	Post Ref.	Debit	Credit	Balance	
						Debit	Credit

SIT PAYABLE   ACCOUNT NO. 2050

Date		Explanation	Post Ref.	Debit	Credit	Balance	
						Debit	Credit

FUTA PAYABLE   ACCOUNT NO. 2060

Date		Explanation	Post Ref.	Debit	Credit	Balance	
						Debit	Credit

SUTA PAYABLE   ACCOUNT NO. 2070

Date		Explanation	Post Ref.	Debit	Credit	Balance	
						Debit	Credit

T. FREEDMAN, CAPITAL   ACCOUNT NO. 3000

Date		Explanation	Post Ref.	Debit	Credit	Balance	
						Debit	Credit
3/1	0X	Balance forward	√				7 4 0 6 00

T. FREEDMAN WITHDRAWALS   ACCOUNT NO. 3010

Date		Explanation	Post Ref.	Debit	Credit	Balance Debit	Balance Credit
3/1	0X	Balance forward	√			2 015 00	

INCOME SUMMARY   ACCOUNT NO. 3020

Date		Explanation	Post Ref.	Debit	Credit	Balance Debit	Balance Credit

SERVICE REVENUE   ACCOUNT NO. 4000

Date		Explanation	Post Ref.	Debit	Credit	Balance Debit	Balance Credit
3/1	0X	Balance forward	√				19 800 00

SALES   ACCOUNT NO. 4010

Date		Explanation	Post Ref.	Debit	Credit	Balance Debit	Balance Credit
3/1	0X	Balance forward	√				9 700 00

GENERAL LEDGER

SALES RETURN AND ALLOWANCES   ACCOUNT NO. 4020

Date		Explanation	Post Ref.	Debit	Credit	Balance	
						Debit	Credit
3/1	0X	Balance forward	√			4 0 0 00	

SALES DISCOUNTS   ACCOUNT NO. 4030

Date		Explanation	Post Ref.	Debit	Credit	Balance	
						Debit	Credit
3/1	0X	Balance forward	√			2 2 0 00	

ADVERTISING EXPENSE   ACCOUNT NO. 5010

Date		Explanation	Post Ref.	Debit	Credit	Balance	
						Debit	Credit
3/1	0X	Balance forward	√			8 0 0 00	

RENT EXPENSE   ACCOUNT NO. 5020

Date		Explanation	Post Ref.	Debit	Credit	Balance	
						Debit	Credit

UTILITIES EXPENSE   ACCOUNT NO. 5030

Date		Explanation	Post Ref.	Debit	Credit	Balance	
						Debit	Credit
3/1	0X	Balance forward	√			2 9 0 00	

PHONE EXPENSE   ACCOUNT NO. 5040

Date		Explanation	Post Ref.	Debit	Credit	Balance Debit	Balance Credit
3/1	0X	Balance forward	√			1 5 0 00	

SUPPLIES EXPENSE   ACCOUNT NO. 5050

Date		Explanation	Post Ref.	Debit	Credit	Balance Debit	Balance Credit

INSURANCE EXPENSE   ACCOUNT NO. 5060

Date		Explanation	Post Ref.	Debit	Credit	Balance Debit	Balance Credit
3/1	0X	Balance forward	√			1 0 0 00	

POSTAGE EXPENSE   ACCOUNT NO. 5070

Date		Explanation	Post Ref.	Debit	Credit	Balance Debit	Balance Credit
3/1	0X	Balance forward	√			1 7 5 00	

DEPRECIATION EXPENSE C.S. EQUIPMENT   ACCOUNT NO. 5080

Date		Explanation	Post Ref.	Debit	Credit	Balance Debit	Balance Credit

DEPRECIATION EXPENSE OFFICE EQUIPMENT   ACCOUNT NO. 5090

Date		Explanation	Post Ref.	Debit	Credit	Balance	
						Debit	Credit

MISCELLANEOUS EXPENSE   ACCOUNT NO. 5100

Date		Explanation	Post Ref.	Debit	Credit	Balance	
						Debit	Credit
3/1	0X	Balance forward	√			1 0 00	

WAGE EXPENSE   ACCOUNT NO. 5110

Date		Explanation	Post Ref.	Debit	Credit	Balance	
						Debit	Credit
3/1	0X	Balance forward	√			2 0 3 0 00	

PAYROLL TAX EXPENSE   ACCOUNT NO. 5120

Date		Explanation	Post Ref.	Debit	Credit	Balance	
						Debit	Credit
3/1	0X	Balance forward	√			2 2 6 35	

INTEREST EXPENSE   ACCOUNT NO. 5130

Date		Explanation	Post Ref.	Debit	Credit	Balance	
						Debit	Credit

BAD DEBT EXPENSE   ACCOUNT NO. 5140

Date		Explanation	Post Ref.	Debit	Credit	Balance	
						Debit	Credit

PURCHASES   ACCOUNT NO. 6000

Date		Explanation	Post Ref.	Debit	Credit	Balance	
						Debit	Credit
3/1	0X	Balance forward	√			9 5 0 00	

PURCHASE RETURNS AND ALLOWANCES   ACCOUNT NO. 6010

Date		Explanation	Post Ref.	Debit	Credit	Balance	
						Debit	Credit
3/1	0X	Balance forward	√				1 0 0 00

PURCHASE DISCOUNTS   ACCOUNT NO. 6020

Date		Explanation	Post Ref.	Debit	Credit	Balance	
						Debit	Credit

FREIGHT IN   ACCOUNT NO. 6030

Date		Explanation	Post Ref.	Debit	Credit	Balance	
						Debit	Credit

CONTINUING PROBLEM FOR CHAPTER 12

ELDORADO COMPUTER CENTER
INCOME STATEMENT
FOR THE SIX MONTHS ENDED MARCH 31, 200X

ELDORADO COMPUTER CENTER
STATEMENT OF OWNER'S EQUITY
FOR THE SIX MONTHS ENDED MARCH 31, 200X

ELDORADO COMPUTER CENTER
BALANCE SHEET
MARCH 31, 200X

MINI PRACTICE SET

THE CORNER DRESS SHOP
GENERAL JOURNAL

PAGE 4

Date		Account Titles and Description	PR	Dr.	Cr.

COMPREHENSIVE REVIEW PROBLEM:
THE CORNER DRESS SHOP

Use a blank fold-out worksheet and the blank payroll register located at the end of this study guide.

MINI PRACTICE SET

THE CORNER DRESS SHOP
GENERAL JOURNAL

Date	Account Titles and Description	PR	Dr.	Cr.

MINI PRACTICE SET

THE CORNER DRESS SHOP
AUXILIARY PETTY CASH RECORD

Date	Voucher No.	Description	Receipts	Payment	Category of Payment				
					Postage Expense	Delivery Expense	Sundry		
							Account	Amount	

MINI PRACTICE SET

THE CORNER DRESS SHOP
SALES JOURNAL

Date		Invoice No.	Terms	Accounts Debited	PR.		Accounts Rec. - Dr. Sales - Cr.			

Name _____ Class _____ Date _____

MINI PRACTICE SET

THE CORNER DRESS SHOP
CASH RECEIPTS JOURNAL

PAGE 6

Date	Cash Dr.	Sales Discounts Dr.	Accounts Receivable Cr.	Sales Cr.	Sundry Cr		
					Account	PR	Amount

MINI PRACTICE SET

PURCHASES JOURNAL

PAGE 4

Date 190X	Account Credited	Date of Invoice	Inv. No.	Terms	PR	Accounts Payable Cr.	Purchases Dr.	Sundry Dr. Account	PR.	Amount

MINI PRACTICE SET:

THE CORNER DRESS SHOP
CASH PAYMENTS JOURNAL

PAGE 7

Date	Check No.	Accounts Debited	PR.	Sundry Dr.	Accounts Payable Dr.	Salaries Payable Dr.	Purchases Discount Cr.	Cash Cr.

MINI PRACTICE SET:

ACCOUNTS PAYABLE SUBSIDIARY LEDGER

NAME   BLEW CO.

Date 190X		Explanation	Post Ref.	Debit	Credit	Credit Balance
MAR	1	Balance	√			1 9 0 0 00

NAME   JONES CO.

Date 190X		Explanation	Post Ref.	Debit	Credit	Credit Balance

NAME   MOE'S GARAGE

Date 190X		Explanation	Post Ref.	Debit	Credit	Credit Balance

MINI PRACTICE SET

NAME   MORRIS CO. _____

Date 200X		Explanation	Post Ref.	Debit	Credit	Credit Balance

ACCOUNTS RECEIVABLE SUBSIDIARY LEDGER

NAME   BING CO. _____

Date 200X		Explanation	Post Ref.	Debit	Credit	Debit Balance
MAR	1	Balance	√			2 2 0 0 00

NAME   BLEW CO. _____

Date 200X		Explanation	Post Ref.	Debit	Credit	Debit Balance

MINI PRACTICE SET

NAME   RONALD CO. _____

Date 200X		Explanation	Post Ref.	Debit	Credit	Debit Balance

GENERAL LEDGER

CASH   ACCOUNT NO. 110

Date 200X		Explanation	Post Ref.	Debit	Credit	Balance Debit	Balance Credit
MAR	1	Balance	√			2 5 0 2 30	

ACCOUNTS RECEIVABLE   ACCOUNT NO. 111

Date 200X		Explanation	Post Ref.	Debit	Credit	Balance Debit	Balance Credit
MAR	1	Balance	√			2 2 0 0 00	

MINI PRACTICE SET

PETTY CASH   ACCOUNT NO. 112

Date 200X		Explanation	Post Ref.	Debit	Credit	Balance Debit	Balance Credit
MAR	1	Balance	√			3 5 00	

MERCHANDISE INVENTORY   ACCOUNT NO. 114

Date 200X		Explanation	Post Ref.	Debit	Credit	Balance Debit	Balance Credit
MAR	1	Balance	√			5 6 0 0 00	

PREPAID RENT   ACCOUNT NO. 116

Date 200X		Explanation	Post Ref.	Debit	Credit	Balance Debit	Balance Credit
MAR	1	Balance	√			1 8 0 0 00	

DELIVERY TRUCK   ACCOUNT NO. 120

Date 200X		Explanation	Post Ref.	Debit	Credit	Balance Debit	Balance Credit
MAR	1	Balance	√			6 0 0 0 00	

MINI PRACTICE SET

ACCUMULATED DEPRECIATION, TRUCK   ACCOUNT NO. 121

Date 200X		Explanation	Post Ref.	Debit	Credit	Balance Debit	Balance Credit
MAR	1	Balance	√				1 5 0 0 00

ACCOUNTS PAYABLE   ACCOUNT NO. 210

Date 200X		Explanation	Post Ref.	Debit	Credit	Balance Debit	Balance Credit
MAR	1	Balance	√				1 9 0 0 00

SALARIES PAYABLE   ACCOUNT NO. 212

Date 200X		Explanation	Post Ref.	Debit	Credit	Balance Debit	Balance Credit

FIT PAYABLE   ACCOUNT NO. 214

Date 200X		Explanation	Post Ref.	Debit	Credit	Balance Debit	Balance Credit
MAR	1	Balance	√				1 2 8 4 00

MINI PRACTICE SET:

FICA-SOCIAL SECURITY PAYABLE   ACCOUNT NO. 216

Date 200X		Explanation	Post Ref.	Debit	Credit	Balance	
						Debit	Credit
MAR	1	Balance	√				1 3 3 9 20

FICA-MEDICARE PAYABLE   ACCOUNT NO. 218

Date 200X		Explanation	Post Ref.	Debit	Credit	Balance	
						Debit	Credit
MAR	1	Balance	√				3 1 3 20

SIT PAYABLE   ACCOUNT NO. 220

Date 200X		Explanation	Post Ref.	Debit	Credit	Balance	
						Debit	Credit
MAR	1	Balance	√				7 5 6 00

SUTA TAX PAYABLE   ACCOUNT NO. 222

Date 200X		Explanation	Post Ref.	Debit	Credit	Balance	
						Debit	Credit
MAR	1	Balance	√				9 7 9 20

FUTA TAX PAYABLE   ACCOUNT NO. 224

Date 200X		Explanation	Post Ref.	Debit	Credit	Balance	
						Debit	Credit
MAR	1	Balance	√				1 6 3 20

UNEARNED RENT   ACCOUNT NO. 226

Date 200X		Explanation	Post Ref.	Debit	Credit	Balance	
						Debit	Credit
MAR	1	Balance	√				8 0 0 00

MINI PRACTICE SET:

B. LOEB, CAPITAL · ACCOUNT NO. 310

Date 200X		Explanation	Post Ref.	Debit	Credit	Balance Debit	Balance Credit
MAR	1	Balance	√				9 1 0 3 10

B. LOEB, WITHDRAWALS · ACCOUNT NO. 320

Date 200X		Explanation	Post Ref.	Debit	Credit	Balance Debit	Balance Credit

INCOME SUMMARY · ACCOUNT NO. 330

Date 200X		Explanation	Post Ref.	Debit	Credit	Balance Debit	Balance Credit

SALES · ACCOUNT NO. 410

Date 200X		Explanation	Post Ref.	Debit	Credit	Balance Debit	Balance Credit

SALES RETURNS AND ALLOWANCES · ACCOUNT NO. 412

Date 200X		Explanation	Post Ref.	Debit	Credit	Balance Debit	Balance Credit

MINI PRACTICE SET

SALES DISCOUNT   ACCOUNT NO. 414

Date 200X	Explanation	Post Ref.	Debit	Credit	Balance Debit	Balance Credit

RENTAL INCOME   ACCOUNT NO. 416

Date 200X	Explanation	Post Ref.	Debit	Credit	Balance Debit	Balance Credit

PURCHASES   ACCOUNT NO. 510

Date 200X	Explanation	Post Ref.	Debit	Credit	Balance Debit	Balance Credit

PURCHASES RETURNS AND ALLOWANCES   ACCOUNT NO. 512

Date 200X	Explanation	Post Ref.	Debit	Credit	Balance Debit	Balance Credit

PURCHASES DISCOUNT   ACCOUNT NO. 514

Date 200X	Explanation	Post Ref.	Debit	Credit	Balance Debit	Balance Credit

MINI PRACTICE SET

SALES SALARY EXPENSE — ACCOUNT NO. 610

Date 200X	Explanation	Post Ref.	Debit	Credit	Balance Debit	Balance Credit

OFFICE SALARY EXPENSE — ACCOUNT NO. 611

Date 200X	Explanation	Post Ref.	Debit	Credit	Balance Debit	Balance Credit

PAYROLL TAX EXPENSE — ACCOUNT NO. 612

Date 200X	Explanation	Post Ref.	Debit	Credit	Balance Debit	Balance Credit

CLEANING EXPENSE — ACCOUNT NO. 614

Date 200X	Explanation	Post Ref.	Debit	Credit	Balance Debit	Balance Credit

DEPRECIATION EXPENSE, TRUCK — ACCOUNT NO. 616

Date 200X	Explanation	Post Ref.	Debit	Credit	Balance Debit	Balance Credit

MINI PRACTICE SET

RENT EXPENSE   ACCOUNT NO. 618

Date 200X	Explanation	Post Ref.	Debit	Credit	Balance Debit	Balance Credit

POSTAGE EXPENSE   ACCOUNT NO. 620

Date 200X	Explanation	Post Ref.	Debit	Credit	Balance Debit	Balance Credit

DELIVERY EXPENSE   ACCOUNT NO. 622

Date 200X	Explanation	Post Ref.	Debit	Credit	Balance Debit	Balance Credit

MISCELLANEOUS EXPENSE   ACCOUNT NO. 624

Date 200X	Explanation	Post Ref.	Debit	Credit	Balance Debit	Balance Credit

MINI PRACTICE SET

THE CORNER DRESS SHOP
SCHEDULE OF ACCOUNTS RECEIVABLE
MARCH 31, 200X

THE CORNER DRESS SHOP
SCHEDULE OF ACCOUNTS PAYABLE
MARCH 31, 200X

MINI PRACTICE SET

THE CORNER DRESS SHOP
INCOME STATEMENT
FOR MONTH ENDED MARCH 31, 200X

MINI PRACTICE SET

THE CORNER DRESS SHOP
STATEMENT OF OWNER'S EQUITY
FOR MONTH ENDED MARCH 31, 200X

MINI PRACTICE SET

THE CORNER DRESS SHOP
BALANCE SHEET
MARCH 31, 200X

MINI PRACTICE SET

THE CORNER DRESS SHOP
POST-CLOSING TRIAL BALANCE
MARCH 31, 200X

Form **941**	**Employer's Quarterly Federal Tax Return**
(Rev. January 2003)	► See separate instructions revised January 2003 for information on completing this return.
Department of the Treasury Internal Revenue Service (99)	**Please type or print.**

Enter state code for state in which deposits were made **only** if different from state in address to the right ► (see page 2 of separate instructions).

Name (as distinguished from trade name)	Date quarter ended	OMB No. 1545-0029
		T
Trade name, if any	Employer identification number	FF
		FD
Address (number and street)	City, state, and ZIP code	FP
		I
		T

If address is different from prior return, check here

IRS Use

1 1 1 1 1 1 1 1 1 1   2   3 3 3 3 3 3 3 3   4 4 4   5 5 5

6   7   8 8 8 8 8 8 8   9 9 9 9 9   10 10 10 10 10 10 10 10 10 10

A If you **do not have to file** returns in the future, check here ► ☐ and enter date final wages paid ►

B If you are a seasonal employer, see **Seasonal employers** on page 1 of the instructions and check here ► ☐

1	Number of employees in the pay period that includes March 12th . ►	1	
2	Total wages and tips, plus other compensation	**2**	
3	Total income tax withheld from wages, tips, and sick pay	**3**	
4	Adjustment of withheld income tax for preceding quarters of **this calendar year**	**4**	
5	Adjusted total of income tax withheld (line 3 as adjusted by line 4)	**5**	

6	Taxable social security wages	**6a**		× 12.4% (.124) =	**6b**
	Taxable social security tips	**6c**		× 12.4% (.124) =	**6d**
7	Taxable Medicare wages and tips . . .	**7a**		× 2.9% (.029) =	**7b**

8	Total social security and Medicare taxes (add lines 6b, 6d, and 7b). **Check here if wages are not subject to social security and/or Medicare tax** . . . . ► ☐	**8**	
9	Adjustment of social security and Medicare taxes (see instructions for required explanation) Sick Pay $ _____ ± Fractions of Cents $ _____ ± Other $ _____ =	**9**	
10	Adjusted total of social security and Medicare taxes (line 8 as adjusted by line 9)	**10**	
11	**Total taxes** (add lines 5 and 10)	**11**	
12	Advance earned income credit (EIC) payments made to employees (see instructions) . . .	**12**	
13	Net taxes (subtract line 12 from line 11). **If $2,500 or more, this must equal line 17, column (d) below (or line D of Schedule B (Form 941))**	**13**	
14	Total deposits for quarter, including overpayment applied from a prior quarter	**14**	
15	**Balance due** (subtract line 14 from line 13). See instructions	**15**	

16 **Overpayment.** If line 14 is more than line 13, enter excess here ► $ _____

and check if to be: ☐ Applied to next return **or** ☐ Refunded.

- **All filers:** If line 13 is less than $2,500, **do not** complete line 17 or Schedule B (Form 941).
- **Semiweekly schedule depositors:** Complete Schedule B (Form 941) and check here . . . . ► ☐
- **Monthly schedule depositors:** Complete line 17, columns (a) through (d), and check here . . . . ► ☐

17	**Monthly Summary of Federal Tax Liability.** (Complete **Schedule B (Form 941)** instead, if you were a semiweekly schedule depositor.)		
(a) First month liability	**(b)** Second month liability	**(c)** Third month liability	**(d)** Total liability for quarter

Third Party Designee	Do you want to allow another person to discuss this return with the IRS (see separate instructions)? ☐ **Yes.** Complete the following. ☐ **No**
	Designee's name ► _____ Phone no. ► ( ) Personal identification number (PIN) ► ☐☐☐☐☐

Sign Here	Under penalties of perjury, I declare that I have examined this return, including accompanying schedules and statements, and to the best of my knowledge and belief, it is true, correct, and complete.
	Signature ► Print Your Name and Title ► Date ►

For Privacy Act and Paperwork Reduction Act Notice, see back of Payment Voucher.   Cat. No. 17001Z   Form **941** (Rev. 1-2003)